Handbook of Drug Control in the United States

Handbook of Drug Control in the United States ⸺

Edited by

⸺ James A. Inciardi

Foreword by

⸺ Joseph R. Biden, Jr.

GREENWOOD PRESS
New York • Westport, Connecticut • London ⸺

Library of Congress Cataloging-in-Publication Data

Handbook of drug control in the United States / edited by James A.
  Inciardi / foreword by Joseph R. Biden, Jr.
      p.   cm.
  Includes bibliographical references.
  ISBN 0–313–26190–3 (lib. bdg. : alk. paper)
  1. Narcotics, Control of—United States.   I. Inciardi, James A.
HV5825.H215   1990
363.4'5'0973—dc20   90–2736

British Library Cataloguing in Publication Data is available.

Library of Congress Catalog Card Number: 90–2736
ISBN: 0–313–26190–3

First published in 1990

Greenwood Press, 88 Post Road West, Westport, CT 06881
An imprint of Greenwood Publishing Group, Inc.

Printed in the United States of America

The paper used in this book complies with the
Permanent Paper Standard issued by the National
Information Standards Organization (Z39.48–1984).

10 9 8 7 6 5 4 3 2 1

To the memory of Carl D. Chambers (1934–1989),
pioneer, mentor, and friend

Contents

Foreword

At a time when the first director of national drug control policy has been appointed to that new federal cabinet position, James A. Inciardi, director of the Division of Criminal Justice at the University of Delaware, has provided an unusually valuable service in compiling the *Handbook of Drug Control in the United States*.

Despite the how-to-do-it connotations of the term handbook, and despite the expert and comprehensive span of the chapters Dr. Inciardi has assembled here, he has wisely avoided the trap into which so many have fallen in attempting to deal with our major national problem of drug trafficking and drug abuse. There is no suggestion here of a one-and-only solution to the problem of illegal drugs. There is no echo of the grandiose wars on drugs that have allowed us to deceive ourselves into believing, more than once over the past twenty years, that if we just mount one last grand campaign, we can eliminate drug abuse and drug trafficking and, in good American fashion, turn our attention to the next item on our national list of problems to be solved. The scale of our problem with illegal drugs tempts us to that analogy with war, but the war-making psychology it engenders—to get it over with as quickly as possible and move on—has invariably led us astray. That temptation and that psychology are absent from this handbook. Dr. Inciardi offers both wiser advice and harder work.

The makings of an effective national antidrug policy are here—from the history and evolution of drug abuse and drug control in the United States, through surveys of supply-reduction and demand-reduction strategies, to a frank scrutiny of the drug control controversies before us today, and finally to the direction drug control may take in the future—but there is no prefabricated solution to the problem, no formula that will free us as a nation from the labor of controlling the abuse and trafficking in illegal drugs.

Instead, Dr. Inciardi and the contributing authors offer us something far more valuable and, in the long run, far more promising—a useful way of thinking about the problem. What we find here is a catalog of the tools we need to undertake not an overnight solution, not a blitzkrieg on drugs that sweeps every-thing before it, but the thoughtful, careful development of a national policy that defines the drug problem in realistic and manageable terms; a policy that mar-shals, balances, and coordinates all of the resources we can bring to bear as a nation; and a policy that measures and adapts itself, step by step, as it builds toward more effective drug control.

It is precisely such a national policy that is, by law, the first priority of the newest officer in the federal cabinet, the director for national drug control policy. For that reason alone, as the author of the legislation that created that new cabinet office, I welcome this timely volume, and I do, indeed, recommend it to the new director. But the comprehensive character of the handbook itself makes it clear that simply creating that new office will not solve anything. Even making a realistic *beginning* toward gaining control of illegal drugs will also require the prompt development of a truly national strategy, the full cooperation and co-ordination of the numerous departments and agencies of government at all levels that have antidrug responsibilities, and, by no means least of all, the full support of a president determined to make that strategy work.

In the end, however, this *Handbook of Drug Control in the United States* obliges us to recognize that the single most effective resource we have in our national struggle to overcome the scourge of illegal drugs and the crime they spawn—the one absolutely irreplaceable ingredient in any remotely effective response to this moral national challenge—is the will of the American people, their own determination that their children and their children's children shall not inherit this problem from our hands. Drug abuse cannot continue to grow and the drug traffickers cannot continue to fatten upon our substance as a nation in a moral environment that militantly and massively opposes them.

I believe that moral impulse already beats strongly in the hearts of the vast majority of Americans, needing only to be brought to a focus by effective moral leadership, in the office of the director of national drug control policy and throughout our institutions of public and private life, and to be given the kind of realistic leverage on the problem offered by this invaluable handbook.

Joseph R. Biden, Jr.

Preface

American drug policy has a relatively long history, spanning the better part of the twentieth century. Drug control efforts, furthermore, have been the result not of one single policy approach, but rather of an outgrowth of numerous competing and often conflicting perspectives on the "drug problem."

It is generally believed that drug use in the United States was widespread throughout the latter part of the nineteenth century, primarily the result of lack of control over the use of opium, morphine, heroin, and cocaine in over-the-counter medications. By the early 1900s, however, the steady progress of medical science provided physicians with a better understanding of these drugs. One result was the passage of the Pure Food and Drug Act in 1906. Another was the Harrison Anti-Narcotics Act in 1914. Collectively, these served to place controls over the manufacture, sale, and distribution of a variety of substances.

During this same period of history, representatives of law enforcement and the courts in major urban areas began noticing an increasing number of narcotics and cocaine users within criminal justice populations. In response, researchers in the fields of medicine, law, and the social sciences began to examine the sequential patterns of drug use and crime, attempting to answer these questions: Is crime the result of, or perhaps some response to, a special set of life circumstances brought about by addiction to narcotics? Conversely, is addiction per se some deviant tendency characteristic of individuals already prone to criminal activity?

The findings that emerged from these research inquiries led to a series of inconstant perspectives. Some researchers found that the criminal histories of their sampled cases preceded any evidence of drug use. They concluded that the narcotics user was indeed a criminal. Other research found the temporal sequence of the initiation of drug use and crime in a reverse direction. Still a third research segment found that portions of their samples had been criminals first, with the remainder having been drug users first.

As perhaps a logical and natural consequence of these findings, various levels of interpretation of the data began to appear in professional and popular literature. Many commentators and analysts spoke of a *criminal model of drug abuse*, in which they suggested that addicts ought to be the objects of vigorous police activity because the vast majority were members of the "dangerous and criminal classes." Drug use was but a later phase in their already developed careers in crime. By contrast, there were those who argued for a *medical model of drug abuse*. Addiction, they contended, was a chronic and relapsing disease, and the addict, they continued, should be dealt with as any patient suffering from some physical or psychological disorder. Although the medical model resulted in a few government-sponsored treatment programs, throughout the first half of the twentieth century the criminal model predominated. As such, American drug policy followed the classic deterrence model: Through legislation and criminal penalties, it was expected that individuals would be discouraged from using drugs; by making an example of traffickers, it was expected that potential drug dealers would seek out other, and hopefully lawful, economic pursuits.

When drug use appeared to be declining during the depression years of the 1930s and the war years of the 1940s, it was believed that the model was working. When drug use began to expand in the inner cities during the economic boom of the 1950s and in the middle class during the social revolution of the 1960s, it was felt that although the deterrence model was basically sound, it had to be strengthened and augmented. During those years the current demand- and supply-reduction strategies became more articulated aspects of American drug control policy.

Demand reduction essentially involves treatment for the user, education and prevention for the would-be user, and research to determine how to best develop and implement plans for treatment, education, and prevention. *Supply reduction* involves federal interdiction and foreign assistance initiatives, aimed at intercepting drugs before they reach U.S. shores or eradicating them at their sources. Supply- and demand-reduction strategies, of course, are not mutually exclusive for they tend to overlap in numerous areas. State and local law enforcement efforts designed to capture criminally involved addicts and user-dealers, for example, often result in coercion into treatment in lieu of or in addition to incarceration. As such, both supply- and demand-reduction goals were approached.

Whereas the 1950s and 1960s witnessed increased drug use and expanded supply- and demand-reduction efforts, the 1970s and 1980s experienced increasingly widespread and diverse drug use, combined with a number of "wars" on drugs. There was President Richard M. Nixon's war on drugs, precipitated by the heroin epidemics of the late 1960s and early 1970s, combined with concerns over the widespread use of methaqualone, amphetamines, and PCP. There was President Ronald Reagan's war on drugs, spirited by the cocaine epidemic of the late 1970s and the 1980s, combined with the crack epidemic following the drug's popularity during the late 1980s. And most currently there is President

George Bush's war on drugs, motivated by the continued use of crack and the high levels of violence that have come to be a significant part of black-market drug distribution.

In presenting a reference volume on drug control in the United States, it would be difficult to present any single coherent statement encompassing the nature, thrust, and content of policy initiatives. Policy efforts have a history, as do drug use patterns and epidemics. Similarly, drug abuse treatment and prevention strategies evolved within a historical context of changing social conditions and priorities. Moreover, research into the nature of the drugs/crime connection, the effectiveness of treatment, the appropriateness of drug testing, and other intervention efforts all occurred against a backdrop of shifting political and economic concerns. As such, this volume is both historical and contemporary in scope.

The "Introduction" and Part I of this *Handbook of Drug Control in the United States* are composed of four chapters intended to provide the reader with a sense of the history of the drug problem in the United States, the roots of the current policy effort, and the emergence of drug abuse treatment as a mechanism of demand reduction, followed by focused examination of what is known about the links between drug use and crime. Part II offers detailed accounts of contemporary efforts at supply and demand reduction—prevention, intervention, treatment, and international assistance initiatives. Part III targets problematic sectors and controversies in contemporary drug control efforts—foreign policy implications, drug testing, the AIDS/intravenous drug use connection, and the legalization of drugs. The appendices offer background on drug scheduling, drug paraphernalia laws, and extradition, plus a summary of the National Drug Control Strategy released by the White House in March 1990. And, finally, the volume closes with exhaustive name and subject indexes, compiled to enhance the reference nature of this volume.

James A. Inciardi

Handbook of Drug Control
in the
United States

Introduction: The Evolution of Drug Abuse in America

James A. Inciardi

The drug problem as it is understood here in the 1990s has a relatively short history. Although marijuana, opium, the coca leaf, and other organic substances with psychoactive properties have been known for thousands of years, their use on a large scale for the enhancement of pleasure and performance spans less than two centuries. The abuse of drugs as such can be traced to a number of factors—advances in chemistry and medicine, the discovery of new intoxicants, and a variety of social and political changes—all of which combined to make drugs readily available for the relief of many ills, both physical and psychological.

OPIUM AND ITS DERIVATIVES

The specific beginnings of drug abuse in the United States are probably buried in antiquity, but in great part were tied to the introduction of over-the-counter patent medicines during the early 1700s. Opium was a common ingredient in these preparations, and by the close of that century medications containing the narcotic were readily available throughout urban and rural America. They were sold in pharmacies, in grocery and general stores, at traveling medicine shows, and through the mail—marketed under such labels as *Ayer's Cherry Pectoral, Mrs. Winslow's Soothing Syrup, McMunn's Elixer, Godfrey's Cordial, Scott's Emulsion,* and *Dover's Powder.* Many of these remedies were seductively advertised as "painkillers," "cough mixtures," "soothing syrups," "consumption cures," and "women's friends." Others were promoted for the treatment of such varied ailments as diarrhea, dysentery, colds, fever, teething, cholera, rheumatism, pelvic disorders, athlete's foot, and even baldness and cancer.[1]

The medical profession also fostered the use of opium. Dr. William Buchan's *Domestic Medicine,* for example, first published in Philadelphia in 1784 as a practical handbook on simple medicines for home use, recommended tincture of opium for the treatment of numerous common ailments, to be prepared as follows:

Take of crude opium, two ounces; spirituous aromatic water, and mountain wine, of each ten ounces. Dissolve the opium, sliced, in the wine, with a gentle heat, frequently stirring it; afterward add the spirit, and strain off the tincture.[2]

Yet the mere appearance of patent medicines in America was only minimally related to the evolution of drug-taking; other more potent social forces had been of considerably greater significance. Remedies were initially shipped to the colonies from London, as were most of the medications of the period. They were available from physicians, or over the counter from apothecaries, grocers, postmasters, and printers, but only in modest quantities. When trade with England was disrupted during the Revolutionary War, a patent medicine industry emerged in the United States. Expansions in the industry were related to the growth of the American press. The manufacturers of the "medicines" were the first business entrepreneurs to seek national markets through widespread advertising. They were the first hucksters to use psychological lures to entice customers to buy their merchandise. They were the first manufacturers to help the local merchants who retailed their wares by going directly to consumers with a message about their products. In total national advertising, this segment of the drug industry ranked highest in expenditures. During the post–Civil War decades, some individual proprietors spent in excess of $500,000 each year for advertising. As to the number of different varieties of patent medicines available, an 1804 New York catalog listed some ninety brands of elixers, a 1857 Boston periodical included almost 600, in 1858 one newspaper account totaled over 1,500 patent medicines, and by 1905 the list had stretched to more than 28,000.[3]

While for the longest time opium had been the only known product of the Oriental poppy, in 1803 a young German pharmacist, Frederick Serturner, isolated the chief alkaloid of opium.[4] Serturner had hit upon morphine, which he so named after Morpheus, the Greek god of dreams. The discovery was to have profound effects on both medicine and society for morphine was, and still is, the greatest single pain reliever the world has ever known. Then the hypodermic syringe was invented, and the use of morphine by injection in military medicine during the Civil War and the Franco-Prussian War granted the procedure legitimacy and familiarity to both physicians and the public.[5] Furthermore, hypodermic medication had its pragmatic aspects—it brought quick local relief, its dosage could be regulated, and it was effective when oral medication was impractical. The regimen, however, was used promiscuously for many physicians were anxious to illustrate their ability to quell the pain suffered by their patients, who, in turn, expected instant relief from discomfort.

The use of morphine by needle had become so pervasive by the 1890s that technology soon responded with the production of inexpensive equipment for mass use. In the 1897 edition of the Sears Roebuck catalog, for example, hypodermic kits, which included a syringe, two needles, two vials, and a carrying case, were advertised for $1.50, with extra needles available at 25¢ each or $2.75 per dozen.[6]

As to the full volume of opium and morphine actually consumed during the nineteenth century, the picture is not altogether clear. Estimates as to the number of individuals actually addicted to opium during the latter part of the nineteenth century tended to be compiled rather loosely, ranging as high as 3 million.[7] Yet other, more rigorously collected data for the period did indicate that the use of narcotic drugs was indeed pervasive. In 1888, for example, one examination of 10,000 prescriptions from Boston-area pharmacies found that some 15 percent contained opiates,[8] and that was only in Boston. In 1900 it was estimated that in the small state of Vermont 3.3 million doses of opium were sold each month.[9]

COCAINE

Beyond opium and morphine, the patent medicine industry branched even further. Although chewing coca leaves for their mild stimulant effects had been a part of the Andean cultures of South America for perhaps a thousand years, for some obscure reason the practice had never become popular in either Europe or the United States. Moreover, the full potency of the coca leaf remained unknown until 1860 when cocaine was first isolated in its pure form. Yet little use was made of the new alkaloid until 1883 when Dr. Theodor Aschenbrandt secured a supply of the drug and issued it to Bavarian soldiers during maneuvers. Aschenbrandt, a German military physician, noted the beneficial effects of cocaine, particularly its ability to suppress fatigue.

Among those who read Aschenbrandt's account with fascination was a struggling young Viennese neurologist, Sigmund Freud. Suffering from chronic fatigue, depression, and various neurotic symptoms, Freud obtained a measure of cocaine and tried it himself. He also offered it to a colleague who was suffering from both a disease of the nervous system and morphine addiction and to a patient with a chronic and painful gastric disorder. Finding the initial results to be quite favorable in all three cases, Freud decided that cocaine was a "magical drug." In a letter to his fiancee, Martha Bernays, in 1884, Freud commented on his experiences with cocaine:

If all goes well I will write an essay on it and I expect it will win its place in therapeutics by the side of morphine and superior to it. I have other hopes and intentions about it. I take very small doses of it regularly against depression and against indigestion, and with the most brilliant success. . . . In short it is only now that I feel that I am a doctor, since I have helped one patient and hope to help more.[10]

Freud then pressed the drug on his friends and colleagues, urging that they use it both for themselves and for their patients; he gave it to his sisters and his fiancee and continued to use it himself. By the close of the 1880s, however,

Freud and the others who had praised cocaine as an all-purpose wonder drug began to withdraw their support for it in light of an increasing number of reports of compulsive use and undesirable side effects. Yet by 1890 the patent medicine industry in the United States had also discovered the benefits of the unregulated use of cocaine. The industry quickly added the drug to its reservoir of home remedies, touting it as helpful not only for everything from alcoholism to venereal disease, but also as a cure for addiction to other patent medicines. Since the new tonics contained substantial amounts of cocaine, they did indeed make users feel better, at least initially, thus spiriting the patent medicine industry into its golden age of popularity.

HEROIN

Research into the mysteries of opium during the nineteenth century led not only to Serturner's discovery of morphine in 1806, but also to the discovery of more than two dozen other alkaloids, including codeine in 1831. Yet more importantly, in an 1874 issue of the *Journal of the Chemical Society*, British chemist C.R.A. Wright described a series of experiments he had carried out to determine the effect of combining various acids with morphine. Wright produced a series of new morphinelike compounds, including what became known in the scientific literature as diacetylmorphine.[11]

Wright's work, however, went for the most part unnoticed. Some twenty-four years later though, in 1898, pharmacologist Heinrich Dreser reported on a series of experiments he had conducted with diacetylmorphine for Friedrich Bayer and Company of Elberfeld, Germany, noting that the drug was highly effective in the treatment of coughs, chest pains, and the discomforts associated with pneumonia and tuberculosis.[12] Dreser's commentary received immediate notice for it had come at a time when antibiotics were still unknown, and pneumonia and tuberculosis were among the leading causes of death. He claimed that diacetylmorphine had a stronger sedative effect on respiration than either morphine or codeine did, that therapeutic relief came quickly, and that the potential for a fatal overdose was almost nil. In response to such favorable reports, Bayer and Company began marketing diacetylmorphine under the trade name of Heroin— so named from the German *heroisch*, meaning heroic and powerful.

Although Bayer's Heroin was promoted as a sedative for coughs and as a chest and lung medicine, it was advocated by some as a treatment for morphine addiction. This situation seems to have arisen from three somewhat-related phenomena. The first was the belief that Heroin was nonaddicting. As one physician wrote in the *New York Medical Journal* in 1900:

Habituation [with Heroin] has been noted in a small percentage of the cases. All observers are agreed, however, that none of the patients suffer in any way from this habituation, and that none of the symptoms which are so characteristic of chronic morphinism have ever been observed. On the other hand, a large number of the reports refer to the fact that the same dose may be used for a long time without any habituation.[13]

Second, since the drug had a greater potency than that of morphine, only small dosages were required for the desired medical effects, thus reducing the potential for the rapid onset of addiction. And third, at the turn of the twentieth century, the medical community did not fully understand the dynamics of cross dependence. Cross dependence refers to the phenomenon that among certain pharmacologically related drugs, physical dependence on one will carry over to all the others. As such, for the patient suffering from the unpleasant effects of morphine withdrawal, the administration of Heroin would have the consequence of one or more doses of morphine. The dependence was maintained and withdrawal disappeared, the two combining to give the appearance of a cure.

Given the endorsement of the medical community, with little mention of its potential dangers, Heroin quickly found its way into routine medical therapeutics and over-the-counter patent medicines.

EARLY DRUG CONTROL MEASURES

By the early years of the twentieth century, the steady progress of medical science had provided physicians with a better understanding of the long-term effects of the drugs they had been advocating. Sigmund Freud had already recognized his poor judgment in the claims he had made about cocaine, the addiction potential and abuse liability of morphine had been well established, and the dependence-producing properties of Bayer's Heroin were being noticed. Yet these drugs—cocaine, morphine, and heroin—often combined with alcohol, were still readily available from a totally unregulated patent medicine industry. Not only were they unregulated, but many were highly potent as well. *Birney's Catarrah Cure*, for example, was 4 percent cocaine. *Colonel Hoestetter's Bitters* had such a generous amount of C_2H_5OH (alcohol) in its formula "to preserve the medicine" that the fumes from just one tablespoonful fed through a gas burner could maintain a bright flame for almost five minutes.

In 1906 the Pure Food and Drug Act was passed, prohibiting the interstate transportation of adulterated or misbranded food and drugs. The act brought about the decline of the patent medicine industry because henceforth the proportions of alcohol, opium, morphine, heroin, cocaine, and a number of other substances in each preparation had to be indicated. Thus, because of the medical profession's emphasis on the negative effects of these ingredients, a number of the remedies lost their appeal. Moreover, it suddenly became difficult to market as a cure for morphine addiction a preparation that contained one or more other addicting drugs.

The new legislation merely imposed standards for quality, packaging, and labeling; it did not actually outlaw the use of cocaine and opiate drugs. The Harrison Act, sponsored by New York Representative Francis Burton Harrison and passed in 1914, ultimately served in that behalf and at the same time altered the nature of drug use in the United States once and for all.

The Harrison Act required all people who imported, manufactured, produced, compounded, sold, dispensed, or otherwise distributed cocaine and opiate drugs to register with the Treasury Department, pay special taxes, and keep records of all transactions. As such, it was a revenue code designed to exercise some measure of public control over drugs, rather than to penalize the estimated 200,000 users of narcotics in the United States. In effect, however, penalization is specifically what occurred.

Certain provisions of the Harrison Act permitted physicians to prescribe, dispense, or administer narcotics to their patients for "legitimate medical purposes" and "in the course of professional practice." But how these two phrases were interpreted by the courts ultimately defined narcotics use as a crime.

Many commentators on the history of drug use in the United States have argued that the Harrison Act snatched addicts from legitimate society and forced them into the underworld. But such a cause-and-effect interpretation tends to be an oversimplification. Without question, at the beginning of the twentieth century, most users of narcotics were members of legitimate society. In fact, the vast majority had first encountered the effects of narcotics through their family physician or local pharmacist or grocer. In other words, their addiction had been medically induced during the course of treatment for some other perceived ailment.

Yet long before the Harrison Act had been passed, there were indications that this population of users had begun to shrink.[14] Agitation had existed in both the medical and the religious communities against the haphazard use of narcotics, defining much of it as a moral disease. For many, the sheer force of social stigma and pressure served to alter their use of drugs. Similarly, the decline of the patent medicine industry after the passage of the Pure Food and Drug Act was believed to have substantially reduced the number of narcotics and cocaine users. Moreover, by 1912 most state governments had enacted legislative controls over the dispensing and selling of narcotics. Thus, it is plausible to assert that the size of the drug-using population had started to decline years before the Harrison Act had become the subject of court interpretation.

Then, too, the combined effects of stigma, social pressure, the Pure Food and Drug Act, and state controls had also served to create an underworld of drug users and black-market drugs. By 1914 a number of commentators had noted this change. Some, however melodramatically, targeted the subterranean economy of narcotics use:

Several individuals have come to the conclusion that selling "dope" is a very profitable business. These individuals have sent their agents among the gangs frequenting our city corners, instructing them to make friends with the members and induce them to take the drug. Janitors, bartenders, and cabmen have also been employed to help sell the habit. The plan has worked so well that there is scarcely a poolroom in New York that may not be called a meeting place for dope fiends. The drug has been made up in candy and sold to school children. The conspiring individuals, being familiar with the habit-forming action of the drugs, believe that the increased number of "fiends" will create a larger demand for the drug, and in this way build up profitable business.[15]

During the latter part of the decade other observers were noting that although the medically induced addict was still prominent, a new population had recently emerged.[16] It was an underworld population, composed principally of heroin and cocaine users who had initiated drug use as the result of associations with other criminals. Thus, it would appear that the emergence of the criminal addict was not simply the result of a cause-and-effect criminalization process—the Harrison Act's definition of narcotics use as criminal. Rather, it was probably the result of the effects of legislation combined with the creation of a new class of users who were already within the underworld.

Although accurate data on the incidence and prevalence of drug use have been available only recently, by the early 1920s readers of the popular media were confronted, almost on a daily basis, with how drug use, and particularly heroin use, had become a national epidemic. Estimates were placed as high as 5 million, with any number of explanations for the increased number of users. Some blamed it on the greed of drug traffickers, others on the inadequate personalities of the users. A few even argued that it was a natural consequence of the Prohibition amendment.[17]

MARIJUANA

By the 1930s the national concern over the use of drugs was not focused solely on heroin for another substance was considered by some to represent an even greater evil. One might expect that it was cocaine since the drug's stimulant effects had been promoted in the United States well before the introduction of Bayer's Heroin. But this was not the case. The new drug was marijuana, alternatively called the "devil drug," the "assassin of youth," and the "weed of madness."

Marijuana, typically referred to a century ago as cannabis or hashish, was introduced to the American public in essentially the same manner that opium, morphine, cocaine, and heroin were. A derivative of the Indian hemp plant *Cannabis sativa*, the drug appeared among the patent medicines hawked from the tailgates of medicine show wagons and was sold as a cure for depression, convulsions, hysteria, insanity, mental retardation, and impotence. Moreover, during the late 1800s such well-known pharmaceutical companies as Parke-Davis and Squibb produced tincture of cannabis for the family pharmacist to dispense. As a medicinal agent, however, the drug quickly fell into disfavor. Because of its insolubility, it could not be injected, and taken orally, it was slow and generally ineffective. Moreover, its potency was variable, making dosage standardization difficult. Yet as a recreational drug, marijuana had its devotees. By the middle of the 1880s every major American city had its clandestine hashish clubs, catering to a rather well-to-do clientele.[18]

At the beginning of the twentieth century what was referred to in Mexico as marijuana (also marihuana and mariguana) began to appear in New Orleans and a number of the Texas border towns. Having been used in South America and

Central America for quite some time, it was a substance less potent than the hashish that was first smoked in the underground clubs decades earlier. Whereas hashish is the resinous extract of the hemp plant, marijuana is composed of the plant's dried leaves, stems, and flowering tops.

By 1920 the use of marijuana had become visible among members of minority groups—blacks in the South and "wetback" Mexicans in the Southwest. Given the social and political climate of the period, it is not at all surprising that the use of the drug became a matter of immediate concern. The agitation for reform that had resulted in the passage of the Harrison Act and the Pure Food and Drug Act was still active, and the movement for national prohibition of alcohol was at its peak. Moreover, not only was marijuana viewed by many as an "intoxicant of blacks and wetbacks" that might have a corrupting influence on white society, but also it was considered particularly dangerous because of its *alien* (spelled "Mexican") and un-American origins.

Through the early 1930s state after state enacted antimarijuana laws, usually instigated by lurid newspaper articles depicting the madness and horror attributed to the drug's use. Even the prestigious *New York Times*, with its claim of "All the News That's Fit to Print," helped to reinforce the growing body of beliefs surrounding marijuana use. In an article headlined "Mexican Family Goes Insane," and datelined Mexico City, July 6, 1927, the *New York Times* reported:

A widow and her four children have been driven insane by eating the Marijuana plant, according to doctors, who say that there is no hope of saving the children's lives and that the mother will be insane for the rest of her life.

The mother was without money to buy other food for the children, whose ages range from 3 to 15, so they gathered some herbs and vegetables growing in the yard for their dinner. Two hours after the mother and children had eaten the plants, they were stricken. Neighbors, hearing outbursts of crazed laughter, rushed to the house to find the entire family insane.

Examination revealed that the narcotic marijuana was growing among the garden vegetables.[19]

A crusade against marijuana ensued, culminating on August 2, 1937 with the passage of the Marijuana Tax Act—a piece of legislation that classified the scraggly tramp of the vegetable world as a narcotic and placed it under essentially the same controls as the Harrison Act had placed on opium and coca products.

THE POSTWAR HEROIN EPIDEMIC

The crusade against marijuana during the 1930s had attributed to drug-taking a level of wickedness that could only have been matched by the Victorian imagery of masturbation and its consequences. The 1940s all but ignored the drug problem, principally because if it was indeed a problem, it was an invisible one— hardly a topic that should divert attention away from the events of a world at war. Then came the 1950s, a time when the prevailing image of drug use was one of heroin addiction on the streets of the urban ghetto. As summarized by the distinguished author and journalist Max Lerner in his celebrated work *America as a Civilization*:

As a case in point we may take the known fact of the prevalence of reefer-and-dope addiction in Negro areas. This is essentially explained in terms of poverty, slum living, and broken families, yet it would be easy to show the lack of drug addiction among other ethnic groups where the same conditions apply.[20]

Lerner went on to explain that addiction among blacks was due to the adjustment problems associated with their rapid movement from a depressed status to the improved standards and freedoms of the era. Yet Lerner's interpretation was hardly a correct one, and not only about "reefer addiction," but also about the prevalence of drug abuse in other populations—rich and poor, white and black, young and old.

In the popular media a somewhat more detailed (and distorted) portrait of the problem was offered. *Time*, *Life*, *Newsweek*, and other major periodicals spoke of how teenagers, jaded on marijuana, had found greater thrills in heroin. For most, the pattern of initiation had been the same. They began with marijuana, the use of which had become a fad in the ghetto. Then, enticed in schoolyards by brazen Mafia pushers dressed in dark suits, white ties, and wide-brimmed hats, their first dose of heroin was given free. By then, however, it was too late; their fate had been sealed; they were already addicted.[21] Or as the saying went, "It's so good, don't even try it once!"

Hollywood offered a somewhat different image of the situation in the 1955 United Artists release of *The Man with the Golden Arm*. The film was somewhat controversial in its day for the Otto Preminger production had touched on a topic that most Americans felt should remain in the ghetto where it belonged. Cast in the role of a would-be professional musician, singer-actor Frank Sinatra was the hero of the story. Plagued by the evils of heroin addiction, he was unable to get his life together. Finally, however, through the help and understanding of his girlfriend Molly (portrayed by Kim Novak), he was saved from a life of pathetic degradation. As in the case of other media images of the drug scene, *The Man with the Golden Arm* offered only a contorted view, failing to probe even the most basic issues.

Within the scientific community, segments of the literature and research were equally curious. As might be expected, most explanations of drug addiction focused on heroin in the ghetto. Young addicts were believed to be either psychotic or neurotic casualties for whom drugs provided relief from anxiety and a means for withdrawing from the stress of daily struggle in the slums. Among the more celebrated studies of the period was psychologist Isidor Chein's *The Road to H*. Concerning youthful addiction in New York City, Chein concluded

The evidence indicated that all addicts suffer from deep-rooted personality disorders. Although psychiatric diagnoses are apt to vary, a particular set of symptoms seems to be common to most juvenile addicts. They are not able to enter into prolonged, close, friendly relations with either peers or adults; they have difficulties in assuming a masculine role; they are frequently overcome by a sense of futility, expectations of failure, and general depression; they are easily frustrated and made anxious, and they find frustrations and anxiety intolerable.[22]

By focusing on such maladies as "weak ego functioning," "defective superego," and "inadequate masculine identification," Chein suggested a psychological predisposition to drug use—in other words, an addiction-prone personality. The text went on to imply that the series of predispositions could be traced to the addict's family experiences. If the youth received too much love or not enough, or if the parents were overwhelming in terms of their affection or indulgence, then the child would develop inadequately. As a result, the youth would probably be unable to withstand pain and discomfort, to cope with the complexities of life in the neighborhood and community, to assess reality correctly, and to feel competent around others of more varied social experiences. Chein concluded that this type of youth would be more prone to trying drugs than others from more conventional family backgrounds would be.

The prevailing portrait of addiction in the scientific community, then, was one of passive adaptation to stress. Drugs allowed the user to experience fulfillment and the satiation of physical and emotional needs. And this general view became the basis of the drug abuse treatment philosophies that were emerging during this period and of the numerous treatment programs that were being established to treat the nation's addicts.

LSD

The 1960s was a time characterized by civil rights movements, political assassinations, campus and antiwar protests, and ghetto riots. Among the more startling events of the decade was the drug revolution. The use of drugs seemed to have leapt from the more marginal zones of society to the very mainstream of community life. No longer were drugs limited to the inner cities and the half-worlds of the jazz scene and the underground bohemian protocultures. Rather, their use had become suddenly and dramatically apparent among members of the adolescent and young adult populations of rural and urban middle-class America. By the close of the decade commentators on the era were maintaining that ours was "the addicted society," that through drugs millions had become "seekers" of "instant enlightenment," and that drug-taking and drug-seeking would persist as continuing facts of American social life.[23]

In retrospect, what were then considered the logical causes of the new drug phenomenon now seem less clear. A variety of changes in the fabric of American life had occurred during those years, which undoubtedly had profound implications for social consciousness and behavior. Notably, the revolution in the technology and handling of drugs that had begun during the 1950s was of sufficient magnitude to justify the designation of the 1960s as "a new chemical age." Recently compounded psychotropic agents were enthusiastically introduced and effectively promoted, with the consequence of exposing the national consciousness to an impressive catalog of chemical temptations—sedatives, tranquilizers, stimulants, antidepressants, analgesics, and hallucinogens—which could offer fresh inspiration, as well as simple and immediate relief from fear, anxiety, tension, frustration, and boredom.[24]

Concomitant with this emergence of a new chemical age, a new youth ethos had become manifest, one characterized by a widely celebrated generational disaffection, a prejudicial dependence on the self and the peer group for value orientation, a critical view of how the world was being run, and a mistrust of an "establishment" drug policy the "facts" and "warnings" of which ran counter to reported peer experiences.

Whatever the ultimate causes of the drug revolution of the sixties might have been, America's younger generations, or at least noticeable segments of them, had embraced drugs. The drug scene had become the arena of "happening" America; "turning on" to drugs to relax and to share friendship and love seemed to have become commonplace. And the prophet—the "high priest" as he called himself—of the new chemical age was a psychology instructor at Harvard University's Center for Research in Human Personality, Dr. Timothy Leary.

The saga of Timothy Leary had its roots not at Harvard in the 1960s, but in Basel, Switzerland, just before the beginning of World War II. It was there, in 1938, that Dr. Albert Hoffman of Sandoz Research Laboratories first isolated a new chemical compound which he called D-lysergic acid diethylamide. Known now as LSD, it was cast aside in his laboratory where, for five years, it remained unappreciated, its properties awaiting discovery. On April 16, 1943, after absorbing some LSD through the skin of his fingers, Hoffman began to hallucinate. In his diary he explained the effect:

With closed eyes, multihued, metamorphizing, fantastic images overwhelmed me.... Sounds were transposed into visual sensations so that from each tone or noise a comparable colored picture was evoked, changing in form and color kaleidoscopically.[25]

Hoffman had experienced the first LSD "trip."

Dr. Humphrey Osmond of the New Jersey Neuropsychiatric Institute neologized a new name for LSD. He called it "psychedelic," meaning mind-expanding. But outside of the scientific community, LSD was generally unknown— even at the start of the 1960s. This was quickly changed by Leary and his colleague at Harvard, Dr. Richard Alpert. They began experimenting with the drug—on themselves and with colleagues, students, artists, writers, clergymen, and volunteer prisoners. Although their adventures with LSD had earned them dismissals from Harvard by 1963, their message had been heard, and LSD had achieved its reputation. Their messages had been numerous and shocking to the political establishment and to hundreds of thousands of mothers and fathers across the nation.

In *The Realist*, a radical periodical of the 1960s, Leary commented:

I predict that psychedelic drugs will be used in all schools in the near future as educational devices—not only marijuana and LSD, to teach kids how to use their sense organs and other cellular equipment effectively—but new and more powerful psychochemicals. . . . [26]

Elsewhere he wrote of the greatest fear that might be generated by psychedelic drug use—what he called "ontological addiction":

. . . the terror of finding a realm of experience, a new dimension of reality so pleasant that one will not want to return. This fear is based on the unconscious hunch . . . that normal consciousness is a form of sleepwalking and that somewhere there exists a form of awakeness, of reality from which one would not want to return. [27]

And then, perhaps most frightening of all to the older generation, were Leary's comments to some 15,000 cheering San Francisco youths on the afternoon of March 26, 1967. As a modern-day Pied Piper, Leary told his audience

Turn on to the scene, *tune in* to what's happening; and *drop out*—of high school, college, grade school . . . follow me, the hard way. [28]

The hysteria over Leary, LSD, and the other psychedelic substances had been threefold. First, the drug scene was especially frightening to mainstream society because it reflected a willful rejection of rationality, order, and predictability. Second, there was the stigmatized association of drug use with antiwar protests and antiestablishment, long-haired, unwashed, radical "hippie" LSD users. And, third, there were the drug's psychic effects, the reported "bad trips" that seemed to border on mental illness. Particularly in the case of LSD, the rumors of how it could "blow one's mind" became legion. One story told of a youth, high on the drug, who took a swan dive in front of a truck moving at 70 mph. Another spoke of two "tripping" teenagers who stared directly into the sun until they were permanently blinded. A third described how LSD's effects on the chromosomes resulted in fetal abnormalities. The stories were never documented and were probably untrue. What *were* true, however, were the reports of LSD "flashbacks." Occurring with only a small percentage of the users, individuals would re-experience the LSD-induced state days, weeks, and sometimes months after the original "trip," without having taken the drug again.

Despite the lurid reports, as it turned out, LSD was not in fact widely used on a regular basis beyond a few social groups that were fully dedicated to drug experiences. In fact, the psychedelic substances had quickly earned reputations as being dangerous and unpredictable, and most people avoided them. By the close of the 1960s, all hallucinogenic drugs had been placed under strict legal control, and the number of users was minimal.[29]

AMPHETAMINES

Throughout the 1960s heroin remained the most feared drug, and by the close of the decade estimates as to the size of the addict population exceeded 500,000. Yet despite the hysteria about the rising tide of heroin addiction, LSD and the youth rebellion, Timothy Leary and the psychedelic age, and the growing awareness of drug abuse along the Main Streets of white America, no one really knew how many people were actually using drugs. In fact, the estimates of the incidence and prevalence of marijuana, heroin, psychedelic, and other drug use were, at the very best, only vague and impressionistic. Although the reliability of political polling had long since demonstrated that the social sciences indeed had the tools to measure the dimensions of the ''drug problem,'' no one at any time throughout the 1960s had gone so far as to count drug users in a systematic way. Yet several indicators existed. Studies were suggesting that the annual production of barbiturate drugs exceeded 1 million pounds, the equivalent of twenty-four one-and-one-half-grain doses for every man, woman, and child in the nation—enough to kill each person twice.[30] And for amphetamines and amphetaminelike compounds, the manufacturing figures came to some fifty doses per U.S. resident each year, with half the production reaching the illicit marketplace.[31]

The amphetamines were not new drugs, but their appearance on the street had been relatively recent. Having been synthesized in Germany during the 1880s, their first use among Americans had not come until World War II. Thousands of servicemen in all of the military branches had been issued Benzedrine, Dexedrine, and a variety of other amphetamines as a matter of course to relieve their fatigue and anxiety. After the war, amphetamine drugs became more readily available, and they were put to a wider assortment of uses—for students cramming for exams, for truck drivers and others who needed to be alert for extended periods of time, in weight-control programs, and as nasal decongestants. Yet as strong stimulants with pharmacological effects similar to those of cocaine, in time they became popular drugs of abuse.

As the 1970s began, the amphetamines were the first item on the government's agenda for drug reform, with Indiana Senator Birch Bayh conducting hearings. There was a parade of witnesses, and the worst fears about the drugs were confirmed—or so it seemed.[32] Bayh and his committee heard the horror stories of the ''speed freaks'' who injected amphetamine and methamphetamine, who stalked the city streets suffering from paranoid delusions and exhibiting episodes of violent behavior at the onset of their psychotic states. They heard, too, of the hundreds, thousands, and perhaps hundreds of thousands of children and teenagers stoned on ''ups,'' ''bennies,'' ''pinks,'' ''purple hearts,'' ''black beauties,'' and ''King Kong pills.'' By that time, systematic surveys of the general population had finally begun, with the first, conducted in New York, empirically documenting that amphetamine use and abuse were indeed widespread.[33]

Almost immediately, new legislation was proposed by the Bayh committee and pushed through by the Senate. Tighter controls were placed on the prescription and distribution of amphetamines, and legitimate production was ultimately cut by 90 percent. In so doing, it was thought that the drug problem, at least in terms of the dangerous amphetamines, would be measurably solved. And meanwhile the heroin epidemic continued, and a new drug—methaqualone—made its entrance.

METHAQUALONE (QUAALUDE)

Methaqualone was initially synthesized in India during the early 1950s as a possible antimalarial agent. When its *hypnotic* (sleep-producing) properties were discovered later in the decade, many hoped that as a *nonbarbiturate* methaqualone might be a safer alternative to the barbiturates.[34]

Barbiturate drugs had been available for the better part of the century. As potent central nervous system depressants, they were the drugs of choice for inducing sleep. Depending on the dosage level, they were also in common use for anesthesia, sedation, and the treatment of tension, anxiety, and convulsions. However, the barbiturates had their problems. They were widely abused for the "high" they could engender. Moreover, they produced addiction after chronic use, were life threatening on withdrawal, and could cause fatal overdoses— particularly when mixed with alcohol.

As an alternative to barbiturates, methaqualone was introduced in England in 1959 and in Germany and Japan in 1960. Despite extensive medical reports of abuse in these three countries, the drug was introduced in the United States under the trade names of Quaalude, Sopor, Parest, Somnafac, and, later, Mequin. Although methaqualone was a prescription drug, the federal drug establishment decided that since there was no evidence of an abuse potential, it need not be monitored, and the number of times a prescription could be refilled need not be restricted. This, combined with an advertising campaign that emphasized that the drug was a "safe alternative to barbiturates," led to the assumption by the medical profession, the lay population, and the media that methaqualone was nonaddicting. Even the prestigious *AMA Drug Evaluations*, as late as 1973, stated no more than "long-term use of larger than therapeutic doses may result in psychic and physical dependence."[35]

The most effective advertising campaign was launched by William H. Rorer Pharmaceuticals. Given the success of the catchy double-a in their antacid Maalox, they named their methaqualone product Quaalude. Their advertising emphasized that it was a nonbarbiturate. Free samples of Quaalude were shipped throughout the country, and physicians began overprescribing the drug.

Looking for a new and safe "high," users sought out methaqualone, and the drug quickly made its way to the street. Rather than a safe alternative to whatever they had been taking previously, street users actually had a drug with the same addiction liability and lethal potential as the barbiturates. What they experienced were a pleasant sense of well-being, an increased pain threshold, and a loss of muscle coordination. The "high" was reputed to enhance sexual performance. Although no actual evidence confirmed that effect, it is likely that the depressant effects of the drug in men were serving to desensitize the nerve endings in the penis, thus permitting intercourse for longer periods without climaxing. Moreover, like alcohol, the drug was acting on the central cortex of the brain to release normal inhibitions. Also common was "luding out"—attaining an intoxicated state rapidly by mixing the drug with wine.

In early 1973, after reports of widespread abuse, acute reactions and fatal overdoses, Birch Bayh convened more Senate hearings, the problems with methaqualone were fully aired, and rigid controls over the drug were put into force.[36] Shortly thereafter the abuses of methaqualone began to decline.[37]

THE RETURN OF MARIJUANA

While legislators, clinicians, and drug educators struggled with the methaqualone problem, marijuana use grew apace. From 1960 through the end of the decade the number of Americans who had used marijuana at least once had increased from a few hundred thousand to an estimated 8 million. By the early 1970s marijuana use had increased geometrically throughout all strata of society.

Given such pervasive use of marijuana and arrests that were affecting the careers and lives of so many otherwise law-abiding citizens, legislation was introduced that reduced the penalties for the simple possession of the drug— first at the federal level and later by the states. In Alabama, judges were no longer required to impose the mandatory minimum sentence of five years for the possession of even one marijuana cigarette, Missouri statutes no longer included life sentences for second possession offenses, and in Georgia second-sale offenses to minors were no longer punishable by death.

Then there was the issue of decriminalization—the removal of criminal penalties for the possession of small amounts of marijuana for personal use. The movement toward decriminalization began in 1973 with Oregon, followed by Colorado, Alaska, Ohio, and California in 1975; Mississippi, North Carolina, and New York in 1977; and Nebraska in 1978. Given the fact that there were an estimated 50 million users of marijuana in the United States by the close of the 1970s, many hoped that decriminalization, and perhaps even the legalization of marijuana use, would become a national affair, but the "movement" suddenly stalled for a variety of reasons.[38] Principally, Congress had failed to pass legislation that would have decriminalized marijuana under federal statutes. The issue had not been salient enough throughout the nation as a whole to result in concerted action in favor of decriminalization. The lobbying on behalf of marijuana law reform had never demonstrated the power and influence necessary for repeal. Perhaps most important of all, marijuana had always been viewed as a drug favored by youth.

By the close of the 1970s and the onset of the 1980s, evidence indicated that marijuana use in the United States had actually declined. In 1975, surveys showed that some 30 million people were users.[39] By the early 1980s this figure had dropped to 20 million, with the most significant declines among people age twenty-five and under.[40] Perhaps the younger generation had begun to realize that although marijuana was not the "devil drug," "assassin of youth," or the "weed of madness," as it had been called earlier, it was not a totally innocuous substance either. Perhaps the change occurred because of the greater concern with health and physical fitness that became so much a part of American culture during the 1980s or as an outgrowth of the antismoking messages that appeared daily in the media. Whatever the reason, it was clear that youthful attitudes had changed. Over the period from 1975 through 1988, moreover, the proportion of seniors in American high schools who believed the regular use of marijuana to be harmful increased from 39 percent to almost 80 percent.[41]

Meanwhile, the heroin problem endured, and cocaine emerged as a new drug of choice.

PHENCYCLIDINE (PCP)

The propaganda campaigns that have periodically emerged to target specific drugs as the root causes of outbreaks of violent crime targeted PCP at various times as a "killer drug" that could change the user into a diabolical monster and a member of the "living dead."

PCP, or more formally phencyclidine, a central nervous system excitant agent having anesthetic, analgesic, and hallucinogenic properties, is not a particularly new drug. It was developed during the 1950s, and following studies on laboratory animals, it was recommended for clinical trials on humans in 1957.[42] Parke, Davis & Company marketed the drug under the trade name of Sernyl. Originally, phencyclidine was used as an anesthetic agent in surgical procedures. Although it was found to be generally effective, the drug often produced a number of unpleasant side effects—extreme excitement, visual disturbances, and delirium. As a result, in 1967 the use of phencyclidine was restricted to "veterinary use only." Under the trade name of Sernylan, it quickly became the most widely used animal tranquilizer.

The street use of PCP (also known as "horse tranquilizer," "elephant juice," "angel dust," "hog," "Tic," "supergrass," and "rocket fuel") occurred initially in the Haight-Ashbury underground community of San Francisco and other West Coast and East Coast cities during 1967. It was first marketed as the PeaCe Pill; hence, the name PCP quickly became popular.

Characteristic of the hallucinogenic drug marketplace has been the mislabeling and promotion of one substance as some other more desirable psychedelic, and for a time PCP occupied a conspicuous position as such a substitute. Samples of mescaline (the hallucinogenic alkaloid found in the peyote cactus) sold in Milwaukee, for example, were invariably PCP.[43] During the late 1960s and early 1970s, tetrahydrocannabinol (THC), the active ingredient in marijuana, was frequently sought after in its pure form as a prestige "fad" drug. Yet THC has *never* been sold on the street because in its isolated form it is so unstable a compound that it quickly loses its potency and effect. During 1970, analyses of "street drugs" from the greater Philadelphia area revealed that PCP was a common THC substitute.[44] In an experiment undertaken in 1971, samples of alleged LSD, THC, mescaline, and PCP were secured from street suppliers in the New York City's Greenwich Village. Laboratory analyses identified the THC and mescaline samples as PCP, and the PCP sample as LSD, with only the LSD sample having accurate labeling. In a second experiment carried out during early 1972 in Miami's Coconut Grove area, twenty-five individual samples of alleged THC were purchased from an equal number of street drug dealers. Under laboratory analysis twenty-two of the THC samples were found to be PCP, one was Darvon (a prescription painkiller), another was an oral contraceptive, and the last was a chocolate-covered peanut.[45] It was quickly learned that these apparent deceptions had been aimed at "plastic," or weekend, hippies and "heads"—those children of two cultures whose social schizophrenia placed them partially in the straight world and partially in the new underground, never fully being a part of either. In both the New York and Miami drug subcultures, however, and probably in most others, THC was simply accepted as another name for PCP, perhaps explaining why the latter drug was called "Tic" for more than a decade in many cities.

The stories describing PCP as a "killer drug" date to its first introduction to the street community. In 1969, for example, a New York City chief of detectives commented: "Let me tell you, this stuff is bad, real bad. One dose of it and we're talking about some serious *instant addiction*."[46]

Similarly, a number of news stories at approximately the same time described PCP as a synthetic drug so powerful that a person could become "high" simply by touching it—instantly absorbing it through the pores. [47] These early reports ran counter to both medical and street experiences,[48] and the drug quickly became relegated to the lengthening catalog of street substances that after their initial appearance received little public attention. Most of those using PCP during those early years were not found among the populations addicted to narcotic drugs. Rather, they were multiple-drug users manifesting patterns of long-term involvement with marijuana and/or hashish, combined with the experimental, social-recreational, or spree use of hallucinogens, sedatives, tranquilizers, and stimulants.

During 1978 the hysteria over PCP emerged once again, but this time in earnest. In one episode of the popular "60 Minutes" television series, CBS News commentator Mike Wallace described PCP as the nation's "number one" drug problem, reporting on bizarre incidents of brutal violence allegedly caused by the new "killer" drug. Shortly thereafter a *People* magazine article touted

PCP as America's most dangerous new drug—the "devil's dust."[49] In these and other reports, violence was always associated with PCP use, as well as the drug's propensity to destroy the user's mind hence to create new recruits to the growing army of the "living dead." During special hearings on August 8, 1978, a senator described PCP as "one of the most insidious drugs known to mankind," and a congressman declared that the drug was "a threat to the national security and that children were playing with death on the installment plan."[50]

Research during 1978 and 1979 quickly demonstrated that comments such as these may have been overstated. In 1978, when PCP was labeled by "60 Minutes" the number one drug problem, responsible for more emergency room admissions than any other drug, estimates from the Drug Abuse Warning Network found PCP to account for only 3 percent of all reported drug emergencies.[51] Furthermore, ethnographic studies of PCP users in Seattle, Miami, Philadelphia, and Chicago demonstrated that the characterizations of users' experiences were slanted and misleading.[52] The studies found something quite different than the monster drug that the media presented as some live enemy so overpowering users that they lost complete control of rationality and helplessly and inescapably moved directly to a psychotic episode, suicide, homicide, or state of suspended confusion, which only an indefinite confinement in a mental hospital would hopefully reverse. Users were typically aware that PCP was a potent drug, and except for the few who sought a heavily anesthetized state, most used it cautiously. They aimed to control its effects. Although some had adverse reactions to the drug, violence was rarely a factor. In fact, among the more than three hundred PCP users contacted during the studies, almost all were baffled by the connection of the drug with violent behavior. The only known episodes of violence occurred during "bad trips" when someone tried to restrain a user, and these were extremely unusual. Furthermore, the few who exhibited aggressive behavior typically had already developed a reputation for violence that was independent of PCP use. None of this should suggest, however, that PCP is a harmless drug. On the contrary, hallucinations, altered mood states, feelings of depersonalization, paranoia, suicidal impulses, and aggressive behavior have been reported, only not to the extent that some commentators have suggested.

In the 1980s it appeared that PCP use had begun to decline. Among national samples of high school seniors surveyed annually, the proportions having used PCP at least once dropped from 13 percent in 1979 to 5 percent in 1984 and to less than 1 percent by 1988.[53] There were indications that additional changes were occurring during the 1980s, changes that appeared to be quite dramatic. More and more reports were appearing in the mass media describing the bizarre behavior that PCP users were exhibiting. PCP-related deaths were increasing, particularly in Washington D.C., and Los Angeles, locales where PCP use seemed to be concentrated.[54] Moreover, the drug put so many of its users into Washington's Saint Elizabeth's Hospital in 1984 that with a grim irony PCP became known in that city as the "key to Saint E's."[55] Yet despite the renewed media attention, all systematic attempts to study the alleged relationship between

PCP use and violent behavior continued to conclude that only a very small minority of users committed bizarre acts while in a PCP-induced state.[56]

CRACK-COCAINE

As America moved through the 1980s, both heroin and cocaine use persisted, and a few new drugs emerged. One of these was "Ecstasy," a synthetic hallucinogen that was quickly outlawed.[57] Of greater concern, however, was the reportedly new drug called "crack"—referred to in the media as a cheap variety of street cocaine that could be smoked and was highly addictive.

Contrary to popular belief, crack is not a new substance, having been first reported in the literature during the early 1970s.[58] At that time, however, knowledge of crack, known then as "base" or "rock" (not to be confused with "rock cocaine"—a cocaine hydrochloride product for intranasal snorting), seemed to be restricted to segments of avid cocaine devotees. Crack is processed from cocaine hydrochloride by adding ammonia or baking soda and water and by heating it to remove the hydrochloride. The result is a pebble-sized crystalline form of cocaine base. And, interestingly, crack gets its name from the fact that the residue of sodium bicarbonate often causes a crackling sound when the substance is smoked.[59]

The rediscovery of crack during the early 1980s seemed to occur simultaneously on the East and West Coasts. As a result of the Colombian government's attempts to reduce the amount of illicit cocaine production within its borders, it apparently, at least for a time, successfully restricted the amount of ether available for transforming coca paste into cocaine hydrochloride. The result was the diversion of coca paste from Colombia, through Central America and the Caribbean, into south Florida for conversion into cocaine. Spillage from shipments through the Caribbean corridor acquainted local island populations with the smoking of coca paste (basuco),[60] which developed the forerunner of crack-cocaine in 1980.[61] Known as "baking-soda base," "base-rock," "gravel," and "roxanne," the prototype was a smokable product composed of coca paste, baking soda, water, and rum. Immigrants from Jamaica, Trinidad, the Leeward and Windward Islands introduced the crack prototype to Caribbean inner-city populations in Miami and New York, where it was ultimately produced from cocaine hydrochloride rather than coca paste. As a Miami-based immigrant from Barbados commented in 1986 about the diffusion of what he referred to as "baking-soda-paste":

Basuco and baking-soda paste seemed to come both at the same time. There was always a little cocaine here and there in the islands, but not too much, and it wasn't cheap. Then 'bout five, maybe six, years ago, the paste hit all of the islands. It seemed to happen overnight—Barbados, Saint Lucia, Dominica, and [Saint] Vincent and [Saint] Kitts—all at the same time.

. . . Then I guess someone started to experiment, and we got the rum-soda-paste concoction. We brought it to Miami when we came in '82, and we saw that the Haitians *too* were into the same combination.[62]

   Apparently at about the same time, a Los Angeles basement chemist redis-covered the rock variety of baking-soda cocaine, and it was initially referred to as "cocaine rock."[63] It was an immediate success, as was the East Coast type, and for a variety of reasons. First, it could be smoked rather than snorted. When cocaine is smoked, it is more rapidly absorbed and reportedly crosses the blood-brain barrier within six seconds—hence, an almost instantaneous high. Second, it was cheap. While a gram of cocaine for snorting may cost $60 or more depending on its purity, the same gram can be transformed into anywhere from five to thirty "rocks." For the user, this meant that individual "rocks" could be purchased for as little as $5, $10, or $20. For the seller, $60 worth of cocaine hydrochloride (purchased wholesale for $30) could generate as much as $150 when sold as rocks. Third, it was easily hidden and transportable, and when hawked in small glass vials, it could be readily scrutinized by potential buyers.

   By the close of 1985 crack had come to the attention of the media and was predicted to be the "wave of the future" among substance abusers,[64] and by mid-1986 national headlines were calling crack a glorified version of cocaine and the major street drug of abuse in the United States.[65] And, too, there was the belief that crack was responsible for rising rates of street crime. As a cover story in *USA Today* put it:

Addicts spend thousands of dollars on binges, smoking the contents of vial after vial in crack or "base" houses—modern-day opium dens—for days at a time without food or sleep. They will do anything to repeat the high, including robbing their families and friends, selling their possessions and bodies.[66]

   As the media blitzed the American people with lurid stories depicting the hazards of crack, Congress and the White House began drawing plans for a more concerted war on crack and other drugs. At the same time, crack use was reported in Canada, England, Finland, Hong Kong, Spain, South Africa, Egypt, India, Mexico, Belize, and Brazil.[67] Simultaneously, a new coca product, space-base, was introduced to the American drug scene. First noticed in New York and Los Angeles during the early months of 1986,[68] space-base was crack doused with liquid PCP, LSD, heroin, or any other drug that might prolong the cocaine high. By midyear, space-base had reached the streets of Miami in the crack-PCP combination.

   By the close of the 1980s crack-cocaine seemed to have emerged as the major drug of concern in many parts of America. Although national surveys were indicating that at the end of the decade only 3 percent of high school students, just over 1 percent of college students, and 3 percent of young adults age 19 to 29 were recent users of crack,[69] the drug appeared to be devastating the social fabric of the inner cities. In New York, Los Angeles, Miami, and numerous other cities, including the nation's capitol, the crack trade had turned many urban street gangs into ghetto-based trafficking organizations, some with direct connections to high-level South American smugglers. In addition, crack distribution rivalries had touched off homicide epidemics that turned entire stretches of urban America into "dead zones"—anarchic badlands written off by law enforcement officials as too dangerous to patrol. And, too, the crack inner cities had other victims as well—the crack users themselves, whose lives revolved around crack-taking and crack-seeking; the "crack babies," born addicted or suffering from syphilis and abandoned in city hospitals; and the neglected or abused children, discarded, beaten, or killed by their crack-addicted parents.[70]

POSTSCRIPT

If anything has been learned from the history of illicit drug use in the United States, it is that it reflects fads, fashions, crazes, and cycles. Various drugs come and go, with their popularities shifting and changing. There have been several so-called "epidemics" involving heroin, cocaine, and numerous other psychotropic agents. For the better part of the 1980s, cocaine and crack were the drugs of the moment. And although their popularity will endure in the 1990s, other drugs will come into prominence—most likely, as was the case with crack, variations on already stylish drugs or, alternatively, rediscoveries of substances previously in vogue.[71]

NOTES

1. E. F. Cook and E. W. Martin, *Remington's Practice of Pharmacy* (Easton, Pa.: Mack Publishing Co., 1951); Charles E. Terry and Mildred Pellens, *The Opium Problem* (New York: Bureau of Social Hygiene, 1968), 56.

2. William Buchan, *Domestic Medicine: or, A Treatise on the Prevention and Cure of Diseases by Regimen and Simple Medicines* (Philadelphia: Crukshank, Bell, and Muir, 1784), 225–26.

3. James Harvey Young, *The Toadstool Millionaires: A Social History of Patent Medicines in America Before Federal Regulation* (Princeton, N.J.: Princeton University Press, 1961), 19–23.

4. Jerome H. Jaffe and William R. Martin, "Narcotic Analgesics and Antagonists," in *The Pharmacological Basis of Therapeutics*, ed. Louis S. Goodman and Alfred Gilman (New York: Macmillan, 1970), 245.

5. See Roberts Bartholow, *A Manual of Hypodermatic Medication* (Philadelphia: Lippincott, 1891).

6. *1897 Sears Roebuck Catalogue* (1897; reprint, New York: Chelsea House, 1968), 32 of insert on drugs.

7. Terry and Pellens, *The Opium Problem*, 1–20. See also H. Wayne Morgan, *Yesterday's Addicts: American Society and Drug Abuse 1865–1920* (Norman: University of Oklahoma Press, 1974).

8. Virgil G. Eaton, "How the Opium Habit Is Acquired," *Popular Science Monthly* 33 (1888): 665–66.

9. A. P. Grinnell, "A Review of Drug Consumption and Alcohol as Found in Proprietary Medicine," *Medical Legal Journal* (1905), cited in Terry and Pellens, *The Opium Problem*, 21–22.

10. Ernest Jones, *The Life and Work of Sigmund Freud*, vol. 1 (New York: Basic Books, 1953), 81; Freud's paper "Uber Coca" (On Coca) has been reprinted in *Cocaine Papers by Sigmund Freud*, ed. Robert Byck (New York: New American Library, 1975), 49–73.

11. C. R. A. Wright, "On the Action of Organic Acids and Their Anhydrides on the Natural Alkaloids," *Journal of the Chemical Society*, 12 July 1874, 1031.

12. See Arnold S. Trebach, *The Heroin Solution* (New Haven, Conn.: Yale University Press, 1982), 39.

13. M. Manges, "A Second Report on the Therapeutics of Heroin," *New York Medical Journal*, 20 January 1900, 82–83.

14. See Morgan, *Yesterday's Addicts*.

15. Perry M. Lichtenstein, "Narcotic Addiction," *New York Medical Journal*, 14 November 1914, 962.

16. G. E. McPherson and J. Cohen, "Survey of 100 Cases of Drug Addiction Entering Camp Upton, New York," *Boston Medical and Surgical Journal*, 5 June 1919; Special Committee of Investigation, *Traffic in Narcotic Drugs* (Washington, D.C.: Department of Treasury, 1919); *Literary Digest*, 26 April 1919, 32; *The Outlook*, 25 June 1919, 315; *The Survey*, 15 March 1919, 867–68; *American Review of Reviews*, July–December 1919, 331–32.

17. *Literary Digest*, 6 March 1920, 27–28; 16 April 1921, 19–20; 24 February 1923, 34–35; 25 August 1923, 22–23.

18. Larry Sloman, *Reefer Madness: A History of Marijuana in America* (Indianapolis: Bobbs-Merrill, 1979), 26. For a description of a late nineteenth century hashish club, see H. H. Kane, "A Hashish-House in New York," *Harper's Monthly*, November 1883, 944–949, reprinted in Morgan, *Yesterday's Addicts*, 159–70.

19. *New York Times*, 6 July 1927, 10.

20. Max Lerner, *America as a Civilization: Life and Thought in the United States Today* (New York: Simon & Schuster, 1957), 666.

21. See *Newsweek*, 20 November 1950, 57–58; 29 January 1951, 23–24; 11 June 1951, 26–27; 25 June 1951, 19–29; 13 August 1951, 50; 17 September 1951, 60; *Life*, 11 June 1951, 116, 119–22; *The Survey*, July 1951, 328–29; *Time*, 26 February 1951, 24; 7 May 1951, 82, 85; *Reader's Digest*, October 1951, 137–40.

22. Isidor Chein, Donald L. Gerard, Robert S. Lee, and Eva Rosenfeld, *The Road to H: Narcotics, Juvenile Delinquency, and Social Policy* (New York: Basic Books, 1964), 14.

23. See Leslie Farber, "Ours Is the Addicted Society," *New York Times Magazine*, 11 December 1966, 43; J. L. Simmons and B. Winograd, *It's Happening: A Portrait of the Youth Scene Today* (Santa Barbara, Calif.: Marc-Laired, 1966); Joel Fort, *The Pleasure Seekers: The Drug Crisis, Youth, and Society* (New York: Grove Press, 1969); A. Geller and M. Boas, *The Drug Beat* (New York: McGraw-Hill, 1969); Helen H. Nowlis, *Drugs on the College Campus* (New York: Doubleday-Anchor, 1969); Richard H. Blum and Associates, *Students and Drugs* (San Francisco: Jossey-Bass, 1970).

24. George Johnson, *The Pill Conspiracy* (Los Angeles: Sherbourne, 1967); James A. Inciardi, "Drugs, Drug-Taking and Drug-Seeking: Notations on the Dynamics of

Myth, Change, and Reality," in *Drugs and the Criminal Justice System*, ed. James A. Inciardi and Carl D. Chambers (Beverly Hills, Calif.: Sage, 1974), 203–22.

25. Cited in William Manchester, *The Glory and the Dream: A Narrative History of America, 1932–1972* (Boston: Little, Brown, 1974), 1362.

26. *The Realist*, September 1966.

27. Timothy Leary, "Introduction," in *LSD: The Consciousness-Expanding Drug*, ed. David Solomon (New York: G. P. Putnam's, 1964), 17.

28. Cited in Manchester, *The Glory*, 1366.

29. National Commission on Marijuana and Drug Abuse, *Drug Abuse in America: Problem in Perspective* (Washington, D.C.: U.S. Government Printing Office, 1973), 81.

30. Carl D. Chambers, Leon Brill, and James A. Inciardi, "Toward Understanding and Managing Nonnarcotic Drug Abusers," *Federal Probation*, March 1972, 50–55.

31. John Griffith, "A Study of Illicit Amphetamine Drug Traffic in Oklahoma City," *American Journal of Psychiatry* 123 (1966): 560–69; John C. Pollard, "Some Comments on Nonnarcotic Drug Abuse" (Paper presented at the Nonnarcotic Drug Institute, Southern Illinois University, Edwardsville, June 1967).

32. U.S. Congress, Senate, Subcommittee to Investigate Juvenile Delinquency of the Committee on the Judiciary, *Legislative Hearings on S. 674, "To Amend the Controlled Substances Act to Move Amphetamines and Certain Other Stimulant Substances from Schedule III of Such Act to Schedule II, and for Other Purposes," July 15 and 16, 1971* (Washington, D.C.: U.S. Government Printing Office, 1972).

33. Carl D. Chambers, *An Assessment of Drug Use in the General Population* (Albany: New York State Narcotic Addiction Control Commission, 1970); James A. Inciardi and Carl D. Chambers, "The Epidemiology of Amphetamine Use in the General Population," *Canadian Journal of Criminology and Corrections*, April 1972, 166–72.

34. For an overview of the history and clinical experiences related to methaqualone, see James A. Inciardi, David M. Petersen, and Carl D. Chambers, "Methaqualone Abuse Patterns, Diversion Paths, and Adverse Reactions," *Journal of the Florida Medical Association* 61 (April 1974): 279–283.

35. AMA Department of Drugs, *AMA Drug Evaluations* (Acton, Mass.: Publishing Sciences Group, 1973), 313.

36. U.S. Congress, Senate Subcommittee to Investigate Juvenile Delinquency of the Committee on the Judiciary, *Legislative Hearings on the Methaqualone Control Act of 1973, S. 1252, November 14 and 16, 1972, February 8, 13, and 14, 1973, April 5, 1973* (Washington, D.C.: U.S. Government Printing Office, 1973).

37. For those who missed the first wave of methaqualone abuse, another began in 1978 and persisted into the early 1980s. In 1980 some four tons of the drug were produced legally in the United States, and it is estimated that another 100 million tons were smuggled in, principally from Colombia. In 1982, when tight restrictions were placed on the importation of methaqualone powder from West Germany to Colombia, trafficking in the drug declined substantially. In 1984 all legal manufacturing of methaqualone was halted in the United States, and since that time, the abuse of the drug has been, at best, modest.

38. See Eric Josephson, "Marijuana Decriminalization: Assessment of Current Legislative Status" (Paper presented at the Technical Review on Methodology in Drug Policy Research, Decriminalization of Marijuana, National Institute on Drug Abuse, Rockville, Md., 20–21 March 1980); James A. Inciardi, "Marijuana Decriminalization Research: A Perspective and Commentary," *Criminology* 19 (May 1981): 145–59.

39. Domestic Council Drug Abuse Task Force, *White Paper on Drug Abuse* (Washington, D.C.: U.S. Government Printing Office, 1975).

40. Drug Abuse Policy Office, Office of Policy Development, The White House, *National Strategy for Prevention of Drug Abuse and Drug Trafficking* (Washington, D.C.: U.S. Government Printing Office, 1984), 19.

41. Lloyd D. Johnston, Patrick M. O'Malley, and Jerald G. Bachman, *Use of Licit and Illicit Drugs by America's High School Students, 1975–1984* (Rockville, Md.: National Institute on Drug Abuse, 1985), 108; University of Michigan news release, 28 February 1989.

42. *Phencyclidine (PCP)*, NCDAI Pub. 18 (Rockville, Md.: National Clearinghouse for Drug Abuse Information, 1973).

43. A. Reed and A. W. Kane, "Phencyclidine (PCP)," *STASH Capsules*, December 1970, 1–2.

44. Sidney H. Schnoll and W. H. Vogel, "Analysis of 'Street Drugs,' " *New England Journal of Medicine* 284 (8 April 1971): 791.

45. The author conducted both experiments.

46. Personal communication, 7 December 1969.

47. *Long Island Press*, 28 November 1970.

48. E. F. Domino, "Neurobiology of Phencyclidine (Sernyl), A Drug with an Unusual Spectrum of Pharmacological Activity," *Internal Review of Neurobiology* 6 (1964): 303–47.

49. Steven Lerner, "So Much for Cocaine and LSD—Angel Dust is America's Most Dangerous New Drug," *People*, 4 September 1978, 46–48. See also Ronald L. Linder, *PCP: The Devil's Dust* (Belmont, Calif.: Wadsworth, 1981).

50. U.S. Congress, Select Committee on Narcotics Abuse Control, *Executive Summary, Hearings on Phencyclidine, August 8* (Washington, D.C.: U.S. Government Printing Office, 1978).

51. The Drug Abuse Warning Network, more commonly known as DAWN, is a large-scale data-collection effort designed to monitor changing patterns of drug abuse in the United States. More than five thousand hospital emergency rooms and county medical examiners report regularly to DAWN. However, since a number of limitations are built into the DAWN data, they are far from representative of the actual character of drug abuse in the United States.

52. Harvey W. Feldman, "PCP Use in Four Cities: An Overview," in *Angel Dust*, ed. Harvey W. Feldman, Michael H. Agar, and George M. Beschner (Lexington, Mass.: Lexington Books, 1979), 29–51.

53. See Johnston et al., note 41.

54. *New York Times*, 9 December 1984, 60.

55. *U.S. News & World Report*, 19 November 1984, 65–66.

56. R. K. Siegel, "PCP and Violent Crime: The People vs. Peace," *Journal of Psychedelic Drugs* 12 (1980): 317–30; Eric D. Wish, "PCP and Crime: Just Another Illicit Drug?" in *Proceedings of the National Institute on Drug Abuse Technical Review on Phencyclidine* (Rockville, Md.: NIDA, May 1985).

57. *Time*, 10 June 1985, 64. See also *USA Today*, 30 May 1985, D1; *New York Times*, 1 June 1985, 6.

58. *The Gourmet Cokebook: A Complete Guide to Cocaine* (White Mountain Press, 1972), cited by M. Schatzman, A. Sabbadini, and L. Forti, "Coca and Cocaine," *Journal of Psychedelic Drugs* 8 (April–June 1976): 95–128.

59. It seems warranted to comment on the general belief that crack is "smokable cocaine." In actuality, crack is *not* smoked. "Smoking" implies combustion, burning, and the inhalation of smoke. Tobacco is smoked. Marijuana is smoked. Crack, on the other hand, is actually inhaled. The small pebbles or rocks, which have a relatively low melting point, are placed in a special glass pipe and heated. Rather than burning, crack vaporizes, and the fumes are inhaled.

60. Coca paste, also known as basuco, is an intermediate product in the transformation of the coca leaf into cocaine. An off-white doughy substance, it is typically mixed with either marijuana or tobacco and smoked in cigarette form.

61. James N. Hall, "Hurricane Crack," *Street Pharmacologist* 10 (September 1986): 1–2.

62. James A. Inciardi, "Beyond Cocaine: Basuco, Crack, and Other Coca Products," *Contemporary Drug Problems* (Fall 1987): 461–92.

63. *U.S. News & World Report*, 11 February 1985, 33.

64. See *New York Times*, 29 November 1985, A1.

65. *New York Times*, 16 May 1986, A1; *Time*, 2 June 1986, 16–18; *Newsweek*, 16 June 1986, 15–22; *Newsweek*, 30 June 1986, 52–54; *New York Times*, 25 August 1986, B1; *New York Times*, 13 September 1986, 1.

66. *USA Today*, 16 June 1986, 1A.

67. Rio de Janeiro (Brazil) *O Globo*, 24 May 1986, 6; Windsor (Canada) *The Windsor Star*, 26 June 1986, A13; Belfast (Ireland) *News Letter*, 9 July 1986, 3; Helsinki (Finland) *Uusi Suomi*, 28 July 1986, 8; Hong Kong *South China Morning Post*, 2 August 1986, 16; London *Al-Fursan*, 13 September 1986, 51–53; Madrid (Spain) *El Alcazar*, 14 September 1986, 11; Johannesburg (South Africa) *Star*, 23 September 1986, 1M; Nuevo Laredo (Mexico) *El Diario de Nuevo Laredo*, 12 October 1986, sec. 4, p. 1; Calcutta (India) *Statesman*, 16 October 1986, 1; Belize City (Belize) *Beacon*, 25 October 1986, 1, 14.

68. *Newsweek*, 30 June 1986, 53.

69. University of Michigan news release, 28 February 1989. "Recent use" is referred to here as *any* use during the one-year period prior to the survey.

70. See *Newsweek*, 28 March 1988, 20–26; *Miami Herald*, 31 May 1988, B1; *New York Times*, 23 June 1988, A1, B4; *Time*, 5 December 1988, 32; David A. Bateman and Margaret C. Heagarty, "Passive Freebase ('Crack') Inhalation by Infants and Toddlers," *American Journal of Diseases of Children* 143 (January 1989): 25–27; *New York Doctor*, 10 April 1989, 1; *U.S. News & World Report*, 10 April 1989, 20–31.

71. For a more detailed history of the evolution of drug abuse in the United States, see James A. Inciardi, *The War on Drugs: Heroin, Cocaine, Crime, and Public Policy* (Palo Alto, Calif.: Mayfield, 1986), from which segments of this introduction were adapted.

PART I

BACKGROUND ISSUES

Chapter 1

The History of Drug Control Policies in the United States

John C. McWilliams

The use of drugs has been prevalent in the United States since the earliest settlement. Consumption of marijuana in the American colonies dates back to the founding of Jamestown, and by 1629 the drug had been introduced into the Puritan colonies of New England. By 1765 George Washington was cultivating marijuana at Mount Vernon, presumably to alleviate the agony of an aching tooth. During the nineteenth century, or what Edward M. Brecher has described as a "dope fiend's paradise," opium could be purchased readily and cheaply. Two opium derivatives, morphine and heroin, were in common use by the latter half of the century and "were as freely accessible as aspirin is today."[1]

The distribution of these drugs was not by way of any syndicate or other form of illegal trafficking, but through perfectly legitimate and respectable sources. Physicians nonchalantly prescribed them for patients who did not have to make an office call. Drug stores sold opiates over the counter without a prescription. Grocery stores also stocked the drugs and sold them as casually as fresh produce or hardware items. It was possible also to mail order a dose of heroin or morphine.[2] Neither the importation nor the manufacture of these drugs was restricted. Since these opiates were addictive and used so widely (one New England pharmacist in a town of 10,000 sold three hundred pounds of opium a year), America obviously had a drug problem.

By the first decade of the twentieth century, reformists in the Progressive movement who labored to eradicate America's social ills began to consider the need for some form of regulation. Three factors can be identified as fostering a change in public opinion. First, as a result of the Spanish-American War in 1898, the United States acquired the Philippine Islands and inherited a loose system for licensing addicts and supplying them with legal opium. If the United States was truly going to civilize and extend Western culture, the problem of narcotics addiction had to be brought under control.

The second factor was the growing concern over the harmful effects of such drugs as opium and cocaine. To encourage a greater degree of federal government intervention, Progressive muckraking journalists exposed addiction problems in newspapers and periodicals. All the publicity about drug abuse caused Americans to re-evaluate their thinking about the indiscriminate use of narcotics.

Third, greater than the concern about uplifting the indigenous population of a remote island or the physical harm of drugs were strains of racism and xenophobia. In the early 1900s, when cocaine and opium became closely associated with blacks, Chinese immigrants, and criminal types, white paranoia and anxiety produced a backlash against the use of narcotics. In 1910, testimony before Congress and a federal survey confirmed far-fetched claims about superhuman feats by users of drugs.[3] In the World War I era, wildly exaggerated and disparaging stereotypes convinced many politicians and other public officials that regulation was necessary. The element of racism connected with drug policies cannot be overstated as it would prove to be the cornerstone for such legislation through the 1940s.

To solve the problem of opium addiction in the Philippines, the Reverend Charles H. Brent, Episcopal bishop of the islands, recommended that narcotics be regulated by international laws, which would give the United States greater input, not only in the Far East, but around the globe. Dr. Hamilton Wright shared the Reverend's views and lobbied for stricter domestic legislation and greater participation for the United States in international control. Because of Dr. Wright's influence in the State Department, President Roosevelt appointed the two of them, along with Charles C. Tenney, a China missionary, as American Representatives to an international opium conference the following year in Shanghai.[4]

The delegations from six countries that convened in China did not produce any formal treaties, but a spirit of cooperation developed which led to a second conference at The Hague in 1911; subsequently, The Hague International Opium Convention of 1912 produced the first international opium agreement.[5] Thus, the beginning of the modern movement for the suppression of narcotics trafficking began with U.S. involvement in the Philippines.

EARLY LEGISLATION: THE HARRISON NARCOTIC ACT

Ironically, while the Brent, Tenney, and Wright delegation succeeded in securing restrictions against opium abroad, the United States had no legislation against it at home. To avoid an embarrassing situation, New York Representative Francis B. Harrison introduced two bills on April 8, 1913: H.R. 1966, to ''prohibit the importation and use of opium for other than medicinal purposes,'' and H.R. 1967, to ''regulate the manufacture of smoking opium within the United States.'' In addition to wide congressional backing, the bills also had the influential support of Secretary of State William Jennings Bryan.

Though H.R. 1966 ultimately was recognized as a revenue bill, Representative Harrison responded to Congressman James R. Mann in Illinois on June 24, 1913, that the measure was intended primarily not to generate revenue, but to prevent the manufacture of smoking opium in the United States. Two days later, with no opposition, the bills were presented for House debate. The bills were referred to the Senate Committee on Finance just before the Thanksgiving recess. On December 20 the bills passed the Senate, and a month later, on January 17, 1914, President Wilson signed the bills to take effect March 1.[6]

Under the Harrison narcotic law, the basis for subsequent federal prosecution of narcotics offenses, the maximum penalty that could be imposed was a five-year imprisonment or a $2,000 fine or both. The average prison term through the mid-1930s of one-and-a-half years was considered too low by those who felt it was not severe enough to deter repeat offenders.[7] The law provided the machinery through which the federal government was able to control the distribution of narcotic drugs within the country. Specifically, manufacturers, importers, pharmacists, and physicians prescribing narcotics were required to be licensed and to pay a graduated occupational tax. The most significant provision of the act was for the collection of revenue. The Harrison Act regulated the dispensation of narcotics through a revenue tax, but it did not prohibit the use of narcotics, among which chloral hydrate (a depressant) and most notably cannabis (marijuana) were not included.

In reality, the Harrison Act was little more than a regulatory law for the marketing of opium, morphine, heroin, and other drugs. If the act was passed with the intention of eradicating the narcotics problem, however, it fell woefully short. Not only did the act exclude what would be the most controversial drug in the country in another twenty years, but also it contained ambiguous provisions with regard to the ramifications of its enforcement. Enigmatic wording in the law pertaining to the right of physicians to prescribe drugs to addicts whose supply was suddenly cut off sharply divided the medical profession. Law enforcement officers interpreted the phrase "in the course of his professional practice only" to mean that opiates should not be made available to addicts. Some doctors favored this interpretation, while others felt it was necessary to continue giving prescriptions to addicts as a means of monitoring their habits. Thus began the debate that would remain unresolved into the 1960s: Was drug addiction a crime or a disease, and should the addict be treated as a sick person or a criminal?[8] A more immediate and tangible consequence of the Harrison Act was that it made the regulated drugs much more expensive.

Ironically, the enactment of the Harrison Act caused more drug use problems than it resolved. Its legal status, according to lower court decisions, was that of a revenue measure. The government was not permitted to seize drugs that fell within the law's wording. Eventually one of the cases, *U.S. v. Jin Fuey Moy*, reached the U.S. Supreme Court. In June 1916, in a 7–2 decision, the Court decided that Dr. Jin Fuey Moy had not acted in good faith when he prescribed morphine to an addict who was not registered to deal in narcotics. However, the government's desire to obtain broad enforcement powers was soundly denied.[9]

In addition to questions about the constitutionality of the Harrison Act, controversy erupted over the maintenance program which grew more intense in the post–World War I years, prompting the Secretary of the Treasury to form a committee to investigate the problem. In 1918 the committee's most dramatic finding was that the illicit use of narcotics had increased while the act had been in effect.[10] Instead of more closely examining the weaknesses of the law, its unclear wording, or its enforcement-related problems, the committee simply stiffened the penalties as committees have done repeatedly and ineffectively ever since.[11]

Enforcement of the Harrison Act was initially assigned to the Bureau of Internal Revenue in the Treasury Department and remained there until 1918 when the Volstead Act—legislation that provided for the enforcement of prohibition—passed over President Wilson's veto. With the added burden of enforcing prohibition, Treasury officials realized that the existing bureaucratic apparatus was inadequate for prosecuting both narcotics and liquor law violations. A special committee appointed by Secretary of the Treasury William McAdoo recommended the creation of separate agencies: one to handle the enforcement of the Harrison Act, the other to enforce prohibition. As a result, a special Narcotics Division within the Prohibition Bureau was created.[12] Headed by former pharmacist Levi G. Nutt, the division employed 170 narcotics agents working out of thirteen offices. Unlike Prohibition agents who were notoriously corrupt, Narcotics officers were hired according to Civil Service guidelines.

Throughout the 1920s perplexing questions relative to the treatment of addiction prompted numerous studies and investigations that endeavored to construct a more definitive portrayal of the addict and his addiction. At the forefront of the controversy was Dr. Lawrence Kolb, a surgeon in the U.S. Public Health Service, whose scientific research showed that addicts and "stable persons" may exhibit different effects from the same drug. He refuted the prevailing belief that since addiction was a crime, the addict should be treated as a criminal. He also attacked the unproven argument that there was a direct correlation between drug addiction and violent crime, believing that the immediate effect of an excessive consumption of opium would be to soothe abnormal impulses. Thus, the drug would be more likely to inhibit a psychopathic murderer's impulse to violent crime than to induce it.[13]

Ardent supporters of the Harrison Act who were opposed to maintenance clinics were placated when Nutt's Narcotics Division forced forty-four of them to shut down by the end of 1921. No clinics meant that users could not sustain their habit legally, and addicts were denied ambulatory treatment. The question of what to do with them became a particularly nettlesome issue for Congress by the mid-1920s. Since addiction was not recognized as a crime, it was not constitutional to round up addicts en masse and throw them in jail. Nor was it practical. Then, as now, prison space was severely limited. Both penitentiaries and psychiatric institutions were already seriously overcrowded. In 1928, for example, the federal penitentiaries held 7,598 inmates in 3,738 cells, double the capacity. The prisons were also not designed to handle this kind of criminal, whose association with the general nonaddict population was viewed as detrimental for both groups.[14]

Generally, ardent Prohibitionists, the supporters of the Harrison Act who wanted more legislation, were also pleased in 1922 when Congress passed the Narcotic Drugs Import and Export Act. Sponsored by Senator Homer Jones of Oklahoma and Representative John Miller of Washington, this act authorized the surgeon general to regulate the importation of crude opium and coca leaves which were to be restricted to medicinal and scientific use. To enforce the $5,000 fines and sentences up to ten years for unlawful importation, the Federal Bureau Board was created. As James A. Inciardi has noted, however, in *The War on Drugs*, "the Jones-Miller Act had little impact other than to further inflate the prices of heroin and morphine on the illicit drug marketplace."[15]

As a solution to this problem, Representative Stephen G. Porter, a Pennsylvania Republican and chairman of the House Ways and Means Committee, introduced H. R. 12781 to provide for the construction of two prison hospitals he referred to as "farms." The farms (one east and one west of the Mississippi River) were to function as clearinghouses for addicts already in penitentiaries or state and county jails, as well as for addicts "at large." That was the pragmatic reasoning for the bill. Congressman Porter also seemed sympathetic with the plight of the addict and progressive in his thinking on rehabilitation when he commented that he was thankful that addicts would not be characterized as "drug fiends" since nine out of ten of these unfortunate people acquired the habit through accident and many of them wanted to be cured.[16]

On June 19, 1929, the Porter bill passed unanimously. The first farm opened in Lexington, Kentucky, in 1935, and the second opened three years later in Fort Worth, Texas. With facilities to treat 1,000 addicts, a professional staff provided psychiatric counseling, medical treatment, and vocational training. Addicts could be assigned to one of the farms by a court, or they could apply voluntarily.[17]

THE FEDERAL BUREAU OF NARCOTICS

Once the drug farms were approved, Congressman Porter wasted no time in proposing legislation for the creation of an independent Bureau of Narcotics, which he saw as a logical next step. He wanted the new agency to be separated from the Prohibition Bureau so that it could function more effectively in domestic and international affairs. It would also be more effective since both enforcement and policy-making personnel would be contained in the same bureau.

Hearings on Porter's H.R. 11143 revealed a general lack of enthusiasm for such an agency, but while supporters were few in number, so were opponents.

In early June 1930 Congress passed the bill. Three days later, on June 9, 1930, President Herbert Hoover's signature ended sixteen years of narcotic and liquor law enforcement in the same agency. To head the Treasury Department's new Federal Bureau of Narcotics (FBN), the president was to appoint a commissioner with the consent of the Senate. The primary responsibility of the commissioner was to enforce the Harrison Act with the powers conferred on him as provided in the Jones-Miller Act.[18]

As head of the old Narcotics Division in the Prohibition Bureau, Levi Nutt was virtually assured appointment as the first commissioner of the Federal Narcotics Bureau. However, allegations that he had knowledge of agents padding arrest reports and that his son, Rolland, did some accounting work for the powerful racketeer Arnold Rothstein proved too embarrassing for him to receive serious consideration, and his candidacy was aborted.[19] Among the many candidates under consideration was Harry J. Anslinger of Altoona, Pennsylvania, who was the assistant commissioner of prohibition in charge of narcotics enforcement. Having worked in the State Department's consular service at The Hague during World War I, and later in Germany, Venezuela, and the Bahamas, Anslinger possessed a solid background in diplomacy and was knowledgeable about both domestic and international enforcement problems. He was also related through marriage to Andrew Mellon, the powerful secretary of the treasury.[20] With little opposition the Senate confirmed Anslinger's appointment to the $9,000-a-year position on December 9, 1930.

The first major task confronting the new commissioner was the complete reorganization of the old Narcotics Division in the Prohibition Bureau. This bureaucratic realignment resulted in a changeover from enforcement on a strictly local basis by a little-known unit of the government to the formulation of broad national and international policies.

Prior to 1930 and the creation of the FBN, enforcement efforts had comparatively little effect on curbing illicit traffic. Commissioner Anslinger realized that major enforcement problems included detecting and preventing unlawful importation into the United States. He reasoned correctly that foreign overproduction and low prices were the main factors that created an abundant supply for most of the addicts in the United States. In 1932 Anslinger briefly outlined his concept for the proper policy to be followed by the bureau if it was to achieve a high level of proficiency in controlling drug syndicates and smuggling activities. Rather than concentrating on local peddlers and addicts, Anslinger felt that the federal government should carry out policies to break up international rings of narcotic runners and to stop interstate narcotic traffic.[21] During his first years in office, he attended the League of Nations International Convention on Narcotics in Geneva, enforced the Harrison Act, and made a vigorous appeal to the states to adopt uniform narcotic laws to stop the growth and spread of illicit drug trafficking.

The commissioner's foremost problem, however, was not the control of drugs already covered by legislation, but how to handle the emergence and rapid spread of a "new" unregulated drug. Prior to the 1930s marijuana generated little concern and received little publicity. But the depression years heightened people's anxieties and insecurities; many Americans forced out of their jobs and homes were frustrated and bitter. Since it was not possible to lay the blame for their dismal condition on any one factor, they were inclined to look for a scapegoat. Marijuana was an easy, convenient target.

At first, the "killer weed" was associated almost exclusively with extremely negative images of marijuana-smoking Mexicans who had crossed the Rio Grande River to take low-paying jobs away from American workers. Under the effects of the drug, they became uncontrollable and maniacal.[22]

About the same time, demands for federal legislation began to emanate from city officials in New Orleans, who linked an increase in their crime rate during the 1920s to the use of marijuana. The crime increase might well have been attributed more to Prohibition violations, but since the legalization of alcohol was gaining popular support, attention was shifted to marijuana as a crime-producing drug. Commissioner of Public Safety Dr. Frank R. Gomilla was so alarmed in 1931 about the dangers of marijuana that he assured the Louisiana Medical Society that the New Orleans Police Department would be especially vigilant for locations of the drug which he felt "should be put in the same class as heroin." Physician Dr. A. E. Fossier and District Attorney Eugene Stanley echoed Gomilla's concern and warned the New Orleans citizenry that a drug so deadly should be suppressed before it got out of hand.[23]

They were correct in anticipating the rapid spread of the Mexican weed. Marijuana use spread up the Mississippi River from New Orleans to river ports in the Midwest and branched out into northeastern cities. By the mid-1930s newspapers and popular magazines were headlining the "marijuana menace" in nearly every part of the country. People were growing it in city backyards, in vacant lots, and along roadways, and resourceful inmates even planted it in the fields of federal prisons. No longer associated exclusively with migrant Mexicans, by 1936 it was said to have replaced liquor in Harlem and was considered chic as a new diversion in affluent Westchester County, New York. It even found its way into New Deal work relief programs when it was discovered that men in the Civilian Conservation Corps in New Hampshire and Works Progress Administration employees in New York were smoking it.[24]

As long as marijuana was confined to Mexicans in the Southwest and to other illegal aliens, the Narcotics Bureau gave it little notice. But when it began to spread into midwestern and northern states, Anslinger mobilized his narcotics force into a nationwide crusade against a drug the properties and effects of which were more feared than understood. The biological effects of the drug were fiercely debated throughout the decade by noted scientists and physicians who were unable to form a clear consensus. When any of them did express uncertainty as to its potency, Anslinger turned a deaf ear, arguing that while some were inclined to minimize the harmfulness of the drug, ample evidence confirmed its disastrous effect on many of its users. More outlandish than the "assassin of youth"

propaganda were the fantastic reports of marijuana's horrible effects. No research at the time proved or disproved the influence marijuana had on the
user's personality or behavior, but it was easy to believe the worst. The editorial outcry against the evil of cannabis claimed the weed caused sex crimes,
murder, and, indeed, almost anything else.[25] Even when Dr. Michael V. Ball,
a physician from Warren, Pennsylvania, attested that marijuana alone was not
responsible for producing the devastating effects attributed to it by the bureau,
Anslinger remained inflexible in his view that marijuana was capable of turning sane and otherwise law-abiding citizens into criminals who wantonly committed dastardly acts.[26]

To shape public opinion and inform the citizenry about the "killer weed,"
Anslinger manipulated the media. Aware of how the marijuana controversy might
reap political benefits, he also enlisted the help of organizations sympathetic to
his crusade against the drug, including the Hearst newspaper chain and moralist
groups such as the General Federation of Women's Clubs, the Woman's Christian
Temperance Union, and the World Narcotics Defense Association. In 1936 he
categorized the marijuana controversy as "one of the most troublesome problems
which confronts us today in the United States." During appropriations hearings
that December, he confirmed Congressman Louis Ludlow's supposition that
marijuana was "about as hellish as heroin," even though Anslinger had admitted
only a year earlier that it was not even addictive.[27]

Realizing how limited his resources were, Anslinger was reluctant, however,
to actively sponsor a federal antimarijuana law. Moreover, legal complexities
loomed. The Harrison Act had been declared constitutional, but it had also been
subjected to judicial review on five occasions, and contemporary observers seriously questioned the merit of the legislation. In 1934 an editorial in the *St.
Louis Post-Dispatch* commented that the Harrison Act "has been a greater failure
than the eighteenth amendment." Worse, the writer argued, the act "made
trafficking in narcotics so profitable it led to the establishment of vast underworld
rings." The column concluded with the assessment that the act "cost taxpayers
millions of dollars a year and aggravated a problem it was designed to correct."[28]

By 1937 the Treasury Department was ready to introduce a federal antimarijuana bill and invited fourteen government officials to participate in a conference
to identify the physiological effects and legal definitions of marijuana. The
discussions were dominated by scientists and lawyers. Alfred L. Tennyson, the
bureau's legal counsel, stressed that in the hearings the department would have
to justify why marijuana should be prohibited and to defend the proposed legislation to those industries that used various parts of the plant for commercial
purposes, such as varnish (Sherwin-Williams) and birdseed companies.[29]

On April 14, 1937, the Treasury Department's proposal to control marijuana
was finally presented in the House of Representatives where Robert L. Doughton
of North Carolina introduced H.R. 6385 to impose a transfer and occupational
excise tax on dealers. The provisions of the bill were threefold: (1) it required
that all manufacturers, importers, dealers, and practitioners register and pay a

special occupational tax; (2) it mandated that all transactions be accomplished through use of written order forms; and (3) it imposed a tax in the amount of $1 an ounce on all transfers to unregistered persons. The key departure of the marijuana tax scheme from that of the Harrison Act was the concept of a prohibitive tax. Under the Harrison Act a nonmedical user could not legitimately buy or possess narcotics.

The House Ways and Means Committee hearings continued for five days through May 4. These hearings accurately reflected both the attitude and the depth of understanding that contributed to this momentous piece of federal narcotics legislation. It also established what was to be a legacy of applying punitive measures as a solution to a complex problem. Not only did the committee members possess little knowledge about marijuana, including its physical appearance and habitat, but also, as became evident during the hearings, they knew no more about its properties and effects beyond what they read in the newspapers. Anslinger and the Treasury Department could not have asked for a more naive and gullible audience. Getting H.R. 6385 out of committee was little more than a matter of going through the motions.

The only serious critic of the bill who appeared before the committee was Dr. William C. Woodward, legislative counsel for the American Medical Association. He never denied that narcotics addiction was a problem, but he did express surprise that the committee had not sought more substantial evidence.[30] If the use of marijuana did cause crime, he asked, why did the committee not invite authorities in related fields to offer their opinions on the matter? Much of the prison population was said to have been addicted to the drug, yet no one from the Bureau of Prisons was asked to testify. Nor was anyone summoned from the Children's Bureau of the Office of Education to discuss the alleged prevalence of marijuana smoking among the adolescent population. Had representatives from these agencies been given the opportunity to testify, they probably would have refuted the Treasury Department's claims that drug addiction among inmates and schoolchildren was a growing problem.[31]

Essentially the point Woodward was trying to make was that more legislation in this situation was not necessarily better. He argued that sufficient laws designed to control marijuana were already in effect. On the federal level was Title 21, Section 198 of the United States Code, the same statute that created the Bureau of Narcotics in 1930. As Woodward pointed out, the secretary of the treasury was to blame for not exercising stricter enforcement during the seven years it had been in effect.

One week after the hearings, on May 11, Chairman Doughton reported the marijuana tax bill, restyled with amendments as H.R. 6906, to the Committee of the Whole House. A month later he presented it for debate on the floor of Congress. The same congressmen who were determined not to allow Woodward's dissenting point of view to sway their judgment in committee hearings participated in the debate on the regulation of marijuana. They exhibited a cavalier attitude in debating the bill and approached it with an aloofness and indifference not commonly associated with the enactment of narcotics laws; it was almost as if they were annoyed with having to discuss it. At least one of the congressmen, future legendary Speaker of the House Sam Rayburn, commented that the bill "has something to do with marijuana . . . a narcotic of some kind."[32]

The Senate hearings, simply an abbreviated version of the House Ways and Means hearings, were relatively brief, requiring just one session to examine only six witnesses, including Anslinger. No new testimony or new evidence was presented. The hearings concluded with less than thirty pages of testimony. In the next few days the bill was reported favorably out of committee, passed with minor amendments, and sent back to the House where it was considered again. The Senate suggestions were quickly adopted. In August President Roosevelt signed the bill into law, and it took effect on October 1, 1937.

The law that banned a plant most people perceived as an "evil weed" imposed an occupational tax on importers, sellers, dealers, and anyone handling cannabis. A transfer tax fixed at $1 per ounce was charged for registered persons and $100 per ounce for those not registered with the government. Of course, no illegal dealers would register. Unlike alcohol during Prohibition, possession was outlawed with penalties to fit an "assassin": Violations were punishable by a $2,000 fine, five years' imprisonment, or both. Unlike the Prohibition amendment and its advocates, this law marked only the beginning of controversial federal drug policies. Ironically the model for repressive narcotics legislation, which was to foster a heated debate over the next forty years, received only minimal attention in the press.

World War II seriously interrupted the normal patterns of international drug distribution which created a "starving time" for addicts; consequently, Anslinger anticipated a marijuana epidemic that he was certain would emerge in the postwar period, just as it had in the years following World War I; he was not concerned with any of the opium compounds that seemed to be enjoying a renewed popularity. In 1943 an editorial in *Military Medicine* addressed the use of marijuana among American soldiers and concluded that the drug was found to be especially appealing to "recruits of low mentality."[33] A year and a half later two doctors in the Army Medical Corps reported the results of a study they conducted with thirty-five marijuana "addicts," who revealed "pronounced disturbances" in the Rorschach tests, exhibited homosexual traits, conveyed a "deprecatory attitude" toward women, frequently engaged in self-mutilation, and were "overly hostile, provocative, and intransigent." It should be noted that of the thirty-five subjects who participated in the study, only one was white, and "nearly all were of low or very low social and economic backgrounds."[34] This kind of research did little to provide a clearer understanding of either the use of marijuana or the drug's effects.

Whatever political and social changes were to occur after the war, Anslinger was convinced that it was critical that the United States take an active role in maintaining the international control and regulation of narcotics, which he helped to accomplish in London as a delegate to the new United Nations organization.

Convinced in 1942 that Japan had started its war on Western civilization ten years earlier by using narcotics as weapons, Anslinger claimed that Japan was working on the theory that a "drug-sullen nation is an easy conquest and cannot offer adequate resistance to attack."[35] The government was still associating narcotics with minority groups, and with the Japanese scare, Anslinger realized the political advantages of identifying global "hot spots" as sources of international distribution.

MAYOR LaGUARDIA'S COMMITTEE

Much discussion and little research about marijuana smoking in the 1930s provided little knowledge and only muddied the controversy to the point that among the relatively limited number of Americans who were aware of a problem, few possessed any clear understanding of what marijuana was. Jazz musicians, who were predominantly black, did more to promote marijuana's popularity than did any other single group. They generated publicity not so much by smoking the weed (though many did), but by using its terminology in their music. Provocative song titles such as "Sweet Marijuana Brown," "If You're a Viper," "Reefer Song," "Sendin' the Viper," and "That Funny Reefer Man" glamorized marijuana smoking. Of course these songs did not escape Anslinger's attention, and neither did many of the musicians who performed them, including Count Basie, Cab Calloway, Duke Ellington, and Louis Armstrong.[36] One of the most popular performers of jazz in the 1930s, Milton "Mezz" Mezzrow, a white Jewish clarinetist, provided a glimpse into the deviant practice of marijuana smoking within the subculture of musicians in his 1946 autobiography *Really the Blues*. He described the effects of marijuana and contradicted nearly every argument the Bureau of Narcotics made against its use. Mezzrow wrote that none of his fellow musicians who smoked the weed ever thought it was addictive, and he felt that it had been erroneously classified as a narcotic. He and his fellow musicians were also convinced that a marijuana cigarette was no more "dangerous or habit-forming than those other great American vices, the five-cent Coke and ice-cream cone, only it gave you more kick for the money."[37]

The increasing number of lurid reports of Harlem "tea pads," or apartments where black jazz devotees congregated to listen to music and share a marijuana cigarette, impelled New York City Mayor Fiorello H. LaGuardia to uncover the facts and fallacies about the "weed of madness." Personally skeptical that marijuana was capable of causing the bizarre behavior that had been attributed to smoking the drug, Mayor LaGuardia was determined to organize an impartial, scientific citywide investigation. To conduct the study the popular LaGuardia appealed to the prestigious New York Academy of Medicine. In October 1938 the academy's Committee on Public Health established a special subcommittee composed of two internists; three psychiatrists; two pharmacologists; one public health expert; the commissioners of Health, Hospitals, and Corrections; and the director of the Division of Psychiatry.[38]

The mayor's committee either challenged or refuted virtually every view about marijuana advanced by Anslinger and the Bureau of Narcotics over the previous decade. One of the committee members visited a Harlem tea pad where he observed that the individuals were relaxed and "free from the anxieties and cares of the realities of life."[39] Contrary to the belief that marijuana smokers in tea pads were aggressive and belligerent, the investigation found that "a boisterous, rowdy atmosphere did not prevail." Nor was it evident that marijuana stimulated erotic behavior. As to its relationship to crime and juvenile delinquency, marijuana was not identified as a significant contributing factor. Interviews of police officers furnished no proof that major crimes were associated with smoking marijuana. They did state that petty crimes were committed, but that the criminal's career usually existed prior to the time the individual smoked his first marijuana cigarette. The committee found that marijuana smoking did not lead to addiction, in the medical sense of the word, to morphine, heroin, or cocaine; it was not widespread in schoolyards and among school-age children; nor was the committee able to establish a direct link between the use of marijuana and cocaine. In what represented perhaps the most serious challenge to Anslinger, the committee found that "the publicity concerning the catastrophic effects of marijuana in New York City is unfounded."[40]

The Mayor's Report was subjected to bitter attack by the Bureau of Narcotics. Rumors of the report's suppression surfaced even before its release. When two members of the mayor's committee, Doctors Samuel Allentuck and Karl B. Bowman, published a preliminary article entitled "The Psychiatric Aspects of Marijuana Intoxication" in the *American Journal of Psychiatry* in 1942, suggesting there might be more reason for concern about tobacco or alcohol than about cannabis, Anslinger openly attacked the authors and the report.[41]

A December 1942 editorial in the *Journal of the American Medical Association* (JAMA) referred to the mayor's report as a "careful study" and mentioned the therapeutic possibilities of marijuana.[42] Throughout 1943 and 1944 an exchange of views on the marijuana controversy continued in JAMA, involving Anslinger, Allentuck, Bowman, and Jules Bouquet of the Narcotics Commission of the League of Nations. By 1945, when the mayor's committee report was finally released, JAMA had published numerous articles from "experts" eager to register their support or criticism of the report.[43] In the end the report had a negligible impact.

THE BOGGS ACT

The Narcotics Bureau's scare tactics, a prevailing fear of Communism in the McCarthy era, and congressional response to the public's anxiety about drug addiction prevented any significant advances in either treating drug addicts or slowing illegal narcotics trafficking. The common and popular solution was to regard the addict as a fugitive and to adopt tougher sentencing laws that would deter drug smugglers. Neither approach alleviated the problem of drug abuse.

Despite evidence that further narcotics legislation was unwarranted, two factors led to the enactment of the Boggs Act, sponsored by Congressman Hale Boggs of Louisiana: Anslinger's testimony during the 1950 Kefauver committee hearings on Organized Crime in Interstate Commerce, during which he claimed that organized crime syndicates were heavily involved in drug trafficking, and a flurry of antinarcotics bills in 1951. Reflecting Anslinger's "get tough" attitude and growing congressional support for a more punitive approach, this legislation increased the already severe penalties against narcotics violators. Not only did the act make it easier for prosecuting attorneys to secure convictions, but also it stipulated that the first-time offender would be subject to a sentence of not less than two years or more than five with the possibility of probation. Second offenders received a mandatory five to ten years with no probation or suspension of the sentence permitted. Three-time losers faced a mandatory twenty years with no probation or suspension of the sentence (prior to the Boggs Act the maximum penalty was a ten-year sentence). All offenses also carried fines up to $2,000.[44]

Those who criticized the Boggs legislation argued that the penalties were inordinately oppressive and were a reflection of attitudes more prevalent in ancient times than in the mid-twentieth century. They also challenged the language and effectiveness of the act because its penalties fell primarily on the victims of the drug trafficking—the addicts—and not on the dealers and distributors. One of the bill's critics in the House of Representatives, Congressman Victor L. Anfuso of New York, agreed that the Boggs penalties were misdirected and argued that imposing severe jail sentences would not prevent the traffic because the profits were too lucrative not to take the risk.[45] The hearings lasted three days. The first witness, Congresswoman Edith Nourse Rogers of Massachusetts, wanted the regulation of over-the-counter sales of barbiturates assigned to the Bureau of Narcotics.[46] Anslinger was not opposed to such regulation; however, knowing that his already overburdened agents could not possibly enforce the laws pertaining to barbiturates with any degree of efficiency or effectiveness, he felt that these activities should be assigned to the Food and Drug Administration. When asked who he thought was most responsible for the traffic in narcotics, Anslinger stated that it was "all underworld" and lamented that the "big fellows" were not given long enough prison sentences, chastising the judiciary system for not keeping them in confinement. The judges, Anslinger argued, were too easy on peddlers, who served light sentences and went right back into dealing. "We are on a merry-go-round," he remarked, and he implored Congress to pass legislation with longer minimum sentences.[47]

By the time the bill was debated on the House floor, opposition to some of its provisions had become substantial. The most vocal opponents, Congressmen Emanuel Celler of New York and Richard M. Simpson of Pennsylvania, agreed that the penalties should be increased, but expressed misgivings about the mandatory minimum sentences. They expressed concern that the bill would make it impossible for a judge to have any discretionary power and to impose any sentence less than two years. In addition, juries would be reluctant to convict a small-time peddler who faced such a harsh mandatory minimum sentence. In defending his bill Congressman Boggs assured his colleagues that he did not intend to encroach on judicial authority, but Celler remained unconvinced and refused to support the bill.[48] By the conclusion of the debate, opposition to H.R. 3490 cut across party lines, with both Democrats and Republicans arguing that though the penalties were not too severe for the professional trafficker in narcotics, they might be an injustice to helpless addicts who fell victim to the drugs. Nevertheless, the bill was approved by a voice vote and sent to the Senate. On November 2, 1951, it was signed into law by President Harry S. Truman.

Almost immediately Anslinger reported a "startling decline" in the illicit use of narcotics by juveniles. While appearing on the television show "Battle Report," he attributed the drop-off in the number of juveniles requesting treatment to the heavier penalties imposed in the new Boggs Act. Because the new law provided heavier penalties, the Commissioner said, law enforcement agencies could reduce the sale and use of narcotics so that one day they will "no longer be a danger or threat to our society."[49]

Yet Anslinger began to agitate for even tougher laws. During the 1951 hearings he had referred to Communist China as a point of origin for heroin and twice had made formal charges against the Chinese Communist regime before the United Nations Commission on Narcotic Drugs for selling heroin and opium as a means of subverting free countries. By 1955 the fear of being overrun by Communists wielding hypodermic needles rather than atomic weaponry had become a major concern of Washington politicians. In 1954 seven members of Congress spoke on the floor about the evils of Communism and either cited Anslinger directly or included articles written by him to be entered in the *Congressional Record*. To get "at the very heart of the whole treacherous narcotics problem," Congressman Fred E. Busbey of Illinois introduced H.R. 8700, which would make mandatory the death penalty or life imprisonment for anyone convicted of selling narcotics to persons under twenty-one years old.[50] The bill did not reach a vote in 1954, but it was indicative of the public's frustration with what it perceived to be an addiction problem of epidemic proportions which threatened American young people.

While Congress continued to debate the most effective methods for dealing with drug offenders, the American Bar Association (ABA) created a special committee to study federal narcotics policies in 1954 and the following year joined with the AMA to urge a congressional investigation of the Harrison Act and the Narcotics Bureau.[51] Instead, on January 14, 1955, forty-two senators cosponsored a bill that provided for even stiffer sentences, including the death penalty for second offenders who supplied drugs to teenagers. But two months later, on March 18, 1955, the Senate did adopt S. Res. 67 which authorized the first nationwide investigation of the illicit narcotics traffic, drug addiction, and the treatment of drug addicts, with the objective of improving the Federal Criminal Code and enforcement procedures dealing with marijuana and other drugs.[52]

Beginning in late May 1955, the testimony at the hearings, chaired by Senator Price Daniel of Texas, indicated that the review of narcotics traffic in the postwar era was almost a replay of past investigations. The FBN—represented by Anslinger and Malachi Harney, the "brain trust" behind the Bureau's enforcement policies—enthusiastically favored the resolution. Just as with the Marijuana Tax Act hearings in 1937, "outside" expert witnesses corroborated Anslinger's assertions about how dangerous narcotics addiction was to the future of the United States. A number of invited public officials offered variations of the exaggerated effects of marijuana.[53] With the exception of Dr. Woodward, who opposed the bill, the only "official" testimony given at the hearings was from Treasury Department personnel who inititated the legislation.

The resulting Narcotic Control Act (NCA) was the most severe antidrug legislation put into effect. In addition to making the possession of marijuana a felony offense, the NCA doubled the lengthy sentences in the Boggs Act and included mandatory minimum sentences for the first conviction. Its most notable feature, however, was the inclusion of the death penalty in some cases.[54] At the time that both Congressman Boggs and Senator Daniel were sponsoring more severe antinarcotics legislation—reflecting the desire of their constituents—they were running for their respective statehouses. Projecting themselves as strong law-and-order advocates of a safe nonpolitical issue would enhance their electability. Obviously these two politicians, like Commissioner Anslinger, were mindful of how valuable a drug epidemic could be in advancing their careers. Not only was the narcotics menace a convenient weapon for minority oppression, but also it was easy to exploit as a political issue.

Anslinger's successor at the FBN, Commissioner Henry L. Giordano, revealed the government's inconsistent policies on federal drug legislation when he was asked during an interview why marijuana was illegal and alcohol—the most abused drug in the country—was not. His response was that "alcohol has been socially accepted for many, many years. Smoking marijuana was never socially accepted."[55] It did not seem to matter that alcohol can be just as deleterious and have effects on the mind and perception similar to those of marijuana. What matters is if a drug is acceptable to the mainstream.

The provisions of the Marijuana Tax Act, of course, were not really designed to raise revenue or even regulate the use of marijuana. Their purpose was to provide the legal mechanisms to enforce the prohibition of all use of marijuana. The bureau accelerated its educational campaign, and within a few years every state had passed laws against marijuana that were often equated with laws concerning murder, rape, and other heinous offenses. These laws also failed to distinguish one drug from another. Immediately following the Marijuana Tax Act, most states had specified that marijuana and heroin penalties should be identical. Consequently, as heroin sentences were increased over the years, marijuana penalties were automatically readjusted upward.

The Marijuana Tax Act, which is now a part of the Internal Revenue Code, has not produced any significant revenue since few marijuana tax stamps have been issued to those wishing to officially register under the act. Still, as late as 1970, the Internal Revenue Service has tried to collect $100,000 per ounce of illegally possessed marijuana from those who have violated the act.[56]

CONTROVERSY OVER MARIJUANA PROHIBITION

The history of marijuana prohibition since the enactment of the Marijuana Tax Act has provoked enormous controversy, resulting in dramatic modifications. Many people viewed the original legislation as a hastily adopted attempt to restrain individual behavior that the government, or agencies of the government, had determined was harmful and objectionable. Many have argued, however, that the "cure" was more detrimental to the user's health than was the "ailment." The actual enforcement of the marijuana prohibition was in many ways more threatening to society than were the problems the drug created.

Drugs stayed on the fringes of society throughout the 1950s, but by the next decade Harvard professor Timothy Leary enticed students to "turn on, tune in, and drop out" with LSD. The volatile baby-boom generation of the 1960s, who flocked to "hothouse" campuses in greater numbers than ever before, was attracted to drugs for the simple reason that their parents condemned them. The counterculture was already convinced of the establishment's hypocrisy with re-gard to coinciding high rates of prosperity, crime, and poverty.[57] When the depression-raised parents condemned marijuana while imbibing martinis over lunch, the generation gap became an unbridgeable chasm.

Because marijuana had become one of the most popular drugs in the 1960s, particularly among the rebellious college student population and counterculture, the federal government devised a plan to crack down on the influx of the drug. In September 1969 Operation Intercept attempted to cut off marijuana trafficking at the Mexican border. Closer inspection of automobiles and over 1,800 strip searches resulted in only thirty-three arrests in its first week. The operation also backed up traffic for three miles or more and offended the Mexican government which protested that its citizens were humiliated and suffered the indignities of a common suspect. Three weeks later the project was canceled. Operation Intercept was replaced by Operation Cooperation which was designed to minimize "unnecessary inconvenience, delay, and irritation in inspections."[58]

In 1963, a year after Anslinger ended his long tenure as head of the Federal Narcotics Bureau, the Presidential Commission on Narcotics and Drug Abuse reversed the long-standing trend of harsh penalties when it advocated a repeal of the mandatory minimum sentences, which clearly were not achieving the desired results.[59]

To deal more effectively with a rapidly growing problem of drug usage among young people in the 1960s, the Bureau of Drug Abuse Control (BDAC) was created, and in 1967 the Presidential Commission on Law Enforcement and Administration of Justice conducted a close study of the drug problem. For more effective bureaucratic handling of the situation, the FBN was transferred to the

Department of Justice in 1968 and merged with BDAC to become the new Bureau of Narcotics and Other Dangerous Drugs (BNDD).

In 1968 Richard Nixon centered his presidential campaign around a law-and-order theme. He also declared war on drugs. To wage that war, he created the Office of Drug Abuse and Law Enforcement (ODALE) and the Office of National Narcotics Intelligence (ONNI), and in 1973 he initiated Reorganization Plan No. 2. Under this plan the five-year-old BNDD became the Drug Enforcement Administration.

During the Nixon administration, various substances were viewed in terms of their physical and mental effects and their propensity for addiction.[60] Greater scientific study revealed a wide disparity in the harmful effects of various drugs. The Comprehensive Drug Abuse Prevention and Control Act in 1970 created five schedules that categorized drugs according to their effects and availability by prescription.

THE OMNIBUS DRUG ENFORCEMENT, EDUCATION, AND CONTROL ACT

For thirty years after the Narcotic Control Act in 1956, Congress passed no significant revisions in the criminal code pertaining to drug usage. In this period Congress did pass two pieces of legislation that provided for the treatment of addicts, three implementing preventative measures, and three bureaucratic or enforcement directives.[61] But in 1986, in an attempt to strengthen efforts to eradicate the drug traffic, Congress responded to increasing public concern by introducing H.R. 5484, the Omnibus Drug Enforcement, Education, and Control Act of 1986.

In an election year the bill enjoyed wide support in Congress as members competed with each other to get their names attached to an effective piece of legislation.[62] Introduced by Democratic Majority Leader Jim Wright of Texas on September 8, the bill stiffened penalties for pushers, increased customs and border patrols, outlawed synthetic drugs, and improved treatment and prevention programs. In a scenario reminiscent of a political poker game, others wanted to "see" the Democrats' penalties and "raise" the ante. Republican Representative Duncan L. Hunter of California and Democratic Representative Tommy Robinson of Arkansas proposed an amendment to provide for military personnel to prevent the entry of aircraft and boats transporting drugs. It passed 237 to 177. California Republican Don Lundgren introduced an amendment to eliminate the exclusionary rule in criminal cases, in effect allowing the use of evidence obtained through improper searches and seizures. The move to abrogate civil liberties also passed by a lop-sided vote of 259 to 153. The most controversial amendment, proposed by George Gekas, a Republican representative from Pennsylvania, imposed the "death penalty for individuals involved in a continuing criminal enterprise who intentionally cause the death of another individual." In an atmosphere of fear and frustration the amendment was adopted on September 11. H.R. 5484 passed the House by an overwhelming margin of 392 to 16.[63]

In the Senate, Democratic Minority Leader Robert C. Byrd of West Virginia introduced a bipartisan measure, S. 2787, that would authorize $1.4 billion for the war on drugs by increasing the penalties for drug offenses, among other lesser provisions. Interestingly, these programs would be paid for with taxes on two other drugs, cigarettes and alcohol.[64] The Senate passed the bill with a 97–2 vote. The death penalty was removed in favor of a mandatory life sentence without parole for drug-related murder cases.[65]

Since 1986, opponents of imposing extremely severe penalties or involving the military in drug interdiction have been silent. Fighting drug abuse, a problem that permeates every socioeconomic group and level, has met with little opposition. According to an August 1986 *Newsweek* survey, 56 percent of those polled were even willing to pay for fighting drug abuse when they felt that the government was spending too little. People were also more supportive of spending money on fighting drugs than they were of spending for President Reagan's Star Wars defense project.[66]

Drug historian and psychiatrist David Musto has stated that the drug problem will diminish proportionately to the degree that the public becomes more outraged about it. He cautions, however, that this process may take ten years. Harvard psychiatrist Lester Grinspoon has expressed a more pessimistic—and perhaps more realistic—view that "people have used, do use, and will always use drugs."[67] The truth may lie somewhere in between. Regardless, it is a certainty that America's history of failed drug control has caught up with it, and the drug problem is likely to accelerate before any improvement is seen.

NOTES

1. Edward M. Brecher, *Licit and Illicit Drugs* (Boston: Little, Brown, 1972), 3; Evan Thomas, "America's Crusade: What Is Behind the Latest War on Drugs," *Time*, 15 September 1986, 64.

2. Brecher, *Licit and Illicit Drugs*, 3. For a more extensive discussion of drug addiction in the nineteenth century, see David F. Musto, *The American Disease: Origins of Narcotic Control* (New York: Oxford University Press, 1973), 1–9; H. Wayne Morgan, *Drugs in America: A Social History, 1800–1980* (Syracuse, N.Y.: Syracuse University Press, 1981), 29–87; and James A. Inciardi, *The War on Drugs: Heroin, Cocaine, Crime, and Public Policy* (Palo Alto, Calif.: Mayfield Publishing Co., 1986), 1–15.

Drugs were in such widespread use that in 1886 John Styth Pemberton used the extract of the kola nut—that was about 2 percent caffeine—to produce a syrup he called Coca-Cola. The cocaine extract was used in the popular drink until 1906 when the Bureau of Food and Drugs initiated a court case that eventually forced the manufacturer to discontinue using the drug. Caffeine was used as a substitute. Also see Brecher, *Licit and Illicit Drugs*, 270–71.

3. Thomas, "America's Crusade," 64. For a discussion of public attitudes and stereotypes as they pertained to drug users, see David Courtwright, *Dark Paradise: Opiate*

Addiction in America Before 1940 (Cambridge, Mass.: Harvard University Press, 1982), 1–4.

4. Morgan, *Drugs in America*, 98–99.

5. Harry J. Anslinger, "Address Before the *New York Herald Tribune*," 25 October 1938, Harry J. Anslinger Papers, Box 4, The Pennsylvania State University, University Park, Pennsylvania [hereafter referred to as HJA]; Harry J. Anslinger, "The Implementation of Treaty Obligations in Regulating the Traffic in Narcotic Drugs," *American University Law Review* 7–8 (1958–1959): 112.

6. See U.S. Congress, 63d Cong.: House, special sess., 3 April 1913, 134; House, 1st sess., 24 June 1913, 2168; House, 26 June 1913, 2191–2201; Senate, 20 December 1913, 1288; Senate, 13 January 1914, 1559; House, 26 January 1914, 2329, in the *Congressional Record*.

Dr. Wright was adamant about restricting the use of narcotics, but apparently felt that alcohol was less detrimental. In 1914 Wright was dismissed from the State Department by Secretary Bryan when he refused to take a pledge of abstinence. Musto, *The American Disease*, 61.

7. Harry J. Anslinger, "The Need For Narcotic Education" (Address, 24 February 1936, HJA, Box 1.

8. Morgan, *Drugs in America*, 109; Brecher, *Licit and Illicit Drugs*, 49–50.

9. U.S. v. Jin Fuey Moy, 241 U.S. 394 (1916). Musto, *The American Disease*, 128–30; Morgan, *Drugs in America*, 110. In the 1919 case of Doremus v. U.S., 253 U.S. 487 (1919), the U.S. Supreme Court held that the Harrison Act was constitutional, as it did again in 1928 in Nigro v. U.S., 276 U.S. 332 (1928).

10. Brecher, *Licit and Illicit Drugs*, 51.

11. Ibid.

12. Musto, *The American Disease*, 135. Secretary McAdoo appointed the special committee in March 1918 to study the future of narcotics enforcement. Committee members were Democratic Congressman Henry T. Rainey of Illinois; Dr. Reid Hunt, professor of pharmacology at Harvard; B. C. Keith, deputy commissioner of the Internal Revenue Bureau; and A. G. DuMez of the Public Health Service.

13. Lawrence Kolb, "Drug Addiction in Its Relation to Crime," *Mental Hygiene* 9 (January 1925): 74–89; Lawrence Kolb, "Types and Characteristics of Drug Addicts," *Mental Hygiene* 9 (April 1925): 300–13; Lawrence Kolb, "Pleasure and Deterioration from Narcotic Addiction," *Mental Hygiene* 9 (October 1925): 699–724. In the 1930s, after the maintenance treatment plan was abandoned, Kolb continued to defend a more humane approach to drug addiction. See Lawrence Kolb, "The Narcotic: His Treatment," *Federal Probation* 1–3 (1937–1939): 19–23.

Typical of the opposition to Dr. Kolb's thinking was a 1919 article that asserted "There would be no question that National and State investigation, and the more rigid enforcement of existing laws, are seriously needed." See "Drug Addicts in America," *Outlook*, 25 June 1919, 315.

14. U.S. Congress, House Committee on the Judiciary, *Establishment of Two Federal Narcotics Farms, Hearings Before the Committee on the Judiciary on H. R. 12781*, 70th Cong., 1st sess., 1928, 12; Courtwright, *Dark Paradise*, 141. For a broader discussion of the maintenance programs and narcotics clinics, see Musto, *The American Disease*, 121–82.

15. Harry J. Anslinger, "The Need for Narcotic Education"; Donald E. Miller, "Nar-

cotic Drug and Marijuana Controls," *Journal of Psychedelic Drugs* 1 & 2 (1967–1969): 27; Inciardi, *The War on Drugs*, 17.

16. U.S. Congress, *Establishment of Two Narcotics Farms, Hearings*, 12–13.

17. "Work to Begin Saturday on First Narcotic Farm," *Washington Herald*, 27 July 1933, HJA, Box 8; John F. Landis, "U.S. Narcotic Farm," *Federal Probation* 1 (April 1937): 25.

18. U.S. Congress, House Committee on Ways and Means, *Bureau of Narcotics, Hearings Before the Committee on Ways and Means in H.R. 10561*, 71st Cong., 2nd sess., 1930, 3–6.

19. "Narcotics Official Suspected Addict," undated article, HJA, Box 6. The scandal in the Narcotics Bureau and the alleged Rothstein connection to Colonel Nutt's relatives is taken from *New York Times* clippings in the Anslinger papers (Box 6). See also U.S. Congress, *Bureau of Narcotics, Hearings*, 73–77; Leo Katcher, *The Big Bankroll: The Life and Times of Arnold Rothstein* (New York: Harper & Brothers, 1958), 290–99; Stanley Meisler, "Federal Narcotics Czar," *Nation* 190 (January–June 1960): 160.

20. "Urge Altoonan as Narcotics Chief," *Altoona Mirror*, 8 May 1930. Anslinger's wife was the former Martha Denniston, member of a wealthy mining family in western Pennsylvania.

21. "Narcotic Agent Lectures Here," *The Dickinsonian*, 15 December 1932, HJA, Box 6.

22. James Sterba, "The Politics of Pot," *Esquire*, August 1968, 59.

23. A. E. Fossier, "The Marijuana Menace," *New Orleans Medical and Surgical Journal* 84 (1931): 247; Eugene Stanley, "Marijuana as a Developer of Criminals," *American Journal of Police Science* 2 (1931): 256.

24. "Use of New Narcotics Reported Spreading," March 1931, HJA, Box 6; Untitled correspondence, HJA, Box 3.

25. Linking drugs with sex was common in the 1930s since a sex-crime panic developed in the middle of the decade and continued until the end of World War II. See Estell B. Freedman, "Uncontrolled Desires: The Response to the Sexual Psychopath, 1920–1960," *Journal of American History* 74 (June 1987): 83–106.

The phrase "assassin of youth" is taken from *Assassin of Youth*, a low-budget movie produced in the 1930s. Anslinger borrowed the title for an article he coauthored with Courtney Riley Cooper in *American Magazine*, July 1937, 18–19, 150–53.

26. Letter from Dr. Michael V. Ball to Will S. Wood, 7 October 1936, and letter from Harry J. Anslinger to Dr. Michael V. Ball, 18 October 1936, HJA, Box 9.

27. Speech to the World Narcotics Defense Association, 13 April 1936, HJA, Box 1.

28. "The Harrison Act's Failure (editorial)," *St. Louis Post-Dispatch*, 17 December 1934.

29. See "Conference on 'Cannabis Sativa,' " 14 January 1937, HJA, Box 6.

30. U.S. Congress: House. *Taxation of Marijuana, Hearings before the Committee on Ways and Means on H.R. 6385*, 75th Cong., 1st sess., 1937, 87.

31. Ibid., 92.

32. Ibid., 118–21.

33. "Narcotics Traffic Is Curbed by War," *New York Times*, 27 September 1942, 51; "The Marijuana Bugaboo," *Military Medicine* 93 (July 1943): 94–95.

34. Eli Markovitz and Henry J. Myers, "The Marijuana Addict in the Army," *War Medicine* 6 (December 1944): 382–91.

35. U.S. Department of the Treasury, *Traffic in Opium and Other Dangerous Drugs*

for the Year Ended December 31, 1942 (Washington, D.C.: U.S. Government Printing Office, 1942), 6–7; Anslinger interview on radio station WFBR, Baltimore, Maryland, 28 February 1947, HJA, Box 1.

36. File: "Marijuana Users—Musicians, 1933–1937," HJA, Box 9; Dan Wakefield, "The Prodigal Powers of Pot," *Playboy*, August 1962, 58.

37. Milton "Mezz" Mezzrow and Bernard Wolfe, *Really the Blues* (New York: Random House, 1946), 85–86.

38. Lester Grinspoon, *Marijuana Reconsidered* (Cambridge, Mass.: Harvard University Press, 1971), 26. See also Mayor LaGuardia's Committee on Marijuana, *The Marijuana Problem in the City of New York* (Lancaster, Pa.: Jacque Cattell Press, 1944; Metuchen, N.J.: Scarecrow Reprint Corporation, 1973).

39. Mayor LaGuardia's Committee, *The Marijuana Problem*, 10.

40. *The Marijuana Problem*, p. 10–12.

41. Samuel Allentuck and Karl R. Bowman, "The Psychiatric Aspects of Marijuana Intoxication," *American Journal of Psychiatry* 99 (1942): 248–50.

42. "Recent Investigation of Marijuana," *JAMA* 120 (1942): 1128–29.

43. See, for example, J. Bouquet, "Marijuana Intoxication (letter to the editor)," *JAMA* 124 (1944): 1010; J. D. Reichard, "The Marijuana Problem (editorial)," *JAMA* 125 (1944): 594; "Marijuana Problems (editorial)," *JAMA* 127 (1945): 1129; Robert P. Walton, "Marijuana Problems (letter to the editor)," *JAMA* 128 (1945): 283; Karl B. Bowman, "Marijuana Problems (letter to the editor)," *JAMA* 128 (1945): 889–90; Eli Markovitz, "Marijuana Problems (letter to the editor)," *JAMA* 129 (1945): 378.

For additional reactions to the LaGuardia report other than in JAMA, see "What Happens to Marijuana Smokers," *Science Digest* 17 (January–June 1940): 35–40; "Marijuana Found Useful in Certain Mental Ills," *Science News Letter* 41–42 (1942): 341–42; George B. Wallace, "The Marijuana Problem in New York City," *American Journal of Corrections* 5–6 (1943–1944): 7, 24–26; Arnold E. Esrati, "How Mild Is Marijuana?" *Magazine Digest* (June 1945): 80–86; "The Marijuana Problem," *Federal Probation* 9–10 (1945–1946): 15–22; "Marijuana and Mentality," *Newsweek*, 18 November 1946, 70–71.

44. U.S. Congress, House Committee on Ways and Means, *Control of Narcotics, Marijuana, and Barbiturates, Hearings Before a Subcommittee of the Committee on Ways and Means, House of Representatives, on H.R. 3490*, 82nd Cong., 1st sess., 1951, pp. 1–2.

45. U.S. Congress, Congressman Victor L. Anfuso Commenting on H.R. 3490, 82d Cong., 1st sess., 21 June 1951, *Congressional Record* 97:6931.

46. U.S. Congress, *Control of Narcotics, Hearings*, 1–2.

47. Ibid., 206; *New York Times*, 15 April 1955, 59.

48. U.S. Congress, Congressman Emanuel Celler Debating H.R. 3490, 82d Cong., 1st sess., 16 July 1951, *Congressional Record* 97: 8205.

49. "Narcotics Drop Reported," *New York Times*, 21 January 1952, 22.

50. U.S. Congress, Congressman Fred E. Busbey Commenting on H.R. 8700, 83d Cong., 2d sess., 2 April 1954, *Congressional Record* 100: 4540–41.

51. Richard J. Bonnie and Charles H. Whitebread II, *The Marijuana Conviction: A History of Marijuana Prohibition in the United States* (Charlottesville: University Press of Virginia, 1974), 215–17.

52. "Bill Sinks Teeth in Narcotics Code," *New York Times*, 15 January 1955, 9; U.S.

Congress, Senator Price Daniel Introducing S. Res. 67, 84th Cong., 1st sess., 18 March 1955, *Congressional Record* 101: 6875.

53. U.S. Congress, Senate Committee on the Judiciary, *Illicit Narcotics Traffic Hearings, Before the Subcommittee on Improvements in the Federal Criminal Code of the Committee of the Judiciary, Senate, on S. Res. 67,* 84th Cong., 1st sess., Part I, 1955, 173, 230.

54. Ibid.

55. Interview with Henry L. Giordano, Washington, D.C., 25 March 1985.

56. Roger Smith, "U.S. Marijuana Legislation and the Creation of a Social Problem," *Journal of Psychedelic Drugs* 1–2 (1967–1969): 97.

57. See, for example, James Q. Wilson, "Crime Amidst Plenty: The Paradox of the Sixties," in *Thinking About Crime* (New York: Vintage Books, 1985), 13–25.

58. Brecher, *Licit and Illicit Drugs*, 434–40; Inciardi, *The War on Drugs*, 34–35.

59. Musto, *The American Disease*, 238.

60. Ibid., 260. The first Federal Strategy for Drug Abuse and Drug Traffic Prevention, created in 1973, demonstrated no appreciable progressive thinking when it acknowledged that alcohol and tobacco were serious problems, but that those drugs have become part of this country's "rituals and customs."

61. Legislation for addicts included the Narcotic Addict Rehabilitation Act of 1966 and the Narcotic Addict Treatment Act of 1974; for prevention there was the Comprehensive Drug Abuse Prevention and Control Act of 1972 and the Drug Abuse Prevention and Treatment Amendments of 1978. The enforcement directives were the Crime Control Act of 1976, which placed the Law Enforcement Assistance Administration (LEAA) under the direction of the attorney general; the Organized Crime Drug Enforcement Program of 1982, in which the attorney general was given concurrent jurisdiction with DEA officials to investigate drug law violations; and a 1986 National Security Decision Directive, which resulted in sending Army helicopters and 160 support troops to Bolivia to raid cocaine-processing facilities. At the same time, Operation Alliance activated six hundred agents along the Mexican-American border to combat drug trafficking. See "Evolution of Current Drug Legislation," *Congressional Digest*, November 1986, 260, 288.

62. "Trying to Say 'No,' " *Newsweek*, 11 August 1986, 14–15. More than eighty pieces of legislation were proposed. "Drugs: Now Prime Time," *U.S. News & World Report*, 11 August 1986, 16.

63. "Recent Action in Congress," *Congressional Digest*, November 1986, 263, 288. Congressman Wright was startled to learn that 82 percent of those polled in his Ft. Worth, Texas, district believed that drug use was a serious problem in their neighborhood. "Drugs: Now Prime Time," 17. See also "Drug Fever in Washington," *Newsweek*, 22 September 1986, 39.

64. "Grabbing the Drug Issue," *Newsweek*, 23 June 1986, 31.

65. "Recent Action in Congress," 288.

66. "Trying to Say 'No,' " 16. In another poll taken a month later, 69 percent of the public said they would favor a highly controversial drug-testing program at their company. "Rolling Out the Big Guns," *Time*, 22 September 1986, 25.

67. Ted Gest, "The Latest Antidrug War: Better Luck This Time?" *U.S. News & World Report*, 25 August 1986, 18.

_____

Chapter 2

The Growth of Drug Abuse Treatment Systems

Barry S. Brown

MAKING OPIATE USE A CRIME

To a significant degree the recent history of drug abuse treatment in the United States has reflected an ambivalence as to whether the drug abuser is properly regarded as a concern of the health care system or of the criminal justice system. The beginnings of that dilemma may be placed at various points in time. One reasonable choice might be the passage of the Pure Food and Drug Act in 1906. Until that time the chief vehicle for abusable substances appears to have been the patent medicines widely available and dispensed for the cure and/or ameliora-tion of a host of complaints. The preparations available frequently contained alcohol and opiates in a combination (laudanum) likely to bring the user a clear sense of relief. The numbers of people who became dependent on the medicines available is, of course, an unknown. However, it has been speculated that this may be the only time in our history when the largest part of the opiate-dependent population was made up of white females.[1]

Concern about the deleterious effects of patent medicines appears to have been stimulated by two contemporaneous movements. On the one hand, the Progres-sive movement in politics had successfully advocated a role for government in the regulation of commerce when there appeared to be a risk to the public well-being. On the other, the medical profession was initiating action to install itself as the profession of choice for health concerns. The ready availability of patent medicines of unknown, but suspicious, content was inimical to the interests of both movements.[2] The passage of the Pure Food and Drug Act began an effort to bring drugs under control; the passage of the Harrison Act in 1914 not only hastened that process, but also led to a casting of the drug user into the shadows of concealment and ostracism.

The Harrison Act made illegal the importation, sale, or possession of opiates under other than medical auspices. On its face the law permitted the dispensing of opiates by physicians for all medical conditions including opiate dependence. Indeed, into the 1920s some physicians and clinics did exactly that, prescribing opiates to permit drug-dependent patients to avert withdrawal.[3] However, actions by the courts, culminating in action by the U.S. Supreme Court in 1928, eventually forbade physicians from prescribing opiates in support of their patients' addictions. The die was cast. Treatment for opiate addiction would in the end be removed from the jurisdiction of the medical profession and placed under the jurisdiction of the underworld. In the process the form in which heroin was available would pass from opium and cumbersome medicines to a form that lent itself to greater concealment and more rapid administration, a practice that would be repeated with other illicit drugs, and the criminal addict would replace the consumer of medicinal aids.

TREATMENT DOWN ON THE FARM

With opiate addiction—now almost exclusively heroin addiction—emerging as an issue in the populations of federal penitentiaries, the federal government established narcotics farms, first in Lexington, Kentucky, in 1935 and later in Ft. Worth, Texas, in 1938. These programs treated only persons dependent on narcotics as legally defined (i.e., opiates, cocaine, and marijuana); the Lexington program treated males from east of the Mississippi and females from all over the country, while the Ft. Worth program admitted males from west of the Mississippi and from New Orleans. While open to nonincarcerated patients, less than 20 percent of the patients admitted themselves voluntarily.[4] Addicts were viewed as "experts in malingering, chicanery, and subterfuge,"[5] and because of that reason, and the need for carefully regulated withdrawal and a lengthy period of rehabilitation, it was seen as beneficial to treat addicts in controlled residential settings.[6]

Treatment during the period from 1935 through the mid-1950s was most likely to consist of medical withdrawal using codeine for mild addictions[7] and subcutaneous morphine and later (1948) subcutaneous methadone for more serious addiction;[8] group therapy and psychotherapy,[9] but without great confidence in either;[10] and rehabilitative experiences generally involving an effort to inculcate good work habits and a sense of responsibility.[11] Follow-up was viewed as of great importance by some,[12] with the belief that a job, a supportive home, and some continued monitoring of the former addict's behaviors were all key to success.[13] In 1947 Addicts Anonymous, later to be renamed Narcotics Anonymous, emerged as a community organization dedicated to the support of addicts' efforts to free themselves of drug use through the mutual support of addicts for addicts in a structure that combined the spiritual and the secular.[14]

THE DEVELOPMENT OF A VARIED
TREATMENT RESPONSE

By the mid-1950s the significant numbers of heroin addicts in the nation's large cities began to spark some significant interest in drug abuse treatment outside the "narcotics farms" and in the urban communities most affected.[15] In New York City space was allotted at Kings County and Bellevue Hospitals for the short-term treatment of adolescent addicts. Long-term treatment was provided at Riverside Hospital beginning in 1952. Treatment included a school in addition to a full range of medical and psychosocial treatment as well as follow-up. During this same time period three clinics dedicated to drug abuse treatment were also opened in Chicago.[16]

The Therapeutic Community

In 1958 there was established in Santa Monica, California, a treatment program destined to have a profound impact on drug abuse treatment throughout the succeeding decades. Charles Dederich, a successful alumnus of Alcoholics Anonymous, had been meeting in his home with other AA members and later some narcotic addicts. Dederich observed that some of the latter who became a part of Dederich's "extended family" showed an ability to give up their use of drugs. Out of that modest in-home experience was born Synanon and the therapeutic community movement.[17]

In time, the therapeutic community would become a national and then an international force, exerting an influence on drug abuse programming well beyond the large number of residential programs that the movement spawned. The therapeutic community asserted not only that the drug abuse client could be rehabilitated, but also that the addict who had successfully completed rehabilitation was central to the treatment and rehabilitation of others. Therapeutic community graduates came to serve at levels up to and including program administrators. Therapeutic community personnel view the new residents (and all drug abusers) as immature, inadequate persons, lacking a capacity to respond appropriately or responsibly to life's challenges. To achieve a level of maturity and responsibility requires the carefully planned use of community pressures and supports within a closed setting (i.e., a setting that for some period permits no external and undesirable influences on the individual's growth and behaviors). The therapeutic community is designed as a hierarchy such that residents are accorded gradually increasing levels of responsibility for the life and functioning of the community commensurate with increasing status within that community and increasing reward. Success, and status, is thus earned by the assumption of responsibility within the community.

Not only is there growth through a training in life experience, but also there is opportunity for growth through interaction with counselors in individual and group sessions. Indeed, it is the group sessions that receive the largest attention in descriptions of therapeutic community programming. Those sessions may involve confrontation intended to force the resident to face his or her efforts at denial or subterfuge and may be designed to permit a gaining of insight and an understanding of behaviors, but group sessions will virtually always involve support from the community for efforts at responsibility-taking and growth.

The therapeutic community views drug abuse as a disorder capable of being

treated through a use of psychosocial and rehabilitative strategies. It views graduation from the residential facility as completion of the rehabilitation (i.e.,
growth, process). In contrast, methadone treatment views the drug abuse it treats
as a disease and defines that disease as chronic and relapsing. As we will see,
this marks one of several points of difference between the therapeutic community
and methadone treatment.

Methadone Treatment

In 1963 there came the first reports of the efficacy of methadone hydrochloride
as a maintenance drug for heroin addiction. Heretofore the drug had been in use
for detoxification of addicts, but now came reports from the Rockefeller Institute
that this World War II–inspired synthetic opiate could allow heroin addicts to
become stabilized physiologically to a point that they ceased craving heroin and
could begin to avail themselves of treatment services.[18] Particular emphasis was
placed on the utility of methadone maintenance with the criminal justice population.[19]

Not only did methadone maintenance treatment add a new and increasingly
influential treatment resource, but also its innovators established a research par-
adigm that came to exert an equally profound influence on the drug abuse field.[20]
They established three core behavioral measures of treatment effectiveness: (1)
reduction in drug use, (2) reduction in criminal activity, and (3) increase in
socially productive activity. While additional measures have been added in accord
with investigators' interests and concerns, these three outcome criteria have
remained central to the field of program evaluation, allowing a degree of comparability across studies of different treatment modalities. It may be particularly
noteworthy that these outcome measures, now universally employed, represent
an evaluation of the extent to which clients' behaviors have become more socially
appropriate (i.e., the client is less invested in illicit activities), as opposed to a
concern with changes in psychiatric or psychological functioning.

Moreover, because Vincent P. Dole, Marie E. Nyswander, and their colleagues
placed an emphasis on examining the efficacy of the treatment modality they
had pioneered, there was established an expectation of treatment evaluation which
has been applied to drug abuse treatment programs generally. In particular,
follow-up evaluation (i.e., the study of former clients' functioning after they
have returned to the community) has come to be seen as essential to an understanding of the effectiveness of a treatment program in rehabilitating clients.
The art and science of follow-up evaluation were extended first by George E.
Valliant[21] and then by John A. O'Donnell,[22] and were developed finally into a
replicable research model by Saul B. Sells, D. Dwayne Simpson, and their
colleagues.[23]

Not long after the introduction of methadone as a maintenance drug, work
began on the study of another class of drugs that many felt could prove important
to the treatment and rehabilitation of heroin addicts. In 1966 it was reported that

cyclazocine, a drug with narcotic antagonist properties, could block the effects of opiate drugs for a period of twenty-four hours. By 1973, with the discovery of the brain's opiate receptors, it would be understood that the action of the narcotic antagonists was such as to occupy those receptors and prevent entry by the metabolites of opiate drugs taken after the antagonist drug had been ingested.[24] However, cyclazocine also produced negative side effects[25] and eventually came to be replaced as an antagonist drug of choice by naltrexone,[26] a drug still available for use today.

In part, the search for an effective antagonist drug represents the continuing effort to find new and more effective strategies of treatment for opiate addiction. In addition, the emphasis on antagonists is consistent with a long-standing public ambivalence about the use of methadone in the treatment of drug addiction. Thus, in 1971 the U.S. Congress took the somewhat unusual step of mandating research in the narrow area of efficacy of narcotic antagonist drugs for treatment of heroin addiction[27] at the same time it called for regulation specific to the provision of methadone treatment.

Conflict over the wisdom and indeed the ethics of methadone maintenance treatment has been a constant in the drug abuse field. While there has been little argument about the capacity of methadone to attract clients, to retain clients in treatment, and to permit clients to adopt prosocial behaviors while in treatment, none of those oft-repeated findings[28] has acted to overcome concerns about the appropriateness of administering methadone in the treatment of heroin addiction. Methadone is most frequently criticized as a simple substitution of one opiate for another (e.g., of whiskey for gin), leaving the addict still an addict.[29] In this argument it is viewed as pointless at best to perpetuate an open-ended dependency on an opiate in the name of rehabilitation and cure. The counterargument by supporters of methadone treatment has been that methadone, unlike other opiates, allows the individual to become accessible to a body of treatment services that permit change in life style and functioning. To buttress their argument, they point to the studies described above, indicating diminution in both heroin use and crime and increases in employment consequent to involvement in methadone treatment. While many clinicians argue against any restriction on the length of methadone maintenance treatment,[30] all but a distinct minority of addict-clients elect to free themselves of methadone at some point in treatment.

In the early days of its availability, methadone treatment was also tied to the political climate of the times and was characterized by some portion of the black community as a "colonial device" and as a "genocidal" initiative.[31] Indeed, one prominent medical administrator reported that "the area [of Bedford-Stuyvesant] was rather hostile to methadone maintenance. People there decided that I was the black man who been chosen by the white man to deliver the white man's poison to that community, which sort of alienated me from the segment of the population that I had been identified with in the past."[32]

Over the years much of the heat has been removed from the controversy surrounding the provision of methadone treatment and, more specifically, methadone maintenance. Nonetheless, the controversy continues and, as will be discussed below, continues to impact on the delivery of treatment services.

Outpatient Drug-Free Treatment

In 1963 the Congress passed the Community Mental Health Centers Act which provided funds for the development of mental health centers at the community level and, within those centers, treatment for drug abuse clients.[33] While there is little indication that the passage of the act stimulated any substantial increase in services to drug abuse clients, it seems likely that the act did exert an influence on the delivery of drug abuse treatment in the decade that followed its passage. The emphasis on the delivery of services to clients at the local level and the reliance on individual counseling strategies—joined as appropriate with vocational, educational, and other community assistance—were carried over to the structure and functioning of the drug-free outpatient programs of the 1970s. While much of the mental health establishment held drug abuse at arm's length—or beyond—through both the 1960s and the 1970s, the community mental health center program provided an important model of service delivery even as the centers themselves were only rarely involved in the treatment of drug abuse clients.

LINKS TO THE CRIMINAL JUSTICE SYSTEM

The 1960s also marked a period in which legislative initiatives were introduced to guarantee continuing supervision/treatment to drug abusers located through the work of the criminal justice system. In 1961 the state of California instituted a civil commitment authority, and in 1966 the state of New York followed suit. Civil commitment programs assert that the inappropriate and criminal behaviors being shown by individuals are a consequence of factors—for example, heroin addiction—which may be more effectively treated through medical/psychosocial interventions than through a reliance on the criminal justice system. Thus, in developing these programs, California and New York implicitly were accepting a position that drug abusers, and more particularly heroin addicts, could be rehabilitated using the programs and personnel of health care.

In practice, civil commitment programs will often use the facilities and staff of the criminal justice system and maintain addict-clients in closed residential facilities. This was the case in both the California and the New York programs.[34] Nonetheless, the message was clear. Drug abusers were subject to services different from those available to other criminal justice clients, and they were subject to those services because they were drug abusers. In both California and New York the services included community aftercare programming and in California methadone treatment. In 1966 the federal government also threw its weight behind civil commitment programs with the passage of the Narcotic Addict

Rehabilitation Act (NARA), and with that action, federal funds could be used to provide drug abuse services through the country.

The Narcotic Addict Rehabilitation Act was divided into four parts.[35] Under Title 1 the surgeon general of the U.S. Public Health Service was empowered to act on behalf of "persons charged with or convicted of violating Federal criminal laws . . . addicted to narcotic drugs, and likely to be rehabilitated through treatment, [who] should, in lieu of prosecution or sentencing, be civilly committed for confinement and treatment designed to effect the restoration to health, and return to society. . . . " Title 2 provided for the treatment of addicts who have been convicted of federal crimes. For Title 2 clients, treatment services were provided by the Federal Bureau of Prisons. Title 3 clients were those committing themselves voluntarily for treatment, and their services were again under the control of the Public Health Service. Title 4 established funding for community-based (i.e., local) drug abuse treatment programs. As such, it placed the federal government and the federal purse in the position of supporting neighborhood programming for drug abuse. While NARA has been phased out, the federal role in community drug abuse treatment has grown. At the same time, the New York civil commitment program has been retrenched to focus its rehabilitative efforts on prison inmates,[36] while the California program continues to be a significant aspect of that state's total treatment programming.[37]

RESPONDING TO AN EPIDEMIC

Through the late 1960s substance abuse, and more particularly heroin addiction, was little more than a curiosity to mainstream America. It had remained, it appeared, safely remote. Confined to ghetto neighborhoods, to despicable elements of the criminal underclass, to the most bohemian of musicians and artists, it was a part of community life that need never impact on the lives and functioning of responsible individuals. By the early 1970s complacency had disappeared. It would never return. In a poll taken in the spring of 1971 only Vietnam and the economy were rated as more significant national problems than was drug addiction;[38] in the summer of that same year a Gallup poll showed drug addiction to be the nation's most significant national problem.[39] The Nixon administration and the nation were about to declare war on drugs, and drug abuse was about to become an obsession that would ebb and flow in the national conscious, but would never again recede into the background of national concerns. Why then did drug abuse become of such overwhelming importance by the summer of 1971, and what were the implications for treatment programming?

There appear to have been two main concerns driving the new drug abuse initiative. On the one hand, the country had only recently been sensitized to the issue of rapidly increasing rates of street crime. Now, increasing numbers of newspaper reports appeared to suggest that much of that crime was drug related.[40] Moreover, there was the clear threat that much of that crime was transportable from its origins in the inner city. As stated by Senator Harold E. Hughes, "whereas formerly [heroin] was *only* a ghetto drug, it has been increasingly used in suburban areas and in our colleges and universities" (emphasis added).[41] Moreover, with the need of heroin addicts to steal the money that would support their habits, the ordinary citizen could no longer feel safe even in his or her own home or neighborhood. And with heroin addiction suddenly seen as having achieved epidemic proportions,[42] the need to contain this threat to the public safety assumed a position of major importance both in the minds of the public and in the minds of their elected officials.

The second main concern triggering the drug abuse initiative had to do with events occurring more than 10,000 miles away. Heroin use was not just a phenomenon of Americans on the streets of New York or Chicago or Los Angeles; it was a phenomenon of Americans on the streets of Saigon and in the rice paddies of Vietnam—Americans who were at long last coming home. According to newspapers as highly regarded as the *New York Times*, coming home would involve "carrying the [heroin] problem into every corner of the country."[43] *Time* magazine was even more graphic in its concerns and envisioned "the specter of weapons-trained addicted combat veterans joining the deadly struggle for drugs."[44] The administration and the Congress were called on to do something to counter the clear threat that 30,000 addicted veterans would join an estimated 250,000 civilian addicts in an attack on the health and safety of a nation.[45] Only later would it become evident that these fears were groundless as returning veterans only rarely maintained a pattern of drug use when removed from the environment in which drug-taking had occurred and from their contacts for obtaining those drugs.[46]

From these concerns was born the Special Action Office for Drug Abuse Prevention. It was mandated to coordinate and direct all government efforts designed to contain drug abuse and to wage the first (or perhaps the continuing) War on Drugs. Thus, too, was born the concept of demand reduction (i.e., the effort to limit the number of drug consumers) and with that the greatly expanded role of government in the treatment and prevention of drug abuse. The first two, and the only, heads of the Special Action Office were both community psychiatrists, signaling the role that health concerns were to play in the response to the heroin crisis. Health and safety had been joined in the war, but health had been made the general. Moreover, while the Special Action Office was concerned with initiating prevention programming, as well as with greatly augmenting the national drug abuse research effort, its major concern and activity were in the area of drug abuse treatment. With evidence that the concerns about heroin use spreading from cities to suburbs and to small towns were indeed justified,[47] the Special Action Office helped to develop community-based treatment programming to serve addict-clients throughout the country. The number of publicly funded treatment programs grew from approximately 50 in 1969 to more than 3,000 in 1974, with more than 100,000 clients in treatment.[48] The District of Columbia was treating 10 drug abuse clients at any one time in 1969 and 4,400 within the next five years. Indeed, program administrators were preparing earnestly to "treat all the heroin addicts in a community."[49]

As implied in the latter quote, the treatment model was drawn from public health and, at least in larger communities, envisioned readily accessible services, speedily delivered, to a mass audience. Central intake facilities were employed in several large cities such that all individuals applying for treatment could be processed in a single location and referred to the community treatment program that appeared best suited to their needs. The treatment programs, as described earlier, were of four major types, although more than one treatment form might be delivered in a single facility, described thereby as a multimodality facility. The four treatment modalities offered were methadone maintenance, methadone detoxification, outpatient drug-free treatment, and residential drug-free treatment (typically therapeutic community programs).

THE FOUR MODALITIES—CONFLICTS AND COOPERATION

The four modalities were allied in their objectives (reduced drug use and crime, increased employment), but differed, often heatedly, in several aspects of process. All were developed with a primary concern for the 80 percent of drug abuse clients who, in the early 1970s, were heroin addicts. Methadone maintenance programs were far more likely to be open-ended with regard to the length of time for treatment. Methadone detoxification, in 1972, came to be limited to a twenty-one-day period of service and was viewed by many as an ameliorative form of care, designed to allow the individual to wean him/herself from heroin, but providing no long-term benefit in terms of increased capabilities or changed psychological functioning. Drug-free treatment forms were allied in excoriating methadone, an agreement that papered over their differences in terms of an emphasis on counseling/psychotherapy and individualized treatment in outpatient programs and on group process and community living in residential programs. The key issue dividing programs, however, lay in the attitude toward methadone. One could either view it as a major program element or reject it outright. There was no middle ground.

In a real sense this conflict over methadone within the drug abuse treatment community reflects the continuing conflict in the larger community. Communities provide funds to support methadone maintenance programs, but then may set limits on the length of time anyone can remain on methadone maintenance or decree that every client has to come daily to obtain their medication for however long they remain in treatment. Still other communities simply have never made methadone available.[50] Some aspects of the conflict have faded. Graduates of methadone and therapeutic community programs fill the counseling ranks of each other's programs, and therapeutic community programs may even provide methadone in association with detoxification.[51] Nonetheless, concerns about the use of an addictive drug in the treatment of drug abuse seem unlikely to fade completely from the public mind or to cease to influence the behaviors of public officials.

Whatever their disagreement about pharmacologic aids, the treatment programs of the early 1970s clearly agreed on a substantial investment in rehabilitative treatment. The drug abuse client of this period was not seen as psychologically impaired so much as s/he was believed to be socially impaired.[52] Addict-clients were overwhelmingly black, inner-city males with limited work histories or skills and with sometimes extensive criminal justice histories. The civil rights movement and the War on Poverty remained significant influences on the new service programs. Many of the early drug abuse treatment programs were funded with dollars from the Office of Economic Opportunity and the Model Cities Act. In this context it is not surprising that much of the effort of treatment programs was directed toward an empowerment of the client population, providing opportunity and skills that could permit deprived individuals to become a part of the American mainstream. As described by Dole and his colleagues to their methadone maintenance program, "the slum-born, minority group, criminal addict needed help to become a productive member of society. Many of these individuals came to us from jail with no vocational skills, no family and no financial resources. They were further handicapped by racial discrimination and by their police records."[53] Little wonder that the first—but not the prototypic—methadone maintenance program provided vocational, educational, and legal assistance in addition to psychosocial support and counseling, and even help in obtaining those financial benefits or services to which an individual was legally entitled.[54]

The persons largely entrusted to provide treatment services to the addict-client were very frequently themselves graduates of drug abuse treatment. To a greater extent than has probably been true of any other large-scale service delivery system, drug abuse treatment has relied on the services of its own former clients. The ex-addict counselor became, and has largely remained, a fixture in the treatment community. The ex-addict counselor was seen as having strengths in relating to the addict-clients that were simply unavailable to professionally trained staff. On the one hand, by virtue of being of the addict-client's world, the ex-addict counselor could be aware of efforts by the client to manipulate the counselor and to control the treatment process. Thus, the ex-addict counselor could forestall those efforts and maintain control over the treatment more easily than could the professional who was naive about the addict's experiences and behaviors. Not only did the opiate client need to have opportunities made available to him or her to partake of the straight life, but also the opiate client needed prodding to take advantage of those opportunities. In addition, the ex-addict counselor could be a role model for the drug abuse client—a clear example that change was possible and that societal acceptance could be achieved. In short, the counselor, having an understanding of what it took to obtain change, could be guide and irritant to its achievement. In recognition of the need to assist the paraprofessional counselor in assuming his/her duties, there was organized a national training program under largely, but not exclusively, federal auspices, devoted to counselor training.

Drug abuse treatment could be seen as derived from mental health treatment, but with differences so profound that it could be viewed as an independent field. Its emphasis on decreasing social deficit, rather than on increasing psychological functioning, and its use of ex-addict paraprofessionals to achieve client change differentiated drug abuse treatment from much of mental health. Drug abuse treatment was further differentiated from traditional mental health practices by its use of monitoring strategies appropriate to clients whose backgrounds involved significant investment in antisocial activities. In particular, programs developed systems of "urine surveillance" designed to clarify the extent to which drug abuse clients continued to abuse drugs while in treatment. Urines were gathered regularly—typically once a week—and were to be used for research and in support of rehabilitation. Only therapeutic community programs objected that the gathering of urines under observation was demeaning on the one hand and unnecessary on the other (since any good counselor should know whether or not a client is using drugs). Nonetheless, therapeutic communities also took it as their responsibility to track drug use, reasoning that not all their members were resident in the facility twenty-four hours a day and that drugs could find a way into virtually any setting. The nature of the client and the nature of the client's problem dictated that close supervision was essential; moreover, it was seen by most as inappropriate simply to take the client's word for his or her functioning. Whereas much of traditional mental health practice emphasizes the development of a trusting relationship between client and therapist, in drug abuse treatment the message from the counselor was "I don't trust you—not until you've earned my trust, and even then. . . . ''

With the creation of the National Institute on Drug Abuse (NIDA), which replaced the Special Action Office, a federal structure was set up to provide funds and assistance to the states in association with the federal funds appropriated for the development and maintenance of treatment programming. NIDA funded community treatment and gave technical assistance to the states in program administration. The Food and Drug Administration monitored the delivery of methadone by the states. Throughout the 1970s it was the particular role of the federal government to join with the states in support of the treatment community, both through its monitoring/technical assistance function and through the funding of a body of research designed to increase the effectiveness of treatment. That research took two forms: the evaluation of treatment programs already available and the study of innovative treatment forms that gave promise of improving the delivery of treatment services. The former allowed the treatment community to assess the effectiveness of current efforts, while the latter allowed for modification of those treatment forms in accord with the acquisition of new information.

Throughout much of the 1970s focus remained on the opiate user (i.e., on a client who was male, minority, inner city, disadvantaged, and no stranger to the criminal justice system). There was a concern with strategies of vocational rehabilitation and job placement,[55] with efforts to understand the impact of treatment programming on drug abusers who remained a part of the criminal justice system[56] and on drug abusers who were referred from that system,[57] and with programming for "special populations," the latter phrase being a euphemism for minority ethnic groups.[58] Aftercare strategies designed to support the exiting client during his/her transition from client status to independence and/or to build new skills for coping with the "straight" community were also being developed and studied.[59]

NEW CLIENTS AND NEW STRATEGIES

By the latter part of the 1970s treatment programming was being developed and studied that made use of mental health strategies that appeared appropriate to the newly emerging drug abuse client. The psychotherapies, the value of which had long been questioned in drug abuse programming,[60] became the subject of a major study at sites in New Haven and Philadelphia.[61] While successful at only one of those sites,[62] the study was seen as calling attention to the importance of dealing with psychological dysfunction in the lives of at least some number of drug abusers and of the utility of mental health strategies in accomplishing that objective.

Studies of opiate clients[63] suggested higher rates of psychopathology, and most particularly of depression, among opiate clients seen in the 1980s than was true of clients seen a decade earlier. This has awakened renewed efforts to employ not only psychotherapy, but other tools of mental health therapy as well. Family therapy,[64] long a staple of alcohol and mental health services, and the behavioral therapies,[65] similarly important to alcohol and mental health services, have become major areas of interest in drug abuse treatment and research.

Nonetheless, the core modalities remain, albeit in somewhat modified form. Methadone treatment now embraces both maintenance and long-term detoxification. In 1984 legislation was passed to extend the period of detoxification from 21 to 180 days, making it possible for the full weight of treatment and rehabilitation programming to be exercised on behalf of opiate clients. Therapeutic community programming has gone through changes as well, most notably perhaps in proposing the efficacy of a brief residential stay (e.g., several months), as opposed to up to two years as had been advocated earlier. Outpatient drug-free programming now is particularly more likely to embrace a range of mental health strategies and to show a lessened reliance on the services of ex-addict personnel.[66]

Today, while a plurality of clients remain opiate involved, it is not the overwhelming majority, as was the case in the early 1970s. Clients are involved with a multitude of nonopiate drugs, sometimes in addition to opiates, but frequently independent of any use of opiates.[67] To date, their needs and their treatment have consumed far less attention than has been given to those of opiate-involved clients.[68] While increasing effort is now being made to study as well as serve these populations, we lag well behind in the information needed to provide effective treatment to nonopiate drug abusers.

THE CRISIS POSED BY AIDS

It might have been expected that the work of the next decade of drug abuse treatment and the study of that treatment would have been consumed with the task of responding to the changing client population by constructing that mix of drug abuse treatment/rehabilitation strategies and mental health programming that appears appropriate to the needs of the drug abuse clients now entering treatment. However, a new drug abuse crisis has emerged and threatens to engulf virtually all other treatment concerns. AIDS is now widely recognized as a threat to the very lives of many drug abuse clients, and of their loved ones, and has thereby become a central issue in drug abuse treatment. Twenty-five percent of those who contract AIDS are intravenous drug users, and all are fated to die. Moreover, the majorities of both heterosexual AIDS cases and pediatric AIDS cases are traceable to intravenous drug users.[69] Thus, intravenous drug use is a particularly significant vector in the spread of this lethal disease.

Drug abuse treatment programs must now face a complex set of new responsibilities and questions. What is the drug abuse treatment program's responsibility for testing clients for the presence of disease? How should clients be cautioned with regard to risk reduction behavior to prevent infection? Should programs discuss with clients "safe" methods for using needles? Should programs make an effort to contact the client's spouse or sex partner if the program has reason to believe the client is carrying the disease? What, if any, special precautions must the program take with its own personnel? What training will the program need to provide to staff to assure accurate understanding and communication of the risk of AIDS infection and of the strategies for reducing that risk?

Drug abuse treatment programs, organized to rehabilitate drug users and to effect their re-entry into society, now find they deal with issues of death and dying, comforting those for whom rehabilitation may no longer be the major concern, and allaying the fears and depression of others. Grief counseling must now take a role beside vocational rehabilitation in the extraordinary amalgam of services these programs are called on to provide.[70]

THE FUNDING OF TREATMENT

Coincident with the changing focus of drug abuse treatment and with the emergency of AIDS, there has been a significant shift in the fiscal responsibility for drug abuse treatment. Since 1980 the states and local governments have been expected to bear a larger share of the financial burden for both drug abuse treatment and prevention, although significant federal funding continues to be provided. However, whereas prior to 1980 that funding was made available to each state in a package that made it specific to the area of drug abuse, money is now provided by the federal government in the form of block grants to each state such that each block contains money for programs and activities in the areas of drug abuse, alcohol abuse, and mental health. It then becomes the responsibility of state officials to apportion the funds in accord with the issues they see as of paramount concern for their state and in relation to the state and local funds they already have available.

There appears as well to have been an increase in private treatment programs and in the purchase of treatment through health insurance plans and individual efforts. Most of that effort has been directed at the nonopiate user, sometimes referred through the efforts of employee assistance programs located at work sites, sometimes through the intercession of concerned family, and sometimes based wholly on the individual's own concern about the effect drugs are having on his or her own functioning and resources. These programs will typically provide outpatient counseling, frequently in association with an initial period of brief hospitalization. Often these private treatment initiatives are adapted from the Alcoholics Anonymous (AA) model and are structured to move the individual through AA's twelve steps from a statement of powerlessness over drugs to a resolution that the individual will carry the message of help to others and will practice the principles learned in all affairs.

CHANGE AS A CONSTANT

Thus, during this century the drug abuse client has moved from a position not far distant from mainstream America (the patent medicine user early in this century) to criminal and pariah (the heroin user of the 1930s and 1940s) to gradual acceptance as a client of the health care system (the heroin user during the period from 1950 to 1980). The direction of drug abuse treatment in the 1990s may well follow two streams based on the presence or absence of intravenous drug use. The opiate (intravenous) user seems destined to continue to receive the treatment/rehabilitation services developed over the course of the past two decades, now increasingly augmented by risk-reduction counseling and services directed at protecting the individual and the community from the spread of a fatal disease. The nonopiate nonintravenous user seems likely to grow farther apart from his/her opiate-using counterpart and may be more likely to receive drug abuse services that will have an increasingly heavy overlay of mental health programming and personnel and that will be available from the private as well as the public sector. However, in risking any prognostication it is well to remember that the drug abuser and drug abuse treatment have gone through numerous changes over the years, few of them easily predictable. There appears to be no reason to believe that the process of change as it relates to drug abuse will become any more predictable in the future.

NOTES

The opinions expressed herein are those of the author and do not necessarily reflect the official position of the National Institute on Drug Abuse or any other part of the U.S. Department of Health and Human Services.

1. John Kaplan, *The Hardest Drug—Heroin and Public Policy* (Chicago: University of Chicago, 1983), 62.

2. Ibid., 62–63.

3. David S. Musto, *The American Disease* (New Haven, Conn.: Yale University Press, 1973).

4. M. J. Pescor, "A Statistical Analysis of the Clinical Record of Hospitalized Drug Addicts," *Public Health Reports*, Supp. 143 (1938).

5. David P. Ausubel, *Drug Addiction: Physiological, Psychological, and Sociological Aspects* (New York: Random House, 1958), 78.

6. Ibid., 77–79.

7. Lawrence Kolb and C. K. Himmelsbach, "Clinical Studies of Drug Addiction: A Critical Review of Withdrawal Treatment with Method of Evaluating Abstinence," *American Journal of Psychiatry*, 94 (1938): 759–799.

8. Alfred R. Lindesmith, *Opiate Addiction* (Bloomington, Ind.: Principia Press, 1947).

9. Abraham Wickler, *Opiate Addiction* (Springfield, Ill.: Charles E. Thomas, 1963).

10. Harold P. Conrad, "Psychiatric Treatment with Narcotic Addiction," in *Drug Addiction I*, ed. William Martin (New York: Springer-Verlag, 1977).

11. David P. Ausubel, "The Psychopathology and Treatment of Drug Addiction in Relation to the Mental Hygiene Movement," *Psychiatric Quarterly Supplement* Part 2 (1948): 119–50.

12. Ausubel, *Drug Addiction*, 84–86.

13. Pescor, "A Statistical Analysis."

14. E. Sagarin, *Odd Man In: Society of Deviants in America* (Chicago: Quadrangle Press, 1969).

15. Jerome H. Jaffe, "The Swinging Pendulum: The Treatment of Drug Users in America," in *Handbook on Drug Abuse*, ed. Robert L. DuPont, Avram Goldstein, and John O'Donnell (Washington, D.C.: National Institute on Drug Abuse and Office of Drug Abuse Policy, 1979), 3–16.

16. Raymond M. Glasscote, James Sussex, Jerome H. Jaffe, John C. Ball, and Leon Brill, *The Treatment of Drug Abuse—Programs, Problems, Prospects* (Washington, D.C.: American Psychiatric Association, 1972).

17. Ibid., 35–36.

18. Vincent P. Dole and Marie A. Nyswander, "A Medical Treatment of Morphine Diacetylmorphine (Heroin) Addiction and Clinical Trial with Methadone Hydrochloride," *Journal of the American Medical Association* 193 (1965): 646–50; Vincent P. Dole, Marie E. Nyswander, and Mary Jean Kreek, "Narcotic Blockade," *Archives of Internal Medicine* 118 (1966): 304–309.

19. Vincent P. Dole, Marie E. Nyswander, and Alan Warner, "Successful Treatment of 750 Criminal Addicts," *Journal of the American Medical Association* 206 (1968): 2707–11.

20. Frances R. Gearing, "Progress Report of the Validation of Treatment Programs—

as of March 31, 1968," in *Proceedings of the First National Conference on Methadone Treatment* (New York: Rockefeller University, 1968), 1–10B.

21. George E. Vaillant, "A 12-Year Followup of New York Addicts: The Relation of Treatment to Outcome," *American Journal of Psychiatry* 122 (1966): 727–37; George E. Vaillant, "A 12-Year Followup of New York Addicts: The Natural History of the Chronic Disease," *New England Journal of Medicine* 275 (1966): 1282–88; George E. Vaillant, "A 12-Year Followup of New York Addicts: Some Social and Psychiatric Characteristics," *Archives of General Psychiatry* 15 (1966): 599–609; George E. Vaillant, "A 12-Year Followup of New York Addicts: Some Determinants and Characteristics of Abstinence," *American Journal of Psychiatry* 123 (1966): 573–84.

22. John A. O'Donnell, *Narcotic Addicts in Kentucky* (Washington, D.C.: U.S. Government Printing Office, 1969).

23. Saul B. Sells and D. Dwayne Simpson, *The Effectiveness of Drug Abuse Treatment: Early Studies of Drug Users Treatment, and Assessment of Outcome During Treatment in the DARP*, vol. 3 (Cambridge, Mass.: Ballinger, 1976); Saul B. Sells and D. Dwayne Simpson, *The Effectiveness of Drug Abuse Treatment: Evaluation of Treatment Outcome for the 1972–1973 DARP Admission Cohort*, vol. 4 (Cambridge, Mass.: Ballinger, 1976); Saul B. Sells, Robert G. Demaree, D. Dwayne Simpson, George W. Joe, and Robert L. Gorsuch, "Issues in the Evaluation of Drug Abuse Treatment," *Professional Psychology* 8 (1977): 609–40.

24. Avram Goldstein, "Recent Advances in Basic Research Relevant to Drug Abuse," in *Handbook on Drug Abuse*, ed. Robert L. DuPont, Avram Goldstein, and John O'Donnell (Washington, D.C.: National Institute on Drug Abuse and Office of Drug Abuse Policy, 1979), 439–46.

25. Jerome H. Jaffe and Leon Brill, "Cyclazocine, A Long-Acting Narcotic Antagonist: Its Voluntary Acceptance as a Treatment Modality by Narcotic Abusers," *International Journal of the Addictions* 1 (1966): 99–123; A. M. Freedman, M. Fink, R. Sharoff, and A. Zaks, "Cyclazocine and Methadone in Narcotic Addiction," *Journal of the American Medical Association* 202 (1967): 191–94; A. M. Freedman, "Clinical Studies of Cyclazocine in the Treatment of Narcotic Addiction," *American Journal of Psychiatry* 124 (1968): 1499–1504.

26. Richard D. Resnick, Elaine Schuyten-Resnick, and Arnold M. Washton, "Treatment of Opioid Dependence with Narcotic Antagonists: A Review and Commentary," in *Handbook on Drug Abuse*, ed. Robert L. DuPont, Avram Goldstein, and John O'Donnell (Washington, D.C.: National Institute on Drug Abuse and Office of Drug Abuse Policy, 1979): 97–104.

27. Resnick, Schuyten-Resnick, and Washton, "Treatment of Opioid Dependence," 98.

28. Saul B. Sells, "Treatment Effectiveness," in *Handbook on Drug Abuse*, ed. Robert L. DuPont, Avram Goldstein, and John O'Donnell (Washington, D.C.: National Institute on Drug Abuse and Office of Drug Abuse Policy, 1979) 105–18; Marvin R. Burt, Barry S. Brown, and Robert L. DuPont, "Followup of Former Clients of a Large Multimodality Drug Treatment Program," *International Journal of the Addictions* 15 (1980): 391–408; D. Dwayne Simpson, George W. Joe, and Sharon A. Bracy, "Six-Year Follow-Up of Opioid Addicts After Admission to Treatment," *Archives of General Psychiatry* 39 (1982): 1318–23; A. Thomas McLellan, Lester Luborsky, Charles P. O'Brien, George D. Woody, and K. A. Druley, "Is Treatment for Substance Abuse Effective," *Journal of the American Medical Association*, 247 (1982): 1423–27; Edward C. Senay, "Meth-

adone Maintenance Treatment," *International Journal of the Addictions* 20 (1985): 803–21.

29. D. Nelkin, *Methadone Maintenance: A Technological Fix* (New York: Braziller, 1973).

30. James R. Cooper, Fred Altman, and Kim Keeley, "Discussion Summary," in *Research on the Treatment of Narcotic Addiction—State of the Art*, ed. James R. Cooper, Fred Altman, Barry Brown, and Dorynne Czechowicz (Washington, D.C.: U.S. Government Printing Office, 1983), 92–94.

31. Nelkin, *Methadone Maintenance*.

32. Beny J. Primm, "Ancillary Services in Methadone Treatment: The Bedford Stuyvesant Experience," in *Proceedings of the Third National Conference on Methadone Treatment*, (Washington, D.C.: U.S. Government Printing Office, 1970), 66–69.

33. Steven E. Katz, "Partial Hospitalization and Comprehensive Community Services," in *Comprehensive Textbook of Psychiatry/IV*, ed. Harold I. Kaplan and Benjamin J. Sadock (Baltimore: Williams & Wilkins, 1985), 1582–87.

34. Glasscote, Sussex, Jaffe, Ball, and Brill, *The Treatment of Drug Abuse*, 104–26; James A. Inciardi, *Criminal Justice* (New York: Academic Press, 1984), 695.

35. Carl G. Leukefeld, "The Clinical Connection: Drugs and Crime," *International Journal of the Addictions* 20 (1985): 1049–64.

36. James A. Inciardi, "Some Considerations on the Clinical Efficacy of Compulsory Treatment: Reviewing the New York Experience," in *Compulsory Treatment of Drug Abuse: Research and Clinical Practice*, ed. Carl G. Leukefeld and Frank M. Tims (Washington, D.C.: U.S. Government Printing Office, 1988), 126–38.

37. M. Douglas Anglin, "The Efficacy of Civil Commitment in Treating Narcotic Addiction," in *Compulsory Treatment of Drug Abuse: Research and Clinical Practice*, ed. Carl G. Leukefeld and Frank M. Tims (Washington, D.C.: U.S. Government Printing Office, 1988), 8–34.

38. "Poll Finds Drugs No. 3 Issue in U.S.," *New York Times*, 17 June 1971.

39. Nelkin, *Methadone Maintenance*.

40. A. Ginsberg, "Documents on Police Bureaucracy Conspiracy Against Human Rights of Opiate Addicts and Constitutional Rights of Medical Profession Causing Mass Break Down of Urban Law and Order," *Journal of Psychedelic Drugs* 4 (1971): 104–11.

41. Harold E. Hughes, "U.S. Senate Report 92–509, Drug Abuse Office, Control and Treatment Act of 1971," in *Legislative History of the Drug Abuse Office and Treatment Act of 1972*, (Washington, D.C.: U.S. Government Printing Office, 1972), 56.

42. Leon Hunt and Carl Chambers, *Heroin Epidemics: A Study of Heroin Use in the United States, 1965–1975* (New York: Spectrum, 1977).

43. *New York Times*, 17 June 1971.

44. *Time*, 28 June 1971.

45. *New York Times*, 19 June 1971.

46. Lee N. Robins, *The Vietnam Drug User Returns* (Washington, D.C.: U.S. Government Printing Office, 1973).

47. Leon Hunt, *Recent Spread of Heroin Use in the United States: Unanswered Questions* (Washington, D.C.: Drug Abuse Council, 1974); Peter Bourne, Leon Hunt, and J. Vogt, *A Study of Heroin Use in the State of Wyoming* (Washington, D.C.: Foundation for International Resources, 1975).

48. Jerome H. Jaffe, "Opioid Dependence," in *Comprehensive Textbook of Psychiatry/IV* (Baltimore: Williams & Wilkens, 1985), 987–1002.

49. Robert L. DuPont, "Trying to Treat All the Heroin Addicts in a Community," in *Proceedings of the Fourth National Conference on Methadone Treatment* (New York: NAPAN, 1972), 77–80.

50. Marsha Rosenbaum, Sheigla Murphy, and Jerome Beck, "Money for Methadone: Preliminary Findings from a Study of Alameda County's New Maintenance Policy," *Journal of Psychoactive Drugs* 19 (1987), 13–19.

51. James L. Sorenson, Alphonso Acampora, and Dana Iscoff, "From Maintenance to Abstinence in a Therapeutic Community: Clinical Treatment Methods," *Journal of Psychoactive Drugs* 16 (1984): 229–39.

52. Lee N. Robins, "Addict Careers," in *Handbook on Drug Abuse*, ed. Robert L. DuPont, Avram Goldstein, and John O'Donnell (Washington, D.C.: National Institute on Drug Abuse and Office of Drug Abuse Policy, 1979), 325–336.

53. Vincent P. Dole, Marie E. Nyswander, and Alan Warner, "Successful Treatment of 750 Criminal Addicts," in *Proceedings of the First National Conference on Methadone Treatment* (New York: Rockefeller University, 1968), 15.

54. Gearing, "Progress Report," 1–10.

55. MARDA, *Manpower Assistance for Rehabilitated Drug Abusers: Report on Pilot Project to Develop and Operate a Manpower and Service Component to Supplement Drug Treatment Programs for Drug Addicted Offenders* (Washington, D.C.: Sam Harris, 1975); VERA Institute of Justice, *Third Annual Research Report on Supported Employment* (New York: VERA Institute, 1975); Sharon M. Hall, P. Loeb, J. W. Norton, and R. Yang, "Improving Vocational Placement in Drug Treatment Clients: A Pilot Study," *Addictive Behaviors* 15 (1977): 438–41; Urbane F. Bass and J. A. Woodward, *Skills Training and Employment for Ex-Addicts in Washington, D.C.: A Report on TREAT* (Rockville, Md.: National Institute on Drug Abuse, 1978); Eileen Wolkstein and Deborah Hastings-Black, "Vocational Rehabilitation," in *Handbook on Drug Abuse*, ed. Robert L. DuPont, Avram Goldstein, and John O'Donnell (Washington, D.C.: National Institute on Drug Abuse and Office of Drug Abuse Policy, 1979), 159–64.

56. George Nash, *The Impact of Drug Abuse Treatment upon Criminality: A Look at Nineteen Programs* (Upper Montclair, N.J.: Montclair State College, 1973).

57. W. F. Wieland and J. L. Novack, "A Comparison of Criminal Justice and Non-Criminal Justice Related Patients in a Methadone Treatment Program," in *Proceedings of the Fifth National Conference on Methadone Maintenance* (New York: NATAN, 1973); David M. Peterson, "Some Reflections on Compulsory Treatment of Addiction," in *Drugs and the Criminal Justice System*, ed. James A. Inciardi and Carl Chambers (Beverly Hills, Calif.: Sage, 1974); R. J. Harford, J. C. Ungerer, and J. K. Kinsella, "Effects of Legal Pressure on Prognosis for Treatment of Drug Dependence," *American Journal of Psychiatry* 133 (1976): 1399–1404; V. J. Rinella, "Rehabilitation or Bust: The Impact of Criminal Justice System Referrals on the Treatment of Drug Addicts and Alcoholics in a Therapeutic Community (Eagleville's Experience)," *American Journal of Drug and Alcohol Abuse* 3 (1976): 53–58; William H. McGlothlin, M. Douglas Anglin, and D. Wilson, "A Followup of Admissions to the California Civil Addict Program," *American Journal of Drug and Alcohol Abuse* 4 (1977): 179–99.

58. Frank S. Espada, "The Drug Abuse Industry and the 'Minority' Communities: Time for Change," in *Handbook on Drug Abuse*, ed. Robert L. DuPont, Avram Goldstein,

and John O'Donnell (Washington, D.C.: National Institute on Drug Abuse and Office of Drug Abuse Policy, 1979), 293–302.

59. Barry S. Brown and Rebecca S. Ashery, "Aftercare in Drug Abuse Programming," in *Handbook on Drug Abuse*, ed. Robert L. DuPont, Avram Goldstein, and John O'Donnell (Washington, D.C.: National Institute on Drug Aubse and Office of Drug Abuse Policy, 1979), 165–74.

60. Conrad, "Psychiatric Treatment."

61. Bruce J. Rounsaville and Herbert D. Kleber, "Psychotherapy/Counseling for Opiate Addicts: Strategies for Use in Different Treatment Settings," *International Journal of the Addictions* 20 (1985): 869–96.

62. George E. Woody, Lester Luborsky, A. Thomas McLellan, Charles P. O'Brien, Aaron T. Beck, Jack Blaine, I. Herman, and A. Hale, "Psychotherapy for Opiate Addicts: Does It Help?" *Archives of General Psychiatry* 40 (1983): 639–45.

63. Bruce J. Rounsaville, Miriam M. Weissman, Herbert Kleber, and Paul H. Wilber, "Heterogeneity of Psychiatric Diagnosis in Treated Opiate Addicts," *Archives of General Psychiatry* 39 (1982): 161–66; A. Thomas McLellan, Lester Luborsky, George E. Woody, Charles P. O'Brien, and K. A. Druley, "Predicting Response to Alcohol and Drug Abuse Treatment, Role of Psychiatric Severity," *Archives of General Psychiatry* 40 (1983): 620–25; George De Leon, Nancy Jainchill, and Mitchell Rosenthal, "Addiction and Psychiatric Disorder: The Problem of Differential Diagnosis," World Conference of Therapeutic Communities (June 1985); David Nurco, unpublished data (1985).

64. Edward Kaufman, "Family System and Family Therapy of Substance Abuse: An Overview of Two Different Decades of Research and Clinical Experience," *International Journal of the Addictions* 20 (1985): 897–916.

65. Anna Rose Childress, A. Thomas McLellan, and Charles P. O'Brien, "Behavioral Therapy for Substance Abuse," *International Journal of the Addictions* 20 (1985): 947–69.

66. Karen M. Greenberg and Barry S. Brown, "Agency Director/Staff Views of the Changing Nature of Drug Abuse and Drug Abuse Treatment," *Clinical Research Notes* (Rockville, Md.: National Institute on Drug Abuse, February 1984), 10–12.

67. National Institute on Drug Abuse, *Demographic Characteristics and Patterns of Use of Clients Admitted to Drug Abuse Treatment Programs in Selected States: Trend Data 1979–1984* (Rockville, Md.: National Institute on Drug Abuse, 1988), 5.

68. Barry S. Brown, "Treatment of Nonopiate Dependency: Issues and Outcomes," in *Research Advances in Alcohol and Drug Problems*, vol. 8, ed. Reginald G. Smart, Howard D. Cappell, Frederick B. Glaser, Yedy Israel, Harold Kalant, Robert E. Popham, Wolfgang Schmidt, and Edward M. Sellers (New York: Plenum, 1984), 291–308.

69. James W. Curran, H. W. Jaffe, A. M. Hardy, W. M. Morgan, R. M. Selik, and T. J. Dondero, "Epidemiology of HIV Infection and AIDS in the United States," *Science*, 239 (1988): 610–16.

70. Barry S. Brown and George M. Beschner, "AIDS and HIV Infection: Implications for Treatment," *Journal of Drug Issues*, 19 (1989): 141–62.

Chapter 3

The Drugs-Crime Connection

David N. Nurco, Timothy W. Kinlock,
and Thomas E. Hanlon

HISTORICAL BACKGROUND

The first recorded speculation regarding a link between narcotic drugs and crime appeared more than a hundred years ago.[1] Since that time there has been a long and continuing controversy in the United States about the relationship between narcotic addiction and crime. On one side were those advocating the "criminal model of addiction,"[2] who regarded addicts as confirmed criminals who endanger society by their antisocial behavior. This viewpoint was epitomized by the late Harry J. Anslinger, the first head of the Federal Bureau of Narcotics, who served in this capacity from 1930 to 1962. Similar viewpoints were publicly expressed as early as 1924. As David Musto noted in his comprehensive historical account *The American Disease*, it was stated in testimony before Congress that heroin was a stimulus to the commission of crime.[3] In this testimony, Dr. Alexander Lambert, the head of the Mayor's Committee on Drug Addiction for New York City, expressed the view that heroin tended to destroy the sense of responsibility to the herd. The commissioner of health of Chicago, Dr. Herman Bundesen, went even further, stating that "the root of the social evil is essentially in our dope, our habit-forming drugs [the] main cause of prostitution and crime."[4] Although there were differences in emphasis and interpretation among those who held that heroin use promoted crime, it was generally agreed that heroin was destructive and criminogenic.

The other side in this historical controversy took the position that narcotic addicts were not criminals, but deprived or mentally ill individuals who were "forced" into the commission of petty theft in order to support their habit. This viewpoint was emphatically presented by Harry Barnes and Negley Teeters of Temple University in their 1945 textbook *New Horizons in Criminology*:

It is now definitely demonstrated that most serious cases of drug addiction are the result of neurotic conditions, namely, mental and nervous disorders growing out of deep-seated mental conflicts in the individual. . . . It is not likely, however, that a normal person will become an addict. . . . Alarmist literature and the propaganda of the crusaders against drug addiction have created a grotesquely exaggerated impression of the danger to society from the drug addict.[5]

This notion has been frequently referred to as the "enslavement theory of addiction."[6] It was based on a medical model, and the proponents of this view advocated the treatment of narcotic addiction by psychiatrists or other physicians. Those who supported this idea included many clinicians and social scientists of the 1950s and 1960s.

Regardless of which side one took in this controversy, it was often assumed that all narcotic addicts were alike. This concept of uniformity was tacitly assumed by most researchers of the drugs-crime connection before the 1970s. As researchers from the National Institute of Justice summarized in a comprehensive literature review published in 1980, the majority of studies concentrated on how certain factors affect most addicts, largely ignoring the fact that "these factors all affect addicts differently" and that addicts "should not be viewed as a homogeneous group that follow the same career paths."[7] This appears to be one of the major flaws inherent in earlier research.

RESEARCH ON THE DRUGS-CRIME CONNECTION

Literature reviews have documented that hundreds of studies of the relationship between addiction and crime were performed from the 1920s to the late 1970s.[8] Several reviewers have commented that these studies contained numerous flaws. As James A. Inciardi has summarized elsewhere,[9] the theories, hypotheses, conclusions, and other findings generated by these studies were of little value since there were considerable biases and deficiencies in their designs. Given the many methodological difficulties, it was impossible to draw reliable conclusions about the magnitude, shape, scope, or direction of drug-related crime.

In their 1987 review article "Characterizing Criminal Careers," Alfred Blumstein and Jacqueline Cohen maintained that "even though the subjects of crime and crime control have been major issues of public debate, and despite their regular appearance as one of the nation's most serious problems, significant advances in empirical research related to these issues is relatively recent. . . . " They also emphasized that "more effectively disentangling the apparent drug-crime nexus is of particular concern."[10]

Not until the 1970s and 1980s were more sophisticated studies of the relationship between drug use and crime finally undertaken. In their book *Taking Care of Business*,[11] published in 1985, Bruce D. Johnson and his associates at the New York State Division of Substance Abuse Services noted that earlier literature reviews had concluded that little was known about the crime rates of heroin abusers and emphasized the need for improved information about the criminal behavior of drug users. They cited the 1967 report of the President's

Commission on Law Enforcement and the Administration of Justice: "Only minimal comprehensive data are available relative to the issue of the drugs/crime relationship";[12] and the 1976 Panel on Drug Use and Criminal Behavior: "Convincing empirical data on drug abuse and crime . . . are generally unavailable— the principal reason being the lack of a long-term, research program in the area."[13]

While there were some notable exceptions, the results of studies revealing differential characteristics among narcotic addicts were usually ignored by policy makers. Examples of these exceptions were the works of Edward Sendoz at the Municipal Court of Boston and Lawrence Holt from the U.S. Public Health Service.[14] Both series of studies suggested that there were different types of addicts. Some were habitual criminals and were so before becoming addicted. On the other hand, others were simply violators of the Harrison Act, having been arrested for illegal possession of narcotics. Unfortunately, the notion of heterogeneity of addicts did not become evident until much later.

METHODOLOGICAL DEFICIENCIES OF EARLY STUDIES

Evidence of criminal activity among narcotic users is longstanding and abundant; however, it is apparent that relationships among the important variables involved are much more complex than were initially believed. As mentioned, literature reviews of studies conducted on the relationship between narcotic addiction and crime found that these investigations contained several important methodological deficiencies. Among the most commonly mentioned problems were the following:

1. the employment of seriously deficient measures of criminality
2. the preoccupation with the single-cause issue or the "chicken-egg" question of which came first, crime or drugs
3. the use of "captive" samples of narcotic addicts
4. the failure to apply measures of criminal activity over time
5. the failure to correctly identify the empirical precursors, correlates, possible determinants, and patterns of criminality and the ignoring of the covariation of such factors within an addict population

MEASUREMENT OF CRIME AMONG NARCOTIC ADDICTS

Probably the most serious methodological problem contained in early studies of the relationship between drug use and crime has been the use of official arrest records, or "rap sheets," as indicators of criminal activity. In a review of sixty-five studies to determine the methods of measuring individual criminal behavior, James J. Collins and his coworkers concluded that "arrest data are a seriously deficient indicator of criminal involvement—in fact it is more accurate to view arrest data as an indicator of criminal justice *system* involvement.''[15] In other words, arrest data more properly measure how often one *gets caught* for committing crime, and there is far from a one-to-one relationship between how often someone is caught and how much crime he or she commits.[16]

Several studies employing confidential self-report interview methods have shown that the use of arrest data as an indicator of the amounts and types of crimes actually committed results in gross underestimates.[17] These investigations have found that less than 1 percent of all offenses reported by addicts resulted in arrest. Typical of findings emphasizing the inadequacy of official statistics as measures of the incidence and prevalence of criminal behavior are those of Inciardi.[18] In one of his studies, Inciardi noted that his sample of 573 Miami narcotic abusers had engaged in criminal activity for an average of two years before their first arrest. Also, he indicated that subsequent arrest rates were extremely low. Of 215,105 offenses reported by the respondents over a one-year period, only 609, or one arrest for every 353 crimes committed (0.3 percent), resulted in arrest.[19]

A common finding of the research of Jan M. Chaiken and Marcia R. Chaiken has been that number of arrests is a poor predictor of who the most dangerous criminals are. Analyzing arrest data and self-reported crime in a Rand Corporation study of over two thousand offenders in three states, these investigators concluded that it was impossible to identify serious and frequent offenders from official records since "the vast majority of those who do commit all of these crimes (robbery, assault, and drug sales) have not been convicted of them."[20] Although all respondents had been arrested, it was found that arrests were so infrequent and the official records so inadequate that it was impossible to distinguish the serious and persistent offenders from the less serious ones. Chaiken and Chaiken found that only about 10 percent of self-reported violent predators could be so identified by arrest records.[21]

In our studies of narcotic addicts in Baltimore, we have obtained similar results.[22] In one of these studies, we analyzed the self-reports and arrest data of a sample of 243 addicts. While these addicts had a total of 2,869 arrests over an eleven-year period, they also had accumulated 473,738 days of crime, resulting in a ratio of arrests to crime days of .006. Not only were arrests an extreme underestimate of how much crime was committed, but also the arrests were biased with regard to both the type of offense committed and the frequency of offenses. Violent crimes were more likely than other crimes to result in arrest, and the probability of arrest decreased for addicts with high crime rates.[23]

THE VALIDITY OF SELF-REPORTED CRIME

Any study relying primarily on informant self-disclosure must eventually come to grips with the issue of the accuracy, or veridicality, of such information.[24] In this context, the self-reports of drug addicts are particularly suspect because of the deviant and illegal nature of their life styles. In addition to possible distortions introduced in order to conceal unsavory aspects of their lives, genuine errors in recalling information about events that occurred years earlier can further affect the accuracy of the information obtained. However, evidence in the literature indicates that addicts, as a group, tend to be surprisingly truthful and accurate in their replies to a wide range of questions when interviewed under nonthreatening conditions.[25] Validation studies that have been conducted have used the following methods: comparing self-reports of arrests with official records, comparing information on drug use with urinalysis results, and using repeat interview procedures.

It is, of course, clear that the social context and the conditions under which interviews are conducted may affect the addicts' motivation to be candid, equivocal, or deceitful. Thus, even though interview information is obtained in the context of research, it would be just as unwarranted to maintain that addicts' responses are invariably valid as it would be to assume that they are invalid. Research procedures that appear to be particularly important to the securing of valid interview data include the following: the addict's recognition of the availability of an official record (that allows corroboration of self-report information); the interviewer's thorough knowledge of the addict subculture, as well as his or her competence, experience, and training in interviewing procedures; the absence of an authoritarian or retribution function in the interview; the assurance of confidentiality; and the use of a structured instrument that enables internal consistency checks and the offering of meaningful time reference points to assist in the recall of information. (The "addict career" interview, which will be discussed in more detail later, is especially useful in this respect.)

THE CRIME-DAYS PER YEAR-AT-RISK CONCEPT

Several investigators of the drugs-crime connection have been striving to develop a meaningful application of what has been termed "lambda"—the rate of offending per unit of time (usually a year) for a given population at risk. Our own calculations involving a variation of this index have used self-reported information from narcotic addicts covering varying periods while addicted and not addicted to narcotics over a lifetime of narcotic drug use. Because narcotic addicts may engage in hundreds of offenses per year, it has proved useful to express the magnitude of their criminal behavior in terms of the number of crime-days per year-at-risk (while at large in the community), rather than in terms of the total number of offenses committed per year. A *crime-day* is conceptually defined as a twenty-four-hour period during which one or more crimes are committed by a given individual. Thus, crime-days per year-at-risk is a rate of occurrence that varies from 0 to 365.

Our use of the crime-days per year-at-risk measure has served to document the continuity of high crime rates among narcotic addicts over extended periods. Although there are differences in the types of crimes that individual addicts engage in, their overall high rates of criminality characteristically persist throughout their periods of addiction. The continuity of these high crime rates is remarkable. An analysis of crime-days per year-at-risk for 354 addicts interviewed between 1973 and 1978 revealed that the crime-day means for the first seven addiction periods were 255, 244, 259, 257, 254, 336, and 236, respectively. Thus, the high rate of criminality reported not only was persistent on a day-to-day basis, but also tended to continue over an extended number of years and periods of addiction.[26]

Use of the crime-days per year-at-risk approach has also enabled us to document a reduction in crime when individuals are not actively addicted. Inasmuch as the life course of narcotic addiction, or ''addict career,'' while in the community is characterized by numerous periods of addiction and nonaddiction, it is feasible to compare the amounts of crime committed by individuals when they are addicted and when they are not.[27] When crime rates were compared in this manner, it was found that the number of crime-days per year-at-risk averaged 255 during periods of active addiction and only 65 during periods of nonaddiction.[28] There was, then, a 75 percent decrease in criminality from addiction to nonaddiction. Further analysis showed that there was a decline in annualized crime rates during successive nonaddiction periods as well. Conversely, crime rates during successive addiction periods remained high.

A subsequent study of 250 addicts in Baltimore and New York, whom our staff interviewed between 1983 and 1984, provided similar results. It was found that the number of overall crime-days per year-at-risk during periods of addiction averaged 259, while the rate for periods of nonaddiction was 108.[29]

NARCOTIC ADDICT TYPES

There has long been a nagging concern about the order of first occurrence of drug abuse and crime and about the directional nature of the relationship between the two. Many early studies of the drugs-crime connection were preoccupied with this question. The inquiry was typically stated as an either-or, mutually exclusive one. Addicts either committed crimes to support their habits or were criminals to begin with, addiction merely being one more manifestation of a deviant life style. As mentioned, regardless of whatever side one took, there was general consensus that addicts basically comprised a homogeneous group. Only recently (since the 1970s) have researchers begun to systematically evaluate the differential characteristics of narcotic addicts. A major outgrowth of research based on an assumption of heterogeneity has been the derivation of narcotic addict types. Such information is just beginning to be available for consideration by policy makers.

Our own work in this area of research has determined that addicts vary along a host of dimensions, including the degree to which they engage in crime.[30] Some individuals are extremely criminal before they become addicted, while others turn to criminal behavior only as a result of their addiction. There are addicts who do not commit any crime except for possession of illegal drugs, while others commit several crimes per day and carry weapons while doing so. Certain addicts may maintain rather stable levels of crime, while the criminal behavior of others may trend upward or downward as addiction careers extend over time. Also, many addicts undergo treatment for their addictions, while others remain addicted for long periods of time with no intention of being treated for their drug problems. Only by carefully examining the various kinds of narcotic addicts will more effective use be made of treatment facilities and correctional resources.

In one of our studies of addicts, we classified a sample of 460 individuals according to criminality, employment, and adequacy of income to meet needs.[31] Two of the types generated by this classification were so different from one another that they suggested two distinct ways of dealing with drug activities. The first type, the "successful criminal," is accustomed to having more than enough money from illicit sources to meet his needs. The second type, the "working addict," is employed at least eight hours a day and is only involved minimally in criminal activities. The successful criminal would appear to be a poor candidate for treatment that counsels him to seek a legitimate job paying far less than his illegal income. For such a strategy to succeed, this type of addict would have to be monitored closely to ascertain whether or not he was returning to drug abuse and crime. Should reinvolvement occur, he should be promptly referred back to the court for disposition. In contrast, the working addict attempts to live in two worlds, the "straight world" and the drug subculture; his struggle to maintain this precarious balance makes him a prime candidate for receiving help in planning for a more legitimate life style. It is believed that such meaningful, pragmatic typologies will ultimately serve to increase the effectiveness of prevention, rehabilitation, and correctional efforts with respect to the individual at risk.

USE OF "CAPTIVE" SAMPLES

Several literature reviews have reported that most investigations of the criminal behavior of narcotic addicts have ignored the problem of population representativeness.[32] Many researchers have studied only "captive" addicts (those in jail or in treatment) who may possess characteristics quite different from those of addicts at large in the community. This fact obviously compromises the generalizability of results.

While a truly random sample of narcotic addicts is apparently impossible to achieve since the activity is illegal and therefore often unseen, making the population incapable of complete enumeration, in the 1970s attempts were begun to minimize these difficulties. One example was our own study, which employed a "community-wide" population consisting of all individuals identified as narcotic addicts by the Baltimore City Police over a twenty-year period.[33] Another approach to the representativeness problem has been the use of samples of narcotic abusers "on the street." In this type of research, ethnographic methods

have been used. Often researchers employ ex-addicts or become familiar themselves with the addict subculture in various ways. An example of the latter, the
setting up of "storefronts," is exemplified by the work in New York City of
Edward A. Preble and John J. Casey[34] in the 1960s and of Bruce Johnson, Paul
Goldstein, and others in the 1970s and 1980s.[35]

Ethnographic research may provide a means of obtaining valuable insights
into the procurement of information regarding the drugs-crime connection that
has not been possible through traditional research. As Goldstein summarized in
1982,

Careful and probing research is needed to explicate the dynamics underlying both drugs
and crime, and the multifaceted relationship between the two phenomena. Ethnographic
techniques may well hold the most promise in this regard. Interviewing subjects in
institutional settings, or perusing official statistics, is a poor substitute for being with
subjects on a daily basis.[36]

MEASURES OF CRIMINAL ACTIVITY OVER TIME

Career patterns of criminal behavior and drug use were typically ignored in
earlier research,[37] most studies having dealt with single-event, pre- and postin-
tervention comparisons of criminal behavior.[38] Systematically measuring criminal activity over time is a relatively new development. As William H.
McGlothlin[39] and other reviewers have noted, however, unless suitable adjustments are made, the age of the addict may become a confounding variable. Since
research has shown that many individuals tend to "mature out" of both crime
and addiction over time, the decreased prevalence of illicit behavior among older
(more experienced) addicts may be a phenomenon associated with age. One way
of dealing with this methodologically, as Blumstein and Cohen have suggested,
is by "tracking carefully the patterns of offending by individual criminals in
order to collect reliable data" which "involves the characterization of the longitudinal pattern of crime events for offenders and assessment of factors that
affect that pattern."[40]

A way of applying this method to the joint study of crime and addiction over
time has centered around the notion of "addict careers." As mentioned earlier,
the addict career, or the time from the first regular narcotic use to the present,
is divided into periods of addiction and nonaddiction. Using this longitudinal
method, crime rates can be compared between different addiction status periods
as well as over successive periods of addiction and nonaddiction.[41] This form
of interview schedule has also been successfully used by McGlothlin, and later
by Douglas Anglin, at UCLA in their follow-up studies of addicts.[42]

TYPES AND EXTENT OF DRUG-RELATED CRIME

Many researchers have concluded that the prevalence and diversity of criminal
involvement by narcotic addicts are high and that this involvement is primarily

for the purpose of supporting the use of drugs. Further, it has been a consistent finding that initiation into both substance abuse and criminal activity occurs at an early age. In particular, several investigators have found that among samples of drug-using offenders, those who reported the most crime as adults, including the most violent crime, were characteristically precocious in their drug use and illegal activity.[43]

It has also been a uniform finding that frequency of narcotic use is generally associated with higher crime rates. Johnson and his associates[44] found that the heaviest heroin users were more likely to be classified as serious offenders. In their research, such individuals were found to be disproportionately represented in the highest categories of criminal involvement and had the highest incomes from major crime. Examining a broader range of drug abusers, the Research Triangle Institute group[45] reported that "expensive" drug use was at least a partial explanation for income-generating crime. These investigators found that more-than-once-a-day heroin and cocaine use predicted comparatively high levels of illegal income. Further examination of the drug-use-frequency/income-from-crime relationship suggested that whereas low-use levels are supportable without resort to illegal activity, frequent daily use rarely is. And Chaiken and Chaiken,[46] classifying prison and jail inmates as addicted heroin users, nonaddicted heroin users, nonheroin drug users, and nondrug users, found that addicted heroin users had markedly higher levels of criminal activity than did nonheroin drug users.

In explanation of the above results, one might argue that those individuals prone to be heavy drug users are also innately prone to become involved in criminal activity. Evidence of a more direct relationship between narcotic drug use frequency and crime requires longitudinal, intrasubject information on narcotic-abusing individuals over periods varying with respect to frequency of narcotic drug use. In our own studies of addict careers, the consistently high rates of criminality associated with addiction periods and the markedly lower rates found in the nonaddiction periods provide substantial support for a causal component in the relationship of drug use to crime. The most parsimonious explanation of these within-group changes in crime rates with varying amounts of narcotic use is that narcotic addiction contributes to an increase in crime. Without engaging in a discussion of causal analysis, it seems evident from the totality of the data that heroin addiction is criminogenic in the same sense that cigarette smoking or air pollutants are carcinogenic—they can, and often do, lead to increased incidence, although they are not the only causal agents.

Although individual addicts vary with respect to the crime they engage in, narcotic addicts as a group engage in many different types of criminal activity. Examining a sample of male and female narcotic users in Miami between 1978 and 1981, Inciardi found that over a preceding twelve-month period, the 573 individuals in this sample were responsible for over 82,000 drug sales, nearly 6,000 robberies and assaults, 6,700 burglaries, and 900 car thefts, as well as for more than 25,000 instances of shoplifting and 46,000 other types of larceny and fraud. Overall, they were responsible for a total of 215,105 criminal offenses of all types during the twelve-month reporting period, or an average of 375 offenses per narcotic user.[47]

Drug Distribution Crimes

Drug distribution crimes (e.g., dealing, copping, tasting) appear to account for a sizable proportion of all crimes performed by narcotic abusers. For Inciardi's sample, drug sales was by far the most frequent crime, accounting for 38 percent of all offenses. The respondents averaged 144 drug sales per year.[48] A sample of 201 heroin abusers studied by Johnson reported committing, on the average, 828 crimes per year per user. The most frequent crime was drug sales, or dealing, which accounted for 34 percent of all crimes. The second most frequent crime was copping (buying for others), which constituted 28 percent of all crimes. Taken together, these and other drug distribution offenses accounted for 65 percent of all crimes reported.[49]

Our recent studies of addicts interviewed in Baltimore and New York during 1983 and 1984 also documented the dominance of drug distribution crimes. This sample of 250 male addicts reported performing drug distribution crimes on nearly 48,000 days while addicted, the average time spent addicted being nearly eight years. On average, the addicts were involved in drug distribution crimes 191 days per year. For the entire sample, drug distribution crimes accounted for 48.3 percent of all crime-days. Comparisons of crime-days frequencies with those reported by an earlier sample of addicts interviewed during 1973–1978 revealed a higher proportion of drug distribution crimes and a lower proportion of theft crimes in the more recent sample. In the earlier sample, drug distribution crimes accounted for only 27 percent of the crime-days, while theft crimes made up 38 percent of the crime-days.[50]

The 100 subjects interviewed in Baltimore were also examined in a separate series of analyses, comparing crime-days results with those for an earlier sample of Baltimore addicts.[51] It was found that for both black and white addicts, crime increased overall, with the greatest area of increase in drug distribution crimes. This was true of crimes committed during both addiction periods and nonaddiction periods. Minor differences in study procedures, however, render these findings tentative rather than conclusive.

Violent Crimes

Obviously, because of their severe consequences to victims, policy makers and the media have emphasized violent drug-related crimes. While investigations by us and others have reported that violent crimes make up a small proportion of all crimes committed by addicts, the actual number of such offenses is still large since addicts commit so many crimes. For example, in Inciardi's sample of 573 narcotic users, the proportion of violent crimes committed in the year before the interview constituted only 2.8 percent of all offenses, but this amounted to nearly six thousand offenses since a total of 215,105 crimes were committed.[52]

Paul Goldstein[53] has recorded many ethnographic accounts of violent drug-related acts from both perpetrators and victims in New York City. Resulting from this research is his theory that violent crime and drugs can be related in three different ways. The psychopharmacological model of violence implies that individuals act violently because of the short- or long-term effects of the ingestion of certain substances. Crimes resulting from withdrawal effects of heroin or directly related to barbiturate or PCP use are examples of this. The economically compulsive model suggests that violent crime is committed to obtain money to purchase drugs. This applies primarily to expensive drugs such as heroin and cocaine. The systemic model purports that violence results from the traditionally aggressive patterns of interaction within the drug distribution system. Killing or assaulting someone for distributing "bad" drugs is an example of this.

A study of 578 homicides in Manhattan in 1981 found that 38 percent of the male victims and 14 percent of the female victims were murdered as result of drug-related activity.[54] This report, published in 1986, stated that the observed proportion of homicides related to drug and other criminal activities was higher than had been reported previously in the United States. The authors concluded that rather than being related to pharmacological actions producing aggressive and homicidal behavior, the effects of drugs were probably indirect and related to drug-seeking activities. They concluded that "the fact that over one-third of male homicide victims in Manhattan in 1981 died in drug-related homicides attests to the magnitude and the impact of the drug problem, particularly with narcotics."[55]

NON-NARCOTIC DRUG USE AND CRIME

While it has been acknowledged that a substantial relationship exists between narcotic addiction and crime, the situation has been somewhat less clear with regard to non-narcotic drugs. In a comprehensive review of the literature published in 1980, Robert P. Gandossy and his associates found the evidence connecting the use of various non-narcotic drugs to crime to be inconclusive.[56] A further problem concerning this issue is that narcotic and non-narcotic drugs are often used in combination. Thus, disentangling their joint relationship to criminal behavior, let alone resolving the issue of cause and effect, is problematical. Research endeavors in the past decade, however, have made several advances in addressing these difficulties.

One method of approaching the issue has been to study the crime rates of individuals during a particular period in which they were strictly non-narcotic users and had never become addicted to narcotics. Inciardi interviewed a sample of 429 such individuals in the years 1978–1981.[57] Reporting both a high prevalence and a diversity of crimes, these individuals admitted to committing a total of 137,076 offenses, for an average of 320 crimes per user, over a one-year period. This rate was slightly lower and the diversity of crimes somewhat less than those found for a sample of narcotic users interviewed during the same period. Of the crimes committed by the non-narcotic users, drug sales accounted for 28 percent, prostitution for 18 percent, and shoplifting for 16 percent.[58]

Another way of studying the non-narcotic drug-crime relationship has been to correlate rates of various types of crime with the use of non-narcotic drugs during periods of addiction and nonaddiction to narcotics. Our own findings from this type of approach have consistently indicated that the use of certain non-narcotic drugs by narcotic addicts is associated with the commission of certain types of crime, although this varied somewhat by ethnic group and narcotic addiction status.[59] Cocaine use was found to have a particularly high association with several different types of crime, including theft, violent crimes, drug dealing, and confidence games. This association appeared to be stronger in black and Hispanic addicts than in white addicts.[60]

TREATMENT AND REHABILITATION

Most of the addicts we have studied in over twenty years of research have been arrested a number of times and have spent considerable time in prison. Many addicts have also had at least one treatment experience for narcotic drug abuse. However, these arrests, periods of incarceration, and treatment experiences appear to have had little deterrent effect on subsequent criminal behavior in the community for a good many addicts. As we have indicated elsewhere,[61] the finding of continuity and persistence of criminal behavior among narcotic addicts stands out as a major conclusion of our research.

Some encouraging findings concerning rehabilitation efforts have involved the use of legal pressures accompanied by a monitoring or surveillance component. Studies of the California Civil Addict Program by McGlothlin and Anglin[62] found that court-ordered, drug-free outpatient treatment accompanied by supervision, including urine testing and weekly visits to a parole officer, was associated with reduced criminal activity. Other studies, conducted by investigators at the Research Triangle Institute (RTI) in North Carolina, found that legal pressure was positively related to retention in treatment programs and that time in treatment was a significant factor in the reduction of criminal behavior following treatment.[63] And, encouraged by their findings in a recently reported study of legal pressure and methadone maintenance outcome, Anglin and his colleagues[64] argue for greater utilization of community drug treatment by pretrial, probation, and parole agencies.

By far the most ambitious series of studies of the influence of treatment on the behavior of the narcotic addict has been that conducted by the Institute of Behavioral Research at Texas Christian University in Ft. Worth.[65] Based on a client reporting system for community-based drug abuse programs, titled Drug Abuse Reporting Program (DARP), this treatment outcome evaluation research involved a comparison of the effectiveness of methadone maintenance programs, therapeutic communities, outpatient drug-free treatments, outpatient detoxification clinics, and intake only (i.e., no treatment). Major criteria of effectiveness included illicit drug use and criminality, along with alcohol use, employment, and need for further treatment. Post-treatment results over a three-year follow-up period were available for four to five thousand clients, with many individuals being followed for as long as six years after treatment admission.

Findings of the DARP revealed a clear-cut superiority of methadone maintenance, therapeutic community, and outpatient drug-free treatment over outpatient detoxification and no treatment. No further differentiation was made among the three effective treatment approaches, all of which produced a marked reduction in self-reported narcotic drug use and criminal behavior. Regardless of treatment type, outcomes associated with treatments of less than ninety days tended to be poor. Persons with less criminal involvement before treatment and persons employed before treatment were more likely to demonstrate favorable outcomes. As apparent in our own research, criminal activity during follow-up was related to daily drug use. And, consistent with the results of other studies, there was no obvious interaction between client and treatment types in terms of outcome.[66]

For DARP clients, during-treatment performance, including longer program involvement and completion of the program, was also positively related to outcome. As in the RTI studies, the marked improvement that tended to occur after the first few months of treatment, particularly with methadone maintenance, suggested a compliance factor associated with coercive entry and program surveillance. After this marked change, there was continued improvement over time in treatment, which suggested a therapeutic effect due to the development of motivation that was also instrumental in the clients' remaining in treatment.[67]

POLICY IMPLICATIONS

Although narcotic addicts as a group extensively engage in crime, the amounts and types of crimes committed vary considerably across individuals. The criminal activity of most addicts is strongly influenced by current addiction status. Narcotic addicts commit millions of crimes per year in the United States, and many of these offenses are of a serious nature. In a very real sense, it can be said that illicit narcotic drugs "drive" crime. Therefore, there is a pressing need to address the problem by continuing to inform the public and its leaders concerning the magnitude and perseverance of criminal behavior among heroin addicts.

As several recent writers have suggested,[68] one approach to a solution involves the early identification of those individuals prone to commit large numbers of serious crimes. Our studies, as well as those by Chaiken and Chaiken, have indicated that, among offenders, those who are precocious in crime and polydrug use will most likely become the most dangerous, long-term criminals.[69] In addition, we are currently studying the etiology of drug abuse, with the goal of determining the distinguishing characteristics of those individuals who later become addicts, as opposed to their peers who do not. Such information will eventually be useful in planning prevention and intervention strategies.

Another policy with regard to drug abuse and crime centers on the targeted reduction of the amounts of illicit drugs, especially heroin and cocaine, consumed by daily users. Implementation of this policy would involve identifying criminally active, daily heroin and cocaine users and ensuring that they are treated and closely monitored in order to alter their drug abuse patterns. Our studies suggest that this particular strategy may work best with addicts minimally involved in crime before becoming addicted and during periods of nonaddiction (i.e., those whose criminal activity is more exclusively related to supporting a habit).[70]

In determining an appropriate disposition of a narcotic drug abuser after arrest, it should again be emphasized that there is not a one-to-one relationship between official arrest records and extent of criminal activity. For a more accurate estimate of the latter, it is important that frequency of narcotic abuse also be determined. From our experiences and those of Johnson and his associates, it appears that the more criminally prone, heaviest narcotic abusers are "slipping through the cracks of the criminal justice system."[71] These individuals are committing more crimes per arrest and are managing to avoid involvement in drug abuse treatment efforts.

Identifying the "heavy" drug abuser is, however, problematic. While individuals tend to be truthful in reporting drug use in research situations where confidentiality and immunity from prosecution are ordinarily guaranteed, there is evidence that on arrest they are likely to conceal their recent drug use.[72] As a result of this finding, urine testing of arrestees has been recommended as an additional means of identifying those who are habitual drug users. Urine testing has therefore been utilized in many jurisdictions as an additional means of identifying arrestees who are drug users. It has recently been estimated that approximately 70 percent of those arrested for serious crimes in major U.S. cities test positive for at least one illicit drug.[73] However, while a single positive urinalysis result is a valid indicator of recent drug use, it is not sufficient to identify an individual as a frequent and persistent drug user. As several researchers have indicated, a series of positive results over a long period of time tends to be a more accurate indicator.[74]

At the very least, it would be advisable for criminal justice authorities to give more concerted attention to evidence concerning the drug activity of individuals who are arrested. One useful approach to this task would be to develop a triage/liaison service within the criminal justice system that would deal exclusively with the disposition of drug-abusing offenders. This service would provide a much needed link between the criminal justice system and a variety of drug abuse treatment programs available for rehabilitation. Major functions of the service would include participation in decisions regarding sentencing, parole, and probation, as well as in implementation of procedures for the appropriate placement, monitoring, and evaluation of outcome for all narcotic addict arrestees. Thus, this service would be an important resource to clinicians who treat drug abusers, as well as to judges and other criminal justice system officials who are involved in the disposition of individual cases.

It is important to reiterate that all narcotic addicts are not alike. What works with one type of addict may not work with another. Some addicts commit a considerable amount of crime, regardless of whether they are addicted, and they may engage in crime several years before becoming addicted to narcotics. On the other hand, other addicts may not commit much crime and may only commit crimes directly related to their use of drugs; during periods of nonaddiction, their criminal activities may drop to trivial levels. As we have emphasized, there are clearly different types of addicts and different pathways to addiction. Effective strategies for dealing with the drugs-crime problem will depend to a significant extent on recognizing this diversity among addicts and on tailoring countermeasures, both therapeutic and judicial, to individual requirements.

Legalizing Drug Use

Some policy makers have proposed that drug-related crime be curtailed by legalizing the use of illicit drugs, making them openly available at little or no cost. This is offered as an admittedly simplistic solution that requires the development of strategies aimed at preserving the smooth functioning of society and mitigating damage to addiction-prone individuals. Outlandish as it may seem, this is an intriguing notion, the ramifications of which bear consideration in view of the lack of effectiveness of current methods of controlling drug use that largely involve attempts at cutting off the sources of drug supply.

A look at history is particularly helpful in conceptualizing the polarity of this issue. During the era of prohibition of alcohol use in this country, emphasis was placed on eliminating sources of supply. As a consequence, alcoholism became less of a national problem, but organized crime flourished in its nearly exclusive role as distributor of alcoholic products. The subsequent repeal of the prohibition, while dealing a significant blow to the underworld, undeniably increased the number of alcoholics and problematic drinkers in our society.[75]

We are now faced with an analogous situation. Unless innovative strategies are developed, the alternative to the high level of drug-related crime associated with strict drug control appears to be an inevitable rise in the number of drug-dependent individuals in society. Ignoring ethical and moral issues for the moment, from a purely pragmatic standpoint, there is the question of how many drug-dependent individuals society can tolerate.

Basic unresolved questions make any position taken with regard to the impact of the legalization of drugs a matter of educated opinion at best. No one knows for certain the extent to which legalization of drugs in this country would increase the number of addicts, nor whether such a strategy would eventually undermine the integrity of our society. Few would deny, however, that the greater availability of, and easier access to, drugs would increase drug use (and addiction) beyond current levels. Whether this nation can be adequately prepared to deal with the consequences of this increase is, again, a matter of conjecture that is beyond the scope of this chapter. More pertinent is this question: What would be the impact of open drug availability on drug-related crime?

To a large extent, the amount of drug-related crime committed is proportional to the costs of drugs, and the latter depend to a large extent on supply and demand. On the supply side, there are two important considerations with regard to legalization, both of which have to do with the effects of a vigorously enforced policy of interdiction. When it is most effective, a policy of interdiction reduces the supply of drugs and, as a consequence, raises the prices people have to pay for them. It also increases the risks associated with drug production and distribution and thus increases the compensation demanded by drug suppliers for their services. Again, the end result is higher drug prices. Assuming that interdiction will never entirely eliminate the supply of drugs, the ironic conclusion is that vigorously enforced interdiction may very well be instrumental in increasing drug-related crime.

In view of the above, some would argue that legalizing drugs would lead to substantial reductions in drug costs and a corresponding reduction in drug-related crime. Such an argument, however, assumes exclusive, trouble-free governmental regulation of the drug supply. Such an assumption would appear to be untenable. The possibility of providing a more desirable drug price and/or purity, unrestricted quantity, personal anonymity, lack of restrictions with regard to age, and other similar inducements could readily lead to black-market competition in drug sales and thus continue the involvement of illegitimate sources of drug supply. Also, the argument ignores the impulsivity and lack of control associated with the use of certain drugs and the crime-linked effects of such drugs as PCP (which produces both self-destructive and assaultive behavior) and cocaine (the excessive use of which has been associated with violence stemming from affective disturbance and paranoid ideation).

This leads us to a consideration of the demand side of the equation, relating supply and demand to drug cost and attendant crime. In view of the above, and the fact that greater demand is associated with increased cost, adoption of intervention strategies aimed at diminishing demand for illicit drugs appears to be the most suitable approach to dealing with the issue of drugs and crime. Consequently, an appropriate policy recommendation would be that concerted attempts be made to dissuade individuals from becoming involved with drugs, along with persistent efforts to wean them off drugs when and if they do become involved. Drug prevention and treatment programs employing both novel and already proven approaches should therefore be targeted for increased support on a national level by both governmental agencies and private funding sources. To the extent that it is drug related, criminal activity in this country should show discernible signs of abatement with any subsequent decrease in drug demand that can thus be effected.

NOTES

1. James A. Inciardi, ed., *The Drugs-Crime Connection* (Beverly Hills, Calif.: Sage, 1981), 7.

2. James A. Inciardi, *The War on Drugs: Heroin, Cocaine, and Public Policy* (Palo Alto, Calif.: Mayfield, 1986), 106.

3. David F. Musto, *The American Disease: Origins of Narcotic Control* (New Haven, Conn.: Yale University Press, 1973).

4. Ibid., 326.

5. Harry E. Barnes and Negley K. Teeters, *New Horizons in Criminology* (New York: Prentice-Hall, 1945), 877.

6. Inciardi, *The War on Drugs*, 148.

7. Robert P. Gandossy, Jay R. Williams, Jo Cohen, and Henrick J. Harwood, *Drugs and Crime: A Survey and Analysis of the Literature* (Washington, D.C.: U.S. Department of Justice, National Institute of Justice, 1980), 67.

8. See Harold Finestone, "Narcotics and Criminality," *Law and Contemporary Problems* 22 (Winter 1957): 72–85; Gregory A. Austin and Dan J. Lettieri, *Drugs and Crime: The Relationship of Drug Use and Concomitant Criminal Behavior* (Rockville, Md.: National Institute on Drug Abuse, 1976); Inciardi, *The Drugs-Crime Connection*; David N. Nurco, John C. Ball, John W. Shaffer, and Thomas E. Hanlon, "The Criminality of Narcotic Addicts," *Journal of Nervous and Mental Disease* 173 (1985): 94–102; Inciardi, *The War on Drugs*.

9. Inciardi, *The War on Drugs*.

10. Alfred Blumstein and Jacqueline Cohen, "Characterizing Criminal Careers," *Science* 237 (1987): 985–91.

11. Bruce D. Johnson, Paul J. Goldstein, Edward Preble, James Schmeidler, Douglas S. Lipton, Barry Spunt, and Thomas Miller, *Taking Care of Business: The Economics of Crime by Heroin Abusers* (Lexington, Mass.: Lexington, 1985).

12. President's Commission on Law Enforcement and the Administration of Justice, *The Challenge of Crime in a Free Society* (Washington, D.C.: U.S. Government Printing Office, 1967), 229.

13. Robert Shellow, ed., *Drug Use and Crime: Report of the Panel on Drug Use and Criminal Behavior* (Washington, D.C.: National Technical Information Service, 1976), 5.

14. Inciardi, *The War on Drugs*.

15. James J. Collins, J. Valley Rachal, Robert L. Hubbard, Elizabeth R. Cavanaugh, S. Gail Craddock, and Patricia L. Kristiansen, *Criminality in a Drug Treatment Sample: Measurement Issues and Initial Findings* (Research Triangle Park, N.C.: Research Triangle Institute, 1982), 27.

16. Jan M. Chaiken and Marcia R. Chaiken, *Who Gets Caught Doing Crime?* (Los Angeles: Hamilton, Rabinovitz, Szanton, and Alschuler, Inc., 1985).

17. See James A. Inciardi and Carl D. Chambers, "Unreported Criminal Involvement of Narcotic Addicts," *Journal of Drug Issues* 2 (1972): 57–64; William H. McGlothlin, M. Douglas Anglin, and Bruce D. Wilson, "Narcotic Addiction and Crime," *Criminology* 16 (1978): 293–316; John C. Ball, Lawrence Rosen, John A. Flueck, and David N. Nurco, "Lifetime Criminality of Heroin Addicts in the United States," *Journal of Drug Issues* 12 (1982): 225–39.

18. Inciardi, *The War on Drugs*.

19. Ibid., 127.

20. Jan M. Chaiken and Marcia R. Chaiken, *Varieties of Criminal Behavior: Summary and Policy Implications* (Santa Monica, Calif.: Rand, 1982), 18.

21. Chaiken and Chaiken, *Who Gets Caught Doing Crime?*

22. Ball, Rosen, Flueck, and Nurco, "Lifetime Criminality of Heroin Addicts."

23. Ibid.

24. Richard C. Stephens, "The Truthfulness of Addict Respondents in Research Projects," *International Journal of the Addictions* 7 (1972): 549–58.

25. See John C. Ball, "The Reliability and Validity of Interview Data Obtained from 59 Narcotic Drug Addicts," *American Journal of Sociology* 72 (1972): 549–58; Stephens, "The Truthfulness"; Arthur J. Bonito, David N. Nurco, and John W. Shaffer, "The Veridicality of Addicts' Self-Reports in Social Research," *International Journal of the Addictions* 11 (1976): 719–24.

26. John C. Ball, John W. Shaffer, and David N. Nurco, "The Day-to-Day Criminality of Heroin Addicts in Baltimore—A Study in the Continuity of Offense Rates," *Drug and Alcohol Dependence* 12 (1983): 119–42.

27. See Ball, Rosen, Flueck, and Nurco, "Lifetime Criminality of Heroin Addicts"; Ball, Shaffer, and Nurco, "The Day-to-Day Criminality"; John W. Shaffer, David N. Nurco, and Timothy W. Kinlock, "A New Classification of Narcotic Addicts," *Comprehensive Psychiatry* 25 (1984): 315–28; David N. Nurco, John W. Shaffer, John C. Ball, Timothy W. Kinlock, and John Langrod, "A Comparison by Ethnic Group and City of the Criminal Activities of Narcotic Addicts," *Journal of Nervous and Mental Disease* 174 (1986): 112–16.

28. Ball, Shaffer, and Nurco, "The Day-to-Day Criminality," 123.

29. Ibid.

30. See David N. Nurco, Ira H. Cisin, and Mitchell B. Balter, "Addict Careers II: The First Ten Years," *International Journal of the Addictions* 8 (1981): 1305–25; "Addict Careers II: The First Ten Years," *International Journal of the Addictions* 8 (1981): 1327–56; "Addict Careers III: Trends Across Time," *International Journal of the Addictions* 8 (1981): 1357–72; David N. Nurco and John W. Shaffer, "Types and Characteristics of Addicts in the Community," *Drug and Alcohol Dependence* 9 (1982): 43–78; Shaffer, Nurco, and Kinlock, "A New Classification"; David N. Nurco, Thomas E. Hanlon, Mitchell B. Balter, Timothy W. Kinlock, and Evelyn Slaght, "A Classification of Narcotic Addicts Based on Type, Amount, and Severity of Crime," *Journal of Drug Issues* (in press).

31. Nurco and Shaffer, "Types and Characteristics."

32. See Gandossy, Williams, Cohen, and Harwood, *Drugs and Crime*; Anne E. Pottieger, "Sample Bias in Drugs/Crime Research: An Empirical Study," in *The Drugs-Crime Connection*, ed. James A. Inciardi (Beverly Hills, Calif.: Sage, 1981), 207–38; George Speckart and M. Douglas Anglin, "Narcotics and Crime: An Analysis of Existing Evidence for a Causal Relationship," *Behavioral Sciences and the Law* 3 (1985): 259–82.

33. David N. Nurco and Robert L. DuPont, "A Preliminary Report on Crime and Addiction Within a Community-Wide Population of Narcotic Addicts," *Drug and Alcohol Dependence* 2 (1977): 109–21.

34. Edward A. Preble and John J. Casey, Jr., "Taking Care of Business: The Heroin User's Life on the Street," *International Journal of the Addictions* 4 (1969): 1–24.

35. See Paul J. Goldstein, "Getting Over: Economic Alternatives to Predating Crime Among Street Drug Users," in *The Drugs-Crime Connection*, ed. James A. Inciardi (Beverly Hills, Calif.: Sage, 1981), 67–84; Johnson et al., *Taking Care of Business*.

36. Goldstein, "Getting Over," 82–83.

37. Gandossy, Williams, Cohen, and Harwood, *Drugs and Crime*, 67.

38. See William H. McGlothlin, "Drugs and Crime," in *Handbook on Drug Abuse*, ed. Robert L. DuPont, Avram Goldstein, and John O'Donnell (Washington, D.C.: National Institute on Drug Abuse and Office of Drug Policy, 1979), 357–64; Gandossy, Williams, Cohen, and Harwood, *Drugs and Crime*, 110.

39. McGlothlin, "Drugs and Crime."

40. Blumstein and Cohen, "Characterizing Criminal Careers," 985.

41. See David N. Nurco, "A Discussion of Validity," in *Self-Reporting Methods in Estimating Drug Abuse*, ed. Beatrice A. Rouse, Nicholas J. Kozel, and Louise G. Richards (Rockville, Md.: National Institute on Drug Abuse, 1985), 4–11.

42. See McGlothlin, Anglin, and Wilson, "Narcotic Addiction and Crime"; M. Douglas Anglin and George Speckart, "Narcotics Use, Property Crime, and Dealing: Structural Dynamics Across the Addiction Career," *Journal of Quantitative Criminology* 2 (1986): 355–75.

43. See Chaiken and Chaiken, *Varieties of Criminal Behavior*; Shaffer, Nurco, and Kinlock, "A New Classification."

44. Johnson et al., *Taking Care of Business*.

45. James J. Collins, Robert L. Hubbard, and J. Valley Rachal, *Heroin and Cocaine Use and Illegal Income* (Research Triangle Park, N.C.: Research Triangle Institute, 1984).

46. Chaiken and Chaiken, *Varieties of Criminal Behavior*.

47. Ibid.

48. Ibid.

49. Johnson et al., *Taking Care of Business*, 77.

50. Nurco, Shaffer, Ball, Kinlock, and Langrod, "A Comparison by Ethnic Group and City."

51. Ibid.

52. Chaiken and Chaiken, *Varieties of Criminal Behavior*.

53. Paul J. Goldstein, "Drugs and Violent Behavior" (Paper presented at the annual meeting of the Academy of Criminal Justice Sciences, Louisville, Ky., 28 April 1982).

54. Kenneth Tardiff, Elliot M. Gross, and Steven F. Messner, "A Study of Homicide in Manhattan, 1981," *American Journal of Public Health* 76 (1986): 139–43.

55. Ibid., 143.

56. Gandossy, Williams, Cohen, and Harwood, *Drugs and Crime*.

57. Inciardi, *The War on Drugs*, 128–30.

58. Ibid.

59. See John W. Shaffer, David N. Nurco, John C. Ball, and Timothy W. Kinlock, "The Frequency of Nonnarcotic Drug Use and Its Relationship to Criminal Activity Among Narcotic Addicts," *Comprehensive Psychiatry* 26 (1985): 558–66; David N. Nurco, Timothy W. Kinlock, Thomas E. Hanlon, and John C. Ball, "Nonnarcotic Drug Use Over an Addiction Career—A Study of Heroin Addicts in Baltimore and New York City," *Comprehensive Psychiatry* 29 (1988): 450–59.

60. Ibid.

61. Nurco, Ball, Shaffer, and Hanlon, "The Criminality of Narcotic Addicts."

62. See William H. McGlothlin, M. Douglas Anglin, and Bruce D. Wilson, *An*

Evaluation of the California Civil Addict Program (Washington, D.C.: U.S. Government Printing Office, 1977); M. Douglas Anglin and William H. McGlothlin, "Outcome of Narcotic Addict Treatment in California," in *Drug Abuse Treatment Evaluation: Strategies, Progress, and Prospects*, ed. Frank Tims and Jacqueline P. Ludford (Washington, D.C.: U.S. Government Printing Office, 1984), 106–28.

63. See James J. Collins and Margaret Allison, "Legal Coercion and Retention in Drug Abuse Treatment," *Hospital and Community Psychiatry* 34 (1983): 1145–49; Robert L. Hubbard, J. Valley Rachal, S. Gail Craddock, and Elizabeth R. Cavanaugh, "Treatment Outcome Prospective Study (TOPS): Client Characteristics and Behaviors Before, During, and After Treatment," in *Drug Abuse Treatment Evaluation: Strategies, Progress, and Prospects*, ed. Frank Tims and Jacqueline P. Ludford (Washington, D.C.: U.S. Government Printing Office, 1984), 42–68.

64. M. Douglas Anglin, Mary-Lynn Brecht, and Ebrahim Maddahian, "Pretreatment Characteristics and Treatment Performance of Legally Coerced Versus Voluntary Methadone Maintenance Admissions," *Criminology* 27 (1989): 537–57.

65. D. Dwayne Simpson and Saul B. Sells, *Highlights of the DARP Follow-Up Research on the Evaluation of Drug Abuse Treatment Effectiveness* (Ft. Worth: Institute of Behavioral Research, Texas Christian University, 1981).

66. Shaffer, Nurco, Ball, and Kinlock, "The Frequency of Nonnarcotic Drug Use and Its Relationship to Criminal Activity among Narcotics Addicts."

67. Simpson and Sells, *Highlights of the DARP*.

68. See Chaiken and Chaiken, *Varieties of Criminal Behavior*; Peter W. Greenwood, *Selective Incapacitation* (Santa Monica, Calif.: Rand, 1982); Nurco, Ball, Shaffer, and Hanlon, "The Criminality of Narcotic Addicts."

69. Ibid.

70. See David N. Nurco, Thomas E. Hanlon, Timothy W. Kinlock, and Karen R. Duszynski, "Differential Patterns of Criminal Activity Over an Addiction Career," *Criminology* (in press).

71. Bruce D. Johnson, Paul Goldstein, Edward Preble, James Schneidler, Douglas S. Lipton, Barry Spunt, Nina Duchaine, Reuben Norman, Thomas Miller, Nancy Meggett, Andrea Kale, and Deborah Hand, *Economic Behavior of Street Opiate Users: Final Report* (New York: Narcotic and Drug Research, Inc., 1983), 232.

72. Eric Wish, "Drug Use Forecasting: New York 1984 to 1986," *National Institute of Justice Research in Action*, February 1987.

73. James R. Stewart (director, National Institute of Justice), *NIJ Reports*, no. 213 (Washington: U.S. Department of Justice, March–April 1989), 1–3.

74. See Chaiken and Chaiken, *Varieties of Criminal Behavior* ; Eric D. Wish, Mary A. Toborg, and John P. Bellasai, *Identifying Drug Users and Monitoring Them During Conditional Release* (Washington, D.C.: U.S. Department of Justice, 1987); Marcia R. Chaiken and Bruce D. Johnson, *Characteristics of Different Types of Drug-Involved Offenders* (Washington: U.S. Department of Justice, 1988).

75. Mark Moore and Dean Gerston, eds., *Alcohol and Public Policy: Beyond the Shadow of Prohibition* (Washington, D.C.: National Academy Press, 1981).

PART II

DRUG CONTROL STRATEGIES

Chapter 4

The Federal Approach to Primary Drug Abuse Prevention and Education

William J. Bukoski

ORIGINS OF PRIMARY DRUG ABUSE PREVENTION AT THE FEDERAL LEVEL

While the concept of primary prevention has been traditionally recognized in public health as an essential program approach for addressing physical and mental health problems, federally supported programs focused specifically on primary drug abuse prevention have had a relatively short history, dating from the late 1960s and early 1970s. The purpose of primary prevention is to reduce the incidence of drug use and to halt progression to drug abuse and associated problem behaviors. Traditionally, it represents but one part of the concept of drug abuse demand reduction which generally also includes treatment (secondary prevention) and rehabilitation (tertiary prevention) research and service programs.

During the 1960s public concern focused on a number of drug abuse problems—particularly heroin addiction, the perceived association between drug abuse and social disorder, the relationship between criminal activity and drug abuse, and the reported widespread recreational use of psychoactive drugs, especially marijuana. The federal response to these issues was relatively modest in scope and provided support for treatment of heroin addiction and treatment research as authorized under the Narcotic Addict Rehabilitation Act of 1966. Limited treatment demonstration project funds were made available through the Department of Housing and Urban Development and as part of the poverty program in the Department of Health, Education, and Welfare. A limited number of grants and contracts were awarded to community-based programs to treat heroin addicts. Drug treatment for heroin addiction was also provided at federal hospitals in Lexington, Kentucky, and Ft. Worth, Texas, which had been functioning in this capacity since the 1930s. The Center for the Studies of Narcotics and Drug Abuse provided the initial base for the emergence of efforts to conduct drug abuse research.[1]

Division of Narcotic Addiction and Drug Abuse (DNADA)

In 1970 federal efforts to respond to the suspected linkage between drug use and street crime resulted in the consolidation of law enforcement activities in drug abuse with the creation of the Bureau of Narcotics and Dangerous Drugs in the Department of Justice. To provide for treatment services and address drug treatment research issues, the Division of Narcotic Addiction and Drug Abuse was created within the National Institute on Mental Health.

Office of Education (OE)

One of the earliest efforts in primary drug abuse prevention and education was initiated by the Department of Health, Education, and Welfare, Office of Education, in the development of training programs for educators to combat drug abuse in the schools. In 1970 the president of the United States instructed the Office of Education to initiate a grant program that would offer funds on a formula basis to provide drug education training for educators in every school system in the country.[2] Approximately $2.8 million was spent on the program in fiscal year 1970 and $2.0 million in fiscal year 1971. In addition, twenty-eight community drug education grants were funded ($2.3 million) in 1970, as were nineteen college-based drug education programs ($659,000). Under Title III funding (Supplementary Educational Services of the Elementary and Secondary Education Act), eleven school-community drug projects were supported at $1.3 million. In December 1970 the Congress formalized this drug education/ training effort with passage of the Drug Abuse Education Act. By fiscal year 1972 the funding for educational programs in drug abuse had reached $13 million, with another $13 million planned for fiscal year 1973.[3]

Over the course of these early years the focus of the projects expanded from training school staff in drug education to providing technical assistance to communities that wished to solve their drug problems. The primary strategy selected by the OE was the school teams approach. Team membership varied, but usually included the superintendent of schools, community officials, teachers, and, in later years, parents and students. To accomplish this training effort, training centers were funded by the OE (for a total of $2.4 million) to train approximately six hundred community teams the first year. Since the 1970s the school teams approach has been successfully continued by the OE and now the Department of Education. Most recently, in 1988, the department funded five regional training centers for the purpose of school teams training and technical assistance in primary drug abuse prevention.

Special Action Office for Drug Abuse Prevention (SAODAP)

To better coordinate federal drug abuse initiatives and to better respond to the increased alarm about the perceived threat of criminal activity of drug addicts, the civil unrest generated by the antiwar movement, and the fear of widespread use of heroin by American soldiers returning home from Vietnam, the president in 1971 created by executive order the Special Action Office for Drug Abuse Prevention.[4] This office was responsible for planning a rational and coordinated approach to the treatment and rehabilitation of heroin addicts. In cooperation with federal agencies, a treatment system was created to treat and rehabilitate heroin addicts. The rhetoric of the day characterized the treatment objectives of this federal action within the global term of drug abuse "prevention." The concepts of primary prevention, secondary prevention (treatment), and tertiary prevention (rehabilitation) as defined by the public health model were not presented as separate and distinct program approaches. Rather, any and all efforts to deal with the heroin epidemic were considered in the published reports of the day to be within the global concept of prevention. In reality, the majority of federal funding supported the delivery of drug treatment services to heroin addicts, and limited funds were available to provide primary prevention education.

National Commission on Marijuana and Drug Abuse

A number of significant reports helped shape the federal government's response to the drug abuse problem. In 1972, consistent with Public Law 91–513, the National Commission on Marijuana and Drug Abuse submitted the first of two reports to the president and the Congress on the status of marijuana use in the country. The first report was entitled *Marijuana: A Signal of Misunderstanding*.[5] The study provided a global assessment of the known risks of marijuana use, the extent of use, prevention programs in operation, an analysis of existing laws and regulations, and social consequences of use. In 1973 the commission turned its attention to the general problem of drug abuse and published the second report entitled *Drug Use in America: Problem in Perspective*.[6]

Both reports questioned the traditional deterrent-based drug policy implemented by the federal and state governments and instead advocated a policy focused on the social rather than the health or criminal consequences of the use of marijuana and other drugs. The commission reports advocated a drug policy that would "minimize irresponsible drug-using behavior."[7] According to the 1973 report, drug use was irresponsible when "the manner or circumstance of use poses a threat to the safety or welfare of others; the pattern of use substantially impedes or risks the impairment of the individual's social and economic functioning; and, the pattern of use reduces the individual's options for self-fulfillment by impairing his faculties or retarding his development."[8]

Though use of marijuana was not advocated by the reports, the tone and content indicated that personal marijuana use was a matter of individual choice and responsible decision making. According to the commission, rather than continuing to emphasize the health risks of drug use, a more realistic policy should focus on the perceived attractions of drug use and the perceived needs that drugs appear to fulfill. A drug policy built on this premise would then offer a greater chance of modifying individual and group behavior through the identification of more positive outlets for self-expression.[9] It was the intent of the commission to provide a more rational and realistic rather than emotional response to a difficult social problem.

The three principal recommendations for the federal government from the first report (published in 1972) on marijuana illustrate the general thrust of the commission's approach to rationalize individual use of marijuana and to decriminalize this personally determined behavior:

1. Possession of marijuana for personal use should no longer be an offense, but marijuana possessed in public would remain contraband subject to summary seizure and forfeiture.

2. Casual distribution of small amounts of marijuana for no remuneration or insignificant remuneration not involving profit should no longer be an offense.

3. A plea of marijuana intoxication should not be a defense to any criminal act committed under its influence, nor should proof of such intoxication constitute a negation of specific intent.[10]

Recommendations from the second report (published in 1973) called for the development of an extensive treatment service and enforcement system at the federal and state level. But the most striking of all the recommendations for prevention called for a moratorium of new drug information programs that dealt with the health risks of drug use and a repeal of mandatory drug education in schools until programs had been evaluated and a more realistic approach to drug education could be developed:

(c) That a moratorium be declared on the production and dissemination of new drug information materials. This step, presently being considered by SAODAP, will enable the federal government to develop necessary standards for accuracy and concept, and allow sufficient time to conduct a critical inventory of presently existing materials.

(d) That policy makers, in recognition of ignorance about the impact of drug education, seriously consider declaring a moratorium on all drug education programs in the schools, at least until programs already in operation have been evaluated and a coherent approach with realistic objectives has been developed. At the very least, state legislatures should repeal all statutes which now require drug education courses to be included in the public school curriculum.[11]

At the time the report was controversial because it appeared to many to signal to the nation that marijuana use was neither physically harmful nor connected in any way known at that time to the progression in use of other "hard" drugs. With today's scientific knowledge of the harmful consequences of marijuana use, the contemporary criticism of the commission's findings appears to have merit. Because of the timing of the report and its emphasis on responsible use, one is tempted to speculate whether the commission's reports may have added to and in part authenticated a social environment conducive to drug use and as a result may have contributed to the increase in marijuana and other drug use that occurred through the middle and late 1970s. Despite the criticism of the commission's reports, they did provoke a thoughtful reconsideration of a number of assumptions concerning the nature of drug abuse by expanding the discussion and debate to include the social and behavioral antecedents and consequences of drug use and abuse.

Relevant to the history of prevention, however, the commission findings on the efficacy of drug abuse education provided a chilling effect on a fragile and scientifically evolving discipline. At least one of the recommendations was immediately initiated. In 1973, concerned about the increasing drug problem, the SAODAP declared a moratorium on the production of drug information[12] and the following year issued new guidelines on media and drug abuse messages for all federal agencies publishing drug abuse information materials.[13] As a result of the 1973 moratorium, federal funding to develop and disseminate drug education materials and teacher training decreased significantly, awaiting the initiation of the new media/drug education guidelines. However, the drug use problem continued.

On a more positive note, the recommendations of the second commission report provided specific support for the development of an effective collaboration of federal, state, and local governments to develop and fund drug treatment, research, and prevention activities and services. The view that federal government action was both essential and appropriate in the face of the heroin epidemic was underscored by the work of the commission, despite its self-admonishment against the development of an unwieldy and unresponsive bureaucracy at the federal level.

Drug Abuse Office and Treatment Act

Prompted by the continuing heroin epidemic, Congress in 1972 passed the Drug Abuse Office and Treatment Act of 1972 (Public Law 92–255). This legislation formalized the SAODAP in the executive branch as the vehicle to provide federal leadership in the fight against drug abuse; instituted the single state agencies for drug abuse treatment, prevention, and control; and recommended the establishment of a separate drug agency within the Department of Health, Education, and Welfare. This agency would provide federal funding to state and community agencies through formula grants and service contracts to fund drug treatment programs at the state and local levels. This agency was also charged with the responsibility to conduct basic and applied drug research on the causes and consequences of drug abuse, evaluate prevention education, provide training for treatment service providers, and monitor national drug use trends.

Alcohol, Drug Abuse, and Mental Health Administration (ADAMHA), National Institute on Drug Abuse (NIDA)

In May 1974 the lead drug abuse agency referenced in Public Law 92–255 was formally created in the Alcohol, Drug Abuse, and Mental Health Administration as the National Institute on Drug Abuse. Joining the NIDA in the ADAMHA were the National Institute On Alcohol Abuse and Alcoholism, which had been created in 1970 by Congress with passage of the Hughes Act, and the National Institute on Mental Health.

The creation of NIDA in 1974 was a benchmark for primary prevention of substance abuse because it established for the first time an operational unit within the federal government that had as its mission the development and enhancement of the concept of primary prevention. In many ways the overall federal approach to primary prevention of drug abuse was reflected in the formation and activity of NIDA's prevention program. The Prevention Branch was established to provide technical assistance in primary prevention program planning and implementation and to develop innovative prevention models through its prevention education grants program. Staffing of the branch reflected an amalgamation of unique talent with expertise in public health planning, education, mass communication, and community development. Funds for this branch were quite limited and were not delineated under a separate line item in the NIDA budget, but instead were included within the line item for the Division of Community Assistance, the unit responsible for administering and monitoring the NIDA's treatment service program of grants and contracts.

At this stage, primary prevention was still emerging as an authentic program entity within the drug abuse field and distinct from the treatment system. Substantial federal efforts were devoted to simply defining the term *prevention* and describing possible prevention approaches that could be implemented at the local level. Through a series of "delphi" meetings, groups of experts were convened by the branch to clarify critical prevention concepts, define terms, and develop recommendations for the implementation of prevention programming at the federal, state, and local levels. The resulting publication entitled *Toward a National Strategy for Primary Drug Abuse Prevention*[14] served to coalesce current thinking on prevention, establish a mutually agreed on lexicon of prevention terms, and set forward a common framework or blueprint for future action.

Over the succeeding years, a number of technical assistance, media, and evaluation projects were developed by the NIDA and the Prevention Branch.[15] For example, technical assistance to state and local prevention programs was provided by Project Pyramid through the development of high-quality prevention publications and the provision of on-site consultation offered by the best experts available to the field at the local, regional, or national level. Another contract involving the Center for Multicultural Awareness provided comparable high-quality technical assistance and multilanguage prevention publications with a special focus on encouraging better understanding of and addressing the special prevention needs of minority populations. Technical assistance in evaluation of primary prevention programs was provided by the National Prevention Evaluation Resource Network (NPERN) which was operated under a NIDA contract awarded to a consortium of three single state agencies. Though the project operated for only several years, significant advances were made in the development of prevention evaluation publications; the elaboration of a prevention evaluation model that included process, outcome, and impact assessment; and the establishment of a skilled cadre of prevention evaluation experts who provided on-site technical assistance to a number of state and local prevention programs. Through its prevention education program (designated as EO7 grants by the Public Health Service), the Prevention Branch was able to competitively review and fund a number of innovative prevention education approaches ranging from the development of school-based models to the support of community action programs that would provide youth with positive alternatives to drug use and abuse. These early demonstration prevention projects provided seed money to local agencies and voluntary groups that wished to prevent substance abuse in their community. The program supported prototypic prevention evaluation efforts that would later emerge at the NIDA as a separate unit (i.e., the Prevention Research Branch).

These early federal efforts in primary prevention appear to reflect the emergence of two trends. The first was the evolution of sanctioned units within the federal government with prevention program staff and funds to combat drug abuse and to prevent the onset and progression of drug use by American youth. This bureaucratization of primary prevention was important because it provided a national focal point for discussing the importance of primary prevention and an organizational unit from which leadership in the field and program funds would emanate. This small cadre of federal officials assigned to work in this fledgling field of primary prevention offered a mechanism by which to respond to congressional interest in prevention, provided within the drug treatment system a primary prevention perspective in the discussion of potential drug abuse policy at the national level, and offered a vehicle for providing training, technical assistance, and developmental dollars for the implementation of primary prevention programs at the state and local levels.

A second trend was the building of a scientific base for both prevention theory and program models derived from studies of the correlates or etiologic factors for drug use onset and from prevention evaluation studies that employed quasi-experimental and experimental designs. Substantial efforts were devoted to describing the psychosocial correlates of drug use onset and progression with the expectation that this basic research knowledge would reveal those potential causes of drug use that might be amenable to change through program intervention. Results from these studies could then be used by the prevention practitioners at the state and local levels to design potentially more effective *theory-based* drug education strategies for use in schools and the community at large. During this time period a number of evaluations of drug education models were attempted with both federal and state funding. Many of these studies were rudimentary in research design and statistical analyses, given today's standards. These evaluations attempted to determine if exposure to drug education and prevention models actually changed drug use knowledge, attitudes, and behaviors. On completion of individual projects, the findings were reported to the funding agency. A number of these reports were also submitted to peer-reviewed drug abuse journals for publication and hopefully dissemination of the research findings to the prevention field. A number of reviews of the evaluations of primary prevention programs were also completed and shared with the field of prevention in the form of either a final report or a journal article. As with the results of correlation research studies, it was expected that the results of the primary prevention evaluations would help prevention program staff at the state or local level make informed choices concerning the selection and promotion of specific prevention models. Intense interest in determining the efficacy of primary prevention programs continues today and has become the focus of primary prevention research sponsored by the NIDA.

With the creation of the NIDA, primary drug abuse prevention began to emerge as a program entity separate and distinct from drug treatment, with efforts focused on the definition of program modalities, the institutionalization of a cadre of prevention specialists at the federal and state levels, and the building of a scientific basis for the development of theory-based prevention programs and controlled testing to determine the efficacy of a particular prevention model.

White House Reports on Drug Abuse and
Drug Abuse Prevention

As indicated earlier, as part of the federal reorganization that occurred in 1974 some of the functions of the SAODAP and all of the program elements of the DNADA were formally transferred to the NIDA. However, the SAODAP continued its drug coordination function, operating from the White House.

In September 1975 the Domestic Council Drug Abuse Task Force released on behalf of the executive branch a *White Paper on Drug Abuse*.[16] The report indicated that the perception emanating from the White House and reported in late 1973 that the nation may have "turned the corner on drug abuse" actually reflected a temporary and regional phenomenon. Concerned by the evidence of continued drug use increases, President Ford in the spring of 1974 directed the Domestic Council to assess the national drug problem and to make recommendations for further federal action. On behalf of the council, representatives from over twenty government agencies participated in the work sessions designed not to critique the current drug abuse efforts of government agencies, but instead to provide a more rational and effective plan for future programs.

Consistent with the spirit of the Drug Abuse Office and Treatment Act of

1972, the *White Paper* acknowledged the importance of a balanced strategy for containing drug abuse, to include equal emphasis on both the control of the supply of drugs through tough antinarcotic laws/enforcement and the reduction of the demand for drugs. According to the report,

The demand reduction program is intended to: (1) dissuade the nonuser from experimenting with drugs; (2) deter the occasional user or experimenter from progressing to the abuse of drugs; (3) make treatment available for abusers of drugs who seek it; and (4) help the former abuser regain his place as a productive member of society.[17]

Not only did the *White Paper* endorse the concept of demand reduction, but also it recommended that it become the cornerstone of the federal approach to drug control. In many ways the *White Paper* began to restore confidence in the concept of primary prevention and served to encourage federal agencies to initiate drug demand programs through treatment, education, training, and technical assistance. Of interest is the fact that the *White Paper* recommended more focus on the prevention component in addition to the treatment component of the demand-reduction approach.

The current treatment focus of demand reduction efforts should be supplemented with increased attention to prevention and vocational rehabilitation. The bulk of Federal resources and attention have gone for treatment since the drug program was elevated to a high priority. In light of the acute need which existed at that time, this focus was clearly necessary.

Yet, treatment is a response to a problem which has already developed. Given the difficulties of successful treatment, it is obvious that effective programs which prevent the problem before it develops are highly desirable. Similarly, vocational rehabilitation during and after treatment which enhances the probability that a former abuser will not return to drug use should be given priority. The task force believes both these areas should be important parts of the overall demand reduction program.[18]

According to the report, primary prevention programs should not just focus on drugs, but also deal with a broad range of adolescent problems, such as school dropouts, alcoholism, and delinquency. It recommended that prevention programs be community based and designed to meet the unique needs of that community. On the other hand, the federal government's prevention role should be "catalytic in nature, providing technical assistance, training, and limited seed money."[19]

The report acknowledged the NIDA's prevention education grant program which in 1975 was supporting approximately forty community- and school-based approaches, including peer counseling, interpersonal communication skill development, drug information, and problem-solving and decision-making skill development.[20]

Of importance to drug education programs, the report, unlike that of the earlier

Marijuana Commission, acknowledged the importance of providing youth with objective basic information on drug effects.

Future Federal media efforts aimed at this audience should: provide basic information about drugs and their effects, not in a "scare" sense, but with an objective presentation of "best information"; and emphasize successful and productive lifestyles of non-drug users.

  Additional media efforts should be directed at parents, teachers, police, clergy, and others whose relations with drug-prone youths have a major influence on whether or not they decide to use drugs.[21]

The *White Paper* made one other important and perhaps novel recommendation that helped shape the role of the federal government in primary drug abuse prevention. In addition to providing technical assistance, training materials and guidebooks, and seed money for creative new prevention programs, the federal government should "rigorously evaluate existing programs; and, make the results of these evaluations widely available for use by States and local communities in designing or improving their own programs."[22]

As indicated above, the NIDA Prevention Branch had taken these recommendations seriously and had launched a technical assistance, public information, capacity building, and evaluation research program through its EO7 drug education grants and later through the initiation of the National Prevention Evaluation Resource Network.

According to Public Law 92–255, the SAODAP was due to terminate in 1975. However, since the drug crisis had not relented, Congress in 1976 re-established the function under the name of the Office of Drug Abuse Policy. With a change in administrations, the office was later terminated, but at the insistence of Congress, the drug coordination council activities were taken over by the president's domestic policy staff. Given that over twenty federal agencies were participating in the federal drug abuse effort, either by attempting to stop the supply of drugs from entering the country through law enforcement and interdiction or by reducing the demand for drugs through treatment of heroin addiction and prevention education, this coordination and policy-making function was deemed essential by both the Congress and the executive branch.

White House Cabinet Committee on Drug Abuse Prevention, Treatment, and Rehabilitation: Report of the Subcommittee on Prevention

The White House subcommittee report on primary prevention[23] was prompted by recommendations provided by the *White Paper* in 1975 and mandated by the Cabinet Committee on Drug Abuse Prevention, Treatment, and Rehabilitation. The report assessed federal efforts in drug prevention and articulated a blueprint for further federal prevention policy and action. Program staff from a number of federal agencies with ongoing drug prevention activities participated in the review process. The objective of the review was to build on prior federal drug abuse and drug prevention planning activities as reflected in a series of annual reports to Congress entitled *The Federal Strategy for Drug Abuse and Drug Traffic Prevention*, which had been published in March 1973, June 1974, June 1975, November 1976, and June 1977.

The Subcommittee on Prevention report indicated that the time was right for further federal planning and action in primary prevention because the crisis that demanded treatment services for addicts was being addressed and because local communities were looking for federal leadership in primary drug abuse prevention. In addition, Congress in passing Public Law 94–237 had placed priority on funding primary prevention programs in both the Department of Health, Education, and Welfare and the Law Enforcement Assistance Administration, Department of Justice. The report presented a number of key themes for drug abuse prevention that helped establish a conceptual framework for subsequent policy and program recommendations. These themes reflected the current thinking of the day and served as a consensus statement for those working in primary prevention at the federal, state, or local level. Highlights of the themes presented in the report follow:

- Prevention activities should be targeted on that drug use which is believed to have the highest social cost as well as on the general drug-taking experience;
- While we are concerned about the causes of drug abuse, our efforts must be primarily focused on moderating the effects of drug taking;
- The population at risk is essentially that group of individuals not yet using drugs or those who are experimenting or just beginning sustained drug use;
- We believe this target population consists essentially of young people between the ages of 8 and 20;
- The Subcommittee supports the promotion of early health education efforts in the home and school . . . ;
- There are a variety of opportunity settings through which prevention programs can be channeled. These include family, peer group, and the school as primary units, and the church, media, and other community institutions such as public service organizations . . . as secondary units;
- Knowledge development must receive high priority so that we can better target populations at risk . . . through careful evaluation of new applied research efforts. . . . outcomes must be better linked to actual program events;
- There should be clearly defined and differentiated roles among the various levels of government . . . the Federal role should be one of leadership and national catalyst. . . . Further, the Federal Government is the only entity which can marshal adequate resources to assure that an adequate knowledge development strategy is promoted. . . . The States should collaborate in the leadership role and be the primary resource targeting and program coordination mechanism . . . local communities should be the primary deliverers of services; and,

• It is important that alcohol and tobacco be included in these prevention activities. These are the first two psychoactive substances used by most people.[24]

Probably, the most significant effect of the report was its emphasis on knowledge development through prevention research. The report stressed the importance of research to guide both program planning and implementation, as well as to expand our scientific knowledge of the causes and consequences of drug abuse and to assess the efficacy under controlled conditions of specific preventive interventions. To further this recommendation, the report included a model prevention research program. For example, the report recommended formative research of drug-using behavior, communications research, the study of invulnerables, and the assessment of program goal setting. The report suggested a variety of impact research studies that would focus on the short- and long-range effects of media, the longitudinal study of attitude change on drug-taking behavior, and the short- and long-range impacts of a variety of prevention strategies to include drug education, and intervention programs for high-risk youth. Also, the report called for systematic and controlled research of community-based prevention programming where the unit of research assignment and analysis would be the community, rather than the individual or school.

Congressionally Mandated Set-Asides for Prevention

In an effort to accentuate and enhance the development of the federal primary prevention effort, Congress mandated in the NIDA's reauthorization legislation (the Drug Abuse, Prevention, Treatment, and Rehabilitation Amendments of 1979—Public Law 96–181) for fiscal years 1980 and 1981 that the NIDA provide set-aside funding for prevention activities from the budget of its Division of Community Assistance (DCA).[25] In fiscal year 1980 this set-aside was 7 percent of the total DCA budget, and in fiscal year 1981 it was 10 percent. Though these funds were not extraordinarily large, they did represent a substantial increase in funding for targeted prevention services from preceding budget periods. In fiscal year 1979 the NIDA's funding for prevention-oriented service grants and contracts was $6.226 million. With the 7 percent set-aside of community assistance funding, expeditures for primary prevention program services doubled to $12.844 million, and in fiscal year 1981 the NIDA's funding for primary prevention service grants and contracts increased to $16.131 million.[26] Thus, over a three-year period, prevention-services funding at the NIDA increased nearly threefold.

As its primary prevention budget increased, the NIDA expanded its efforts to fund the position of state prevention coordinator (SPC) in every single state agency through the development and administration of the State Prevention Coordinator Program (SPCP).[27] Under this program, single state agencies applied to the NIDA for federal grant funds to support the state's SPC position and to compete for funds to implement specific prevention approaches, such as the Channel 1 alternatives project and other educational programs designed to assist parents and families in preventing drug use and abuse. The SPCP incorporated both a competitive review approach and a formula allocation model to guide the award of these innovative federal prevention grants. In many ways this grant program was the first substantial building block in the institutionalization of a viable primary prevention capacity within the single state agency drug abuse system.

The Omnibus Budget Reconciliation Act of 1981

In 1981 the funding of drug abuse treatment and primary prevention was radically altered by congressional enactment of the Omnibus Budget Reconciliation Act of 1981 (Public Law 97–35, enacted 13 August 1981). This legislation provided states and local authorities with the opportunity to better provide health services and social services by shifting federal support from categorical funding provided by specific federal agencies to a series of block grants.

Under the legislation ten categorical programs were folded into the Alcohol, Drug Abuse, and Mental Health Services Block Grant.[28] The legislation shifted the responsibility for planning and administration of treatment and primary prevention services to state governments. Federal funding was provided directly to the states based on a funding formula and could be obtained in a straightforward fashion by a written request from state authorities to the Department of Health and Human Services. Direct federal oversight and policy guidance that influenced the nature of treatment and prevention expenditures were replaced by the state planning and decision-making process. However, the legislation did mandate that states spend at least 35 percent of their ADMS funds on alcohol programs, 35 percent on drug programs, and 20 percent on drug and alcohol prevention services.[29]

As a result of the block grant, the NIDA's budget decreased from $243.893 million in fiscal year 1981 to $56.414 in fiscal year 1982,[30] and the NIDA's program mission shifted accordingly to focus primarily on basic and applied research, to include basic biomedical, treatment, prevention, and drug abuse liability studies. Although drug research had become its primary mission, the NIDA still retained its responsibility for monitoring national drug use trends, providing limited technical assistance in prevention through the Prevention Branch, and supporting and directing drug media campaigns and the drug abuse clearinghouse function.[31]

The legislation also affected the organizational structure of the NIDA and its role in prevention in that the reorganization of the NIDA that followed included the development of the Division of Clinical Research with a Prevention Research Branch responsible for prevention-related etiologic studies and controlled research to test the efficacy of specific preventive interventions. In addition, prevention technical assistance was provided to the field from the Division of Prevention and Communications, specifically from the Prevention Branch. Thus, the NIDA had established both a Prevention Research Branch to meet the research needs of primary prevention and a Prevention Branch to meet the program needs of the field.

As a result, the NIDA increased the visibility and viability of primary prevention research. The NIDA had for the first time a Prevention Research Branch with program staff and budget targeted to the development of scientific knowledge directly relevant to primary prevention. Toward this end, several prevention research grant announcements were developed to support prevention research in selected areas of investigation. In April 1983 the NIDA released the *Drug Abuse Prevention Research Announcement*[32] which invited well-designed and -controlled studies in a number of prevention-related areas, to include

1. primary disease prevention and health promotion interventions aimed at reducing the incidence of drug abuse;
2. outreach and early intervention programs for novice drug users and abusers who have not been clinically identified;
3. methods for early identification and screening of persons at risk of drug abuse; and
4. risk factors as a basis for the design of preventive interventions.

The announcement prompted a number of prevention research studies that were funded by the NIDA in the area of school-based interventions, parent/family skills training, risk factor research through cross-sectional and longitudinal research designs, and secondary data analysis.

In August 1984 the NIDA released the *Community Prevention Research in Alcohol and Drug Abuse Announcement.*[33] This grant program of controlled research encouraged rigorous scientific study of multiple component drug and alcohol abuse prevention to be implemented at multiple levels in the community (individual, peer group, family, school, work place, and community). The grant announcement requested that research proposals include study designs that would test the effects of both individual and various combinations of program components as measured at the community level. The unit of sampling and data analysis would be the community. This program of research addressed persistent efforts at the federal level to assess under controlled field conditions community-based prevention programming, a recommendation proposed earlier in 1977 by the Subcommittee on Prevention. As a result of the community research announcement, four research grant awards have been made, and all studies are currently in progress.

Subsequently, the NIDA gradually increased the budget for prevention research. This growth reflects the slow, but positive development of scientific expertise by the community of prevention researchers, the increased research productivity through the publication of prevention-oriented peer-reviewed journal articles that have emanated from these studies, and the growth in credibility and confidence of the emerging science of prevention research within the greater scientific community.

Given the importance of primary prevention, the NIDA allocations to the

Prevention Research Branch have systematically increased since 1982, as shown
by its budgetary history:[34]

FY1982	$ 2,874,000
FY1983	$ 3,944,544
FY1984	$ 4,574,957
FY1985	$ 5,945,979
FY1986	$ 6,191,369
FY1987	$10,125,290

Programmatic accomplishments include the development of several significant
new program areas of research, to include the following grant announcements:

- DA–87–17   Drug and Alcohol Abuse Prevention Research
- DA–84–01   Community Prevention Research in Alcohol and Drug Abuse
- DA–86–05   Research on the Etiology of Drug Abuse Among Ethnic and Minority
             Juvenile Populations
- DA–87–09   Vulnerability to Drug Abuse
- DA–87–21   Research Center on Drug Abuse Vulnerability
- DA–87–10   Acquired Immunodeficiency Syndrome (AIDS) and the Prevention of
             Intravenous Drug Abuse
- DA–87–15   Drug Abuse Prevention Research Centers

As of 1988 the Prevention Research Branch's portfolio included over fifty active
research and research-training grants that reflect the major and emerging research
areas of interest to the NIDA and the prevention field.

The Anti-Drug Abuse Act

During late 1985 and the spring, summer, and fall of 1986 the country was
inundated with media coverage of the crack-cocaine epidemic that was threatening the fabric of American society. The extent, repetitiveness, intensity, and
authenticity of the media coverage alerted the public and public policy makers
to the threat of drug abuse, and particularly cocaine use and abuse. Though the
media were accused by some of overplaying the story, the death of University
of Maryland basketball star and future Boston Celtic Len Bias from cardiac arrest
due to cocaine ingestion in late spring of 1986, followed shortly by the death
of Don Rogers, a promising player from the San Diego Chargers professional
football team, due to cocaine ingestion, helped shake the nation from its possible
skepticism of the crack-cocaine threat.[35]

It was also speculated that prompt federal action would be taken because the
deleterious effects of cocaine use were seen firsthand by some congressional

policy makers, promising politicians, and members of the media. Many had learned that no one was immune from the seductive power of this drug. Political action to combat the crack-cocaine problem was promised by both sides of the aisle in Congress and by the administration. The debate was focused and intense, and action was fast in coming with passage of the Anti-Drug Abuse Act of 1986 (Public Law 99–570) on October 27 of that year.

Of significance for primary prevention, the legislation created the Office of Substance Abuse Prevention (OSAP) within the Alcohol, Drug Abuse, and Mental Health Administration which would have as its mission the prevention of drug use and abuse, particularly by high-risk youth. New and extensive primary drug abuse prevention responsibilities were also given to the Department of Education through the passage of the Drug-Free Schools and Communities Act, Title IV, Subtitle B of the Anti-Drug Abuse Act.[36]

The Anti-Drug Abuse Act of 1986 provided massive increases in drug abuse funding—$1.7 billion at the federal and state levels for law enforcement, drug education, treatment, and rehabilitation programs. The act increased total federal spending for prevention from $24 million in fiscal year 1986 to $249 million in fiscal year 1987. Under the legislation the Department of Education would receive $200 million in fiscal year 1987 for school-based drug education, administered through grants to both states and local school systems. ACTION, the federal program aimed at enhancing voluntarism in America, would receive $3 million in fiscal year 1987 and $3 million in fiscal year 1988 to support, coordinate, and stimulate private-sector drug abuse prevention activities. Finally, $43 million would be provided to the ADAMHA, with the creation of OSAP. OSAP would provide national leadership in the development of model prevention/treatment demonstration programs for high-risk youth, deliver technical assistance in drug abuse programming at the state and local levels, and continue in a consolidated communications program the excellent work of information dissemination provided by the formerly separate clearinghouses for alcohol and for drug information.[37]

LAW ENFORCEMENT, DRUG EDUCATION, TREATMENT, AND REHABILITATION PROGRAMS

Alcohol, Drug Abuse, and Mental Health Administration (ADAMHA)

The Anti-Drug Abuse Act of 1986 provided substantial additional funding ($262 million) for drug abuse research and drug treatment and prevention programming at the ADAMHA. As a result of the legislation, the Alcohol, Drug Abuse, and Mental Health Services Block Grant was enhanced by $13.86 million, increasing the state allocation to $509 million for fiscal year 1987. These funds were to be used by states for drug, alcohol, and mental health service programs, to include treatment and prevention. Of the total, $162.86 million were earmarked for states to enhance their drug treatment services, with 45 percent of these funds allocated on the basis of population and distributed concurrent with their block grant allotment and 55 percent allocated and distributed on the basis of need as determined by the Department of Health and Human Services.

The legislation provided that 1 percent of the funds ($2.3 million) would be used to evaluate alcohol and drug treatment programs. And, as part of the law, $10.4 million was transferred to the Veterans Administration to increase and enhance outpatient treatment and prevention education programs for veterans. Finally, the legislation mandated that the ADAMHA establish a centralized prevention education program to be called the Office of Substance Abuse Prevention. This office would unify prevention activities across the National Institute on Drug Abuse and the National Institute on Alcohol Abuse and Alcoholism and develop a single combined clearinghouse for disseminating drug and alcohol information.[38]

Office of Substance Abuse Prevention (OSAP)

Since its creation in the fall of 1986, OSAP has formalized a vigorous program aimed at facilitating technology transfer, awarding demonstration grants, forming partnerships with parent and community groups, operating the alcohol and drug abuse clearinghouse, and coordinating with the state and local drug abuse service system. The current organization of OSAP includes the office of the director and three divisions: Communication Program, Prevention Implementation, and Demonstrations and Evaluation. The budget for fiscal year 1987 was $41.5 million and $34.2 million for fiscal year 1988.[39]

The first year of operation focused substantial effort on the solicitation of comprehensive and targeted prevention and treatment grant proposals to provide innovative prevention services to high-risk youth.[40] Of the 863 applications, OSAP funded 131 demonstration programs distributed across the country. The awards totaled over $24 million for both one- and two-year projects.

The 1986 legislation also established within OSAP a national alcohol and drug abuse clearinghouse to develop and distribute prevention program and research publications and to offer reference retrieval services to the alcohol and drug field. A number of significant technical assistance efforts are also underway at OSAP, with a special focus on program development and capacity building to involve parents, youth, and communities through regional workshops for information dissemination, prevention training for members and staff of minority organizations, and model community-based prevention contracts. OSAP has initiated several evaluation initiatives to assess its demonstration grants program, including a multiyear process evaluation contract. Also, OSAP is pursuing an assessment of prevention efforts in conjunction with the Department of Education's mandated programs.

National Institute on Drug Abuse (NIDA)

The Anti-Drug Abuse Act of 1986 provided an additional $27 million to the NIDA in fiscal year 1987 to expand its drug research program.[41] These monies permitted the initiation of a number of new primary prevention projects (and treatment and basic research projects) that would not have been otherwise supported. For example, the NIDA released in January 1987 a new prevention research grant announcement[42] and a prevention research centers grant announcement.[43] The centers announcement called for center applications that would

1. improve our understanding of etiologic factors that predispose individuals to initiate drug use;

2. identify factors involved in the progression from initial drug use to drug dependence;

3. develop criteria and early identification methodologies for use with children and adolescents at high risk for drug abuse;

4. design and test preventive interventions at the individual and small group level through controlled randomized studies; and,

5. assess the progression of drug use through prospective longitudinal studies of high-risk populations.

After extensive peer review of a number of center applications submitted in response to the announcement, a prevention center grant award was made to the University of Kentucky at Lexington (Grant No. P50 DA05312–01). The center provides a national focal point for leadership and excellence in drug abuse prevention research approached from a mulitdisciplinary perspective. The center not only will contribute to the scientific knowledge base in primary prevention through the conduct of individual research projects, but also will promote and enhance the capacity of research, clinical, and program professionals in the field of prevention to better integrate new advances, technologies, and theory into drug abuse prevention programming.

The fiscal year 1986 antidrug abuse funds provided to the NIDA supported a number of significant basic, applied, and epidemiologic research studies. Each division within NIDA benefited. The Division of Preclinical Research expended $8.7 million; the Division of Clinical Research, which includes the NIDA's drug treatment and prevention research programs, recieved $9.8 million; the Division of Epidemiology and Statistical Analysis expended $3.2 million; and the Addictions Research Center, the NIDA's intramural research program, received $3.0 million. In total, the NIDA funded or supplemented a total of 114 important research studies as a direct result of the Anti-Drug Abuse Act of 1986.[44]

The Department of Education

Under the Drug-Free Schools and Communities Act of 1986, enacted as Title IV, Subtitle B of the Anti-Drug Abuse Act of 1986, the Department of Education was authorized $200 million for fiscal year 1987 and $250 million each year for fiscal years 1988 and 1989. Of the $200 million, $5.5 million was allocated to the development of audiovisual drug education materials. Of the remainder, approximately $161 million was provided to state and local educational agencies, and $33.4 million was provided to federally directed drug education initiatives, such as the development of programs for higher education, Indian youth, and native Hawaiians and the establishment of regional training centers for school teams ($8.7 million). Of the state and local funds, $1.9 million was allocated to the U.S. territories and $159.1 million to state grants provided to either the offices of the governors ($47.7 million) or the state and local education agencies ($111.3 million).[45]

The Department of Education has initiated a vigorous antidrug campaign which was launched with the publication of *Schools Without Drugs*.[46] In addition, the department publishes a newsletter entitled "The Challenge." Both publications describe successful model drug education programs that are currently in operation in elementary, middle, and secondary schools across the country. With the additional funding, the Department of Education has substantially expanded its efforts directly and in cooperation with state and local education agencies to provide effective drug education to schools throughout the country and to offer effective drug-related family-based education, counseling, referral, training, and public awareness campaigns. The department has also initiated an antidrug education program for schools of higher education with two grant programs designed to fund drug education projects for college students and to provide teacher training, summer institutes, workshops, and the development of model curricula for implementation in colleges and universities.[47]

With funds from the antidrug legislation, the department also continued and enhanced its longstanding and highly effective regional training center program to train school teams to fight drug abuse at the local level. Five grants were awarded in the fall of 1987 to fund training centers to meet the prevention education needs of schools and communities in the northeastern, southeastern, midwestern, southwestern, and western regions.[48] The school-teams approach to drug education has been well received by local school and community drug education specialists as a federal prevention program that meets local needs through the process of training to increase local capacity for self-help and through the delivery of post-training technical assistance to local teams that have completed training at the department's regional centers.

As a result of the antidrug abuse legislation of 1986, federal efforts in demand-side programs (drug abuse treatment, primary prevention, and rehabilitation) were dramatically increased in scope and mission. Research on and programs aimed at primary prevention of drug abuse appeared to make important gains as the result of the legislation. At this point, the actual return on this federal investment has yet to be determined, although the prospects for improving the prevention and treatment service delivery system have substantially increased.

At this point, federal efforts in drug abuse prevention are at a crossroads. The Anti-Drug Abuse Act of 1986 provided time-limited funding through 1988. The future direction of drug abuse prevention activities at the federal level will be dependent in part on the success of current activities, public concern about the drug problem, and the outcomes of the political process. There is no doubt that affirmation of the importance of prevention will continue. Prevention program technical support and prevention research have demonstrated efficacy and effectiveness and have become a permanent element of the federal approach to the drug abuse problem. What is not clear at this time is the future mission and scope of federal prevention activities. Needs assessment of the prevention field clearly delineates specific gaps in our scientific knowledge and deficits in the capacity of the health care delivery system to provide youth, parents, and communities with effective prevention services. A number of prevention strategies offer promise for the future development and diffusion of research-based prevention programs. Federal efforts to enhance and expand the involvement of the voluntary and private sectors in drug abuse prevention have had encouraging results that augur a better future for prevention. Yet serious questions have been raised about the actual efficacy of drug prevention program services and the capacity of the service system to reach high-risk youth, families, and communities. Questions remain concerning the best roles for federal, state, and local governments in their efforts to prevent drug abuse. Effective leadership is needed, yet the commitment to prevention is not clearly established. The momentum from current prevention action may be reaching its ebb, while the plans for the future of prevention may still be on the drawing boards. Prevention is at a crossroads. Federal initiatives will be a part of the future of prevention, but their nature and scope are unclear.

NOTES

This chapter was prepared by a federal government employee as part of official duties; the ideas expressed in it represent the author's interpretation and do not represent the official position of the National Institute on Drug Abuse, its employees, or any other part of the U.S. Department of Health and Human Services.

1. Office of Drug Abuse Policy, *Drug Use Patterns, Consequences, and the Federal Response: A Policy Review* (Washington, D.C.: Executive Office of the President, March 1978).

2. Stanley Einstein, Marvin Lavenhar, Edward Wolfson, Donald Louria, Mark Quinones, and Gerald McAteer, "The Training of Teachers for Drug Abuse Education Programs: Preliminary Considerations," *Journal of Drug Education* 1, no. 4 (December 1971): 323–45.

3. National Commission on Marijuana and Drug Abuse, *Marijuana: A Signal of*

Misunderstanding, vol. II (Washington, D.C.: U.S. Government Printing Office, 1972), 1198–1230.

4. Office of Drug Abuse Policy, *Drug Use Patterns*, 2.

5. National Commission on Marijuana and Drug Abuse, *Marijuana*.

6. National Commission on Marijuana and Drug Abuse, *Drug Use in America: Problem in Perspective* (Washington, D.C.: U.S. Government Printing Office, 1973).

7. Ibid., 205.

8. Ibid., 205–206.

9. Ibid., 270.

10. Office of Drug Use Policy, *Drug Use Patterns*, 458.

11. Ibid., 475.

12. National Institute on Drug Abuse, *Recommendations for Future Federal Activities in Drug Abuse Prevention: Cabinet Committee on Drug Abuse Prevention, Treatment, and Rehabilitation: Report of the Subcommittee on Prevention* (Washington, D.C.: U.S. Government Printing Office, 1977), 4.

13. Special Action Office, *The Media and Drug Abuse Messages* (Washington, D.C.: Executive Office of the President, April 1974).

14. National Institute on Drug Abuse, *Toward a National Strategy for Primary Drug Abuse Prevention: Final Report Delphi II* (Rockville, Md.: NIDA, 1975).

15. Department of Health, Education, and Welfare, *Drug Abuse Prevention, Treatment, and Rehabilitation: Second Annual Report to the President and Congress of the United States, Fiscal Year 1979* (Washington, D.C.: HEW, 1979), 143–58.

16. Domestic Council Drug Abuse Task Force, *White Paper on Drug Abuse* (Washington, D.C.: U.S. Government Printing Office, 1975).

17. Ibid., 1.

18. Ibid., 7.

19. Ibid.

20. Ibid., 66.

21. Ibid.

22. Ibid., 67.

23. National Institute on Drug Abuse, *Recommendations for Future Federal Activities—Report of the Subcommittee on Prevention* (Washington, D.C.: U.S. Government Printing Office, 1977).

24. Ibid., 9–11.

25. Alcohol, Drug Abuse, and Mental Health Administration, *ADAMHA Prevention Policy and Programs—1979–1982*, DHHS Pub. no. (ADM) 81-1038 (Washington, D.C.: U.S. Government Printing Office, 1981), 52.

26. National Institute on Drug Abuse, *NIDA Prevention Funding by Budget Activity* (Rockville, Md.: Financial Management Branch, NIDA, 1988).

27. Alcohol, Drug Abuse, and Mental Health Administration, *ADAMHA Prevention Policy and Programs*, 57.

28. William J. Bukoski, "Drug Abuse Prevention Funding Resulting from the Omnibus Budget Reconciliation Act of 1981," *Journal of Drug Education* 16, no. 1 (1986): 51–55.

29. Alcohol, Drug Abuse, and Mental Health Administration, *Alcohol and Drug Abuse and Mental Health Services Block Grant Report to Congress* (Washington, D.C.: Department of Health and Human Services, October 1983), Appendix B, 33.

30. Alcohol, Drug Abuse, and Mental Health Administration, National Institute on

Drug Abuse, *Fiscal Year 1984 Budget Request* (Rockville, Md.: National Institute on Drug Abuse, 1983).

31. National Institute on Drug Abuse, *Fifth Annual Report, Drug Abuse Prevention, Treatment, and Rehabilitation in Fiscal Year 1982* (Rockville, Md.: National Institute on Drug Abuse, 1983), 10.

32. National Institute on Drug Abuse, *Drug Abuse Prevention Research Announcement* (Rockville, Md.: National Institute on Drug Abuse, April 1983), 1.

33. National Institute on Drug Abuse, *Community Prevention Research in Alcohol and Drug Abuse Announcement* August (Rockville, Md.: National Institute on Drug Abuse, 1984).

34. National Institute on Drug Abuse, *Prevention Funding by Budget Activity* (Rockville, Md.: National Institute on Drug Abuse, 1988).

35. "The Enemy Within," *Time*, 15 September 1986, 59–68.

36. National Association of State Alcohol and Drug Abuse Directors, *Alcohol and Drug Abuse Report* (Washington, D.C.: NASADAD, December 1986).

37. U.S. General Accounting Office, *Drug Abuse Prevention: Further Efforts Needed to Identify Programs That Work*, GAO/HRD–88–26 (Washington, D.C.: GAO, 1988), 21–22.

38. National Institute on Drug Abuse, *NIDA Notes*, DHHS Pub. no. (ADM) 86-1488 (Rockville, Md.: NIDA, December 1986), 1–3.

39. National Drug Information Center of Families in Action, *Drug Abuse Update* 24 (March 1988): 6–7.

40. Office of Substance Abuse Prevention, ADAMHA, *Alcohol and Drug Abuse Demonstration Grants Announcement No. AD-87-01*, (Rockville, Md.: National Institute on Drug Abuse, February 1987).

41. National Institute on Drug Abuse, Financial Management Branch, *Summary of the Fiscal Year 1987 Drug Initiative* (Rockville, Md.: National Institute on Drug Abuse, 1987).

42. National Institute on Drug Abuse, *Drug and Alcohol Abuse Prevention Research Grant Announcement—DA-87-17* (Rockville, Md.: National Institute on Drug Abuse, January 1987).

43. National Institute on Drug Abuse, *Drug Abuse Prevention Research Centers— DA-87-15* (Rockville, Md.: National Institute on Drug Abuse, January 1987).

44. National Institute on Drug Abuse, *Summary of Fiscal Year 1987 Drug Initiative* (Rockville, Md.: National Institute on Drug Abuse, 1987).

45. Department of Education, *Drug Free Schools and Communities Act of 1986–1987 Appropriations* (chart) October 1986; National Institute on Drug Abuse, *NIDA Notes* (Washington, D.C.: U.S. Government Printing Office, 1986), 1; Program Information Associates, *Federal Alcohol and Drug Abuse Initiatives: A Special Report* (Honolulu: Program Information Associates, 1987), 30–37.

46. Department of Education, *Schools Without Drugs* (Washington, D.C.: Department of Education, 1986).

47. National Institute on Drug Abuse, *NIDA Notes* 2, no. 3 (Fall 1987): 4.

48. National Association of State Alcohol and Drug Abuse Directors, *National Prevention Network News* 2, no.9 (February 1988), 5.

Chapter 5

Treatment Strategies

George De Leon

Two major epidemics of drug abuse actually occurred during the decades from 1965 to 1985. The first, commonly defined as the heroin epidemic in terms of rates of new addicts, reached its peak in the early 1970s. This epidemic galvanized a major federal response, leading to the development of four major treatment modalities: detoxification, methadone maintenance, drug-free outpatient centers, and drug-free residential therapeutic communities.

The second epidemic of drug abuse reflects a complex social-psychological phenomenon that may be termed the *enculturation* of drug use, evident in the wider spectrum of drug abusers, the increased variety of substances used, and the decreased age of onset of drug use. Thus, more people are involved with more drugs at an early age and for a longer time than were previous (pre-1975) generations. Currently at its high point, this epidemic involves polydrug, alcohol, and cocaine/crack-cocaine abuse which has fostered the development of a variety of treatment strategies in addition to the four major modalities.

The major objective of this chapter is to depict the current status of drug abuse treatment in the United States with a focus on the four major treatment modalities. Although material is presented on the newer treatment strategies, particularly for cocaine abuse, the latter have not been sufficiently evaluated to provide firm conclusions concerning their effectiveness. (Fuller discussion of the growth of treatment systems in the United States is provided elsewhere in this volume.)

The literature surveyed was not exhaustive, but rather was limited by several considerations. First, the main findings and conclusions are presented from published research. Clinical reports and research in progress are not included, although some exceptions are noted. Several existing reviews served as primary sources from which a consensus could be drawn concerning the effectiveness of treatment.[1] Evaluation research included studies of individual programs and national multimodality, multiprogram surveys.

Second, evaluation has focused on treatment of opiate addicts since this group constituted the vast majority of drug abusers who presented a significant social problem in terms of crime and health care (now currently evident in the AIDS crisis). Thus, most of what is known about the effectiveness of drug treatment is derived from research on opiate addicts in the four major treatment modalities.

Third, alcohol abuse has been documented to be the number one substance abuse health problem (with the possible exception of cigarette addiction). However, review of the considerable literature on the treatment of alcohol abuse is beyond the purview of this effort, requiring a chapter in its own right. Nevertheless, some conclusions are offered from the research that has assessed treatment effects on substance abuse patterns, including alcohol use.

The initial section of the chapter provides an overview of the approach and effectiveness of the four major modalities. Success rates are presented in terms of the principal aims of the different modalities, with a focus on opiate abusers. Included are subsections on new treatment strategies for both opiate and cocaine abusers. There follows a review of several key issues that remain to be resolved concerning treatment issues and policy concerns.

THE MAJOR MODALITIES

A considerable literature documents the effectiveness of the four major modalities of substance abuse treatment: detoxification, methadone maintenance, drug-free outpatient settings, and residential therapeutic communities (TCs).[2] Each modality has its view of drug abuse, each impacts the drug abuser in different ways, and the effectiveness of each must be evaluated in terms of its principal aims.

Detoxification

These programs are usually conducted in inpatient hospital settings and are of short-term duration—seven to twenty-one days. While not grounded in any theoretical view of drug abuse, an essential rationale underlying this approach is that sudden withdrawal from narcotics results in characteristic physical and psychological states of extreme discomfort. This negative abstinence syndrome discourages many addicts from attempting withdrawal. Indeed, avoidance of the abstinence syndrome may reinforce continued use of illicit narcotics. Thus, the principal aim of detoxification is the elimination of physiological dependence through a medically safe and inexpensive procedure.[3]

Methadone has been the medication of choice for detoxification from opiates. Generally, a starting dose (e.g., 30 milligrams) of methadone is gradually reduced in small increments until the body adjusts to a drug-free state.

Practically all opiate abusers have undergone at least one hospital detoxification, making this modality the most active. With virtually no mortality or morbidity reported, detoxification is an effective temporary treatment for safe withdrawal from opiate dependency. However, relapse to opiate use occurs in over 95% of detoxified clients. Occasionally, long-term cessation of use follows, but rehabilitative effects are rare.

A secondary objective of detoxification programs is to provide a temporary legal alternative to illicit drug use and referral to more extensive treatment modalities. Studies indicate, however, that less than 15% of detoxification admissions are successfully referred to other treatments.[4]

Given its high relapse rates, the rationale for detoxification programs requires re-examination. For many opiate abusers this option lessens the motivation to abstain or seek entry into a more demanding treatment regime. However, detoxification is justified as a means to recruit addicts into temporary treatment. This is of particular relevance to the current AIDS crisis since detoxification programs can interrupt needle use and provide counseling to reduce AIDS-related risk behaviors.

Methadone Maintenance

These programs have been guided by the general view that opiate addiction is a recurring disease which may relate to physiological or metabolic anomalies, and that addiction to illicit opiates assures involvement in a criminal life style. The principal aim of this treatment is to foster a prosocial life style undistracted by the illegal pursuit of narcotics. Abstinence from chemical dependency is not a primary goal, although it eventually occurs for some clients.

Methadone maintenance clinics have generally operated on an outpatient basis, although some hospitals and community-based residential centers have incorporated methadone as part of a multimodality approach. Many clinics recognize that methadone itself is not sufficient to facilitate rehabilitation. Therefore, counseling services are offered for educational, vocational, family, and legal assistance.

The initial phase of methadone treatment, detoxification, is designed to withdraw the client from heroin on dosages of methadone sufficient to block a negative abstinence syndrome without euphoria or sedation. In maintenance, the next phase, an optimal dose of methadone is stabilized which prevents the syndrome and eliminates subjective craving for heroin. During this phase the intention is to help the patient establish a good relationship with the clinic in order to utilize other available services.[5]

When effectiveness is defined in terms of heroin and methadone abstinence, less than 10 percent are judged successful ten years after treatment.[6] Most clients followed show histories of recurrent relapse to use of heroin or illicit methadone and to alcohol abuse, and/or they have required retreatment. When success includes those remaining on legal methadone, however, results are brighter. One-year retention rates are highest among all the modalities. About 27 to 41 percent in the national samples reveal favorable to highly favorable outcomes (employment, no arrests plus abstinence or continued use of licit methadone).[7]

Figure 5.1
First-Year Outcome of DARP Patients

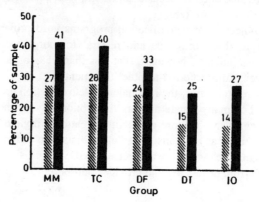

Source: D. D. Simpson, "National Treatment System Evaluation Based on the DARP Follow-Up Research," in *Drug Abuse Treatment Evaluation: Strategies, Progress, and Prospects*, ed. F. Tims and J. Ludford, NIDA Research Analysis and Utilization System (RAUS) Monograph Series (Washington, D.C.: U.S. Government Printing Office, 1984), 444.

(See Figure 5.1.) Thus, methadone maintenance offers an effective treatment for blocking illicit opiate dependency. Moreover, its ancillary services can facilitate rehabilitation effects for a number of others if abstinence is excluded as a criterion of success.

Drug-Free Outpatient Treatment

This umbrella term describes a diversity of ambulatory (and day care) programs with little in common except that they are not residential and do not regularly employ methadone or other pharmacotherapeutic agents. However, drugs may be used for medical problems or psychopharmacological adjuncts.

Originally offered for relatively well socialized opiate abusers, outpatient settings evolved into a modality attracting nonopiate, alcohol, and/or polydrug abusers, most recently centering on cocaine use. The target clients include those undergoing a first treatment experience, completees from other treatment modalities who need aftercare, relapsed clients from other treatments, and those requiring intervention and/or transitional services after prison or a hospital stay. These groups vary widely in demography and economic status, as well as in terms of the length and severity of their drug problem.

Usually based on a mental health perspective, counseling (individual and group) is the fundamental service in most outpatient programs, although many include other services (e.g., family therapy, contingency contracting as treatment for substance abuse).

Evaluating the effectiveness of the outpatient modality is particularly difficult because of the variety of programs and clients served. The national survey studies indicate that favorable to highly favorable outcomes occur in 24 to 33 percent of the sample.[8] (See Figure 5.1.) Ambulatory settings are generally successful in reducing opiate drug use; however, the research indicates that there is little effect on alcohol or marijuana use. Nor is the modality seen as particularly appropriate for the more antisocial drug abuser.[9]

Therapeutic Communities

The term *therapeutic communities* (TCs) for substance abuse is generic, describing a spectrum of over five hundred residential programs. Though diverse in size and clientele served, about a third of these programs incorporate the regime of traditional therapeutic communities (e.g., Amity, Inc., Daytop Village, Gateway House, Phoenix House, etc.).

The traditional TC provides a residential setting for drug abusers, criminal offenders, and the socially dislocated in order to acquire a complete change in life style. While the optimal residential stay varies somewhat across programs, most clients require fifteen to twenty-four months for completion or graduation. However, some TCs have incorporated shorter periods of stay based on client needs and progress.

Traditional TCs have accommodated a broad spectrum of drug abusers— mainly male, white, and in their midtwenties. Originally they attracted a majority of opiate addicts. Currently, however, most TC clients are nonopiate, multiple drug abusers.[10] Thus, this modality has responded to clients with drug problems of varying severity, and with different life styles, and from different economic and ethnic backgrounds.

Fuller accounts of the perspective and approach of the TC are contained in other writings.[11] Briefly, the TC views drug abuse as deviant behavior, reflecting impeded personality development and deficits in social, educational, and economic skills. Its antecedents may lie in socioeconomic disadvantage, poor family effectiveness, and psychological factors. In this perspective, substance abuse is a disorder of the whole person. Addiction is a symptom, not the essence of a disorder. The problem is not the drug, but the person. The goal of treatment is a global change in the individual through an integration of conduct, feelings, values, and attitudes associated with a socially productive, drug-free life style.

Although drug abuse arises from personal and social conditions, recovery is always the responsibility of the individual. The structure and practices of the TC facilitate self-help change through sequenced stages of learning, characterized as growing up or maturation. Its social organization is a family surrogate system, vertically stratified. Primary staff, clinical and custodial, are paraprofessionals, consisting of ex-offenders or ex-drug addicts successfully rehabilitated in therapeutic community programs. Ancillary staff include educational, mental health, and vocational service professionals, as well as fiscal administrators and medical and legal personnel.

The daily regime is full and varied, including encounter group therapy, staff and peer counseling, tutorial learning sessions, remedial and formal educational classes, special projects, residential job functions, and, in the later stages, conventional occupations for clients in a living-out situation. Completion of all phases of the regime marks the end of treatment, but signifies a continued involvement in a self-help process of change.

The principle aim of the TC is to effect social and psychological change consistent with a drug-free life style. This includes abstinence from illicit substance use, elimination of antisocial behavior, employability, and development of prosocial attitudes and values that reflect honesty, responsibility, nonviolence, and self-reliance. In terms of this aim, national surveys indicate that 28 to 40 percent of the clients achieve favorable to highly favorable outcomes (no crime, no illicit drug use, and prosocial behavior).[12] (See Figure 5.1.)

Results from studies of specific TC programs reveal that success rates among graduates (completees) followed seven years after treatment exceed 75 percent.[13] Among dropouts, success rates average 33 percent, but percentages relate directly to time spent in treatment. (See Figure 5.2.) Approximately 50 percent of those who remain a year or longer in residence are successful across all years of follow-up, compared to about 25 percent who stayed less than a year.[14] Additionally, psychological improvements post-treatment are highly correlated with prosocial behavior changes.[15]

Factors Associated with Successful Outcomes

Does success or improvement relate to certain client factors? Despite considerable research, this question remains unanswered. There has been relatively little investigation of the nontreatment factors that contribute to sustained recovery. Studies have focused on predicting outcome status from client characteristics. Some statistical correlations have been obtained involving demography and pretreatment behavior (drug use, criminality, psychological disorder). Generally, favorable outcomes are similar across age, sex, race, and primary drug, although studies report somewhat better results for females and opiate addicts.[16] Though significant, these correlations remain small predictors of outcome, compared with length of time in drug treatment. Based on the variables studied thus far, there is no typical client profile which predicts success in treatment.[17]

Summary

Research provides convincing evidence for the effectiveness of treatment for drug abuse. Significant improvements occur during and following treatment on separate outcome measures of social adjustment (drug use, criminal activity, and employment) and on composite indices measuring individual change. With few exceptions, follow-up studies report a positive relationship between length of stay in treatment and post-treatment outcome status. In addition, therapeutic

Figure 5.2
Outcome of Therapeutic Community Clients

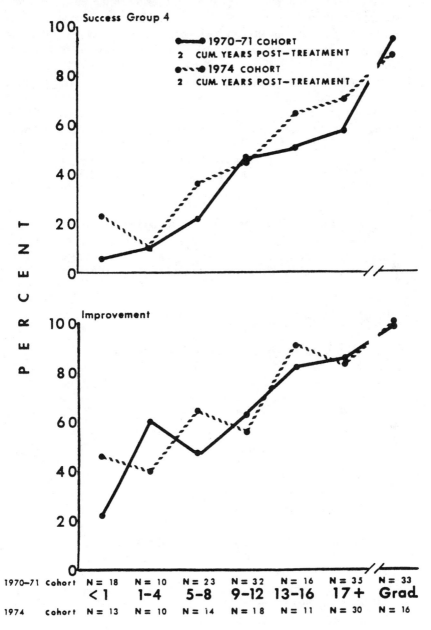

Source: G. De Leon, *The Therapeutic Community: Study of Effectiveness*. Treatment Research Monograph Series DHHS Pub. no. (ADM) 84–1286 (Rockville, Md.: National Institute on Drug Abuse, 1984).

community studies show psychological improvements during treatment and at follow-up; and, there appears to be a direct correlation with behavioral success in terms of drug use, criminality, and psychological improvement at follow-up. Finally, studies in all modalities reveal few consistent predictors of successful outcome other than length of stay in treatment.

Thus, the four major modalities appear reasonably effective, depending on their principal aims. Detoxification provides a temporary safe treatment for withdrawal, while services in outpatient settings yield positive socialization. Methadone maintenance is an effective substitute for illicit opiate addiction, but rarely leads to total abstinence. When global rehabilitation is the aim for the seriously dependent abuser, the drug-free therapeutic community is particularly effective.

OTHER TREATMENTS FOR OPIATE ABUSE

Several strategies other than the four major modalities have been the focus of clinical research for use with opiate abusers. In general, the effectiveness of these has yet to be firmly documented, although work thus far suggests they are promising. These include short-term psychotherapy, family approaches, and relapse prevention. Each of these is briefly reviewed.

Psychotherapies for Addictions

Historically, traditional psychotherapies were not successfully applied to opiate addicts. Some reasons for this are elaborated in other writings.[18] Mainly these relate to characteristics of addicts and the addictive disorder. For example, clinical research and experience have shown that addiction must be viewed as a disorder of the "whole person," and treatment must emphasize goals of personality change, maturation, and socialization. These may be contrasted with goals of traditional psychotherapy which focus on symptom relief, general adjustment, and personal growth.

Moreover, addict populations have been overrepresented among the socially disadvantaged, particularly those from the black and Hispanic minorities. These groups have been unreceptive to, unresponsive to, or unreached by psychotherapy. Indeed, it was the relative ineffectiveness of conventional treatments including psychotherapy for the rapidly rising substance abuse problem in the epidemic of the mid-1960s that spawned the four major modalities.

Recently, psychotherapy has been re-evaluated in clinical trials with opiate addicts in methadone maintenance settings. The results appear favorable, but somewhat tentative. For example, limited outcome (six-month) studies compare the effectiveness of two forms of short-term psychotherapy (supportive expressive therapy, and cognitive therapy) and drug counseling, implemented with Veterans Administration patients enrolled in an outpatient methadone maintenance clinic. Results indicated that the clients who received either form of therapy in addition to counseling and methadone showed better improvements than did clients who received counseling and methadone alone. However, these findings were not replicated in similar studies at a New Haven substance abuse clinic.[19]

Family Approaches

There are varieties of family approaches used in the treatment of addicts of which three distinct forms may be noted: family systems therapy, family support groups, and family education groups. Family therapy refers to treatment activities in which the client (addict) and the family are viewed as the targets of the treatment: interventions are directed at modifying pathological or dysfunctional interpersonal patterns among the family members that relate to the chemically dependent client. Usually conducted by mental health professionals, the number of sessions and the specific intervention strategies and assumptions differ somewhat, although most are based on a family system perspective.[20]

Family support groups are mutual self-help aggregates, typified by Al-Anon for the families of alcoholics who usually are participating in Alcoholics Anonymous. These groups utilize shared experience to facilitate the family members' adjustment to the addict's treatment and recovery. They assist in developing positive coping behaviors and in modifying behaviors and attitudes that may inadvertently enable the addict to continue his or her chemical dependency. There is little emphasis on identifying family dysfunction or psychopathology or on modifying complex interpersonal patterns or personality. Traditional professionals play no significant roles in these groups; the number and schedule of meetings vary, often in conjunction with the addict's separate treatment.

Family education groups provide orientation to family members concerning the treatment of the addict (e.g., course of treatment, typical problems with the clients, requirements and expectations of the family members, etc.). The major aim of these groups is to forge an alliance between the treatment agency and the significant others in the addict's life in order to strengthen family support for the primary treatment. Orientation is usually conducted in groups by a special staff member during a fixed number of sessions. Although family problems are not the focus of these groups, some self-help activity occurs, and referral for assistance is provided by the treatment program. A recent example of the use of these orientation groups is described in other writings.[21] Preliminary findings suggest that these could lessen early dropout from treatment.

Overall, research has still not fully clarified the effectiveness of any of these family approaches to the treatment of opiate addicts in particular or of substance abusers in general. Studies of the short-term version of family systems therapy do indicate improvements for those addicts in regular treatment;[22] family support and education groups are essentially unevaluated. Despite the status of research, however, family involvement is viewed as essential in the treatment of abusers, particularly adolescents.

Relapse Prevention

Relapse prevention (RP) is a generic term, describing a variety of perspectives and methodologies utilized to minimize the return to drug use by those who have achieved abstinence or significant reductions as a result of treatment. Such clients require a special program or intervention, instructions, fellowship, support, and guidance to maintain their sobriety or improved status. Thus, RP provides services that complement those used routinely during primary treatment.

Relapse prevention thinking and methods emerged primarily from treatment designed to maintain treatment-produced change among alcoholics. A fundamental assumption about RP is that relapse problems are somewhat different from those encountered in primary treatment.

A review of the extensive research in relapse prevention for alcoholism is contained in the literature.[23] Generally studies document that clients undergoing systematic RP training show significantly better maintenance of sobriety or reduction in alcohol use than do those who do not receive such training.

The development of RP methods for other substance abusers, particularly opiate addicts, is relatively recent. Two prominent approaches focus on skills training[24] and recovery training.[25] Briefly, recovery training employs four basic types of elements: fellowship meetings, recovery training group sessions, drug-free recreational activities, and a network of senior ex-addicts. The program is planned for at least a six-month period.

The skills training approach is based on a theory of rehabilitation that makes social control the central issue in successful client re-entry. A ten-month, three-phase program strengthens the addicts' rebonding to the mainstream society through attachment to conventional others, commitment to conventional lines of activities, behavior skills training, social activities, and social network development.

Both of these strategies have been evaluated. Results show that clients undergoing these procedures have lower relapse rates than do comparison groups.

Summary

Studies indicate that family approaches, relapse prevention, and certain forms of psychotherapy are promising. Although their effectiveness remains to be further researched, they do not appear to be substitutes for primary treatment strategies, nor are they readily applicable to all opiate abusers. Their value, however, is to enhance the effectiveness of primary treatment approaches.

TREATMENT STRATEGIES FOR COCAINE AND OTHER SUBSTANCE ABUSE

The recent decade is marked by pervasive polydrug abuse, centering around cocaine/crack-cocaine, alcohol, and marijuana abuse. A number of polydrug clients appear in the major drug-free modalities. For example, cocaine/crack-cocaine was the primary drug of abuse in over 60 percent of the admissions to therapeutic communities in 1987–1988, compared to less than 15 percent in 1979.[26] Illicit use of cocaine and excessive use of alcohol have been documented in a considerable proportion of methadone-maintained clients.

However, increasing numbers of polydrug/cocaine abusers enter short-term residential treatment. These settings, while standard for the treatment of alcohol problems, have recently proliferated in response to the growing numbers of cocaine abusers. They are separately described here since they are frequently offered as a primary modality or in conjunction with outpatient treatment.

Short-Term Residential Treatments

These consist of a variety of programs, hospital or community based, many of which are operated as private psychiatric or drug abuse treatment centers. Primarily they serve the more socially advantaged substance abusers, with their fees for services generally covered by insurance, in contrast to the major modalities, the costs of which are mainly tax subsidized. The treatment orientation of these programs is also varied, but mainly reflects a mix of traditional mental health and twelve-step perspectives. They offer a broad menu of services (e.g., education, nutrition, relaxation training, recreation, counseling/psychotherapy, psychopharmacologic adjuncts, and self-help groups).

There is no clear research evidence concerning the efficacy of short-term residential treatment for cocaine abuse or, for that matter, for short-term treatment in general, regardless of the modality (inpatient or outpatient) for any drug of abuse. Given what is known about the importance of length of stay in treatment and the complexity of the recovery process in addiction, there is little likelihood that twenty-eight-day clinics or short-term modalities (one to six months) will yield stable positive outcomes. As centers for assessment, diagnosis, crisis intervention, and referral, however, these programs appear to be useful.

In addition to those discussed, several other strategies and methods have been employed with opiate addicts or adapted for abuses of cocaine and other drugs. They may be utilized in conjunction with methadone (e.g., contingency management),[27] and during detoxification (e.g., acupuncture). Some are in a developmental stage (e.g., neurobehavioral programming) or of limited clinical utility in addiction treatment (e.g., narcotic antagonists for opiate abuse). Two prominent treatment strategies are pharmacotherapy and self-help groups.

Pharmacotherapy

Although not requiring detoxification procedures such as those for opiate abuse, medical and psychological methods have evolved for management of cocaine withdrawal. These focus on reducing the discomforts of cocaine "craving" and moderating the depression often associated with withdrawal. Procedures

are conducted in both inpatient and outpatient settings and often use pharmacologic adjuncts such as tranquilizers and antidepressants. Although not rigorously evaluated, studies thus far indicate their clinical utility in conjunction with
other forms of therapy.[28]

Self-Help Groups

These groups have emerged as part of a general movement emphasizing self-
help in health care. The prototypical self-help group is Alcoholics Anonymous
(AA), based on a well-described twelve-step approach to the recovery process,
from which most other self-help groups have derived. The more familiar of these
for substance abuse are Cocaine Anonymous (CA), Narcotics Anonymous (NA),
and Drugs Anonymous (DA).

The effectiveness of twelve-step-oriented self-help groups has not been sufficiently documented to meet the conventional scientific standards, largely because of client self-selection factors and the philosophical disinclination of these
groups to undergo rigorous evaluation. Nevertheless, the weight of clinical and
observational evidence along with some research data support the conclusion
that self-help groups appear to be essential in facilitating recoveries in a number
of substance abusers.

Some self-help groups (not necessarily twelve-step oriented) have been implemented and studied as adjuncts to or following primary treatment for opiate
abuse. Findings indicate that such groups do lessen relapse in the aftercare phase
of post-treatment.[29] The application of these groups for cocaine abuse is currently
being evaluated.

Summary

Recent years have witnessed an increase in the number and variety of therapeutic approaches for opiate and polydrug/cocaine abusers. Most of these have
been implemented in combinations, as a main treatment strategy, or in conjunction with the major modalities. The effectiveness of these has not been
adequately documented, although findings indicate that pharmacotherapy and
self-help groups are important adjuncts to primary treatment approaches, particularly for cocaine abuse.

CURRENT TREATMENT ISSUES

The knowledge base developed mainly from evaluation of the four major
modalities has yielded a broad research agenda of questions and issues that
remain to be resolved. These are relevant for all treatment strategies and bear
on policy matters as well.

Relapse

Although treatments are effective, relapse to drug use is the rule, particularly among clients who prematurely leave the treatment setting or who are in the re-entry or aftercare stages of their recovery. Research and clinical observation have focused on the temporal aspects of relapse and the social and psychological conditions related to the relapse event. Among clients who completely achieve abstinence from their primary drug, the risk of relapse is highest in the first six to twelve months thereafter, usually within the first ninety days.[30] The duration of the relapse episode varies, depending mainly on the stability of the primary treatment effects, particularly the length of stay in treatment.

For a particular individual the probability of relapse decreases after the first year of abstinence. However, cumulative relapse rates across people understandably increase over time, reflecting the increasing number of different individuals who relapse with the passage of time.

The conditions relating to relapse vary, including circumstances, social settings, psychological stress, or use of alcohol, regardless of the addict's primary drug. The specific cues or triggers to relapse are often the people, places, and events most associated with drug use. Research is now developing on identification of the conditions associated with relapse.

There are important distinctions with respect to the relapse issue that bear on the selection of relapse prevention or retreatment strategies.[31] First, the term *relapse* itself refers to the reoccurrence of drug use after a period of abstinence. However, the pattern of reuse varies, ranging from a single reoccurrence ("slip") to episodes of multiple reoccurrence ("binges") to a return to the frequent pattern of use prior to abstinence ("relapse"). Second, even if full relapse occurs, the individual may not display the behavior and attitudes associated with a drug abuse life style, but may seek help or retreatment. Thus, relapse must be distinguished from regression and should be treated accordingly. The central conclusion from the literature on relapse emphasizes the importance of a continued program for maintaining treatment gains with respect to sobriety.[32]

Retreatment

Outcome studies indicate that approximately 40 percent of those treated in the major modalities (excluding detoxification centers) return to treatment at least once after their initial treatment experience, and a substantial number of these are multiple admissions.[33] Among the opiate readmissions, most choose methadone maintenance regardless of their initial treatment modality.

Interpretation of retreatment is difficult since election to re-enter treatment appears to be a positive alternative to cope with relapse, compared with no treatment. Indeed, the evidence suggests that for many substance abusers stable recovery requires several treatment experiences, a point emphasized further in the sections on relapse prevention and aftercare.

Aftercare. Evidence shows that the recovery process can be sustained with continued programming beyond that of primary treatment. Aftercare refers to the variety of interventions, services, and assistance provided for chemical abusers after they leave primary treatment to facilitate the recovery process, for example, educational remediation, vocational counseling, life skill training, family assistance, relapse prevention. Such services are most effectively carried out in the context of fellowship, client advocacy, and mutual self-help. The implementation of coherent aftercare models in conjunction with a primary treatment program is only a recent development which awaits evaluation.[34]

Retention in Treatment

The most consistent predictor of successful outcome in all modalities is retention in treatment. However, most admissions leave treatment before the optimal time needed to effect maximal improvement. Indeed, dropping out is the rule across all major treatment modalities.[35]

Despite its importance, retention was not systematically investigated until relatively recently.[36] The general conclusions from this work can be summarized in terms of the three main questions concerning retention. First, what are the retention rates, and when does dropout occur? Precise percentages are difficult to provide because of a variety of factors (e.g., reporting problems, program and regional differences, yearly changes, etc.). National surveys of admissions during 1979–1980 show that one-year retention rates are generally highest for methadone maintenance (22 to 40 percent) and lowest for drug-free outpatients and traditional (two-year) therapeutic communities (7 to 15 percent). Evidence points to an increasing trend in yearly retention rates, particularly in therapeutic communities.[37]

Retention rates vary, but the temporal pattern of dropping out is remarkably uniform. Figure 5.3, for example, presents retention curves for the residential drug-free modality drawn from several data systems. Dropout is highest within the first fifteen days of admission and declines thereafter, indicating that the majority of dropouts leave within the first three months. Beyond ninety days, however, the likelihood of continued retention in treatment increases with the longer stay in treatment itself.[38] Though not shown, the pattern of dropping out is the same in methadone and drug-free outpatient programs.[39] Although the absolute level of retention may vary (with higher retention for methadone maintenance), the shape of the dropout curve is similar.

Second, who are the dropouts? Overall, research indicates that no typical profile has emerged that predicts retention in treatment. Correlates of retention are generally weak and sporadic, depending on the study and the modality. Evidence suggests that shorter retention is associated with severe criminal or psychiatric histories and with voluntary admissions to drug-free outpatient and residential treatment that involve no legal pressure.[40]

Why do clients drop out of treatment? This question has not been adequately

Figure 5.3
Retention Curves for Drug-Free Residential Programs

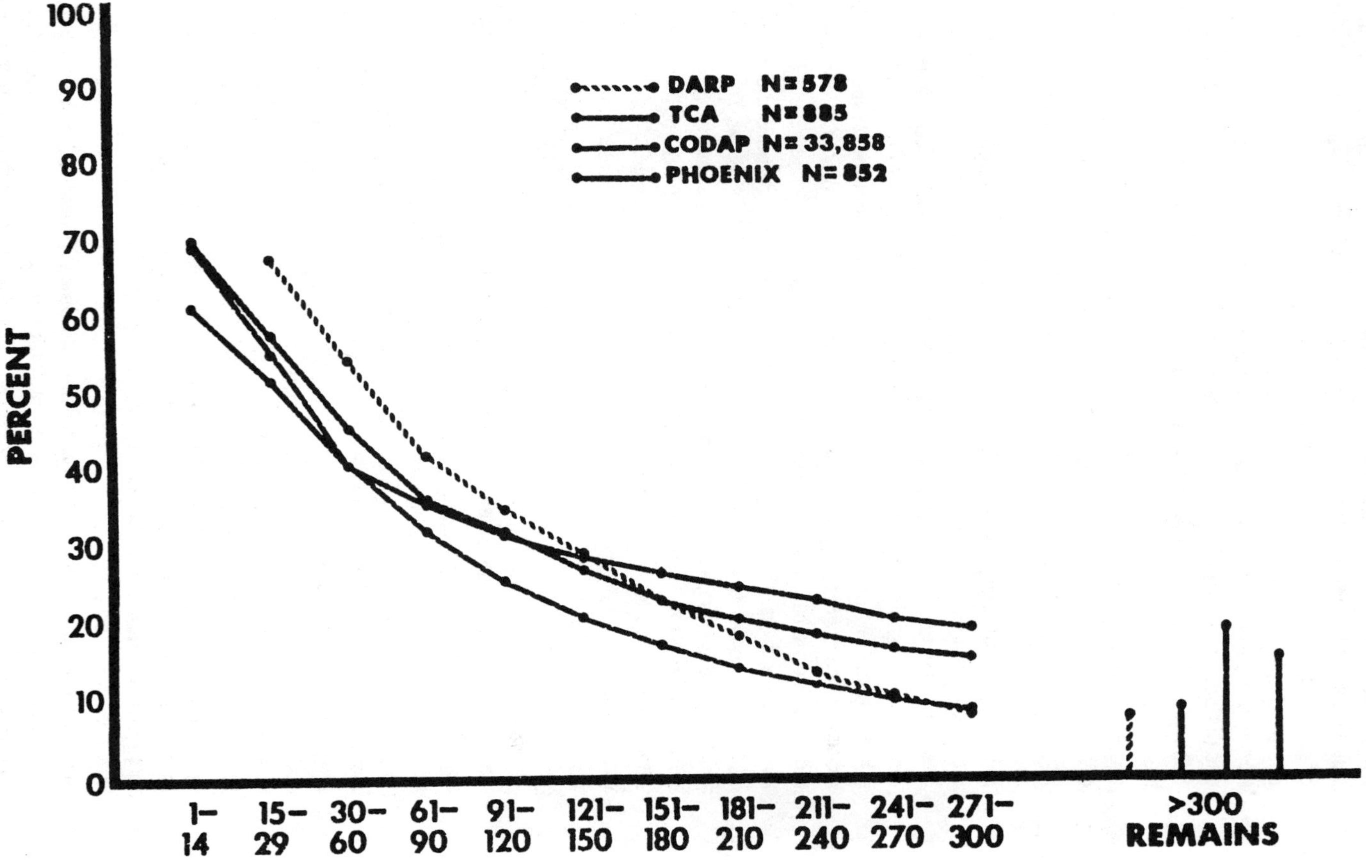

investigated, although research is currently exploring this aspect of retention.[41] Therapeutic community studies have assessed the relationship between the client's status at follow-up and his or her retrospective perceptions of the treatment experience and reasons for leaving treatment prematurely.[42] Longer retention in treatment and a successful outcome are directly related to client ratings of satisfaction with treatment and the relevance of specific program components.[43] Lack of motivation, readiness, and suitability for treatment appear to be reasons for premature terminations.[44]

Treatment Process. The importance of understanding treatment process is evident to most investigators. To a large extent the conclusions concerning treatment effectiveness and retention highlight the need to clarify treatment process. For example, the relationship between length of stay and treatment outcome indirectly infers the influence of treatment elements on client status. It is this interplay between treatment elements and client change that defines process.

Notwithstanding its importance, treatment process has been the least investigated problem in drug abuse treatment research. Studies have indirectly examined process through longitudinal investigations of treatment change, clients' retrospective perceptions of their treatment experience, and, in a few instances, the correlation between program components and client change.[45] In general, the findings from these studies support inferences concerning the process of change, although the process itself remains to be studied directly.

Methodological and Cost Benefit Issues. Conclusions concerning treatment effectiveness have to be interpreted in light of certain methodological limits, the most serious of which stems from the lack of control groups. Follow-up samples may be self-selected to seek, remain in, and benefit from treatment, or perhaps to improve without any treatment. Thus far, however, solutions to these selection problems have eluded research strategies. Assembling untreated matched controls or comparative treatment groups through random assignment has not been feasible. There are ethical and practical problems in withholding treatment, and random assignment to different treatment modalities requires huge samples to absorb attrition rates arising from client-treatment mismatch.[46]

Does treatment significantly reduce the social costs of drug abuse? An answer to this question requires some clarification of the terms *cost effectiveness* and *cost benefits. Costs* are private (e.g., labor, productivity, and life span) and social (e.g., publicly born medical expenditures associated with law enforcement and medical services resulting from drug-related crime). *Cost effectiveness* refers to reductions in the costs associated with producing successes or cures. *Cost benefits* refers to improvements in client status, such as decreases in drug use, criminality, and medical care. Though not a cure, client improvement can result in significant reductions in private and social costs.

A precise assessment of the cost effectiveness or benefit of treatment is difficult to obtain because of conceptual and methodological problems. Nevertheless, the findings from cost of treatment studies support a general conclusion that the major treatment modalities do show an attenuation in both private and social costs.[47] However, the cost gains from the newer treatment strategies await evaluation of their impact.

EMERGING TREATMENT ISSUES AND INITIATIVES

Complex treatment issues and initiatives are now emerging with the wide diversity of drugs and drug users. Three are discussed in this section: special populations, client treatment matching, and recent federal initiatives.

Special Populations

Although all segments of the society are affected by drug use, there are three large subpopulations that are a new focus of treatment initiatives: criminal drug users in the prison system, adolescents, and substance abusers with psychiatric disorders. Considerable resources are beginning to be directed toward developing appropriate treatment strategies for these groups.

Criminal Justice Drug Offenders. The association between crime and drug use is well documented. Indeed, it was this correlation that galvanized the federal effort to expand the drug treatment system in the mid-1960s as part of its war on crime.

Most drug abusers admitted to the major treatment modalities have criminal histories, and, more importantly, community-based treatments are effective in reducing or eliminating criminal activity as well as drug use. However, significant numbers of criminal offenders with drug problems (estimated as high as 70 percent) are detained or serving sentences within the prison systems (see Chapter 11 by Eric D. Wish).

Until recently, relatively little treatment was available for drug abusers within prison. Driven by the mandate to minimize AIDS-related problems and to reduce overcrowding in the prisons, new efforts have been implemented to expand drug treatment services within prisons and jails. Treatment strategies include individual and group counseling; self-help groups such as Alcoholics, Narcotics, and Cocaine Anonymous (i.e., AA, NA, CA); and therapeutic communities.

The effectiveness of these approaches with prison populations is only beginning to be established. For example, studies of the adaptation of the therapeutic community within state correctional institutions document significant reductions in drug use and recidivism two years after release from prison.[48] Based on this and related research, federal criminal justice agencies are supporting the development of comprehensive drug treatment systems within the prison systems, many of which will include therapeutic communities.

Adolescent Substance Abusers. The need for a strenuous treatment effort for adolescent substance abuse has been acknowledged (see Chapter 8 by Alfred S. Friedman and George Beschner). What is known about treatment effectiveness for the young client comes from a few studies of drug-free outpatient and residential TCs. Generally the outcomes are similar to those for adults. However, more young people require legal and/or family pressure to seek and remain in treatment, and adolescents require more time in treatment to achieve favorable outcomes compared with adult clients.[49]

Surveys indicate a decreasing trend in drug use in national samples of high school seniors. However, the current pool of adolescent substance abuse casualties is deep, and the casualty rate will assuredly continue well into the future, imposing a constant demand for adolescent treatments.

Although TCs and drug-free outpatient settings are effective for some adolescents, new treatment strategies have to be developed that are appropriate for the special needs of these drug users. For example, a number of TCs are modifying the classical model for the young client in both inpatient and outpatient settings.[50] Though promising, these efforts await rigorous evaluations.

The Dual Diagnosis Abuser. Considerable data document the increased prevalence of drug abuse in psychiatric populations[51] and, correspondingly, a worsening psychological profile among substance abusers who enter drug treatment settings.[52] These two subpopulations of drug abusers have been labeled. The first group is comprised of mentally ill chemical abusers (MICAs), whose primary disorder is a psychiatric condition in addition to substance abuse. Their main treatment resource has been the mental health system. The second group consists of chemical abusers who are mentally ill (CAMI), for whom the primary disorder is substance abuse in addition to another psychiatric condition. Their main resource has been the drug abuse treatment system (i.e., the major modalities). (A third group consists of homeless substance abusers, many of whom have other psychiatric conditions.)

Treatment in these systems has been inappropriate for both groups. The conventional psychiatric hospital and mental health treatment approaches are unsuitable, as are the major drug treatment modalities. Needs assessment surveys have described this circumstance as one in which the MICA and, to a lesser extent, the CAMI client "fall through the cracks," inadequately served by both the mental health and the drug treatment systems. In response to this, several community-based agencies have launched residential treatment programs, utilizing adaptations of the therapeutic community model for the dual diagnosis client. These efforts must be viewed as encouraging demonstration projects that await evaluation.

Client-Treatment Matching

Given the widening spectrum of clients and treatment strategies, we must ask this question: Can we match particular clients to specific treatment modalities to maximize overall success rates? The empirical data bearing on the issue of matching have been developed from the prediction studies of outcome and retention referred to earlier. These showed that there are few client predictors of success or retention that are specific to any treatment modality. Thus, client characteristics may be of limited utility for matching to treatment.

The matching issue is complex. Methodological and ethical problems make matching and random assignment studies extremely difficult to conduct, much less evaluate. Moreover, matching is obscured by factors associated with treatment programs, unmeasured client differences, and the recovery process itself. A fuller discussion of these issues is contained in other writings.[53] Two main points may be briefly summarized.

First, treatment programs may differ in experience, staffing, funding, resources, philosophy, etc. Such differences affect the quality as well as the effectiveness of treatment, which in turn contributes to the difficulty in matching. In this regard, efficacy studies on newer treatment alternatives must be completed before client treatment matching efforts for these can be undertaken. Second, which treatment a client needs may depend on where he or she is in terms of recovery. Thus, matching studies must focus on new client variables—those relating to the changing characteristics of individuals in the recovery process.

Federal Initiatives

The enculturation of drug abuse with its sequelae of persistent crime, AIDS, and other health problems at all levels of the society has reshaped policy with respect to treatment strategies. The omnibus drug bills for 1988 and 1989 have supported several major treatment initiatives, some specific examples of which are briefly illustrated.

Expanding Treatment Accessibility and Improving Quality. Federal resources have expanded considerably to make treatment more available (offering increased options through more programs and more treatment slots) and accessible (providing ease of entry through reduced waiting lists and minimal eligibility requirements). Additionally, research funding has been extended to enhance retention in treatment, to develop new interventions, and to improve the quality of existing treatment modalities.

Compulsory Treatment. In addition to efforts to expand treatment resources within the prison system, current policy deliberations focus on drug treatment alternatives to incarceration (i.e., treatment "outside of the walls"). Compulsory treatment issues are discussed in more detail in Chapters 6 and 7 in this volume. Research in this area is reviewed in *Compulsory Treatment of Drug Abuse*,[54] a recent publication the main conclusions from which can be briefly summarized.

In general, there is little evidence for differential outcomes between legally referred and nonlegally referred clients. Significant improvements in drug use, criminality, and employment occur for both groups and are directly related to time spent in treatment. As noted earlier, research does indicate that legal pressure increases retention in drug-free ambulatory and residential treatment, a factor that increases the likelihood of positive treatment effects. Thus, legal referral to treatment for some drug abuse offenders may be a useful alternative to incarceration.

However, the efficacy of compulsory treatment strategies depends on several factors. For example, important client differences must be clarified, particularly with respect to perceived legal pressure, motivation, readiness, and suitability for different treatment options. Also, implementation of an effective compulsory treatment policy requires firm linkages between the criminal justice system and the treatment system.[55]

TREATMENT IN THE LARGER CONTEXT

The current knowledge base firmly supports the conclusion that drug treatments offer an effective strategy for reducing the demand for drugs in several ways. The considerable number of successes and improvements indicates that treatment significantly decreases drug use and associated criminal activity among former drug abusers. An increasing pool of recovered drug abusers provides visible role models of former casualties who have changed positively and who mediate messages to active users of the value of treatment.

Moreover, treatment and prevention are interrelated demand-reduction strategies. Prevention efforts are often conducted by treatment agencies at the local community level; and it is commonly observed that prevention campaigns often uncover previously undetected treatment needs. Conversely, data indicate that early intervention (treatment) is perhaps the most direct strategy for preventing later substance abuse and deviancy.

Nevertheless, the social forces associated with drug use prevail. The positive effects of treatment should not be confused with the continuing presence of substance abuse. Treatments may produce recovery, but not reduce the drug problem.

Thus, treatment alone will not cure drug abuse. To a considerable extent the efficacy of treatment and the recovery process itself depend on influences that fundamentally reflect the fabric of society in terms of its attitudes, values, and conduct with respect to drug use. For example, rehabilitation can be undermined by the social climate of drug use. Use of alcohol, marijuana, cocaine, and other "recreational" drugs exerts counterrehabilitative influences. Recovering clients must affiliate with a network of others that reinforces the conduct and values of a drug-free life style. Such a network is increasingly difficult to identify in a social climate that sends a message that altered consciousness or quick relief from discomfort, if not preferred, is acceptable. Thus, the efficacy of treatment has been subverted by a culture that has redefined the norms of its own drug involvement.

Recent indicators are brighter. Society appears to be moving toward consensus in rejecting the chemical alternative. The expansion of federal resources has paralleled a proliferation of private-sector drug treatment centers, changes in insurance coverage for substance abuse treatment, and the growth of employee assistance programs (EAPs). These developments testify to society's reluctant, but clear acceptance of an entrenched drug abuse problem. Moreover, evidence for a broader change in social attitudes is seen in the effective parents' movements against drug and alcohol use, and most hopeful is the declining trend in drug use among high school seniors.

These trends, however, do not obscure the necessity for society's long-term commitment to support treatment. The small, but steady decline in student use is defined in terms of 1979, the recorded peak year of youth drug use. However, the 1987 level is nearly five times higher than that reported in 1962, an early year for which there are statistics.[56] This current base level of drug use, clearly elevated over earlier generations, is perhaps the most sobering measure of the enculturation of drug use. Notwithstanding brighter signs, society's drug treatment needs will continue to grow, reflecting the casualties of the past, the present, and the future.

NOTES

1. D. D. Simpson and S. Sells, "Effectiveness of Treatment for Drug Abuse: An Overview of the DARP Research Program," *Advances in Alcohol and Substance Abuse* 2 (1982): 7–29; G. De Leon, "The Therapeutic Community: Status and Evolution," *International Journal of the Addictions* 20 (1985): 823–44.

2. Ibid.

3. "The Young Adult Chronic Patient and Substance Abuse," *Tie-Lines* 1 (1984).

4. R. Newman, "Detoxification Treatment for Narcotic Addicts" in *Handbook on Drug Abuse*, ed. R. Dupont, A. Goldstein, and J. O'Donnell (Rockville, Md.: National Institute on Drug Abuse, 1979), 21–29.

5. E. C. Senay, "Methadone Maintenance Treatment," *International Journal of the Addictions* 20 (1985): 803–21.

6. V. P. Dole and H. Joseph, "Longterm Outcome of Patients Treated with Methadone Maintenance," *Annals of the New York Academy of Science* 311 (1978): 181–89.

7. Simpson and Sells, "Effectiveness of Treatment."

8. Ibid.

9. R. L. Hubbard, J. J. Collins, J. Valley Rachal, and E. R. Cavanaugh, "The Criminal Justice Client in Drug Abuse Treatment," in *Compulsory Treatment of Drug Abuse: Research and Clinical Practice*, ed. C. G. Leukefeld and F. M. Tims, DHHS Pub. no. (ADM) 88-1578 (Rockville, Md.: National Institute on Drug Abuse, 1988).

10. G. De Leon and M. S. Rosenthal, *Treatment in Residential Communities in Treatments of Psychiatric Disorders*, ed. T. B. Karasu (Washington, D.C.: American Psychiatric Association Press, 1989), 1379–1396.

11. Ibid.; G. De Leon, "The Therapeutic Community for Substance Abuse: Perspective and Approach," in *Therapeutic Communities for Addictions: Readings in Theory, Research and Practice*, ed. G. De Leon and J. Ziegenfuss (Springfield, Ill.: Charles C. Thomas, 1986).

12. Simpson and Sells, "Effectiveness of Treatment."

13. G. De Leon, *The Therapeutic Community: Study of Effectiveness*, Research Monograph Series, DHHS Pub. no. (ADM) 85-1286 (Rockville, Md.: National Institute on Drug Abuse, 1984).

14. Ibid.

15. Ibid. De Leon, "The Therapeutic Community: Status and Evolution."

16. Ibid.

17. "Predicting Retention and Follow-Up Status," De Leon, *The Therapeutic Community: Study of Effectiveness* ; G. De Leon, "Socio-Demographic Predictors of Outcomes in Drug Abuse Treatment: Implications for Client Treatment Matching" (Paper presented to National Institute on Drug Abuse Technical Review Meeting on Matching Clients to Treatment: A Critical Review, 1986); Simpson and Sells, "Effectiveness of Treatment"; D. D. Simpson, G. Joe, and W. Lehman, *Addiction Careers: Summary of Studies Based on the DARP 12 Year Follow-Up*, Treatment Research Report, DHHS Pub. no. 2 (ADM) 86-1420 (Rockville, Md.: National Institute on Drug Abuse, 1986).

18. G. De Leon, *Therapeutic Communities: Psychopathology and Substance Abuse*, Final Report on Project Activities, Grant no. R01-DA0-3860 (Rockville, Md.: National Institute on Drug Abuse, 1988).

19. B. Rounsaville and H. Kleber, "Psychotherapy/Counseling for the Opiate Addict: Strategies for Use in Different Treatment Settings," *International Journal of the Addictions*, 20 (1985): 869–896.

20. J. L. Sorenson, D. Gibson, G. Bemal, and D. Deitch, "Methadone Applicant Dropouts: Impact of Requiring Involvement of Friends and Family in Treatment," *International Journal of the Addictions* 20 (1985): 73; H. Joseph, "The Criminal Justice System and Opiate Addiction: A Historical Perspective," in *Compulsory Treatment of Drug Abuse: Research and Clinical Practice*, ed. C. G. Leukefeld and F. M. Tims, DHHS Pub. no. (ADM) 88-1578 (Rockville, Md.: National Institute on Drug Abuse, 1988).

21. G. De Leon, *The Therapeutic Community: Enhancing Retention in Treatment.* Final Report of Project Activities, Grant no. R01-DA0-3617 (Rockville, Md.: National Institute on Drug Abuse, 1988).

22. Sorenson, Gibson, Bemal, and Deitch, "Methadone Applicant Dropouts"; Joseph, "The Criminal Justice System."

23. A. Marlatt and J. Gordon, *Relapse Prevention* (New York: Pergamon Press, 1985).

24. J. D. Hawkins and R. Catalano, "Aftercare in Drug Abuse Treatment," *International Journal of the Addictions* 20 (1985): 917–45.

25. F. Zackon, E. E. McAuliffe, and J. Chien, *Addict Aftercare: Recovery Training and Self-Help*, Research Monograph Series, DHHS Pub. no. (ADM) 85-1341 (Rockville, Md.: National Institute on Drug Abuse, 1985).

26. TCA Feedback Series (New York: Therapeutic Communities of America, Division of Research and Training, 1988).

27. S. Hall, "Clinical Trials in Drug Treatment," in *Drug Abuse Treatment Evaluation: Strategies, Progress and Prospects*, ed. F. Tims and J. Ludford, DHHS Pub. no. (ADM) 88–1329 (Rockville, Md.: National Institute on Drug Abuse, 1984).

28. F. Gawin and H. Kleber, "Pharmacological Treatment of Cocaine Abuse," *Psychiatric Clinics of North America* 9 (1986): 573-83.

29. D. M. Nurco, N. Wegner, P. Stephenson, A. Makofsky, and J. W. Shaffer, *Ex-Addicts Self-Help Groups* (New York: Praeger, 1983); Senay, "Methadone Maintenance Treatment."

30. Simpson and Sells, "Effectiveness of Treatment"; De Leon, *The Therapeutic Community: Study of Effectiveness*; Simpson, Joe, and Lehman, *Addiction Careers*.

31. G. De Leon, "Retention in Drug-Free Therapeutic Communities." Paper presented at the National Institute on Drug Abuse RAUS Technical Review Meeting on "Improving Drug Treatment." Bethesda, Md.: NIH, 1989.

32. B. S. Brown, *Addicts and Aftercare: Community Integration of the Former Drug*

User (Beverly Hills, Calif.: Sage, 1979); Hawkings and Catalano, "Aftercare in Drug Abuse Treatment."

33. Simpson and Sells, "Effectiveness of Treatment."

34. Brown, *Addicts and Aftercare* ; Zackon, McAuliffe, and Chien, *Addict Aftercare*; Gawin and Kleber, "Pharmacological Treatment of Cocaine Abuse."

35. G. De Leon and S. Schwartz, "The Therapeutic Community: What Are the Retention Rates?" *American Journal of Drug and Alcohol Abuse* 10 (1984): 267–84.

36. Ibid.; De Leon, *The Therapeutic Community: Enhancing Retention in Treatment*.

37. TCA Rapid Feedback Series,

38. De Leon and Schwartz, "The Therapeutic Community: What Are the Retention Rates?"

39. De Leon and Schwartz, "The Therapeutic Community."

40. Hubbard, Collins, Rachal, and Cavanaugh, "The Criminal Justice System Client in Drug Abuse Treatment."

41. Wexler and De Leon, "Perceived Quality of Adjustment 5 Years after Therapeutic Community Treatment"; De Leon, *The Therapeutic Community: Enhancing Retention in Treatment*.

42. Wexler and De Leon, "Perceived Quality of Adjustment 5 Years after Therapeutic Community Treatment."

43. "Predicting Retention and Follow-up Status," Wexler and De Leon, "Perceived Quality of Adjustment 5 Years after Therapeutic Community Treatment."

44. G. De Leon and N. Jainchill, "Circumstances, Motivation, Readiness and Suitability as Correlates of Treatment Tenure," *Journal of Psychoactive Drugs* 18 (1986): 203–208.

45. De Leon, *The Therapeutic Community: Study of Effectiveness*; De Leon, "The Therapeutic Community: Status and Evolution."

46. R. N. Bales, D. W. Van Stone, J. N. Kuldau, T. M. Engelsing, R. M. Elashoff, and V. P. Zarcone, "Therapeutic Communities Versus Methadone Maintenance: A Prospective Controlled Study of Narcotic Addiction Treatment," *Archives of General Psychiatry* 37 (1980): 179–93; G. De Leon, *Evaluating Treatment Effectiveness: Proving Treatment Influence May Be a Non-Issue*. (Washington, D.C.: National Alcohol and Drug Abuse Conference, 1980).

47. V. P. Dole, H. Joseph, and D. Des Jarlais, *Costs and Benefits of Treating Chronic Users of Heroin and Methadone Maintenance*, Internal Report (New York: New York State Division of Substance Abuse Services Bureau of Research, 1981); H. J. Harwood, R. L. Hubbard, J. J. Collins, and J. Valley Rachal, "The Costs of Crime and the Benefits of Drug Abuse Treatment: A Cost-Benefit Analysis Using TOPS Data," in *Compulsory Treatment of Drug Abuse: Research and Clinical Practice*, ed. C. G. Leukefeld and F. M. Tims, DHHS Pub. no. (ADM) 88-1578 (Rockville, Md.: National Institute of Drug Abuse, 1988).

48. H. K. Wexler, D. S. Lipton, and K. Foster, "Outcome Evaluation of a Prison Therapeutic Community for Substance Abuse Treatment: Preliminary Results." Paper presented at the American Society for Criminology, 1985.

49. G. M. Beschner and A. S. Friedman, "Treatment of Adolescent Drug Abusers," *International Journal of the Addictions* 20 (1985): 971–73; G. De Leon, "Adolescent Abusers in the Therapeutic Community: Treatment Outcomes," in *Proceedings on the Ninth World Conference on Therapeutic Communities*, ed. A. Acampura and E. Nebelkopf

(San Francisco: Abacus Press, 1986); Hubbard, Collins, Rachal, and Cavanaugh, "The Criminal Justice Client in Drug Abuse Treatment."

50. G. De Leon, "The Therapeutic Community Perspective and Approach for Adolescent Substance Abusers," in *Adolescent Psychiatry: Developmental and Clinical Studies*, ed. S. Feinstein (Chicago: University of Chicago, 1988).

51. H. E. Rose, F. B. Glaser, and T. Germanson, "The Prevalence of Psychiatric Disorders in Patients with Alcohol and Other Drug Problems," *Archives of General Psychiatry* 45 (1988): 1023–31.

52. N. Jainchill, G. De Leon, and L. Pinkham, "Psychiatric Diagnosis Among Substance Abusers in Therapeutic Community Treatment," *Journal of Psychoactive Drugs* 18 (1986): 209–13; B. J. Rounsaville, M. M. Weissman, H. Kleber, and C. Wilber, "Heterogeneity of Psychiatric Diagnosis in Mental Opiate Addicts," *Archives of General Psychiatry* 39 (1982): 161–66; R. L. Hubbard, J. V. Rachal, S. G. Craddock, and E. R. Cavanaugh, "Treatment Outcome Prospective Study (TOPS): Client Characteristics and Behaviors Before, During, and After Treatment," in *Drug Abuse Treatment Evaluation: Strategies, Progress and Prospects*, Research Monograph 51, DHHS Pub. no. (ADM) 84-1329 (Rockville, Md.: National Institute on Drug Abuse, 1984); Rose, Glaser, and Germanson, "The Prevalence of Psychiatric Disorders"; G. De Leon, "Psychopathology and Substance Abuse: What are We Learning from Research in Therapeutic Communities," *Journal of Psychoactive Drugs* 21 (1989), 177–188.

53. A. T. McLellan, "Increased Effectiveness of Substance Abusers Treatment: A Prospective Study of Patient-Treatment 'Matching,' " *Journal of Nervous and Mental Diseases* 17 (1983): 587–605; G. De Leon, *Demographic Predictors of Outcomes in Drug Abuse Treatment, NIDA Technical Review Meeting on Matching Clients to Treatments: A Critical Review*. (Rockville, Md.: National Institute of Drug Abuse, 1986).

54. C. G. Leukefeld and F. M. Tims, eds., *Compulsory Treatment of Drug Abuse: Research and Clinical Practice*, DHHS Pub. no. (ADM) 88-1578 (Rockville, Md.: National Institute on Drug Abuse, 1988).

55. G. De Leon, "Legal Pressure in Therapeutic Communities," in *Compulsory Treatment of Drug Abuse: Research and Clinical Practice*, eds. C. G. Leukefeld and F. Tims (Rockville, Md.: National Institute of Drug Abuse, 1988).

56. G. De Leon, data drawn from several sources by the author.

Chapter 6

Treatment Alternatives to Street Crime (TASC)

Beth A. Weinman

TASC HISTORY

Robinson v. California,[1] decided by the U.S. Supreme Court in 1962, is considered a landmark case that offered a new approach to the Eighth Amendment's ban on "cruel and unusual punishments." The case involved a petitioner's appeal of his conviction as a narcotic addict under a section of the California Health and Safety Code that read:

No person shall use, or be under the influence, or be addicted to the use of narcotics, excepting when administered by or under the direction of a person licensed by the State to prescribe and administer narcotics. It shall be the burden of the defense to show that it comes within the exception. Any person convicted of violating any provision of this section is guilty of a misdemeanor and shall be sentenced to serve a term of not less than 90 days nor more than a year in the county jail.[2]

The Supreme Court reversed Robinson's conviction, declaring that status offenses such as "being addicted to narcotic drugs" were unconstitutional and that imprisonment for such an offense was a violation of the Eighth Amendment. A lesser known aspect of the decision in *Robinson* was that in viewing addiction as a "disease," the Court also held that a state could establish a program of compulsory treatment for narcotic addiction. And further, the Court held that such compulsory treatment could involve periods of voluntary confinement, with penal sanctions imposed for the failure to comply with compulsory treatment procedures.

In the years following the decision in *Robinson*, several conceptual and strategic models were developed to implement this new understanding. By the early seventies, a presidentially appointed Special Study Commission on Drugs established that there was a definite link between drug use and crime, and particularly between narcotic addiction and crime. More specifically, it had become a matter of empirical fact that a small number of addicts were responsible for a significant proportion of urban street crimes and that a disproportionate share of criminal justice system resources were being absorbed by their recidivism.[3]

Discussions on how to link treatment and the judicial process and how to interrupt the relationship between drug use and criminal behavior were held by the Law Enforcement Assistance Administration (LEAA), the White House Special Action Office for Drug Abuse Prevention (SAODAP), and the National Institute on Mental Health's Division of Narcotic Addiction and Drug Abuse (DNADA)—the predecessor to the National Institute on Drug Abuse (NIDA). The resulting federal initiative, modeled after earlier experiments with compulsory treatment,[4] was funded under the Drug Abuse Office and Treatment Act of 1972 and christened TASC—Treatment Alternatives to Street Crime. The first TASC project, opened in Wilmington, Delaware, in August 1972, provided pretrial diversion for opiate addicts who were facing charges for nonviolent crimes and who were identified in jail by urine tests and interviews. After assessment of their treatment suitability and needs, arrestees who volunteered for TASC were referred and escorted to appropriate community-based treatment and monitored for continued compliance with treatment requirements. Successful completion of the program typically resulted in the dismissal of charges.[5]

LEAA issued program guidelines for replication of the TASC model, focusing on pretrial diversion and sentencing alternatives for drug-dependent offenders, and awarded seed grants with the understanding that successful demonstration projects would gain local and state funding to continue the programs within a three-year period. In 1972–1973, thirteen TASC projects were initiated by local jurisdictions in eleven states. By 1975 nineteen more such projects were underway, making a total of twenty-nine operational sites in twenty-four states. Before federal funding was withdrawn in 1982, TASC projects were developed in 130 sites in 39 states and Puerto Rico.[6] All of the LEAA-funded TASC programs were required to conduct independent evaluations of their effectiveness, and more than forty of these local assessments were completed over the ten-year period of LEAA oversight. Although a few evaluators found that some TASC programs had unduly optimistic expectations for client success or were underutilized, the majority concluded that local TASC efforts effectively

• intervened with clients to reduce drug abuse and criminal activity;
• linked the criminal justice and treatment systems; and
• identified previously untreated drug-dependent offenders.

THE BENEFITS OF TASC

TASC provides an objective and effective bridge between two separate institutions: the justice system and the treatment community. The justice system's legal sanctions reflect community concerns for public safety and punishment, whereas the treatment system emphasizes therapeutic relationships as a means for changing individuals who would otherwise burden the justice system with their persistent criminality.

The mission of TASC is to participate in justice system processing as early in the continuum as is acceptable to participating agencies. TASC identifies, assesses, and refers appropriate drug- and/or alcohol-dependent defendants accused or convicted of nonviolent crimes to community-based substance abuse treatment as an alternative or supplement to existing justice system sanctions and procedures. TASC then monitors the drug-dependent subject's compliance with individually tailored progress expectations for abstinence, employment, and improved social-personal functioning. It then reports treatment results back to the referring justice system component. Clients who violate conditions of their justice mandate—TASC—or treatment agreement are usually sent back to the justice system for continued processing or sanctions.

TASC combines the influence of legal sanctions for probable or proven crimes with the appeal of such innovative justice system dispositions as deferred prosecution, creative community sentencing, diversion, pretrial intervention, probation, and parole supervision to motivate treatment cooperation by the substance abuser. Through treatment referral and closely supervised community reintegration, TASC aims to permanently interrupt the vicious cycle of addiction, criminality, arrest, prosecution, conviction, incarceration, release, readdiction, criminality, and rearrest.

TASC programs not only offer renewed hope to drug- and alcohol-dependent clients by encouraging them to alter their life styles while remaining in their own communities, but also provide important incentives to the justice and treatment system participants. For the justice system, TASC can reduce the costs and relieve many substance-abuse-related processing burdens through assistance with such services as addiction-related medical situation, pretrial screening, and post-trial supervision. The treatment community also benefits from TASC's legal focus, which seems to motivate and prolong clients' treatment cooperation and ensures clear definition and observation of criteria for treatment dismissal or completion. Public safety is also increased through TASC's careful supervision of criminally involved clients during their community-based treatment.[7]

Specifically, TASC has the ability to create a system of communication between the criminal justice and treatment systems. Historically, these systems have had difficulties in both communication and coordination of activities. Several of these difficulties are the result of the two systems' perceptions of having vastly different goals with the same offender population. While the criminal justice system has the objective of providing offender control to enhance community safety and to provide appropriate punishment, in the final analysis the criminal justice system also seeks to change individual behavior and reduce community affliction, as does the drug treatment system.

Difficulties in communication between the two systems have also developed through the perceptions and stereotypes held by justice professionals that those who work in the drug intervention/treatment/rehabilitation field are very young, nervous looking, liberals, inappropriate dressers, ex-felons, drug users, and/or not motivated enough to become a true professional (i.e., doctors, lawyers, accountants). As such, the treatment provider is often treated with suspicion, fear, and something less than respect.

Treatment people, often unaware of these criminal justice perceptions, typically respond with suspicion. Treatment personnel perceive the criminal justice system as lacking the expertise to work with the drug-dependent offender in a way that accelerates the offender rehabilitation. Experience with the criminal justice system is often fraught with role conflicts for both the treatment provider and the criminal justice participant, resulting in a perception that the justice system interferes with the treatment process, rather than actually providing assistance by means of legal intervention and thus retention in treatment.

The language that each system uses creates further barriers and distance, making it harder for the two systems to cooperate. (See Table 6.1.)

As these systems perceive different goals for themselves and have languages that oppose one another, their ability to communicate, while serving the exact same individual, has at the very least remained difficult.

The TASC case management model, incorporating critical program elements, focuses on specific strategies to overcome these barriers in effective communication and coordination between the criminal justice and treatment systems. In breaking down these barriers, TASC programming ensures offender accountability through specific performance standards that compel offender compliance with both the criminal justice mandate and the designated treatment plan. The TASC program in its discrete function reduces the potential for offender manipulation of the two systems, coordinates the alternative system goals, and reduces the perceived system differences. As a result, the necessary comprehensive case management is provided to the criminal justice system, the treatment system, the drug-dependent individual, and the community.

NATIONAL TASC PROGRAMMING

Nationally, TASC programs have been involved in an effort to define and document the specific steps, or *critical elements,* necessary for a "successful" TASC program effort. This documentation will also afford the TASC field the benefit of standardization across sites and provide a common language to use to bring a complex program concept into an operational program framework. These "proven effective" elements are divided into two sections: those that need to be in place prior to beginning actual TASC program operations and those that assure successful TASC program operations. Specifically, the TASC critical elements are these:

I. Organizational

1. A broad base of support within the justice system with a protocol for continued and effective communication

Table 6.1
System Terminology

CRIMINAL JUSTICE	NEUTRAL	DRUG TREATMENT
Defendant,	Human Subject	Client,
Offender		Patient
Court,	Facility	Treatment Program
Jail,		Therapeutic Community
Prison,		
Surveillance,	Direction	Counseling,
Supervision		Advocacy
Sentence	Period of Time	Treatment Phrase
Criminal Behavior	Presenting Problem	Addiction
Completion of	Goal	Recovery,
Sentence		Abstinence
Pre-Sentence	Report	"Case Notes"
Investigation		

2. A broad base of support within the treatment system with a protocol for continued and effective communication

3. An independent TASC unit with a designated administrator

4. Policies and procedures for required staff training

5. A data collection system to be used in program management and evaluation

II. Operational

6. Agreed-on eligibility criteria

7. Procedures for the identification of eligible offenders

8. Documented procedures for assessment and referral

9. Documented policies and procedures for random urinalysis and other physical tests

10. Procedures for offender monitoring that include criteria for success and failure, required frequency of contact, schedule of reporting, and notification of termination to the justice system[8]

These critical elements represent the nationally accepted model for case management of the drug-dependent offender.

TASC ENHANCEMENTS

The TASC program model can be effected at any point within the criminal justice continuum and has the potential of further expansion that services "special populations." Among these special populations that the TASC case management model has proven effective in impacting are juveniles, driving under the influence (DUI) offenders, mentally ill offenders, and perpetrators of domestic violence.

While one of the benefits of the TASC case management model is its transferability to varying populations, it is important to point out some additional elements and considerations that are required when dealing with these special populations.

I. Juveniles

1. Juvenile court intervention points vary from those points in the adult court.
2. Family involvement and consent are essential.
3. Differentiations in diagnosis must be considered.
4. Separate referrals are necessary for education/intervention/treatment.

II. DUI Offenders

1. Considerations for the monitoring of alcohol use and/or antabuse (the administration of medication) must be made.
2. Relationships with traffic court must be established.
3. A thorough review of systems for assessment and referral of DUI offenders must be made to avoid duplication of services.

III. Mentally Ill Offenders

1. Mentally ill offenders may have a higher potential for violence.
2. Special expertise in client assessment and referral is required.
3. Smaller case management caseloads must be considered.
4. Urinalysis would be required to monitor use of prescribed medications as well as illicit drugs.
5. Knowledge of the mental health system is required.
6. An extensive social service network needs to be sought.
7. Civil commitment procedures must be researched.

IV. Perpetrators of Domestic Violence

1. This population requires linkages with family court.

2. Specialized treatment services must be available.

3. They are potentially violent clientele.

4. An emphasis on family relations and family involvement is required.

5. Victim involvement is essential.

After review and clarification of these distinctive considerations, the TASC case management model is easily transferable to these special populations.

THE FUTURE OF TASC

Within the context of federal supply- and-demand-reduction strategies, TASC programs are touted as an approach to *user accountability* for drug abuse. The user accountability thesis is this: If there were no drug abusers, there would be no drug problem, and as such, all drug abusers must be held accountable for their actions. Within this context, TASC programs have a demonstrated value for reducing the flow of cases through overburdened criminal justice systems by interrupting the cycle of addiction, criminality, arrest, prosecution, conviction, incarceration, release, readdiction, criminality, and rearrest. During the latter part of the 1980s, states began funding TASC programs within their departments of correction to manage parolees after release. Furthermore, given the research documenting the viability of urinalysis as a means of reducing pretrial misconduct and pretrial rearrest,[9] the TASC critical element of urine monitoring has taken on greater significance for the criminal justice decision maker. With urinalysis monitoring combined with the support of individual offender case management, courts are looking toward funding TASC programs through their administrative offices.

TASC's next effort must focus on evaluation and demonstrations of program efficacy. In this behalf, continued efforts to confirm the results of the Treatment Outcome Prospective Study (TOPS) have been initiated.[10] The TOPS study found that participation in treatment with a TASC referral contributed to longer retention, and the research has clearly demonstrated that retention in treatment is an important contributor to treatment effectiveness.[11]

To this end, a TASC assessment protocol has been developed to evaluate how the TASC critical elements are implemented and operating at each site; it also details

• the numbers and types of TASC system participants and how each relates to program operations;

• problems that have been or are being encountered and effective strategies developed to overcome these difficulties;

- individual site organization and administration and how these interact with the criminal justice and treatment systems; and
- characteristics of the TASC, criminal justice, and treatment participants at each site and the impact each of these has on TASC program functioning and potential client outcome.

The assessment protocol assists TASC programs to both implement and develop the proven process of TASC operations. Taking this assessment one step further, it was then necessary to establish outcome measures that evaluate the effectiveness of TASC program goals.

As all TASC professionals realize, measuring the outcome of a service or intervention when there are a myriad of uncontrolled variables cannot produce hard and fast results, but rather only indications as to the likely direction of the effect of the intervention.[12] For programs such as TASC, it is true that outcome measures are not absolute measures for, except in a few instances, it is impossible to say conclusively what would have happened had an individual not been a part of a TASC program. Yet it is also true that anecdotal measures of effectiveness can no longer substantiate TASC's "proven effectiveness." What can be measured is the achievement of each of the TASC program's stated goals.

The goals of TASC programs were articulated by a special advisory board of the National Association of State Alcohol and Drug Abuse Directors (NASA-DAD) during 1987. These goals were adopted by the National Consortium of TASC Programs in February of 1989. The TASC goals are to

- reduce the criminality of the alcohol- and other-drug-dependent offender;
- maximize the rehabilitative aspects of the criminal justice system; and
- maximize the rehabilitative aspects of the treatment system.

With these goals in mind, outcome measures for TASC programs were then developed.

Recommended Outcome Measure #1: Rearrest Rates

The relationship between drug use and criminal behavior is a very complex one. Some, but certainly not all, crimes committed by TASC clients can be attributed to the need for drugs. It would be unrealistic to expect criminal activity to cease in a group so entrenched in the criminal life style, but it can be expected that the level of criminal activity will diminish.

Given that addicts chronically relapse, measures other than rearrest rates are often thought to be more appropriate. After all, intervention with the drug-dependent population requires a lengthy management program.[13] While it is true that the myriad of interventions provided by TASC programs assists the criminal justice decision maker to manage the drug-dependent-offender caseload, it is also true that the point of the offender's actual re-entry into the criminal justice system is what is most significant to criminal justice decision makers. Overall, the criminal justice system's interest in the drug-dependent-offender population hinges on law enforcement and safety, rather than on a concern for the individual's alcohol and/or drug problem. The rehabilitation philosophy of the criminal justice system rests on the premises that persons who commit crimes have identifiable reasons for doing so and that these can be discovered, addressed, and altered. Its aim is to modify behavior and reintegrate the lawbreaker into the wider society as a productive citizen.[14] In fact, the National Academy of Criminal Justice has defined rehabilitation as no further criminal justice involvement.[15]

While rearrest does not necessarily presume criminal reinvolvement because the individual has yet to be proven guilty, rearrest does presume re-entry into the criminal justice system and therefore resumption of the use of the local jurisdiction's criminal justice resources. Through examination of rearrest rates, acceptable or "successful" levels can be determined over time.

Recommended Outcome Measure #2: Retention in Treatment

The precise process of case management under the auspices of TASC is associated with longer retention in treatment. Further, it is accepted that treatment retention is an important contributor to treatment effectiveness.[16] The problem of retention reflects the chronic and severe nature of drug dependence. For example, a study of seven therapeutic communities in six states found that twelve-month retention rates averaged only 12 percent of admitted clients.[17] Research, primarily completed with heroin addicts, indicates that treatment lengths of six months or more are necessary to produce significant changes in offender characteristics and conditions that are related to reducing drug use.[18] And, finally, research also suggests that criminal behavior has been found to diminish while individuals are in treatment.[19]

Given the importance of retention and the findings of TASC's contribution to longer retention rates as reported in the TOPS—that participation in treatment with a TASC referral contributes to longer retention—it is incumbent on TASC programs to continue to measure the offender's retention in treatment as a means of strengthening the TASC position.

While it would certainly be easier to choose a six-month retention rate as the measure for this particular TASC goal, the countless treatment options, lengths, and diverse factors contributing to retention rates would convolute this outcome measure, so much so that in the final analysis it might be worthless. The proportion of time the individual is retained in treatment presents a more accurate picture of offender outcome for this specific TASC program goal. To measure retention in treatment one must look at the percentage of time TASC clients remain in their *assigned or recommended* treatment modality, whether it is twenty-six days or twenty-six months. TASC programs would need to generate individual treatment "program profiles" that document specific and intended treatment lengths of each facility to which TASC refers. On successful or unsuccessful termination from TASC, the client's rate of retention, within his/her designated treatment facility, may then be recorded for future study and comparison.

Recommended Outcome Measure #3: Drug-Free Status

In recent years urinalysis tests have received considerable attention as a source of information about an offender's drug use. Since its inception in 1972, TASC has used urine testing as a means of gathering information for both the identification and the monitoring of the drug-dependent offender. To this day urinalysis continues to be a critical element for TASC programs. With the increasing use of urinalysis testing throughout the 1980s, substantial information collected from diverse client populations has converged to show that addicted offenders are likely to commit both drug and nondrug crimes at high rates.[20] And research further indicates that with the use of urinalysis, treatment-induced reduction in narcotics use is associated with concurrent reductions in individual crime rates.[21] Historically, much of what has been learned about the relationship between drug use and crime has come from studies that have relied heavily on offenders' self-reports.[22] Confidential interviews for research purposes only have verified that the criminally involved population is also significantly involved in drug use. However, when the interviews are obtained in conjunction with criminal justice auspices, the validity of self-reports is much less reliable.[23] The evidence is convincing that detainees will severely underreport their drug use, even in a voluntary, confidential research interview. If valid self-reports of recent drug use cannot be obtained in a voluntary, confidential research interview held within the criminal justice system, it seems obvious that they cannot be obtained when the information is to be reported to the criminal justice system. As it is the obligation of TASC to report to the criminal justice system regarding the offender's progress in treatment, the use of urinalysis has become an extremely important vehicle for confirming or denying the validity of offender self-reports on drug use.

To measure the rehabilitative aspects of the treatment system in conjunction with the rehabilitative aspects of the criminal justice system, it is necessary to include the condition of the offender's drug-free status. Through the use of urinalysis testing as an outcome measure, TASC programs are provided with a technologically sound and credible method to determine offender compliance with this goal and with their treatment plan.

Once again, only after these outcome measures are recorded by TASC programs for a significant period of time will a true measure of program effectiveness become available for discussion. After data are collected using these measures by a number of TASC programs over a specific period of time specific questions regarding TASC's effectiveness can begin to be answered. These questions include the following: How high a percentage of TASC client rearrest is too high for TASC program effectiveness? How low is too low for TASC clients' retention in treatment before a program is considered ineffective?

In order to achieve an accurate evaluation of TASC programs, this information must be gathered, compared, and clearly documented to ensure program effectiveness for the criminal justice system, the treatment community, and the drug-involved offender.

NOTES

1. *Robinson v. California*, 370 U.S. 660 (1962).

2. Ibid,.

3. See Research Triangle Institute, *Drug Use and Crime: Report of the Panel on Drug Use and Criminal Behavior* (Springfield, Va.: National Technical Information Service, 1976).

4. For a discussion of early compulsory treatment efforts, see William H. McGlothlin, M. Douglas Anglin, and Bruce D. Wilson, *An Evaluation of the California Civil Addict Program* (Rockville, Md.: National Institute on Drug Abuse, 1977), 4.

5. *Treatment Alternatives to Street Crime: Program Brief*, Prepared under cooperative agreement number 86-SA-CX-K026 by the National Association of State Alcohol and Drug Abuse Directors, Inc. (Washington, D.C.: Bureau of Justice Assistance, 1988).

6. Ibid.

7. L. Foster Cook and Beth A. Weinman, "Treatment Alternatives to Street Crime," in *Compulsory Treatment of Drug Abuse: Research and Clinical Practice*, ed. Carl G. Leukefeld and Frank M. Tims (Rockville, Md.: National Institute on Drug Abuse, 1988), 99–105.

8. *Treatment Alternatives to Street Crime*, Bureau of Justice Assistance.

9. See Chapter 11 by Eric D. Wish.

10. J. J. Collins, R. L. Hubbard, J. V. Rachal, and E. R. Cavanaugh, "The Drug Abuse Treatment Client in the Criminal Justice System 1979–1980 TOPS Admission Cohorts," in *Compulsory Treatment of Drug Abuse: Research and Clinical Practice*, ed. Carl G. Leukefeld and Frank M. Tims (Rockville, Md.: National Institute on Drug Abuse, 1988), 57–79.

11. D. D. Simpson, "Treatment for Drug Abuse: Follow-Up Outcomes and Length of Time Spent," *Archives of General Psychiatry* 38 (1981): 875–80; R. L. Hubbard, M. E. Marsden, E. R. Cavanaugh, J. V. Rachal, and H. M. Ginzburg, "The Role of Drug Abuse in Limiting the Spread of AIDS," *Review of Infectious Disease* 10 (1988): 377–84.

12. M. D. Anglin, *The Efficacy to Civil Commitment in Treating Narcotics Addiction*, National Institute on Drug Abuse Monograph Series (Rockville, Md.: National Institute on Drug Abuse, 1986).

13. Fazey, C. S. J., "The Evaluation of the Liverpool Drug Dependency Clinic: The First Two Years, 1985–1987." Liverpool, England, 1988, 3.

14. Inciardi, James A., *Criminal Justice*, 2nd ed. (Harcourt Brace, 1988).

15. National Academy of Criminal Justice, 1978.

16. D. D. Simpson, "Treatment for Drug Abuse: Follow-Up Outcomes and Length of Time Spent," *Arch Ge Psychiatry* 38, no. 8 (1981): 875–80; R. L. Hubbard, M. E.

Marsden, E. R. Cavanaugh, J. V. Rachal, and H. M. Ginzburg, "The Role of Drug Abuse in Limiting the Spread of AIDS," *Rev Infect Dis* 10, no. 2, (1988): 377–84.

17. G. De Leon and S. Schwartz, "The Therapeutic Community: What Are the Retention Rates?" *American Journal of Drug and Alcohol Abuse* 10, no. 2 (1984).

18. Ibid.

19. Henrick J. Harwood, "The Cost of Crime and the Benefits of Drug Abuse Treatment: Cost-Benefit Analysis Using TOPS Data," *Compulsory Treatment of Drug Abuse: Research and Clinical Practice*, ed. Carl G. Leukefeld and Frank M. Tims (Rockville, Md.: National Institute on Drug Abuse, 1988), 209–35.

20. W. H. McGlothlin, M. D. Anglin, and B. D. Wilson, *An Evaluation of the California Civil Addict Program*, Services Research Issues Studies (Rockville, Md.: National Institute on Drug Abuse, 1977).

21. E. D. Wish, and B. D. Johnson, "The Impact of Substance Abuse on Criminal Careers," in *Criminal Careers and Career Criminals*, vol. 2, ed. A. Blumstein, J. Cohen, and C. A. Visher (Washington, D.C.: National Academy Press, 1986).

22. Eric D. Wish, "Identifying Drug-Abusing Criminals," in *Compulsory Treatment of Drug Abuse: Research and Clinical Practice*, ed. Carl G. Leukefeld and Frank M. Tims (Rockville, Md.: National Institute on Drug Abuse, 1988), 139–59.

23. Ibid.

Chapter 7 _____

Legal Coercion and Drug Abuse Treatment: Research Findings and Social Policy Implications

M. Douglas Anglin and Yih-Ing Hser

Discussions about drugs and social policy designed to resolve drug abuse problems are filled with hyperbole and speculation, regardless of whether the discussion occurs within governmental agencies, in the media, or in public (Goldberg & Meyers 1980). Philosophical positions taken by the discussants, whether from personal conviction or for public consumption, often disregard empirical data and analyses as well as theoretical interpretations. A particularly obfuscating belief is that legal solutions or enacted legal measures by themselves will produce significant change in the world's current drug situation. Given that the legal efforts in the United States for over sixty years have had limited social effect and that production, distribution, and consumption of illicit drugs throughout the world has actually increased, this perspective is untenable (Drug Abuse Council 1980). Although many solutions have been proposed, no consensus has consistently emerged as to what alternative strategies should be undertaken (Eldridge 1962; Lindesmith 1965; Duster 1970; Meyers 1980; Trebach 1982).

One concept that has repeatedly surfaced as a strategy for reducing drug demand is to combine legal coercion with drug treatment efforts as a dual approach with both rehabilitation and social control elements. Such approaches, with different degrees of emphasis on either element, have recurred as social policy for most of the present century. Examples include the morphine maintenance clinics established by some communities in the 1920s, the federal narcotic treatment farms situated at Ft. Worth and Lexington in the 1930s, the 1960s experiments with civil commitment in California and New York and at the federal level, and the present system, commencing in the 1970s, of criminal justice system reliance on community drug treatment programs as alternatives to incarceration or as adjuncts to legal supervision.

The civil commitment programs of the 1960s were designed to provide legal coercion into inpatient treatment, which included vocational and educational development and a strong program of aftercare with continual monitoring for drug use. As implemented, however, some of these programs fell short of their design, and many observers assumed that the civil commitment approach had failed. Even so, the principle of combining legal coercion with treatment was adapted and used in conjunction with the community treatment system that developed during the 1970s. As currently applied, legal coercion, broadly defined, is a common reason for addicts to enter treatment—but this present-day coercion is inconsistently applied.

Histories of civil commitment programs are available from several sources (Musto 1973; Maddux 1986; Inciardi 1988). This chapter will focus on the recent history and evaluation results of civil commitment programs as established in the United States and on the development and outcomes of later legal coercion efforts. Further, the principal features of successful civil commitment and other legal programs will be discussed, and a comprehensive model for the use of civil commitment and other legal system procedures to control and rehabilitate narcotics addicts will be proposed.

WHAT IS CIVIL COMMITMENT?

Civil commitment is a legal procedure that allows narcotics addicts or other drug addicts to be committed to a compulsory drug treatment program, typically involving a residential period and an aftercare period in the community. Provisions are included for helping clients with education and employment and for responding promptly to signs of readdiction, usually detected by a regular program of monitoring through urinalysis. Civil commitment is frequently used with addicts who are arrested for criminal activity; with criminal charges pending, the addict can be coerced into treatment and retained long enough to receive the benefits of a treatment program.

THE CIVIL COMMITMENT IN THE UNITED STATES

Three major civil commitment programs have been established in the United States in the last thirty years: the California Civil Addict Program (CAP), the New York Civil Commitment Program (CCP), and programs under the federal Narcotic Addict Rehabilitation Act (NARA). The intent and the enabling legislation for these programs were quite similar, but their implementation and outcomes were different in many respects (McGlothlin & Anglin in press). In general, similar procedures were mandated for all three programs: diversion during criminal adjudication from incarceration in jail or prison to a narcotics treatment facility or program. There was also provision for the involuntary commitment of addicted individuals who had not been charged with a crime. This provision, however, was used relatively infrequently in the three programs and is not used at all today except in rare instances.

California (CAP)

The commitment procedure stipulated by the 1961 legislation establishing the CAP was straightforward: Any individual who was found by medical examination to be addicted to drugs could be committed to the program. In practice, however, the majority of those committed had been arrested for property crimes or drug trafficking and were diverted from conventional criminal processing. The CAP was administered by the California Department of Corrections, which employed rehabilitation professionals as well as correctional staff. The seven-year commitment period was divided into two phases: a period of incarceration at a special minimum security facility, the California Rehabilitation Center, followed by parole—monitored release into the community. Addicts could be reincarcerated for infractions of program and parole regulations. During both the incarceration and the parole phases under the Department of Corrections' supervision, the major target of intervention was the drug-using behavior of the individuals committed to the program. Because of reasonably effective monitoring by urine testing, any return to compulsive patterns of narcotics use could be identified early in the relapse and a proper intervention effected (often including a "dry-out" incarceration).

Throughout the 1960s and into the early 1970s, program results were not spectacular, but behavioral outcomes were as good as, or better than, those for other intervention attempts with narcotics addicts. To some extent, overall outcomes were better because the program could be imposed on any identified addict at any time; thus, many antisocial addicts participated who were not likely to enter conventional treatment programs. Most alternative programs attracted only certain segments of the addict population—namely, those who were less antisocial—and then only in certain periods of their involvement with narcotics, usually later in their addiction careers. That the CAP produced equivalent outcomes with less desirable addicts speaks well of the approach.

Evaluation of the California CAP. Two evaluations of the California Civil Addict Program illustrate the effectiveness of civil commitment programs. The first study, conducted by W. H. McGlothlin, M. D. Anglin, and B. D. Wilson (1977), compared (1) addicts admitted to the program and subsequently released into the community under supervision with (2) addicts admitted to the program and discharged after a short time because of legal errors in the commitment procedures. Table 7.1 summarizes the effects of the program on multiple outcome measures. The comparison shows that during the seven years after commitment, the program group reduced daily narcotics use by 21.8 percent, while the discharged group reduced daily use by only 6.8 percent. Furthermore, the program group reported that its criminal activities were reduced by 18.6 percent, while the discharged group reported a reduction of 6.7 percent.

A second evaluation by Anglin and McGlothlin (1985) focused on the program group. From this group, three subsamples were identified according to narcotics use and treatment status at the time of the interview, which was some twelve

Table 7.1
Summary of Mean Precommitment and Postcommitment Status and Behavior for Comparison (C) and Treatment (T) Samples[a]

Status or Behavior	Comparison Period I	II	III	Treatment Period I	II	III	Mean Differences Between Change Scores $(T_{II}-T_I)-(C_{II}-C_I)$ Diff.	T-Ratio	$(T_{III}-T_I)-(C_{III}-C_I)$ Diff.	T-Ratio
Mean arrests per year[b]										
Drug arrests	1.06	0.95	0.67	0.83	0.53	0.70	-.19	1.69	0.26	1.27
Nondrug arrests	1.13	1.18	0.90	1.15	0.80	0.72	-.40	2.82e	-.20	1.29
Parole violations	0.10	0.31	0.32	0.12	0.67	0.16	0.34	5.34e	-.18	2.69e
Mean % of time incarcerated	23.2	50.9	31.7	20.7	50.5	24.5	2.1	0.91	-4.7	1.56
Mean % of nonincarcerated time										
Under legal supervision	31.7	52.6	60.0	35.4	86.1	44.2	29.8	7.16e	-19.5	4.05e
Using narcotics daily	54.5	47.7	28.4	52.8	31.0	20.9	-15.0	3.88e	-5.8	1.49
Dealing drugs (with or without profit)	46.9	38.2	25.1	42.1	28.2	18.4	-5.3	1.41	-1.9	0.47
Employed (full or part time)	44.8	48.8	53.0	50.3	61.5	61.1	7.2	2.09d	2.6	0.65
Alcohol abuse[c]	30.0	36.8	37.4	36.2	39.7	45.5	-3.3	0.88	1.9	0.43
Criminal activities	49.8	43.1	30.5	47.2	28.6	21.0	-11.9	2.91e	-6.9	1.46
Mean no. self-reported crimes/yr.[b]	66	77	52	70	44	33	-36	3.29e	-23	1.88
Mean income ($00) from crime/yr.[b]	45	72	48	49	45	30	-32	2.93e	-23	2.06d
Composite score: % of time alive, not incarcerated, and not using narcotics daily	35.3	27.9	45.9	36.6	36.1	57.2	6.9	2.49d	10.0	2.72e

Note:
Period I   = First narcotic use (N1) to civil commitment (A).
Period II = A to (A + 7 years) the legislated period of commitment.
Period III = (A + 7 years) to time of interview (I).

[a]The percentages in this table are the mean of individual percentages for the respective periods, not the percentage of the overall person-months.

[b]Data on arrests, self-reported crimes, and income from crime are rates per nonincarcerated person-year. Crime income does not include drug dealing, gambling, etc.

[c]Alcohol abuse is defined as drinking at least a six-pack of beer, or a bottle of wine, or seven drinks of liquor over a six-hour period two or more times per week.

[d]Significant beyond the .05 level of confidence.

[e]Significant beyond the .01 level of confidence.

* Source: An Evaluation of the California Civil Addict Program, NIDA, 1977.

years after admission to the program: (1) a maturing-out sample (Winick 1962), (2) a subsequent treatment (methadone maintenance) sample, and (3) a chronic street addict sample.

Figure 7.1 demonstrates the addiction career history of these three groups for four critical periods: (1) the period before commitment to the CAP, (2) the stipulated commitment period, (3) an early postdischarge period, and (4) a later postdischarge period in which the subsequent treatment group entered methadone maintenance (MM). The commitment period is indicated by the dashed line along the lower portion of the figure. The entry to MM is indicated by the letter *M*.

Prior to commitment, the three groups were relatively similar in terms of their levels of daily narcotics use. Admission to the CAP, however, caused a differential change in the level of daily use. The maturing-out sample, approximately 40 percent of the program group, steadily reduced daily narcotics consumption during the commitment period and did not resume addicted use after discharge from commitment. However, at the time of the interview, many in this sample used narcotics occasionally.

The subsequent methadone treatment sample, approximately 30 percent of the program group, showed a large decrease (approximately 25 percent) in daily drug use during the commitment period. However, after discharge, addicted use by this group had reached its precommitment level. Addicted use continued at that level until the group re-entered long-term treatment, this time with methadone maintenance.

The chronic street addict sample, approximately 30 percent of the program group, showed a moderate reduction (approximately 10 percent) in daily narcotics use during the commitment period. However, after discharge, addicted use rose to a level exceeding that reported in the precommitment period[1] and was still high in the year preceding the interview; for that year the chronic street addicts described themselves as addicted 55 percent of their nonincarcerated time. Figure 7.2 shows a similar temporal pattern for levels of criminal activity among the three groups.

These studies have at least two important findings. First, civil commitment as implemented in the California Civil Addict Program reduced daily narcotics use and associated property crime by program participants three times as much as was achieved with similar addicts who were not in the program. Second, while the program's effects differed across three types of addicts, narcotics use and crime were suppressed to some degree in all three groups. Unfortunately, these results were not available to California corrections planners in a timely fashion, and the CAP, although still utilized, decreased in size and programming effort in the late 1970s.

New York (CCP)[2]

During the same historical period as the CAP, the 1959 Metcalf-Volker Narcotic Addict Commitment Act was enacted by New York State. The act provided

Figure 7.1
Percentage of Nonincarcerated Time Using Narcotics Daily: CAP Inactive, Active, and Methadone Subsamples

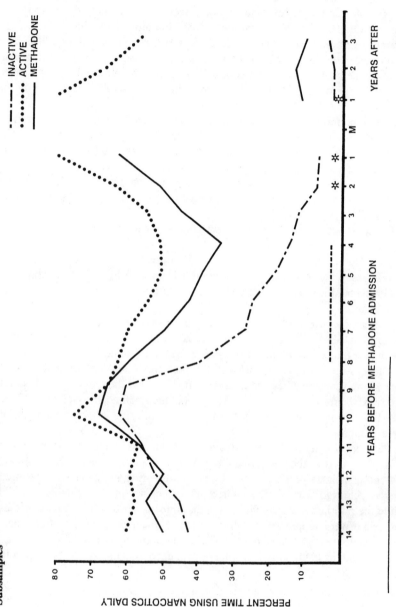

156

Figure 7.2
Percentage of Nonincarcerated Time Involved in Property Crime: CAP Inactive, Active, and Methadone Subsamples

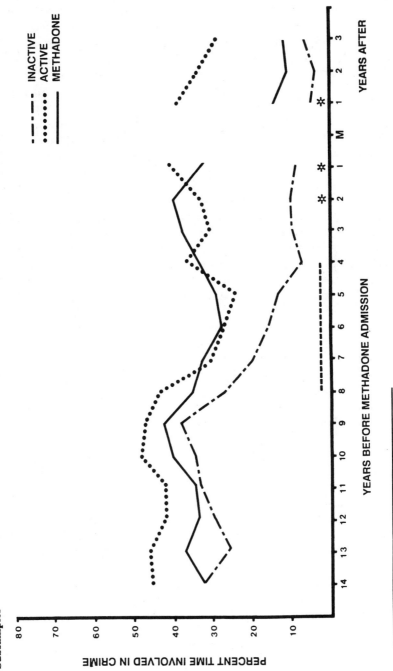

funds to plan and develop facilities for the prevention and control of narcotics addiction. Under the act, narcotics addicts arrested on criminal charges could elect to be transferred to the care of the Department of Mental Hygiene for a maximum period of thirty-six months while the criminal charge was held in abeyance. The intent of the Metcalf-Volker legislation was to reach arrested narcotics addicts who showed a potential for rehabilitation and whose crimes were not serious. The impact of the program proved disappointing. Many eligible addicts preferred the (generally shorter) prison sentence to the longer period of supervision under the treatment program. Furthermore, most addicts who were admitted did not complete the program. Studies reported a high rate of rearrest and abscondence. The program's chief flaw was thought to be its essentially voluntary nature, combined with the lack of adverse consequences for leaving treatment.

Given these results, new legislation was enacted in 1966 and provided that persons convicted of crimes be committed, on proof of addiction, to a compulsory program of rehabilitation and treatment. Narcotics rehabilitation centers and aftercare services providing close supervision were to be operated by the state, and a central agency was created with the power to develop, conduct, and coordinate a comprehensive antiaddiction program.

The key provision of the 1966 legislation was the program of compulsory treatment. Three methods of admission were provided: (1) civil certification of nonarrested addicts, whereby an addict or someone believing a person to be an addict could petition a judge for voluntary or nonvoluntary certification to the program; (2) civil certification of arrested addicts, whereby addicts arrested for certain crimes who satisfied eligibility requirements could apply for civil certi- fication rather than submit to the criminal charge; and (3) civil certification of convicted addicts, whereby defendants found guilty of a misdemeanor or pros- titution and also found to be narcotics addicts were required to be certified to the custody of the narcotics authority. Convicted felons could also be so com- mitted at the discretion of the judge.

A study by the New York Legislative Commission on Expenditure Review in 1971 concluded that the certification process in the civil courts was generally working as the legislature had intended. However, the percentage of arrested or convicted addicts certified over the life of the program steadily declined. The number of addicts convicted of misdemeanors who were certified for compulsory treatment was particularly small, considering that such referral was mandated by law.

The New York CCP was operated through a variety of centers, using different treatment approaches and philosophies. The costs of maintaining these facilities were high, partly because new or revamped facilities required high capital ex- penditures and partly because each center was operated separately, thus pre- venting economies of scale. Staff costs were also high, with a staff-to-patient ratio of 1:1. The average length of patient supervision under the program was two years and one month, of which approximately ten months were residential.

Evaluations of the New York Program. Findings from a number of studies of individual treatment centers conducted by various evaluating agencies are available, and most point out the lack of a cohesive policy guiding the overall program.

A study of abscondence, defined as escape from residential facilities or as "lost to contact" during aftercare, found that the proportion of absconding clients increased steadily during the program period; as the proportion of clients in aftercare increased, so did the proportion absconding (Babst & Diamond 1972).

A 1970 study by the New York State Office of Substance Abuse Services of clients who had been treated for up to three years and discharged by that agency followed the clients for three years after discharge to determine changes in drug use, criminal activity, employment patterns, and involvement in subsequent treatment. Over the three-year follow-up period, the self-reported use of heroin and cocaine declined sharply. However, the number of subjects employed showed little variation, although the mean number of months worked increased slightly, from 8.3 months in the first year to 9.6 months in the third year. Almost half the subjects reported engaging in some kind of criminal activity during the first follow-up year, compared with 26 percent in the third year. The offense that declined the most over the three-year period was burglary.

An evaluation conducted by the New York State Commission of Investigation in 1976 reported dissatisfaction with many aspects of the CCP; the report called for a "sweeping top to bottom review" of the program, with introduction of cost-effectiveness studies, written management procedures, better staff training, more attention to planning for release, and other improvements. Within the next three years the civil commitment residential program was essentially abolished, even though the laws remained on the books. The residential treatment centers were thought to be too expensive and not effective enough in the fight against drug addiction. State policy in subsequent years de-emphasized long-term residential programs in favor of community-oriented treatment, methadone maintenance, and short-term detoxification.

The Federal Narcotic Addiction Rehabilitation Act (NARA)[3]

In response to recommendations from a 1963 Presidential Advisory Commission on Narcotic and Drug Abuse, the federal government passed the Narcotic Addiction Rehabilitation Act (NARA) in 1966. The basic purpose of NARA was to supervise and rehabilitate addicts by providing treatment and aftercare in the addicts' home communities. The NARA legislation contained four titles: Title I authorized the federal courts to impose civil commitment for treatment on any addict charged with certain nonviolent federal offenses. Title II provided for addicts already convicted of a crime (and thus in the custody of the Federal Bureau of Prisons) to be committed to the custody of the Attorney General for treatment in a Bureau of Prisons facility, followed by parole to outpatient aftercare in the community. Title III provided for the involuntary civil commitment of addicts not charged with a federal offense. Title IV authorized funding for the establishment of aftercare services in local communities.

The implementation of NARA was divided between two major government systems, representing two very different sets of treatment assumptions: Titles I and III were implemented through the public health system and Title II through the federal criminal justice system, in particular the Bureau of Prisons. Program participants under Titles I and III were to be given inpatient care for six months at the public health hospitals at Lexington, Kentucky, and Ft. Worth, Texas. On leaving the hospital they would be returned to their communities for aftercare, which was to be provided by the existing community mental health center network through funding provided by Title IV. The client could be declared rehabilitated and discharged only through the courts.

Between 1967 and 1973, 10,151 patients were admitted to the NARA programs. Despite an anticipated wider use, only 5 percent were committed under Title I, Title II resulted in 2 percent of admissions, and the other 93 percent were admitted under Title III.

The initial problems that occurred during the implementation of NARA Titles I and III were caused by a complex and unwieldy administrative structure in which every move of the addict through the system had to be accomplished through the courts; specific reports had to be filed, hearings held, and examinations made. Files on addicts with pending criminal charges or convictions had to be maintained for years. For every hearing or change of status, these addicts had to be transported to and from the courts with full precautions against escape. All of these complexities made the program an administrative nightmare.

Early Title I and III implementation efforts were also hampered by the U.S. attorneys' lack of training in applying the provisions of NARA, by the lack of readiness of the inpatient and outpatient programs at the start of implementation, and by the community social service agencies' unwillingness to serve addicts and their insufficient training in working with addicts.

Title II, the portion of the program administered by the federal criminal justice system, slowly, but steadily increased in size. More institutions for inpatient care were added, and the Bureau of Prisons, the administering agency, developed its own aftercare program. Although Title II was similar to the other titles in most respects, it had an additional feature: The patient could not enter aftercare until he or she had been released from criminal sentence; this required recommendations by both the staff of the inpatient facility and the U.S. Board of Parole. Because many convicted addicts could not meet the eligibility requirements under Title II, the Bureau of Prisons began establishing "non-NARA" treatment units for a variety of drug-dependent offenders, including those dependent on drugs other than narcotics. As of 1979, twenty-three NARA or similar programs operated under Title II. Although the number of clients subsequently declined somewhat, the program was considered a success.

The Title I and Title III programs on the other hand grew rapidly, but were relatively short-lived. After only four years, in 1970, NARA programs under both titles began to decline. These two NARA titles were perceived as expensive, administratively cumbersome, and restrictive, and they were superseded by other federal and community drug treatment programs.

A major contribution to this perception occurred because the way NARA Titles I and III were implemented forced an uneasy cooperation between the criminal justice system and the health delivery system. The cooperation was difficult because guidelines were lacking and because the assumptions of the criminal justice system about addicts were very different from those of the community health centers.

In addition to high costs and administrative difficulties, several more specific problems surfaced in Title I and Title III Implementation.

1. Because the need for care was far greater than the capacity of the program, attempts were made to accept only those addicts most likely to succeed. The resulting high rejection rate caused the court system to lose respect for the NARA program and to withdraw its cooperation to some extent.

2. Addicts were not slow to develop a "racket" in which they shuffled back and forth between the treatment program and the courts until in many cases their files or the courts' witnesses would be lost and the criminal charges would be dropped.

3. Methods of treatment used in the centers were more appropriate for some patient populations than for others; many addicts found the group approach, in which they were expected to "talk about their feelings," to be worse than prison.

4. Courts in some states declared that the NARA treatment centers could not hold patients in treatment if they wanted to leave or keep them under nonvoluntary supervision in the community, thus removing the important compulsory aspect of the civil commitment procedures.

Because of these problems, Titles I and III of NARA were underused and never served the large number of addicts for which they had been designed.

Although many factors contributed to the decline of the NARA programs, the most important was the growth of the drug abuse community treatment network. Before NARA was passed, there were no more than a few community-centered treatment agencies; by the end of 1972 there were sixty-eight community grant programs, many supported by NARA, for the treatment of drug abuse. One exception was methadone maintenance, a treatment modality which had gained popularity during the early years of NARA, but which, under NARA regulations, could not be used. To be discharged from the program as rehabilitated, the client had to be free of addiction to drugs, including methadone. Thus, NARA patients were excluded from a form of treatment that was showing effective results for a broad spectrum of addicts.

Although NARA itself did not succeed, its emphasis on aftercare led to a thriving community treatment network that subsequently made drug abuse treatment more widely available and less expensive.

Summary of Civil Commitment Effectiveness

The general consensus of several authors is that the New York program was pretty much a failure (Inciardi 1988). Titles I and III of the federal NARA also did not fare well on evaluation (Lindblad & Besteman in press). But Title II, administered by the Federal Bureau of Prisons, was more efficacious (Kitchener & Teitelbaum in press). California's CAP was perhaps the most successful of the three efforts (McGlothlin, Anglin, & Wilson 1977). The outcome differences for the various civil commitment programs can, for the most part, be attributed to implementation strategy. While it is possible to develop reasonable social intervention policies that achieve good behavioral outcomes when they are properly applied, methods of implementing the policies can ensure or sabotage success.

An important reason for the lack of success of New York's program was that it was implemented through the state's welfare agency, rather than through an established agency with experience in dealing with addicts and addicted behavior. The federal NARA program had minimal results for Title I and III commitments for similar reasons. In contrast, NARA's Title II program and the California CAP were implemented through the criminal justice system—specifically, the Federal Bureau of Prisons and the California Department of Corrections—and both worked reasonably well—or as well as any other type of intervention has worked for narcotics addicts.

LEGAL COERCION AND CIVIL COMMITMENT ISSUES

Although the California and New York civil addict programs and the federal NARA were in full operation for only about a decade (1965–1975), their development bridged an important period in the national response to the drug abuse crisis of the post–Vietnam War era. The transition was made in that period from mainly a criminal justice system approach for dealing with illicit drug consumers, which had predominated before 1965, to an extensive network of community drug treatment programs, which developed in the 1970s. In fact, the funds allocated to the implementation of the federal Narcotic Addict Rehabilitation Act assisted in the development of many community drug treatment programs (Lindblad & Besteman in press).

EFFECTS OF LEGAL COERCION INTO TREATMENT

With the rise of community-based treatment systems, the original civil commitment concepts and programs fell into disuse, to be replaced by a looser arrangement in which many individuals were referred, but not committed, to drug treatment by the courts or by the probation or parole system. In essence a de facto coercive structure in court, probation, and parole referrals to drug treatment developed; this emergent arrangement was similar to compulsory treatment efforts, but was somewhat more haphazard and less coordinated. Because of this development, more recent research has not involved civil commitment per se, but instead has studied criminal justice system referrals to treatment (Anglin, Brechet & Maddahian 1988). The following section is based on research conducted in southern California by the authors.

Types of Legal Coercion

To find out what types of legal coercion had substituted for the civil commitment procedures of the 1970s, subjects from two cohorts of southern California methadone maintenance clients were asked why they had entered methadone maintenance or therapeutic community treatment programs. The two cohorts were a cohort of 1971–1973 admissions to methadone maintenance and a 1976–78 cross-section cohort of clients in methadone maintenance (Anglin & McGlothlin 1985; Anglin et al. 1989). For each cohort the total number of treatment entries for methadone maintenance and therapeutic communities and the self-reported reasons for entry were determined. The results are shown in Table 7.2.

The 296 subjects in the admission cohort produced 499 methadone maintenance entries and 40 therapeutic community entries. Forty-six percent of the methadone maintenance entries involved a legal reason that motivated entry. These legal reasons could be subdivided into pressure from police, pressure from probation or parole staff, pressure from the courts, and indirect pressure presupposing eventual legal problems. All of these situations represented some level of legal coercion into treatment.

Among those from the admissions cohort who entered therapeutic communities—which represented a less desirable situation for the addicts because they were, in effect, restricted to a residential facility for a period of time—legal coercion was reported as the main reason for 73 percent of the entries. Thus, the threshold level of coercion for motivating someone to enter treatment is higher for therapeutic communities than for methadone maintenance programs.

The same pattern was observed for the 331 men and 236 women in the cross-section sample. In this cohort 36 percent of methadone maintenance entries for men and 21 percent for women resulted, in part, from legal coercion. For therapeutic community entries 66 percent of those for men and 54 percent of those for women involved legal coercion (Anglin et al., 1988).

Other reasons for entering treatment were more varied, and some of the classifications represented broad categories of open-ended types of answers. The answers may have been as vague as a desire to use less heroin. It is clear from the table that, after legal reasons, the most important reason is either an attempt to lower heroin use or a reflection of "burn-out" with the addict life style.

Table 7.2
Major Self-Reported Reasons for Treatment Entries for Southern California Programs

Treatment Program	1971-73 Admissions		1976-78 Cross Section			
	MM	TC	MM		TC	
	Male	Male	Male	Female	Male	Female
No. of Treatment Entries	N = 499	N = 40	N=727	N=598	N=64	N=71
Reasons:	%	%	%	%	%	%
Legal Reasons	46	73	36	21	66	54
Police Pressure	1	-	1	1	-	-
P.O. Pressure	16	23	15	7	22	15
Court Pressure	6	35	2	4	38	32
Indirect Legal Pressure	9	10	15	8	5	7
General Legal Pressure	14	5	3	2	1	-
Other Reasons	54	27	64	79	34	46
Use Less Heroin	29	7	14	16	9	7
External Factors	5	3	8	7	-	4
Reduce Crime	2	-	1	1	-	-
Health Problems	1	-	1	2	1	-
Family & Friends	5	-	5	4	3	13
Spouse Encouragement	N/A	N/A	6	5	1	1
Child Related	N/A	N/A	1	8	-	-
Tired of Life Style	7	15	22	28	14	14
Fear of Readdiction	1	-	1	2	-	-
Others	5	3	6	7	5	7

Note: MM = Methadone Maintenance; TC = Therapeutic Community.
[a]P.O. = Probation or parole officer
Percentages may not total due to rounding

Outcome Effects of Legal Coercion

To test the common belief that people entering treatment under legal coercion do not do as well as volunteer admissions do, the admissions cohort was sub-divided into three smaller groups: those who came in under high legal coercion, those entering under moderate legal coercion, and those who reported no legal coercion and thus entered for "more voluntary reasons." High legal coercion was defined as having both active legal supervision with urine monitoring at entry and self-perceived legal coercion. Moderate legal coercion required active monitoring under legal supervision, but did not require either the testing condition or the self-perception of coercion.

Differences in performance among these groups during their first methadone maintenance treatment episode were examined. Table 7.3 presents behavioral

Table 7.3
During-Treatment Behavior of MM Admissions Entering Under No, Moderate, and High Legal Coercion[a]

Variables	Legal Coercion Level			
	none	moderate	high	F-value
N	84	101	111	
#Months MI-MD	30	31	27	0.42
CJS Legal Supervision	5	83	87	331.21**
Criminal Activities				
Property crime	15.76	18.40	18.64	0.19
Number crimes/mo.	2.59	3.71	2.89	0.58
Crime income/mo.	151.72	360.39	205.29	2.48
Dealing	25.93	23.13	28.48	0.48
Dealing income/wk.	50.93	52.13	40.37	0.11
Drug Involvement				
Narcotics use				
Daily use	11.38	14.96	14.20	0.01
Irregular use	40.91	37.42	38.78	0.18
No use	47.71	47.61	47.02	0.01
Other drug use				
Heavy alcohol use	39.27	40.61	41.08	0.04
Daily marijuana use	14.68	7.10	12.88	1.63
Social Activities				
Working	56.59	57.67	54.50	0.15
Work income/wk.	93.77	101.81	91.74	0.34
Married	40.89	42.63	35.31	0.69
Common-law relationship	33.81	35.92	44.46	1.59

Note: MI = Entry into first treatment episode of MM; MD = discharge from first treatment episode of MM; MI-MD = months of receiving MM during first treatment.
[a]Unless otherwise noted, all measures represent percent of nonincarcerated time in the indicated status.
[b]$p < .001$

variables under the three levels of legal coercion. As can be seen, no significant differences were found for the period during treatment other than for the percentage of time under criminal justice system supervision.

The difference with respect to supervision level is to be expected because it is an artifact of the way legal coercion groups were defined. However, in terms of criminal activities, drug involvement, and social functioning, these groups were essentially the same. The three groups cannot be distinguished in terms of these behaviors.

Since the groups cannot be differentiated other than on the level of coercion used to bring them into treatment, the findings have important social policy implications. The results provide a powerful argument for a general social policy of using legal coercion to bring into treatment as many people as possible by whatever legal means are available. After all, until addicts are exposed to an environment where intervention can occur and are retained for a sufficient period to produce and maintain positive outcomes, change cannot be expected.

The advent of AIDS, where treatment seems to act as a buffer against the probability of infection, is an added incentive for following this policy. Based on the cumulative findings presented above, civil commitment and other forms of legal coercion, when properly implemented, work—and seem to work for a majority of addicts. Such efforts should be considered for much stronger implementation, both in isolation, for addict offenders reluctant to enter community treatment programs, and in cooperation with treatment, as in the federal Treatment Alternatives to Street Crime (TASC) program (Cook et al. 1986).

An overall conclusion from the studies previously discussed is that civil commitment and other drug treatment involving legal coercion, particularly methadone maintenance, are effective ways to reduce narcotics addiction and to minimize the adverse social effects associated with it. How an individual is exposed to treatment seems to be irrelevant. What is important is that the narcotics addict must be brought into an environment where intervention can occur over time. Civil commitment and other legally coercive measures are useful and proven strategies to get people into a treatment program when they will not enter voluntarily. The use of such measures, in a better coordinated and expanded fashion, could produce significant individual and social benefits.[4]

Important Features of Legal Coercion Models

From the accumulated experience of the three major civil commitment programs and from observations of the current system of informal and somewhat uneasy partnership between the criminal justice and treatment systems, a number of features can be identified the presence of which would be necessary in any legally coercive or civil commitment approaches intended to reduce demand for narcotics. Before discussing these, however, two caveats must be considered.

The first caveat is basically a philosophical one. Opiate dependence is a chronic relapsing condition. No social intervention effort has more than modified the time course of addiction or moderated the level of addiction intensity. Lasting cures for opiate dependence do not exist for the large majority of addicts (Anglin & McGlothlin 1985). Thus, expectations for the outcomes of legal coercion or civil commitment programs, like those for other treatment programs for opiate dependence, should be kept at a reasonable level.

A second caveat has to do with the danger of rigidly basing program features and implementation on any one theory. The etiology of opiate dependence is complex, and the population of opiate-dependent individuals is heterogeneous. No single personality or behavioral theory has been particularly helpful in structuring social interventions to modify addict behavior.

Two approaches, however, have been more useful than others in providing a pragmatic basis for designing appropriate interventions (Anglin & McGlothlin 1985). The first is applied social systems analysis—that is, examining all immediate resources pertaining to the individual addict that may be brought into play to help reach an intervention program objective. These resources include the personal resources of the addict: education, individual capabilities, and vocational skills useful for attaining and maintaining employment. Also included are social resources such as family, community support, and other social service agency assistance that can be combined with the ongoing work of the intervention program itself.

The second approach that may be useful when applied in employing legal coercion programs is a behavior modification orientation (Anglin & McGlothlin 1985). Given the time, expense, and debatable effectiveness of counseling and various forms of psychotherapy, a reasonable and cost-effective way to operate an intervention program is to focus only on behavior—the behaviors that are expected within the program, the initial behaviors of persons committed to the program, and the long-range methods by which the initial behaviors can be changed and the desired behaviors achieved and maintained.

Design elements for programs employing legal coercion fall into two categories: administrative and program structure. The importance of the administrative aspects of such programs should not be underestimated. For example, the fact that the New York Civil Commitment Program and Titles I and III of the federal NARA program were placed in inappropriate administrative structures contributed substantially to the lack of demonstrable success of these programs (Brill & Winick in press; Mandell in press). Title II of NARA and the California Civil Addict Program achieved better results because they were assigned to pre-existing unified administrative departments in their respective criminal justice systems. The establishment of new and separate administrative agencies or the use of welfare or other social service agency structures unaccustomed to dealing with an opiate-dependent population should be avoided. The most practical administrative structure is found in probation and parole agencies, which have extensive experience dealing with opiate-dependent individuals. Moreover, their existing administrative apparatus can be easily modified to meet program objectives.

Four structural program features are of greatest importance in legal coercion efforts. First, the period of legal supervision must be a lengthy one, certainly not less than five years. Opiate dependence is a chronically relapsing condition. Except in a minority of cases, several rounds of treatment, aftercare, and relapse are to be expected. The typical successful intervention attains longer periods in which the dependency is controlled and shorter periods of relapse. Because most addicts have had several years of addicted use before coming to the attention of treatment or criminal justice system authorities, it is not unreasonable to expect that several more years will be necessary to control, reduce, or eliminate their drug dependence.

Second, the program must be conducted in two phases. The first must provide a significant level of control—such as a residential stay in a controlled setting or very close monitoring in an outpatient setting—so that the addict can be detoxified from illicit drugs and assessed and an individual program plan can be instituted. The initial period of control, especially in an inpatient setting, need not necessarily be a long one, except for individuals who need educational or vocational training. For many addicts the personal benefits gained from educational and vocational training are important over the long term in preventing or reducing relapse (Anglin et al. 1986).

The second phase is community release under observation, with objective means for monitoring drug use (e.g., urine testing). If the program plan for the opiate-dependent individual includes methadone maintenance or naltrexone blocking treatment in conjunction with legal supervision, then treatment participation should be monitored in the community release phase, and the individual should be tested often and randomly for drug use. Other interventions—such as job training—that might be useful in prolonging the community aftercare phase and preventing relapse should be effected on an individual basis.

The community phase of a legal coercion program must be flexible. Some level of continued drug use is to be expected from the majority of those in community aftercare (McGlothlin, Anglin & Wilson 1977; Anglin & McGlothlin 1985). Authority to deal with program infractions such as occasional drug use should reside with the field agency directly responsible for supervising the addict. Intermittent drug use that does not seriously disrupt the individual's program plan, as well as other program infractions, should be dealt with on an individual basis in the context of the addict's overall adjustment. Any detected readdiction, however, would require immediate placement under strong control, either in a residential setting for detoxification or in a methadone maintenance or naltrexone blocking treatment program. Commission of property crime could also result in return to the controlled environment.

The third structural program feature is a provision for early discharge from the program for good behavior. The minimum period before early discharge is possible cannot be too short; a minimum of two years of community supervision should be completed without relapse to addicted use and with progress in employment and in meeting other social responsibilities adequately. In this regard, the timing of release from external control resides (after a minimal time period) with the addict. Thus, such an approach does not have to be perceived as unnecessarily restrictive of civil liberties.

Finally, any intervention program must undergo regular evaluation to determine its level of effectiveness and to determine whether the changing population characteristics of addicts require compensatory changes in the program. Program staff and policies must be kept current with developments in the treatment of opiate dependence so that suitable new methods can be adopted.

AN INTEGRATED DYNAMIC SYSTEM OF SOCIAL INTERVENTION

What have we learned from these findings, from parallel findings in the research literature, and from the accumulated experience of clinical researchers and practitioners in the field? We know that community treatment, particularly methadone maintenance, produces significant short-term and long-term improvements in levels of drug use and crime (Powers et al. 1988) and, to a lesser degree, improvements in employment and social functioning. We know that criminal justice supervision has similar effects, although not to the same degree, during periods of its imposition (Anglin, Deschenes & Speckart 1987). However, we have not been able to demonstrate long-term effects when such supervision is removed. We also know that the current interaction between legal supervision and community drug treatment is one by which imposed supervision encourages, or even coerces, criminal offenders with drug abuse problems into community treatment.

To date, the interaction between legal supervision and community treatment, while beneficial, has often been haphazard and coincidental. Social implications then, by our current understanding, seem to be fairly straightforward: (1) policy should be developed for the early detection of drug abuse, (2) assessment should be made at the individual level for an integrated system intervention, (3) such intervention should be made available or even imposed, and (4) individuals should be monitored for compliance.

Figure 7.3 presents a simplified model for an integrated dynamic system of social intervention for drug abuse. The figure delineates three aspects of the model: (1) the level of addiction, moving from the global perspective of the general population to a level addressing the most recalcitrant of drug-abusing offenders; (2) the intervention strategies that are reasonable to apply at each level; and (3) the movement of drug-using individuals through the various levels of addiction and the points at which practical strategies can be applied to these individuals.

First, the levels of addiction need explication. The most global level, of course, is that of the general population; most individuals either do not become involved with illicit drugs or do so in a limited way. Of those who ever try an illicit drug, a small proportion escalate their use to a casual or even regular level for a period

Figure 7.3
Dynamic System of Intervention Integration

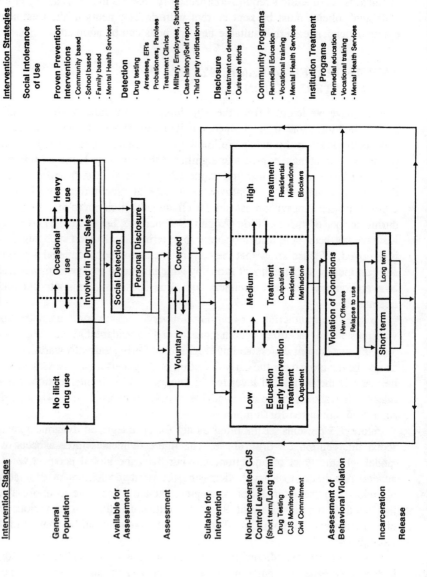

of time. From this group, certain individuals escalate into habitual, dependent, or addicted use, and the proportions of those doing so vary depending on the particular drug with which they become involved.

The first problem for a rational intervention approach is detection of those using. Detection typically occurs either through social agencies or by self-disclosure. Social agencies where detection occurs include hospital emergency rooms, where a certain proportion of cases are brought in because of problems associated with drug use; criminal justice enforcement agencies, where arrestees show extremely high levels of drug use (Carver 1986); and third parties such as employers, parents, or school officials who have reason to suspect drug abuse. Detection by self-disclosure occurs when drug use becomes a problem for an individual who discloses to a third party or seeks treatment.

Once a drug user has been identified, careful assessment should be made of the user's drug use history, current level of use, and problems existing because of the use of drugs. Such assessment should be designed to (1) allow a choice of intervention strategies that includes both community treatment (imposed, if necessary) and criminal justice alternatives and (2) provide for enough flexibility and sufficient ancillary services to achieve the highest probability of success in both short- and long-term behavior change.

The social intervention efforts proposed in the integrated dynamic system depicted in Figure 7.3 involve various levels of criminal justice supervision as well as various levels of community treatment intervention. On the criminal justice side, the lowest levels of intervention may involve diversion of individuals from court processing into treatment; the imposition of treatment as a condition of probation, as a condition of early release from incarceration, or as an adjunct to parole after incarceration; or the imposition of treatment as a condition of remaining unincarcerated should a violation of parole or early release conditions be detected. On the community treatment side, interventions can range from simple educational approaches or outpatient counseling to methadone maintenance and other pharmacotherapies to residential treatment. The integration of these two dimensions of intervention can provide nearly any level of monitored control and intensity of treatment that may be desired for a given individual.

One concept embedded in this model needs further exposition. Involvement with drugs can be a chronic condition that requires protracted intervention to resolve. This prolongation is particularly evident in the treatment of narcotics addiction, where ten- to thirty-year histories of abuse are not uncommon. The treatment outcome studies on which this model is partially based indicate that long-term investment in habilitation or rehabilitation will be necessary in many cases. Some proportion of drug users will require a number of years of treatment, or even permanent case management in treatment. In addition, for most drug-using individuals, there are periods of control in which prosocial behavior becomes established, but these periods can be interrupted by conditions that produce relapse. The model proposed here is designed to anticipate and intervene early in the relapse cycle. Under such real-world conditions, it is evident that monitoring the behavior of drug offenders is necessary, not only to sustain the prosocial gains obtained from successful interventions, but also to identify potential relapse conditions early in the cycle so that additional assessments can be made for revised intervention strategies. The lines and arrows connecting the various states in the model depict the flow of constant monitoring and the dynamic intervention strategy as it applies to individuals coming through the system.

While it is always hoped that any one intervention will produce results, the model also allows for a flexible response so that if the original intervention strategy is not producing the desired results, a higher level of control with a greater intensity of treatment can be applied. For example, at the lower levels of drug involvement, simple diversion with criminal justice monitoring that includes drug testing and/or community treatment intervention involving education or outpatient counseling can be required for a predetermined period of time. If, under these conditions, individuals can demonstrate for a sufficiently long period that personal control has been achieved, then these constraints can be removed. At the other extreme, for the chronically relapsing offender, intense legal supervision after a period of incarceration or inpatient treatment may be necessary, together with a high intensity of community treatment such as methadone maintenance or residential care. The individual will also need very careful monitoring for a longer prescribed period, during which the individual may demonstrate sufficient control so that constraints can be removed.

The model proposed here is similar in a number of respects to that used by the mental health delivery system in managing the chronically mentally ill. Reasonable goals are to minimize the numbers of individuals entering higher-restriction states, to minimize the more serious and costly options of long-term incarceration or residential treatment, and to maximize time in the community with behavior at an acceptable level. For many drug-abusing offenders, this process may be accomplished in a few years; for others, long-term intervention or lifetime case management may be necessary.

With the social policies now in place, all the elements for developing the proposed system are available (see note 4). The criminal justice system has relied on community treatment since treatment became generally available. Community delivery of drug treatment has matured from a sparse scattering of programs developed in the late 1960s and early 1970s to a well-established nationwide network. However, despite the advances of the last two decades, a number of problems will have to be resolved before the system is sufficiently efficient and effective.

The first and most serious of these problems is the current level of funding of treatment programs. At present, there are long waiting lists for treatment slots in most communities. This situation can be remedied partly by an increase in funding for such slots and partly by the provision of other resources to enhance the current delivery system. Such resources would include better salaries for practitioners, better continuing education resources, and greater access to ancillary resources such as educational and vocational programming. Any increases in funding and training must not be temporary phenomena, but instead must represent a long-term commitment to dealing with the treatment of drug abuse.

Second, no widespread outreach efforts are in place to induce drug abusers to come into treatment voluntarily. Such efforts would certainly increase the population in treatment at a lesser implementation cost—especially in terms of judicial expense—than legal coercion or civil commitment requires. In this respect, studies have shown that outreach efforts, particularly since the advent of AIDS, can successfully bring more voluntary entrants into treatment—if the intended population is reached and if treatment is accessible.

Without these two changes, increases in legal coercion or civil commitment efforts would be appropriate only for a limited number of addicts who are unlikely to enter treatment otherwise and who are sufficiently problematic in their behavior to warrant criminal justice system involvement.

The criminal justice system presents different problems. Many members of this system have not been educated to the benefits of community treatment; a substantial number may believe that community treatment is ineffectual or coddles the addict and may sabotage the process because of these beliefs. In addition, the communication and coordination between the criminal justice system and the community treatment system must be improved. Members of these systems need to move out of their adversarial stance toward the realization that by collaborating in producing the desired behavior changes, they can significantly improve outcomes for individuals under their care and for society as a whole.

CONCLUSION

The overall processes related to the cessation of narcotics use, or maturing out, are probabilistic and time-related ones (Winick 1962; Anglin et al. 1986; Brecht et al. 1987). A small, but accumulating percentage of identified addicts will stop using narcotics on an addicted basis in each year after intervention. Some parameters that differentially influence that percentage can be specified, but their effect is not very large in the short term. The chronic relapsing nature of narcotics addiction requires a long-term monitoring effort like civil commitment or other legal coercion efforts in combination with community treatment so that the percentage ceasing addicted use in any year can be maximized and the duration of individual addiction careers—and their cost to society—can be minimized.

The integrated model, while initially proposed for heroin addicts, should be considered for intervention with abusers of other drugs—for example, alcohol and cocaine. Application of the model to abusers of other drugs, while reasonable at the construct level, should proceed carefully by including relevant research findings and planning for evaluation research in any proposed implementations.

NOTES

This research was supported in part by the National Institute of Justice under Grants 86-IJ-CX-0069 and 87-IJ-CX-0042 and by USPHS Grant DA-04268 from the National

Institute on Drug Abuse. Further support was obtained from Contract D-0001-8 from the California Department of Alcohol and Drug Programs.

We would like to thank Kean Mantius for her editorial assistance and Tina Stewart for manuscript preparation.

1. This high rise in use corresponded to a period of high heroin availability in the United States. This period is indicated by asterisks along the lower portion of the figure.

2. Material in this section is summarized from Brill and Winick (in press).

3. Material in this section is summarized from Lindblad and Besteman (in press).

4. Although the first laws permitting involuntary treatment of opiate addicts were enacted in the nineteenth century, it was not until the California and New York civil commitment legislation in the late 1960s that enough addicts were committed under involuntary treatment laws to produce court tests of the constitutionality of such legislation.

Civil commitment represents a substantial deprivation of liberty for the individual. The constitutionality of civil commitment must be discussed in terms of society's intent. Are we committing addicts because addiction itself is a crime? Because the use of illicit drugs is a crime? To protect addicts against themselves? To restrict social damage related to addiction, such as increased nondrug-related crime and the "spreading" of addiction to others? How do we define "addiction" or "treatment"?

After civil commitment legislation was enacted in California and New York, the courts were called on to decide whether involuntary treatment was constitutional. Both the California and New York courts decided that it was. These decisions were heavily influenced by statements made by the U.S. Supreme Court in *Robinson v. California*, 370 U.S. 660 (1962). Although the constitutionality of civil commitment was not at issue in the *Robinson* case, the court stated (in dictum) that a state might establish a program of compulsory treatment for opiate addicts, either to discourage violation of its criminal laws against narcotics trafficking or to safeguard the general health or welfare of its inhabitants. Possibly because the constitutionality of civil commitment was not an issue in the case at hand, the court did not examine thoroughly the constitutional issues involved in its statement. The California and New York courts, relying on the dictum in the *Robinson* opinion, do not appear to have explored the issues thoroughly either.

At present, then, we have a number of legal opinions on the record saying that states may establish programs to coerce or commit addicts to treatment without their consent; however, none of these opinions provides a thorough explication of the constitutional basis for such programs. (*Source*: Rosenthal in press.)

REFERENCES

Anglin, M. D.; Brecht, M.; and Maddahian, E. 1988. Pre-treatment characteristics and treatment performance of legally coerced versus voluntary methadone maintenance admissions. *Criminology* 27(3):537–57.

Anglin, M. D.; Brecht, M. L.; Woodward, J. A.; and Bonett, D. G. 1986. An empirical study of maturing out: Conditional factors. *International Journal of the Addictions* 21:233–46.

Anglin, M. D.; Deschenes, E. P.; and Speckart, G. 1987. The effect of legal supervision on narcotic addiction and criminal behavior. Paper presented at the annual meeting of the American Society of Criminology, Montreal, November 1987.

Anglin, M. D., and McGlothlin, W. H. 1985. Methadone maintenance in California: A decade's experience. In *The yearbook of substance use and abuse*. Vol. 3, ed. L. Brill and C. Winick, 219–80. New York: Human Sciences Press, Inc.

Anglin, M. D.; Speckart, G. R.; Booth, M. W.; and Ryan, T. M. 1989. Consequences and costs of shutting off methadone. *Addictive Behaviors* 14:307–26.

Babst, D. V., and Diamond, S. 1972. *Abscondence trends for NACC certified clients*. New York: Narcotic Addiction Control Commission.

Brecht, M. L.; Anglin, M. D.; Woodward, J. A.; and Bonett, D. G. 1987. Conditional factors of maturing out: Personal resources and preaddiction sociopathy. *International Journal of the Addictions* 22(1):55–69.

Brill, L., and Winick, C. In press. The New York civil commitment program. In *The compulsory treatment of opiate dependence*, ed. W. H. McGlothlin and M. D. Anglin.

Carver, J. A. 1986. Drugs and crime: Controlling use and reducing risk through testing. *NIJ Reports*, SNI 199, September/October. Washington, D.C.: U.S. Department of Justice.

Cook, L. F.; Weinman, B. A.; et al. 1986. Treatment alternatives to street crime. In *The compulsory treatment of drug abuse: Research and clinical practice*, NIDA Research Monograph 86. DHHS Pub. no. (ADM) 88-1578. Rockville, Md.: NIDA.

Drug Abuse Council, ed. 1980. *The facts about drug abuse*. Final report of the Drug Abuse Council. New York: Free Press.

Duster, T. 1970. *The legislation of morality: Law, drugs, and moral judgment*. New York: Free Press.

Eldridge, W. B. 1962. *Narcotics and the law: A critique of the American experiment in narcotic drug control*. New York: American Bar Association and New York University Press.

Goldberg, P. B., and Meyers, E. J. 1980. The influence of public understanding and attitudes of drug education and prevention. In *The facts about drug abuse*, ed. Drug Abuse Council. New York: Free Press.

Inciardi, J. A. 1988. Compulsory treatment in New York: A brief narrative history of misjudgment, mismanagement, and misrepresentation. *Journal of Drug Issues* 18(4):547–60.

Kitchener, H. L., and Teitelbaum, H. E. In press. A review of research on implementation of NARA Title II in the Federal Bureau of Prisons. In *The compulsory treatment of opiate dependence*, ed. W. H. McGlothlin & M. D. Anglin.

Lindblad, R. A., and Besteman, K. J. In press. A national civil commitment program for treatment of drug addiction. In *The compulsory treatment of opiate dependence*, ed. W. H. McGlothlin and M. D. Anglin.

Lindesmith, A. R. 1965. *The addict and the law*. Bloomington, Ind.: Indiana University Press.

McGlothlin, W. H.; Anglin, M. D.; and Wilson, B. D. 1977. *An evaluation of the California civil addict program*. National Institute on Drug Abuse Services Research Monograph Series. DHEW Pub. no. (ADM) 78-558. Washington, D.C.: U.S. Government Printing Office.

McGlothlin, W. H., and Anglin, M. D. In press. *The compulsory treatment of opiate dependence*. New York: Haworth Press.

Maddux, J. F. 1986. Clinical experience with civil commitment. In *The compulsory treatment of drug abuse: Research and clinical practice*. NIDA Research Monograph 86. DHHS Pub. no. (ADM) 88-1578. Rockville, Md.: NIDA.

Mandell, W. In press. Evaluation of the federal civil commitment program for narcotics addicts. In *The compulsory treatment of opiate dependence*, ed. W. H. McGlothlin and M. D. Anglin.

Meyers, E. J. 1980. American heroin policy: Some alternatives. In *The facts about drug abuse*, ed. Drug Abuse Council. New York: Free Press.

Musto, D. 1973. *The American disease: Origins of narcotics control*. New Haven, Conn.: Yale University Press.

New York Office of Drug Abuse Services. 1976. *Three Years Later: A follow-up of decertified ODAS Clients*. New York: Author.

Powers, K.; Hser, Y.; Hanssens, D. M.; and Anglin, M. D. In press. Measuring the long-term effects of public policy: The case of narcotics use and property crime. *Management Science*, in submission.

Rosenthal, M. P. In press. The constitutionality of involuntary civil commitment of opiate addicts. In *The compulsory treatment of opiate dependence*, ed. W. H. McGlothlin & M. D. Anglin.

Trebach, A. S. 1982. *The heroin solution*. New Haven, Conn.: Yale University Press.

Weil, A. 1972. *The natural mind*. Boston: Houghton Mifflin.

Winick, C. 1962. Maturing out of narcotic addiction. *U.N. Bulletin on Narcotics* 14: 1–7.

Chapter 8

Intervention Strategies for Youthful Drug Abusers

Alfred S. Friedman and George Beschner

Adolescent drug abuse is acknowledged to be a major national problem, yet little is known about adolescent drug treatment programs and their effectiveness. More research needs to be done on treatment effects to determine *what* treatment works for *whom*.

The challenge is not so simple. To understand adolescent drug abuse and how to treat it, one must understand the nature of adolescence, a time of experimentation and defiance. One also must understand the tremendous influence of peer pressure; the damaging effects of living in a family where the children are either misused or not properly supervised, or where the parents are poor role models, or where the children may be exposed to substance-abusing role models; and the provocative appeal of the drugs themselves.

Adolescence is a complicated and often a chaotic phase of life, involving efforts to resolve the counterdependency struggle with parents, the challenge of the initial efforts to make the heterosexual adjustment, and the challenge of graduating from high school and of planning or starting a career.

Of particular concern (for treatment) are the compulsive drug users who have serious personal problems and take drugs to avoid reality (the real problems in their life situation) or to get relief from psychic pain, anxiety, tensions, anger, etc. Unable to handle the pressure and responsibilities of growing up, many of these adolescents are confused and have a low self-image.

On the other hand, we have observed that many drug-using adolescents are more satisfied with their social life and tend to have more peer and heterosexual relationships than do those who do not use drugs. For youngsters who use drugs to relieve the boredom they feel about school, attending school while "high" or while involved in drug use results in diminished school performance and failure. One controlled study shows that drug use contributes to a very significant degree to dropping out and to failing to graduate from high school—regardless of whatever other school behavior or learning problems the youngster might have.[1] Failure in school and problems with school authorities compound the problems that most of these adolescents already have in their relationships with their parents. This adds to other conflicts that already exist in the family. In a national survey that we conducted of adolescent drug treatment programs, 49 percent of the clients reported at the time of admission to treatment that there were serious conflicts in their families and gave this as a reason for coming into treatment.[2]

The position of the adolescent drug abuser vis-à-vis parents and other adult figures (such as treatment personnel) involves mistrust, misunderstanding, and fear of restriction, punishments, rejection, or abandonment.

Drawing from the literature and our own research, this chapter reviews what is now known about adolescent drug abusers and their treatment needs and about what kinds of adolescent treatment programs are available. It also reviews what has been learned about the effectiveness of adolescent programs.

Compared to the heroin addiction epidemic of the 1960s and early 1970s, adolescent drug abuse today is more broadly based; it cuts across all socioeconomic strata and involves a wider array of chemical substances. It also is the result of complex underlying problems inextricably bound to the psychology of adolescence, which is itself a challenge.

Six percent of high school seniors in the United States are *daily* users of either alcohol or marijuana. The majority of adolescents who come to drug treatment use more than one illicit substance. Marijuana is frequently used in combination with other substances. Approximately 57 percent of high school seniors had at some time in their lives experimented with marijuana, and some 20 percent had used stimulants. In addition, seniors had experimented with many other drugs—cocaine (16 percent), methaqualone (10 percent), tranquilizers (13 percent), barbiturates (10 percent), phencyclidine (PCP) (6 percent), and inhalants (19 percent).

Research shows that adolescents use drugs for a host of reasons. Drugs (1) are often readily available; (2) provide a quick, easy, and cheap way to feel good; (3) offer a means of gaining acceptance in peer relationships; (4) may help modify unpleasant feelings, reduce disturbing emotions, alleviate depression, reduce tension, and aid in coping with life pressures.[3]

For some adolescents, experimentation with drugs is merely part of a rite of passage through their challenging teen years.[4] Most adolescent drug users fall into a category called "experimental," "situational," or "recreational" users. Such individuals, influenced to use drugs mainly by their peers, tend to use drugs infrequently and in small amounts to get high, have fun, and relax. They generally do not have serious problems with drugs or require treatment. For others, however, drug use goes well beyond experimentation and signals serious adjustment problems.[5] These are generally compulsive, dedicated users with serious personal problems. They rely on drugs as self-medication to cope with their problems, not unlike some adults.[6] These adolescents—possibly as much as 5 percent of teens aged 14 to 18—have serious drug and drug-related problems and generally need treatment.

Most teenage experimenters will not become habitual users or require treatment for drug-related problems. However, a great many will.

Why do some youngsters become more seriously involved in using drugs than others do? Why do some become drug dependent? There is no single answer. Reasons for drug involvement and drug dependency are varied and complex. There are many different types of drug use patterns and many different types of drug users. One potent factor that seems to lead to drug dependency in adolescents as well as in adults is the psychoactive or tranquilizing effects of drugs that provide relief for pain.

Most popular drugs relieve stress and anxiety. Tranquilizers have become one of the most accepted and widely prescribed types of drugs because they calm anxiety. Heroin, like morphine and other opiate derivatives, is effective as a tranquilizing agent, also relieving feelings of worthlessness and despair. For addicts in ghetto communities, heroin provides a feeling of ''normalcy''—a chance to feel good about oneself and escape the feelings of hopelessness that come from living in poverty and lacking opportunities. Cocaine produces stimulation and euphoria. Marijuana can produce a dreamy, relaxed feeling similar to the effects that some get from alcohol. Alcohol can produce a wide range of effects—it can depress, stimulate, tranquilize, or agitate, depending on the personality of the user, the environment, and the concentrations and mixtures used.

So is it any wonder that in facing problems that sometime seem insurmountable, many adolescents would find drugs appealing? Once they start using drugs to relieve anxiety and stress and to escape from life's pressures, there is an increased likelihood of returning to such use, especially if problems persist and there are no alternative ways of relieving pressures and pain.

Drug use, however, can and usually does exacerbate the problems, especially if a youngster's performance is impaired or his/her behavior changes—which is likely with drugs. The youngster experiences more pressure from parents and sometimes from school authorities and, as a result, is more likely to seek relief/escape through drugs.

Fewer adolescent abusers than adult addicts are physiologically addicted to narcotics. Consequently, their treatment is less likely to include the medical procedures that accompany addiction, such as detoxification, pharmacological substitutions (e.g., methadone), and the use of narcotic blocking agents (e.g., naltrexone).

About two-thirds of the adolescent males in residential treatment and one-half of the males in outpatient drug treatment (OPDT) committed crimes during the year prior to treatment. While they may often engage in minor stealing and selling of drugs, it is unlikely that they will become imprisoned or come into regular contact with the more hard-core criminal elements. As might be expected, adult drug abusers and addicts are more likely to have been arrested, convicted, and jailed. Thus, adolescent drug users who either seek or are referred to treatment usually present a multiplicity of problems beyond drug use per se. In any attempt to treat adolescent drug abusers, attention must be given to these underlying problems and usually to the family situation as well. Educational needs and the need for parental and family support, as well as the need to provide education assistance and alternative activities and interests, play a large role in the treatment of adolescents.

In one study of high school students, drug users were more likely to be involved in gang activity, to have more problems with police (including arrests for offenses of violence), and to have more problems in school (more grades repeated, less "enjoyment" and "satisfaction" with school, more lack of motivation to achieve in school, more suspensions or expulsions from school). Adolescent drug users reported more time spent "hanging out" with peers, more time sleeping, less time discussing problems with parents, less time reading or watching TV or doing homework, and less time participating in religious activities. They expressed more satisfaction with the number of friends and the amount of social contact they had. Thus, these adolescent drug users appeared to be more dissociated from the adult world and more involved with their own particular peer group.[7]

Since adolescence is a critical developmental period of life, heavy drug use and involvement in a drug life style have a greater negative impact on the development, the maturation, and the future of adolescents than they do on adults. Drugs divert the adolescent's interest, energy, and effort from more constructive life tasks and challenges.

FAMILY

Families of adolescent drug users differ significantly from families in which the adolescent offspring either do not use drugs or only have used marijuana experimentally. In contrast to experimental drug users or nonusers, adolescents with serious drug problems come from families with the following characteristics:

- There is more discrepancy between how the parents would ideally like their children to be and how they perceive them actually to be.[8]
- Parents are perceived as having relatively less influence than peers do. Both parents are perceived to be more approving of drug use.[9]
- Offspring perceive less love and support from both parents, particularly fathers.[10]

Kandel reported that adolescent initiation into the use of illicit drugs, other than marijuana, appears to be strongly related to parental influences.[11] The adolescent's feelings of closeness to the family predicted to the low likelihood of initiation into these other illicit drugs, while strict controls imposed by parents and parental disagreement about discipline predicted to their likelihood of initiation. Use of drugs by parents was also found to be an important predictor.

Some of the findings of the National Youth Polydrug Study on the relationship of family factors to adolescent drug abuse are as follows:

- Adolescents whose parents had drug problems, alcohol problems, psychiatric problems, or problems with the law were found to be more heavily involved in drug abuse than were adolescents whose parents were not reported to have such problems.
- There is a significant positive correlation between the number of problems reported in the family and the number of different types of drugs abused by the adolescent offspring.
- There is less shared authority and poorer communication in the family.[12]
- There is less spontaneous problem solving in structured family interaction tasks.[13]

By the time parents discover the adolescent's drug problem, it is likely to be serious. Like their adult alcoholic counterparts, teens confronted with their drug abuse almost always resort to denial, regardless of how long or how frequently they have been using drugs. Some parents "buy into" this denial for a time, wanting to believe that there is not a problem; some over-react and thus risk worsening the problem they are hoping to correct. Eventually, most parents begin to face the truth rationally and find their children's refusals to do so hard to understand.

On finding that their children are using drugs, many parents feel hurt, betrayed, or guilty. Some feel helpless because they have a limited understanding of adolescent rebellion or of drug abuse and do not know where to turn or what to do. Others feel frustrated because after learning about the problem and reaching out for help, they find there is no simple (or "right") approach or answer. Each family's problem is unique in some ways.

In a study by Glickman and Utada,[14] the most prevalent concerns expressed about parent(s) by the clients in both outpatient and residential treatment settings were these: "objects to my friends," "is disappointed in me," "complains too much," and "does not trust me." Half of the adolescents claimed ten of thirty-five items on a family problems list. Their primary family concerns were as follows: "the family is too curious about what I do" (58 percent residential, 40 percent outpatient), "fights with brothers and/or sisters" (48 percent residential, 34 percent outpatient), and "my friends are not welcome at home" (47 percent residential, 34 percent outpatient).

In addition to drug and alcohol problems and family problems (conflicts with parents, etc.), the reasons given by adolescent clients in the National Youth Polydrug Study (N = 1,750) for applying for treatment were (in rank order): (2) school-related problems (39.5 percent), (3) legal problems—involvement in criminal justice system (35.3 percent), and (4) emotional or psychiatric problems—need for counseling, etc. (27.7 percent). Almost a third (32.7 percent) of the adolescents surveyed had experienced one or more previous overdose episodes, 15.9 percent had made one or more previous suicide attempts, and 20.4 percent had received treatment for a mental health problem on one or more occasions.

On admission to residential and outpatient treatment programs, adolescents were asked to identify (from a list of thirty-five) their own personal problems. During this initial phase of treatment, most of the adolescents identified negative feelings/attitudes they had about themselves. For example, the most prevalent problems identified by adolescents in residential programs were "hard to express feelings" (77 percent), "feeling bored" (72 percent), and "getting angry often" (58 percent). Adolescent outpatient clients, at admission, most often reported "feeling bored" (63 percent), "feeling restless" (56 percent), and "daydreaming a lot" (50 percent). Obviously, it is important for counselors to assess how adolescents, on entering treatment, feel about themselves; to gain some impression of their self-concept; and to be prepared to engage these clients about feelings of alienation, anger, loneliness, and self-doubt.

Thus, adolescent drug users who seek or are referred to treatment usually present a multiplicity of problems beyond drug use per se. In any attempt to treat adolescent drug abusers, attention must be given to these underlying problems and usually to the family situation as well.

Parents who decide, or are required by the school or the court, to seek professional treatment for their children have several options. A clergyman, family physician, or school counselor may be able to provide some guidance for the family in finding an appropriate resource since it is likely that professional help will be needed from someone who is trained to treat adolescent substance abusers. Initially, the family should seek the advice of someone who has an understanding of the overall problem and who can provide information about the various treatment options that are available. Good diagnosis and a careful evaluation of the youngster are the keys to selecting an appropriate approach and should be done before treatment is initiated. Substance abusers are more likely than nonabusers to be depressed, to have other emotional and psychological problems, or to have serious physical problems. In developing a treatment plan, these problems, in addition to family history and the youngster's social functioning, must be considered.

If youngsters are not motivated to seek treatment and are outside the control of their parents, there are few treatment options. In extreme cases they can be legally committed to a hospital (inpatient) facility which provides diagnostic services, detoxification treatment, and psychological counseling, if such a facility exists in the community. In some states it is difficult to work out the involuntary commitment procedure.

In recognition of the growing need for detoxification and emergency treatment for overdoses, private hospital (inpatient) treatment programs have been started in many communities across the country. But these programs are very expensive, costing as much as $5,000 per patient per month, and, therefore, they are available only to families with comprehensive health insurance. Some state and local governments support public inpatient treatment programs which are less expensive, but the capacity of these programs is usually limited.

Most hospital programs offer only short-term care, essentially to treat crisis situations and to diagnose medical and psychological problems. If long-term treatment is needed, the hospital will usually try to refer adolescents to less expensive outpatient, daycare, or residential (nonhospital) programs.

Nationally, only a small number of residential treatment programs are designed especially for adolescent substance abusers, and, therefore, adolescents are likely to receive the same treatment that adults do. Twelve percent of adolescent drug clients enter residential programs. Compared to adolescents who enter outpatient programs, residential clients generally (1) have a lower educational level, (2) are more likely to have been referred to treatment by the criminal justice system, and (3) are more likely to have had previous treatment episodes. Patients usually stay in residential treatment for six months to one year. Compared to inpatient programs, residential programs are far less costly, averaging between $9,000 and $10,000 per year. Residential programs generally provide individual and group therapy, educational classes, parent participation, confrontational meetings, recreational activities, and shared responsibility for managing the facility; they generally lack the medical, psychological, and diagnostic services offered by hospital programs.

Residential programs may not be appropriate for teens who are in treatment against their will. Most do not have closed, locked wards to prevent youngsters from running away. Many are located in remote areas to discourage escape attempts, but these locations make it difficult for parents to be involved in regular family sessions. For a number of reasons, residential programs tend to have high dropout rates (about 80 percent leave in the first few months), but those who do stay in these programs are likely to show improvement; progress is roughly proportionate to the length of time in treatment.[15]

Daycare treatment programs offer many of the same services that residential programs do, but without overnight accommodations. Some school systems support alternative education programs or daycare programs for substance-abusing high school students. The drug treatment programs operate during school hours, serving adolescents until they are drug-free and able to return to regular classrooms. Five percent of young clients participate in these daycare programs, which provide more extended treatment activity than do outpatient clinics. One type of day program—which offers educational services—can lead to high school certificates for dropouts from public school. Unfortunately, only about fifty such programs have been established in the United States.

Almost all communities have outpatient drug treatment and counseling programs or community mental health centers supported by the state, county, or city government. These programs, which treat more than 80 percent of the adolescent substance abusers admitted to treatment, generally provide drug counseling services to adults and adolescents in addition to treating a broad range of psychological and behavioral problems. Outpatient clinics have very few controls and relatively little structure. Thus, patients must be highly motivated to benefit from the counseling provided and must make a personal commitment to attend regularly and participate actively. As in other treatment settings, family participation may be needed for treatment to be effective, and unfortunately few adolescent outpatient programs have family therapy specialists.

Aftercare programs are based on the recognition that the treatment process should not end abruptly at discharge from a daycare, inpatient, or residential program. Aftercare programs usually have professional counselors or other support persons available when problems arise, anxieties build, and peer pressure or temptation to use drugs increases. Some aftercare programs make use of peer groups to provide support during the re-entry process. These groups, consisting of other teens going through recovery, are organized and led by both professional and peer counselors. Teens often feel more comfortable talking openly to peers about their families, friends, and other relationships and also may be more receptive to feedback from their peers.

In our national survey comparing thirty-one adolescent residential programs with forty-three adolescent outpatient programs, we learned the following:

Drug-free outpatient programs devoted more staff time to counseling and psychotherapy, than did residential programs (69 versus 40 percent). DFOPs devoted more staff time to individual counseling and family counseling, and less time to group counseling, medical services, or to educational and recreational programs. The residential counselors utilized "confrontation," "rap sessions" and "assertiveness therapy" more, while outpatient counselors utilized "long-term psychotherapy," "values clarification" and "gestalt therapy," more.

Family participation may be needed for treatment to be effective in outpatient clinics; but unfortunately few adolescent outpatient programs have family therapy specialists.

Counselors in outpatient programs were more likely to have obtained a masters or doctoral degree (54 percent to 29 percent). Counselors in both types of settings perceived the following five characteristics in more than half of their adolescent clients:

1. "consider the use of marijuana and alcohol to be acceptable and normal activity";

2. "have psychological and situational problems which predate their drug use";

3. "are failing in their formal societal roles especially as students";

4. "come to treatment non-voluntarily, someone or some agency pressures them";

5. "do not come to treatment seeking help to stop taking drugs."

The residential counselors agreed with statements 3 and 4 more often than did the outpatient counselors.[16]

On the MOOS Program Environment Scale both clients and staff of residential programs were found to rate their programs more positively than did clients and staff of outpatient programs; in the following specific ways: (1) "encourage and provide more support"; (2) "provide more practical help," such as job training; and (3) "more concern with clients' personal problems." The only COPES factor on which the outpatient programs were perceived as superior to residential programs, was on "spontaneity" ("The program encourages clients to act openly and to express their feelings openly").

THE CLINICAL PICTURE

Thus, the presenting clinical picture at intake to treatment includes poor school performance, lack of interest in extracurricular activities, nonstraight friends, loss of interest in or conflict with family, hostile/aggressive and resistant behavior, brushes with the law, and sometimes physical signs of being "high" or "stoned." They have negative feelings, alienation, anger, loneliness, and self-doubt. There is among them a fairly high rate of suicidal attempts and of crises related to drug overdoses. Counselors view their adolescent clients as presenting many complex problems, requiring different intervention strategies.

These youngsters ostensibly seek pleasure in drugs, and for a period of time, the drugs may work for them, but they are often miserable underneath—they hurt. Sometimes, when you get to know them, you see and hear their pain under their bravado and denial. As they struggle to achieve an identity, they frequently doubt whether they are going to make it in life.

In the early stages of treatment, youngsters are usually defiant, angry, and mistrusting of the adult staff. They can be gotten through this stage, but one has to work fairly long and hard to establish a relationship of trust and to get their cooperation in treatment. After engaging the adolescent client in a relationship of trust, the counselor tries to develop the experience of "being" and "staying" with the young client, of creating a holding relationship of listening and maintaining a secure treatment frame in which the client can feel safe.

Gradually the counselor helps the young client express intense feelings—which may be under the surface—of fear, rage, sadness, anxiety, worry, frustration, despair, hopelessness, or helplessness. Once these feelings are expressed and in the open, the counselor helps the adolescent to understand them, how and why they came about, and how to deal or cope with them without having to resort to drugs.

Counselors agreed (in our survey) that the following are effective counseling approaches:

1. "An understanding and empathic attitude."
2. "Confronting the client with his/her self-destructive and maladaptive behavior."
3. "Provide emotional support."
4. "Providing practical assistance in solving the client's real life problems."

These clients need to be helped to own the responsibility for causing some of their own problems.

EFFECTS OF TREATMENT (TREATMENT OUTCOME)

Treatment usually has to be *drug-free*, without prescribing a drug for anxiety or depression. Whether one deals directly with the drop problems first and foremost (or requires abstinence as a condition for psychotherapy) or also deals with the other problems may depend on the circumstances of the individual case. (Thus, the treatment usually consists of more than the A-A program.) However, at some point in the treatment process the issue of the client's continuing use of drugs needs to be confronted. Also, most clients need a support system (usually the family, and sometimes a nonusing boyfriend, girlfriend, or some other caring, interested person).

The clinical impressions of many drug counselors and therapists in drug treatment programs is that while it may be difficult to initially engage adolescent polydrug abusers in a constructive therapeutic working relationship, a significant percentage of these young clients *do* get some help from their participation in the treatment programs. The clinicians report that many such clients improve their life situations. Gradually they become less anxious, less tense, less depressed, and less confused—and also less defensive and challenging, less hostile/aggressive, and less self-destructive. They start to face their problems, to bear some of the pain (a little at a time), and gradually to give up using drugs.

The two large-scale, multiprogram studies of drug treatment outcome, the DARP and the TOPS studies,[17] reported significant reductions in drug use for adolescent clients in drug-free outpatient treatment, except for the use of alcohol and marijuana. There was, in fact, a reported increase of marijuana use. The DARP and the TOPS studies also reported a significant improvement in employment and a significant degree of "satisfaction" with the treatment programs reported by the adolescent clients of the outpatient drugfree programs.

In the TOPS study, considering only those who stayed in treatment at least three months, there (1) were more daily marijuana users at follow-up (54 percent) than during the year preceding treatment (48 percent), (2) were fewer heavy alcohol users (54 percent prior to treatment versus 41 percent at follow-up), and (3) was less involvement in criminal activities (53 percent before and 36 percent after). About two of five clients reported being "very satisfied" with the treatment they had received.

The TOPS residential program clients fared better: (1) the number of daily marijuana users dropped (from 79 percent of the sample at pretreatment to 12 percent at follow-up), (2) the number of heavy alcohol users declined (from 56 percent to 29 percent), and (3) the number of clients involved in illegal acts declined (from 71 percent to 36 percent). Almost half of the former residential clients were "very satisfied" with the treatment they had received.

Dropping out, rather than completing or graduating, is the rule for most residential treatment programs, for adolescent as well as for adult clients. But some of the dropouts show improvement.

How much of the improvement reported by these two studies was due to the treatment per se and how much was due to other factors (maturation of the subjects, changes in their life situations, etc.) is not clear since none of the studies referred to had a no-treatment control group. (Because of the ethical question involved in deferring or denying treatment to those who apply for help, studies with no-treatment control groups, based on assignment to a waiting list, are difficult to arrange today.)

An evaluation of the effects of a supportive life skills program for court-committed adolescent male substance abusers, conducted in a private vocational high school setting, showed many statistically significant and impressive types of improvement (benefits) at follow-up evaluation. The most pronounced or dramatic degree of improvement was found to occur in decreases in problems related to school. These findings include the following:

- A significant improvement (increase) in surveyed items on attitudes and behavior in relation to school: school enjoyment and satisfaction with classes.

- A decrease in the prevalence of personal problems and a statistically significant decrease in gang-related problems.

- A statistically significant improvement for Rosenberg Self-Esteem Scale items: "I am able to do things as well as other people," "I feel that I am a person of worth. . . . " The summary subscale score for the five positively stated items on the scale also showed an increase (improvement).

- A statistically significant decrease in the number of negative behaviors the subjects reported they engaged in at home within the family context. Similarly, a significant decrease (improvement) in the total negative behaviors score was derived by adding the ratings on the four-point rating scales for each item.

- Regarding legal offenses, there was a statistically significant decrease in property offenses and victim offenses.

- Also observed were statistically significant decreases for two of the substances reported (PCP and hallucinogens) and a significant decrease in the self-reported frequency of getting drunk. There was little change in drug use patterns overall, which, in view of the other positive changes, is surprising.[18]

A recently completed evaluation study compared the outcome for a family therapy method with the outcome for a parent group method.[19] Of the families of 190 adolescent drug abuse outpatient clients, in six different drug treatment clinics, assigned to a family therapy or a parent group procedure, 166 (or 87 percent) were retrieved for follow-up evaluation fifteen months later (after a six-month course of treatment and a nine-month follow-up period). The clients in both groups also were offered individual counseling sessions and peer group counseling sessions, in addition to the type of family treatment to which they were assigned. There was no significant difference between the two groups in the number of individual and group sessions attended by the clients. The mean number of family therapy sessions attended was thirteen, and the mean number of parent group sessions attended was eleven, although a course of twenty-four weekly sessions was offered to each family in each of the two groups.

In 93 percent of the families assigned to family therapy, one or both parents participated; but in only 67 percent of the families assigned to a parent group did one or both parents participate. In this regard, it appears to be more effective for a program to offer the family therapy modality than to offer the parent group modality.

After 65 treatment outcome criteria were analyzed by paired "t" tests, a significant degree of improvement was found, from pretreatment to follow-up, for the parent group method on fifty-five of these criteria and for the family therapy method on fifty-eight of these criteria. This is an impressive improvement, and it included a highly significant degree of reduction in drug use by the clients in both groups. It is not possible, however, to determine how much of this improvement is the result of the participation of the family in treatment since nearly all clients participated in some individual and peer group sessions and since a no-treatment control group was not included in the study.

Only on two of the sixty-five outcome criteria was there a significant difference between the family therapy clients and the parent group clients on the degree of improvement, and these were in favor of the parent group.

COMBINED DISORDERS (OR CO-MORBIDITY)

Many adult drug abusers and addicts have been found to have high rates of psychiatric symptomatology, particularly depression and personality disorders. This is apparently somewhat less true for adolescent abusers than it is for adult abusers. For adult drug and alcohol abusers, a global measure of the severity of psychiatric problems at pretreatment was found by McLellan and his colleagues to be the single best predictor of treatment response, compared to five other types of problems at pretreatment.[20] Those adult abusers and addicts with relatively severe psychiatric symptoms showed lower levels of improvement, or improved relatively little from treatment, unless treated in a psychiatric hospital. On the other hand, abusers with a *low* severity of psychiatric symptoms did quite well, regardless of what type of treatment setting they were treated in. It might therefore not be cost effective to admit such a patient to the hospital. It would appear that a drug abuser with moderately severe or very severe psychiatric problems should be admitted to the hospital unless, at least, the other types of treatment settings (outpatient, daycare and residential) develop special staff well trained to treat psychiatric problems.

The current authors had recently decided to investigate whether the findings regarding treatment outcome for adolescents with combined drug abuse and psychiatric problems would be the same as those reported above for the adult patients. We found, unexpectedly, that there was a tendency for young delinquent male clients referred by the family court to a day-treatment program, to improve *more, rather than less*, when they had reported more psychiatric symptoms at intake. We have three speculations regarding this finding: (1) Relatively few clients in this sample reported severe psychiatric problems; (2) those who were more self-evaluative and more open and revealing regarding disturbing inner thoughts and feelings might have been more trusting, more ready, and better motivated for counseling or therapy; (3) these delinquent boys tend to "act out" and to externalize, rather than to internalize, their frustrations, tensions, anxieties, and problems.

We have recently cross-validated this finding in a study of adolescent drug abusers in six different outpatient drug treatment programs. Only about 25 percent of this sample was referred to treatment from the criminal justice system. We found, again, with this second sample (which was more representative of adolescent abusers usually admitted to outpatient drug-free programs) that those who reported more psychiatric symptoms at pretreatment showed significantly greater improvement at follow-up on seven of eight different treatment outcome criteria. Thus, these findings for adolescents in outpatient programs are not the same as, and possibly the opposite of, those for adults in outpatient programs.

Nevertheless, it must be true for adolescent clients, as well as for adult clients, that different clients require different treatment settings and different programs. Adolescent drug abuse is a complex condition, and the various types of abusers require multiple treatment approaches and a coordinated community network of services. These programs should be more complementary than competitive. Also required are a careful initial differential diagnostic study and a determination of the client's capacity for change and readiness for certain specific treatment methods and treatment goals. It seems important to explore the potential for better patient-treatment matching in treating drug abusers, and very little systematic work of this type has been done.

SUCCESSFUL TREATMENT OF ADOLESCENT DRUG ABUSERS

The relationship to treatment outcome, as measured by reduction in drug use, of specific characteristics and elements of thirty drug-free outpatient programs for adolescents has been reported by the authors of this chapter by analyzing separately two annual client subsamples.[21] The program, not the individual clients, was the unit of analysis. While controlling for differences between programs in terms of their client populations, multiple regression analysis indicated that the following characteristics of programs were found to predict the outcome criterion variable (a summary score of substance use) to a statistically significant degree: (1) treat a large number of adolescent clients; (2) have a special school for school dropouts; (3) have a relatively large budget; (4) employ counselors or therapists who have at least two years' experience in working with *adolescent* drug abusers; (5) provide special services such as vocational counseling, recreational services, and birth control services; (6) use such therapy methods as crisis intervention, gestalt therapy, music/art therapy, and group confrontation; and (7) are perceived by the clients as allowing and encouraging free expression and spontaneous action by clients.

There was a high degree of replication of these findings across the two annual subsamples of clients, and the amount of variance in the treatment outcome criterion variable accounted for by the above-listed program characteristics was quite impressive.

Similar findings were obtained in a comparison study of twenty-two drug-free residential programs. Data were obtained on 2,532 adolescent clients in these programs. The following characteristics of programs were found to predict to a lower case failure rate to a statistically significant degree: (1) the number of years that the counselors had worked in the programs; (2) the number of volunteer staff in direct service (client contact); (3) the proportion of clients receiving bodily and mental relaxation techniques; (4) the counselors' perceptions that their programs accept or encourage relatively more spontaneous personal expressiveness, including expression of anger by clients, in staff-client relationships, but encourage less client "autonomy" (self-sufficiency and independence in regard to making their own decisions); and (5) counselors' reports that providing practical assistance in solving clients' real life problems is useful.

Only two of these program characteristics were found to be associated with successful treatment for both types of treatment settings: (1) the number of volunteer staff and (2) the counselors' reports that the program has a "practical orientation" (provides assistance in solving clients' real-life problems). In addition to the similar findings on two of the program characteristics for both outpatient and residential programs, there was also an interesting similarity in the findings regarding the client (rather than the program) characteristics that predicted to treatment outcome. For both types of treatment settings there was a higher rate of case failure for black clients and a lower rate of case failure for clients in small towns. In regard to client socioeconomic status, the middle-class clients in outpatient programs had a *lower* rate of case failure, while lower-middle-class clients in residential programs had a *greater* rate of case failure. The greater rate of case failure for black clients could possibly be accounted for, at least in part, by a high rate of opiate use, which has often been reported for both adolescent and adult black clients, compared to white clients.

Two of ten client characteristics recorded in the NIDA-CODAP national data file were found to predict, to a significant degree, to the degree of reduction in drug use at the time of discharge from treatment. For adolescent clients admitted to 30 outpatient clinics in each of two calendar years, 1979 (N = 2,509) and 1980 (N = 3,094), these two predictor variables were number of prior admissions and marijuana as the primary drug of abuse. Marijuana as the primary drug of abuse was the only client variable to account for more than 1 percent (4.4 percent) of the variance in the reduction in drug use. The primary marijuana users showed *less* reduction in the amount of drug use and were less often considered to have completed the course of treatment.[22] This finding of less improvement for marijuana users is consistent with findings reported above for the adolescent subsamples of the DARP and TOPS studies. In general, client demographic and background variables, obtained at intake, are not very effective in predicting to treatment outcome.

OUTSTANDING TREATMENT PROGRAMS FOR
ADOLESCENT DRUG ABUSERS

The Door

The Door—a comprehensive, "broad brush," community-based delivery system for adolescents—is possibly the best known and most regarded youth-oriented agency in the country that provides treatment for drug abuse. It has become recognized as a model for comprehensive, holistic, integrated, multi-disciplinary service programs for youth. The staff of this program include drug and alcohol counselors, internists, gynecologists and pediatricians, family planning and sex counselors, nutritionists, nurses, health educators, psychiatrists and psychologists, social workers, caseworkers and mental health workers, lawyers, teachers, craftsmen, youth workers, and educational, job, theater, dance, and music instructors.

The Door treatment program comprises five general components, the most central of which is the counseling services and support activities which include a full range of psychiatric and social services, comprehensive medical services, a very large and popular sex counseling and birth control service, a complete educational program called "The Learning Laboratory" (including remediation and tutoring in basic skills, high school equivalency and training, legal counseling services, a recreation program, vocational training workshops, creative and manual arts and crafts training, life skills workshops, "alternative programs," "milieu programs," youth awareness seminars, and a food program). At follow-up evaluation, 43 percent of The Door's Learning Laboratory participants were involved in education or training programs, 56 percent had furthered their education, and 50 percent had decreased their drug use.[23]

Straight, Inc.

Straight, Inc., is a privately funded outpatient program servicing 280 clients located in St. Petersburg, Florida, and Springfield, Virginia. Clients progress through a series of five phases of treatment. During the first phase, the client lives with a foster family. This family is that of an "oldcomer" (a client who has progressed farther in the program). When the client has progressed to the second phase, a decision is made by the professional staff and clients who have staff positions to allow the client to return home to work on family issues. Parents are required to follow a strict set of rules for the remainder of their child's involvement in the Straight program. For example, no drugs or alcohol are to be used by anyone in the home, and anyone visiting the home must be approved by the Straight staff. Parents are involved in therapy groups, both with other parents and with adolescents (not with their own children though). The child's participation in Straight is from 9:00 A.M. to 9:00 P.M.

On graduation to phase three, the client returns to his or her prior school environment. During this phase, participation in the Straight program occurs after school. Clients are not allowed to socialize with other students who use drugs while at school or at home. In effect, this rule encourages clients to interact primarily with other Straight clients. Some clients are chosen to become staff trainees. Success in this position leads to a junior staff position which is a paid, part-time job. The principles that Straight encourages include (1) total abstinence from drugs and sex (no dating is allowed at any time during the program), (2) a focus on the child's responsibility for his or her behavior, and (3) a strong emphasis on religious beliefs and moral values.

A systematic follow-up study in 1986 of 222 clients of this rather unique program, admitted consecutively from November 1982 to June 1984, reported these findings: Only 35 percent of the clients reported using alcohol, and only 26 percent reported using marijuana during the follow-up period, compared to reports of 99 percent and 97 percent, respectively, for the period before admission to the program. There were also large reductions in the rates reported by the clients for use of all other types of illicit substances. Follow-up reports by parents agreed quite well with the clients' self-reports, indicating a statistically significant decrease in the proportion of clients who were still involved in substance use at followup.

Statistically significant improvement at follow-up was also reported by clients on seven of eight other selected outcome criteria (e.g., suicidal thoughts, physical violence, number of arrests). The majority of the clients reported that they were "satisfied" with the program (70 percent), that the program "helped" them (74 percent), and specifically that the program helped them with their relationship with their parents (69 percent).

Although the graduates from the program, compared to the dropouts, report significantly greater satisfaction with, and help from, the program, the graduates did not report a significantly greater reduction in substance use at follow-up. Retention (number of months in treatment) had no significant effect on improvement as measured by reduction in substance use at followup.[24]

NOTES

1. A. S. Friedman, N. Glickman, and A. Utada, "Does Drug and Alcohol Use Lead to Failure to Graduate from High School?" *Journal of Drug Education* 15, no. 4 (1985).

2. A. S Friedman, E. Pomerance, R. Sanders, et al. "The Structure and Problems of the Families of Adolescent Drug Abusers," *Contemporary Drug Problems* (Fall 1980).

3. G. B. Beschner and A. S. Friedman, in *Youth Drug Abuse: Problems, Issues and Treatment*, ed G. B. Beschner and A. S. Friedman (Lexington, Mass.: D.C. Heath, 1979).

4. H. W. Feldman, M. H. Agar, and G. M. Bescher, *Angel Dust: An Ethnographic Study of PCP Users* (Lexington, Mass.: Lexington Books, 1979).

5. B. Jalali, M. Jalali, G. Crocette, et al. "Adolescents and Drug Use: Toward a

More Comprehensive Approach," *American Journal of Orthopsychiatry* 51, no. 1 (January 1981).

6. D. R. Wesson, A. S. Carlin, K. M Adams, and G. M Bescher, *Polydrug Abuse* (New York: Academic Press, 1977). D. Kandel, "Epidemiological and Psychosocial Perspectives on Adolescent Drug Abuse," *Journal of American Academic Child Psychiatry* 21, no. 4 (1982): 328–47.

7. N. Glickman, A. Utada, and A. Friedman, "Characteristics of Drug Users in Urban Public High Schools," in *Clinical Notes*, Grant no. H81-DA-01657 (Rockville, Md.: National Institute on Drug Abuse, August 1983).

8. B. K. Alexander and G. S. Dibb, "Interpersonal Perception in Addict Families," *Family Process* 16 (1977): 17–28.

9. R. Jessor, "Predicting Time of Onset of Marijuana Use: A Developmental Study of High School Youth," in *Predicting Adolescent Drug Abuse: A Review of Issues, Methods and Correlates*, ed. D. Lettiere, DHEW Pub. No. (ADM) 76-299 (Washington, D.C.: U.S. Government Printing Office, 1975).

10. F. Streit, D. Halsted, and P. Pascale, "Differences Among Youthful Users and Non-Users of Drugs Based on Their Perceptions of Parental Behavior," *International Journal of Addiction* 9, no. 5 (1974): 749–55; G. D. Mellinger, R. H. Somers, and D. I. Manheimer, "Drug Use Research Items Pertaining to Personality and Interpersonal Relations: A Working Paper for Research Investigators," in *Predicting Adolescent Drug Abuse: A Review of Issues, Methods and Correlates*, ed. D. J. Lettiere, DHEW Pub. No. (ADM) 76-299 (Washington, D.C.: U.S. Government Printing Office, 1975).

11. D. Kandel, "Inter- and Intragenerational Influences of Adolescent Marijuana Use," *Journal of Social Issues* 30, no. 2 (1974): 107–35.

12. D. G. Hunt, "Parental Permissiveness as Perceived by the Offspring and the Degree of Marijuana Usage Among Offspring," *Human Relations* 27 (1974): 267–85; S. R. Cannon, *Social Functioning Patterns in Families of Offspring Receiving Treatment for Drug Abuse* (Rosyln Heights, N.Y.: Libra Publications, 1976).

13. D. E. Mead, and S. S. Campbell, "Decision Making and Interaction by Families with and Without a Drug Abusing Child," *Family Process* 11 (1972): 487–98.

14. N. Glickman, A. Utada, and A. Friedman, "Characteristics of Drug Users in Urban Public High Schools."

15. G. DeLeon and D. Deitch, "Treatment of the Adolescent Abuser in a Therapeutic Community," in *Treatment Services for Adolescent Drug Abusers* (Rockville, Md.: National Institute on Drug Abuse, 1984).

16. A. Friedman, "Adolescent Drug Abuse Treatment Programs," *Treatment Research Notes* (September 1982), 2.

17. S. B. Sells and D. D. Simpson, "Evaluation of Treatment Outcome for Youths in the Drug Abuse Reporting Program (DARP): A Follow-Up Study," in *Youth Drug Abuse: Problems, Issues and Treatment*, ed. G. M. Beschner and A. S. Friedman (Lexington, Mass.: D.C. Heath, 1979), 571–613; R. L Hubbard, E. R. Cavanaugh, S. G. Craddock, et al. "Characteristics, Behaviors, and Outcomes for Youth in the TOPS," in *Treatment Services for Adolescent Substance Abusers*, DHHS Pub. no. (ADM) 85-1342 (Rockville, Md.: National Institute on Drug Abuse, 1985).

18. S. Gaus and Gilbert T. Henderson, "Supportive Life Skills Program for Court-Committed Adolescent Substance Abusers," in *Treatment Services for Adolescent Substance Abusers*, DHHS Pub. no. (ADM) 85-1342 (Rockville, Md.: National Institute on Drug Abuse, 1985).

19. A. S Friedman, S. Granick, A. Utada, and N. Glickman, "Family Therapy vs. Parent Groups: Effects on Adolescent Drug Abusers," *Family Process* (in press).

20. A. T. McLellan, G. E. Woody, L. Luborsky, et al. "Increased Effectiveness of Substance Abuse Treatment: A Prospective Study of Patient-Treatment 'Matching,' " *Journal of Nervous and Mental Disease* 174, no. 11 (1986): 669–79.

21. A. S. Friedman, and N. W. Glickman, "Program Characteristics for Successful Treatment of Adolescent Drug Abuse," *Journal of Nervous and Mental Disease* 174, no. 11 (1986): 669–79.

22. A. S. Friedman, N. W. Glickman, and M. R. Morrissey, "Prediction to Successful Treatment Outcome by Client Characteristics and Retention in Treatment in Adolescent Drug Treatment Programs: A Large-Scale Cross Validation Study," *Journal of Drug Education* 16 (1980): 149–65.

23. L. Mai, S. Pedrick, and M. Greene, *The Learning Laboratory, Treatment Research Monograph*, DHHS Pub. no. (ADM) 80-928 (Rockville, Md.: National Institute on Drug Abuse, 1980).

24. A. S. Friedman, R. Schwartz, A. Utada, and N. W. Glickman, "A Follow-Up Study of Clients of the Straight, Inc. Program: An Evaluation of Treatment Outcome," *Journal of Nervous and Mental Disease* (in press).

Chapter 9

Research and Prevention Assistance in the International Sector

Richard A. Lindblad

During the 1980s there was a major shift in the way many countries posited themselves as drug-producing or drug-consuming nations. In prior years many drug-producing countries saw North America as responsible for the world's drug problem. After all, if there were no market, there would be no demand: Cartels would then have no motivation to produce illicit drugs. In fact, except for some endemic chewing of coca leaves in the Andes, some "medicinal" ganja use in Jamaica, and some opium smoking in certain Asian countries, the United States was the major drug-consuming country. Currently, however, many if not all drug-producing countries see themselves as having a drug consumption problem as well. It is not uncommon for foreign governments to describe the nature and extent of their drug problem as being proportional to that of the United States, sometimes with a lag of three to five years.

The United States' dubious distinction of leading the world in drug consumption also provides the corollary that it leads the world in efforts to combat the disorder. No other nation has devoted such resources to drug abuse research, prevention, education, and treatment. In fiscal year 1989 the federal government allocated $1.5 billion to reduce the demand for drugs—$940 million to educate the nation's youth and $621 million to provide drug abuse treatment. The National Institute on Drug Abuse (NIDA) managed a $290 million budget to research the epidemiology, causality, treatment, and prevention of drug abuse. The Office of Substance Abuse Prevention (OSAP) had in excess of $69 million for prevention and public education activities including managing a national clearinghouse for the distribution of prevention materials and research findings. The knowledge, technology, and expertise produced by such expenditures benefits the international community as initiatives to reduce demand emerge throughout the world. Other nations recognize the technological and scientific leadership of the United States; its research publications are sought everywhere, and hundreds of international scientists and country representatives visit U.S. drug control agencies each year to learn from their successes and failures. The United States is asked to provide technical assistance and training, to participate in collaborative research, to help with educational placements, and to develop a knowledge base on specific drug abuse issues.

ORGANIZATIONAL AND PROGRAMMATIC ISSUES

Legislative Mandate

The National Institute on Drug Abuse, the Office of Substance Abuse Prevention, and the National Institute on Alcohol Abuse and Alcoholism (NIAAA), which are all part of the Alcohol, Drug Abuse, and Mental Health Administration (ADAMHA), receive legal authority to participate in international activities by an indirect mandate. Each of these organizations has been created under specific legislation directing that resources be allocated to national drug abuse programs. None of the enabling acts designates international programming. However, ADAMHA, as a component of the U.S. Public Health Service (PHS), has indirect authority for international programs from the PHS Act (42 U.S.C. §§ 241, 242b) and the International Health Research Act of 1960. The PHS Act grants authority to participate in and fund international activities as long as the efforts "benefit or advance the health of the American people."[1] This broad authority has resulted in the active participation of PHS and ADAMHA in many international activities, including the responsibilities arising from international treaties.

This broad legislative mandate and the awareness that drug abuse is a global problem notwithstanding, the international research and prevention activities of ADAMHA have been limited to relatively few programs. The urgent need to focus on domestic drug abuse issues, the limited research expertise in other countries, and the world community's lack of awareness of research opportunities have all limited the agency's international demand reduction portfolio.

Funding

Because funding for drug abuse prevention and research in the United States remains inadequate to meet its research, prevention, and treatment needs, priority is given to domestic projects. Program directors and The National Drug Abuse Advisory Council discourage the use of NIDA's funds for international research unless the opportunity is unique and the issue cannot be studied domestically. Favorable consideration has been given to such recent unique research opportunities as a study of the natural history of coca paste smoking in Colombia and an assessment of the health consequences of chronic drug-specific marijuana use in Jamaica.

The policy of giving priority to domestic research has led to an increase in collaborative efforts between U.S. institutions and foreign governments. A U.S.

university may include in its research design a binational component to assess the cross-cultural aspects of its investigations, and indeed the inclusion of cultural influence factors in the study design may strengthen the rigor of the application.

Although foreign researchers are eligible to compete independently for ADAMHA extramural funding, they submit few proposals. All applications are critically examined by U.S. scientists in a peer review process and assigned competitive priority scores. Traditionally, proposals from foreign scientists have not competed well against those of domestic researchers. Foreign researchers face difficulties arising from such complex issues as communication barriers, lack of awareness of procedural requirements, inaccessibility to the agencies' technical advisors in grant development, limited scientific peer recognition, and the submission of inadequate scientific design. Even carefully prepared applications can be refused funding if the nature of the proposed research is determined by the reviewer to be unimportant. Foreign researchers would improve their likelihood of competing if they responded only to formal grant announcements issued by funding agencies.

OFFICE OF SUBSTANCE ABUSE PREVENTION

The ever-increasing demand for prevention technology and programming led to the creation of the Office of Substance Abuse Prevention in 1986. OSAP is charged with developing prevention materials, operating a clearinghouse, managing a demonstration grant program, coordinating prevention research findings, and implementing government policy on substance abuse prevention.

The OSAP Clearinghouse disseminates all of NIDA's research publications, as well as NIAAA's. It dispatches materials regularly to both the national and the international communities.

OSAP's international technical assistance and grant program is growing. In conjunction with NIDA, OSAP recently funded a U.S./Mexico Border Health Initiative to conduct research and provide prevention services in that area. OSAP experts are available to provide technical assistance to international bodies: OSAP recently helped develop a manual and workshop presentation on media campaigns to prevent drug abuse for the U.S. State Department to use in assisting foreign governments that wish to launch such campaigns. At the International Conference on Drug Abuse and Illicit Trafficking (ICDAIT), sponsored by the United Nations (UN), OSAP was designated to display and promote U.S. prevention materials and efforts.

NIDA'S INTERNATIONAL COOPERATIVE EFFORTS

Despite domestic barriers to funding international research, NIDA is supporting a number of international projects: In 1988, studies from Israel, China, Scotland, England, Canada, and Jamaica on such topics as prenatal cannabis exposure, the neural substrates of cocaine abuse, and opioid peptides were funded.

In the future the number of international researchers receiving federal funds will probably increase as a result of improved global communications and awareness of drug abuse issues, as well as expanded international collaboration on technical problems. Also, in 1989, NIDA expanded its special population research training program to include limited numbers of international trainees: Potential grantees are taught how to design research protocols and prepare research applications that can more successfully compete in the peer review process.

Four years after its establishment in 1974, NIDA became a World Health Organization (WHO) collaborating center on drug abuse, one of five pursuing the following objectives:

• developing coordinated planning mechanisms for exchange of knowledge and experience,

• promoting efforts for research and training,

• addressing the needs of developing countries in fields related to drug abuse, and

• reviewing and evaluating policies and programs to reduce the supply of and demand for illicit drugs.

As a drug abuse collaborating center, NIDA is a part of a network that facilitates the pursuit of research goals on an international basis. The mechanism expedites the dispatch of resources so funds and technical assistance can be quickly assigned to meet pressing programmatic needs.

The WHO collaborating center concept is being used to train international researchers and to initiate international research studies in priority areas. For example, preliminary planning is underway for NIDA and another WHO collaborating center in South America to study the cross-cultural comparability of specific risk factors that appear to predict those youthful subjects who will later abuse drugs. Examples of previous joint projects undertaken with WHO include studying the diagnosis and classification of mental disorders (including drug abuse), participating in an international meeting of experts to review the question of AIDS and intravenous drug use, and cosponsoring a meeting of experts on cocaine abuse.

TECHNICAL ASSISTANCE

Because of their prominence in drug abuse research and prevention, ADAMHA and NIDA scientists and grantees are often asked to provide technical assistance to foreign ministries and international organizations. Requests come through international organizations or the U.S. State Department, which can provide the travel funds. In many countries, limited funds make it impossible to acquire technical assistance from the private sector. As a government agency, NIDA makes its scientists available to foreign governments at no expense. If NIDA scientists are not available, the institute can usually identify grantees who can respond to the request, and many grantees, if provided travel, are willing to consult at no cost to the requesting government.

Technical Assistance in Epidemiology

While NIDA attempts to respond at some level to all formal requests for assistance, the institute has designated epidemiology as a priority for international consultation. Basic, comparable data to describe the nature and extent of drug abuse are essential in planning programs, initiating prevention efforts, and measuring the success of intervention. Without some standardization of data collection procedures, it is not possible to assess the problem in different geographical areas. As more and more nations face a drug abuse problem, they look to the United States for assistance in developing their data collection skills. NIDA has provided technical assistance in epidemiology to dozens of countries and international organizations. Its survey methods and data collection instruments are rapidly setting the standard for excellence in the field.

The type and amount of NIDA's epidemiological assistance vary both by the nature and the source of the request. As a regular invitee, NIDA participates in regional epidemiological meetings of the Pan American Health Organization (PAHO), the Organization of American States, and the Council of Europe and provides intermittent short-term consultation. Countries also request short-term assistance, and during the 1980s Mexico, Ecuador, Peru, Colombia, Trinidad, Brazil, Argentina, and several African nations received technical help in epidemiology from NIDA.

Intense and long-term assistance sometimes results due to special circumstances. NIDA provided extended technical assistance and training in epidemiology to Jamaican scientists for two national surveys. This comprehensive project was possible because although the request came from the Jamaican government, it was endorsed and partially funded by the U.S. Agency for International Development. NIDA conducted a two-month training program for the researchers and, as the studies were implemented, provided ongoing technical assistance and oversight.

Another example of long-term epidemiological assistance grew out of the 1987 UN International Conference on Drug Abuse and Illicit Trafficking. The U.S. delegation at the meeting promoted a recommendation for international collaboration in developing comparable international data collection methods. The following year, at the meeting of the UN Commission on Narcotic Drugs, the U.S. delegation introduced and successfully promoted a resolution to establish an International Drug Abuse Assessment System (IDAAS) within the UN Division of Narcotics. As part of both U.S. delegations, NIDA was instrumental in getting the resolution approved, and NIDA provides the ongoing technical oversight as IDAAS is implemented. IDAAS will result in a major change in the procedures and instruments that the United Nations uses to collect, analyze, and report the nature and extent of drug abuse among member countries. The new system will be able to compile information from nations having advanced data collection programs, but its unique characteristic will be the ability to report reliable information from all members—even if they lack advanced programs. To accomplish this goal, IDAAS data collection instruments will focus on minimal data sets (such as police or health care reports) that exist in less developed countries. Essential to the new system will be a network of reporters who will develop common definitions and will be regularly trained in reporting and maintaining quality assurance procedures.

Binational Agreements

Binational or regional agreements between the United States and other countries provide an administrative structure for technical assistance. For example, the United States and Israel have a bilateral agreement to cooperate in the field of health. The 1989 binational symposium focused on drug abuse treatment, prevention, and research, and NIDA scientists traveled to Israel to meet with their counterparts and exchange scientific papers and information.

An agreement with India for cooperation in science and technology has been in existence since 1982. This agreement fosters collaboration in basic and applied research on drug abuse and related problems. Under this agreement NIDA scientists have participated in technical exchanges with the National Institute of Mental Health in Bangalor and with the Central Drug Research Institute of Lucknow.

Similarly, an agreement exists with the Polish Institute of Psychology and Neurology for exchange of scientific information in epidemiology, biomedical research, and drug abuse prevention. A PHS bilateral agreement also provides for technical exchange with the Chinese Academy of Medical Science, and the Public Health Service has a drug-abuse-related binational agreement with the Finnish Ministry of Social Affairs. Further, in May 1988 an accord for collaboration on biomedical problems of alcohol and drug abuse was signed by the All-Union Research Center on Medico-Biological Problems of Narcology (USSR) and by NIDA and NIAAA.

The formal binational agreement provides a more enduring mechanism for collaborative technical exchange than does a specific request by an individual country. The binational agreement usually spans several years and emphasizes generic concepts of cooperation. Regardless of their origin or nature, all technical requests are coordinated with the U.S. Department of State, and all formal agreements receive State Department clearance before they become official.

THE ROLES OF OTHER U.S. GOVERNMENT AGENCIES IN REDUCING INTERNATIONAL DEMAND

Bureau of International Narcotic Matters (INM)

Congress has charged the State Department's Bureau of International Narcotic Matters with coordinating and overseeing the efforts of agencies of the U.S. government to curb international drug abuse. Most INM funds ($101 million in fiscal year 1989) are directed toward reducing the supply (through control of illicit crops and drug interdiction); however, a small portion ($2 million in fiscal year 1989) has been designated for efforts to reduce demand. The goal is to promote efforts that help countries become more aware of, and better able to respond to, their drug problems, so the program centers on diplomatic initiatives to establish social and political environments within which the problems of drug abuse are better understood by foreign officials. INM arranges for technical assistance and provides training to countries on request, giving priority to drug-producing and drug transit nations. INM produces a monthly newsletter called the *International Network Bulletin* (Box 15121, Washington, DC 20003) and sponsors a series of training workshops on such topics as epidemiology and the use of media to promote public awareness of drug abuse. INM often facilitates the travel of international visitors to the United States so that they can participate in training opportunities at NIDA, OSAP, or other institutions.

U.S. Information Agency (USIA)

Other U.S. government agencies have active programs to assist in reducing the demand for illicit drugs. The U.S. Information Agency, for example, has an aggressive program for the dissemination of information on drug abuse prevention and control. The USIA usually conducts country-specific opinion surveys and then uses the results to target its technical assistance efforts. The response can include sponsoring public awareness campaigns, providing grants for international visitors, making experts available to speak abroad, holding satellite interactive press conferences, and funding specific training programs. The USIA demand-reduction efforts emerge from country-specific initiatives requested by U.S. embassy staff in each country.

Agency for International Development (AID)

The U.S. Agency for International Development is active in promoting efforts to reduce the demand for illicit drugs in certain less developed countries. AID has given antidrug use programs priority because of the drain on economic development that results from the production and consumption of illicit drugs. In the 1980s AID has focused on promoting drug awareness programs by sponsoring major public education and media programs in Bolivia, Pakistan, Peru, and Thailand, for example. In Peru and Jamaica, AID funded public awareness efforts that also included national studies of the epidemiology of drug abuse. In most of these projects, technical direction and expertise come from the United States, but the responsibility for project execution rests with foreign governments. In the Jamaican epidemiology studies NIDA provided technical oversight of the effort, PAHO facilitated administrative issues, and the Jamaican government actually conducted the studies. In the Peruvian studies a private U.S. contractor provided technical assistance and supervision, but the Peruvian government carried out the studies.

AID has also planned a major program to reduce demand in less developed countries of Latin America. This initiative, the most comprehensive prevention program AID has ever funded, is designed to strengthen the capabilities of countries to plan, implement, and assess drug awareness and prevention programs. The effort includes the use of epidemiologic studies, technical assistance, and the mass media. A regional center for prevention, a regional clearinghouse for materials on drug abuse, and a series of directed educational and training initiatives is part of this comprehensive program. NIDA and OSAP have been asked to sign cooperative agreements to provide technical assistance in the program.

TRAINING OPPORTUNITIES FOR
INTERNATIONAL VISITORS

Many universities, institutions, and organizations sponsor training in drug abuse research and prevention for international visitors, but because the training opportunities are so diverse, it is often difficult for interested persons to learn of programs that might fit their needs.

Some organizations, such as INM, the USIA Office of Programs, and AID, provide a brokeragelike service for international visitors, both groups and individuals, who seek training. Trainees apply through the U.S. mission, and programs are arranged to meet their needs. Currently, about 40 percent of AID trainees are studying for degrees at institutions of higher learning. Often, however, the service these organizations provide is short term, giving only an overview of U.S. technical capabilities.

Fellowships and Individual Grants

Fellowships and individual grants are generally available to foreign visitors only at the graduate level. The training is provided through academic institutions with the sponsorship of government agencies or private foundations. One of the best sources of information about scholarships, fellowships, and individual grant awards is the USIA; its libraries offer guides and lists of funding available for international visitors. The USIA also has individual and group grant programs, which are administered by the Institute of International Education (IIE), 809 United Nations Plaza, New York, NY 10017.

Many of the fellowship opportunities available for the study of drug abuse have traditionally not been used by researchers. For example, the John E. Fogarty International Center of the National Institutes of Health provides fellowships for U.S. scientists to study in other countries and for foreign scientists to come to the United States. The Fogarty program is available for qualified biomedical, behavioral, or health scientists, but scholars wishing to pursue research on drug abuse have not applied. Similarly, fellowships from WHO and its regional office have seldom been used to support training in drug abuse, although they could be.

The Hubert H. Humphrey Fellowships

The number of grants awarded by both AID and the USIA for the study of drug abuse has grown steadily, and in 1987 a special drug abuse scholarship program was initiated as part of the Hubert H. Humphrey North-South Fellowship Program. A Fulbright Exchange Activity funded by the USIA and administered nationally by IIE, the Humphrey Fellowship Program brings accomplished professionals from developing countries to the United States for a year of graduate study and related experience at selected universities. Fields of study include planning and resource management, public administration, agriculture, health, and nutrition. Humphrey Drug Abuse Fellowships are awarded to English-speaking postdoctoral applicants who have a strong academic background, a minimum of five years of experience, and strong references from professional colleagues and supervisors. The fellowships are generally offered to administrators and planners with a public service orientation. Grants provide for living expenses, international travel, training costs, and health insurance. A typical program includes guided projects, seminars, field trips, meetings and conferences, consultations, and professional affiliations with government agencies or private organizations. Fellows have been assigned to such organizations as NIDA, PAHO, state drug abuse agencies, and private treatment or prevention programs, according to their needs.

NIDA Training

NIDA's training service may result from national agreements or requests from organizations such as WHO, the United Nations, or the U.S. Department of State. Because of its leadership in research, prevention, and treatment of drug abuse, NIDA has an extensive network of professionals and organizations. Thus, it can place trainees with grantees, state agencies, or its own scientists. In recent years many such training opportunities have been facilitated: A toxicologist from India was placed in a NIDA-affiliated laboratory, epidemiologists from Jamaica were placed with NIDA survey researchers, a sociologist from Japan was placed with a NIDA treatment research grantee, and a survey researcher from China was assigned to a NIDA epidemiology grantee.

NIDA's Addiction Research Center (ARC) maintains a Visitors Fellowship Program for scientists who have at least three years of postdoctoral experience in research on substance abuse. Fellowships are granted for thirteen months, and they can be renewed once. The program is restricted to those who have demonstrated competency in research and who desire to promote their study in an eminent institution in collaboration with the nation's leading drug abuse scientists. The ARC Visitors Fellowship Program carefully selects candidates who have the qualifications and research interests needed to work closely with NIDA intramural scientists on studies deemed to be of major importance in building scientific knowledge on drug abuse.

SUMMARY

The United States has assumed a position of international leadership in research on and prevention of drug abuse. The international community seeks technical assistance from U.S. government agencies and academic institutions, and although there has been no formal plan for an organized response to these many requests, the United States has made a substantial commitment. Often technical assistance results from formal agreements between the United States and other nations or international organizations. Because of the ever-increasing demand for U.S. expertise, agencies such as INM, AID, and the USIA have country-specific criteria that they use to respond to international requests, and agencies such as NIDA have had to establish programmatic priorities for consultants (such as epidemiology).

Many U.S. agencies provide brokerage services for international visitors by arranging specific training in U.S. institutions. The number of fellowships for study related to drug abuse is increasing; however, many of these scholarship opportunities have not been explored by potential trainees. Opportunities for international technical exchange and research will probably increase greatly in the near future as policy makers from other nations see that the problems of drug abuse have no geographical boundaries.

NOTE

1. Office of General Counsel, PHS. Interoffice memorandum to Deputy Assistant Secretary for International Health, 15 August 1979.

PART III

ISSUES AND PROBLEMS IN DRUG CONTROL

Chapter 10

South American Drug Traffic: Domestic Impacts and Foreign Policy Implications

Richard B. Craig

No anthology on drug control would be complete without reference to source countries. This chapter analyzes the domestic and international implications of narcotics production and trafficking for three South American nations. While it focuses on Bolivia, Peru, and Colombia, it must be emphasized that no country in the hemisphere has managed to avoid entirely the multiple impacts of *narcotráfico*. Illicit narcotics have in fact affected virtually every Latin American and Caribbean country politically, economically, socially, psychologically, and diplomatically. Governments at all levels have been corrupted, challenged, assaulted, and destabilized. Economies have been subverted by or become dependent on narcodollars. Traditional social structures have been threatened by a new narcotics elite that seeks to buy and bully its way into social respectability. Drug abuse has become a serious health problem. National images have been transformed in the eyes of the outside world. And drug trafficking has become the most sensitive issue between Washington and La Paz, Lima, and Bogotá. It is the flashpoint and shows no signs of losing its spark.

BOLIVIA

Bolivia is the quintessential coca nation; it is a veritable *cocalandia*. It also exemplifies America's frustration with the centerpiece of its international narcotics control policy—crop eradication. Most Bolivianos are involved, either directly or indirectly, in a *cocacultura*. They grow the leaf, ceremonialize it, chew it, drink it, cook it, stomp it, refine it, smoke it, sell it, and seek to eradicate it. Coca's impact on Bolivian culture is such as to render it a vital national resource.

The hearty coca tree often thrives where other vegetation cannot survive and remains productive for twenty to thirty years. Harvested two to four times annually, one hectare of coca trees produces approximately one and a half tons of leaves. Once they are dried, the leaves are mixed with one or several chemicals to form coca paste. The dried paste is then converted to cocaine base by mixing it with precursor chemicals. Conversion from base to cocaine hydrochloride requires caution, skill, and a final filtering.

Under Bolivian law it is legal to grow coca, but illegal to manufacture coca derivatives. According to the State Department's Bureau of International Narcotics Matters, approximately 40,000 hectares of Bolivian coca yielded roughly 56,000 metric tons of leaf in 1987. Some 10,000 leaf tons were estimated to have been consumed domestically, leaving roughly 46,000 tons available for potential conversion to 80 tons of cocaine hydrochloride.[1] The majority of the nation's leaf production is today being converted domestically to cocaine for smuggling abroad, ultimately to the United States and Europe.

The social impacts of Bolivia's transition from a land of traditional coca chewers to a major producer of cocaine for export have been profound. Estimates vary as to how many individuals are involved in the coca-cocaine cycle, ranging from 200,000 coca farmers and their families to half a million employed in the enterprise from cultivation to smuggling.[2] No one, however, debates the role of coca in traditional Indian life and the cocaine boom's negative impacts.

In the wake of mass migration from the highlands into Bolivia's Chapare region, which now grows most of the nation's coca and processes the great majority of its cocaine, the leaf's pivotal social and religious position, like the Chapare itself, is under siege. Kevin Healy delineates the multiple repercussions for native people of this cocaine metamorphosis. In the wake of the Chapare's coca-cocaine boom, labor shortages have developed in traditional agriculture, with a resultant drop in the production of staple crops. Monetization of coca as a cash crop has eroded mutual support systems based on reciprocal labor patterns. The ecosystem is threatened as processing chemicals are dumped into streams and irrigation ditches.[3] Like the land, the Indian, too, is being corrupted as he becomes part of the vicious, illicit cycle.

With the exception of small plot coca farming, all facets of the cocaine enterprise are illegal. Still, hundreds of peasants are employed as *pisadores*, individuals who stomp the coca leaf–kerosene mixture in crude paste laboratories. Others work as *cepes*, men who carry large loads of coca leaf or paste to processing labs. Still others smuggle the indispensable precursor chemicals. Predictably, when the state responds, it is the Indian who bears the brunt of most police efforts. It is the Indian, too, who has become the principal victim of his own product.

Bolivia, like all source nations, is now plagued with an escalating drug abuse problem. Overproduction, glutted markets, and poor law enforcement have combined to spawn the devastating smoking of *pitillo*, tobacco laced with coca paste. Bolivia's *pitillo* addict is being ravaged both physically and psychologically by the impurities contained in the unrefined coca paste. Paste smoking has spread rapidly from processing zones into urban areas, particularly among students. A burgeoning abuse problem in a country with virtually no treatment and rehabilitation program has serious implications for national authorities. Today's estimated 100,000 young coca paste addicts may well be only a portent of things to come. The same holds true for drug-related violence and corruption.

Corruption and violence are endemic to Bolivian drug processing zones. Each is buttressed by an influx of external traffickers and widespread illicit commerce in automatic weapons. Most residents, government officials, and even the leaders of Bolivia's rural police narcotics strike force have been compromised by *narcodólares*. As is the case in other source countries, the nearer the drug scene, the greater the corruption.

In macroeconomic terms the impact of Bolivian narcotics is glaringly obvious: Without drug dollars, the economy, already a basket case, would be virtually bankrupt. U.S. government studies have consistently pegged annual export earnings from coca-cocaine at approximately $1 billion, yet Bolivian sources cite figures more than twice that amount.[4] Admittedly conservative, the American estimate still leaves illicit drugs far and away Bolivia's largest export and foremost earner of foreign exchange. What remains unclear is how much of these illicit earnings are repatriated.

During the late 1970s and early 1980s, when Bolivia's cocaine capos worked hand in hand with selected government officials, "an ideal political and economic climate existed for the investment of narco-dollars."[5] Most of these funds went into cattle, land, real estate, and legitimate businesses. With the economy's downturn and spectacular inflationary spiral of the mid-1980s, *traficantes* lost confidence in the local economy and began investing most of their profits abroad. Nevertheless, Bolivia's interior minister noted in January 1986 that "more than 50% of the dollars entering the country come from drug trafficking."[6] Central Bank President Miguel Fabri was even more emphatic: "Whoever controls more than 50% of the supply of something also controls its price. The traffickers are leading Bolivia's economy by the nose."[7] And considering the fact that La Paz does not tax repatriated illicit dollars, one might conclude the government acquiesces to being led.

No area of the country has escaped unscathed from the coca bonanza. U.S. government sources estimate that 5 percent of all Bolivians depend directly on coca for their livelihood. That figure probably exceeds 50 percent in such key growing/processing zones as the Yungas, the Chapare, and the upper Cochabamba Valley. In the mid-1980s the grower and his family could gross $5,000–$9,000 annually by tending only one hectare of coca, a small fortune by Bolivian standards. Others in the coca-cocaine cycle earn exceptionally high wages vis-à-vis legitimate laborers.[8] But with prosperity has come a serious economic side effect: The nation and many of its people have been hooked on the fickle *cocaeconomía*.

At the regional level this dependency is again epitomized by the Chapare where, in typical boom-town fashion, prices skyrocketed in the 1980s. Cochabamba has traditionally been the city having the lowest cost of living in Bolivia, but in 1984 it became the most expensive. The campesino spent his coca dollars on luxury imports instead of investing in land and animals. The market in contraband merchandise, always a problem, exploded. With everyone buying black-market goods, legitimate businesses saw their sales dwindle, and as a consequence tax revenues dried up. Labor for noncoca-related jobs became scarce. Most ironically, the Indian could no longer afford coca for chewing, so expensive had it become. And all the while the quality of life in terms of health care, education, and cultural values stagnated.[9]

Like the Cochabamba department, the nation, too, has become dependent on coca and the foreign demand for cocaine. The 61 percent growth rate in Bolivia's agrarian sector between 1980 and 1986, for example, was due primarily if not entirely to accelerated coca production.[10] This supply-side dependency is even more precarious than anything Bolivia experienced with tin. Should, for reasons of lagging external demand and/or internal law enforcement, the coca boom become a bust, Bolivia could be thrown into a serious crisis. Here as elsewhere, illicit drugs are pre-eminently a political issue.

Bolivia played a minor role in international narcotics until the 1970s. With the rise in external demand in the mid-1970s, rural elites from Santa Cruz and the Beni organized the first major processing centers and through collusion with particular military authorities were soon shipping ever larger amounts of paste and base to syndicates in Colombia for final processing. Bolivia's narcoentrepreneurs were joined in the 1980s by a major faction of the Bolivian military led by the president, General Luis García Meza, and his interior minister, Colonel Luis Arce Gómez. Together they formed the world's first official "narcocracy," a government controlled by individuals dedicated to making cocaine Bolivia's premier export and themselves narco nouveau riche. García Meza was ousted in August 1981, and following a fourteen-month holding action, Hernán Siles Suazo became the country's first elected civilian president in eighteen years. During his approximately three years in office a gradual, yet fundamental change took place in Bolivia's drug scene, the ramifications of which continue to this day.

Originally controlled by major traffickers and then by professional intermediaries, the processing of coca paste and cocaine base came under the control of the peasants themselves in hundreds of cooperative ventures throughout the coca zones and most poignantly in the Chapare. In effect, the nuclear or extended family has come to monopolize coca farming and paste production. As a result, the campesino's profits and concomitantly the government's challenge are much greater.

Bolivia's peasants are unique in the Latin American context. Independent and impressively well organized into *sindicatos* with connecting links to other regional and national workers' syndicates, their organizational skills and political clout are epitomized by the Chapare's peasant coca producers. The *Federración Especial del Chapare* (FEC) is a highly disciplined grouping of *sindicatos*, the primary raison d'être of which is opposition to government controls over coca production and acreage. Supported by the Confederation of Bolivian Peasant

Workers and the national Bolivian Workers Congress with its more than one million members, the FEC has repeatedly thwarted government crop control and law enforcement efforts. Massive demonstrations, road blocks, marches, building occupations, and violent clashes have virtually stymied the government's antidrug program. The political clout of peasant growers and their impressive support linkages and aggressive tactics eventually forced the administration of Víctor Paz Estenssoro to rethink its approach to illicit drug control.

Plagued with unprecedented economic problems, the Paz Estenssoro government altered the very character of Bolivia's antidrug program and changed its thrust from eradication to cooperative law enforcement and interdiction. Operation Blast Furnace, the highly publicized and politically precarious Bolivian-U.S. initiative against processing labs in Santa Cruz and the Beni, all but ended cocaine production during the fall of 1986. With most labs destroyed or dismantled and moved outside the country, demand for coca leaves was reduced to the point of rendering coca farming financially unattractive. The Bolivian position on drug control was thus vindicated, at least during a six-month period.

Success will prove fleeting, however, if interdiction is not coupled with eradication. In league with Washington, La Paz formulated a medium-range, three-part initiative: continuous law enforcement/interdiction, legislation prohibiting all but traditional coca cultivation, and one year of voluntary crop destruction to be followed by forced eradication. As regards traditional cultivation, an executive decree has been on the books since May 1985 which designates specific zones adequate to meet the demand of coca leaf chewers and declares illegal all other coca farming. Unfortunately, the decree was never enforced. The key independent variables still remained enactment of legislation and eradication/crop substitution. Passage of the former proved excruciatingly difficult, given the strength of the campesino *sindicatos* and their powerful allies. Successful implementation of the latter may simply prove to be a political impossibility.

Bolivia, it must be recalled, is noted for its political instability. Remaining in office for a full term, even during the best of times, is highly problematic. For any Bolivian chief executive the combination of severe economic recession, nationalistic reaction to the U.S. military presence, campesino political clout, and the virtual impossibility of finding a financially adequate replacement crop for coca may prove to be insurmountable barriers.

To make feasible a successful crop substitution program, Bolivia turned in early 1987 to the international community for support. The plan called for La Paz to furnish 20 percent of a $300 million fund over a three-year period, with the remaining $240 million to come from outside donors. Washington pledged $115 million to this undertaking which pays campesinos to eradicate their coca crops and replace them with legal ones or to relocate outside coca-growing zones. The goal was to reduce coca plantings to 15,000 hectares within eighteen months through positive and negative incentives. Reaction from the campesinos to the three-year scheme? The Bolivian Workers Congress, which has long been in an undeclared state of war with the national government, declared its own ''state of emergency'' in early March 1987 and called on peasants to block the roads. More ominously, in late May some 10,000 coca-growing peasants blocked highways in the Santa Cruz, Cochabamba, and La Paz provinces, demanding that the government cancel its eradication program.[11]

Realistically, neither La Paz nor Washington could believe that $300 million over three years would eliminate Bolivian cocaine. Achievement of that goal, notes one authoritative source, would require *far* more: $600 million a year for several years in compensation for planting legitimate crops; $300 million annually for several years to replace cocaine's importance to the economy; a well-trained, uncorrupted army of 40,000; and, assuming the above conditions are met, a three- to four-year period of violence that could cost the lives of 10,000 Bolivians.[12] Thus, for $300 million the realist looks for a reduction in, not an elimination of, coca cultivation and cocaine processing.

The government has made clear that it will no longer tolerate the *cocainización* of the nation. The majority of Bolivians support their leaders; so, too, does the State Department. It is the U.S. Congress that has remained most skeptical and on occasion financially vindictive, imposing economic sanctions on Bolivia for its failure to reach specified eradication goals. Yet even such politically opportune legislators have been encouraged by recent events on the Bolivian drug scene.

Bolivia has made progress in reaching objectives specified under a Principles of Narcotics Cooperation agreement finalized with Washington in August 1987. Under the pact La Paz agreed to implement an accelerated interdiction program, eradicate under a voluntary system 1,800 hectares of coca by 13 August 1988, force the eradication of all remaining illicit coca, and attempt in earnest to enact legislation banning the cultivation of all coca destined for use in cocaine processing. The Bolivian government has since developed, with U.S. assistance, an improved law enforcement/interdiction strategy, Operation Snowcap, which has led to the dismantling of several major cocaine labs; has voluntarily eradicated more than the specified 1,800 hectares of coca; has created a new narcotics administration organization; and has arrested several major *traficantes*, including the nation's most notorious capo, Roberto Suárez.[13]

Short-term successes notwithstanding, the ultimate fate of Bolivia's antidrug program and harmonious U.S.-Bolivian narcopolitics rests in the implementation of recently enacted coca control legislation. The law, which limits coca cultivation to traditional growing areas and authorizes the manual destruction of all other coca crops, took effect on 23 July 1989, but not before peasant growers succeeded in crippling its implementation. Faced with a series of massive protests, the government agreed to grower participation in defining and implementing the eradication statute, a concession that does not bode well either for Bolivia as a major source of cocaine or for U.S.-Bolivian relations.

PERU

Bolivia and Peru are in many respects quite similar. Both are Andean, largely Indian, poverty striken, politically unstable, dependent states. Each has undergone an agrarian revolution in recent years which politicized the Indian and raised hopes that have since been frustrated. Each has seen the military surrender power to civilian politicians who must contend with this highly politicized, indignant populace in a time of economic calamity. Together they constitute the source of most of the world's cocaine. Despite these similarities, however, Peru and Bolivia are in key respects very different. So, too, is Washington's narcotics control program with each nation.

Peru's 1968 revolution was led by a left-leaning military that distributed land to campesinos in the form of cooperatives and then, in an effort to pacify the countryside, proceeded to integrate them vertically into the government. However, as the 1970s drew to a close, the campesino was still living in poverty and bordering on rebellion. Predictably, the military returned power to the civilians, and in 1980 Fernando Belaúnde Terry again became president in a landmark democratic election. Belaúnde Terry inherited a country in economic disarray and a disgruntled, well-organized, politically powerful rural sector.

During his term in office (1980–1985), things economic went from bad to much worse; while Peru's illicit drug production skyrocketed, narcocorruption became ingrained, and Latin America's most violent revolutionary group, *Sendero Luminoso*, grew and spread through the countryside and into the capital. Such was the state of Peruvian affairs when an audacious young Alan García became president in mid-1985.

Heir to a legacy of economic nationalism, political populism, and independent foreign policy, García faced three principal challenges: economic chaos, powerful drug traffickers, and *Sendero Luminoso* revolutionaries. Alan García, like Paz Estenssoro in Bolivia, initially chose a bold economic strategy. But unlike Paz Estenssoro's orthodoxy, he would opt for growth with austerity. García's economics made him Don Quixote to fellow debt-shackled Latin Americans. By limiting debt service to no more than 10 percent of exports, however, García incurred the wrath of international lenders, and by opposing U.S. Latin American policy at every turn, he did not endear himself to Washington. On the other hand, his frontal approach to both narcotics and *Sendero* generally pleased the State Department.

During his election campaign García vowed to give no quarter to the *traficante*. Addressing the United Nations as Peru's new chief executive, he pledged to take the offensive via interdiction, law enforcement, eradication, and anticorruption measures. His initial actions proved García to be a man of his word, particularly as regards interdiction and moral renovation. But he now faces a very formidable drug challenge exacerbated by economic desperation and escalating violence.

Peru is the world's largest coca producer. Hectarage estimates for 1987 ranged from a high 135,000 by Peruvian sources to a composite 109,000 by the State Department. Utilizing the lower figure it is calculated that some 109,000 metric tons of leaves were harvested which, after domestic consumption in leaf and paste form, converted to approximately 530 tons of paste and base primarily for export to Colombia and other neighboring countries where it is converted to cocaine hydrochloride.[14]

Approximately two million Peruvians are coca chewers. Like Bolivia, Peru's Indian culture is inexorably linked to coca. The department of Cusco, like the Yungas in Bolivia, has long been the heart of Peru's traditional coca production. In recent years, however, coca growing has increased dramatically in response to foreign demand, with most of the cultivation and processing now taking place in the Upper Huallaga Valley. The valley, some 300 miles north of Lima, is to Peru what the Chapare is to Bolivia, but larger. This 500-square-mile jungle area supplies perhaps 50 percent of the world's crude cocaine and has thus received the greatest attention from Lima and Washington.

Peruvian authorities have opted for a strategy reminiscent of Bolivia's. Through interdiction and law enforcement, the principal goal has been to deprive coca of its economic incentive by constricting the illicit market. García has coupled this with an aggressive campaign against corruption and, with U.S. and international assistance, with a precarious coca eradication/crop substitution program. The president has every reason for caution in his approach for while drug cultivation/trafficking poses a threat to the nation's political system, it also contributes to economic stability and rural peace.

Socially, the negative manifestations of Peru's narcotics boom are exemplified by three inseparable phenomena: violence, corruption, and drug abuse. In Peru, drugs and corruption have always gone hand in hand, but the recent linkage of *Sendero Luminoso* guerrillas with grower and trafficker opponents to crop eradication poses an ominous development.

Peruvian-U.S. eradication/substitution efforts predate all others, but it was not until 1983 that they actually got off the ground in the Upper Huallaga. It appeared initially that the project would become the long-sought model. From a modest total of 703 hectares destroyed in 1983, the total jumped to 3,200 in 1984 and then to 4,830 in 1985, only to slump to a reported 2,575 hectares in 1986 and 355 hectares in 1987.[15] The 1985 figure still constitutes the most successful coca eradication program to date in any country, and the cumulative total would have been far greater had bureaucratic rivalries, grower resistance, corruption, and terroristic violence not interceded.

Peasant resistance is understandable and predictable. In the Huallaga alone, an estimated 100,000 campesino families earn exceptionally good livings in the coca/cocaine cycle.[16] Thus, what farmer would not resist government efforts to destroy his and his family's livelihood? His traditional life style may be endangered by *cocainización*, but the peasant has never had it so good. Few have failed to resist physically when government crop eradicators arrive with their armed escorts. The majority, however, have remained relatively nonviolent vis-à-vis hired narcothugs and guerrilla cadre.

Sendero Luminoso guerrillas began filtering into the Upper Huallaga in late 1983. Sensing a potential alliance between *traficante* and guerrilla and facing an escalating level of violence against its coca eradicators, the government declared a state of emergency and ordered the army into the valley in August 1984. From Lima's perspective the move was necessary to thwart a serious antisystem threat, *Sendero*, and to support the eradication program by preserving the lives of its practitioners. It appears, in retrospect, to have achieved neither goal.

Until December 1985, when the state of emergency was lifted, the army was the Huallaga's de facto government. During that year and a half it brushed aside the antinarcotics police force, actually confining them to the barracks on several occasions. This often left eradicators unprotected. From November 1984, when nineteen workers and surveyors were massacred, until the army was pulled out of the Upper Huallaga Valley, they were all too often left unprotected. The military viewed its task as eliminating the guerrilla, not uprooting coca bushes and thereby antagonizing peasant growers whose allegiance was needed against *Sendero*. "We have to have popular support to fight terrorism," noted an anonymous army official. "We have to have a friend in the population. You can't do that by eradicating coca."[17] What the officer failed to add was that one surely cannot accomplish any goal of an antidrug operation when one's own ranks are narcocorrupted. The convergence of guerrilla forces, angry coca farmers, and military corruption has come to pose the government's most serious problem. Having cleansed the ranks of Peru's drug-tainted police forces by early on removing more than 2,000 of their number, Alan García finds himself on the horns of a narcoterror dilemma in the Upper Huallaga.

A second important social variable in Peru's drug scene is domestic abuse. Like other Latin American leaders, President García, while never failing to emphasize the fundamental culpability of American consumers, has come to admit that substance abuse is a serious, growing problem at home. Traditional coca mastication is not the issue. It is the alarming increase in derivative smoking that has Peruvians most concerned.

Whether by design or as the result of overproduction, literally thousands of urbanites and increasing numbers of campesinos, particularly in drug zones, are smoking coca paste. Longitudinal analyses reveal alarming increases in the use of coca paste as well as marijuana and cocaine between 1979 and 1986. The number of Peruvians, most of them young, who have used illicit drugs at least once has been pegged at 600,000.[18] The nation's drug abuse problem, despite increased government efforts to publicize its growing dangers, shows no sign of abating. Neither do Peru's underground economy and the role of narcodollars therein.

The nation's economy registered marked improvement during President García's first two years in office. Unfortunately, the lot of Peru's poverty-stricken masses did not improve. It may in fact have worsened in many respects, rendering even more precarious the government's crop eradication program. Writing in early 1987, one analyst noted, "today, 75% of the population is either unemployed or underemployed, while half the remaining 25% earn the minimum wage of $56 per month. Seventy percent of the population is undernourished, while 52% are living at 'high nutritional risk.' "[19] What the author left unsaid is the fact that more than half of all working Peruvians survive because of their role in the nation's amazing "informal sector," which functions entirely outside the official economy. A major pillar, if not the very foundation, of Peru's parallel economy appears to be illicit *cocadólares*.

Alan García was not merely jesting when he once termed the cocaine industry Latin America's "only successful multinational." With its contribution to Peru's underground economy put officially (and conservatively) at $600 million in 1986, one can appreciate cocaine's impact on an economy which saw its reserves slip to $1 billion in 1987.[20] Understandably, these totals never appear in the government's economic figures. "The invisible injection of coca dollars," wrote one journalist, "lends a boost to the economy that the Peruvian authorities pretend not to take into consideration in their statistics, but in reality it represents a significant contribution."[21]

The full economic impact of coca-cocaine is most clearly evidenced in such boom towns as Tingo María, Tocache, and Aucayacu in the Upper Huallaga. Like their Bolivian counterparts, the residents of Peru's drug zones seldom invest their illicit earnings in land, livestock, and tangibles. They waste them on expensive, flashy luxuries, all the while laying no base for a better standard of legitimate living in the future. There are exceptions, of course, but they are rare. So, too, are politically viable solutions to Peru's narcodilemma.

Peru's foremost political problem is terrorism, not illicit coca. On the other hand, narcotics may now be classified by association as one with terrorism. Narcoterrorism has become an undeniable reality as *Sendero Luminoso* cadre have moved into major drug zones, and trafficker assaults on government representatives in these regions have become so brutal as to qualify de facto as terroristic. Narcothugs and guerrilla cadres are tactically so similar in the Upper Huallaga that most distinctions between the two become speculative. The object of their attention is the campesino cultivator. This potentially explosive synthesis of fanatic revolutionary, *traficante*, and peasant drug entrepreneur has long been the ultimate fear of Lima and Washington.

Centered far to the south in the Ayacucho region, *Sendero Luminoso* leaders came to view the Upper Huallaga, with its Indian base and unpopular foreign presence, as fertile recruiting grounds. By depicting the eradication campaign as government collusion with an imperialistic power designed to deprive the native of his livelihood, the guerrillas have verified their own dialectical theory. The government's antidrug program in Peru's coca heartland presented an ideal opportunity for *Sendero* guerrillas. They simply took advantage of it. Today, they *are* the government in the Upper Huallaga.

During its occupation of the valley from August 1984 to December 1985, the army's performance constituted both a blessing and a curse. Its antiterrorist campaign was generally successful. *Sendero* activity was kept to a minimum. On the other hand, its impact on Peru's antidrug campaign, and the coca eradication program in particular, was decidedly negative. In a word, the army was narcocorrupted. Fully cognizant of this reality, President García rescinded the emergency decree for the Upper Huallaga and dispatched the troops to more traditional guerrilla strongholds, whereupon two patterns emerged. First, government workers went back to destroying coca seedlings, while antinarcotics police protected them and simultaneously sought to clean up trafficker enclaves. Second, guerrilla cadres returned in increasing numbers to pose as the peasant's only true friend and protector. Perhaps more ominously for the future of coca eradication, Latin America's most fanatical revolutionaries sacrificed doctrinal purity for a piece of the coca action.

One of *Sendero*'s major problems has always been a lack of funds. No amount of revolutionary zeal can replace a steady cash flow, particularly when it comes to acquiring more weaponry. Peru's revolutionary leaders have now decided to emulate Colombian guerrillas by levying a form of war tax on the coca farmer in exchange for protection against crop eradicators. One author contends that as the de facto government in much of the Upper Huallaga, the rebels, like the Crown centuries ago, are demanding one-fifth of the Indian's coca harvest. They then convert the leaves to paste and sell it to traffickers for cash or barter it for high-powered weapons.[22]

In addition to becoming narcomiddlemen, the rebels are actively organizing peasants to defend themselves and their coca. *Sendero* cadres and narcotics dealers have formed joint militia forces and established training centers near Tingo María.[23] Thus, not only have these guerrillas compromised their revolutionary doctrine by becoming the worst kind of "bourgeois capitalists," but also they have emerged as leaders of makeshift grower/trafficker syndicates. Both developments bode ill for Peru.

President García's public support, which initially topped 80 percent, has slumped dramatically. His repeated clashes with the armed forces, the crumbling base of support within his own party, the nation's precarious economic outlook, and Peru's stark poverty are causes for serious concern. As regards the Upper Huallaga and its rebel-trafficker-peasant nexus, García is caught between the proverbial rock and hard place. The Huallaga is a classic example of a state within a state, a region beyond the central government's reach. The army alone is truly capable of pacifying the area. Unfortunately, its definition of pacification also implies leaving the coca farmer at peace and receiving a fair share of the illicit drug profits. However, when the army's presence was reduced, *Sendero* cadres returned in ever larger numbers. The Peruvian government now faces both problems, *narcotráfico* and revolutionaries, simultaneously. Washington, meanwhile, is caught in a somewhat different Catch–22 by these same developments.

The Bureau of International Narcotics Matters is the driving force behind Peru's antidrug campaign, having contributed some $5 million to the effort in FY 1987 and $5.5 million in FY 1988. In addition, the Agency for International Development is involved in a long-term $23 million crop substitution/rural development program in the Upper Huallaga.[24] For all practical purposes, Peru's program is financed by the United States. For Washington, the rock is seeing its antidrug dollars, and particularly its coca eradication funds, deprive the Indian of his livelihood and drive him into the ranks of a stridently anti-American revolutionary group. The hard place is a return to the Huallaga by the army and a repeat of the 1984–1985 events. Meanwhile, the campesino cultivator clearly prefers the army to *Sendero*—the soldier will tend to the rebel and ignore the coca—and he fears the rebel's asking price: 20 percent of his crop if he co-operates, his life if he does not.

In summarizing the multiple ramifications for Peru of illicit narcotics production and trafficking, one must first acknowledge the early accomplishment of the García administration under very trying circumstances. Peru under Alan García has accomplished more in the interdiction/law enforcement phase of its antidrug campaign than did all previous governments combined. The president's anticorruption campaign is unprecedented, particularly in light of the narcocorruption that wracked the preceding Belaúnde Terry government. García has also become a recognized leader in promoting regional cooperation against illicit drug processing and smuggling. Peru currently works closely with five South American states and Mexico in various antinarcotics programs.

Such accomplishments would have proved far more difficult, if not impossible, had García not initially enjoyed the strong support of the Peruvian people and the U.S. government. Ironically, Lima and Washington have been at loggerheads on most issues other than narcotics since García came to power in mid-1985. Yet despite these differences, the young president senses correctly the challenge posed by powerful *traficantes* to the populace and the political system. In league with guerrillas or on their own, they virtually are the government in several departments. The Upper Huallaga presents a particularly delicate challenge for any Peruvian administration.

An astute politician, García has opted for a strategy of denial, while not totally neglecting crop eradication and substitution. Attacking the trafficker, seizing his product, dismantling his labs, and destroying his runways constitute a can't lose proposition politically since most of the *traficantes* are Colombians. Destroying the peasants' small coca plots is another matter. It involves both direct and indirect risks. So the goal has been to deprive coca of its economic allure by constricting the market. In theory, if the price of leaves falls low enough as the result of a glutted market, campesinos will cease raising coca and opt for substitute crops sponsored by the government. In practice, such a strategy can enjoy only limited success.

Any long-term solution to Peru's problems as a source of illicit narcotics must perforce include two developments: in-country eradication and demand reduction in major consumer nations. Unfortunately, neither appears likely in the near future, and this leaves rational Peruvian authorities with little or no choice. They must reduce substantially the growing of coca. If cultivation is not curtailed in the Upper Huallaga and kept from spreading elsewhere, Peru could literally drown politically, economically, socially, and diplomatically in a sea of coca.

COLOMBIA

No source country better epitomizes the domestic and international ramifications of drug trafficking than does Colombia. Its rise to prominence as the world's drug smuggling capital has been well documented.[25] Unlike Peru and Bolivia, there is no legal coca cultivation in Colombia despite its centuries-old use by native Indians. Nevertheless, at least 25,000 hectares are currently under cultivation, primarily in the south. More importantly, up to 90 metric tons of cocaine base were smuggled into Colombia from Peru and Bolivia in both 1987 and 1988. Hundreds of "kitchen" labs convert domestic coca leaves to paste, while several large, relatively sophisticated laboratories refine the base to cocaine hydrochloride for export, primarily to the United States. As regards marijuana, Colombia still ranks as a major producer, with an estimated 13,000 hectares producing a net of some 5,500 tons in 1987. Most cocaine trafficking is monopolized either directly or indirectly at all stages by the infamous Medellín and Cali cartels, but marijuana trafficking is controlled by as many as three dozen groups.[26]

The cumulative impact of illicit narcotics on Colombian society, economics, politics, and foreign policy has been nothing short of profound. Violence and drug smuggling are synonymous, and Colombia has long enjoyed an infamous reputation for the former. In a profession known for its violence, Colombian *traficantes* stand out. As a rule, death is meted out to those who cannot be bought off, who prove "uncooperative." Given the price of recalcitrance, the wonder is not how many Colombian officials, journalists, and innocent bystanders have been narcocompromised, but how many have not and lived to tell about it. For many, *narcotráfico* has changed fundamentally their very way of life.

Several areas along the north coast, in the eastern plains, and in the Amazon have been transformed, as coca and marijuana industries have replaced the traditional pursuits of farming, pasturing, mining, and fishing. Whole life styles have been altered by all-embracing drug cultures that permit few deviations from the norm. In several instances traditional Indian communities have undergone forced draft changes almost overnight. Introduction of commercial drug economies has removed the peasant from subsistence agriculture and transformed him into a rural wage earner. Villages have become boom towns the principal trademarks of which are violence and conspicuous consumption. Under seige are reciprocal labor obligations, social mores, and, when the police arrive, the Indians themselves. On the opposite end of the social spectrum, the phenomenal wealth generated by cocaine has enabled selected major traffickers to buy their way into social respectability in a very brief time span. All the while, the capos have produced a surplus of marijuana and cocaine which is being dumped on the local market at bargain prices. The result: Colombia currently faces a *serious*, escalating abuse problem.

Particularly frightening is the smoking of *basuco*, cocaine paste or base mixed with marijuana and/or tobacco. Introduced in the late 1970s when excess coca glutted trafficker refining capacity, basuco smoking accounts for more than half of all drug treatment cases. By mid-1989, Colombian drug abuse experts estimated that some 500,000 individuals were regular users of cocaine in one form or another. In a country of some 30 million, this figure is proportionately equal to cocaine consumption in the United States. Of greater importance to class-conscious Colombians, ever-increasing numbers of cocaine abusers are middle- and upper-class teenagers.[27]

A final social issue in Colombia's drug scenario, that of legalization, differs from abuse in one critical respect: It stands little to no chance of becoming a reality. In search of possible solutions to the nation's drug problems, several highly respected Colombians have suggested legalization, initially of marijuana and most recently of cocaine. In December 1980 a proposal to legalize marijuana was pigeonholed in the Congress and never reached the floor for debate. Six years later a highly respected judge, who also presided over the Council of State at the time, went on television to defend his proposal for legalization of marijuana *and* cocaine and the establishment of a government monopoly. Speaking only for himself and coupling his appeal with a recommendation to abrogate the U.S.-Colombian extradition treaty, Samuel Buitrago opined, ''You've got to look at the question more objectively.''[28]

While controversy inevitably surrounds legalization proposals, there is no doubt that illicit narcotics have deeply affected the Colombian economy. The only question is one of degree. In truth no one really knows how much is earned by Colombian traffickers, although the value of their cocaine and marijuana exports probably totals $3–4 billion annually. More importantly, there are no reliable repatriation studies. United States officials tend to underestimate the probable total, while most journalists overstate it in much the same manner. A reliable ''guesstimate'' would be that some $2 billion in illicit narcotics earnings find their way back into the economy each year. The multiple impacts of such funds are profound. Their effects are both positive and negative.

On the credit side, one may begin with the 1970s during which marijuana and coca/cocaine were critical variables in the impressive growth of Colombia's agrarian sector. Narcodollars were equally crucial to the nation's large trade surplus, which increased some tenfold from the mid to late 1970s and continues to this day. Government officials often feign ignorance regarding the source of these funds, but it is undeniable that (1) most are narcodollars, (2) they add substantially to Colombia's foreign exchange reserve, and (3) their acceptance renders the government an admitted party to illicit money laundering.

An additional positive economic spinoff from illicit drug trafficking is employment. Colombia's narcotics industries employed an estimated 200,000 people in the 1970s. Today that figure may approach 500,000 individuals who work in one phase or another of the marijuana-cocaine enterprise.[29] With high unemployment and underemployment rates, *traficantes* have an abundant labor pool from which to draw. Even in the best of times there will be no shortage of hands, so well paid are narcoproletarians.

As regards the economic debits of Colombia's narcotics phenomenon, it must be concluded on balance that they overshadow the credits. Beginning at the micro level of the peasant, one witnesses a repeat of the Bolivian and Peruvian scenarios: narco boom towns, conspicuous consumption, no sound investment of earnings, and serious discontent when the illicit market changes, moves, or dries up. Slash-and-burn farming is the rule, with its resultant ecological damage as the trafficker moves his operation from one remote locale to another in response to government eradication efforts. Illicit drug farming has contributed substantially to Colombia's becoming a net food importer through the conversion of crop lands to marijuana and coca fields and the recruitment of campesinos to grow, process, and smuggle these products. Labor shortages in legitimate agriculture and business are the rule in drug zones.

Narcotráfico's negative impacts are equally clear at the macroeconomic level. While the practice of accepting, without question, dollars at the national bank's "side window" augments Colombia's cash reserves, it also leaves the door open to trafficker inroads into legitimate businesses. Probably "laundering" no more than 20 percent of their earnings through "the window," capos still were able to threaten legitimate control of several banks and credit companies in the early 1980s. They have purchased outright numerous major businesses including banks, textile mills, and even football teams. The influx of narcodollars has been so great that Colombia is one of the very few countries in which black-market dollars are worth less than the official exchange rate. Finally, the "side window" policy has contributed immeasurably to Colombia's booming and highly destabilizing underground economy. In brief, drug money so permeates the entire financial system as to render it vulnerable to trafficker whims. That kind of economic clout leads inexorably to political power.

Narcotics traffic has affected the nation's political process at all levels: international, national, regional, and local. A most insidious effect of drugs on the Colombian body politic is psychological, difficult to document, yet undeniably real. This author calls it compound cynicism because Colombians were political cynics long before the drug bonanza and will remain so if and when it disappears. Accusations and revelations concerning prominent political officials' involvement in narcotics traffic, however, have broken the barrier of tolerability for the average citizen.

By 1980 even the minister of justice lamented that the Congress contained known representatives of trafficking groups. While narcotics were not an important issue in the presidential elections of 1982 and 1986, drug money has surely played a role in electoral campaigns at all levels during the 1980s. As recently as March 1987, a father-son political pair was indicted by a North Carolina grand jury for cocaine smuggling. The father is an alternate member of the Congress, while the son is a full-time congressman. Then there is the well-known case of Pablo Escobar, one of the Medellín cartel's most prominent capos, who was elected as an alternate to the House of Representatives in 1982. Admittedly unique, Escobar's effort pales alongside Carlos Lehder's imaginative political ventures.[30]

Having earlier made unsuccessful bids for the national senate and Bogotá's municipal council, the notorious smuggler first purchased a newspaper and then created his own political party. The latter was targeted specifically at Washington's narcotics assistance program, Bogotá's antidrug campaign, and the U.S.-Colombian extradition treaty, an instrument that led to his conviction in a Florida courtroom.

Lehder's third political venture has proved more durable and far more deadly. In December 1981 he joined other major traffickers to fund the infamous paramilitary group MAS, or Death to Kidnappers. Aimed originally at any revolutionary group or common criminal foolhardy enough to kidnap a member of the drug trafficking fraternity, MAS has since come to be recognized as a notorious death squad, specializing in the assassination of left-wing politicians, students, and party members.

Trafficker inroads at the national level, though at times highly publicized, are minimal, considering the potential. The same cannot be said regarding regional and local areas, some of which are effectively beyond Bogotá's control. In such zones it is hardly surprising that department supervisors, municipal lawmakers, judges, and entire local constabularies are involved in illicit drugs. Either they work for the trafficker, or they are the *traficantes*. More fundamentally for the future of Colombian politics, some departmental and local political systems have been so permeated by the illicit drug business that the two are often indistinguishable.

In their defense, many Colombian magistrates and politicians work under a twin burden not borne by their American counterparts—extremely low salaries and the virtual certainty of physical liquidation should they not "cooperate." Colombian *traficantes* have raised the practice of intimidation to unprecedented levels. The results have been devastating in both human and political terms.

The murder on April 30, 1984, of Minister of Justice Rodrigo Lara Bonilla stands as a benchmark. Gunned down by trafficker-hired motorized assassins, Lara Bonilla was the first prominent national figure to accept publicly the trafficker challenge. Sadly, he was not the last to pay the ultimate price. The "hit list" appears shockingly endless: Hernando Baquero, a member of the Supreme Court's penal chamber and one of the delegates who negotiated the 1979 U.S.-Colombia extradition treaty; Avianca Airlines Security Chief Carlos Arturo Luna; Raúl Echeverría, deputy director of Cali's leading daily *El Occidente*; Gustavo Zuluaga, Medellín Superior Tribunal magistrate; Colonel Jaime Ramírez, the highly respected former head of Colombia's antinarcotics police; Guillermo Cano, owner of the nation's second largest newspaper and a vocal critic of the Medellín cartel; Enrique Parejo, ambassador to Hungary and ex-minister of justice (who, though shot five times, miraculously survived); Carlos Hoyos, attorney general; more than half of the members of the Supreme Court, murdered during a November 1985 seige of the national Palace of Justice by narcotics-tainted revolutionaries; and most recently, Luis Carlos Galán, the very popular Liberal presidential aspirant, murdered in August 1989.

Ties between terrorist groups and drug smugglers have proven mutually ben-eficial. Such is the case with Colombia's and Latin America's oldest revolutionary movement, the *Fuerzas Armadas Revolucionarias de Colombia* (FARC), the armed wing of the Communist party. Roughly half of FARC's 33 "fronts" are active in marijuana- and coca-growing areas where its cadres collect tribute for protecting illicit plots, cocaine laboratories, and landing strips.

Colombia's second most publicized insurgent group, the M-19, continues its ties with Cuba. The movement was involved in a guns-for-dope relationship in the early 1980s when a noted Colombian drug runner supplied the M-19 with weapons. He, in return, was aided in the drug smuggling venture by Cuban officials who allegedly provided the arms and safe havens for drug cargoes in return for cash payments. Far more controversial is the connection among drugs, extradition, the M-19, and the aforementioned Palace of Justice seige. The United States has drawn a direct link between the bloody assault and the destruction of extradition files on major *traficantes*, claiming that the operation was financed by the Medellín cartel. However, spokesmen for the M-19 have denied any drug connection to the seizure.

Perhaps the key point to be made in analyzing the role of insurgent groups in Colombia's drug scene is not whether there exists a verifiable conspiracy between trafficker and revolutionary, but rather what the modus operandi is of each of the two camps and what their *tactics* are that render cocaine capos and guerrillas kindred spirits. Both are terrorists because they use violent strategies and tactics. Alone or in concert they pose a bona fide challenge to both the nation's political system and U.S.-Colombian relations.

Despite the fact that the drug question has recently become a serious threat to harmonious relations between Bogotá and Washington, Colombia remains today the linchpin of America's international narcopolitics. It can, within reason, be called one of the three authentic "success stories" resulting from that policy, the other two being Turkey and Mexico. Colombia, in fact, represents a micro-cosm of three core elements in Washington's international narcotics program: (1) crop eradication at the foreign source, hopefully through an aerial herbicide program; (2) interdiction in the source nation or in route to the United States, preferably in cooperation with source state security forces; and (3) elimination/immobilization of major traffickers, again on a cooperative basis. Dating back at least to the early 1970s, U.S. policy has shown marked continuity in goal and strategy: Keep illicit Colombian drugs out of the United States through eradication, interdiction, and immobilization *in Colombia*! Continuity notwith-standing, U.S.-Colombian narcotics relations have been cyclical in nature and often unilateral, incident-prone, and highly contentious. Illicit drug traffic has been the most acrimonious of issues between the two countries since the mid-1970s.

In practice, Colombia-U.S. narcopolitics have been cyclical in nature. This ebb and flow has been determined without exception by the American drug scene and Washington's interpretation of Colombia's role therein. Put another way, the relationship's tone depends on Colombia's share of the U.S. illicit drug market, particularly its cocaine component. The larger Colombia's share, the greater Washington's pressure to eradicate, dismantle, and interdict. The greater the pressure, the more confrontational U.S.-Colombian narcopolitics and bilateral relations in general. Conversely, when market share indicators are favorable, so, too, are relations writ small and large. It is important to note that this interrelationship has held constant for many years, the nature of leadership in either country notwithstanding.[31]

The United States' narcotics policy toward Colombia contains several inherent contradictions, one of the most obvious and diplomatically precarious being the tendency toward unilateral decision making within a bilateral, cooperative framework. As a rule, Washington has tended to rely on a cooperative approach during the "peaks" of its narcopolitics with Colombia. Consultation and mutual decision making are the rules in harmonious times. However, it is during the "valleys" of the relationship, those periods when Colombia's share of America's drug market increases and/or in the wake of unfortunate personal incidents, that Washington abandons its binational cooperative stance and acts unilaterally without consulting or even warning Bogotá. To put it more bluntly, in times of exasperation over perceived Colombian inaction, American officials (all too often those not directly involved in the day-to-day antidrug program) shift to a go-it-alone-and-damn-the-torpedoes mode.

Such a response is epitomized by U.S. reaction to the release in December 1987 of Jorge Ochoa, perhaps Colombia's most notorious cocaine capo, from a Colombian jail. Not only did Bogotá come in for scathing criticism and ridicule, but also Colombian products and travelers were subjected to special and often humiliating Customs checks at U.S. ports of entry. Such was the case despite the lack of Colombian government jurisdiction over the judge who signed Ochoa's release form.

While wholly consistent with the prerogatives of an independent nation and perhaps effective in the short term, such unilateral actions do little in the long run to benefit either Washington's narcopolitics or U.S.-Colombian relations. In fact, not only was the American response in the Ochoa case ill conceived (Ochoa was under extraordinary government security and Washington's actions surely will not result in his reincarceration), but also it rendered the government's antidrug campaign even more unpopular with the public and effectively destroyed at that time any hope of reviving the moribund extradition treaty, a critical factor in U.S.-Colombian narcopolitics.

It is noteworthy, particularly from a policy viewpoint, how little has been

learned by both parties to this incident-prone, up-and-down relationship. Neither Washington nor Bogotá has developed a strategy to resolve these crises. It
is almost as if both sides precariously await such events for their cathartic effect. Sequentially, the pattern is roughly as follows: worsening narcorelations,
unilateral American initiative and/or damaging incident, charge-countercharge,
spillover into relations in general, escalating rhetoric from officials and media,
mediation by cooler heads, binational conferences followed by words of praise
for one side by the other, and improved cooperative efforts.

One of the first questions that arises from a study of this cyclical relationship
involves commitment: Just how serious is the United States' determination to
solve its drug abuse problem? More pointedly for comparative purposes, how
determined is its effort vis-à-vis those of Colombia, Bolivia, or Peru? To his
credit, Ronald Reagan budgeted more funds and assigned more personnel to the
U.S. antidrug program than did any of his predecessors. The Bush administration
has loosened the antinarcotics purse strings even more. Considering the problem's
scope, however, it still amounts to a small drop in a very large bucket.

The overall results of Washington's international control program have been
discouraging. Abuse figures, despite some tentatively encouraging trends, are
disappointing across the board. Of the three major illicit drugs, none is in short
supply. Latin America's role in America's drug scene has reached major status.
As a result, critics and curers abound.

The most logical U.S. policy option involves a balancing of priorities between
supply and demand. Washington must place more emphasis on the problem's
demand side. This need not mean neglecting the role of source countries, but it
will clearly require *far* more funding, less rhetoric, and new ways of conceiving
the nation's abuse problem. A second politically feasible option would couple
demand reduction efforts with stepped-up law enforcement in the United States.
Its backers argue, in very Reaganesque terms, for a draconian "get tough"
approach to trafficker *and* user.

Ironically, I have yet to meet a Latin American official who does not favor
such stringent law-and-order policies. In effect, most of them want American
officials to "practice what they preach," to do unto their narcotics lawbreakers
what they demand that the Latin Americans do unto theirs. They reason that if
Washington couples a concerted demand reduction program with accelerated law
enforcement efforts against grower, trafficker, and abuser, America's drug problem will be substantially reduced. There would then be no reason for Washington's "big stick" diplomacy when it comes to America's drug abuse problem.

As regards the two policy options, several caveats are in order. First, there
can be no doubt regarding the demand side of the question. As long as the profit
incentive remains so great, illicit drugs will be smuggled into the country.
Second, the suggestion of coupling demand reduction with stepped-up law enforcement is perhaps logical. But it is also fraught with dangers, particularly for
source countries.

In the real world of U.S. narcopolitics such a policy would admittedly amount to greater emphasis on demand reduction and domestic law enforcement, but it would also mean at least as much, and probably more, emphasis on source country components: eradication, interdiction, and immobilization. Given the realities of civil liberties, criminal procedure, and Gramm-Rudman, it is likely that "get tough" legislation in the United States will mean "get tough" with Bolivia, Peru, and Colombia.

NOTES

1. U.S. Department of State, Bureau of International Narcotics Matters, *International Narcotics Control Strategy Report* (Washington D.C.: U.S. Government Printing Office, 1988), 78.

2. Kevin Healy, "Coca, the State, and the Peasantry in Bolivia, 1982–1988." *Journal of Interamerican Studies and World Affairs* 30 (Summer-Fall 1988): 106.

3. See, in particular, Kevin Healy's seminal analysis, "Coca, the State, and the Peasantry in Bolivia, 1982–1988," *Journal of Interamerican Studies and World Affairs* 30 (Summer–Fall 1988): 105–26.

4. Note, for example, "On the Path to Privatization," *Latin American Regional Report, Andean Group*, 9 April 1987, 7.

5. Ray Henkel, "Coca and Cocaine: The Industry and Its Impact" (Department of Geography, Arizona State University, Tempe, Ariz. n.d., manuscript).

6. "Economic Policy Makes Water." *Latin American Weekly Report*, 17 January 1986, 3.

7. "Economic Policy Makes Water." *Latin America Weekly Report*, 17 January 1986, 2–3.

8. Richard B. Craig, "Illicit Drug Traffic: Implications for South American Source Countries," *Journal of Interamerican Studies and World Affairs* 29 (Summer 1987):6.

9. Healy, "Coca the State."

10. Craig, "Illicit Drug Traffic," 7.

11. "The Left's Alternative Plan for Bolivia," *Latin America Weekly Report*, 11 June 1987, 2.

12. *Latin America Regional Report, Andean Group*, 11 December 1986, 4–5.

13. U.S. Department of State, *International Narcotics* (1988), 71–74.

14. Ibid., 109.

15. U. S. Department of State, Bureau of International Narcotics Matters, *International Narcotics Control Strategy Report* (1986, 1987, 1988), passim.

16. Craig, "Illicit Drug Traffic," 13.

17. Jackson Diehl, "Model Antidrug Drive Fails in Peru," *Washington Post*, 29 December 1984.

18. U.S. Department of State, *International Narcotics* (1987), 119.

19. Thomas Davies, Jr., "The Shining Path to Peruvian Democratization" (Paper presented at the meeting of the Rocky Mountain Council of Latin American Studies, Santa Fe, April 1987).

20. Marcel Niedergang, "Some See Answer to Colombia's Problems in Legal Drugs," *Le Monde/Manchester Guardian Weekly*, 11 January 1987, 13.

21. Niedergang, "Some See Answer," 13.

22. Tyler Bridges, "Peruvian Rebels Supplant Army as Shield for Drug Producers," *Wall Street Journal*, 1 May 1987, 17.

23. "Peru: A New Alliance," *Latin America Weekly Report*, 11 June 1987, 2.

24. Interview, Bureau of International Narcotic Matters, U.S. Department of State, 25 April 1989.

25. For background, see the author's "Colombian Narcotics and United States-Colombian Relations," *Journal of Interamerican Studies and World Affairs* 36 (August 1981): 243–70; and "Domestic Implications of Illicit Drug Cultivation, Processing, and Trafficking in Colombia," *Journal of Interamerican Studies and World Affairs* 8 (August 1983): 325–50. Also note Bruce M. Bagley, "Colombia and the War on Drugs," *Foreign Affairs* 67 (Fall 1988): 70–92.

26. U.S. Department of State, "International Narcotics . . . 1989," 75.

27. Joseph B. Treaster, "Colombia Strains to Stem Rampant Cocaine Abuse," *New York Times*, 15 September 1989, p.1.

28. Niedergang, "Some See Answer."

29. Interview, Bureau of International Narcotic Matters, U.S. Department of State, 25 April 1989.

30. The most revealing account of the Medellín cartel's multidimensional empire is Fabio Castillo's *Los jinetes de la cocaína* (Bogotá: Editorial Documentos Periodísticos, 1987).

31. Regarding U.S. narcotics policy with Colombia, see the author's aforementioned works and two studies by Rensselaer W. Lee III: "The Latin American Drug Connection," *Foreign Policy* no. 61 (Winter 1985–1986): 143-59; and "Why the United States Cannot Stop South American Cocaine," *Orbis* 32 (Fall 1988): 499–520.

Chapter 11 ───────────────────────────────

Drug Testing and the Identification of Drug-Abusing Criminals

Eric D. Wish

This chapter describes issues relevant to the identification of drug abusers within the criminal justice system. This topic takes on special significance in light of the national drug control strategy requirement that states initiate drug-testing programs for arrestees, probationers, and parolees in order to remain eligible to receive federal criminal justice funds.[1] In the first section some of the reasons why the identification of drug-abusing offenders may be an important role for the criminal justice system are discussed. This is followed by a review and comparison of available methods for screening large numbers of offenders for recent drug use.

WHY IDENTIFY THE DRUG-ABUSING OFFENDER?

To Identify Active Criminals

During the past decade, substantial information collected from diverse offender populations has converged to show that hard-drug-abusing offenders are especially likely to commit both drug- and nondrug-related crimes at high rates.[2] Heroin addicts in Baltimore reported committing six times as many crimes during periods when they used narcotics frequently as during periods of lesser use.[3] Violent predators, the most criminally active class of incarcerated persons, were distinguishable by their histories of juvenile drug abuse and adult high-cost heroin habits.[4] Drug abuse in an offender has been a prominent item in many of the more useful criminologic scales designed to predict recidivism.[5] Studies of arrestees in Washington, D.C., and New York City have found that persons who test positive by urinalysis at arrest for one or more hard drugs (usually cocaine, heroin, or PCP) had a greater number of rearrests than did arrestees with a negative test result.[6] And perhaps most important, treatment-induced reductions in narcotics use have been found to be associated with concomitant reductions in individual crime rates.[7] While early research focused primarily on the link between heroin use and crime, a number of recent studies have documented a growing role of cocaine in street crime.[8]

There are a number of reasons why drug abuse and crime are associated. In some instances, persons are so dependent on a drug that they are driven to commit income-generating crimes like theft, robbery, drug selling, and prostitution. For other persons, the drug abuse appears to be merely one of many deviant behaviors they engage in, while for yet others, the crime may be the result of a violent, bizarre reaction to a drug. In planning effective responses for each person, it may be necessary to understand which of the above motives apply.

Because drug-abusing offenders account for a disproportionate share of all crime, a policy that focuses on identifying drug-abusing offenders and applying appropriate interventions has promise for producing a substantial impact on community crime and the overburdened criminal justice system. Certainly one would prefer to apply limited criminal justice resources to the most active offenders. There is growing evidence that criminal justice referral of offenders to drug abuse treatment programs, often accompanied by urine monitoring, can result in persons' remaining longer in treatment and in a reduction in both drug use and crime.[9] There is also the possibility that one might reduce jail and prison overcrowding by referring drug-abusing detainees to treatment and/or urine monitoring programs. In addition, because younger offenders are less likely to inject hard drugs and to use heroin, identification of the youthful offender who is abusing such drugs as marijuana, PCP, or cocaine has promise for enabling society to intervene in and prevent the progression to more extensive drug use.[10]

To Identify Persons in Need of Drug Abuse Treatment and Health Care

Abusers of hard drugs, and especially persons who inject drugs, are at high risk for health problems.[11] Intravenous drug users are especially at high risk for contracting AIDS by sharing dirty needles that contain blood from infected fellow addicts.[12] Prostitutes are also likely to have serious drug abuse and associated health problems. The probability of a urine positive for drugs was higher for female arrestees in New York City than for male arrestees.[13] More than 69 percent of the prostitutes among the female arrestees studied in New York City in 1984 were positive for cocaine. These females frequently reported instances of childhood sexual abuse and protracted histories of emotional and health problems. Because prostitutes usually receive fines or very short sentences (often as time served), they are usually back on the streets of New York within hours of arrest, with no effort made to identify and treat their drug abuse or health problems. Given that more than one-half of the arrestees in Washington, D.C., and in New York City have been found to test positive for one or more drugs, it would seem that the criminal justice system offers an unusual opportunity to society for identifying persons in need of immediate health care.

To Monitor Community Drug Use Trends

As illicit drugs become available in a community, the more deviant persons can be expected to be among those who first use them. In time, use spreads to the larger society. One might therefore predict that changes in the level of illicit drug use in an offender population would be a leading indicator of community drug use. A comparison of urine test results for arrestees in Washington D.C., with the traditional indicators of community drug use showed this to be the case.[14] The rise in heroin use in Washington, D.C., between 1977 and 1980 showed up in the statistics from the arrestee urine-testing program one to one and a half years before it appeared in local statistics on overdose deaths, hospital emergency room admissions, and drug abuse treatment program admissions. The results from the arrestee urine-testing program in Washington and our research in New York have also documented the rising use of cocaine in these cities in the eighties.[15]

By operating a program of drug testing of arrestees on a regular basis, communities may derive secondary bonuses of being able to detect drug epidemics earlier and being able to plan community responses. The potential benefit of urine testing of offenders for tracking drug crime trends has prompted the National Institute of Justice to establish a national drug use forecasting (DUF) system based on urine samples obtained periodically from arrestees in large cities.[16] The impact of law enforcement and other interventions designed to reduce drug use and production can also be measured by an ongoing drug-testing program. A study of the feasibility of establishing urine screening in jail facilities conducted in the 1970s serendipitously uncovered the availability of propoxyphene in the area. These results alerted law enforcement agencies to the problem so that action to locate the suppliers could be taken.[17]

HOW CAN ONE IDENTIFY THE
DRUG-ABUSING OFFENDER?

For a civil commitment program to operate within the criminal justice system, there must be a feasible means available for screening large numbers of persons for recent drug use. The methods utilized must be low in cost, accurate, and capable of being implemented with minimum disruption to the already over-burdened criminal justice systems in most large cities. We focus on four methods: offenders' self-reports, criminal justice records, urinalysis tests, and radioimmunoassay of hair (RIAH). We have excluded blood tests from consideration because of the general difficulty presented by drawing blood from large numbers of detainees as well as the fears of transmission of AIDS. We also have excluded breathalyzer tests because alcohol is a licit drug and is not in itself an indicator of high rates of criminal activity.[18] We also excluded physical and behavioral signs of drug use and intoxication, primarily because they are already widely employed to identify the sick drug-abusing offender who is experiencing withdrawal symptoms or strong drug reactions, but are of less utility for identifying other users. We do discuss hair analysis, even though it is at an experimental stage and still very expensive, because it has some interesting potential advantages over the other techniques.[19]

Offenders' Self-Reports

There is a long tradition in social science research of being able to obtain valid self-reports about deviant behaviors, including illicit drug use. Some of the best estimates of drug use have come from studies involving personal interviews or self-administered questionnaires.[20] Much of what we know about the relationship of drug abuse to crime has also come from studies that have relied on offenders' self-reports. The validity of the information obtained in these studies has usually been tested and affirmed by comparing the respondent's self-reports with information in official records or the results of a urinalysis of a specimen obtained at the conclusion of the interview.[21] Even when we have interviewed active criminals in our secure, confidential research storefront in East Harlem, we have found considerable agreement between self-reported drug use and the urine tests.[22] Among the most important reasons why the respondents in these studies appear willing to disclose sensitive information about themselves are that the data are collected voluntarily for research purposes only in a safe environment and that the anonymity and confidentiality of the information are assured.

These conditions do not exist when attempting to identify drug-using offenders detained in the threatening criminal justice system. The evidence is convincing that detainees will severely underreport their recent drug use, even in a voluntary, confidential research interview. Table 11.1 compares the estimates of drug use obtained in an arrestee population from self-reports in a research interview with their urine specimens analyzed by EMIT. It is clear that twice as many arrestees were found positive for any drug by urinalysis than admitted to recent use in a confidential voluntary research interview in Manhattan Central Booking. The arrestees who refused to participate in the confidential research interview had a high likelihood of rearrest, similar to that found for arrestees who provided a urine that was positive for multiple drugs. When the pretrial release interview information was compared with their urinalysis test results, arrestees in Washington, D.C., were also found to underreport their recent use of drugs by about one-half.[23] Findings from the drug use forecasting programs in twenty-one cities have shown that arrestees across the country underreport recent drug use, especially use of cocaine, even in an anonymous research interview.[24]

Similar findings were obtained from a recent study of probationers assigned to the intensive supervision probation program in New York City.[25] In that study

Table 11.1
Underreporting of Drug Use by Arrestees in a Confidential Research Interview

	REPORTED USING DRUG 24-48 HRS. BEFORE ARREST (n=4847)	POSITIVE BY EMIT AT ARREST (n=4847)
Cocaine	20%	42%
Opiates	14%	21%
Methadone	6%	8%
PCP	3%	12%
Any of the above:	28%	56%
2+ of above:	11%	23%

Table 11.2
Estimates of Recent Drug Use in Probationers from Self-Reports, Urine Tests, and Probation Officer Ratings (N = 66 interviewed probationers with urine test and officer's rating)

	Probationer Reported Using In 24-48 Hours Before Interview	Percent of Probationers Rated By PO As Using Drug In Past Month	Urine Test At Interview
Marijuana	24%	21%	42%
Cocaine	3%	9%	52%
Heroin	3%	3%	2%
PCP	0	0	2%
Methadone	2%	3%	0
Any of above	24%	23%	68%

only 24 percent of the probationers admitted to recent use of a drug in a research interview held in a private area in the probation department office, while 68 percent tested positive by urinalysis (Table 11.2). Moreover, probation officers who indicated that they relied most on the probationer for information about his current drug use also underestimated (23 percent) the prevalence of current drug use in their cases.

If one cannot obtain valid self-reports of recent drug use in a voluntary confidential research interview held within the criminal justice system, it is obvious that one could not do so when the information is to be used by someone to commit the person to treatment or urine monitoring.

In spite of these limitations, there are important uses for self-reports for identifying drug abusers detained by the criminal justice system. Although self-reports would detect only a small portion of drug users, the persons who do admit to drug use are a bona fide group for further action. A study of juvenile detainees found that youths who tested negative for marijuana, but who admitted to recent marijuana use had detention records that were more similar to those of persons who tested positive than to those of youths who were negative by test and self-report.[26] The authors conclude that it would be beneficial to select out for further assessment youths who were positive by urine test *or* who reported recent drug use.

Furthermore, in our study of arrestees in New York City we found that self-reports of current dependence on drugs or of a need for treatment were valuable in differentiating which persons who tested positive were more seriously involved with drugs and crime. Table 11.3 shows that among all arrestees who tested positive, those who admitted to dependence on drugs or alcohol at arrest or to a need for treatment were much more likely to have reported the recent use of drugs, injection of cocaine, and prior treatment. The dependent persons also had more extensive criminal records than did the nondependent persons.

Thus, while many drug abusers will conceal their drug problems, those who do report serious drug problems while in the criminal justice system may be a valid group for further assessment and diversion to treatment. Jurisdictions wishing to implement some immediate, low-cost action to identify drug abusers could assign persons to interview detainees and refer them to treatment programs. Although many drug abusers would go undetected, the number of persons identified would probably be all that most cities could handle anyway, given the usually overburdened and limited treatment resources.

In summary, self-report information can be very valuable for obtaining in-depth details about drug abuse if the offender is willing to disclose the information. It is a poor method to rely on as the primary tool for screening for drug users detained in the criminal justice system. The most promising use for offender self-reports in the criminal justice setting is probably in conjunction with other evidence of drug use that can be used to motivate the offender to discuss his behavior.

Criminal Justice Records

The criminal justice system maintains extensive files of information on offenders. Given our discussion above, and given that much of the information in

Table 11.3
Drug Use and Criminal History in Arrestees Who Tested Positive for Drugs, by Self-Reported Dependence or Need for Treatment

	Positive, Not Dependent (n=1651)	Positive, Dependent* (n=926)
DRUG USE (from self-reports)		
Reported using 24-48 Hrs prior to arrest:		
Cocaine	15%	61%
Heroin	6%	53%
Marijuana	34%	36%
Downers	2%	12%
Illicit Methadone	1%	8%
PCP	3%	6%
Injects cocaine:	9%	61%
Ever received drug treatment:	11%	60%
CRIMINAL HISTORY (from records)		
Ever arrested before:	78%	91%
2+ prior misdemeanor convictions:	32%	60%
2+ prior felony convictions:	10%	14%
Prior arrest for a drug-related offense:	33%	59%

*Male arrestees who tested positive for one or more drugs (opiates, cocaine, PCP, or methadone) and who reported current dependence on drugs or alcohol or a need for treatment.

these records is obtained from the offender, it is not surprising to find that information about the offender's involvement in drugs is often minimal and unreliable.[27]

Even when an arrest report has a place to enter information about the arrestee's drug use, it typically is not completed. This is probably because the police officer often is unaware of the arrestee's involvement with drugs and because information not of immediate relevance to an officer tends not to be reliably entered into a data system. Even in Washington, D.C., where the U.S. Attorney General has installed PROMIS (Prosecutor's Management Information System) to track case information, the arresting officers identified as drug involved only 22 percent of the persons who were found positive for drugs at arrest by urinalysis.[28] Presentence investigation reports should contain more information about the offender's background. However, in the absence of urine tests, the investigator must rely on the defendant's admission of drug use or that from a family member. And in large cities, the time and resources available for soliciting such information are limited.

If records do not contain detailed information about drug involvement, can a person's record of arrest or convictions for a drug offense serve as an accurate indicator of drug use? The evidence indicates that persons charged with the sale or possession of controlled substances are most likely to be drug users (Table 11.4).

Almost three-quarters of male arrestees in New York City (and of arrestees in Washington, D.C.) charged with these offenses in 1984 tested positive for opiates, cocaine, methadone, or PCP. However, more than one-half the persons charged with robbery, burglary, larceny, or murder were also positive for drugs.[29] And 56 percent of the arrestees were positive for a drug when only 20 percent of the sample were charged with a drug offense. Only 10 percent of the 17,000 male and female arrestees found to be drug positive by urinalysis in Washington, D.C., in 1973–1974 were charged with a drug offense.[30] Thus, while offenders with a history of drug offenses are most likely to be using drugs, it is clear that offenders charged with a variety of other offenses may be drug users. By relying solely on a drug offense to identify the drug user, one would miss the majority of users.

Urinalysis Tests

In recent years urinalysis tests have received considerable attention as a source of information about an offender's drug use.[31] It should be noted, however, that researchers have been using the tests for the past fifteen years as a means to validate information obtained in interviews about recent drug use. And drug abuse treatment programs have often monitored patients' drug use by urinalysis.[32] Urine tests were employed successfully by the Department of Defense to screen army personnel before they left Vietnam for the United States in the 1970s and in recent years to combat a growing drug use problem. Furthermore, in the initial years of the federally sponsored TASC (Treatment Alternatives to Street Crime) program, urinalysis was used to identify drug-using offenders for diversion into treatment programs. Urine tests have been used by the U.S. Department of Probation and by local probation departments to screen suspected drug users. Mass screening of offender populations for drugs has been used only in Washington, D.C., however, where all arrestees detained in the Superior Court lockup prior to court appearance have been tested since 1971.

There are a number of possible urinalysis techniques, and a common error

Table 11.4
What Charges Were Most Associated with Having a Positive Urine Test?

Arrest Charge	(N)	Percent Positive*
Possession of drugs	(615)	76%
Sale of drugs	(355)	71%
Poss. stolen property	(474)	61%
Forgery	(94)	60%
Burglary	(348)	59%
Murder/manslaughter	(64)	56%
Larceny	(667)	56%
Robbery	(676)	54%
Weapons	(157)	53%
Stolen credit cards	(56)	52%
Criminal mischief	(66)	48%
Gambling	(147)	45%
Sexual assault	(79)	41%
Public disorder	(108)	37%
Assault	(506)	37%
Fare beating	(98)	37%
Fraud	(54)	30%
Other offenses	(269)	45%
Total:	(4833)	56%

*Positive by EMIT for opiates, cocaine, PCP, or methadone.

made by persons when assessing the validity of drug testing is to fail to consider the type of test used. Until recently, most urine testing of offenders in the criminal justice system and in treatment programs was conducted using a thin layer chromatography (TLC) general screen. This technique is especially economical because it can screen for a variety of drugs, but it is a very subjective process, requiring experienced technicians to interpret the results.

Primarily because of their low cost, sensitivity, and ease of use, the most commonly used urine tests today is the EMIT (enzyme multiplied immunoassay test). This test involves a chemical reaction of the specimen with an antibody designed to react to a specific drug. The chemical reaction causes a change in the specimen's transmission of light. This change in transmissibility is detected by a machine that provides a quantitative reading that is compared with the

Table 11.5
Drugs Detected in Urine Specimens from Male Arrestees, by Type of Test
(n = 4,847 Specimens)

Drug Detected	TLC	EMIT
Cocaine	14%	42%
Opiates (morphine)	9%	21%
PCP	NA	12%
Methadone	4%	8%

reading from a standard solution containing a known concentration of the drug. If the reading from the specimen is higher than that of the standard, the specimen is positive for that drug. Because the determination of a positive is based on specific numbers, the level of subjectivity required by the EMIT is less than that required by TLC. Certainly, TLC looks more economical because for approximately $2 one can screen for as many as twenty different types of drugs. EMITs are specific to one drug and cost between $1 and $5 for each drug tested. (These are high-volume, reduced rates charged to researchers by the New York State Division of Substance Abuse Testing Laboratory.)

Table 11.5 presents a comparison of the results from 4,847 specimens obtained from arrestees in New York City and tested by TLC and the comparable EMIT technique by the New York State Testing Laboratory. It is clear that the TLC test underdetects the common street drugs by almost two-thirds.[33] Many laboratories have used a two-test approach to identifying drugs. They would first screen for drugs using TLC and then confirm any positive result by an EMIT. Such a procedure would clearly result in many drug users' escaping detection. As a result of the findings above, EMITs are being substituted for TLC tests across the country.

The growing popularity of the EMITs has made them the object of several legal challenges. The primary criticism is that the EMITs have too high a rate of false positive errors. That is, the tests falsely indicate the presence of a drug. Much of the debate surrounds the possibility that some common *licit* drugs can cross-react with the test's reagents to produce a positive result.[34] The ingestion of poppy seed bagels has been found to produce a positive test result for opiates. Furthermore, the EMIT for opiates will detect heroin (morphine) as well as prescribed drugs such as codeine. Sloppy recording procedures by laboratory staff and failure to maintain the chain of custody of the specimen can also produce serious test errors.

Other urinalysis techniques are available for detecting drugs, including radioimmunoassay and gas chromatography/mass spectrometry (GC/MS).[35] Some of these techniques have not been used frequently in the criminal justice system, and sufficient case law does not exist regarding whether the courts consider them to be valid. At present, GC/MS is too costly and time consuming to be used as the initial test in large-scale screening programs, although it has been required by some courts as a confirmation test.

A study by the Centers for Disease Control (CDC) has been cited for its report of substantial errors in the results from the thirteen labs that were surveyed.[36] In a blind experiment the CDC sent a group of blank urine specimens as well as specimens containing known quantities of drugs to the labs for analysis (the particular urinalysis tests used by the labs were not specified). The study found that while some labs failed to detect specific drugs contained in the specimens, few instances occurred where a lab reported a drug in one of the blank specimens. In fact, the average accuracy of the analyses of the blank specimens was 99 percent, and there were so few false positive results that the analyses of this issue were limited.

Our experience using urine tests in offender populations also indicates that the problem of false negatives is much larger than is that of false positive errors. In contrast to controlled laboratory experiments, when one tests for illicit drugs in offenders, one cannot control for many of the factors that influence the concentration of the drug in the urine. The quantity of the drug taken, its purity, and the time since its ingestion are unknown. It is therefore somewhat amazing when a test does detect a drug! Our studies show that even when a person admits to taking a drug during the prior one or two days covered by the test, it is found in only 70 to 80 percent of the cases. Many drug users will thus escape detection by urinalysis.

It is probable that the future of urine testing in the criminal justice system will depend on a satisfactory solution to the problem of false positive errors. The NIDA guidelines for work place testing, which do not apply to testing conducted by the criminal justice system, state that all positive test results from immunoassay tests should be confirmed by GC/MS.[37] The most accurate technique available for identifying drugs in the urine is GC/MS, but it costs about $70–$100 per specimen. It seems appropriate to require such a procedure when a single test result may cause a person to lose his or her job or liberty. However, when a test result is used solely to trigger further investigation of whether a person is involved with drugs, it may be that confirmation by other methods (urine monitoring or diagnostic interview) would be equally acceptable. The courts have yet to decide this issue.

Even though urine tests do contain some degree of error, the evidence is strong that the tests have a high degree of validity. The EMITs have been ruled valid by judges, although courts have differed on the need for confirmation of positive results.[38] Furthermore, the construct validity of urine tests, the evidence that the the relationships found with the tests are consistent with the current knowledge about drug use, is impressive. Studies of arrestees and probationers in New York City and Washington, D.C., have found hypothesized relationships between

Figure 11.1
Mean Number of Rearrests, by Urine Test and Age

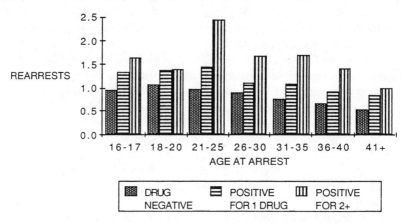

Measures rearrests in an 11–17 month period after the index arrest. These findings do not control for time at risk on the street. Differences would be expected to be more extreme, however, because drug users were somewhat more likely to be remanded after arraignment than were nonusers.

detected drug use and age, prior arrest history, type of arrest charge, and recidivism.[39] And a positive test for marijuana was related to a greater lifetime use of marijuana and a greater number of juvenile detentions in juveniles in Tampa.[40] In fact, we first discovered the lesser sensitivity of the TLC test in our research because the analyses of specimens from unapprehended offenders interviewed in a research storefront in East Harlem did not confirm the heavy drug use that these persons were reporting! Only after the EMITs were used was the claimed drug use verified by the urine tests.[41] Perhaps of primary significance is the finding from studies in Washington, D.C., and New York that not only the presence of a drug, but also the *number* of drugs detected was related to criminal behavior. For all age groups, arrestees positive for two or more drugs (usually cocaine and opiates) had the greatest number of rearrests. Furthermore, 60 percent of the rearrests for multiple drug users were for offenses other than the sale or possession of drugs.[42]

It is unknown what proportion of offenders who are found positive is seriously involved with drugs. For this reason, a positive urine test should be used with other information (self-reports, criminal justice records, or repeated urine testings) to determine whether the offender chronically abuses drugs and is in need of treatment.

Radioimmunoassay of Hair

Radioimmunoassay of hair (RIAH) is an experimental procedure with potential for drug detection.[43] As hair is formed in the scalp, the cells are nourished by the blood, and drugs present in the blood are deposited in the cells at the root level. One can extract the drugs from the hair and analyze them by radioimmunoassay. Researchers have found that the level of the drug taken is correlated with the amount deposited in the hair cells. Perhaps of most importance is that one can obtain a historical record of the level of drug use of the person. While hair at the scalp level contains evidence of current use, hair further from the root contains evidence of use months ago when it was formed. Thus, by analyzing sections of hair (especially in persons with long hair!), one can discern a trend in drug use over time.[44] Procedures are available for detecting the most commonly abused drugs.

One possible advantage of RIAH is that one cannot easily fake the test. For example, one cannot suspend use before a scheduled test to avoid detection. Once the drug is stored in the hair, it remains there permanently. And the technique of obtaining hair is noninvasive and less objectionable to some persons than is that of obtaining urine. The analysis may provide evidence of the level and trend of use over time. In addition, if the test is inconclusive or a retest is required, one can obtain a similar sample for analysis more easily than with urine testing. The largest drawbacks to the test include the fact that it requires radioactive materials and the types of precautions usually needed in handling such substances, the cost (roughly $50 per drug tested), the turnaround time of approximately twenty-four hours, and the unavailability of standardized and accepted extraction techniques. In addition, there is some possibility that the content of the hair can be influenced by environmental contaminants[45] and that the potential for measuring use patterns over time has yet to be conclusively demonstrated.[46]

Even if current research confirms the utility of RIAH, the long turnaround time for the analysis and the cost may prohibit the adoption of the method for large-scale screening of offenders. In addition, it will take considerable time for the courts and the scientific community to acknowledge the validity of the new technique. If the technique is eventually accepted and the analysis time remains long, the technique will most likely be less useful than are other techniques for testing arrestees pretrial, where the judge typically requires the results quickly at the time of arraignment. Perhaps the most valuable use for RIAH with offenders will be for the confirmation of the results of other tests and for the verification of changes in the person's use.

SUMMARY

In a criminal justice setting, urine testing is the most feasible and accurate method now available for screening large numbers of offenders for drug use. Self-report and record information can be effectively used to verify and extend information about the seriousness of use in persons who test positive. The newer RIAH methods offer promise for delineating patterns of drug use over time if the method is valid, can be standardized, and gains acceptance from the scientific and judicial communities.

NOTES

1. *National Drug Control Strategy* (Washington, D.C.: The White House, 1989).

2. Eric D. Wish and B. D. Johnson, "The Impact of Substance Abuse on Criminal Careers," in *Criminal Careers and "Career Criminals"*, vol. 2, ed. A. Blumstein, J. Cohen, and Christy A. Visher (Washington, D.C.: National Academy Press, 1986).

3. John C. Ball, Lawrence Rosen, John A. Flueck, and David N. Nurco, "The Criminality of Heroin Addicts When Addicted and When Off Opiates," in *The Drugs-Crime Connection*, ed. James A. Inciardi (Beverly Hills, Calif.: Sage, 1981), 39–66.

4. Jan Chaiken and Marcia Chaiken, *Varieties of Criminal Behavior* (Santa Monica, Calif.: Rand, 1982).

5. Alfred Blumstein, J. Cohen, J. A. Roth, and C. A. Visher, *Criminal Careers and "Career Criminals,"* vol. 1 (Washington, D.C.: National Academy Press, 1986).

6. Mary Toborg, J. P. Bellassai, and A. M. J. Yeger, "The Washington, D.C. Urine Testing Program for Arrestees and Defendants Awaiting Trial: A Summary of Interim Findings" (Paper presented at the NIJ-sponsored conference on Drugs and Crime: Detecting Use and Reducing Risk, Washington, D.C., 5 June 1986); Eric D. Wish, E. Brady, and M. Cuadrado, "Urine Testing of Arrestees: Findings from Manhattan" (Paper presented at the NIJ-sponsored conference on Drugs and Crime: Detecting Use and Reducing Risk, Washington, D.C., 5 June 1986); J. K. Stewart, "Quid Pro Quo: Stay Drug-Free and Stay on Release," *George Washington Law Review* 57 (1988); D. A. Smith, E. D. Wish, and G. R. Jarjoura, "Drug Use and Pretrial Misconduct in New York City," *Journal of Quantitative Criminology* (1989).

7. William H. McGlothlin, M. Douglas Anglin, and Bruce D. Wilson, *An Evaluation of the California Civil Addict Program* (Rockville, Md.: National Institute on Drug Abuse, 1977).

8. Dana Hunt, Douglas S. Lipton, and Barry Spunt, "Patterns of Criminal Activity Among Methadone Clients and Current Narcotics Users Not in Treatment," *Journal of Drug Issues* 14 (1984): 687–702; James J. Collins, Robert Hubbard, and J. Valley Rachal, "Expensive Drug Use and Illegal Income: A Test of Explanatory Hypotheses," *Criminology* 23 (1985): 743–764; Bruce D. Johnson, Paul Goldstein, Edward Preble, James Schmeidler, Douglas S. Lipton, Barry Spunt, and Thomas Miller, *Taking Care of Business: The Economics of Crime by Heroin Abusers* (Lexington, Mass.: Lexington Books, 1985).

9. James J. Collins and Margret Allison, "Legal Coercion and Retention in Drug Abuse Treatment," *Hospital and Community Psychiatry* 14 (1983): 1145–49; M. D. Anglin and W. H. McGlothlin, "Outcome on Narcotic Addict Treatment in California," in *Drug Abuse Treatment Evaluation: Strategy, Progress, and Prospects*, ed. F. M. Tims and J. Ludford (Washington, D.C.: U.S. Government Printing Office, 1984); Maxine Stitzer and Mary E. McCaul, "Criminal Justice Interventions with Drug and Alcohol Abusers: The Role of Compulsory Treatment," in *Behavioral Approaches to Crime and Delinquency*, ed. Curtis J. Braukman and Edward K. Morris (New York: Plenum Press, 1987).

10. Wish, Brady, and Cuadrado, "Urine Testing of Arrestees"; Richard Dembo, M.

Washburn, E. D. Wish, H. Yeung, A. Getreu, E. Berry, and W. Blount, "Heavy Marijuana Use and Crime Among Youths Entering a Juvenile Detention Center," *Journal of Psychoactive Drugs* 19 (1987).

11. P. J. Goldstein and D. E. Hunt. "Health Consequences of Drug Use," *Final Report to the Carter Center of Emory University*, (Atlanta: 1984).

12. Michael Marmor, Don C. Des Jarlais, Samuel R. Friedman, Margaret Lyden, and Wafaa El-Sadr, "The Epidemic of Acquired Immunodeficiency Syndrome (AIDS) and Suggestions for Its Control in Drug Abusers," *Journal of Substance Abuse Treatment* 1 (1984): 237–47.

13. Wish, Brady, and Cuadrado, "Urine Testing of Arrestees"; E. D. Wish, J. Oneil, and V. Baldau, *Lose Opportunity to Combat AIDS: Drug Abusers in the Criminal Justice System*, (National Institute of Justice, 1988).

14. Eric D. Wish, "Urine Testing of Arrestees: A Tool for Reducing Drug Abuse and Crime" (Paper presented at the annual meeting of the American Psychological Association, Washington, D.C., August 1982); Brian Forst and Eric Wish, "Drug Use and Crime: Providing a Missing Link," in *Violent Crime in America*, ed. Kenneth R. Feinberg (Washington, D.C.: National Policy Exchange, 1983), 84–95.

15. Eric D. Wish, "Identification of Drug Abusing Offenders: A Guide for Practitioners" (Paper presented at the National Research Council Workshop on Drugs and Crime, Atlanta, December 1986).

16. "Growing Focus on Criminal Careers," *Science* 233 (1986): 1377–78; *NIJ Reports*, SNI 202, National Institute of Justice, March–April, 1987.

17. National Institute on Drug Abuse, *Monitoring Drug Abuse in the Community Through a Jail Urine Screening Program*, (ADM) 80-903 (Washington, D.C.: U.S. Government Printing Office, 1979).

18. Eric D. Wish, M. Chedekel, E. Brady, and M. Cuadrado, "Alcohol Use and Crime in Arrestees in Manhattan" (Paper presented at the annual meeting of the American Academy of Forensic Sciences, New Orleans, February 1986).

19. A more detailed description of these techniques can be found in Wish, "Identification of Drug Abusing Offenders."

20. John A. O'Donnell, Harwin L. Voss, Richard Clayton, Gerald T. Slatin, and Robin G. Room, *Young Men and Drugs—A Nationwide Survey* (Rockville, Md.: National Institute on Drug Abuse, 1976); Lloyd D. Johnston, J. G. Bachman, and P. M. O'Malley, *Drug Use Among American High School Students, 1975–77* (Washington, D.C.: U. S. Government Printing Office, 1977).

21. Adele V. Harrell, "Validation of Self-Report: The Research Record," in *Self-Report Methods of Estimating Drug Use*, ed. B. A. Rouse, N. Kozel, and L. Richards, *NIDA Research Monograph No. 57* (Washington D.C., U.S. Government Printing Office, 1985).

22. Eric D. Wish, B. Johnson, D. Strug, K. Anderson, and T. Miller, "Concordance Between Self-Reports of Drug Use and Urinalysis Test Results from Active Unapprehended Criminals" (1983, manuscript); Eric D. Wish, D. Strug, K. Anderson, T. Miller, and B. Johnson, "Are Urine Tests Good Indicators of the Validity of Self-Reports of Drug Use? It Depends on the Test" (Paper presented at the annual meeting of the American Society of Criminology, Denver, November 1983).

23. Toborg, Bellassai, and Yeger, "The Washington, D.C. Urine Testing Program."

24. National Institute of Justice, *Drug Use Forecasting*, Research in Action Report, January to March 1989 (September 1989).

25. Eric D. Wish, M. Cuadrado, and J. Martorana, "Estimates of Drug Use in Intensive Supervision Probationers: Results from a Pilot Study," *Federal Probation* 50 (1986).

26. Richard Dembo, E. D. Wish, A. Getreu, M. Washburn, J. Schmeidler, B. Estrellita, and W. R. Blount, "Further Examination of the Association Between Heavy Marijuana Use and Crime Among Youths Entering a Juvenile Detention Center" (Paper presented at the annual meeting of the American Society of Criminology, Atlanta, November 1986).

27. Paul J. Goldstein, "Homicide Related to Drug Traffic," *Bulletin of the New York Academy of Medicine* 62 (1986): 509–16.

28. Eric D. Wish, K. A. Klumpp, A. H. Moorer, E. Brady, and K. M. Williams, *An Analysis of Drugs and Crime Among Arrestees in the District of Columbia, Executive Summary*, Pub. no. 1982-361-233/6346, (Washington, D.C.: U.S. Department of Justice, December 1981).

29. Wish, Brady, and Cuadrado, "Urine Testing of Arrestees."

30. Ibid.

31. Eric D. Wish, "Urine Testing of Arrestees: A Tool."

32. McGlothlin, Anglin, and Wilson, *An Evaluation*.

33. S. Magura, D. Goldsmith, C. Casriel, P. J. Goldstein, and D. S. Lipton, "The Validity of Methadone Clients' Self-Reported Drug Use," *International Journal of the Addictions* 22 (1987): 727–49.

34. John P. Morgan, "Problems of Mass Screening for Misused Drugs," *Journal of Psychoactive Drugs* 16 (1984): 305–17.

35. Richard L. Hawks and C. Nora Chiang, eds., *Urine Testing for Drugs of Abuse* (Rockville, Md.: National Institute on Drug Abuse, 1986).

36. Hugh B. Hansen, Samuel P. Caudill, and D. Joe Boone, "Crisis in Drug Testing: Results of CDC Blind Study," *Journal of the American Medical Association* 253 (1985): 2382–87.

37. "Mandatory Guidelines for Federal Workplace Drug Testing Programs," *Federal Register* (11 April 1988).

38. Jones vs. United States, No. 86–31 (D.C. Ct. App. 9 September 1988).

39. Wish, Brady, and Cuadrado, "Urine Testing of Arrestees."

40. Dembo et al., "Further Examination."

41. Eric D. Wish, et al., supra note 29.

42. Ibid.

43. M. R. Harkey and G. L. Henderson, *Hair Analysis for Drugs of Abuse: A Critical Review of the Technology*, Final Report Submitted to the California Department of Alcohol and Drug Programs (Sacramento, Calif.: 1988).

44. Lynn R. Witherspoon and Joseph S. Trapani, "Forensic Radioimmunoassay—A New Area," *Journal of Nuclear Medicine* 20 (1983): 796–97; Susan Thanepohn, "A New Wrinkle: Testing Hair for Drugs," *U.S. Journal*, 10 (April 1986).

45. K. Puschel, P. Thomasch, and W. Arnold, "Opiate Levels in Hair," *Forensic Science International* 21 (1983): 181–86.

46. Harkey and Henderson, *Hair Analysis*.

Chapter 12

Drug Testing and the Constitution

Kenneth C. Haas

The use of illegal drugs by employees appears to be a growing problem in the workplace. It has been estimated that 10 to 23 percent of all employees use drugs at work.[1] These employees have three to four times as many accidents as do other employees, and many of these accidents result in death, injuries, or substantial property loss.[2] Drug abusers cost employers billions of dollars annually as a result of poor job performance, higher insurance costs, increased claims made on company health plans, high absenteeism, damage to company property, and employee theft.[3] The cost to the economy may well exceed $60 billion a year.[4]

Heightened awareness of this problem has led employers to implement various types of drug-testing programs, many of which include urine testing.[5] The Bush administration has called for the urinalysis of approximately 1.1 million federal employees in "sensitive" jobs, from railroad workers to Justice Department attorneys.[6] State and local governments also have embarked on ambitious urinalysis programs, ranging from pre-employment testing of job applicants to random testing of incumbent employees.[7]

Not surprisingly, such programs have prompted the filing of numerous lawsuits in federal and state courts. Private employers, however, are not bound by the Bill of Rights or other provisions of the Constitution, all of which explicitly limit only the actions of government entities and government employers.[8] Thus, the large majority of the drug-testing suits filed in American courts have attacked testing conducted by government agencies and government-regulated industries such as railroads and airlines.[9] Nearly all of these suits have challenged urine-testing programs and other drug-testing plans under the theory that such testing violates the Fourth Amendment's prohibition of unreasonable searches and seizures.

On 21 March 1989, the U.S. Supreme Court announced its first two decisions on the constitutionality of drug testing. In the first case, *Skinner v. Railway Labor Executives' Association*, the Court assessed the validity of Federal Railroad

Administration regulations mandating breath, blood, and urine testing of railroad employees after major train accidents. The second case, *National Treasury Employees Union v. Von Raab*, focused on the constitutionality of a U.S. Customs Service program requiring all employees seeking promotion or transfer to drug enforcement jobs to undergo urinalysis. This chapter will examine these two decisions in detail, with an emphasis on the divergent approaches taken by the majority and dissenting Justices in the *Von Raab* case. The analysis will demonstrate that the *Railway Labor Executives* and *Von Raab* decisions resolved some of the constitutional questions surrounding drug testing, but that several important questions remain unanswered.

THE FOURTH AMENDMENT

Drug-testing programs have been challenged as violative of several provisions of the Constitution, but only Fourth Amendment challenges have been consistently successful. Some public employees, for example, have brought lawsuits attacking drug testing on the theory that it violates employees' Fifth Amendment protection against self-incrimination.[10] However, it is settled law that the self-incrimination clause applies only to testimonial evidence, not to bodily fluids.[11] Equally important, the protection against self-incrimination applies only in criminal cases and thus cannot be used to challenge blood or urine tests that are conducted solely for civil purposes.[12]

In several cases plaintiffs have asserted that drug testing violates a general constitutional right of privacy.[13] This contention is based on the landmark case of *Griswold v. Connecticut*,[14] in which the U.S. Supreme Court invalidated a Connecticut law making it a crime to use a contraceptive device on the ground that the law violated a right to privacy that is implicit in the Constitution as a result of "zones of privacy" created by the "liberty" safeguards in the due process clauses of the Fifth and Fourteenth Amendments and by the "penumbras" surrounding the First, Third, Fourth, Fifth, and Ninth Amendments. Although *Griswold* has not been overturned, the general constitutional right to privacy has not played a major role in drug-testing litigation and is not likely to do so in the future. To be sure, an employee can reasonably argue that the process of obtaining and testing a urine sample violates his or her most basic privacy rights, especially when the testing reveals evidence of off-the-job substance use that may have no effect on a worker's job performance. The Supreme Court, however, has construed the constitutional right of privacy to apply only in cases involving marriage, procreation, abortion, contraception, family relationships, and child rearing and education.[15] Since governmental efforts to detect the use of illicit drugs do not invade the privacy our society recognizes in marriage, procreation, and family relationships, courts are unlikely to strike down drug-testing programs on "pure privacy" grounds.

However, those who challenge drug-testing schemes can make a Fourth Amendment claim that rests on much stronger doctrinal grounds. The Supreme

Court recently made it clear that government employee urinalysis is a search within the meaning of the Fourth Amendment.[16] Thus, the future of public employee drug testing is likely to be shaped by court decisions that will apply Fourth Amendment guidelines to distinguish between the constitutional drug-testing program and the unconstitutional one.

The Fourth Amendment states that

The right of the people to be secure in their persons, houses, papers, and effects, against unreasonable searches and seizures, shall not be violated, and no Warrants shall issue, but upon probable cause, supported by Oath or affirmation, and particularly describing the place to be searched, and the persons or things to be seized.[17]

This amendment was the response of the framers of the Constitution to the general warrants (authorizing searches of anyone or anything at any time) and other abuses of personal liberty engendered by the search and seizure practices of the time.[18] The framers clearly intended "[t]he Bill of Rights in general and the Fourth Amendment, in particular [to be] profoundly anti-government documents."[19] Throughout its history, the Supreme Court has recognized that the basic purpose of the Fourth Amendment is to protect the privacy and dignity of the individual against unreasonable intrusions by the state and "all of its creatures."[20]

Central to the analysis of the constitutionality of drug testing is the relationship between the two clauses that make up the Fourth Amendment. The first clause contains a general guarantee of freedom from unreasonable searches and seizures, and the second clause specifies the conditions under which search warrants can be issued. The relationship between the two clauses has always been unclear,[21] but in the 1967 case of *Katz v. United States*,[22] the Supreme Court, stressing the importance of protecting the individual's "reasonable expectation of privacy," articulated the fundamental principle that "searches conducted outside the judicial process without prior approval by judge or magistrate are *per se* unreasonable under the Fourth Amendment—subject only to a few specifically established and well-delineated exceptions."[23] Although the Court has been retreating from strict adherence to the warrant requirement in recent years by expanding the number of exceptions to the requirement,[24] the *Katz* principle remains intact.[25] The Supreme Court continues to require that a warrant be obtained unless the search fits into an established exception or is deemed not to have invaded one's reasonable expectation of privacy.[26]

For the opponents of drug testing, a particularly disquieting trend has been the Supreme Court's growing willingness to waive both the warrant requirement and the traditional understanding that even a search that may permissibly be conducted without a warrant must be based on probable cause to believe that a crime has been committed.[27] This has been accomplished through the use of a "reasonableness" test. Whereas the probable-cause standard places the individual's right to privacy above the government's interest in conducting a search,[28] the reasonableness test weighs both interests equally and balances them against each other in light of the totality of the circumstances surrounding each case.[29]

The first clear sign that the Supreme Court was likely to embrace the reasonableness test as the appropriate Fourth Amendment standard in drug-testing cases came in 1985. In *New Jersey v. T.L.O.*[30] the Court held that public school officials need neither a search warrant nor circumstances constituting probable cause before searching a student. Since this was a case involving the special needs of a school environment, not a case involving ordinary street crime, the reasonableness test, according to the *T.L.O.* Court, should replace the traditional warrant and probable-cause analysis. The two-part reasonableness test approved in *T.L.O.* requires only (1) that school officials have reasonable grounds to suspect that a search will turn up evidence of violations of law or school rules and (2) that the search be reasonably related in scope to the circumstances that justified the search in the first place.[31]

The same two-pronged reasonableness test was employed two years later in *Griffin v. Wisconsin*.[32] In permitting probation officers to conduct warrantless searches of probationers' homes, the Court noted that exceptions to the warrant and probable-cause requirements can be permitted in situations in which "special needs, beyond the normal need for law enforcement, make [these requirements] impractical."[33] This "special needs" argument also carried the day in *O'Connor v. Ortega*,[34] a 1987 decision that authorizes government employers to conduct searches of their employees' offices without search warrants or probable cause. Writing for a four-Justice plurality, Justice O'Connor began by acknowledging that public employees have a reasonable expectation of privacy in their offices[35] and that government employers are limited by the Fourth Amendment when they conduct searches that infringe on these privacy expectations.[36] However, she also asserted that requiring an employer to obtain a search warrant whenever he or she wished to search an employee's office for work-related reasons would "disrupt the routine conduct of business and unduly burden agency supervisors."[37]

The *Ortega* decision makes it clear that workplace searches (presumably including public employee drug-testing programs) are similar to school searches conducted by school officials in that they must be analyzed in terms of "special needs" that go beyond the normal need for law enforcement.[38] In place of the warrant and probable-cause requirements, the plurality created a special reasonableness test to be used on a case-by-case basis to judge the constitutionality of workplace searches—"the standard of reasonableness under all the circumstances."[39] Under this standard, an employer may conduct a warrantless search "when there are reasonable grounds for suspecting that the search will turn up evidence that the employee is guilty of work-related misconduct, or that the search is necessary for a noninvestigatory work-related purpose such as to retrieve a needed file."[40] Once begun, the search will be permissible in scope if it is limited to the objectives of the search and is "not excessively intrusive," given the nature of the misconduct.[41]

Although *Ortega* was not a drug-testing case, the Court's adoption of still another "special needs" exception to traditional Fourth Amendment requirements could only be seen as encouraging employers to implement drug-testing plans. Some legal scholars predicted that the Supreme Court would, in effect, create a "drug-testing" exception when the Justices announced their first decisions in this new area of law.[42] As previously mentioned, the Court did, in fact, reach decisions in two drug-testing cases in the 1988–1989 term. We now turn to an examination of these cases.

SKINNER V. RAILWAY LABOR EXECUTIVES' ASSOCIATION

The threshold question in any case in which a plaintiff asserts a violation of Fourth Amendment rights is whether a challenged governmental activity amounts to a search covered by the Fourth Amendment. In the first of two drug-testing cases decided on 21 March 1989, the Supreme Court established that public employee urinalysis is indeed a search within the meaning of the Fourth Amendment. In *Skinner v. Railway Labor Executives' Association*,[43] the Court, speaking through Justice Kennedy's majority opinion, pointed out that compelled blood testing had already been recognized by the Court as a search because it implicates legitimate societal concerns about bodily integrity.[44] Blood testing involves a physical penetration of the skin and an ensuing chemical analysis of the blood sample, both of which infringe on "expectation(s) of privacy that society is prepared to recognize as reasonable."[45] Similarly, compelling a person to produce aveolar or "deep lung" breath and subsequently analyzing the breath are intrusions that trigger understandable concerns about personal privacy.[46] Although urine testing, unlike blood testing, does not involve a physical penetration of the skin,[47] it was indisputable, Justice Kennedy asserted, that the chemical analysis of urine, like that of blood, "can reveal a host of private medical facts about an employee, including whether she is epileptic, pregnant, or diabetic."[48] Moreover, he stressed, urine-testing procedures usually include visual or aural monitoring of the act of urination—a highly personal and private function that, as a matter of law and social custom, is "traditionally performed without public observation."[49] The Justices therefore were in unanimous agreement that urine testing intrudes on expectations of privacy long recognized by our society as reasonable and thus must be deemed a search under the Fourth Amendment.[50]

Having determined that urine testing, like blood and breathalyzer testing, constitutes a Fourth Amendment search, Justice Kennedy turned to the major issue presented in the *Railway Labor Executives* case—the constitutionality of Federal Railroad Administration (FRA) regulations mandating urine, blood, and breath tests of employees after serious train accidents or rule violations. The regulations in question require the prompt collection of blood and urine samples from all crew members of trains involved in accidents that include a fatality, the release of hazardous material accompanied by either evacuation or injury, or damage to railroad property of $500,000 or more. The regulations also mandate blood and urine testing after any "train incident" that involves a fatality to any on-duty railroad employee and after any "impact accident," which is defined as any collision that results in a reportable injury or in damage to railroad property of $50,000 or more. Finally, the regulations provide for breath or urine tests when a supervisor has reasonable suspicion that an employee's acts or omissions contributed to an accident, when two supervisors agree that there is reasonable suspicion to believe that an employee is under the influence of alcohol or other drugs, or when the employee violates speeding regulations or other railroad operating rules.[51]

A seven-Justice majority held these regulations to be constitutionally valid even though they contained no warrant requirement and permitted testing under circumstances in which there would sometimes be neither probable cause nor reasonable suspicion to believe that a particular employee was under the influence of alcohol or illegal drugs. Equally important in terms of the future of public employee drug testing, the Court upheld the FRA regulations by employing a reasonableness or "multifactor balancing test" similar to the ones used in *O'Connor v. Ortega* and other cases that arguably present "special needs, beyond the normal need for law enforcement."[52]

Justice Kennedy began his analysis by stating that the Court was not abandoning its traditional probable-cause analysis—requiring a judicial warrant based on probable cause except in certain well-defined circumstances—for routine criminal cases.[53] However, the Court analogized the government's need to regulate the railroads and other safety-sensitive industries to the government's interests in maintaining the efficient operation of schools and government offices and in supervising probationers and prisoners.[54] Since these activities present "special needs [that] make the warrant and probable-cause requirements impractical,"[55] the majority Justices determined that the appropriate standard for reviewing the FRA regulations was a reasonableness test.[56] This, in and of itself, portended the outcome of the case. Whereas a more traditional probable-cause analysis would have started with the assumption that the railroad employees' interests in privacy ranked at least slightly ahead of the government's interests, the majority's reasonableness analysis started with the assumption that the employees' privacy interests and the government's interests were equally important. The decision thus would turn on the majority's balancing of the probable benefits of implementing the FRA regulations against the costs imposed on the personal privacy of employees.

Perhaps in an effort to emphasize that the warrant requirement remains an essential element of Fourth Amendment jurisprudence, Justice Kennedy briefly paid homage to the warrant requirement's role in protecting citizens against random and arbitrary governmental actions in ordinary law enforcement situations.[57] He contended, however, that the FRA regulations were written in such a narrow and specific way that a warrant requirement was not necessary to protect employees against abuse and arbitrariness by their supervisors.[58] For the most part, only employees involved in certain accidents or incidents could be tested. Some discretion may have to be used in determining whether an employee's acts or omissions contributed to an accident, but supervisors would have to use objective criteria to make these determinations, thus minimizing the likelihood of abuse of discretion.[59] Justice Kennedy emphasized that since some drugs do not remain in the urine or the bloodstream for long periods of time, the delay necessary to obtain a search warrant could result in the loss of valuable evidence.[60] Furthermore, requiring railroad supervisors to become familiar with the details of Fourth Amendment warrant procedures "is simply unreasonable."[61] Accordingly, the majority concluded that the absence of a warrant requirement did not undermine the constitutionality of the FRA regulations.[62]

Justice Kennedy next considered the question of whether postaccident testing could be conducted in the absence of probable cause or at least some quantum of reasonable or individualized suspicion that a particular employee was under the influence of alcohol or some other drug. Conceding that "even a search that may be performed without a warrant must be based, as a general matter, on probable cause (or at least individualized suspicion) to believe that the person to be searched has violated the law,"[63] Justice Kennedy nevertheless proceeded to explain why a showing of individualized suspicion was not necessary. Noting that the regulations governing postaccident testing do not require that urine samples be furnished under the direct observation of a monitor[64] and that railroad employees in safety-sensitive positions have diminished expectations of privacy as a result of their "participation in an industry that is regulated pervasively to ensure safety,"[65] Justice Kennedy reasoned that the postaccident testing procedures "pose only limited threats to the justifiable expectations of privacy of covered employees."[66]

The government, according to Justice Kennedy, can point to several compelling reasons for carrying out postaccident testing without having to prove the existence of individualized suspicion.[67] Railroad employees must discharge duties fraught with risks of injury to others and could potentially "cause great human loss before any signs of impairment become noticeable to supervisors or others."[68] Furthermore, the postaccident testing procedures are intended not only to provide valuable information that can help to pinpoint the causes of an accident, but also to deter drug use by ensuring that employees know that "they will be tested upon the occurrence of a triggering event, the timing of which no employee can predict with certainty."[69]

Requiring supervisors to establish the existence of individualized suspicion in the aftermath of an accident, argued Justice Kennedy, would defeat the government's goals of deterring drug use, investigating accidents, and protecting public safety.[70] The scene at a serious railroad accident is typically confused and chaotic, and investigators often find it very difficult to determine which crew members may have contributed in one way or another to the accident.[71] The delay caused by the need to identify suspected crew members and gather sufficient evidence to support the existence of individualized suspicion probably would result in the deterioration or loss of the evidence provided by the tests.[72] Thus, the compelling governmental interests served by the postaccident testing regulations would be seriously hindered if railroad supervisors were forced to gather specific facts amounting to an individualized suspicion of impairment before testing a particular employee.[73] Under these circumstances, concluded Justice Kennedy, the government's compelling interests in deterring drug use and promoting rail safety clearly outweigh the privacy interests of railroad workers.[74] Accordingly, the majority upheld all of the FRA's drug-testing regulations.

Justice Brennan, joined by Justice Marshall, submitted a stinging dissenting opinion, criticizing the majority for utilizing "a formless and unguided 'reasonableness' balancing inquiry" rather than the traditional analytic framework used in Fourth Amendment cases.[75] Justice Brennan repudiated the majority's "special needs" rationale as "unprincipled and dangerous," and pointed out that this was the first "special needs" case to sanction searches that could not be supported by at least some quantum of individualized evidence of culpability on the part of those subjected to a search.[76] He added that even if he had accepted the majority's view that the FRA's regulations should be analyzed under a reasonableness test, he would have found the regulations to be constitutionally infirm.[77] The majority, he declared, had inflated the likely efficacy of the FRA's testing program and had erroneously found the privacy and dignity interests of the employees to be minimal.[78] He described the majority as having been "swept away by society's obsession with stopping the scourge of illegal drugs" and concluded by predicting that ultimately "today's decision will reduce the privacy all citizens may enjoy."[79]

NATIONAL TREASURY EMPLOYEES UNION V. VON RAAB

The Supreme Court's second drug-testing case addressed the constitutionality of a U.S. Customs Service drug-screening program requiring urine testing of all incumbent employees seeking promotion or transfer to positions involving direct interdiction of illegal drugs or requiring the carrying of firearms. Under the program, employees selected conditionally for positions involving drug interdiction or the carrying of firearms are notified by letter that their final selection is contingent on successful completion of a urine test. When the candidates appear at the test site, they must remove any outer clothing, such as a coat or jacket, surrender any personal belongings, and enter a bathroom stall to urinate into a specimen jar. To protect against the substitution of another person's urine or the adulteration of the urine, a monitor of the same sex as the candidate stands next to the stall "to listen for the normal sounds of urination." After receiving the specimen, the monitor inspects it for proper color and temperature, seals and marks the container, and sends it to the testing laboratory. There the enzyme multiplied immunoassay test (EMIT) is used to detect the presence of marijuana, cocaine, opiates, amphetamines, and phencyclidine. If a sample tests positive, it will then be retested with the more accurate gas chromatography/mass spectrometry (GC/MS) test. Employees who test positive on both tests and who offer no satisfactory explanation are subject to dismissal from the Customs Service.[80]

In *National Treasury Employees Union v. Von Raab*,[81] Justice Kennedy, this time writing for a five-Justice majority, once again used a reasonableness test to analyze the challenged regulations and found them to be constitutionally permissible. Indeed, Justice Kennedy's *Von Raab* opinion began by justifying the majority's use of the same kind of reasonableness test used by the majority in the *Railway Labor Executives* case.[82] Like the FRA's postaccident testing regulations, the Customs program "is not designed to serve the ordinary needs of law enforcement."[83] Its purposes are not to bring criminal prosecutions against employees, but to deter drug use among those seeking promotions to sensitive positions and to prevent drug users from attaining such positions.[84] These are precisely the kinds of "special needs," according to Justice Kennedy, that justify a departure from the Fourth Amendment's ordinary warrant and probable-cause requirements.[85] A warrant requirement in the context of the Customs testing program, he argued, would do little to protect personal privacy and serve only to divert valuable resources from the agency's primary mission.[86] In ordinary criminal prosecutions a search warrant interposes a neutral magistrate between the citizen and the police and serves to advise the citizen that a particular search of a particular person or place has been authorized by law.[87] But, under the Customs program, all employees seeking a covered position are fully aware that they must take a drug test.[88] Since Customs Service supervisors do not exercise any discretion whatsoever in deciding which employees must undergo urinalysis, "there are simply 'no special facts for a neutral magistrate to evaluate.' "[89]

The next question to be answered was whether the Customs Service testing program violated the traditional understanding that even a warrantless search must be based on probable cause or at least some articulable facts constituting a basis for reasonable suspicion. Justice Kennedy answered this question in the negative, accepting the government's argument that the Customs Service's need to conduct suspicionless searches outweighs the privacy interests of the covered employees. The Customs Service had made a convincing argument, he explained, that it had a compelling interest in ensuring that employees engaged in drug enforcement efforts "are physically fit, and have unimpeachable integrity and judgment."[90] Front-line interdiction personnel are frequently offered bribes, and several employees have been arrested for accepting bribes and committing other integrity violations in recent years.[91] This problem could worsen if Customs employees, "because of their own drug use, were to become unsympathetic to their mission of interdicting narcotics" or, even worse, were tempted to accept bribes and help "facilitate importation of sizable drug shipments or block apprehension of dangerous criminals."[92] The Customs Service has an equally compelling interest, according to Justice Kennedy, in preventing the promotion of drug users to jobs that require the employee to carry a firearm.[93] An employee who carries a weapon clearly discharges duties fraught with risks of injury to others and cannot afford to suffer from impaired judgment.[94] The Customs

Service therefore has a duty to protect the public by minimizing the possibility that drug-impaired employees will be promoted to positions in which they may have to use firearms.[95]

Justice Kennedy's reasonableness analysis continued by balancing the Custom Service's compelling interest in preventing drug use among the covered employees against the testing program's interference with the privacy interests of those employees. Acknowledging that the collection and subsequent chemical analysis of an individual's urine sample represented an invasion of privacy that "could be substantial in some circumstances," Justice Kennedy nonetheless concluded that the Customs testing program was not impermissibly intrusive in light of the "operational realities of the workplace."[96] Like those who join the military or who work in the intelligence services, Customs employees who carry weapons and/or work in the drug enforcement field should expect effective inquiries into their fitness and integrity.[97] Those who want to work in this area simply must realize that they "have a diminished expectation of privacy in respect to the intrusions occasioned by a urine test."[98]

The majority was especially critical of two of the arguments proffered by the National Treasury Employees Union. First, the petitioners' brief had stressed that there was little or no evidence of a drug problem among Customs employees and that only five employees out of 3,600 tested so far had tested positive for drugs.[99] But the *Von Raab* majority viewed this contention as evincing "an unduly narrow view of the context in which the Service's testing program was implemented."[100] There can be no doubt, said Justice Kennedy, that drug abuse is a serious problem in the American workplace and that the Customs Service is not immune.[101] Since many Customs agents are not subject to day-to-day supervision, detecting drug impairment among Customs employees is especially difficult.[102] As Justice Kennedy saw it, the fact that all but a few of the employees tested have proved to be innocent of drug abuse should be regarded not as impugning the testing program's validity, but as demonstrating the program's deterrent strength.[103] Nearly all of the people subjected to suspicionless searches when they seek to board commercial airlines also prove to be innocent of any wrongdoing, but that does not prove that airport searches are unnecessary or ineffective.[104] This practice has been held to be constitutional because the government has a compelling interest in guarding against great potential harm and "preventing an otherwise pervasive societal problem from spreading to the particular context."[105] Similar justifications apply to the Customs drug-testing program, declared Justice Kennedy. The importance of preventing the possible harms that would result if drug abuse were to become a significant problem in the Customs Service "furnishes an ample justification for reasonable searches calculated to advance the Government's goal."[106]

The *Von Raab* majority also rejected the second major argument advanced by the attorneys for the Treasury Employees Union. The petitioners' briefs had contended that because drug-abusing employees could easily avoid detection by adulterating their urine samples or by temporary abstinence, the Customs

Service's testing scheme was not a "sufficiently productive mechanism" to justify its intrusions into employee privacy interests.[107] In response, Justice Kennedy maintained that no employee could reasonably expect to succeed in adulterating the sample because of the precautions built into the collection process.[108] Similarly, he argued that employees cannot confidently expect to avoid detection by abstaining after the test date is assigned because they cannot predict their individual patterns of elimination for a particular drug with perfect accuracy. He cited evidence that the length of time it takes for particular drugs to become undetectable in urine varies widely among people and may extend for as long as twenty-two days.[109] Moreover, those with particularly severe drug problems may be unable to abstain even for a short period of time.[110] Having repudiated the plaintiffs' principal arguments, Justice Kennedy concluded that the Customs testing plan was reasonable under the Fourth Amendment: "[W]e believe that the Government has demonstrated that its compelling interests in safeguarding our borders and the public safety outweigh the privacy expectations of employees who seek to be promoted to positions that directly involve the interdiction of illegal drugs or that require the incumbent to carry a firearm."[111]

The *Von Raab* decision prompted two dissenting opinions. First, Justice Marshall, joined by Justice Brennan, wrote a brief opinion referring to his reasons for dissenting in the *Railway Labor Executives* case. He described the *Von Raab* majority's abandonment of the probable-cause requirement as "unprincipled and unjustifiable," averred that the majority had applied its own reasonableness test in an erroneous manner, and stated his agreement with the other *Von Raab* dissenting opinion.[112] The second dissenting opinion was authored by Justice Scalia who, like Justice Kennedy, is a Reagan appointee generally viewed as a judicial "conservative." Nevertheless, in scathing terms, Justice Scalia, joined by Justice Stevens, deplored the Customs testing program as "a kind of immolation of privacy and human dignity in symbolic opposition to drug use."[113]

Central to Justice Scalia's dissent was his disagreement with the majority's dismissal of the union's argument that there was no real evidence of a drug problem among Customs Service employees. He had voted with the *Railway Labor Executives* majority, Justice Scalia explained, because the Federal Railroad Association had provided ample evidence of drug and alcohol abuse among railroad employees and had demonstrated that such abuse could seriously endanger the public safety.[114] It was important to note, he added, that the Court's decision in *New Jersey v. T.L.O.* was reached only after the Justices had reviewed well-documented evidence that drug use was a serious and growing problem in American schools.[115] But in the present case, as Justice Scalia put it, "[t]he Court's opinion . . . will be searched in vain for real evidence of a real problem that will be solved by urine testing of Customs employees."[116]

Justice Kennedy's majority opinion, Justice Scalia charged, was filled with broad generalizations about the severity of the national drug problem, vague references to integrity violations by Customs officers, and speculation that drug-impaired employees could jeopardize public safety or become unsympathetic to their drug enforcement mission.[117] However, what was "revealingly absent" from the government's briefs and the majority opinion "[was] the recitation of *even a single instance* in which any of the speculated horribles actually occurred; an instance, that is, in which the cause of bribe-taking, or of poor aim, or of unsympathetic law enforcement . . . was drug use."[118] It was especially telling, declared Justice Scalia, that William Von Raab, the Commissioner of Customs, had stated that "Customs is largely drug-free" and that "[t]he extent of illegal drug use by Customs employees was not the reason for establishing [the testing] program."[119] And, noted Justice Scalia, the testing results to date, showing that only 5 employees out of 3,600 had tested positive for drugs, had, in effect, demonstrated that the Customs Service was largely drug-free.[120] Justice Scalia was especially critical of Justice Kennedy's argument that "[t]here is little reason to believe that American workplaces are immune from the pervasive social problem" of illegal drug use.[121] Such an overgeneralization, Justice Scalia wrote, might be sufficient to justify suspicionless urine testing of employees in a workplace that "could produce such catastrophic social harm that no risk whatever is tolerable—the secured areas of a nuclear power plant, for example."[122] However, vague generalizations and mere speculation do not justify suspicionless and humiliating bodily searches of all employees who work in any kind of law enforcement capacity.[123]

Justice Scalia expressed doubt that urine testing will prove to be "even marginally more effective in preventing gun-carrying agents from risking 'impaired perception and judgment' than is their current knowledge that, if impaired, they may be shot dead in unequal combat with unimpaired smugglers."[124] The only possible exception, he contended, would be an employee whose drug addiction problem was so severe that "it would be detectable even without benefit of a urine test."[125] Nevertheless, he speculated, the *Von Raab* Court's approval of suspicionless urine testing of weapons-carrying employees would almost certainly be cited as precedent for upholding laws permitting the suspicionless testing of all employees—public and private—whose work, if performed under the influence of drugs, could possibly endanger public safety.[126]

The "feeble justifications" for the Customs testing program that had been accepted by the *Von Raab* majority had convinced him, Justice Scalia concluded, that the real reason for the testing program had been unwittingly disclosed by the Commissioner of Customs in his memorandum to employees announcing the program: "Implementation of the drug screening program would set an important example in our country's struggle with this most serious threat to our national health and security."[127] The program, in other words, was not based on a sincere belief that employee drug use could result in serious public harm; it was actually intended to show that the government was serious about its "war on drugs" and determined to eliminate "this scourge of our society."[128] To Justice Scalia, however, this justification is unacceptable because "the impairment of individual liberties cannot be the means of making a point [and] symbolism, even symbolism for so worthy a cause as the abolition of unlawful drugs, cannot validate an otherwise unreasonable search.''[129] By subjecting its employees to such needless assaults on their privacy and dignity, the government, in Justice Scalia's view, had confirmed the wisdom and insight in Justice Brandeis's often quoted warning: "The greatest dangers to liberty lurk in insidious encroachment by men of zeal, well-meaning but without understanding.''[130]

THE FUTURE OF DRUG-TESTING LITIGATION

The *Railway Labor Executives* and *Von Raab* cases, taken together, arguably create a drug-testing exception to the traditional warrant and probable-cause requirements of the Fourth Amendment. Both decisions uphold mandatory urinalysis of certain categories of public employees in the absence of reasonable or individualized suspicion that particular employees are using drugs or are involved in any kind of drug-related wrongdoing. Although the majority opinions never specifically refer to a drug-testing exception, the majority Justices make it clear that both decisions rest on the idea that under certain circumstances or situations, the warrantless and suspicionless drug testing of government employees falls in the category of a special need that goes beyond the normal need for law enforcement.[131] This, in turn, justifies the Court's use of a "reasonableness" analysis rather than a more traditional probable-cause analysis that would have placed greater emphasis on the individual's right to be left alone. However, neither decision makes it clear whether all public employee drug-testing programs fall in the "special needs" category. If the Court eventually decides that they do, it would not be unrealistic to predict that a wide range of public employee testing programs will win judicial approval.

Without doubt, the The *Railway Labor Executives* and *Von Raab* decisions are important decisions, both for what they tell us about the future of drug testing and for what they tell us about the Court's evolving view of the Fourth Amendment. These cases have established the general guidelines for judicial review of various public employee drug-testing programs, and they have resolved several significant threshold questions concerning the constitutionality of government-sponsored drug testing. In fact, one likely result of these decisions is an increased commitment to drug testing by both public and private employers. As noted previously, private companies are not bound by the commands of the Fourth Amendment. But many private employers may have been reluctant to implement drug testing, with the attendant risks of employee resentment and union opposition, in the absence of a clear signal from the Supreme Court that such programs are permissible in public employment situations.

Nevertheless, it must be stressed that a number of significant drug-testing issues remain unsettled. The *Railway Labor Executives* decision approved only the postaccident testing of employees in safety-sensitive jobs, and the *Von Raab* holding arguably applies only to the prepromotion testing of incumbent employees seeking high-risk law enforcement jobs. While the decisions must be considered major setbacks for public employee unions and anyone else opposed to drug testing, they cannot be read as giving government employers carte blanche to force all employees to undergo urinalysis or other types of drug testing.

Some of the questions not clearly covered by the Supreme Court's decisions have engendered little or no conflict among the lower federal and state courts. For example, there has been virtually unanimous agreement that the Fourth Amendment does not prohibit government agencies from requiring public employees in safety-sensitive positions to submit to urine or blood testing as part of a routine periodic physical examination.[132] Similarly, the lower courts have overwhelmingly concluded that pre-employment drug testing, as part of a physical examination routinely given to prospective government employees who are seeking safety-sensitive jobs, is constitutionally permissible.[133] The Supreme Court can be expected to agree with both of these positions sometime in the near future. Indeed, the Court could go so far as to approve drug testing conducted as part of a regular physical examination for both incumbent and prospective government employees, even if they are not in or seeking a safety-sensitive position.

On the employees' side, the courts have reached a consensus that in the absence of some kind of permissible testing scheme that includes all employees in a certain category, a government employer cannot single out a particular employee on the basis of a mere hunch and force the employee to submit to urine testing. In such a case the employer must be able to cite specific facts that amount to reasonable suspicion that the employee is using illegal drugs.[134] Moreover, the lower courts are also in agreement that if an employer's drug-testing order is found to violate Fourth Amendment standards, it cannot be upheld because the employee signed a form consenting to drug testing at the time he or she was hired.[135] As one court put it, "advance consent to future 'unreasonable' searches is not a reasonable condition of employment."[136] There is no reason to expect the Supreme Court to disagree with those positions.

By far the most difficult drug-testing questions—and those that have prompted the greatest disagreements among the lower courts—are the questions surrounding the constitutionality of random testing programs and uniform testing programs (i.e., programs that involve unannounced or periodic testing of an entire class of incumbent employees). Both kinds of testing raise similar constitutional questions. They indisputably permit the suspicionless testing of employees, but, if properly and fairly administered, eliminate the potential for abuse of discretion by employers.[137] Until the Supreme Court addresses the constitutionality of such programs, conflicts among the lower courts can be expected to multiply. The U.S. Court of Appeals for the Third Circuit, for example, has ruled that police officers can be subjected to random and uniform testing,[138] but the Sixth Circuit has held otherwise.[139] Similarly, the Eighth Circuit has bestowed its constitutional stamp of approval on the random and uniform testing of prison guards,[140] but a federal district court in Illinois recently struck down Cook County's guard-testing plan as violative of the Fourth Amendment.[141]

It is extremely difficult to predict whether (and what kinds of) random and uniform drug-testing programs will eventually gain Supreme Court approval.[142] For one thing, there is no way to know whether any of the five Justices who made up the *Von Raab* majority regarded the Customs Service testing plan as being on or near the line separating legitimate testing programs from illegitimate ones. For the opponents of drug testing the most disturbing aspect of *Von Raab* undoubtedly was that the majority upheld the Customs testing program despite the lack of solid evidence that drug abuse was an appreciable problem among Customs employees.

Accordingly, it would not be unrealistic to predict that the Court will uphold random and uniform testing programs so long as these programs serve a compelling governmental interest. Future decisions will therefore turn on a reasonableness analysis, focusing on the totality of facts and circumstances of each case. Among the most important factors will be the legitimacy of the employees' privacy expectations and whether the employees are in jobs that put them in a position to endanger themselves or others. At this point it seems certain that the courts cannot expect any decrease in drug-testing litigation in the near future.

NOTES

1. See Note, "Employee Drug Testing—Issues Facing Private Sector Employers," *North Carolina Law Review* 65 (1987): 832, 832–33.

2. See "Jar Wars: Drug Testing in the Workplace," *Willamette Law Review* 23 (1987): 529, 529–35. On 4 January 1987, sixteen people were killed near Baltimore in a collision between a Conrail freight train and an Amtrak passenger train. Both the engineer and a crewman on the Conrail train, which had disregarded a stop signal, tested positive for marijuana in postaccident urine tests. See "Drug Testing on Rails Praised as Deterrent," *New York Times*, 19 February 1987, B2.

3. See Michael R. O'Donnell, "Employee Drug Testing—Balancing the Interests in the Workplace: A Reasonable Suspicion Standard," *Virginia Law Review* 74 (1988): 969, 970–71.

4. "Battling the Enemy Within," *Time*, 17 March 1986, 53.

5. About 50 percent of the Fortune 500 companies have implemented some form of drug testing. Most of these programs involve only pre-employment urine testing of job applicants. See *National Law Journal*, 7 April 1986, p. 1; O'Donnell, "Employee Drug Testing," 972.

6. *New York Times*, 26 March 1989, E5.

7. Although the large majority of drug-testing lawsuits have involved employee challenges to employer drug-testing schemes, the controversy over drug testing also extends to efforts to test college, professional, and amateur athletes; prisoners; pretrial detainees; probationers; parolees; and others who are not "employees." See generally Fred Cohen and Kate King, "Drug Testing and Corrections," *Criminal Law Bulletin* 23 (1987): 151–72; Steven F. Brock and Kevin M. McKenna, "Drug Testing in Sports," *Dickinson Law Review* 92 (1988): 505–70.

8. See especially *United States v. Jacobsen*, 466 U.S. 109, 113 (1984) (holding that the Fourth Amendment does not apply to actions by private individuals). See also *Monroe v. Consolidated Freightways, Inc.*, 654 F. Supp. 661, 663 (E.D. Mo. 1987)

(applying *Jacobsen* in the context of private employer drug testing). Although the U.S. Constitution and most state constitutions do not apply to private employers, private-sector employees may have legal redress under some circumstances. For example, private employees who are covered by a collective bargaining agreement may be able to challenge a company's drug testing as a violation of that bargaining agreement. In employee situations lacking a collective bargaining agreement an employee may have a basis for a tort action, claiming wrongful discharge, defamation, invasion of privacy, or some other wrong in cases involving a refusal to submit to urinalysis testing or a false positive result. See generally Andrea M. Kanski, "Employee Drug Testing—Balancing the Employer's Right to Know with the Employee's Right to Privacy," *Detroit College of Law Review* (1987): 27–63. For a discussion of the accuracy of various drug-testing methods, see "Jar Wars," 536–48. Finally, it is noteworthy that some state constitutions contain right-of-privacy clauses that arguably protect against extragovernmental invasions of privacy. For example, the California Constitution has been held to afford protection against both governmental and private violations of privacy. See Thomas L. McGovern III, "Employee Drug-Testing Legislation: Redrawing the Battlelines in the War on Drugs," *Stanford Law Review* 39 (1987): 1453, 1466–67.

9. Whether or not a government subcontractor or some other government-regulated private employer is subject to the strictures of the Constitution will usually depend on a court's analysis of whether and to what extent the government encourages or participates in the actions of the private employer, whether and to what extent the government subsidizes the actions of the private employer, whether and to what extent the government regulates the private employer, whether the private entity is performing a function that is ordinarily the exclusive prerogative of the government, and whether a symbiotic relationship exists between the government and the private entity. See generally *Lustig v. United States*, 338 U.S. 74, 78–79 (1949); *Rendell-Baker v. Kohn*, 457 U.S. 830, 839–43 (1982). In its first drug-testing decision, the Supreme Court held that breath, blood, and urine tests mandated by private railroads in reliance on regulations promulgated by the Federal Railroad Administration clearly implicate the Fourth Amendment because the regulations demonstrate that the federal government has actively encouraged, endorsed and participated in the testing. See *Skinner v. Railway Labor Executives' Association*, *U.S. Law Week* 57 (1989): 4324, 4327.

10. See, e.g., *National Treasury Employees Union v. Von Raab*, 649 F. Supp. 380, 388 (E.D. La. 1986).

11. See *Schmerber v. California*, 384 U.S. 757, 761 (1966).

12. See, e.g., *Burka v. New York City Transit Authority*, 680 F. Supp. 590, 611–12 (S.D. N.Y. 1988).

13. See, e.g., *Capua v. City of Plainfield*, 643 F. Supp. 1507, 1515, (D.N.J. 1986); *Railway Labor Executives' Association v. Burnley*, 839 F.2d 575, 591–92 (1988), *rev'd on other grounds*, 57 U.S.L.W. 4324 (1989).

14. 381 U.S. 479 (1965).

15. See generally *Roe v. Wade*, 410 U.S. 113 (1973) and the cases cited in *Carey v. Population Services International*, 431 U.S. 678, 684–85 (1977).

16. See notes 43–50 and the accompanying text.

17. U.S. CONST. amend. IV.

18. See Stephen A. Saltzburg, *American Criminal Procedure* (St. Paul: West Publishing Co., 1984), 45–51.

19. Anthony Amsterdam, "Perspectives on the Fourth Amendment," *Minnesota Law Review* 58 (1974): 349, 353.

20. See, e.g., *Schmerber v. California*, 384 U.S. 757, 767 (1966); *Camara v. Municipal Court*, 387 U.S. 523, 536–37 (1967); *New Jersey v. T.L.O.*, 469 U.S. 325, 335 (1985).

21. For example, one interpretation is that the "reasonable" search is one conducted pursuant to the warrant requirement of the second clause. A second theory is that the first clause implies that some searches may be "unreasonable" even when conducted pursuant to a warrant. And a third interpretation is that the first clause permits some searches to be adjudged "reasonable" without a warrant. Although all three interpretations can find support in case law, the third theory is predominant today. See Note, "Constitutional Law: Urinalysis and the Public Employer—Another Well-Delineated Exception to the Warrant Requirement?" *Oklahoma Law Review* 39 (1986): 257, 258–60.

22. 389 U.S. 347, 357 (1967).

23. Among the established exceptions to the warrant requirement are the exigent circumstances exception [*Schmerber v. California*, 384 U.S. 757 (1966)], the search incident to arrest exception [*Chimel v. California*, 395 U.S. 752 (1969)], the "stop and frisk" exception [*Terry v. Ohio*, 392 U.S. 1 (1968)], the consent exception [*Schneckloth v. Bustamonte* 412 U.S. 218 (1973)], the automobile exception [*Carroll v. United States*, 267 U.S. 132 (1925)], the hot pursuit exception [*Warden v. Hayden*, 387 U.S. 294 (1967)], the plain view exception [*Coolidge v. New Hampshire*, 403 U.S. 443 (1971)], the "open fields" exception [*Hester v. United States*, 265 U.S. 57 (1924)], the abandoned property exception [*Abel v. United States*, 362 U.S. 217 (1960)], the misplaced trust exception [*United States v. White*, 401 U.S. 745 (1971)], the inventory search exception [*South Dakota v. Opperman*, 428 U.S. 364 (1976)], the border search exception [*Almeida-Sanchez v. United States* (1973)], and the administrative search exception [*Camara v. Municipal Court*, 387 U.S. 523 (1967)]. See generally Geoffrey P. Alpert and Kenneth C. Haas, "Judicial Rulemaking and the Fourth Amendment: Cars, Containers, and Exclusionary Justice," *Alabama Law Review* 35 (1984): 23–61.

24. See note 23. See also *United States v. Leon*, 468 U.S. 897 (1984) (creating a "good faith" exception to exclusionary rule when police conduct a search and seize evidence in reasonable reliance on a search warrant subsequently found to be unsupported by probable cause); *New Jersey v. T.L.O.*, 469 U.S. 325 (1985) (holding that warrant requirement is impractical in school environment); *Murray v. United States*, 108 S. Ct. 2529 (1989) (establishing "independent source" exception to exclusionary rule by holding that evidence discovered by police during initial warrantless entry into warehouse is admissible if same evidence is also "discovered" during a second search pursuant to a search warrant that is based on information obtained wholly independently of the initial illegal search).

25. See, e.g., *Mincey v. Arizona*, 437 U.S. 385, 390 (1978) (stating that *Katz* rule is "a cardinal principle" of Fourth Amendment jurisprudence); *O'Connor v. Ortega*, 480 U.S. 709, 720 (1987) (declaring that searches without warrants are unreasonable except in "certain carefully defined classes of cases").

26. The Supreme Court has demonstrated an increasing willingness to permit warrantless searches on the ground that the police did not violate an expectation of privacy "that society is prepared to recognize as 'reasonable' " [*Katz v. United States*, 389 U.S. 347, 361 (1967) (Harlan, J., concurring)]. See especially *California v. Greenwood*, 486 U.S. 35, 40–41 (1988) (upholding warrantless search and seizure of garbage bags left

for collection outside the curtilage of a house on the theory that such bags are "readily accessible to animals, children, scavengers, snoops and other members of the public" and thus respondents did not have an objectively reasonable expectation of privacy in the contents of the bags).

27. See especially Phyllis T. Bookspan, "Behind Closed Doors: Constitutional Implications of Government Employee Drug Testing," *Nova Law Review* 11 (1987): 329–37.

28. The Supreme Court has always stressed that probable cause must be a flexibly defined concept. Thus, probable cause often is defined as a degree of certainty lying somewhere between "reasonable suspicion," the amount of certainty necessary to justify a police officer's "stop and frisk" [*Terry v. Ohio*, 392 U.S. 1 (1968)] and "beyond a reasonable doubt," the standard of proof in a criminal trial. See generally Charles H. Whitebread and Christopher Slobogin, *Criminal Procedure*, 2d ed. (Mineola, N.Y.: Foundation Press, 1986), 146–47.

29. Chief Justice Rehnquist has long favored expanded use of the reasonableness test. See, e.g., *Michigan v. Tyler*, 436 U.S. 499, 516 (1978) (Rehnquist, J., dissenting); *Michigan v. Clifford*, 464 U.S. 287, 305 (1984) (Rehnquist, J., dissenting).

30. 469 U.S. 325 (1985).

31. *Id.* at 341–42. Applying this test, the Court upheld a vice-principal's search of a fourteen-year-old girl's purse merely because she was caught smoking tobacco cigarettes in a lavatory. He discovered marijuana and other drug paraphernalia in her purse and turned her in to the police.

32. 483 U.S. 868 (1987).

33. *Id.* at 872 [quoting *New Jersey v. T.L.O.*, 469 U.S. 325, 351 (1985) (Blackmun, J., concurring)].

34. 480 U.S. 709 (1987).

35. *Id.* at 717–18.

36. *Id.* at 714.

37. *Id.* at 722.

38. *Id.* at 722–25.

39. *Id.* at 725–26.

40. *Id.* at 726.

41. *Id.*

42. See, for example, Phyllis T. Bookspan, "Jar Wars: Employee Drug Testing, the Constitution, and the American Drug Problem," *American Criminal Law Review* 26 (1988): 359, 375.

43. 57 U.S.L.W. 4324 (1989).

44. *Id.* at 4327–28. See *Schmerber v. California*, 384 U.S. 757, 767–68 (deeming blood testing a Fourth Amendment search). See also *Winston v. Lee*, 470 U.S. 753 (1985) (holding that proposed surgery, under general anesthetic, to remove bullet from suspect's chest would violate the Fourth Amendment).

45. *Skinner v. Railway Labor Executives' Association*, 57 U.S.L.W. at 4328.

46. *Id.*

47. *Id.*

48. *Id.*

49. *Id.* (quoting *National Treasury Employees Union v. Von Raab*, 816 F.2d 170, 175, (5th Cir. 1987).

50. *Id.* For an argument that urinalysis should not be considered a search covered

by the Fourth Amendment, see Comment, " 'Drug Testing of Government Employees Should Not Be a Matter of Fourth Amendment Concern' Cries a Lone Voice in a Wilderness of Opposition," *Brigham Young University Law Review* (1987): 1239–70. Indeed, it should be noted that over the past few years the Court has sometimes ruled that arguably intrusive police actions did not amount to searches. See especially *United States v. Place*, 462 U.S. 696 (1983) (a "sniff test" by a police dog trained to detect illegal drugs is not a search in Fourth Amendment terms); *United States v. Karo*, 468 U.S. 705 (1984) (the warrantless installation of an electronic "beeper" in a container without the owner's consent and the transfer of the container to the defendants for purposes of tracking their movements did not amount to a search).

51. See *Skinner v. Railway Labor Executives' Association*, 57 U.S.L.W. at 4325–26.

52. See notes 30–41 and the accompanying text.

53. *Skinner v. Railway Labor Executives' Association*, 57 U.S.L.W. at 4328.

54. *Id*. at 4328–29.

55. *Id*. at 4328.

56. *Id*. at 4328–29.

57. *Id*. at 4329.

58. *Id*.

59. *Id*. 4329 n. 6.

60. *Id*. at 4329.

61. *Id*. at 4329–30.

62. *Id*. at 4330.

63. *Id*.

64. *Id*.

65. *Id*.

66. *Id*. at 4331.

67. *Id*.

68. *Id*.

69. *Id*.

70. *Id*.

71. *Id*.

72. *Id*. at 4332.

73. *Id*.

74. *Id*.

75. *Id*. at 4334 (Marshall, J., dissenting).

76. *Id*.

77. *Id*. at 4337.

78. *Id*. at 4336–38.

79. *Id*. at 4338.

80. See 57 U.S.L.W. 4338, 4339–40 (1989) for an overview of the Customs Service program. The program also requires urinalysis of first-time applicants seeking drug enforcement jobs. However, the petitioners included only incumbent employees, and the Court therefore considered only the issue of the constitutionality of the drug screening as it applied to current employees seeking promotion or transfer to a covered position. It should also be noted that the Customs program requires urine tests of all prospective or current employees seeking a position involving the handling of "classified" information. However, the Supreme Court declined to assess the validity of the testing of

such employees because the record was not clear as to whether the Customs Service had defined the category of employees required to handle classified material in such a way as to include only those employees likely to gain access to sensitive information. See *id*. at 4344.

81. 57 U.S.L.W. 4338 (1989).

82. *Id*. at 4340–41.

83. *Id*. at 4341.

84. *Id*.

85. *Id*.

86. *Id*.

87. *Id*.

88. *Id*.

89. *Id*. [quoting *South Dakota v. Opperman*, 428 U.S. 364, 383 (1976) (Powell, J., concurring)].

90. *Id*. at 4341–42.

91. *Id*. at 4342. Justice Kennedy cited Customs Service reports that seventy-six employees were arrested from 1985 to 1987. But it is not clear whether all of these arrests involved drug-related crimes.

92. *Id*.

93. *Id*.

94. *Id*.

95. *Id*.

96. *Id*.

97. *Id*.

98. *Id*.

99. *Id*. at 4343.

100. *Id*.

101. *Id*.

102. *Id*.

103. *Id*. at 4343 n. 3.

104. *Id*.

105. *Id*. See *United States v. Edwards*, 498 F.2d 496 (2d Cir. 1974) (upholding the validity of suspicionless searches of all passengers seeking to board commercial flights as well as searches of carry-on luggage).

106. *National Treasury Employees Union v. Von Raab*, 57 U.S.L.W. at 4343.

107. *Id*.

108. *Id*. at 4344.

109. *Id*. at 4343.

110. *Id*.

111. *Id*. at 4344.

112. *Id*. (Marshall, J., dissenting).

113. *Id*. at 4345 (Scalia, J., dissenting).

114. *Id*.

115. *Id*. See *New Jersey v. T.L.O.*, 469 U.S. 325, 339 (1985).

116. *National Treasury Employees Union v. Von Raab*, 57 U.S.L.W. at 4345.

117. *Id*.

118. *Id*. Although the majority opinion alluded to cases of bribe-taking and other

integrity violations by Customs Officers, none of these cases was clearly linked to drug use by employees. See *id*. at 4338, 4342.

119. *Id*. at 4345.

120. *Id*. at 4345–46.

121. *Id*. at 4346. See *id*. at 4338, 4343.

122. *Id*. at 4346.

123. *Id*.

124. *Id*. at 4345. Justice Scalia pointed out that the *Von Raab* holding arguably could be cited in support of urine testing of all public employees who carry weapons. See *id*.

125. *Id*.

126. *Id*. at 4346.

127. *Id*.

128. *Id*.

129. *Id*.

130. *Id* .at 4346–47 [quoti..g *Olmstead v. United States*, 277 U.S. 438, 485 (1928) (Brandeis, J., dissenting)].

131. See notes 53–56 and the accompanying text, and notes 81–85 and the accompanying text.

132. See, e.g., *Policeman's Benevolent Association of New Jersey v. Washington Township*, 850 F.2d 133 (3d Cir. 1988); *Jones v. McKenzie*, 833 F.2d 335 (D.C. Cir. 1987); *McDonell v. Hunter*, 612 F. Supp. 1122, 1130 n. 6 (S.D. Iowa 1985), *modified on other grounds*, 809 F.2d 1302 (8th Cir. 1987); *Wrightsell v. City of Chicago*, 678 F. Supp. 727, 733 (N.D. Ill. 1988); *City of Palm Bay v. Bauman*, 475 So. 2d 1322, 1324 (Fla. Dist. Ct. App. 1985).

133. See, e.g., *Lovvorn v. City of Chattanooga*, 647 F. Supp. 875, 881 n.7 (E.D. Tenn. 1986), *aff'd on other grounds*, 846 F.2d 1539 (6th Cir. 1988); *Dozier v. New York City*, 130 A.D.2d 128, 519 N.Y.S.2d 135 (1987); *Alverado v. Washington Public Power Supply*, 759 P.2d 427 (Wash. 1988).

134. See, e.g., *McDonell v. Hunter*, 809 F.2d 1302, 1308–09 (8th Cir. 1987); *Copeland v. Philadelphia Police Department* 840 F.2d 1139, 1144 (3d Cir. 1988); *Smith v. White*, 666 F. Supp 1085, 1089 (E.D. Tenn. 1987); *Egloff v. New Jersey Air National Guard*, 684 F. Supp. 1275, 1280 (D. N.J. 1988); *Turner v. Fraternal Order of Police*, 500 A.2d 1005, 1008–09 (D.C. 1985); *King v. McMickens*, 120 A.D.2d 351, 353, 501 N.Y.S. 2d 679, 681 (1986).

135. See, e.g., *National Federation of Federal Employees v. Weinberger*, 818 F.2d 935, 943 (D.C. Cir. 1987); *Taylor v. O'Grady*, 669 F. Supp. 1422, 1443 (N.D. Ill. 1987); *City of Palm Bay v. Bauman*, 475 So. 2d 1322, 1324–25 (Fla. Dist. Ct. App. 1985).

136. *McDonell v. Hunter*, 612 F. Supp. 1122, 1131 (D.C. Iowa 1985), *aff'd*, 809 F.2d 1302, 1310 (8th Cir. 1987).

137. In evaluating the constitutionality of search and seizure practices, the Supreme Court has condemned the standardless—and thus potentially discriminatory—exercise of discretion by authorities. See especially *Delaware v. Prouse*, 440 U.S. 648 (1979) (holding that police may not pull over a motorist for a spot-check unless they have some articulatable and reasonable suspicion for doing so, but suggesting in dicta that roadblock-type stops or other truly random methods may be acceptable).

138. *Policeman's Benevolent Association of New Jersey v. Washington Township*, 850 F.2d 133 (3d Cir. 1988).

139. *Penny v. Kennedy*, 846 F.2d 1563 (6th Cir. 1988). For a critical analysis of the efficacy of police drug testing, see Roger G. Dunham, Lisa Lewis, and Geoffrey P. Alpert, "Testing the Police for Drugs," *Criminal Law Bulletin* 24 (1988); 155–66.

140. *McDonell v. Hunter*, 809 F.2d 1302 (8th Cir. 1987).

141. *Taylor v. O'Grady*, 669 F. Supp. 1422 (N.D. Ill. 1987). For a discussion of the pros and cons of subjecting prison guards and other correctional personnel to urinalysis, see Cohen and King, "Drug Testing and Corrections," 167–72.

142. In addition to the cases cited in notes 136–139, other prominent decisions on the constitutionality of random and/or uniform drug-testing programs are *Transport Workers' Union v. Southeastern Pennsylvania Transportation Authority*, 863 F.2d 1110 (3d Cir. 1988) (using a reasonableness test to uphold random testing of transportation workers in safety-sensitive jobs); *Rushton v. Nebraska Public Power District*, 844 F.2d 562 (8th Cir. 1988) (upholding both random and uniform testing of nuclear power plant workers under the "administrative search" exception to the warrant requirement); *Shoemaker v. Handel*, 795 F.2d 1136 (3d Cir. 1986), *cert. denied*, 479 U.S. 986 (1986) (holding that random urine testing and daily breathalyzer testing of jockeys are permissible under the "administrative search" exception); *Lovvorn v. City of Chattanooga*, 846 F.2d 1539 (6th Cir. 1988) (enjoining uniform testing of Chattanooga firefighters on the ground that there was no evidence of a widespread drug problem among the city's firefighters); *Patchogue-Medford Congress of Teachers v. Board of Education*, 70 N.Y. 2d 57, 510 N.E. 2d 325, 517 N.Y.S. 2d 456 (1987) (holding that uniform testing of probationary school teachers violates the search and seizure clauses of both the U.S. Constitution and the New York Constitution); and *City of Palm Bay v. Bauman*, 475 So. 2d 1322 (Fla. Dist. Ct. App. 1985) (invalidating random testing of police officers and firefighters as violative of the search and seizure clauses of both the U.S. Constitution and the Florida Constitution).

Chapter 13

AIDS, IV Drug Use, and the
Federal Agenda

Duane C. McBride, Dale D. Chitwood, J. Bryan Page,
Clyde B. McCoy, and James A. Inciardi

The world of the intravenous (IV) drug user has always involved considerable risk. It is a world marked by the violence associated with conflicts over access to drugs, quality of drugs, and drug distribution. These are among the daily concomitants of being an active IV user.[1] The criminal activities of IV drug users directed toward obtaining funds to purchase drugs, as well as possessing, selling, and distributing drugs, place them at risk for arrest and incarceration.[2] In addition, figures from emergency rooms and medical examiners around the country document the risk of drug overdose and death.[3] And, finally, research has demonstrated that IV drug users are at high risk for a variety of bacterial and viral infections, as well as for noninfectious diseases associated with using nonsterile needles and the toxic effects of the drugs themselves.[4] Ethnographers have often observed that managing these risks is an integral part of the status of being a street IV drug user. Being too tough to be the target of violence, finding a stable source of income and quality drugs, and avoiding arrest and sickness are the marks of the successful street drug user.[5]

The 1980s, however, introduced a new and dramatic addition to the risks encountered by IV drug users—Acquired Immune Deficiency Syndrome (AIDS). This risk cannot be successfully managed by having a tough reputation, running a good con, knowing where to get the best quality drugs, or even getting the best medical help once infected. In addition to sexual transmission, the unique AIDS-related risk behavior for IV drug users is the sharing of needles. Researchers have described the use and sharing of needles as a core component of the culture of IV drug users, for it is one of the bonds that provides social meaning to the drug use life style.[6] Thus, a core definitional element of being an IV drug user is a potentially fatal risk behavior.

The risk of AIDS among IV drug users, and consequently among other groups, has led to a major increase, engagement, or re-engagement of national governments around the world in the prevention and treatment of IV drug use and in programs designed to reduce its associated risk behaviors. These programs have run the gamut from simple information distribution to intensive education and even needle exchange programs. Many governments have made IV drug users a major force of public health programs, with a high priority for resources and manpower. Within the framework of such international attention, and the high risk of IV drug for infection with Human Immunodeficiency Virus (HIV)—the virus that causes AIDS—it is the purpose of this chapter to (1) briefly review the nature and scope of HIV and AIDS; (2) describe the AIDS-IV drug connection, its epidemiology, and its impact on the social world of the user; (3) describe federal policies targeting AIDS and IV drug use; and (4) consider possible national policy approaches within the framework of current efforts.

THE NATURE OF HIV AND AIDS

AIDS is a severe manifestation of infection with HIV,[7] and ever since it was first isolated and identified as the cause of AIDS in 1983, there has been a proliferation of material about the origins of HIV, its biochemical structure, and its epidemiological distribution.[8] While these issues are beyond the specific scope of this discussion, it is important to review the major conclusions of research in these areas, particularly as they relate to IV drug use and consequent policy issues.

Concentrating first on the pathology of human immunodeficiency virus, virologists have concluded that HIV attaches itself to the T-lymphocyte, a subset of the T-helper cell group, through an exterior receptor. In addition, HIV can also enter macrophages, another type of immune system cell.[9] Second, HIV is classified as a retrovirus because of its ability to make DNA copies from its RNA. This means that HIV has the ability to take its basic genetic code—RNA—that directs the function of the virus cell and change it into DNA, the basic reproductive instruction code of the human host cell. Thus, once HIV enters human T-cells or macrophages, the genetic functional information encoded in its RNA can be transcripted into the DNA of the human host cell. The now-infected human cell then reproduces the genetic material of the retrovirus as it reproduces its own (now-infected) DNA. Because the T-helper cell is responsible for stimulating and coordinating the body's immune system response, as the infection progresses, the patient is more susceptible to a wide variety of opportunistic infections.[10]

Clinical studies of exposure to HIV generally rely on blood tests that identify the presence of the antibodies to the virus. The assumption is that the presence of HIV antibodies indicates exposure to the virus. Virus isolation is a separate procedure and is not routinely done in clinical assessments or studies of seroprevalence.

Two blood tests are employed to screen for HIV antibodies. The enzyme linked immunosorbent assay (ELISA) is used for initial screening, while the

Western Blot analysis is used for confirmation. The ELISA is reported to be highly sensitive to the presence of antibodies, yielding few false negatives, but some false positives. Generally, when using the ELISA method, if a blood sample tests positive for HIV antibodies twice, the Western Blot analysis is used to confirm sero-status. This procedure is thought to virtually eliminate false sero-status positives. Researchers continue to emphasize, however, that there are problems of interpretation and sero-status definition of test results.[11] In a small percentage of cases indeterminant findings occur, and even more detailed tests are used to ascertain sero-status.

It was during the summer of 1981 that the first clinical reports of opportunistic infections in severely immunodepressed patients began to appear in the medical literature.[12] This was the beginning of what has become known as the "AIDS epidemic," and these early cases were clustered in New York and California. Although these states continue to have the largest number of cases—accounting for more than 40 percent of all AIDS victims, AIDS has been reported in all U.S. states and territories.

From the very beginning of the epidemic, homosexual and bisexual men comprised the largest number of adult/adolescent cases, and as of 30 April 1989 this risk group still constituted 61 percent of all accumulated AIDS cases.[13] There has, however, been a major change in the proportional distribution of AIDS risk categories since the initiation of AIDS surveillance reports by the Centers for Disease Control. During the early years of the epidemic, for example, when there were less than 2,000 reported cases nationwide, homosexual and bisexual men accounted for more than 70 percent of all cases.[14] Yet of the almost 19,000 new cases reported between May 1988 and April 1989, this latter group comprised only 57 percent. By contrast, whereas IV drug users accounted for well under 20 percent of all cases during the early 1980s, they represented almost 30 percent of all new AIDS cases reported during the year ending 30 April 1989.[15] It might be added that among women and minorities, the use of IV drugs is the major risk factor for AIDS.

Among the major public health concerns with AIDS are the mechanisms through which HIV is spread. All accepted clinical and research evidence indicates that the virus is a considerably fragile one. It does not survive for long periods outside of the body, and it appears to be spread only by the entry of blood products and/or semen from an infected person into the circulatory system of a host body.[16] Blood transfusions, because of the direct transfer of a large volume of blood cells, were initially a major means of infection. Since 1985, however, the careful screening of donors and donated blood has virtually eliminated transfusions as a major risk factor.[17] Because HIV is also concentrated in semen, sexual contacts present a risk of infection. While vaginal intercourse may result in HIV infection, particularly if there are abrasions in the vagina, existing research data indicate that the sexual behavior with the highest risk for HIV infection is anal intercourse. More specifically, when the penis penetrates the rectum, sensitive rectal tissues are often torn, and small, open wounds result. Under these circumstances, ejaculated semen has direct access to the bloodstream of the recipient, thus increasing the risk of HIV infection.[18]

The major risk for children of contracting AIDS lies in being born to a woman who is positive for HIV antibodies.[19] As of 30 April 1989, for example, 79 percent of the 1,561 children diagnosed with AIDS had mothers who were either HIV positive or at risk for HIV infection.[20] Although the exact mechanisms of transmission are still under study, it is believed that the virus is transmitted to the fetus through fluid exchange with the mother.

While HIV has been identified in other body fluids, such as tears and saliva, the viability and concentration of the virus in these fluids is reported to be minimal.[21] The concentration of HIV in blood, blood products, and semen appears to make these the primary sources of infection.

THE AIDS-IV CONNECTION

As already noted, epidemiological data indicate that IV drug users contain an increasing proportion of all AIDS cases and a particularly high percentage for females and minorities. While IV drug users—because of their own sexual practices or the prostitution associated with obtaining funds for drugs—are certainly susceptible to infection through sexual transmission, it is the basic pattern of needle use that uniquely promotes the spread of HIV within this population.[22] The problematic activity is needle sharing. The blood that remains in the syringe and needle from an infected person may infect another individual who uses those "works" without cleaning them. The common practice of "booting" enhances the probability of blood remaining in the syringe and needle. Booting is the practice of inserting a needle into a vein, aspirating the blood back into the syringe, mixing the blood with the drug in the syringe, and then shooting the resultant mixture back into the vein. Users believe that this practice enhances the euphoric "high."

Of particular concern to epidemiologists and public health officials is the use of "shooting galleries" by IV drug users. As described by ethnographers, shooting galleries are places where IV drug users go to obtain "works" (needles and syringes) as well as drugs. IV drug users may perceive themselves as less at risk for arrest or harassment by police if they do not carry a needle and syringe. The shooting gallery may also function as a focal point of a drug user's social network—a place where information on the location of the purest drugs and best prices can be obtained, as well as knowledge about new drugs or sources of drugs.[23] Yet, regardless of the particular functional role that shooting galleries play in the world of the IV drug user, they have two characteristics that make them special environments for the spread of HIV. First, they are places where a large number of needles are stored, used, and shared by relatively large numbers of drug users from a variety of IV-drug-using groups. The needles and syringes used in shooting galleries are rarely, if ever, cleaned effectively.

From the earliest years of the AIDS epidemic, researchers have reported a relationship between the use of shooting galleries and AIDS. Data collected during the early 1980s, for example, found that among IV users in drug treatment programs, those who had used shooting galleries were more likely to have AIDS than were those who did not.[24] Similar studies during the second half of the decade had essentially the same findings.[25] As such, the data indicate that needle use and needle sharing are important potential vectors for the spread of HIV and AIDS.

By contrast, however, few studies have focused on the actual presence of HIV antibodies in needles and syringes in use on the street. The first analysis was conducted in Australia, where the investigators found that 3 of 300 needles turned in as part of a needle exchange program contained HIV antibodies.[26] During 1988, in a research investigation conducted by members of the South Florida AIDS Research Consortium, some 200 needles and syringes were collected from three popular "shooting galleries" in Miami.[27] The analysis found that some 10 percent of the needle/syringe combinations contained HIV antibodies. And perhaps most importantly, some 5 percent of the apparently "clean" needles (containing no visible blood or dirt) contained HIV antibodies.

Although the probability of infection from needle use and needle sharing is not fully understood, these data suggest why researchers are reporting relatively high rates of HIV infection among IV drug users. The earliest studies reported high rates of sero-positivity (the presence of HIV antibodies in the blood) and AIDS in the IV drug population. By 1984, studies from New York City were reporting sero-prevalence rates of 40 percent or higher among IV drug users in or entering treatment.[28] Later investigations throughout the United States found that among those entering treatment, rates of sero-positivity ranged from only a few percent in such cities as Tampa, Florida, and Cleveland, Ohio, to over 60 percent in New York City.[29]

Because of the illegal nature of IV drug use, epidemiological data on the prevalence of viral infection is very difficult to estimate. Research has consistently shown that a large proportion of IV drug users successfully function without contact with the treatment and criminal justice systems. Thus, because most of the research reports focus on treatment admissions, epidemiological data are limited. Quite simply, there are no local or national population lists that might be randomly sampled from to provide reliable sero-prevalence estimates.

In an attempt to provide a broader data base of community prevalence information, investigators from the South Florida AIDS Research Consortium began in 1985 to coordinate their efforts to identify different components of the IV-drug-using population in the greater Miami area, so as to focus their epidemiological research efforts on these high-risk groups. The research targeted IV drug users who were active in the street community, in or entering treatment, in local jails, and appearing in the county hospital emergency room for acute drug reactions.[30]

Preliminary findings from these efforts indicated that (1) of the first 514 IV drug users tested at treatment entry, 12.1 percent tested positive for HIV[31] and (2) of 400 IV drug users drawn from the street community and not in treatment, 25 percent tested positive for HIV.[32] Although the data are tentative, from but one community, and not adjusted for sex and ethnicity, they do suggest that the street populations of IV drug users are at higher risk for HIV infection and are important targets for drug treatment and other AIDS prevention/intervention techniques.

In these still relatively early stages of epidemiological research, data suggest that there are considerable differences in HIV infection rates by gender and ethnicity. A 1984 study of 147 IV drug users from methadone maintenance or detoxification programs in New York City found that 58.1 percent of the females were sero-positive, as compared to 48.1 percent of the males.[33] Similarly, a study of 514 IV drug users in treatment programs throughout the greater Miami area found that 15.5 percent of the females, as opposed to 10.5 percent of the males, were sero-positive.[34] While neither the New York nor the Miami data indicated a significant difference in rates of sero-positivity by sex, the studies and the literature in general indicate that among IV drug users, females are slightly and consistently more likely to be sero-positive. Moreover, these studies demonstrate statistical differences in sero-positivity by race/ethnicity, with blacks and Hispanics having higher rates than do whites. Most striking in this regard were the Miami data, in that 6.1 percent of white IV drug users were sero-positive, as compared to 31.6 percent of blacks and 25.5 percent of Hispanics. Perhaps most notable in the data was the finding that black females had a sero-positivity rate of 55.9 percent, as compared to white females at 4.9 percent.[35]

It must be noted here that epidemiological studies of HIV and AIDS are still only in their early stages. Research is still primarily in the counting stages and has only just begun to focus on explaining the count and its distribution. As such, explanations at this point are speculative. Those examining ethnic and gender differences in rates of sero-positivity are focusing on the cultural differences among the groups that might be of any explanatory value. Ethnographic data already suggest that law enforcement practices that focus on arrests for the possession of drug paraphernalia may be causing black IV drug users to minimize their risk of arrest by using shooting galleries or sharing needles.[36] Similarly, ethnographers in the Miami projects are focusing on ethnic differences in both condom use and the sociocultural meanings of needle sharing. Alternatively, work by anthropologist J. Bryan Page in the Miami area reminds us that while rates of infectivity may be higher among Hispanics than among whites in many locales, Hispanics who reside outside of New York City are underrepresented among AIDS cases.[37] As such, it is not that minorities are more AIDS prone, but perhaps that because of certain law enforcement practices, cultural patterns, and/or beliefs about the virus, they are more likely to engage in behaviors that place them at greater risk for HIV infection.

In retrospect, then, the prevalence figures that continue to emerge, the increasing proportion of diagnosed AIDS cases accounted for by IV drug users, the relatively high rates of HIV infectivity among IV drug users in many U.S. cities, and the apparent presence of HIV-infected blood in needles and syringes used in shooting galleries all suggest the significant public health problem of HIV infection that intravenous drug users pose.

DRUGS AND THE IMMUNE SYSTEM

While most of the scientific and public health concern with HIV infection among IV drug users focuses on needle sharing or sexual behaviors, it is important to note that there is evidence that the toxic effects of a variety of drugs may damage or suppress the immune system.

In their classic work *The Opium Problem*, Charles Terry and Mildred Pellens describe immune system studies conducted in 1902 by French researcher L. E. R. Lancelin.[38] Lancelin focused on the immune system effects of morphine and found that rabbits fed nontoxic dosages of morphine died when infected with particular viral agents. The same viral agent dosage level did not kill animals not being given morphine. Lancelin, as well as Terry and Pellens, concluded that morphine reduced the body's resistance to infection. These early twentieth-century conclusions have continued to be a part of the understanding of the consequences of opiate use. For example, research reported by Ezio Tubara and his colleagues led them to conclude that morphine compromises the immune system and potentially makes the body more susceptible to infection.[39]

In addition to the effects of opiates, researchers have also noted that canna-binoids and cocaine may negatively affect the immune system. Research by Herman Friedman and his colleagues indicated that even at relatively low doses, cannabinoids may reduce immunity to retroviruses.[40] Researcher Thomas W. Klein also has reported that cocaine negatively affects the proliferation of cultured T-lymphocytes.[41] A study of cocaine users conducted prior to the beginnings of the AIDS epidemic documented behavioral characteristics of IV cocaine use that led to increased high-risk behavior for exposure to HIV.[42] Similarly, other studies have shown that IV cocaine users are more likely to test positive for antibodies to HIV than are IV users who inject opiates only.[43]

For many years, the research literature has contained a variety of articles suggesting a negative impact of alcohol on the immune system. Studies by Thomas Jerrells and his colleagues, for example, found that even in individuals with good liver functioning, the ingestion of alcohol impaired the immune system response to new viral or bacterial infections and impaired the ability of the body to recognize and respond to agents that it had previously encountered.[44] These studies suggest that an important part of the understanding of the relationship between AIDS and IV drug use, or drug use in general, must include a focus on how the wide variety of drugs used impacts on the immune system and how that impact affects vulnerability to HIV and associated opportunistic infections. Work by R. M. Donahoe and A. Falek has also focused on this issue, suggesting that for some drugs the impact on the immune system can vary from one time to the next—enhancing responses on some occasions while inhibiting on others.[45] As a result, there remains a need to further document the nature of the relationship between drug use and immune system functioning—how drug use makes users (1) more susceptible to HIV infection, (2) more likely to experience faster disease progression, and (3) more likely to experience opportunistic infections.

IV DRUG USE AND THE SECONDARY SPREAD OF HIV AND AIDS

From a public health perspective, what makes the nature and extent of HIV among drug users particularly troublesome is the role of IV drug use and the secondary spread of AIDS. The concept of *secondary spread* refers to HIV infection in heterosexuals who do not engage in IV drug use and its related risk behaviors.

Data presented earlier in this chapter pointed out that in excess of three-fourths of children diagnosed with AIDS had mothers who were IV drug users. As such, the major intergenerational transmission vector of HIV is from the IV-drug-using mother to her fetus.[46] In addition, research on heterosexual transmission indicates that it is the female sexual partners of male IV drug users who are most at risk for heterosexual contagion.[47] Within this context, Don Des Jarlais and his colleagues have reported that in New York City non-IV-drug-using female sexual partners of IV drug users account for 87 percent of all heterosexually transmitted AIDS cases.[48]

In the Miami community outreach project already noted, it was found that among the first 400 individuals interviewed 75 percent of the IV drug users with single sexual partners almost never used condoms and that over 50 percent of those with multiple sexual partners almost never did so. These data indicate that safe practices may not be a routine aspect of IV drug users' sexual activity. Given the needle-sharing practices of IV users, this would suggest that the sexual partners of the IV drug users are at considerable risk for HIV and AIDS.

While IV drug users currently account for only 24 percent of all known adult and adolescent AIDS cases, researchers believe that existing data on intergenerational and heterosexual transmission indicate that IV drug users account for over 40 percent of secondary HIV infection cases.[49] AIDS prevention programs for pregnant women and sexually active individuals who reside in high drug use areas are clearly needed.

AIDS AND PROGRAM POLICIES FOR IV DRUG USERS

Before the impact of AIDS on policies and programs for IV drug users can be examined, it is important to note a number of the changes that have occurred over the years in American drug control strategies. Drug policy in the United States has a rather convoluted history, meandering from (1) a concerted law enforcement approach to (2) a mental health approach to (3) flirtations with some level of legalization of certain drugs to (4) neoprohibition. International policy has also included a variety of initiatives, ranging from crop eradication programs to direct assistance in the areas of interdiction, research, and training.

Contemporary drug control policies began their evolution during the late 1960s when American society was experiencing rapid expansions in the number of drug-related arrests, overdoses, and requests for treatment. One response was the creation of the White House Special Action Office for Drug Abuse Prevention (SAODAP)—a policy-making entity; a second was the establishment of the National Institute on Drug Abuse (NIDA)—a research agency within the Department of Health, Education, and Welfare that was separate from the agencies dealing with mental health and alcoholism. NIDA's charter was to focus on basic and applied research, prevention and education, and the provision of community treatment services. By 1980 NIDA was funding more than 50,000 drug abuse treatment slots across the nation and carrying out an extensive research, prevention, and education effort.

In 1981 the thrust of American drug policy shifted somewhat. Shortly after Ronald Reagan became president of the United States, the federal government began its disengagement from the drug abuse treatment business. At the order of the executive branch and with the support of Congress, by 1982 the National Institute on Drug Abuse no longer provided direct funds for the provision of treatment services for drug abusers. The new administration advocated a community-based and -funded approach to drug treatment and a prevention approach that emphasized "just say no," rather than the more expensive federally funded treatment and prevention efforts. As such, the early 1980s witnessed the dismantling of NIDA's involvement in community treatment and most of its prevention initiatives. In addition, NIDA's research programs experienced annual budget reductions. At the same time, however, funds for interdiction and other supply-reduction strategies were expanded.

The AIDS epidemic, however, effected a dramatic change in drug abuse funding allocations. When early reports noted IV drug users as a major risk group, community and political pressures influenced Congress to increase funding for AIDS research among IV drug users, with NIDA receiving its first major funds in this area in 1985. During the second half of the 1980s, NIDA initiated a whole series of AIDS research and prevention programs.

To a very great extent the AIDS epidemic has served to re-engage the federal government in expanded prevention, research, and community treatment services for the nation's drug abusers—primarily within the framework of AIDS prevention. As NIDA Director Charles Schuster noted in 1988, "the focus of Institute and National policy is a renewed effort to"

- prevent the initiation of drug use.
- reach out to IV drug users and attempt to recruit them into treatment.
- provide funds to establish new drug treatment programs directed toward high-risk IV drug users.

• reduce risk behavior among IV drug users who do not enter treatment.

• conduct basic and applied research on drug use etiology and behavior.[50]

A major effort has been in the risk-reduction area. It has always been clearly recognized that a significant proportion of IV drug users will not seek treatment, even with effective outreach into the community. In response, NIDA developed a program to identify high-risk IV drug users who are active in the street community and to use indigenous outreach workers to recruit them into risk-reduction and treatment programs. The effort was developed and funded through traditional research grant award mechanisms, and in late 1987 the first five cities targeted were Chicago, Miami, New York, Philadelphia, and San Francisco. By 1990 the number of locales involved in the community outreach effort was more than two dozen, with annual funding of some $40 million.[51]

While the specific procedures vary by site, a description of the overall program indicates that it is designed to

• identify IV drug users (and their sex partners) who are not in treatment.

• collect baseline data to (a) describe the extent and type of risk behaviors; (b) determine sero-status, with the referral of those who are HIV positive to appropriate community services; (c) ascertain knowledge of HIV risk and sources of information; (d) obtain relevant sociodemographic data.

• refer IV drug users into treatment.

• recruit those who decline to enter treatment into a risk-reduction program. This program generally consists of information dissemination, role playing, and individual and group counseling techniques. Because participants in this program have refused to enter treatment, the risk-reduction program focuses on maintaining the subjects' existing life style in a way that reduces the risk of HIV infection. Specifically, the focus of the intervention is the elimination of needle sharing, with specific emphases on proper needle cleaning and condom use. In some cities this program involves random assignment to varying levels of intervention intensity, while in others it follows the traditional pre- and post-test examination of the specific target group.[52]

• follow the study population at six-month intervals to determine changes in sero-status, risk behaviors, and knowledge about HIV and AIDS.

A second component of NIDA's risk-reduction effort was the allocation of $30 million a year for five-year projects to develop and test the effectiveness of new and innovative drug abuse treatment strategies for IV drug users and others at high risk for HIV and AIDS. The funding of the twenty specific demonstration projects and five treatment research centers that compose this initiative commenced in late 1989.

NATIONAL POLICY ISSUES

The development of specific policies and programs for drug users at risk for HIV and AIDS takes place within the general discussions of AIDS and AIDS prevention. But there is an additional component as well, involving the illegality of the drug-using behaviors—the possession of controlled substances and the use of drug paraphernalia. By contrast, within the last fifteen years the gay community has been very successful in convincing mental health professionals to define homosexual behavior as an emotionally healthy, biologically based behavior or life style choice. Similarly, gay rights groups have been successful in achieving court-recognized civil rights protections in many locales.[53] Gay community approaches to AIDS education and prevention focus on limiting the number of sexual partners and on safer sexual practices through the use of condoms and other forms of nonfluid exchange during sexual interactions. These AIDS prevention efforts take place within a framework of addressing a group engaged in what has increasingly come to be defined as legal and emotionally acceptable behavior. The debate on this matter certainly continues; although homosexual sodomy constitutes a violation of the law in most state jurisdictions,[54] for the most part AIDS education and prevention efforts in the gay community do not have to address the illegality of the behavior in and of itself.

AIDS prevention among IV drug users, however, must address issues associated with illegal behaviors. Moreover, the illegal status of cocaine, heroin, and other injectable street drugs may well play an important role in the risk of becoming infected with HIV for some users. Because it is a violation of the law to carry syringes in many jurisdictions, drug users often go to shooting galleries to rent "works" (drug paraphernalia). Alternatively, to reduce the risk of arrest it is common for only one member of a drug-using group to carry a needle and syringe and to share it with his or her peers. And it is needle sharing—both in shooting galleries and with friends and peers—that has been identified as placing drug users at high risk for HIV infection.

At the policy level it has been argued that the risk of HIV infection from needle sharing should be dealt with through the legalization of drugs and drug-taking paraphernalia.[55] However, the congressional hearings and national debate on the legalization issue that occurred during 1988 suggested that neither the American political establishment nor the American people as a whole were interested in making heroin, cocaine, crack, marijuana, and other controlled substances more available.[56] However, there has been a concerted willingness, as long as treatment is offered, to use federal funds to provide needle-cleaning information. For example, the NIDA-funded community outreach programs noted earlier include needle-cleaning instruction as a part of their prevention/intervention strategies.

Alternatively, needle exchange programs exist in both the Netherlands and England.[57] The U.S. government, however, has not directly addressed this issue, although a pilot program was initiated by the New York City Health Department during the latter part of 1988.[58] On the whole, however, evaluations indicate that exchange programs are rarely frequented by hard-core drug users. Evaluations of needle exchange programs in Europe indicate that they are used, but that they are not used by many hard-core street IV drug users.[59]

As for the effectiveness of the behavioral risk-reduction programs that were launched during the closing years of the 1980s, this remains to be demonstrated. Whether or not heroin- or cocaine-addicted populations will change their patterns of needle use will not be fully understood for a number of years.

NOTES

This research was supported in part by HHS Grant #R18-AO5349-02 from the National Institute on Drug Abuse. The authors wish to thank Bill Chobotar and April Julian for their editorial assistance.

1. M. H. Agar, *Ripping and Running: A Formal Ethnography of Heroin Addicts* (New York: Seminar Press, 1973); D. C. McBride, "Drugs and Violence," in *The Drugs-Crime Connection*, ed. J. A. Inciardi (Beverly Hills, Calif.: Sage, 1981), 105–23; P. J. Goldstein, "Homicide Behavior Related to Drug Traffic," *Bulletin of the New York Academy of Medicine* 62 (1986): 509–16.

2. J. A. Inciardi, "Heroin Use and Street Crime," *Crime and Delinquency* 25 (July 1979): 335–46; D. N. Nurco, J. C. Ball, J. W. Shaffer, and T. F. Hanlon, "The Criminality of Narcotic Addicts," *Journal of Nervous and Mental Disease* 173 (1985): 94–102.

3. National Institute on Drug Abuse, *Data from the Drug Abuse Warning Network (DAWN)*, Statistical Series 1, no. 7, DHHS Pub. no. 88-1584 (Washington, D.C.: U.S. Government Printing Office, 1988).

4. R. R. Blanck, N. W. Ream, and J. S. Deleese, "Infectious Complications of Illicit Drug Use," *International Journal of the Addictions* 19 (1984): 221–32.

5. E. Preble and J. Casey, "Taking Care of Business: The Heroin User's Life on the Streets," *International Journal of the Addictions* 4 (1969): 1–24; G. M. Beschner and W. Brower, "The Scene," in *Life with Heroin: Voices from the Inner City*, ed. B. Hanson, G. Beschner, J. M. Walters, and E. Bovelle (Lexington, Mass.: Lexington Books, 1985), 19–29.

6. J. A. O'Donnell and J. P. Jones, "Diffusion of the Intravenous Technique Among Narcotic Addicts," *Journal of Health and Social Behavior* 9 (1968): 120–30.

7. Although more than one strain of HIV has been identified, the term *HIV* is used in this chapter to signify all varieties.

8. F. Barre-Simoussi, J. G. Cherman, F. Rey, M. T. Nugeyre, S. Chamaret, J. Gruest, C. Dauget, C. Alexer-Blin, F. Vezinet-Burn, C. Rouzioux, W. Roxenbaum, and L. Montagnier, "Isolation of a T-Lymphotropic Retrovirus from a Patient at Risk for Acquired Immune Deficiency Syndrome (AIDS)," *Science* 220 (1983): 868–71; R. C. Gallo, S. Z. Salahuddin, M. Popovic, G. M. Shearer, M. Kaplan, B. F. Haynes, T. J. Polker, R. Redfield, J. Oleske, B. Safai, G. White, P. Foster, and P. D. Markham, "Frequent Detection and Isolation of Cytopathic Retrovirus (HLTV-III) from Patients with AIDS and at Risk for AIDS," *Science* 224 (1984): 500–503.

9. R. C. Gallo and L. Montagnier, "AIDS in 1988," *Scientific American* 259 (October 1988): 41–48.

10. M. B. Cohen and J. H. Beckstead, "Pathology of AIDS," in *AIDS: Pathogenesis and Treatment*, ed. J. A. Levy (New York: Marcel Dekker, 1989), 305–22.

11. M. R. Proffitt, "The AIDS Retrovirus," in *AIDS: A Health Care Management Response*, ed. K. D. Blanchet (Rockville, Md.: Aspen Publishers, 1988), 19–30.

12. "Kaposi's Sarcoma and Pneumocystis Pneumonia," *Morbidity and Mortality Weekly Report* 30 (3 July 1981): 305–308.

13. *HIV/AIDS Surveillance Report.* Division of HIV/AIDS Center for Infectious Diseases, Centers for Disease Control, Atlanta, Ga. (May 1989), 8, 9.

14. F. P. Siegal and M. Siegal, *AIDS: The Medical Mystery* (New York: Grove Press, 1983).

15. Centers for Disease Control, *HIV/AIDS.*

16. J. W. Curran and W. M. Morgan, "Acquired Immunodeficiency Syndrome: The Beginning, the Present, and the Future," in *AIDS from the Beginning*, ed. H. M. Cole and G. D. Lundberg (Chicago: American Medical Association, 1986), xxi–xxxvi; M. Robert-Guroff and R. C. Gallo, "A Virological Perspective on Acquired Immunodeficiency Syndrome," in *AIDS from the Beginning*, ed. H. M. Cole and G. D. Lundberg (Chicago: American Medical Association, 1986), xxvii–xxxi; L. H. Brooks, *Infection Control in AIDS: A Health Care Management Response* (Rockville, Md.: Aspen Publishers, 1988).

17. H. A. Perkins, "AIDS in Transfusion Recipients," in *AIDS: Pathogenesis and Treatment*, ed. J. A. Levy (New York: Marcel Dekker, 1989), 97–114.

18. W. W. Darrow, D. F. Echenberg, and H. W. Jaffe, P. M. O'Malley, R. H. Byers, J. P. Getchell, and J. W. Curran, "Risk Factors for Human Immunodeficiency Virus (HIV) Infection in Homosexual Men," *American Journal of Public Health* 77 (1987): 479–83.

19. G. B. Scott, M. A. Fischl, and N. K. Klimas, M. A. Fletcher, G. M. Dickinson, R. S. Levine, and W. P. Parks, "Mothers of Infants with AIDS: Evidence for Both Symptomatic and Asymptomatic Carriers," *Journal of the American Medical Association* 253 (1985): 363–66.

20. Centers for Disease Control, *HIV/AIDS.*

21. D. D. Ho, R. E. Byington, R. T. Schooley, T. Flynn, T. R. Rota, and M. S. Hirsch, "Infrequency of Isolation of HTLV-III Virus from Saliva in AIDS," *New England Journal of Medicine* 313 (19 December 1985): 1606.

22. D. C. Des Jarlais, S. R. Friedman, and W. Hopkins, "Risk Reduction for the Acquired Immunodeficiency Syndrome Among IV Drug Users," *Annals of Internal Medicine* 103 (1985): 755–59.

23. J. M. Walters, "Taking Care of Business Updated: A Fresh Look at the Daily Routine of the Heroin User," in *Life with Heroin: Voices from the Inner City*, ed. B. Hanson, G. Beschner, J. M. Walters, and E. Bovelli (Lexington, Mass.: Lexington Books, 1985), 31–48.

24. G. H. Friedland, C. Harris, C. B. Butkus-Small, D. Shine, B. Moll, W. Darrow, and R. Klein, "Intravenous Drug Abusers and the Acquired Immunodeficiency Syndrome (AIDS): Demographic, Drug Use and Needle Sharing Patterns," *Archives of Internal Medicine* 8 (1985): 1413–37.

25. See M. Marmor, D. C. Des Jarlais, H. Cohen, S. T. Beatrice, N. Dubin, W. El-Sadr, D. Mildvan, S. Yancovitz, U. Mathur, and R. Holzman, "Risk Factors with Human Immunodeficiency Virus Among Intravenous Drug Users in New York City," *AIDS* (1987): 39–44; D. D. Chitwood, C. B. McCoy, J. A. Inciardi, D. C. McBride, M. Comerford, E. Trapido, H. V. McCoy, J. B. Page, J. Griffin, M. A. Fletcher, and M. A. Ashman, "HIV, Seropositivity of Needles from Shooting Galleries in South Florida," *American Journal of Public Health* 80 (1990): 150–152.

26. A. Wodak, K. Dolan, A. A. Imrie, J. Gold, J. Wolk, B. M. Wryte, and D. A.

Cooper, "Antibodies in the Human Immunodeficiency Virus in Needles and Syringes Used by Intravenous Drug Abusers," *Medical Journal of Australia* 147 (1987): 275–76.

27. See Chitwood et al., "HIV, Seropositivity."

28. D. M. Novick, M. J. Kreek, D. C. Des Jarlais, T. J. Spira, E. T. Khuri, J. Ragunath, V. S. Kalyarnaraman, A. M. Gelb, and A. Miescher, "LAV Among Parenteral Drug Users: Therapeutic, Historical and Ethical Aspects," in *Problems of Drug Dependence, 1985: Proceedings of the 47th Annual Scientific Meeting, The Committee on Problems of Drug Dependence*, ed. L. J. Harris (Rockville, Md.: National Institute on Drug Abuse, 1986), 318–20.

29. W. R. Lange, F. R. Snyder, D. Zozousky, V. Kaistha, M. A. Kaczaniuk, J. H. Jaffe, and the ARC Epidemiological Collaborating Group, "Geographic Distribution of Human Immunodeficiency Virus Markers in Parenteral Drug Abusers," *American Journal of Public Health* 78 (1988): 443–46.

30. D. D. Chitwood, M. M. Comerford, C. B. McCoy, E. J. Trapido, J. B. Page, D. C. McBride, and J. A. Inciardi, "Epidemiology of HIV Among Intravenous Drug Users in South Florida" (Poster presented at the IV International Conference on AIDS Conference, Abstract no. 4521, Stockholm, Sweden, June 1988); J. B. Page and D. D. Chitwood, "Seropositivity Among Street Recruited IV Drug Users," (Poster presented at the IV International Conference on AIDS, Abstract no. 8005, Stockholm, Sweden, June 1988); C. B. McCoy and D. D. Chitwood, "The Implementation of an Evaluation of AIDS Prevention Among IV Drug Users," *Journal of Drug Issues* (in press).

31. See Chitwood et al., "Epidemiology of HIV."

32. C. B. McCoy, "HIV Infection Among Street Drug Users," *American Behavioral Scientist* (in press).

33. See Marmor et al., "Risk Factors."

34. McCoy, "HIV Infection."

35. Chitwood et al., "Epidemiology of HIV."

36. Walters, "Taking Care."

37. J. B. Page, "Risk of HIV Infection in the Hispanic Population of Dade County Florida," (Paper presented at the annual meeting of the American Psychological Association, Atlanta, 12 August 1988).

38. C. E. Terry and M. Pellens, *The Opium Problem* (Montclair, N.J.: Patterson Smith, 1970), 182–84.

39. E. Tubaro, G. Borelli, C. Croce, G. Cavallo, and G. Santiangeli, "Effect of Morphine on Resistance to Infection," *Journal of Infectious Diseases* 148 (1983): 656–66.

40. H. Friedman, T. Klein, S. Specter, S. Pross, C. Newton, D. K. Blanchard, and R. Widen, in *Psychological, Neuropsychiatric, and Substance Abuse Aspects of AIDS*, ed. T. Bridge, A. F. Mirsky, and F. K. Goodwin (New York: Raven Press, 1988), 125–37.

41. T. W. Klein, C. A. Newton, and H. Friedman, "Suppression of Human and Mouse Lymphocyte Proliferation by Cocaine," in *Psychological Neuropsychiatric, and Substance Abuse Aspects of AIDS*, ed. T. Bridge, A. F. Mirsky, and F. K. Goodwin (New York: Raven Press, 1988), 139–43.

42. D. D. Chitwood, "Patterns and Consequences of Cocaine Use," in *Cocaine Use in America: Epidemiological and Clinical Perspectives*, ed. N. J. Kogel and E. H. Adams (Rockville, Md.: National Institute on Drug Abuse, 1985), 111–29.

43. R. E. Chaisson, P. Bacchetti, D. Osmond, B. Brodie, M. A. Sande, and A. R. Moss, "Cocaine Use and HIV Infection in Intravenous Drug Users in San Francisco," *Journal of the American Medical Association* 261 (1989): 561–65; D. D. Chitwood, C. B. McCoy, and M. Comerford, "Risk Behavior for HIV for Intravenous Cocaine Users: Implications for Intervention," in *AIDS and Intravenous Drug Use: Future Directions for Community Based Peer Research*, ed. C. Leukefeld (Rockville, Md.: National Institute on Drug Abuse, in press).

44. T. R. Jerrels, C. A. Marietta, G. Bone, F. F. Weight, and M. J. Eckardt, "Ethanol-Associated Immunosuppression," in *Psychological, Neuropsychiatric, and Substance Abuse Aspects of AIDS*, ed. T. Bridge, A. F. Mirsky, and F. K. Goodwin (New York: Raven Press, 1988). 173–85.

45. R. M. Donahoe and A. Falek, "Neuroimmunomodulation by Opiates and Other Drugs of Abuse: Relationship to HIV Infection and AIDS," in *Psychological, Neuropsychiatric, and Substance Abuse Aspects of AIDS*, ed. T. Bridge, A. F. Mirsky, and F. K. Goodwin (New York: Raven Press, 1988), 145–58.

46. G. B. Scott, B. F. Buck, J. G. Letterman, F. L. Bloom, and W. P. Parks, "Acquired Immunodeficiency Syndrome in Infants," *New England Journal of Medicine* 310 (1984): 76–81.

47. J. B. Cohen and G. B. Wofsy, "Heterosexual Transmission of HIV," in *AIDS: Pathogenesis and Treatment*, ed. J. A. Levy (New York: Marcel Dekker, 1989), 142, 143.

48. D. C. Des Jarlais, E. Wish, S. R. Friedman, R. Stoneburner, S. R. Yancovitz, D. Mildvan, W. El-Sadr, E. Bradley, and M. Cuadrado, "Intravenous Drug Use and Heterosexual Transmission of the Human Immunodeficiency Virus: Current Trends in New York City," *New York State Journal of Medicine* 87 (1987): 283–86.

49. J. Newmeyer, "Role of the IV Drug User and the Secondary Spread of AIDS," *Street Pharmacologist* 11 (1987): 1–2.

50. C. R. Schuster, "Intravenous Drug Use and AIDS Prevention," *Public Health Reports* 103 (1988): 261–66.

51. "Report of the Working Group on Intravenous Drug Abuse," *Public Health Reports* 103 (Supp. 1) (1988): 66–71.

52. Ibid.

53. J. Foster, "Impact of the AIDS Epidemic on the Gay Political Agenda," in *AIDS: Principles, Practices and Politics*, ed. I. B. Corless and M. Pittman-Lindeman (Washington, D.C.: Hemisphere Publishing Corp., 1988), 209–19.

54. See the U.S. Supreme Court opinion in Bowers v. Hardwick, 39 Crim. L. Rep. (BNA) 3261 (1986).

55. E. A. Nadelmann, "U.S. Drug Policy: A Bad Export," *Foreign Policy* 70 (1988): 83–108.

56. See J. A. Inciardi and D. C. McBride, "Legalization: A High Risk Alternative in the War on Drugs," *American Behavioral Scientist* 32 (1989): 259–89.

57. L. Alldritt, K. Dolan, M. Donaghoe, and G. V. Stimson, "HIV and the Injecting Drug User: Clients of Syringe Exchange Schemes in England and Scotland," (Paper presented at the IV International Conference on AIDS, Abstract no. 8511, Stockholm, Sweden, June 1988); E. C. Buning, C. Hargers, A. D. Verster, G. W. Van Santen, and R. A. Coutinro, "The Evaluation of the Needle/Syringe Exchange in Amsterdam" (Paper

presented at the IV International Conference on AIDS, Abstract no. 8513, Stockholm, Sweden, June 1988).

58. "New York City Swaps Needles to Stop AIDS Spread." *USA Today* (November 7, 1988): 2.

59. Supra note 57.

Chapter 14

Debating the Legalization of Drugs

James A. Inciardi and Duane C. McBride

The history of American drug policy reflects a textbook case in the sociology of law and the dramatization of evil.[1] Largely through the moral enterprises of the medical profession during the 1880s and 1890s, the use of certain types of drugs (initially opium and morphine, followed by cocaine and heroin) came to be defined as sinful, deviant, and outright *wicked*.[2] By the turn of the twentieth century, politicians and police advanced claims that drug use was linked to the underworld. With the passage of the Harrison Act in 1914, narcotics users became defined as criminal offenders. In the decades hence, a variety of new and aggressive opinion makers fought against drug use, and by the close of the 1930s they had constructed an image of drug users as "dope fiends" who faced a lifetime of slavery to drugs.[3]

During these early years of drug policy formation, there seemed to be few critics of the emerging control efforts. A conspicuous exception in this regard was Alfred R. Lindesmith, who during the 1930s was a graduate student at the University of Chicago and in subsequent years a member of the sociology faculty at Indiana University. Lindesmith's first exposure to the drug field was through criminal addicts, but the majority of his thinking was influenced by his research with patients at the U.S. Public Health Service Hospital at Lexington, Kentucky. There the addict population was comprised of individuals addicted to either morphine or paragoric, and their drugs had been obtained from physicians through either legal or quasi-legal means. They were members of neither the criminal underworld nor the street subcultures. As "patients" under treatment for some illness, Lindesmith argued that criminal penalties were inappropriate for those suffering from the chronic and relapsing disease of addiction.[4] Although a direct call for the legalization of drugs was not apparent in Lindesmith's early work, it was clearly implied. His arguments for policy changes were criticized at the federal level[5]—and then essentially ignored.

Arguments for the legalization of drugs came to the forefront during the 1960s. The sixties were a time when drug use seemed to leap from the marginal zones of society to the very center of middle-class community life. As the use of heroin, marijuana, and a variety of hallucinogenic drugs increased, so, too, did the number of arrests on drug charges of apparently otherwise law-abiding citizens. Spirited by the liberalism of the era, discussions about drugs in the social science community often encouraged some form of legalization. By legalizing the possession and sale of the whole spectrum of illicit drugs, it was argued, lives would no longer be disrupted by arrests, the drug black market would shrink, and drug-related crime would eventually disappear. Once again, the calls for legalization were for the most part ignored.

THE BEGINNINGS OF THE DEBATE

By 1988 it had long since been decided by numerous observers that the seventy-four years of federal prohibition since the passage of the Harrison Act of 1914 were not only a costly and abject failure, but a totally doomed effort as well. It was argued that drug laws and drug enforcement had served mainly to create enormous profits for drug dealers and traffickers, overcrowded jails, corruption among police and other government employees, a distorted foreign policy, predatory street crime carried on by users in search of the funds necessary to purchase black-market drugs, and urban areas harassed by street-level drug dealers and terrorized by violent drug gangs.[6]

Much of what these observers were remarking about indeed had been the case. To begin with, expenditures for the war on drugs had been considerable. Federal disbursements for supply- and demand-reduction from 1981 through 1988, for example, had totaled some $16.5 billion.[7] These figures, furthermore, did not include the many more billions of dollars spent by state and local governments on law enforcement and other criminal justice system costs and on prevention, education, treatment, and research.

On the more positive side of the equation, interdiction initiatives had resulted in a somewhat impressive set of figures. From 1981 through 1987 some 5.3 million kilograms of marijuana had been seized. And even more importantly, cocaine seizures had increased dramatically, from 2,000 kilograms in 1981 to almost 60,000 in 1988.[8]

Quite clearly, however, there was a negative side to these figures. Customs, Coast Guard, and Drug Enforcement Administration (DEA) officials readily admitted that these seizures probably reflected only 10 percent of the marijuana and cocaine entering the country.[9] Furthermore, DEA figures indicated that despite the seizures and increased expenditures on interdiction, the growing supply of cocaine in the United States had resulted in increased availability and a dramatic decline in price.[10] To further complicate the picture, the purity of cocaine also had increased significantly over this same period of time.[11] Intimidating as well for the war on drugs was the fact that during the 1980s worldwide production of both marijuana and opium had increased.[12] To this was added the problem that many countries seemed to be unable, or unwilling, to take a stand against drug traffickers. And there were other problems: the continued use of illegal drugs, with many cities seemingly overwhelmed with crack-cocaine; violence in the inner cities and elsewhere, as drug-trafficking gangs competed for distribution territories; street crime, committed by users for the sake of supporting their drug habits; and corruption in law enforcement and other branches of government, brought on by the considerable economic opportunities for those involved in drug distribution.

Within the context of the concerns about the continued extent and consequences of illegal drug use in the United States, the closing years of the 1980s witnessed a renewed call for the *decriminalization*, if not the outright *legalization*, of most or all illicit drugs.[13] Most vocal in this behalf have been Ernest van den Haag, professor of jurisprudence and public policy at Fordham University;[14] Ethan A. Nadelmann from the Woodrow Wilson School of Public and International Affairs at Princeton University;[15] free-market economist Milton Friedman;[16] Gary S. Becker, professor of economics and sociology at the University of Chicago;[17] freelance writer Harry Schwartz;[18] Professor Arnold S. Trebach of The American University;[19] Professor Steven Wisotsky of Nova University Law Center;[20] and Baltimore Mayor Curt L. Schmoke.[21]

ARGUING FOR LEGALIZATION

The arguments posed by the supporters of legalization might be summarized as follows: (1) The drug laws have created evils far worse than the drugs themselves have—corruption, violence, street crime, and disrespect for the law. (2) Legislation passed to control drugs has failed to reduce demand. (3) You cannot have illegal that which a significant segment of the population in any society is committed to doing. You simply cannot arrest, prosecute, and punish such large numbers of people, particularly in a democracy. And specifically in this behalf, in a liberal democracy the government must not interfere with *personal* behavior if liberty is to be maintained. (4) If marijuana, cocaine, heroin, and other drugs were legalized, a number of very positive things would happen:

- Drug prices would fall.
- Users could obtain their drugs at low, government-regulated prices and would no longer be forced to engage in prostitution and street crime to support their habits.
- The fact that the levels of drug-related crime would significantly decline would result in less crowded courts, jails, and prisons and would free law enforcement personnel to focus their energies on the "real criminals" in society.
- Drug production, distribution, and sale would be removed from the criminal arena; no longer would it be within the province of organized crime, and as a result, such criminal syndicates as the Medellín cartel and the Jamaican posses would be decapitalized and the violence associated with drug distribution rivalries eliminated.

• Government corruption and intimidation by traffickers, as well as drug-based foreign policies, would be effectively reduced, if not eliminated entirely.

• The often draconian measures undertaken by police to enforce the drug laws would be curtailed, thus restoring to the American public many of its hard-won civil liberties.

To these contentions has been added the argument that legalization in any form or structure would have only a minimal impact on current drug use levels. There is the assumption that given the existing levels of access to most illegal drugs, current levels of use closely match demand. Thus, there would be no additional health, safety, behavioral, and/or other problems accompanying legalization. And, finally, the point is sometimes argued that through government regulation of drugs, the billions of dollars spent annually on drug enforcement could be better utilized. Moreover, by taxing government-regulated drugs, revenues would be collected that could be used for preventing drug abuse and treating those harmed by drugs.

Perhaps the most articulate and must fully developed arguments for legalizing drugs come from Steven Wisotsky, Arnold S. Trebach, and Ethan A. Nadelmann, whose individual positions are summarized below.

Steven Wisotsky

Professor Wisotsky argues that despite the most recent war on drugs begun in 1982, there has been an increase in drug use, in crime, in police corruption, and in terror and murder, especially in foreign nations. National security has been threatened because there is the incentive to make large amounts of money by breaking the law. All of the tighter laws have led to a repressive type of government that, in order to enforce its laws, has taken away individual rights.

The Crime Control Act of 1984 was a blow to the morale of criminal defendants and interfered with their ability to prepare defenses. Some citizens are being stopped and searched without probable cause, and the government won almost all the drug cases and seriously punished the first-time offenders.

The war on drugs cannot be won. It is destructive to civil liberties and is encouraging and enriching mobsters. Time has proven its failure; now we need to set realistic and principled priorities based on facts. These facts should be researched by a national study commission of experts and leaders.

The goals of this commission should be to decrease drug use and to decrease the black-market pathologies of drug use. These include the street violence associated with the distribution of currently illegal drugs and the corruption of police and other public officials. These goals can be accomplished by defining the real causes of drug use problems, distinguishing between problems that arise from actual drug use and those that emerge from current laws and enforcement practices, and setting realistic, principled priorities that are based on scientific truth. Too often research has been funded to support existing drug policy, failing to provide an accurate picture.

Most drug use does not cause real harm; it is the drug laws that cause the most harm. The Dutch model—in which drug use remains illegal, but is ignored—is a good example of a reasonable national policy. If the legal system would ignore the harmless drug use of adults, attention could be focused on the real issues. These include preventing drug use by children, placing a top priority on the public use of drugs and drug impairment, and treating chronic users who cause harm to themselves and others. In an *un*oppressive society, drug users would be more likely to accept treatment if they were not afraid of the criminal justice system. Addicts should be treated voluntarily, and treatment budgets should be increased.

The best means of dealing with drugs is through regulation. The regulations might include getting tougher on such legal drugs as tobacco and alcohol. Vending machines for cigarettes should be eliminated, and the hours of sale for alcohol and tobacco should be restricted. Taxes should also be raised to reflect the cost of dealing with the consequences of use.

While there have been isolated achievements of current drug laws, a cost-benefit analysis would show that current policy and enforcement have a very minimal benefit, yet an extremely high cost in terms of resources, crime, corruption, and the loss of liberty. Cocaine use is down—not because of law enforcement, but because of education and health concerns. In addition, the heavy drug-using generation is aging and using fewer drugs, while the younger generations are not using as much as their predecessors.

Ultimately, it is not the role of government in a free society to tell its adult citizens what risks to take. To do so is to totalitarian. Bicycles kill 10,000 people a year, and yet no one proposes making them illegal.

In conclusion, Wisotsky holds that national policy should be to maintain zero tolerance for the use of drugs by children, relax drug laws for adults, and initiate more stringent regulations regarding the sale of alcohol and tobacco. Research should focus on the prevalence and frequency of use and on the real consequences of use. This would enable the development of a meaningful index of health and well-being relative to drug use. Such research would also document nonharmful, and even therapeutic, drug use.

Arnold S. Trebach

In 1982 Professor Trebach applauded the British approach to drug addiction, which involved maintaining addicts on heroin as well as using heroin for pain relief for the terminally ill. He noted that the U.S. government ignored the British experience and those Americans who advocated it.

In the years hence Professor Trebach has argued that it is the police who are the victims of violence or the threat of violence, victims of the temptation of easy money and the stress of undercover work. People need drugs, and our society has denied their need. Drug-related deaths are few each year as compared to over 500,000 annually from alcohol and tobacco. There were no reports of marijuana overdose deaths. Children are at greater risk of death from being involved in accidents related to toys and swimming pools and from being murdered by their parents than they are from taking drugs.

Professor Trebach goes on to argue that there are peaceful compromises to the war on drugs: greater controls on the sale of alcohol and tobacco and fewer controls on currently illegal drugs. His reform principles include different forms of legalization, medicalization, decriminalization, the selective and rational enforcement of existing laws, and the need to virtually ignore the simple user and small-scale dealer.

This peace process to end the war on drugs can begin by organizing opposition to extremist officials and policies and by promoting tolerance, compassion, treatment, and educational help for users and abusers. Ending the war on drugs requires federal leadership through existing structures (such as the National Institute on Drug Abuse), focusing on increased funds for treatment and for developing and evaluating model programs such as AIDS prevention, with needle exchange and treatment a top priority.

The peace policy process would recognize that it would probably be impossible to immediately legalize drugs. More pragmatically, small steps could be taken. These positive steps would include adopting the Dutch approach of ignoring nonproblem use and users, adopting the Alaskan approach of allowing marijuana to be grown for private home consumption, and attempting to develop other economic outlets for the marijuana plant. Perhaps products based on the fiber itself, such as rope or even clothing, could be developed.

In the peace process it should be remembered that the most harmful drugs in our society—alcohol and tobacco—should have greater regulatory controls and that increased treatment should be provided for users.

Ethan A. Nadelmann

Professor Nadelmann, clearly the most visible player in the prolegalization debate, argues that America's prohibitions against marijuana, cocaine, heroin, and other drugs impose far too large a cost in terms of tax dollars, crime, and infringements on civil rights and individual liberties.

On the domestic front the criminalization of the drug market has proven to be as counterproductive as was Prohibition sixty years ago—at costs that are becoming unsupportable. He documents how drug cases are clogging the criminal justice system, with the expense of processing and incarcerating drug offenders rising at an astronomical rate. Ironically, he adds, the greatest beneficiaries of drug laws are the traffickers. The criminalization of the drug market effectively imposes a de facto value-added tax paid to dealers.

Legalization would slash the costs to the criminal justice system and reduce the number of crimes committed to buy drugs at artificially high prices. The quality of urban life would rise, the rate of homicide would decline, and American foreign policy would be freed to pursue more realistic goals. The logic of legalization is grounded on two assumptions: that most illegal drugs are not as dangerous as is commonly believed and that the most risky among them are unlikely to prove widely appealing precisely because of their obvious danger. Legalization would be risky, but risk is not a certainty. One thing is certain, Nadelmann concludes: Current control policies have produced little progress and have proven highly counterproductive.

ARGUING AGAINST LEGALIZATION

Those most vocally *opposed* to the legalization of drugs include the Hon. Charles B. Rangel (D–N.Y.), chairman of the House Select Committee on Narcotics Abuse and Control;[22] Charles R. Schuster, director of the National Institute on Drug Abuse;[23] William J. Bennett, director of the Office of National Drug Control Policy;[24] and drug abuse researchers James A. Inciardi of the University of Delaware and Duane C. McBride of Andrews University.[25] Their arguments fall into seven general areas, each of which is addressed below.

The Legalization Proposals Are Not "Proposals" At All Argument

Although legalizing drugs has been debated for quite some time, Rep. Rangel of New York and researchers Inciardi and McBride point out that never has an advocate of the position structured a concrete proposal. Any attempt to legalize drugs would be extremely complex, but all proponents tend to proceed from a simplistic, "shoot-from-the-hip" position without first developing any sophisticated proposals. In this regard, there are many questions that would need to be addressed, including the following:

- What drugs should be legalized? Marijuana? Heroin? Cocaine? And if cocaine is designated for legalization, should proposals include such coca products as crack and other forms of freebase cocaine? Which hallucinogenic drugs should be legalized? LSD? Peyote? Mescaline? What about quaaludes? Should they be returned to the legal market? In short, which drugs should be legalized, according to what criteria, and who should determine the criteria?

- Assuming that some rationally determined slate of drugs could be designated for legalization, what purity and potency levels should be permitted?

- As with alcohol, should there be age limits as to who can and cannot use drugs? Should those old enough to drive be permitted to buy and use drugs?

- Where should the drugs be sold? Over the counter in drug and grocery stores, as is the case with many pharmaceuticals? Through mail-order houses? In special vending machines strategically located in public restrooms, hotel lobbies, and train and bus stations? Should some, or all, of the newly legalized drugs be available only on a prescription basis? How often should these prescriptions be refillable?

- Where should the raw material for drugs originate? Would cultivation be restricted to U.S. lands, or would foreign sources be permitted? Should trade restrictions of any type be imposed—by drug, amount, potency, purity, or country?

- If drugs are to be legalized, should the drug market be a totally free one, with private industry establishing the prices, as well as the levels of purity and potency? What kinds of advertising should be permitted?

- If drugs are to be legalized, what types of restrictions on their use should be structured? Should transportation workers, nuclear plant employees, or other categories of workers be forbidden to use them at all times, or just while they are on duty?

- For any restrictions placed on sales, potency levels, distribution, prices, quantity, and advertising in a legalized drug market, what government bureaucracy should be charged with the enforcement of the legalization statutes? The Federal Bureau of Investigation (FBI)? The Drug Enforcement Administration (DEA)? The Food and Drug Administration (FDA)? The Bureau of Alcohol, Tobacco, and Firearms (ATF)? State and local law enforcement agencies? Or should some new federal bureaucracy be created for the purpose? Going further, what kinds of penalties ought to be established for violation of the legalization restrictions?

The Public Health and Behavioral Consequences Argument

There is considerable evidence to suggest that the legalization of drugs would create behavioral and public health problems to a degree that would far outweigh the current consequences of the drug prohibition. There are some excellent reasons why marijuana, cocaine, heroin, and other drugs are now controlled, and why they ought to remain so.

Marijuana. Recent research suggests that marijuana smoking is a practice that combines the hazardous features of both tobacco and alcohol with a number of pitfalls of its own. Moreover, there are many disturbing questions about marijuana's effect on the vital systems of the body, on the brain and mind, on immunity and resistance, and on sex and reproduction.[26]

Recent research on behavioral aspects suggests that marijuana use severely affects the social perceptions of heavy users. The Center for Psychological Studies in New York City, for example, has found that adults who smoked marijuana daily believed the drug helped them to function better—improving their self-awareness and relationships with others.[27] In reality, however, marijuana had served as a "buffer" so to speak, enabling users to tolerate problems, rather than to face them and make changes that might increase the quality of their social functioning and satisfaction with life. The study reported that the research subjects used marijuana to avoid dealing with their difficulties and that their avoidance inevitably made their problems worse—on the job, at home, and in family and sexual relationships.

It has been argued that what this research documented was what clinicians had been saying for years. Personal growth evolves from learning to cope with stress, anxiety, frustration, and the many other difficulties that life presents, both small and large. Marijuana use (and the use of other drugs as well, including alcohol), particularly among adolescents and young adults, interferes with this process, and the result is a drug-induced arrested development.[28]

Cocaine. The pleasure and feelings of power that cocaine engenders make its use a rather unwise recreational pursuit. In very small and occasional doses it is no more harmful than equally moderate doses of alcohol, but there is a side to cocaine that can be very destructive. That euphoric lift, with its feelings of pleasure, confidence, and being on top of things, that comes from but a few brief snorts is short-lived and invariably followed by a letdown. More specifically, when the elation and grandiose feelings begin to wane, a corresponding deep depression is often felt, which is in such marked contrast to users' previous states that they are strongly motivated to repeat the dose and restore the euphoria. This leads to chronic, compulsive use. And when chronic users try to stop using cocaine, they are typically plunged into a severe depression from which only more cocaine can arouse them. Most clinicians estimate that approximately 10 percent of those who begin to use cocaine "recreationally" will go on to serious, heavy, chronic, compulsive use.[29]

To this can be added what is known as the "cocaine psychosis."[30] As the dose and duration of cocaine use increase, the development of cocaine-related psychopathology is not uncommon. Cocaine psychosis is generally preceded by a transitional period, characterized by increased suspiciousness, compulsive behavior, fault finding, and eventually paranoia. When the psychotic state is reached, individuals may experience visual and/or auditory hallucinations, with persecutory voices commonly heard. Many believe that they are being followed by police or that family, friends, and others are plotting against them. Moreover, everyday events tend to be misinterpreted in a way that supports delusional beliefs. When coupled with the irritability and hyperactivity that the stimulant nature of cocaine tends to generate in almost all of its users, the cocaine-induced paranoia may lead to violent behavior as a means of "self-defense" against imagined persecutors. And to this must be added the potent stimulant effects of cocaine on the heart.

Crack. A form of cocaine base, crack is smoked rather than snorted, and as such, it is more rapidly absorbed than cocaine—reportedly crossing the blood-brain barrier within six seconds.[31] Hence, an instantaneous high. Its low price (as little as $3 per rock in some locales) has made it an attractive drug of abuse for those with limited funds, particularly adolescents. Its rapid absorption brings on a faster onset of dependence than is typical with cocaine, resulting in higher rates of addiction, binge use, and psychoses. The consequences include higher levels of cocaine-related violence and all the same manifestations of personal, familial, and occupational neglect that are associated with other forms of drug dependence.[32]

Heroin. A derivative of morphine, heroin is a highly addictive narcotic, and the drug is historically associated with addiction and street crime. Although heroin overdose is not uncommon, unlike alcohol, cocaine, tobacco, and many prescription drugs, the direct physiological damage caused by heroin use tends to be minimal. And it is for this reason that the protagonists of drug legalization include heroin in their arguments. By making heroin readily available to users, they argue, many problems could be sharply reduced, if not totally eliminated, including the crime associated with supporting a heroin habit; the overdoses resulting from problematic levels of heroin purity and potency; the HIV and hepatitis infections brought about by needle sharing; and the personal, social, and occupational dislocations resulting from the drug-induced criminal life style.[33]

The belief that the legalization of heroin would eliminate crime, overdose, infections, and life dislocations is for the most part delusional for it is likely that the heroin use life style would change little for most addicts, regardless of the legal status of the drug. And there is ample evidence to support this argument—in the biographies and autobiographies of narcotics addicts, in the clinical assessments of heroin addiction, and in the treatment literature.[34] The point is this. Heroin is a highly addictive drug. For the addict it becomes life consuming: It becomes mother, father, spouse, lover, counselor, and confessor. Because heroin is a short-acting drug, with its effects lasting at best four to six hours, it must be taken regularly and repeatedly. Because there is a more rapid onset when taken intravenously, most heroin users inject the drug. Because heroin has depressant effects, a portion of the user's day is spent in a semistupefied state. Collectively, these attributes result in a user who is more concerned with drug-taking than with health, family, work, or anything else.

The Crime and Enslavement Theory Argument

For the better part of the current century there has been a concerted belief in what has become known as the "enslavement theory of addiction"—the conviction that because of the high prices of heroin and cocaine on the drug black market, users are forced to commit crimes in order to support their drug habits.[35] In this regard, supporters of drug legalization argue that if the criminal penalties attached to heroin and cocaine possession and sale were removed, three things would occur: The black market would disappear, the prices of heroin and cocaine would decline significantly, and users would no longer have to engage in street crime in order to support their desired levels of drug intake. Yet there has never been any solid empirical evidence to support the contentions of the enslavement theory. Quite the contrary.

Research since the middle of the 1970s with active drug users in the streets of New York, Miami, Baltimore, and elsewhere has demonstrated that the enslavement theory has little basis in reality and that the contentions of the legalization proponents in this behalf are mistaken.[36] All of these studies of the criminal careers of heroin and other drug users have convincingly documented that while drug use tends to intensify and perpetuate criminal behavior, it usually does not initiate criminal careers. In fact, the evidence suggests that among the majority of street drug users who are involved in crime, their criminal careers were well established prior to the onset of either narcotics or cocaine use.

The Expanded Market Argument

An important argument revolves around the assumption that legalization would have minimal impact on use, that most or all those who would use drugs are already using. Such an assumption appears to ignore one of the most powerful aspects of American tradition: the ability of an entrepreneurial market system to create, expand, and maintain high levels of demand.

There has never been any serious discussion of how the issues of advertising and marketing might be handled. However, if the treatment of such other legal drugs as alcohol and tobacco is used as a model of regulatory control, then it is reasonable to assume an application of free speech rights to legalized drugs. And this indeed would be logical for, after all, the drugs would be *legal* products. And, similarly, it would not seem unreasonable to assume that the American market economy would become strongly involved in expanding and maintaining demand for the legalized substances. The successes of tobacco and alcohol advertising programs are eminently conspicuous. The linking of smoking with women's rights has been masterful. The linking of alcohol with the pursuit of happiness after work, in recreational activities, and in romantic liaisons has been so effective that during 1987 alone Americans spent some $71.9 billion on beer, wine, and distilled spirits.[37]

The issue, then, of whether the market is saturated fails to recognize the ability of a free enterprise system to expand demand. And there are epidemiological data that confirm that there is considerable room for increasing the demand for drugs. Estimates projected from the National Institute on Drug Abuse's most recent household survey of drug abuse suggest that only 6 percent of the population aged 12 years or older are *current users* (any use during the past month) of marijuana and only 2 percent are current users of cocaine.[38] The survey also demonstrated, however, that the majority of adolescents and young adults are current users of the major available legal drug—alcohol—and that, in all, there are no less than 57.1 million current users of cigarettes and more than 105 million current users of alcohol. To assume that the legalization of drugs would maintain the current, relatively low levels of drug use when there are high rates of both alcohol and tobacco use seems rather naive. Moreover, it considerably underestimates the advertising industry's ability to create a context of use that appears integral to a meaningful, successful, liberated life.

The Drugs and Violence Argument

There seem to be three models of drug-related violence—the psychopharmacologic, the economically compulsive, and the systemic.[39] The *psychopharmacological model of violence* suggests that some individuals, as the result of short-term or long-term ingestion of specific substances, may become excitable and irrational and may exhibit violent behavior. The paranoia and aggression associated with the cocaine psychosis fit into the psychopharmacological model, as does most alcohol-related violence.

The *economically compulsive model of violence* holds that some drug users engage in economically oriented violent crime to support drug use. This model is illustrated in the many studies of drug use and criminal behavior that have demonstrated that while drug sales, property crimes, and prostitution are the primary economic offenses committed by users, armed robberies and muggings do indeed occur.[40]

The *systemic model of violence* maintains that violent crime is intrinsic to the very involvement with illicit substances. As such, systemic violence refers to the traditionally aggressive patterns of interaction within systems of illegal drug trafficking and distribution.

It is the systemic violence that has become associated with trafficking in crack in the inner cities that has brought the most attention to drug-related violence in recent years. Moreover, concerns with this same violence have focused the current interest on the possibility of legalizing drugs.[41] And it is certainly logical to assume that if heroin, cocaine, and marijuana were legal substances, systemic drug-related violence would indeed decline significantly. But, too, there are some very troubling considerations. *First*, to achieve the desired declines in systemic violence, it would require that crack be legalized as well. For after all, it is in the crack distribution system that much of the drug-related violence is occurring. *Second*, it is already clear that there is considerable psychopharmacologic violence associated with the cocaine psychosis. Moreover, research has demonstrated that there is far more psychopharmacologic violence connected with heroin use than is generally believed.[42] Given the fact that drug use would certainly increase with legalization, in all likelihood any declines in systemic violence would be accompanied by corresponding increases in psychopharmacologic violence. The United States already pays a high price for alcohol-related violence, a phenomenon well documented by recent research.[43] Why compound the problem with the legalization of additional violence-producing substances?

The Declining Drug Use Trend Argument

It would appear that agitation for such a drastic policy change as would be involved in the legalization of drugs is in great part an outgrowth of frustration. "After having spent billions of dollars on interdiction, education, prevention, treatment, and research," many ask, "what do we have to show for it?" The answer is declining trends in drug use within the general population. Consider the data. First, there is the National Institute on Drug Abuse's annual survey of high school seniors, conducted each year by the University of Michigan.[44] For example, marijuana use has been on a steady decline since its peak usage levels at the close of the 1970s. Whereas 60.4 percent of high school seniors in 1979 had used marijuana at least once in their lives, by 1988 that figure had dropped to 47.2 percent. Even sharper declines are apparent with regard to use in the past year and current use (any use in the past thirty days). Perhaps the most significant drop has been in the daily use of marijuana, from a high of 10.7 percent in 1978 to 2.7 percent in 1988.

The results of the 1988 survey also reflect a significant drop in the use of cocaine after a decade of rising trends in use: a decline from 6.2 percent in 1986 to 4.3 percent in 1987 to 3.4 percent in 1988 in the proportion of seniors who said they were current users of cocaine, and a decline from 12.7 percent in 1986 to 10.3 percent in 1987 to 7.9 percent in 1988 in the proportion of seniors who said they had used the drug at least once in the past year. The proportion of seniors who had "ever used" and who used "daily" also declined.

No clear trend data are available in these surveys regarding crack, but the 1988 figures suggest that crack use may not be all that widespread among America's high school population: 4.8 percent reported having tried crack, 3.1 percent reported having used it in the past year, 1.6 percent reported current use, and only 0.1 percent indicated the current daily use of the drug.

There are other indicators of declining drug use. Since 1980 the University of Michigan survey team has been collecting data on drug use among college students. The proportion of these students reporting "any use during the past year" declined overall. In addition, NIDA's National Household Surveys on Drug Abuse tend to confirm the findings of the high school surveys.

The Public Opinion Argument

The public opinion argument points to the fact that despite what the prolegalization constituency suggests, the American people are opposed to their ideas. Consider the data. *First*, in the Gallup surveys conducted from 1969 through 1985, people were asked: "Do you think the use of marijuana should be made legal or not?" The 1985 response reflected 23 percent in favor, 73 percent opposed, and 4 percent with no opinion.[45] *Second*, surveys of college freshmen conducted each year by the American Council on Education have found that the overwhelming majority of students are opposed to the legalization of marijuana, including some 81 percent of the class of 1991.[46] *Third*, the findings of a *Washington Post* poll conducted during June of 1988 indicated that 90 percent of those surveyed opposed the legalization of drugs.[47] *Fourth*, an ABC News poll conducted at the height of the legalization debate in 1988 found that 90 percent of the American population favored keeping drugs illegal.[48] Finally, a *Time*/CNN poll conducted during October 1989 found that 79 percent of the population would be willing to pay higher taxes if the money were used for fighting the war on drugs.[49]

DISCUSSION

No doubt the legalization of drugs argument will endure for quite some time to come. Regardless of one's position, a useful philosophical framework for examining the arguments might be the notions contained in John Stuart Mill's celebrated essay *On Liberty*,[50] first published in 1859. Mill, an eighteenth-century philosopher and economist, played a significant role in defining both the British and the American concepts of individual liberty and the proper limitation of government intrusion into individual behavioral choices.

Mill's utilitarian ideals might argue that drugs should be legalized if the benefits in doing so would outweigh the harms caused by drug use. The liberty principle implies that government has no right to interfere with adult behaviors that do not harm others. Government may educate, it may inform, and it may even cajole, Mill argued, but its laws must not restrict individual choice, even if the actions in question may be harmful to the individual involved. Whether implicitly or explicitly, all arguments for the legalization of drugs draw on these principles. Perhaps the next step in the debate should revolve around Mill's thesis and how it might apply to the war on drugs and American drug policy.

NOTES

1. See Alfred R. Lindesmith, *The Addict and the Law* (Bloomington: Indiana University Press, 1965); Rufus King, *The Drug Hang-Up: America's Fifty Year Folly* (New York: Norton, 1972); David F. Musto, *The American Disease: Origins of Narcotic Control* (New Haven, Conn.: Yale University Press, 1973).

2. Charles E. Terry and Mildred Pellens, *The Opium Problem* (New York: Bureau of Social Hygiene, 1928).

3. James A. Inciardi, *The War on Drugs: Heroin, Cocaine, Crime, and Public Policy* (Palo Alto, Calif.: Mayfield, 1986), 100.

4. Alfred R. Lindesmith, "A Sociological Theory of Addiction," *American Journal of Sociology* 43 (1938): 593–613; Alfred R. Lindesmith, " 'Dope Fiend' Mythology," *Journal of Criminal Law and Criminology* 31 (1940): 199–208.

5. Twain Michelsen, "Lindesmith's Mythology," *Journal of Criminal Law and Criminology* 31 (1940): 373–400.

6. See, for example, Steven Wisotsky, *Breaking the Impasse in the War on Drugs* (New York: Greenwood Press, 1986); Duane C. McBride, Cindy Burgman-Habermehl, Geoff Alpert, and Dale D. Chitwood, "Drugs and Homicide," *Bulletin of the New York Academy of Medicine* 62 (June 1986): 497–508; Arnold S. Trebach, *The Great Drug War* (New York: Macmillan, 1987); *New York Times*, 20 March 1988, E9; *Time*, 7 March 1988, 24; *Newsweek*, 28 March 1988, 20–29; *Miami Herald, Neighbors*, 24 April 1988, 21–25; Louis Kraar, "The Drug Trade," *Fortune*, 20 June 1988, 27–38. See also Ron Rosenbaum, "Crack Murder: A Detective Story," *New York Times Magazine*, 15 February 1987, 24–33, 57, 60.

7. Figures were provided by the Office of Management and Budget (1988 costs are estimated).

8. *New York Times*, 11 April 1988, A12; *Time*, 13 November 1989, 81.

9. *Drug Smuggling: Large Amounts of Illegal Drugs Not Seized by Federal Authorities* (Washington, D.C.: U.S. General Accounting Office, 1987).

10. Maurice Rinfret, "Cocaine Price, Purity, and Trafficking Trends" (Paper presented at the National Institute on Drug Abuse Technical Review Meeting on the Epidemiology of Cocaine Use and Abuse, Rockville, Maryland, 3–4 May 1988).

11. Ibid.

12. U.S. Department of State, Bureau of International Narcotics Matters, *International Narcotics Control Strategy Report* (Washington, D.C.: Department of State, 1 March 1988).

13. Although the terms *legalization* and *decriminalization* are often used interchangeably in discussions of drug policy, they clearly have different meanings. *Legalizing* a drug would serve to abolish the laws (and associated criminal penalties) that prohibit its production, sale, distribution, and possession. As such, alcohol, tobacco, and aspirin are legal drugs. In contemporary usage, *decriminalizing* a drug is a lesser measure, serving only to remove the criminal penalties associated with possession. Under current marijuana decriminalization statutes, the criminal penalties associated with possession of small amounts for personal use have been removed. However, sale, distribution, production, importation, and certain levels of possession remain prohibited by the criminal law. See James A. Inciardi, "Marijuana Decriminalization Research: A Perspective and Commentary," *Criminology* 19 (May 1981): 145–59.

14. See Ernest van den Haag, "Legalize Those Drugs We Can't Control," *New York Times*, 8 August 1985, 22.

15. See Ethan A. Nadelmann, "The Real International Drug Problem" (Paper presented at the Defense Academic Research Support Conference on "International Drugs: Threat and Response," National Defense College, Defense Intelligence Analysis Center, Washington, D.C., 2–3 June 1987); Ethan A. Nadelmann, "U.S. Drug Policy: A Bad Export," *Foreign Policy* 70 (Spring 1988): 83–108; Ethan A. Nadelmann, "The Case for Legalization," *The Public Interest* 92 (Summer 1988): 3–31; Ethan A. Nadelmann, "Drug Prohibition in the United States: Costs, Consequences, and Alternatives," *Science* 245 (1 September 1989): 939–47.

16. See Milton Friedman and Rose Friedman, *Tyranny of the Status Quo* (San Diego: Harcourt Brace Jovanovich, 1984), 132–41; Milton Friedman, "An Open Letter to Bill Bennett," *Wall Street Journal*, 7 September 1989, A14.

17. See Gary S. Becker, "Should Drug Use Be Legalized?" *Business Week*, 17 August 1987, 22.

18. See Harry Schwartz, "We Can't Win the War, Let's Make Drugs Legal," *USA Today*, 12 October 1987, 12A.

19. Trebach, *The Great Drug War* ; Arnold S. Trebach, "Effects of the Drug War on Constitutional Guaranties," *Drug Law Report* 2 (January–February 1988): 1–10; Arnold S. Trebach, "Tough Choices: The Practical Politics of Drug Policy Reform," *American Behavioral Scientist* 32 (January–February 1989): 248–58.

20. Wisotsky, *Breaking the Impasse*; Steven Wisotsky, "Beyond the War on Drugs," in *The Drug Legalization Debate*, ed. James A. Inciardi (Newbury Park, Calif.: Sage, in press).

21. Kurt L. Schmoke, "Get Our Heads Out of the Sand," *USA Today*, 18 May 1988, 10A; U.S. Congress, House Select Committee on Narcotics Abuse and Control, "Testimony of the Honorable Kurt L. Schmoke," *Legalization of Illicit Drugs: Impact and Feasibility, Part 1, Hearing Before the Select Committee on Narcotics Abuse and Control,*

100th Cong., 2nd sess., 29 September 1988; Kurt L. Schmoke, "War on Drugs Is Lost; Let's Seek New Ideas," *USA Today*, 30 October 1989, 11A.

22. U.S. Congress, House Select Committee, "Testimony of the Honorable Kurt L. Schmoke."

23. Ibid.

24. William J. Bennett, "A Response to Milton Friedman," *Wall Street Journal*, 19 September 1989, A30; William J. Bennett, "Legal Drugs Means More Addicts," *USA Today*, 30 October 1989, 11A.

25. James A. Inciardi and Duane C. McBride, "Legalization: A High-Risk Alternative in the War on Drugs," *American Behavioral Scientist* 32 (January–February 1989): 259–89.

26. For a thorough discussion and analysis of these points, see Helen C. Jones and Paul W. Lovinger, *The Marijuana Question* (New York: Dodd, Mead, 1985).

27. Herbert Hendin, Ann Pollinger Haas, Paul Singer, Melvin Ellner, and Richard Ulman, *Living High: Daily Marijuana Use Among Adults* (New York: Human Sciences Press, 1987).

28. See Robert L. DuPont, *Getting Tough on Gateway Drugs* (Washington, D.C.: American Psychiatric Press, 1984), 80–83.

29. John Grabowski, ed., *Cocaine: Pharmacology, Effects, and Treatment of Abuse* (Rockville, Md.: National Institute on Drug Abuse, 1984); Nicholas J. Kozel and Edgar H. Adams, eds., *Cocaine Use in America: Epidemiologic and Clinical Perspectives* (Rockville, Md.: National Institute on Drug Abuse, 1985); Patricia G. Erickson, Edward M. Adlaf, Glenn F. Murray, and Reginald G. Smart, *The Steel Drug: Cocaine in Perspective* (Lexington, Mass.: Lexington Books, 1987); Henry I. Spitz and Jeffrey S. Rosecan, *Cocaine Abuse: New Directions in Treatment and Research* (New York: Brunner/Mazel, 1987).

30. See Roger D. Weiss and Steven M. Mirin, *Cocaine* (Washington, D.C.: American Psychiatric Press, 1987), 50–53.

31. For a more thorough discussion of crack, see James A. Inciardi, "Beyond Cocaine: Basuco, Crack, and Other Coca Products," *Contemporary Drug Problems* 14 (Fall 1987): 461–92.

32. For example, see *New York Times*, 7 March 1987, 29, 32; *New York Times*, 23 June 1988, A1, B4.

33. This point of view is most thoroughly articulated in Arnold S. Trebach, *The Heroin Solution* (New Haven, Conn.: Yale University Press, 1982).

34. See *Twenty Years in Hell, or the Life, Experience, Trials, and Tribulations of a Morphine Fiend* (Kansas City, Mo.: 1903); William Burroughs, *Junkie* (New York: Ace, 1953); Leroy Street, *I Was a Drug Addict* (New York: Random House, 1953); Marie Nyswander, *The Drug Addict as a Patient* (New York: Grune & Stratton, 1956); Seymour Fiddle, *Portraits From a Shooting Gallery* (New York: Harper & Row, 1967); Phil Hirsch, *Hooked* (New York: Pyramid, 1968); David E. Smith and George R. Gay, eds., *"It's So Good, Don't Even Try It Once"* (Englewood Cliffs, N.J.: Prentice-Hall, 1971); Florrie Fisher, *The Lonely Trip Back* (New York: Bantam, 1972); Leroy Gould, Andrew L. Walker, Lansing E. Crane, and Charles W. Litz, *Connections: Notes from the Heroin World* (New Haven, Conn.: Yale University Press, 1974); Richard P. Rettig, Manual J. Torres, and Gerald R. Garrett, *Manny: A Criminal-Addict's Story* (Boston: Houghton Mifflin, 1977); Marsha Rosenbaum, *Women on Heroin* (New Brunswick, N.J.: Rutgers University Press, 1981); Stanton Peele, *The Meaning of Addiction* (Lexington, Mass.:

Lexington Books, 1985); Jerome J. Platt, *Heroin Addiction* (Malabar, Fla.: Robert E. Krieger, 1986).

35. See Inciardi, *The War on Drugs*, 145–73.

36. See Richard C. Stephens and Duane C. McBride, "Becoming a Street Addict," *Human Organization* 35 (1976): 87–93; Duane C. McBride and Clyde B. McCoy, "Crime and Drugs: The Issues and the Literature," *Journal of Drug Issues* 12 (Spring 1982): 137–52; Bruce D. Johnson, Paul J. Goldstein, Edward Preble, James Schmeidler, Douglas S. Lipton, Barry Spunt, and Thomas Miller, *Taking Care of Business: The Economics of Crime by Heroin Users* (Lexington, Mass.: Lexington Books, 1985); David N. Nurco, John C. Ball, John W. Shaffer, and Thomas F. Hanlon, "The Criminality of Narcotic Addicts," *Journal of Nervous and Mental Disease* 173 (1985): 94–102; Inciardi, *The War on Drugs*, 115–43.

37. *Drug Abuse Update* (June 1988), 5.

38. *National Household Survey on Drug Abuse: Population Estimates 1988* (Rockville, Md.: National Institute on Drug Abuse, 1989).

39. See Paul J. Goldstein, "Homicide Related to Drug Traffic," *Bulletin of the New York Academy of Medicine* 62 (June 1986): 509–16.

40. Supra note 36.

41. See *Wilmington* (Delaware) *News Journal*, 3 April 1988, E2; *Drug Abuse Report*, 6 April 1988, 7–8; *USA Today*, 18 May 1988, 10A; *Newsweek*, 30 May 1988, 36–38; *Time*, 30 May 1988, 12–19; *New York Times*, 2 June 1988, A26; *Fortune*, 20 June 1988, 39–41.

42. See Paul J. Goldstein, *Prostitution and Drugs* (Lexington, Mass.: Lexington Books, 1979), 126; Duane C. McBride, "Drugs and Violence," in *The Drugs-Crime Connection*, ed. James A. Inciardi (Beverly Hills, Calif.: Sage, 1981), 105–23; Inciardi, *The War on Drugs*, 135.

43. See James J. Collins, ed., *Drinking and Crime: Perspectives on the Relationships Between Alcohol Consumption and Criminal Behavior* (New York: Guilford Press, 1981).

44. These surveys have been conducted since 1975, and the data reported here are drawn from Lloyd D. Johnston, Patrick M. O'Malley, and Jerald G. Bachman, *Drug Use, Drinking, and Smoking: National Survey Results from High School, College, and Young Adult Populations: 1975–1988* (Rockville, Md.: National Institute on Drug Abuse, 1989).

45. *The Gallup Poll*, 20 June 1985.

46. Summarized in the *San Diego Union*, 10 April 1988, C-5.

47. *Washington Post*, 26 June 1988, C1, C4.

48. National telephone survey of 2,326 persons ages 16 and over, August 14–26, 1986. Data provided by Roper Center, Storrs, Conn., June 15, 1988.

49. *Time*, 23 October 1989, 34.

50. John Stuart Mill, *On Liberty* (1859; reprint, Boston: Atlantic Monthly Press, 1921).

PART IV

APPENDICES

Appendix A

The Scheduling of MDMA ("Ecstasy")

Jerome Beck and Marsha Rosenbaum

The popularization of MDMA in the mid-1980s has presented a number of challenging dilemmas to the scheduling process. Frequently referred to as "Ecstasy," "XTC," or "Adam," MDMA suddenly became the object of extensive media coverage in 1985, highlighting what appeared to be a dramatic increase in both therapeutic and recreational use. A controversy ensued, providing widely divergent perspectives on the substance. Representing one faction were various psychiatrists who viewed MDMA as a valuable therapeutic adjunct and saw minimal harm associated with carefully monitored use.[1] The other side was largely composed of drug enforcement officials who viewed MDMA as a dangerous "designer drug," possessing potentially harmful actions, with increasing abuse seen outside of the therapeutic community.[2] Alexander Shulgin aptly described the situation in observing that "MDMA has been thrust upon the public awareness as a largely unknown drug which to some is a medical miracle and to others a social devil."[3]

The continuing controversy surrounding the scheduling of MDMA highlights many problems with current drug control policy. In making sense of efforts to control MDMA, we will examine the sequence of events that have contributed to the scheduling controversy. Within this format we will also outline the various justifications offered by both sides in determining the proper legal status of MDMA. Although we provide a brief overview of what is currently known about MDMA, our primary focus involves an examination of various efforts to control this controversial substance.[4]

THE EMERGENCE AND POPULARIZATION OF MDMA

The uniqueness of MDMA (3,4-methylenedioxymethamphetamine) is illustrated by the confusion over the proper terminology to describe its actions. As an N-methyl analogue of MDA, it is related to both the amphetamines and mescaline. Although MDMA has been commonly labeled as a psychedelic drug, it possesses stimulant properties as well. Moreover, it is rarely hallucinogenic and seldom produces the sensory phenomena or mental confusion associated with other psychedelics.[5]

In terms of popular use, MDMA is essentially the successor to MDA, the counterculture "love drug" of the late 1960s and early 1970s. MDA first appeared on the streets in 1967, when its use was noted in the Haight-Ashbury drug subculture.[6] It quickly gained a reputation for producing a sensual, easily managed euphoria. In 1970 MDA was placed in Schedule I of the newly created Controlled Substances Act (CSA).[7] There it joined virtually every other psychedelic drug known at that time. Since MDMA was virtually unknown in 1970, it was not included in the CSA.

Although MDMA first appeared on the street in the early 1970s, use remained limited until the end of the decade. Information about the drug was disseminated largely through word of mouth and anonymously written "flight guides" which provided instructions on proper use. Toward the end of the 1970s a small number of psychiatrists and other therapists began using MDMA as an adjunct for various purposes, particularly in facilitating communication, acceptance, and fear reduction.[8] Both therapeutic and recreational use gradually increased in the early 1980s. Despite their belief in MDMA's efficacy, therapists were reluctant to publicize their preliminary findings for fear that any publicity would inevitably result in its illegality and removal from therapeutic research and use. Although steadily increasing in popularity during this time, its production was generally small scale, with use concentrated in certain urban areas.[9]

The Drug Enforcement Administration (DEA) first encountered MDMA in 1972 through a street sample bought in the Chicago area.[10] Such reports were infrequent, however, and it was not until a decade later that the Drug Control Section of the DEA began soliciting information regarding MDMA.[11] Owing to its structural similarity to MDA, it was to be expected that the DEA would eventually recommend scheduling MDMA as well. In 1982 an early article on MDMA quoted a DEA spokesman: "If we can get enough evidence to be sure there's potential for abuse, we'll ban it."[12]

PROPOSED SCHEDULING

The DEA recommended the placement of MDMA into Schedule I on 27 July 1984.[13] During the same month, the World Health Organization (WHO) requested information and comments regarding MDMA's abuse potential.[14] In support of a Schedule I placement, a DEA chemist concluded that "MDMA has a high potential for abuse based on its chemical and pharmacological similarity to MDA, its self-administration without medical supervision, its clandestine synthesis and its distribution in the illicit drug traffic."[15]

What appeared to be a routine scheduling process of a little-known drug was quickly challenged by a fairly well organized group of psychiatrists and researchers who strongly believed in MDMA's therapeutic potential. Citing LSD as a case example, therapists argued that a Schedule I status would severely hinder any research into the drug's therapeutic potential. The government's surprise at the therapists' reaction was evidenced by a DEA pharmacologist's statement that they "had no idea psychiatrists were using it."[16]

The proposed scheduling and ensuing reaction by therapists soon brought MDMA to national attention. Within a short period of time in mid-1985, almost all the print and electronic media had discovered MDMA. Nearly all the major newspapers and magazines printed stories on the subject, often sensationalizing the reputed euphoric and therapeutic qualities of MDMA.[17]

The rise in publicity was accompanied by what appeared to be an exponential increase in street demand. UCLA psychopharmacologist Ronald Siegel stated that street use "escalated from an estimated 10,000 doses distributed in all of 1976 to 30,000 doses distributed per month in 1985."[18] The DEA found evidence of increased use throughout much of the country and estimated that in one month "30,000 dosage units are distributed in one Texas city alone."[19] Although these estimates (made just before MDMA became illegal) must be considered highly speculative, they attested to MDMA's increasing popularity and/or the power of free publicity.

In response to MDMA proponents' challenges, federal administrative law hearings were held in three cities (Los Angeles, Kansas City, and Washington, D.C.) to determine the final scheduling of MDMA. Two significant events preceded these hearings, which were held in the summer and fall of 1985. In April, at the 1971 Convention on Psychotropic Substances, the 22nd WHO Expert Committee on Drug Dependence recommended that MDMA be placed into Schedule I.[20] The committee's recommendation provided significant support to the DEA's case. However, the committee also urged nations to "facilitate research on this interesting substance."

EMERGENCY SCHEDULING

Shortly before the first hearing, the DEA administrator unexpectedly invoked the emergency scheduling powers granted by the Comprehensive Crime Control Act of 1985. As a result, MDMA was temporarily placed into Schedule I on 1 July 1985.[21] The primary rationale for this federal law was an attempt at counteracting the sudden advent of so-called "designer drugs" (primarily synthetic opiate analogues) in the early 1980s.[22] This amendment to the Controlled Substances Act provides the attorney general with authority to place any substance posing "an imminent hazard to public safety" into Schedule I for a period of one year (plus an additional six months, if necessary) while the final scheduling process is underway.[23]

A number of rationales were provided for the necessity of this action. The primary justification centered on an as-yet-unpublished study associating high dosage, intravenous use of MDA in rats with suspected serotonergic neurotoxicity of unknown significance.[24]

Perhaps an even more significant reason behind the emergency scheduling was the promotion of MDMA as a legally available euphoriant in Texas (primarily in the Dallas area). Beginning in 1984 this mass production and marketing scheme stood in sharp contrast to the relatively small-scale, less overt activities found in other parts of the country.[25] The blatantly open sales of MDMA in numerous bars and nightclubs presented a very public and problematic drug use pattern to authorities. A DEA *Fact Sheet* pointed to the "open promotion of MDMA as a legal euphoriant through fliers, circulars and promotional parties," as well as stating that "30,000 dosage units of MDMA are distributed each month" in Dallas.[26]

The DEA claimed that the emergency scheduling of MDMA was a "completely separate and parallel action from the continued scheduling process regarding the permanent scheduling of MDMA."[27] However, in his opening remarks at the first hearing, Francis Young, the DEA's administrative law judge, criticized the emergency scheduling, both for its poor timing and for its prejudgment of MDMA's therapeutic value.[28]

THE ADMINISTRATIVE LAW HEARINGS

The DEA [together with the Food and Drug Administration (FDA)] clearly believed that MDMA belonged in Schedule I. The DEA's attorneys set out to prove that MDMA fit all three criteria necessary for such a placement: a high potential for abuse, no currently accepted medical use, and a lack of safety for use under medical supervision.[29]

Although virtually everyone at the hearings agreed that there should be at least some controls placed on MDMA (outlawing nonmedical use), therapists and other advocates proposed that it remain available for clinical use and research. They attempted to refute the DEA's contentions by arguing that MDMA has only a low to moderate abuse potential, is safe under medical supervision, and possesses significant therapeutic value. As a consequence, they urged that MDMA be placed into either Schedule III or IV.[30]

Many researchers and therapists feared that a Schedule I status would destroy any hope of evaluating MDMA's therapeutic potential. Therapists argued that their quiescence in publicizing any preliminary findings was justified in light of previous control efforts directed at other psychedelics. Numerous LSD studies involving over 40,000 subjects were conducted throughout the 1950s and early 1960s. Major reviews of these studies concluded that, in general, LSD research had compiled a remarkable safety record with arguable efficacy in at least some studies.[31] Nevertheless, strict controls established in the late 1960s resulted in the discontinuance of practically all LSD research. Once-flourishing explorations into the therapeutic potential of other psychedelic substances (including MDA) also came to a virtual standstill following their placement in Schedule I of the 1970 Controlled Substances Act.[32]

This action was not supported by much of the therapeutic community. According to Lester Grinspoon and James Bakalar, "Almost everyone who has worked with psychedelic drugs, and many who have not, think that their research potential is great; and many who have worked with them also think they have therapeutic potential."[33] They back up their contentions by citing results from surveys of LSD researchers as well as of randomly selected American Psychiatric Association and American Medical Association members.

The DEA attorneys countered therapist concerns by arguing that a Schedule I status does not preclude appropriately conducted research into MDMA's therapeutic potential. Various government officials were called on to testify that such substances could still be studied if the correct protocol is followed.[34] However, citing historical examples, MDMA proponents argued that stringent Schedule I requirements discouraged research and claimed that no substance had ever been removed from Schedule I.[35] Edward Tocus refuted the latter point by noting that sufentanil had been rescheduled from Schedule I to II in 1984.[36] This appears to be one of only two exceptions to the rule, however, with almost all changes in scheduling occurring in the direction of increased control.[37]

Several psychiatrists testified on behalf of MDMA's therapeutic potential at the hearings. In general, therapists argued that a major advantage of MDMA over traditional psychedelics is that it produces far less distortion of sensory perception and fewer unpleasant emotional reactions. The MDMA experience is generally seen as both personal and familiar and seems to differ only in its degree of intensity from that of everyday experience. This is in sharp contrast to the effect of most other psychedelics where the experience is often perceived as unfamiliar and transpersonal.[38] As Grinspoon argued, "MDMA appears to have some of the advantages of LSD-like drugs without most of the corresponding disadvantages."[39]

In countering the optimism expressed by MDMA advocates, DEA attorneys called on various research experts to critique the anecdotal nature of the therapists' testimony.[40] These government witnesses also gave little credence to the two inadequately controlled preliminary studies conducted by proponents. In general, their critique of the therapists' testimony could be summed up in Joe Kleinman's conclusion that "Although these reports make interesting reading, their lack of scientific design, methodology and controls makes them scientifically unsound."[41]

Since MDMA proponents fell far short of meeting the FDA's exacting specifications regarding safety and accepted medical use, the third criterion pertaining to abuse potential became even more significant. Of interest here is the process that determines whether a substance possesses the "high potential for abuse" necessary for inclusion into Schedule I. This was a key concern for both camps as a result of an obvious gap in the Controlled Substances Act.

Of the five schedules, four are reserved entirely for substances that possess demonstrated medical value and safety. These drugs are placed in differing schedules depending on their potential for abuse, with II being the highest and V the lowest. Those attempting to control substances of unproven medical value and safety have only one available option, Schedule I. However, the criteria necessary for inclusion in this schedule specifically state that the substance must possess a *high potential for abuse*.

A number of ill-defined problems arise in any attempt to assess the level of abuse potential for various substances. Should *any* nonmedical use of a psychoactive drug automatically be considered abuse? Even utilizing more exacting definitions of abuse (e.g., problematic use characterized by dysfunction or other negative consequences), one still encounters problems regarding where to draw the lines for low, moderate, and high abuse potential since practically any psychoactive substance (licit or illicit) will be abused by at least some individuals.

In attempting to demonstrate that MDMA does indeed possess a high abuse potential, DEA attorneys cited two animal studies which found that most primates will self-administer MDMA at regular intervals (although less than cocaine).[42] They also relied on commonly accepted drug problem indicators (e.g., drug treatment and emergency room admissions) to support their contention.[43] MDMA advocates, however, turned this argument around by noting the remarkable lack of such reported problems when compared with the DEA's own estimates of MDMA use.[44] Their contention was later supported by John Newmeyer's epidemiological review of drug problem indicators, which concluded that MDMA "has given hardly any indication that it is a problem for Americans, either in terms of adverse reactions, treatment admissions or police involvement."[45]

Despite the paucity of reported problems, the strong euphoria commonly associated with the "Ecstasy" experience certainly suggests a high abuse potential. One could assume that a significant minority of MDMA users would experience major problems from overuse. However, in sharp contrast to cocaine, this does not appear to be the case, at least among current user groups. In testimony submitted on the DEA's behalf, Ronald Siegel noted that the most common patterns of MDMA use were "experimental" (ten times or less in a lifetime) or "social-recreational" (one to four times per month). He also stated that "compulsive patterns marked by escalating dose and frequency of use have not been reported with MDMA users."[46]

Our preliminary findings generally support Siegel's observations.[47] The most frequent use of MDMA tends to occur during the months following the initial experience. After the first exposure, a small minority of users attempt to continually re-experience the positive aspects of the drug. However, this abusive cycle tends to be brief. Within a short period of time the frequent use of MDMA almost invariably produces a strong dysphoric reaction which is only exacerbated with continued use. The increasing number of unpleasant side effects, coupled with an almost total loss of desired effects, appears to occur with greater rapidity and intensity than with other more commonly abused substances.[48] Those respondents in our study who continue to use MDMA tend to do so in a controlled, infrequent manner.

Based on various drug abuse indicators, only minimal problems have been associated with current MDMA use. However, since the popularity of MDMA is fairly recent, more time is needed to see how use patterns develop among new groups introduced to the drug. As Newmeyer cautions:

It may well be that MDMA currently enjoys controlled, careful use by a number of cognoscenti, somewhat as LSD did around 1960. Perhaps in future years, a much larger number of less sophisticated individuals will be drawn in MDMA usage and will find ways to evince adverse reactions, police involvement and other unpleasant consequences from use of the drug.[49]

THE JUDGE'S RULING

From the outset of the hearings, the administrative law judge expressed serious doubts regarding the lawful placement of MDMA into any of the available schedules. In preparation for the actual hearings, the judge reviewed some of the dilemmas involved in attempting to appropriately schedule MDMA. Following an extensive review of relevant legislation and court decisions, he concluded that "to shoe-horn a substance such as we are considering into any of the established schedules requires us to rewrite the statute of Congress."[50]

In addressing the most obvious gap in the Controlled Substances Act, the judge concluded that

The Acting Administrator should decide that a substance which has a potential for abuse less than a *high* potential, and not currently accepted medical use in treatment in the United States, cannot lawfully be placed in any of the five schedules established by the Controlled Substances Act of 1970. The terms of the Act do not permit it. No amount of poring over legislative history empowers us to close the obvious gap left in the statutory scheme.[51]

The judge offered an alternative if the DEA administrator rejected the above recommendation. If a substance such as MDMA was found to have less than a high abuse potential and no currently accepted medical use, then it should be placed into Schedule III, IV, or V depending on its actual abuse potential. He cited federal and circuit court decisions, congressional actions, and the DEA's previous indications to support this recommendation.[52]

After the hearings were completed, the administrative law judge issued his final, nonbinding recommendation on 22 May 1986 to John Lawn, the DEA administrator. Concurring with proponents' arguments, the judge recommended that MDMA be placed into Schedule III, which would allow for human research and therapeutic use by physicians.[53] Based on a systematic review of the evidence presented at the hearings, he concluded that MDMA did not appear to possess a high potential for abuse. In addition, he also concluded that MDMA did have a currently accepted medical use as well as accepted safety of use under medical supervision.[54]

THE DEA'S OVERRULING OF THE JUDGE

In a sharply worded rebuttal, the DEA's attorneys claimed that "the Administrative Law Judge's faulty reasoning, failure to understand the materials presented, and bias led him to arrive at the erroneous conclusion that MDMA should be placed in Schedule III."[55] They then proceeded to systematically critique the judge's analysis and once again called for a Schedule I ruling. The attorneys reemphasized the absence of well-controlled, double-blind studies necessary in meeting the "currently accepted medical use" criteria required of drugs in Schedule II–IV.[56] Relying on these arguments, the DEA administrator subsequently rejected the judge's recommendation (although rejecting DEA attorneys' "bias" allegation) and permanently placed MDMA into Schedule I on 13 November 1986.[57]

APPELLATE COURT DECISIONS AND
THEIR IMPLICATIONS

Four recent appellate court decisions have challenged the validity of the DEA's attempts to temporarily and permanently schedule MDMA in 1985 and 1986.[58] The major consequence of these rulings has been the apparent invalidation of these placements on technical grounds.

Three of the appellate court decisions concerned the validity of prosecutions and convictions resulting from MDMA's temporary placement in Schedule I on 1 July 1985. All three cases (*United States v. Spain*, *United States v. Caudle*, and *United States v. Emerson*) involved defendants convicted as a result of the emergency scheduling. Although differing somewhat as to the challenges and resulting decisions, all three rulings were in basic agreement that the emergency scheduling was invalid. As a consequence, the convictions were overturned. The rationales for all three reversals were based primarily on technicalities associated with faulty implementation of the new law.[59] For example, in May of 1988 the U.S. Court of Appeals for the Ninth Circuit concluded that "The Administrator's temporary scheduling of MDMA was an improper exercise of authority not delegated to him by the Attorney General."[60]

Grinspoon v. Drug Enforcement Administration differed from the other three cases in not challenging a previous conviction. Instead, this appeal to the U.S. Court of Appeals for the First Circuit in late 1986 was a continuation of the therapists' battle to get MDMA out of Schedule I. In appealing the administrator's final schedule, Grinspoon and his colleagues challenged the DEA's rationale regarding all three criteria necessary for a Schedule I placement. In September of 1987 the court overturned the administrator's final scheduling and remanded the case to the DEA to reanalyze its scheduling of MDMA.[61] In so doing, the court ruled that the DEA had erred in narrowly defining the criteria for "currently accepted medical use" as equivalent to an FDA New Drug Application or an Investigational New Drug Protocol approval. The court also found that the DEA erred by equating "lack of accepted safety for use of the drug or other substance under medical supervision" with lack of FDA approval. To address these definitional problems, the court directed the DEA to better define these two scheduling criteria and demonstrate how they apply to MDMA.[62]

The court did concur, however, with the DEA's finding that MDMA possesses a "high potential for abuse." Although the court agreed with the proponents in noting the lack of sufficient evidence demonstrating abuse of MDMA, it went on to note that MDMA clearly had the *potential* for significant abuse. The court acknowledged that a Schedule I placement might impede MDMA research, but concluded that this reason was not sufficient to require moving MDMA out of Schedule I.[63]

Addressing the First Circuit Court's directives, the DEA administrator concluded that MDMA fell far short of meeting the DEA's revised definitions of what constituted medical use. Although acknowledging that "many witnesses in this proceeding, including those presented by the agency, indicated that MDMA may have a potential therapeutic use, such a potential use is not sufficient to establish accepted medical use." Consequently, he once again ordered the placement of MDMA into Schedule I, effective 23 March 1988. [64]

An unforeseen legal complication did ensue, however, as a result of the First Circuit Court's decision. Although temporarily dismissing MDMA's placement in Schedule I, the court's ruling appeared to have little effect on MDMA's legality since it was generally assumed that it would continue to be illegal as a result of the Controlled Substance Analogue Enforcement Act passed in late 1986.[65] The analogue or "designer drug" law makes illegal any substance that is similar in structure or psychological effect to any substance already scheduled, providing it is manufactured, possessed, or sold with the intention that it will be consumed by humans.[66]

It now appears, however, that anyone arrested for MDMA offenses prior to the second rescheduling cannot be prosecuted under the Analogue Act. This conclusion results from the fact that since MDMA had already been made a controlled substance, it could no longer be considered an analogue of a controlled substance.[67]

In sum, the major consequence of these rulings is the likelihood that most, if not all, convictions for MDMA offenses before 23 March 1988 will ultimately be reversed if appealed. As a U.S. Department of Justice lawyer recently concluded, "it appears that all federal prosecutions based upon MDMA's previous status as a Schedule I controlled substance will be subject to challenge and that such challenges are likely to be sustained."[68] It should be noted, however, that although these rulings fault the DEA's actions in attempting to schedule MDMA, they lend little or no support to the therapists' position.

CONCLUSIONS

Barring unforeseen circumstances, it appears that MDMA will remain in Schedule I for an appreciable length of time, pending the outcome of various animal studies conducted to assess the neurotoxicity question. The importance of this research emphasis is highlighted by the fact that its eventual resolution will largely determine if and when needed human studies of MDMA's therapeutic potential are allowed to resume.

At this point in time knowledge regarding almost every aspect of MDMA remains extremely limited. During the hearings both sides of the controversy were largely dependent on testimony based on anecdotal data or extrapolations from preliminary animal studies. The most significant point of agreement between the two camps was the recognition of the need for more research to better determine the potential benefits and risks of a substance that was rapidly becoming popular.

The paucity of epidemiological research continues to prevent a valid assessment of the current extent of patterns or changes in MDMA use.[69] Opinion is divided on whether the overall use of MDMA has increased, decreased, or stayed the same since its scheduling in 1985. With the exception of Perotuka's 1987 survey of 369 Stanford undergraduates (which found that an astonishing 39 percent had reportedly tried MDMA),[70] there have been no additional published estimates of use.

Several professionals in the drug field have dismissed MDMA as a short-term fad. Preliminary findings from our own sociological study, however, suggest that MDMA's perceived therapeutic and euphoric effects, combined with reports of the relative ease commonly associated with the experience, continue to attract new users. The "acid house" phenomenon, with Ecstasy reappearing in nightclubs, indicates that it has an enduring quality.

Regarding scheduling and MDMA's final resolution, the controversy challenged some of the basic precepts underlying the Controlled Substances Act. The administrative law judge was not alone in his frustration regarding the limitations of the five available schedules and the vagaries of the criteria utilized in determining proper placement into them. In concluding that MDMA did not meet *any* of the three criteria necessary for a Schedule I placement (high abuse potential, no currently accepted medical use, and lack of safety for use under medical supervision), the administrative law judge presented a significant challenge to his agency's interpretation of the scheduling process. Although his findings were rejected by the DEA administrator and largely overruled by the First Circuit Court, they nonetheless highlighted the troublesome dilemmas associated with attempting to apply the DEA's and the FDA's understandings of these criteria to MDMA.[71]

NOTES

The authors gratefully acknowledge the assistance of Lynne Jackson, Joel Brown, Rick Doblin, and Alexander Shulgin. This research was supported by NIDA Grant #R01

DA0440801, "Exploring Ecstasy: A Study of MDMA Users," Beatrice Rouse, project officer.

1. "Written Testimony Submitted on Behalf of Drs. Grinspoon and Greer, Professors Bakalar and Roberts," *U.S. Department of Justice, Drug Enforcement Administration Hearings*, Docket no. 84-48: G. Greer, L. Grinspoon, R. D. Lynch (22 April 1985); R. J. Strassman (23 April 1985); P. E. Wolfson (24 April 1985).

2. U.S. Department of Justice, Drug Enforcement Administration, *Fact Sheet* (Washington, D.C.: U.S. Dept. of Justice, 1985); F. Sapienza, "Written Testimony Submitted on Behalf of Drug Enforcement Administration, Professors Bakalar and Roberts," *U.S. Department of Justice, Drug Enforcement Administration Hearings*, Docket no. 84–48 (25 April 1985); D. W. Holsten and D. W. Scheister, "Controls over the Manufacture of MDMA," *California Society for the Treatment of Alcohol and Other Drug Dependencies News* 12 (1985): 14–15; F. Sapienza, "MDMA and the Controlled Substances Act" (Paper presented to MDMA: A Multidisciplinary Conference, San Francisco, May 1986).

3. A. Shulgin, "What Is MDMA?" *PharmChem Newsletter* 14, no. 3 (1985): 3.

4. For more comprehensive discussions of MDMA, its uses, and the scheduling controversy, see J. Beck, "The Popularization and Resultant Implications of a Recently Controlled Psychoactive Substance," *Contemporary Drug Problems* 13, no. 1 (1986): 23–63; R. B. Seymour, *MDMA* (San Francisco: Haight-Ashbury Publications, 1986); R. B. Seymour, D. R. Wesson, and D. E. Smith, eds., "MDMA: Proceedings of the Conference," *Journal of Psychoactive Drugs* 18, no. 4 (1986); J. Beck, "The Public Health Implications of MDMA Use," in *Ecstasy: The Clinical, Pharmacological, and Neurotoxicological Effects of the Drug MDMA*, ed. S. J. Peroutka (Boston: Kluwer Academic Publishers, 1990).

5. Beck, "The Popularization"; Shulgin, "What Is MDMA?"; Seymour, *MDMA*.

6. F. H. Meyers, A. J. Rose, and D. E. Smith, "Incidents Involving the Haight-Ashbury Population and Some Uncommonly Used Drugs," *Journal of Psychedelic Drugs* 1, no. 1 (1967–68): 140–46.

7. Of the five schedules provided by the 1970 Controlled Substances Act (CSA), Schedule I is reserved for those drugs lacking recognized medical use and safety as well as possessing a high potential for abuse (e.g., heroin, LSD, PCP). As it pertains to MDMA, this appendix examines the various schedules and the criteria utilized in determining proper placement into them. For a more comprehensive analysis of the CSA itself, see Alexander Shulgin, *The Controlled Substances Act: A Resource Manual of the Current Status of the Federal Drug Laws* (Berkeley, Calif.: Ronin Publishing, 1988).

8. Beck, "The Popularization"; Seymour, *MDMA*.

9. Beck, "The Popularization"; C. L. Renfroe, "MDMA on the Street: Analysis Anonymous," *Journal of Psychoactive Drugs* 18, no. 4 (1986): 363–69.

10. Seymour, *MDMA*, 27.

11. C. Dye, "XTC: The Chemical Pursuit of Pleasure," *Drug Journal News* 10, no. 5 (1982): 8–9.

12. Ibid., 8.

13. F. M. Mullen, "Schedules of Controlled Substances. Proposed Placement of 3,4-methylenedioxymethamphetamine into Schedule I," *Federal Register* 49, no. 146 (1984): 30210–11.

14. W. F. Randolph, "International Drug Scheduling: Convention on Psychotropic

Substances: Stimulants and/or Hallucinogenic Drugs," *Federal Register*, 49, no. 140 (1984): 29273–74.

15. Sapienza, "Written Testimony," 11.

16. J. Adler, "Getting High on 'Ecstasy,' " *Newsweek*, 15 April 1985, 96.

17. Ibid., J. Leavy, "Ecstasy: The Lure and the Peril," *Washington Post*, 1 June 1985, 1, 4; A. Toufexis, "A Crackdown on Ecstasy," *Time*, 10 June 1985, 64; C. G. Dowling, "The Trouble with Ecstasy," *Life*, September 1985, 88–94.

18. R. K. Siegel, "Direct Testimony Submitted on Behalf of Drug Enforcement Administration," *U.S. Department of Justice, Drug Enforcement Administration Hearings*, Docket no. 84–48 (13 April 1985), 2.

19. U.S. Department of Justice, Drug Enforcement Administration, *Fact Sheet*.

20. World Health Organization, *Excerpt from the Report of the 22nd WHO Expert Committee on Drug Dependence*, Annex 11 (Geneva: World Health Organization, 20 May 1985), 8.

21. J. C. Lawn, "Schedules of Controlled Substances: Temporary Placement of 3,4-methylenedioxymethamphetamine (MDMA) into Schedule I," *Federal Register* 50, no. 105 (1985): 23118–20.

22. The "designer drug" label has been applied to the intentional process of chemically engineering existing controlled substances to create drugs that are not currently illegal. As D. R. Wesson defines them, these are "substances wherein the psychoactive properties of a scheduled drug have been retained, but the molecular structure has been altered in order to avoid prosecution under the Controlled Substances Act" [quoted in D. E. Smith and R. B. Seymour, "Clarification of Designer Drugs," *U.S. Journal of Drug and Alcohol Abuse* (November 1985): 1]. Although MDMA is often referred to as a designer drug, this designation is debatable since it was first synthesized in 1912 and patented in 1914, long before the Controlled Substances Act of 1970. The primary designer drugs are synthetic opiate analogues employed as heroin substitutes. Significant problems have resulted from the use of these substances, with MPTP associated with Parkinson's disease and the fentanyl analogues responsible for a large number of fatal overdoses. MDMA has often been confused with these drugs both in the media and on the street, resulting in a number of erroneous beliefs. See J. Beck and P. A. Morgan, "Designer Drug Confusion: A Focus on MDMA," *Journal of Drug Education* 16, no. 3 (1986): 287–301.

23. Lawn, "Schedules of Controlled Substances: Temporary Placement."

24. G. Ricaurte, G. Bryan, L. Strauss, L. Seiden, and C. Schuster, "Hallucinogenic Amphetamine Selectively Destroys Brain Serotonin Nerve Terminals," *Science* 229 (1985): 986–88.

25. Beck, "The Popularization"; "The Trouble with Ecstasy," *Life*.

26. U.S. Department of Justice, Drug Enforcement Administration, *Fact Sheet*, 1.

27. Ibid., 2.

28. Beck, "The Popularization," 50.

29. Sapienza, "MDMA."

30. See, for example, "Written Testimony on Behalf of Drs. Grinspoon and Greer": Greer; Grinspoon.

A placement into Schedule II was generally regarded as a legal impossibility. This schedule is reserved for substances possessing demonstrated medical value and safety in combination with a high potential for abuse (e.g., cocaine, morphine). Since well-controlled, double-blind therapeutic trials had not been conducted for MDMA, a finding of high abuse potential would result in a Schedule I placement.

31. S. Cohen, "Lysergic Acid Diethylamide: Side Effects and Complications," *Journal of Nervous and Mental Disease* 130 (January 1960): 39; W. McGlothlin and D. Arnold, "LSD Revisited: A Ten-Year Follow-Up of Medical LSD Use," *Archives of General Psychiatry* 24 (January 1971): 35–49. For comprehensive reviews of LSD research, see E. M. Brecher and eds., *Consumer Reports, Licit and Illicit Drugs* (Mt. Vernon, N.Y.: Consumers Union, 1972); and L. Grinspoon and J. B. Bakalar, *Psychedelic Drugs Reconsidered* (New York: Basic Books, 1979).

32. Brecher and eds., *Consumer Reports*; Grinspoon and Bakalar, *Psychedelic Drugs*.

33. Grinspoon and Bakalar, *Psychedelic Drugs*, 293.

34. See "Rebuttal Testimony Submitted on Behalf of Drug Enforcement Administration: Depositions in DEA Hearings," *U.S. Department of Justice, Drug Enforcement Administration Hearings*, Docket no. 84–48: J. M. Sheahan (submitted 20 May 1985); J. E. Kleinman (submitted 18 April 1985); L. Snyder (submitted 16 May 1985).

35. "DEA, Clinicians Disagree on MDMA Scheduling," *Brain/Mind Bulletin*, 15 April 1985, 3.

36. See E. C. Tocus, "Testimony Submitted on Behalf of Drug Enforcement Administration: Depositions in DEA Hearings," *U.S. Department of Justice, Drug Enforcement Administration Hearings*, Docket no. 84–48 (submitted 16 May 1985).

37. A. Shulgin, personal communication, 1 June 1988, 38.

38. Beck, "The Popularization."

39. "Written Testimony Submitted on Behalf of Drs. Grinspoon and Greer": Grinspoon, 3.

40. See "Direct Testimony," *U.S. Department of Justice, Drug Enforcement Administration Hearings*, Docket no. 84–48: J. P. Docherty, E. C. Tocus, and H. E. Shannon (submitted 24 April 1985); "Rebuttal Testimony," Kleinman. The two studies conducted by proponents were J. J. Downing, "The Psychological and Physiological Effects of MDMA on Normal Volunteers," *Journal of Psychoactive Drugs*, 18: 335–40; and G. Greer, *MDMA: A New Psychotropic Compound and Its Effects in Humans* (Santa Fe: G. Greer, 1983).

41. "Rebuttal Testimony," Kleinman, 2.

42. R. R. Griffiths, B. Lamb and J. V. Brady, *A Preliminary Report on the Reinforcing Effects of Racemic 3,4-methylenedioxymethamphetamine in the Baboon*, (submitted as a preprint to the DEA for the MDMA hearings, October 1985); L. S. Harris, *Preliminary Report on the Dependence Liability and Abuse Potential of Methylenedioxmethamphetamine (MDMA)*, (submitted as a preprint to the DEA for the MDMA hearings, October 1985).

43. Sapienza, "MDMA"; Beck, "The Popularization."

44. Beck, "The Popularization"; Seymour, *MDMA*.

45. J. A. Newmeyer, "Some Considerations on the Prevalence of MDMA Use," *Journal of Psychoative Drugs* 18, no.4 (1986): 361–62.

46. Siegel, "Direct Testimony," 3.

47. J. Beck, D. Harlow, D. McDonnell, P. Morgan, M. Rosenbaum, and L. Watson, *Exploring Ecstasy: A Description of MDMA Users*. Final Report to the National Institute of Drug Abuse, Grant #1 RO1 DA04408, September 1989.

48. "Written Testimony Submitted on Behalf of Drs. Grinspoon and Greer": Greer; Beck, "The Popularization"; Seymour, *MDMA*.

49. Newmeyer, "Some Considerations," 362.

50. F. L. Young, "Opinion and Recommended Decision on Preliminary Issue, Submitted in the Matter of MDMA Scheduling," *U.S. Department of Justice, Drug Enforcement Administration Hearings*, Docket no. 84–48 (1 June 1985), 7.

51. Ibid., 21.

52. Ibid., 21.

53. F. L. Young, "Opinion and Recommended Ruling, Findings of Fact, Conclusions of Law and Decision of the Administrative Law Judge, Submitted in the Matter of MDMA Scheduling," *U.S. Department of Justice, Drug Enforcement Administration Hearings*, Docket no. 84–48 (22 May 1986), 68.

54. Ibid., 35, 38, 66.

55. S. E. Stone and C. A. Johnson, "Government's Exceptions to the Opinion and Recommended Ruling, Findings of Fact, Conclusions of Law and Decision of the Administrative Law Judge, Submitted in the Matter of MDMA Scheduling," *U.S. Department of Justice, Drug Enforcement Administration Hearings*, Docket no. 84–48 (13 June 1986), 2.

56. Ibid., 2–11.

57. J. C. Lawn, "Schedules of Controlled Substances: Scheduling of 3,4-methylenedioxymethamphetamine (MDMA) into Schedule I of the Controlled Substances Act," *Federal Register* 51, no. 198 (14 October 1986): 36552–60.

58. H. Harbin, "MDMA," *Narcotics, Forfeiture and Money-Laundering Update* (U.S. Department of Justice) 2, no. 1 (1988): 14–19.

59. Ibid.

60. United States v. William Waldo Emerson, 88 C.D.O.S. 3106, 3109 (9th Cir. 1988).

61. Grinspoon v. Drug Enforcement Administration, 828 F.2d 881 (1st Cir. 1987).

62. Ibid.

63. Ibid.

64. J. C. Lawn, "Schedules of Controlled Substances: Scheduling of 3,4-methylenedioxymethamphetamine (MDMA) into Schedule I of the Controlled Substances Act; Remand," *Federal Register* 53, no. 34 (1986): 5158.

65. Controlled Substances Analogue Enforcement Act, 21 U.S.C. 802(32), 813 (1986).

66. The analogue act appears to eliminate any pressing need for emergency scheduling since practically any drug the DEA might consider scheduling is already illegal by virtue of its similarity to drugs already scheduled. It can be anticipated, however, that numerous challenges to this law (particularly on grounds of vagueness) will encourage continued reliance on the more accepted scheduling process.

67. Harbin, "MDMA."

68. Ibid., 18.

69. There has been only one published estimate of use since the administrative law hearings were held in 1985. S. J. Peroutka, "Incidence of Recreational Use of 3,4-methylenedioxymethamphetamine (MDMA, 'Ecstasy') on an Undergraduate Campus," *New England Journal of Medicine* 317 (1988): 1542. This survey revealed that an astonishing 39 percent of Stanford undergraduates had tried MDMA. However, the fact that this was a convenience sample casts serious doubt on its overall validity.

70. Ibid., 1542.

71. For a broader examination of these "troublesome dilemmas," see Beck, "The Public Health Implications."

Appendix B

Controlling Drug Paraphernalia

Kerry Murphy Healey

In 1980 the Select Committee on Narcotics Abuse and Control charged that the drug paraphernalia industry posed "a severe threat to the educational, social, and emotional development of our youth."[1] Over the past decade a majority of state and local legislators have supported the proposition that laws controlling the sale of drug paraphernalia are an important component of the nation's campaign against drug abuse. At present, forty-nine states and the District of Columbia seek to control the sale of drug paraphernalia under state law or local ordinances. Thirty-eight of these states and the District of Columbia have enacted statutes based on the Drug Enforcement Administration's (DEA's) Model Drug Paraphernalia Act (the Model Act) of 1979. In October of 1986 the federal government addressed the issue of drug paraphernalia control by adopting a Model Act–based law prohibiting the use of the postal service, or any other interstate conveyance, as a part of a scheme to sell drug paraphernalia. The federal law also banned the import of drug paraphernalia.[2] Since it is still too early to gauge the impact of federal antiparaphernalia laws, this appendix will assess the development and efficacy of state-level drug paraphernalia controls.

The DEA's Model Act was drafted to provide the basis for more uniform paraphernalia regulation and to attempt to answer the most difficult question confronted by legislators in this field: What are drug paraphernalia? The Model Act focuses on the *intent* of those who manufacture, sell, or use paraphernalia. Thus, under the Model Act, a pipe is a legal object when manufactured, sold, and used for legal purposes, but becomes drug paraphernalia when it is designed or intended for use with illegal drugs.

The Model Act focuses on the intent of the paraphernalia manufacturer, seller, or user because the range of objects that may be employed as drug paraphernalia is limited only by one's imagination. Many drug paraphernalia are also common household items (e.g., mirrors, razors, baking soda, blenders) or objects used primarily for legal purposes (e.g., pipes, grow-lights for plants, rolling papers, and syringes). Objects such as these that have plausible legal uses are sometimes referred to as "soft-core" or "dual use" drug paraphernalia. A few objects have been invented or promoted primarily to facilitate drug abuse (e.g., glass pipes, bongs, isomerization and drug-testing kits); these items may be called "hard-core" drug paraphernalia. In the absence of illegal drugs, the distinction between ordinary objects and drug paraphernalia is always subjective. Thus, in every case, police and prosecutors must attempt to establish the intent of those engaged in the manufacture, advertisement, delivery, or use of potential drug paraphernalia.

THE RISE OF THE PARAPHERNALIA INDUSTRY AND ANTIPARAPHERNALIA LAWS

The drug paraphernalia industry is thought to have reached its height during the late 1970s. In 1979 the government estimated that drug paraphernalia sales in the United States may have topped $3 billion.[3] Paraphernalia industry estimates for the same period were considerably lower, placing gross annual sales between $350 million and $1 billion.[4] Regardless of the true volume of sales, by the late 1970s the drug paraphernalia industry had grown affluent enough to form trade associations and to reach beyond urban centers into suburban malls and rural towns.

Until 1977 the sale of drug paraphernalia was virtually unregulated by state laws or local ordinances. Although some states had enacted laws controlling the sale of paraphernalia through pharmacists or the possession of drug paraphernalia, no laws existed that were specifically designed to ban the sale of drug paraphernalia in "head shops" (that is, stores that sold primarily drug-related products). Throughout the 1970s head shops and a variety of other merchants openly sold drug paraphernalia in most jurisdictions. In addition, a number of publications dedicated to the drug culture and drug paraphernalia emerged. While some of these publications were short-lived, others—such as *High Times*—continue to flourish.

In 1977 the first antiparaphernalia parent group, Families in Action, was formed in DeKalb, Georgia. The founder was disturbed that head shops and drug culture publications were seeking to glamorize, teach the use of, and provide the paraphernalia necessary to use illegal drugs. It was argued that the legal sale of paraphernalia in head shops implicitly encouraged drug abuse among young people.[5] This implicit encouragement to break or disregard drug laws became known as the "head shop message"—that drug abuse is both socially and legally accepted. Citing the paraphernalia merchants' alliance with an illicit industry, Families in Action lobbied for the enactment of local ordinances banning the sale of drug paraphernalia. These efforts met with success, and shortly thereafter similar parent and citizen lobbies were formed in California, Florida, and New Jersey. By 1980 some seventy-seven antiparaphernalia ordinances had been enacted in thirteen states, and statewide paraphernalia controls had been adopted in three jurisdictions.[6]

The paraphernalia industry did not, however, disband in the face of these new controls. Instead, paraphernalia merchants pooled their resources to fund a number of constitutional challenges to state and local antiparaphernalia laws. This campaign was initially successful: Courts frequently found the new laws to be overbroad or impermissibly vague. In 1979, at the request of the White House, the DEA drafted the Model Drug Paraphernalia Act. The purpose of the Model Act was twofold: first, to correct the constitutional deficiencies of earlier legislation; and, second, to provide a basis for a uniform scheme of paraphernalia regulation. Since that time both of these goals have been met—the DEA's Model Act has been enacted by a majority of states and Model Act laws have been upheld by virtually all U.S. circuit courts of appeal.

Nonetheless, the trend toward banning the sale of drug paraphernalia has been ignored or rejected in nine states. One state permits the unrestricted sale of drug paraphernalia, five states rely on local ordinances to control drug paraphernalia sales, and three others restrict the sale of drug paraphernalia only in reference to minors. Nearly a decade after the introduction of the first antiparaphernalia laws, the drug paraphernalia industry continues to enjoy the freedom to operate in a number of jurisdictions without the threat of prosecution. This foothold, though limited, is presently a source of concern to some legislators, law enforcers, and citizen groups. These groups argue that so long as no uniform regulation of the drug paraphernalia industry exists at the state level, paraphernalia will continue to be available to the citizens, both minors and adults, of all states via mail-order sales. It is as yet too early to predict what effect the newly enacted federal antiparaphernalia law will have on the flow of drug paraphernalia between states.

STATE DRUG PARAPHERNALIA LAWS

As of December 1987, forty-four states and the District of Columbia had passed laws to control the sale of drug paraphernalia. The majority of these laws were patterned on the DEA's Model Act. With the addition of Alabama in April 1986 a total of thirty-eight states and the District of Columbia have adopted Model Act legislation. Six other states—Colorado, New York, Ohio, Oregon, Tennessee, and West Virginia—have antiparaphernalia legislation not patterned on the Model Act. The remaining six states—Alaska, Hawaii, Illinois, Iowa, Michigan, and Wisconsin—impose no state-level sanctions on the sale of drug paraphernalia. (It should be noted, however, that until it was overturned in September 1987, Illinois had a non–Model Act law prohibiting the sale of drug paraphernalia, and the sale of these items is to some degree restricted in Alaska, Illinois, Iowa, Michigan, and Wisconsin by local or county ordinances.)

In those states with non–Model Act laws, a wide variety of legislation is in force. In Colorado and New York, state statutes were intended to resemble the

Model Act in most features, while in Ohio, Oregon, and West Virginia, laws prohibit the sale of drug paraphernalia only to minors. West Virginia requires licensing for drug paraphernalia dealers, and in Ohio the law pertains only to the sale of marijuana paraphernalia. Some non–Model Act statutes impose heavy sanctions on the sale of paraphernalia. For example, in Tennessee the sale of paraphernalia to adults or minors is a felony on the first offense.

Because the Model Act suggests no specific penalties for paraphernalia offenses, there is great variance among state laws. The majority of paraphernalia offenses are punishable as misdemeanors. However, it is common for more severe penalties to be imposed for repeated violations and violations involving minors. Only seven states have made the sale of drug paraphernalia a felony or its equivalent on the first offense. These include Indiana, which amended its paraphernalia laws in 1986 to increase the penalty. Thus, while the sale of drug paraphernalia is prohibited by state law in most jurisdictions, the penalties provided under these laws are often civil and rarely include mandatory prison time or fines.

CONSTITUTIONAL CHALLENGES TO
ANTIPARAPHERNALIA LAWS

The constitutionality of antiparaphernalia laws has been challenged on a wide variety of grounds.[7] However, the majority of early challenges argued that paraphernalia laws were overbroad or too vague to meet constitutional requirements. According to the U.S. Supreme Court, a law is impermissibly vague if it fails to define clearly what is prohibited. Vagueness is a violation of due process for the following reasons:

Vague laws offend several important values. First, because we assume that man is free to steer between lawful and unlawful conduct, we insist that laws give the person of ordinary intelligence a reasonable opportunity to know what is prohibited, so that he may act accordingly. Vague laws may trap the innocent by not providing fair warning. Second, if arbitrary and discriminatory enforcement is to be prevented, laws must provide explicit standards for those who apply them. A vague law impermissibly delegates basic policy matters to policemen, judges, and juries for resolution on an ad hoc and subjective basis, with the attendant dangers of arbitrary and discriminatory application.[8]

Overbreadth challenges frequently involve many of the same issues as those raised in vagueness challenges. However, challenges alleging overbreadth argue from the standpoint that the restrictions placed on the sale of paraphernalia impinge on constitutionally protected conduct. While challenges alleging overbreadth and vagueness were initially the most successful in defeating drug paraphernalia legislation,[9] the value of these doctrines to those seeking to invalidate head shop laws was severely limited following the Supreme Court's 1982 decision in *Hoffman Estates v. Flipside*.[10] In *Hoffman Estates* the Court upheld an Illinois licensing ordinance that was not patterned on the DEA's Model Act. In rejecting charges of vagueness and overbreadth in relation to a statute that was less precise than the Model Act, the Court indirectly buttressed the facial constitutionality of all Model Act legislation. In 1983 the constitutionality of the Model Act was further strengthened when the Supreme Court directed, without specific discussion, the U.S. Court of Appeals for the Sixth Circuit to reverse its ruling in *Record Revolution, No. 6, Inc. v. Parma*,[11] thus upholding the constitutionality of a Model Act ordinance in accordance with *Hoffman Estates*. Because the Supreme Court did not specifically discuss its ruling, it is assumed that the Court's discussion of antiparaphernalia laws in *Hoffman Estates* supports the phrasing of the Model Act. Thus, in *Hoffman Estates* the Supreme Court established a method for determining the facial constitutionality of all types of drug paraphernalia laws. This model was subsequently adopted by a majority of lower courts. Using *Hoffman Estates* as a guide, many of the early rulings of unconstitutionality were reversed, and today the Model Act has been upheld by eight circuit courts and is generally presumed to be facially constitutional.[12]

Although the risk of discriminatory future enforcement is considered insufficient grounds to preclude pre-enforcement validity, the courts have frequently noted that a ruling of facial constitutionality does not guarantee that a law will be constitutional as applied to individual defendants.[13] Thus, the most pressing question concerning the constitutionality of the Model Act has been whether it will be able to withstand applied challenges. The alleged vulnerability of the Model Act to applied constitutional challenges has been a key element in recent arguments for the repeal of existing antiparaphernalia legislation and in the opposition to the mail-order drug paraphernalia bill recently enacted by Congress. It has been suggested that while the facial constitutionality of the Model Act is generally accepted, the enforcement of the Model Act or any act patterned after it will frequently result in the violation of constitutional rights.

Applied Challenges to Antiparaphernalia Laws

Due to the relative youth of the Model Act and the small number of applied challenges that have reached the appellate courts, the applied constitutionality of the Model Act has not as yet been adequately tested. To date, there have been only a handful of state-level cases challenging the constitutionality of the application of the Model Act or other antiparaphernalia statutes. Nonetheless, this limited sample suggests that Model Act legislation may be more resistant to applied challenges than are other state antiparaphernalia laws.[14] While it is too early to disregard the threat of constitutional challenges, other factors, such as adequate resources and familiarity with drug paraphernalia enforcement procedure, currently appear to be more important to the effective enforcement of the Model Act.[15]

IMPACT OF STATE ANTIPARAPHERNALIA LAWS

Scope of the Problem Before Antiparaphernalia Laws

In a study conducted by the National Institute of Justice (NIJ) of the U.S. Department of Justice, 55 percent of the police and sheriffs surveyed reported that head shops had been operating in their jurisdiction before the enactment of antiparaphernalia laws.[16] The presence of head shops was perceived to be a more pressing problem in some jurisdictions than in others. For example, 25 percent of the law enforcement officers considered the drug paraphernalia problem in their jurisdiction to have been "very serious," while another 29 percent characterized the problem in their community as having been only "somewhat serious." The businesses complained of by law enforcement officers and prosecutors ranged from "combination shops" (such as tobacco stores, record stores, convenience stores, and flea markets) that primarily sold legal products to stores geared exclusively toward the sale of drug paraphernalia. In other communities the sale of drug paraphernalia had not been a source of concern— 20 percent of the police and prosecutors interviewed stated that the presence of head shops or other drug paraphernalia outlets had not been a serious problem in their jurisdiction.[17] In this category, the presence of head shops in the community was not always the controlling factor. Some respondents argued that while head shops may have been operating, they had not aroused enough concern in the community to be termed "a problem."

In addition to head shops, drug paraphernalia also was reported to have been available through mail-order firms advertised in drug culture publications. Although Congress has now recognized the mail-order sale of drug paraphernalia as a source of federal concern, mail-order sales were not named by respondents as an original factor contributing to the need for state-level antiparaphernalia laws.

The Impact of Antiparaphernalia Laws on Head Shops

State and local authorities agree that antiparaphernalia legislation has had a significant impact on the availability of drug paraphernalia in head shops. Forty-five percent of those police and sheriffs who reported head shops operating in their community before the enactment of antiparaphernalia laws reported no head shops operating today. In those jurisdictions with antiparaphernalia laws in force, 46 percent of the police and 41 percent of the prosecutors claimed that antiparaphernalia legislation had been very effective in eliminating the open sale and promotion of drug paraphernalia in head shops in their area. These respondents emphasized that many head shops had been closed and that the remaining paraphernalia merchants stocked primarily dual-use items, such as pipes, rolling papers, and "snuff kits." Another 23 percent of all respondents felt that the laws had been at least somewhat effective in curbing the open sale of drug paraphernalia. In general, police and prosecutors were less likely to characterize the laws as "very effective" than were the state attorneys general.

Thirty-one percent of the police and prosecutors were critical of the efficacy of antiparaphernalia laws. Many of these respondents argued that drug paraphernalia laws have been unsuccessful because paraphernalia continues to be available from a number of sources. Police data provided some support for this view: 31 percent of the officers reported the continued operation of head shops in their jurisdiction, 24 percent reported the sale of drug paraphernalia in convenience or variety stores, and 20 percent reported the sale of drug paraphernalia by tobacconists. However, the source of drug paraphernalia named most frequently by police was mail-order catalogs—35 percent of the police interviewed stated that mail-order sales were thought to account for much of the drug paraphernalia found in their jurisdiction. Some respondents attributed the emergence of the mail-order drug paraphernalia industry as a primary supplier of drug paraphernalia to the success of the Model Act in decreasing the number of over-the-counter outlets for these products. Thus, although it was agreed that the enactment of antiparaphernalia laws had succeeded in reducing the number of head shops, some respondents were not satisfied with the law since the closings had not reduced the amount of drug paraphernalia found in the course of drug arrests.

According to the respondents, the primary beneficial effects of the enactment of antiparaphernalia laws have been the closing of many head shops, a significant degree of voluntary compliance with the law,[18] a sharp decline in the sale of hard-core drug paraphernalia (i.e., cocaine freebasing kits, "crack" kits, devices to enhance drug potency, drug purity testing kits, or chemicals to cut controlled substances) in head shops,[19] and the creation of an effective deterrent to the sale of drug paraphernalia by legitimate retailers.

Changes in the Drug Paraphernalia Industry

While opinions expressed concerning any semicovert industry are necessarily speculative and circumstantial, respondents stated that certain changes in the drug paraphernalia industry can be discerned as a result of antiparaphernalia laws.[20] The most fundamental effect of antiparaphernalia laws on the drug paraphernalia industry appears to be a shift in advertising and marketing strategies, specifically a new emphasis on dual use items and mail-order sales. For example, most advertisements for drug paraphernalia in both catalogs and drug culture publications now rely on the fact that the buyer is aware of an illegal use for the item which is not explicitly suggested by the advertising copy. In 1979 an advertisement which was carried by drug culture periodicals read: "The Chemist, Free Base System, the 'Ultimate High,' in Colombia, the natives call their Snow Vapor-Base. For over 100 years, in every village, it's been the Toke of the Town!"[21] At present, no cocaine freebasing kits are advertised in the leading drug culture periodical, *High Times*, or in catalogs examined by NIJ in the course of its study.[22] Instead, catalogs and advertisements for cocaine-related paraphernalia carry such captions as "Executive Snuff Kit," "Standard Snuff Vial," or "Original Deering Snuff, Tea, and Spice Grinder." In addition, product design may have been changed to emphasize a possible legal use.

Respondents with experience in dealing with paraphernalia distributors and mail-order businesses also cite a consolidation of market share by the larger firms. It is thought that the manufacture, distribution, and mail-order sale of drug paraphernalia is no longer a cottage industry. Rather, respondents suggest that those paraphernalia dealers who remain now operate a relatively small number of mid- to large-sized firms. Materials examined by NIJ would tend to support the conclusion that the mail-order sale of drug paraphernalia has become a lucrative and fairly sophisticated industry, dominated by fewer than 20 firms.

Aside from changes in marketing and advertising, in some instances mail-order drug paraphernalia companies and major manufacturers and distributors of paraphernalia have chosen to relocate. Usually, businesses have moved in order to operate from states that have no drug paraphernalia controls or from jurisdictions where drug paraphernalia prosecutions are uncommon. For example, survey respondents report that drug paraphernalia firms prosecuted in Illinois sometimes choose to relocate over the Iowa line to avoid further legal disputes.

The concentration of drug paraphernalia suppliers in unregulated states presents a double challenge to antiparaphernalia laws. First, these businesses are, for all practical purposes, beyond the control of other states' laws, although their products may well reach the citizens of those states. Second, drug paraphernalia businesses clustered in unregulated states are well positioned to lobby against the adoption of the Model Act in those areas. While the new federal antiparaphernalia legislation may help to stop the flow of paraphernalia into regulated states from unregulated areas, the lobbying efforts of the paraphernalia industry are likely only to intensify as antiparaphernalia laws receive more attention.

CONCLUSION

The enactment of the DEA's Model Drug Paraphernalia Act by a majority of states has significantly reduced the number of head shops in operation and the ready availability of hard-core drug paraphernalia. Nonetheless, many problems still exist which inhibit the enforcement of antiparaphernalia laws. The most important of these is a shortage of police and prosecutorial resources. Without adequate resources, low-priority drug laws, including antiparaphernalia laws, go unenforced. Drug paraphernalia investigations and prosecutions are expensive, are complex, and require specialized knowledge. For these reasons, drug paraphernalia enforcement frequently receives the lowest drug enforcement priority.

Antiparaphernalia laws serve several purposes. On the first and most obvious level, they attempt to control the availability of drug paraphernalia. While antiparaphernalia laws can be shown to be successful in curbing the sale and availability of drug paraphernalia, it is difficult—if not impossible—to relate this reduction to a decrease in drug consumption. The absence of a quantifiable connection to drug abuse does not, however, reduce the value of these laws to the overall success of a drug control program. Many of the goals of drug paraphernalia legislation are symbolic: Drug paraphernalia laws contradict the head shop message that drug abuse is socially acceptable and legally tolerated, and they correct the anomaly of a society that outlaws drug abuse, but would allow its merchants to indirectly profit from drug sales. Until police and prosecutors are given resources and training adequate to enforce all drug laws, the primary purpose of drug paraphernalia laws will be to symbolize society's rejection of the drug culture.

NOTES

This appendix is excerpted in part from the author's study *State and Local Experience with Drug Paraphernalia Laws* (Washington, D.C.: U.S. Department of Justice, 1987).

1. *Drug Paraphernalia: A Report of the Select Committee on Narcotics Abuse and Control*, 96th Cong., 2nd sess., 1980, (SCNAC-96-1-6), 17.

2. Anti-Drug Abuse Act of 1986, P.L. 99-570, (codified at 21 U.S.C. § 857).

3. U.S. Congress, House of Representatives, *Hearing Before the Select Committee on Narcotics Abuse and Control*, 96th Cong., 2d. sess., 1 November 1979, SNAC-96-1-12.

4. Ibid., 55, 58.

5. Ibid. See also "Testimony of Sue Rusche, founder, DeKalb Families in Action," 4.

6. U.S. Department of Health, Education, and Welfare. *Community and Legal Responses to Drug Paraphernalia*, DHEW Pub. no. (ADM) 80–963 (Washington, D.C.: U.S. Government Printing Office, 1980), 35.

7. See *Harv. J. on Legis.* 20 (1983): 617, 619.

8. Grayned v. City of Rockford, 408 U.S. 104, 108–109 (1972) (footnotes omitted).

9. Annotation, 69 A.L.R. Fed. 15.

10. 455 U.S. 489, *reh'g denied*, 456 U.S. 950; 72 L. Ed. 2d 476; 102 S. Ct. 2023. See generally 20 *Harv. J. on Legis.* 617.

11. 638 F.2d 916 (6th Cir. 1980), *vacated*, 451 U.S. 1013, *vacated*, 456 U.S. 968.

12. The most recent upholding of the facial constitutionality of the Model Act was handed down by the Supreme Court of Missouri in Missouri v. Munson, 714 S.W.2d 515 (1986), wherein the court rejected arguments alleging vagueness, overbreadth, and the denial of due process. Earlier rulings upholding the facial constitutionality of Model Act laws may be found at 69 A.L.R. Fed. at Annotation, 24.

13. 672 F. 2d 1225; 69 A.L.R. Fed 1.

14. The Model Act has been challenged as applied in Pennsylvania [Cochran v. Commonwealth, 69 Pa. Commw. 74, 450 A.2d 75 (1982); Potter v. Commonwealth, 504 A.2d 243 (1986)]; California [People v. Nelson, Wolf and Vitale, 171 Cal. App. 3d Supp.(1985)]; and Kentucky [McKinney v. Commonwealth (1985), republished by order of the Supreme Court of Kentucky, 12 March 1986 (86-SC-10-D, 84-CA-1172-DG, 83-X-013)]. Non–Model Act laws have been challenged as applied in New York [Franza v. Carey, 115 Misc. 2d 882, 454 N.Y.S.2d 1002 (1982); Franza v. Carey, 102 A.D.2d

780, 478 N.Y.S.2d 873 (1984)] and Illinois [Illinois v. Crow's Nest, Inc., 484 N.E.2d 907, (3d Dist. 1985); Illinois v. Ziegler (Array Distributors, Inc.), 139 Ill. App. 3d 1088, 94 Ill. Dec. 484 (1986); People v. Levin (and Monroe), No. 85 M14880683, Sup. Ct. No. 63724 (June 1986)].

15. Procedural mistakes appear to have been the cause for findings of unconstitutionality in some lower court cases. See, e.g., Florida v. Karpf, No. 83-27442 (Crim. Ct. Div. February 1984); Florida v. McMahon, No. 85-3320 CF SPEISER (Broward County April 1986).

16. The statistics in this section are drawn from surveys conducted by NIJ. See Healey, *State and Local Experience with Drug Paraphernalia Laws*, Washington, D.C.: U.S. Department of Justice, 1987). The number of prosecutors reporting the existence of head shops was over 90 percent; however, since many prosecutors were selected on the basis of their experience with head shop cases, this study assumes that the figures supplied by the randomly selected sample of police and sheriffs are more representative of the true prevalence of head shops before the enactment of antiparaphernalia laws.

17. Sixteen percent of the prosecutors and ten percent of the police did not know how serious the drug paraphernalia problem had been in their jurisdiction before the enactment of antiparaphernalia laws.

18. In 28 percent of the jurisdictions most or all of the head shops closed without prosecution.

19. Sixty-seven percent of police and prosecutors in jurisdictions with antiparaphernalia laws in force reported that these laws had been "effective" in curbing the sale of hard-core drug paraphernalia.

20. Thirty-nine percent of the prosecutors and attorneys general thought that antiparaphernalia legislation had significantly reduced or deterred the covert sale of drug paraphernalia, while 40 percent found the law ineffective in discouraging the continued sale of these items outside head shops in their area.

21. This advertisement, used by Select Industries, Walnut Creek, California, was discussed in U.S. Congress, House of Representatives, *Hearing Before the Select Committee on Narcotics Abuse and Control*, 96th Cong., 1st sess., 1 November 1979, SCNAC-96-1-12, 63.

22. While freebasing equipment is no longer sold as a "kit," all the necessary implements and chemicals are still being sold separately. The items, taken separately, more convincingly retain the protection offered by the dual use classification.

Appendix C

Extradition and Drug Trafficking

Mary Ann Forney

In February 1987, some twenty miles outside of Medellín, Colombia, a special police force captured Carlos Lehder Rivas, a key figure in a drug trafficking organization that was estimated at the time to be supplying over 80 percent of the world's cocaine.[1] Within hours, Lehder was on a plane to Florida, a consequence of the extradition treaty between the United States and Colombia. His arrest and subsequent extradition to the United States stemmed from a 1981 indictment charging him with conspiracy, importation and distribution of cocaine, operation of a continuing criminal enterprise, and tax evasion.[2] The extradition of this particular drug trafficking entrepreneur effectively demonstrated the efforts the U.S. and Colombian governments had made in their war against drugs. Within months, however, the legality of the treaty that brought about Lehder's extradition for trial in federal court was questioned, and by 26 June 1987 the Colombian Supreme Court had ruled the law ratifying the treaty invalid.[3]

The Lehder episode demonstrated that while extradition can be a powerful and sweeping weapon in the war on drugs, it can also be a tentative and fragile one, subject to contingencies well beyond the control of U.S. courts, legislators, and law enforcement groups. Within this context, this appendix will briefly examine the nature of extradition and the U.S./Colombian extradition experience.

THE NATURE OF EXTRADITION

Extradition has been defined as "the surrender by one jurisdiction or nation (*the requested state*) to another (*the requesting state*) of an individual accused or convicted of an offense outside of its own territory (*the requested person*), and within the territorial jurisdiction of the other, which, being competent to try and punish him, demands the surrender."[4] The history of extradition involving jurisdictions within the United States dates back to the earliest days of the American republic. Under most circumstances, for example, every state has always been required to return a fugitive from another state on demand by the requesting state's governor. Article IV, Section 2 of the Constitution of the United States provides as follows:

A Person charged in any State with Treason, Felony, or other Crime, who shall flee from Justice, and be found in another State, shall on Demand of the executive Authority of the State from which he fled, be delivered up, to be removed to the State having Jurisdiction of the Crime.[5]

More currently, there is a Uniform Extradition Act that is accepted by most states as authority on this matter, and the requesting state needs only to charge that the wanted person committed a crime within its borders or even outside its jurisdiction, intentionally resulting in a crime in the state and to state that the requesting state's executive authority is making the demand.[6] Under the authority of either the U.S. Constitution or the Uniform Extradition Act, foreign nations cannot be forced to return persons charged with violating the laws of the United States, a situation that has resulted in the signing of a variety of mutual extradition treaties.

Historically, in 1833 Belgium was the first country to establish an extradition treaty.[7] During the mid–1800s the United States recognized the need for extradition treaties with other nations and since 1842 has negotiated treaties with some ninety countries.[8] Renegotiations of extradition treaties occur, particularly when extraditable crimes need to be clarified and/or updated, as in the cases of drug trafficking, aircraft hijacking, and the international transfer of funds—crimes that were non-existent when the treaties were first negotiated.

While a number of countries may authorize extradition with or without a treaty,[9] the United States can request a fugitive only when an extradition treaty is in force with the requested nation.[10] Although the extradition of foreign nationals to the United States has been negotiated, most countries retain the right to decline the surrender of their own citizens.[11] Most treaties include a *political offense exception* (POE) that precludes a country from surrendering a fugitive if the requesting state charges political offenses against the government of the requesting state; exceptions to the POE are generally determined on an individual case basis.[12]

Generally, extraditable offenses must be crimes in both countries, punishable by a minimum prison term of one year; the fugitive may not be detained, tried, or punished for crimes other that those for which extradition was granted; and extradition is typically denied if the individual has already been prosecuted in the requested state for the same offense charged by the requesting state (prior jeopardy) or if the offense has exceeded the statute of limitations of the requesting or requested state.[13]

Any request for extradition must be made through the appropriate diplomatic channels and may come from state or local jurisdictions or from federal agencies that have accumulated evidence against an individual suspected of criminal activity. Every such request is sent to the Office of International Affairs in the U.S. Justice Department, which, in turn, forwards all documentation of alleged offenses to the U.S. State Department. The extradition request must be accompanied by an indictment (or its equivalent) or a conviction, with either an arrest warrant or a copy of the sentence imposed. The documents—signed by a judge or other judicial authority, authenticated by the official seal of the State Department, and certified by the diplomatic or consular office of the requested state in the United States—are then sent to the requested state for processing through their court system.[14] The amount of time the requested state takes processing the extradition request varies depending on local judicial channels. More important is whether the individual in question is already under arrest in the requested state. In the extradition processing of Carlos Lehder Rivas, for example, once he was under arrest, it was only a matter of hours before he was returned to the United States. However, it took six years for the Colombian police to locate and arrest him.

THE EXTRADITION EXPERIENCE

The threat of extradition to the United States has had no greater impact than in Colombia where the economics of cocaine cultivation and distribution have provided traffickers with significant economic and political powers. In fact, a common consensus among Colombian traffickers has been that it would be "better to be in a Colombian grave than in an American jail."[15] This fear resulted in the systematic assassination of the many Colombian justices, political officials, and journalists who led the fight for extradition. By the close of the 1980s no less than twelve Colombian Supreme Court justices and scores of other judges, hundreds of politicians, a justice minister, and the attorney general had been murdered.[16] In addition, traffickers had threatened to execute five American citizens for every Colombian extradited to the United States.[17]

The Treaty of Extradition with the Republic of Colombia was passed on 14 September 1979 and entered into force on 4 March 1982.[18] Prior to the passage of this 1979 treaty (which replaced the U.S.-Colombia Convention for Reciprocal Extradition of Criminals of 1888 and the Supplementary Convention of Extradition of 1940),[19] there were no provisions to extradite for drug-related offenses. The new document detailed a list of thirty-five crimes, including the following drug-related crimes: offenses against the laws relating to the traffic in or the possession, production, or manufacture of narcotic drugs, cannabis, hallucinogenic drugs, cocaine and its derivatives, and other substances that produce physical or psychological dependence; offenses against public health, such as the illicit manufacture of or traffic in chemical products or substances injurious to health; violations of the laws relating to the importation, exportation, or transit of goods, persons, articles, or merchandise, including violations of the customs laws; offenses relating to the willful evasion of taxes and duties; receiving or transporting any money, valuable securities, or other property, knowing the same to have been unlawfully obtained; and any offense against the laws relating to international trade and transfers of funds.[20]

As soon as the 1979 treaty was put into force, the U.S. Department of Justice began issuing extradition requests for Colombian drug traffickers indicted in U.S. courts for various drug-related offenses. The first successful extradition case occurred in 1985. Until the treaty was invalidated by the Colombian courts a year later, a total of sixteen alleged traffickers, including Carlos Lehder, were extradited to the United States from Colombia on drug-related charges.[21]

The treaty, however, proved to be fragile. Throughout most of the 1980s, cocaine-trafficking revenues were estimated to have exceeded those from all of Colombia's legal exports, including coffee and oil. As a result, and not surprisingly, local traffickers have tended to be intolerant of legal harassment, particularly from agents of the U.S. government. In this regard, Colombian government officials generally have been offered two alternatives: payoffs or death. It is estimated that in the city of Medellín, the center of the Colombian cocaine industry, 80 percent of the police have been corrupted by drug traffickers.[22] In addition, judges and government officials have been paid to release indicted or convicted drug dealers and have been executed if they failed to comply. Resistance, death threats, and murder follow.[23] These activities ultimately resulted in the invalidation of the 1979 extradition treaty between the United States and Colombia.

The Colombian legislation regulating the treaty (Law No. 27 of 1980) was declared invalid in 1986, after the first thirteen extradition cases were successfully executed, on grounds that Article 120–20 of the National Constitution was violated. Article 120–20 held that only the president of Colombia was authorized to direct diplomatic and trade relations with other countries. Since the extradition treaty had been signed by a deputy minister and not then President Julio Turbay Ayala, the Supreme Court of Justice recommended that Law No. 27 be declared unconstitutional. Two days later President Virgilio Barco assumed responsibility and approved the law under a new establishment number, Law 68 of 1986,[24] thus renewing the extradition treaty. However, by June 1987 the Colombian Supreme Court had declared the new law invalid because the president had approved it without the required ratification by the legislative branch of government.[25] The practical result of this action was the need to negotiate a new law with the United States.[26]

Why the Supreme Court of Colombia resorted to the strictest letter of the law in these rulings was well understood by observers both inside and outside Colombia. Cocaine traffickers had effectively intimidated the legislative and judicial branches of that nation's government. A case in point involved Jorge Luis Ochoa Vasquez, a reputed principal in the well-known Medellín cocaine cartel. Twice arrested in Colombia, but released on both occasions as the result of reported payoffs of over $3 million to prison and judicial officials, Ochoa never had to face the threat of prolonged imprisonment in either the United States or his own country. Moreover, in 1988 Colombia Attorney General Carlos Mauro Hoyos was assassinated near Medellín while investigating bribery charges against the warden and judge who signed Ochoa's release. "The war will continue," boasted the drug traffickers, claiming that Hoyos had been executed because of his support of the extradition treaty.[27]

DISCUSSION

Even under circumstances where governments are *not* intimidated by powerful criminal groups, the process of extradition is beset by a variety of limitations that nevertheless impede efforts to bring criminals to the United States for prosecution. For example, most agreements contain articles restricting the extradition of nationals. However, a few treaty negotiations have made innovative adjustments to this restriction. Article 8 of the 1979 treaty between Colombia and the United States notes the following:

Neither Contracting Party shall be bound to deliver up its own nationals, but the Executive Authority of the Requested State shall have the power to deliver them up if, in its discretion it be deemed proper to do so.[28]

On the other hand, if extradition is denied because of nationality, the requested state is obligated to submit the case to its own authorities for prosecution. As such, the requested state cannot ignore the charges. It must either extradite or prosecute the wanted person locally.

The Inter-American Convention on Extradition of 1981 bound member nations of the Organization of American States (OAS) to extradite nationals unless the law of the requested state specifically stated otherwise.[29] This treaty, while not limiting or abrogating other multilateral conventions or extradition treaties in effect between countries, established a simplified process for the extradition of individuals from one country to another. However, neither the United States nor Colombia had been a party to this convention, thus eliminating this avenue of extradition.[30]

A second limitation to extradition as a tool for prosecuting drug traffickers is the political offense exception.[31] Extradition treaties may not require extradition for any act or crime that constitutes a "political offense" against the requesting state. Because POE parameters have been loosely drawn and definitions of political offenses vary among countries, judicial branches of government have had difficulty in consistently determining what separates a crime such as drug trafficking from a political offense.

In 1988, for example, had General Manuel Antonio Noriega of Panama not effectively thwarted American attempts to bring him to justice, it is possible that Panamanian courts might have interpreted the charges against him as no more than political offenses. On more than one occasion the government of the United States had been rather vocal in its condemnation of the Noriega regime, clearly indicating its preferences for democratic leadership. Given this, observers of the extradition process would not have been surprised if the charges of corruption and complicity in cocaine trafficking leveled against the Panamanian general had been treated in that nation as U.S. attempts to remove an undesirable political figure. Noriega was eventually extradited, but his return to the United States for trial was accomplished only after American troops occupied Panama at the close of 1989.

In summary, the use of extradition as a weapon in the war on drugs would appear to be of limited value, particularly when focused as a strategy for combating the drug trade between the United States and Latin America. In addition to the limitations inherent in the treaties themselves, combined with the unwillingness of many governments to exercise them, there is an even more basic difficulty. Unless the *requested* state can effectively apply its own rules of law and take a significant number of suspected traffickers into custody, the extradition of only a few traffickers to the United States will probably have no noticeable effect on the availability of drugs. This was clearly the case with Carlos Lehder Rivas, the only major cocaine trafficker to be extradited to the United States during the 1980s. During the two-year period following his arrest, cocaine imports to the United States not only failed to slow, but actually increased.

POSTSCRIPT

In August 1989, when Colombian Senator Luis Carlos Galán was assassinated by drug traffickers, the extradition treaty with the United States was suddenly reactivated. Senator Galan had been an outspoken antidrug campaigner and the leading candidate in Colombia's presidential election scheduled for 1990. Colombian President Virgilio Barco, holding that the survival of his country was at stake, responded with the announcement that traffickers wanted in the United States would be summarily extradited, bypassing the courts.[32] What followed were a crackdown on the drug traffickers by the government and retaliatory attacks by the traffickers.

Seven weeks after Galán's assassination, the Colombian Supreme Court upheld the legality of Barco's decree,[33] but by then the Colombian people had begun to grow weary of the murders and bombings committed by the traffickers. As the year drew to a close, only six traffickers had been extradited to the United States, none of whom were considered to be key leaders of the cocaine cartels. At the same time, there was talk that the voters might decide on the fate of the extradition treaty and that peace talks with the leaders of the Medellín cartel might be appropriate,[34] once again underscoring the problematic nature of extradition as a drug control strategy.

EXTRADITION TREATY WITH THE REPUBLIC OF COLOMBIA

(Summary Based on the Committee on Foreign Relations Report, January 1985)

ARTICLE 1

Article 1 includes a jurisdictional provision which allows extradition where the offense has been committed outside the territory of the requesting state by a national of that State.

Crimes committed outside the territory of the requesting state may also provide the basis for extradition if the offense so committed would also be punishable under the law of the requested state in similar circumstances. Like provisions are contained in U.S. extradition treaties with the Federal Republic of Germany, Japan, and Mexico. It is anticipated that such provisions would be useful in the areas of narcotics and counterfeiting violations.

ARTICLE 2

Article 2 includes as extraditable offenses those, whether listed or not, that are punishable under the federal laws of the United States and the laws of Colombia and carry a term of imprisonment for a maximum period exceeding one year in both countries, thus expanding the number of extraditable offenses in the present treaty.

Article 2 also authorizes extradition under certain conditions for an attempt to commit or a conspiracy to commit any extraditable offense. This article permits the government of the United States to request the extradition of a person for any extraditable offense when federal jurisdiction is based on the use of the mails or other means of carrying out interstate commerce (Colombian courts, as well as those of other countries, have had difficulty in understanding that these elements are solely jurisdictional and not substantive).

ARTICLE 3

Article 3 defines the territorial application of the treaty.

ARTICLE 4

Article 4 provides that extradition shall not be granted for political or military offenses. It also provides extradition where the request, while involving an offense not political in nature, is made for political purposes.

Article 4 also gives the executive authority of each party the responsibility of determining whether a request for extradition involves a political or military offense, unless the national laws of the requested party grant such powers to its courts. In the United States the laws do not grant such powers to its courts, and the authority therefore would rest with the executive branch. Similar provisions are contained in the new Mexican treaty and the proposed Dutch treaty.

ARTICLE 5

Article 5 is a prior jeopardy provision. It bars extradition when the person requested has been prosecuted in the requested state for the offense for which extradition is sought.

ARTICLE 6

Article 6 precludes extradition where prosecution or enforcement of the penalty for the offense for which extradition is sought has become barred by lapse of time according to the laws of the requested or requesting state.

ARTICLE 7

Article 7 permits refusal of extradition in capital cases unless satisfactory assurances are received that the death penalty will not be imposed or, if imposed, will not be executed for an offense not punishable by death in the country from which extradition is requested. A similar article has been included in most recent treaties.

ARTICLE 8

Article 8 deals with the extradition of nationals. It is similar to the provisions in some of our other recently signed extradition treaties. It grants the executive authority the discretionary power to extradite nationals of the other country. If extradition is denied on the basis of nationality, however, the requested party must undertake to submit the case to its competent authorities for the purpose of prosecution provided that party has jurisdiction over the offense. This article thus takes into account the law of Colombia which normally prohibits extradition of Colombian nationals, but allows for their prosecution in Colombia for offenses committed abroad.

The first paragraph of Article 8 is innovative. It imposes an obligation on the requested state to extradite all persons, including the other country's nationals, in cases where the offense involves acts punishable in both countries and where the offense was intended to be consummated in the requesting state. This provision is especially important in prosecuting exporters of dangerous drugs and narcotics.

ARTICLE 9

Article 9 limits extradition to cases where there is sufficient evidence, according to the laws of the requested state, to bring the person sought to trial had the offense been committed in the requested state or where the person sought is shown to be the person convicted by the courts of the requested state.

Article 9 also provides that the requested party shall make all arrangements necessary for internal extradition procedures and employ all legal means to obtain from the judicial authorities the decisions necessary to perfect the extradition request. The United States expects to continue the present practice under which each country is represented in extradition proceedings by the other's justice department.

ARTICLE 10

Article 10 provides for the request of additional evidence by the executive authority of the requesting state should it be thought that the evidence furnished is not sufficient to fulfill the requirements of the treaty.

Article 10 also states that if the evidence submitted is not sufficient or is not received, the individual in custody shall be released. Since an extradition proceeding is not a trial, there is no double jeopardy bar to resuming a proceeding on the basis of supplemented evidence: Article 10 states these general propositions of extradition law so that there will be no doubt.

ARTICLE 11

Article 11 outlines the means of obtaining a provisional arrest through the diplomatic channel. To cover emergency situations, this article provides for the provisional arrest of a fugitive without the presentation of documentation. However, it is incumbent upon the requesting state to include in its request certain basic information concerning the facts of the case and the existence of a warrant of arrest or judgment of conviction in the requesting state. Sufficient data to identify the fugitive are also required.

ARTICLE 12

Article 12 stresses the need for prompt extradition decisions by the requested state, including reasons for complete or partial rejections of extradition requests. Both countries have statutory limits on how long a person may remain in custody in the requested state after the fugitive has been committed for surrender to the requesting state. In the United States, for example, a court may order a fugitive, who has been found extraditable and certified to the Secretary of State for final review and surrender, discharged from custody if the person is not delivered to the foreign authorities within two months of such commitment, 18 U.S.C. § 3188. Thus, Article 12 conforms to the legal norms of both contracting parties that prohibit prolonged periods of detention after a decision to extradite has been or should have been made.

ARTICLE 13

Article 13 is consistent with current U.S. extradition practice and makes clear that the requested state has the discretion to postpone the surrender of a person found extraditable to the requesting state pending the resolution of ongoing proceedings relating to local charges or until the completion of a sentence rendered pursuant to current or past criminal proceedings.

ARTICLE 14

Article 14 permits the executive authority of the requesting state, when presented the extradition requests from several states at the same time, to determine to which state the fugitive shall be extradited.

ARTICLE 15

Article 15 expounds the Rule of Speciality, which states that, with the exception stated, a person may only be detained, tried, or punished for the offense for which he was extradited. The exception to this rule involves an offense that is legally altered in the course of the proceedings. For this exception to apply, the altered offense would have to be (a) based on the same set of facts contained in the extradition request and its supporting documents and (b) punishable by a penalty no more severe than the offense for which the person was extradited.

As in several modern U.S. treaties, the Rule of Speciality in this treaty permits the requested state to authorize prosecution for offenses in addition to those for which extradition was granted. This provision generally will be used in cases where the requesting state discovers evidence of additional crimes after a fugitive's extradition.

Article 15 will also permit someone surrendered for one offense to be convicted of a lesser included offense.

ARTICLE 16

Article 16 provides for exceptions to the formal extradition process as set forth in 18 U.S.C. § 3184. It allows a person sought for extradition to waive his right to an extradition hearing, thus permitting the immediate transfer of the fugitive to the custody of the requesting state without the need for a formal finding of extraditability by the courts and the executive authority of the requested state.

ARTICLE 17

Article 17 provides for the surrender by the requested state of all property relevant to the offense in question and for its subsequent return. Such provisions allow the requested state to return to the requesting state objects in the possession or control of the person sought that belong to the victim of the underlying crime or that are necessary to establish an element of an offense (e.g., the murder weapon). Article 17 must, however, be read together with the internal law of the requested state, and rights of third parties in the property must be respected.

ARTICLE 18

Article 18 permits, under specified conditions, the transport through a contracting party of an individual who is being surrendered by a third state to the other contracting party.

ARTICLE 19

Article 19 provides that the requesting party shall pay only the costs associated with the transportation of the person sought and with the translation of extradition documents.

ARTICLE 20

Article 20 makes clear that the treaty is retroactive in effect.

ARTICLE 21

Article 21 provides that the treaty will enter into force on the date of exchange of the instruments of ratification. On entry into force, this treaty will terminate the Treaty of Extradition between the United States and Colombia signed on 7 May 1888, and the Supplementary Convention signed on 9 September 1940.

NOTES

1. *Time*, 1 December 1986, 25; *U.S. News and World Report*, 8 February 1988, 28–29.

2. *National Law Journal*, 7 December 1987, p. 6; U.S. v. Lehder, *81-81 CR J-12*; *Time*, 16 February 1987, 37.

3. Lyle Denniston, "Further Extraditions Left in Doubt by a Court Ruling in Colombia," *Drug Enforcement Report*, (July 1987): 4.

4. Terlinder v. Ames, 184 U.S. 270, 289 (1902).

5. Curiously, despite the wording of the Constitution, the federal government has no responsibility for enforcing the extradition clause. In Kentucky v. Dennison, decided by the U.S. Supreme Court in 1861, the Justices unanimously held that while the Constitution imposes a moral obligation on a governor to surrender a fugitive sought and requested by another governor, such obligation cannot be enforced in the federal courts.

6. The Uniform Criminal Extradition Act, 11 *Uniform Laws Annotated*, has been adopted by every state except Mississippi. For statutory citations for every state, see Ill. Rev. Stat., ch. 20, § 12 (West Supp. 1980–1981), and 18 U.S.C. ch. 209.

7. Act of October 1, 1833, *Pasinomie* 1833, vol. 3, 239.

8. U.S. Congress, Senate Committee on Foreign Relations. *Extradition Treaty with the Republic of China*, 97th Cong. 1st sess., 20 November 1981, Executive Report no. 97-34, 140.13; Miriam Sapiro, "Extradition in an Era of Terrorism: The Need to Abolish the Political Offense Exception," *New York University Law Review* 61 (October 1986): 654–702.

9. "Review of Foreign Laws," in *Transnational Aspects of Criminal Procedure: Michigan Yearbook of International Legal Studies* (New York: Clark Boardman Co., 1983), 281–319.

10. Factor v. Laubenheimer, 290 U.S. 276, 287 (1933).

11. *Inter-American Convention on Extradition* (Washington, D.C.: General Secretariat OAS, 1981), 3–16.

12. C. Van den Winjngaert, *The Political Offense Exception to Extradition* (The Netherlands: Kluwer-Deventer, 1980), 27–89.

13. Factor v. Laubenheimer, 290 U.S. at 276; United States v. Raucher, 119 U.S. 407, 423–30 (1986); L. Anderson, "Protecting the Rights of the Requested Person in Extradition Proceedings: An Argument for a Humanitarian Exception," in *Transnational Aspects of Criminal Procedure: Michigan Yearbook of International Legal Studies* (New York: Clark Boardman Co., 1983), 153–70.

14. M. D. Gouldman, "Extradition from Other Countries," in *Transnational Aspects of Criminal Procedure: Michigan Yearbook of International Legal Studies* (New York: Clark Boardman Co., 1983), 173–208.

15. *Miami Herald*, 26 January 1988, 1A.

16. *U.S. News and World Report*, 8 February 1988, 28–29.

17. *U.S. News and World Report*, 16 February 1987, 12.

18. The Treaty of Extradition with the Republic of Colombia is in many ways similar to other extradition treaties between the United States and other foreign governments. A summary of this treaty is provided following this analysis.

19. Treaty of Extradition with the Republic of Colombia § 140.1 (14 September 1979).

20. Ibid., §§ 140.1–140. 11.

21. Denniston, "Further Extraditions," 4.

22. *Time*, 21 March 1988, 45–46.

23. See Bogotá *El Siglo*, 4 October 1985, 1, 8.

24. Bogotá *El Tiempo*, 16 December 1986, 4A; Bogotá *El Tiempo*, 29 May 1987, 1A, 10A.

25. Denniston, "Further Extraditions," 4; Bogotá *El Tiempo*, 4 June 1987, 1A, 8A.

26. Prior to the invalidation of the U.S./Colombian treaty, a rather unique approach taken by Colombian drug traffickers to avoid extradition to the United States was an open proposal to their government, written on behalf of sixty-five "extraditables." The letter claimed that if the government agreed to prosecute them in Colombia, rather than extradite them to the United States for prosecution, these extraditables would (a) cancel their nation's foreign debt of $11 billion, (b) bring back to Colombia any capital they were holding in foreign banks, and, (c) surrender their cocaine-processing laboratories. To the shock and dismay of many Colombian officials, a group of these extraditables met with both former president Alfonso Lopez Michelson and then Attorney General Carlos Jimenez

Gomez in Mexico City and Panama City, asking these officials to serve as mediators between them and their government. However, Colombian President Belisario Betancur and Justice Minister Parejo Gonzalez took a strong stand on the matter and refused to negotiate. See Bogotá *El Tiempo*, 8 May 1986, 3.

27. *Time*, 1 December 1986, 25; *Nation*, 5 September 1987, 189–192; *Miami Herald*, 29 November 1987, 1A, 28A; *Time*, 11 Jan. 1988, 53; *Miami Herald*, 26 January 1988, 1A, 6A; *New York Times*, 26 January 1988, A1, A11; *U.S. News and World Report*, 8 February 1988, 28–29; *Latin American Regional Reports, Andean Group Report*, 3 March 1988, 2–3.

28. Treaty of Extradition 140.5.

29. *Inter-American Convention*, 3–16.

30. *New York Times*, 11 January 1988, A3.

31. Van den Winjngaert, *The Political Offense*, 27–89.

32. *New York Times*, 20 August 1989, 12; *Miami Herald*, 25 August 1989, 1A, 8A; *Newsweek*, 28 August 1989, 37; *Time*, 4 September 1989, 12–15.

33. *Miami Herald*, 4 October 1989, 4A.

34. *Miami Herald*, 6 October 1989, 4A; *Miami Herald*, 5 November 1989, 8A; Latin American Regional Reports, *Andean Group Report*, 9 November 1989, 3.

Appendix D

The National Drug Control Strategy: A Synopsis

Diane M. Canova

On 18 November 1988 President Reagan signed into law the Anti-Drug Abuse Act of 1988 (P.L. 100-690) which created the office of National Drug Control Policy, a new executive branch agency charged with the development of a comprehensive, coordinated national strategy to combat illegal drug-related activities.

As required by law, the first National Drug Control strategy was to be submitted to Congress six months after the confirmation of the director of this new office. Pursuant to this congressional mandate, William J. Bennett, director of the Office of National Drug Control Policy, produced the office's first strategy that was submitted by President George Bush to Congress on 5 September 1989. Henceforth, a revised strategy is to be submitted to Congress by 1 February of each succeeding year.

The following is a summary of the provisions contained in the 1989 National Drug Control Strategy.

BENNETT'S INTRODUCTION

In spite of some positive news contained in the most recent National Household Survey conducted by the National Institute on Drug Abuse, which suggests that the number of current users of the two most common illegal substances—marijuana and cocaine—is down, points to other evidence indicating that the U.S. drug problem is getting worse, not better. Cited are alarming statistics on crime, lost worker productivity, the abundant and cheap availability of drugs, and health threats, such as AIDS, increased emergency hospital admissions, and drug-addicted babies.

Bennett acknowledges that previous federal, state, and local efforts aimed solely at reducing supply failed to measurably impact on both the supply and the use of illegal drugs. One of the central themes of the strategy is that a coordinated strategy focusing on all aspects of the drug crisis—education, treatment, law enforcement—is needed.

The coordinated approach advocated by Bennett includes as its hallmark the need to develop tough policies regarding use of illegal drugs. "[T]he highest priority of our drug policy must be a stubborn determination further to reduce the overall level of drug use nationwide—experimental first use, 'casual use', regular use, and addiction alike" (National Drug Control Strategy, 8). As a result, many of the approaches recommended by Bennett stress accountability for one's drug-using behavior and the need to attack the problem from a variety of perspectives, including criminal sanctions and treatment.

The national priorities in the specific areas of criminal justice; drug treatment; education, community action, and work place; international; interdiction; research; and intelligence are considered below.

CRIMINAL JUSTICE PRIORITIES

- Increased federal funding to states and localities for street-level drug law enforcement.
- Federal funding to states for planning, developing, and implementing alternative sentencing programs for nonviolent drug offenders, including house arrest and boot camps.
- Increased federal funding for federal law enforcement activities (including courts, prisons, prosecutors, and law enforcement officers) and additional resources targeted on federal money-laundering investigations.
- Vigorous prosecution of and increased fines for all misdemeanor state drug offenses.
- Expanded programs to eradicate the domestic marijuana crop.
- Adoption by the states of drug-testing programs throughout their criminal justice systems for arrestees, prisoners, parolees, and those out on bail. Adoption of such programs will be a condition for receipt of federal criminal justice funds.
- Funding through the Department of Housing and Urban Development to establish security systems for public housing projects, including tenant identification cards, guards, and security fences.
- Establishment of a Supply-Reduction Working Group, chaired by the Office of National Drug Control Policy, to carry out the statutory requirement to "coordinate and oversee the implementation by National Drug Control Program agencies of the policies, objectives, and priorities" defined in the National Drug Control Strategy. This group will consider supply-related drug policy issues that are interdepartmental in nature. It will not deal with operational decisions or have line authority or responsibility.
- Revision of federal drug agency personnel evaluation systems, where appropriate, to add a criterion for career advancement and reward that emphasizes cooperation among employees within and across various agencies.

The National Drug Control Strategy criminal justice recommendations target traditional street crime enforcement by stating that "the first challenge facing our criminal justice system is to help reclaim neighborhoods that have been rendered unsafe by drugs'' (National Drug Control Strategy, 19). The strategy calls for vigorous enforcement of laws by employing effective police methods and acknowledges that the support and cooperation of state and local law enforcement agencies is essential if this aspect of the strategy is to succeed. To assist in the renewed importance of state and local law enforcement efforts, the strategy proposes to more than double funding from $150 million to $350 million in 1990.

In addition to promoting enhanced street-level law enforcement efforts, the strategy calls for the development of a variety of criminal sanctions to ensure that punishment is both swift and certain. The strategy acknowledges that undermanned police forces and insufficient numbers of prosecutors, judges, jails, and prisons currently contribute to the inability of most jurisdictions to appropriately punish all offenders. Since the expansion of the entire criminal justice system will take the infusion of much larger financial resources and involve potentially lengthy time delays, the strategy encourages the use of innovative alternative sanctions for nonviolent drug offenders, including house arrest, halfway houses, and boot camps.

First-time and occasional drug users should be faced with less formal sanctions such as driver's license suspension, employer notification, overnight or weekend detention, eviction from public housing, or forfeiture of automobiles. As stated in the strategy, ''whatever the extent of their offense, if they use drugs they should be held accountable'' (National Drug Control Strategy, 25). The strategy's interest in accountability extends to recommending that probation, parole, and court-supervised treatment programs maintain regular drug-testing programs to enforce drug abstinence.

Although the strategy focuses a good deal of attention on state and local law enforcement efforts, it does include specific recommendations for federal government activities and cites the need for a Supply-Reduction Working Group to coordinate federal, state, and local efforts and for expansion of money-laundering investigations and crop eradication projects. Coordination of law enforcement efforts is cited as necessary to resolve ''turf battles,'' to provide policy oversight, and to establish supply-related priorities.

DRUG TREATMENT PRIORITIES

- Increased federal funds for treatment in order to expand the number of treatment slots and the range of treatment methods available.

- Greater state, local, and individual treatment program accountability for effectiveness. Submission of state plans for treatment resource allocation and systemic improvements will be a condition for receipt of federal treatment funds.

- Improved coordination among local treatment facilities so that treatment resources and availability match community needs and so that drug users are referred to the most appropriate treatment provider.

- Improved coordination between treatment facilities and social, health, and employment agencies in order to better assist those drug-dependent persons who need services in addition to treatment. Under some circumstances, treatment facilities will be assisted in the development of their own programs in these areas.

- Increased funding of outreach programs and early treatment for expectant mothers who use drugs.

- State and private insurance company coverage of outpatient and other less intensive forms of treatment for drug use. A thorough review of federal policy will be conducted to determine whether changes in federal coverage are necessary.

- Exploration of ways to increase the use of civil commitment as a means to bring more drug-dependent persons into the treatment system.

- Expanded and improved federal information collection and research. Priority will be given to describing current treatment capacity and needs; evaluating treatment effectiveness for specific populations; and developing methods of the treatment of individuals who are dependent on both cocaine and crack or on cocaine in combination with other substances and of individuals who have both psychiatric and drug problems.

The National Drug Control Strategy recognizes the need to expand and improve drug abuse treatment and to that end calls for increased federal resources to expand the number of treatment slots and the range of treatment methods available. Because federal funding for local treatment programs is provided in block grants to the states, the strategy encourages the states to target the funds to the cities and programs where the greatest needs occur. States will also be required to submit state treatment plans describing how funds will be allocated and how these monies will be used to improve their treatment systems.

The strategy recommends improved coordination among treatment facilities and between treatment facilities and social, health, and employment agencies to facilitate improved client-treatment matching. Since drug users come to treatment with widely varying social and vocational skills, treatment programs must cooperate to provide a full range of social services, counseling, medical treatment, and job training.

The strategy encourages states to explore ways of getting more drug users into treatment, including expanded use of civil commitment by the courts to mandate participation in treatment in lieu of or in addition to incarceration. States are also encouraged to expand prison- and jail-based treatment programs and to make outreach efforts to identify and treat pregnant addicts. Additionally, private employers should establish more employee assistance programs to help employees with drug or alcohol problems that affect job performance.

While recognizing the need to expand treatment capacity, the strategy also calls for expanded and improved data collection and research to fill the gaps in our knowledge of the treatment system; to improve treatment effectiveness, and to develop better methods of treatment for cocaine and crack dependency.

EDUCATION, COMMUNITY ACTION, AND WORK PLACE PRIORITIES

- Implementation of firm drug prevention programs and policies in schools, colleges, and universities. Such programs and policies will be a condition of eligibility for receipt of federal funds.

- Development of model alternative schools for youths with drug problems. Federal assistance to local education agencies will promote such development.

- Federal support for communitywide drug prevention efforts.

- Federal support for development of antidrug media outreach activities that deal with the dangers of using illegal drugs—particularly crack—and with drug-impaired pregnancies.

- Creation of a national program to mobilize volunteer efforts to prevent the illegal use of drugs.

- Implementation of Executive Order 12564 to ensure a drug-free federal work force.

- Drug-free work place policies in the private sector and in state and local governments, providing clear penalties for drug use and including drug-testing where appropriate.

- Establishment of a Demand-Reduction Working Group, chaired by the Office of National Drug Control Policy, to carry out the statutory requirement to "coordinate and oversee the implementation by National Drug Control Program agencies of the policies, objectives, and priorities" defined in the national strategy (National Drug Control Strategy, 58). This group will consider demand-related drug policy issues that are interdepartmental in nature. It will not deal with operational decisions or have line authority or responsibility.

The National Drug Control Strategy calls for the implementation of drug prevention programs in schools, colleges, and universities as a condition of receiving federal aid. School-based prevention programs should be reinforced by tough, but fair school policies on the use, possession, and distribution of drugs. To address the potential increase in the number of students expelled that could result from tough school policies, the strategy recommends the development of alternative education approaches for youths with drug problems and for those who cannot succeed in regular classes.

Local communities are encouraged to "mobilize against drugs" in a number of ways, including additional antidrug media outreach activities; expanded volunteer efforts, and activities involving religious and professional organizations (National Drug Control Strategy, 53). Additionally, the private sector is asked to implement drug-free work place policies, providing clear penalties for drug use and including appropriate drug testing.

The strategy also calls for the establishment of a Demand-Reduction Working Group to coordinate and implement the Office of National Drug Control Policy's programs.

INTERNATIONAL PRIORITIES

• Disruption and dismantling of drug-trafficking organizations.

• Reduced cocaine supply. Law enforcement, military, and economic assistance will be provided to the three Andean cocaine-producing countries to isolate major coca-growing areas; to block the delivery of chemicals used for cocaine processing; to destroy cocaine hydrochloride processing labs; and to dismantle the trafficking organizations. Efforts in transit areas will be improved, and joint intelligence collection centers will be created in the Caribbean Basin.

• Reduced heroin supply through efforts to convince other countries to exert influence on opium growers and reduce heroin processing and distribution.

• Reduced marijuana supply through strengthened foreign law enforcement and eradication and through efforts to discourage minor producing nations from becoming major producers.

• U.S. assistance to and encouragement of European community and multilateral efforts aimed at source country and transit country production and distribution and at European consumption. European community support against international and regional drug organizations will be enlisted.

• Other international objectives:

—Elevation of drugs as a bilateral foreign policy issue.

—U.S. ratification of the United Nations Convention Against Illicit Traffic in Narcotic Drugs and Psychotropic Substances, along with other pending mutual legal assistance treaties. Other nations will be urged to ratify the convention.

—Support for the U.S. foreign aid certification process in order to achieve more effective supply—and transit—country compliance with American drug control objectives.

—Bilateral and multilateral efforts against international money-laundering activities.

The national strategy recognizes the need to develop policies and programs focusing on international drug production and trafficking. As the strategy states, "a cornerstone of our international drug policy must be a determination to work with and motivate other countries to engage their own resources and efforts to defeat trafficking" (National Drug Control Strategy, 61). Efforts must be undertaken to cripple all aspects of illegal drug activity, including production, processing, transportation, distribution, and financial networks.

Cocaine and heroin are acknowledged to be the most serious threats to the United States, and the strategy responds with a call for a comprehensive and long-term effort, involving economic, military, and law enforcement approaches to reduce trafficking of these drugs. Regarding cocaine trafficking, the strategy advocates increased cooperation with the governments of the coca-producing countries that should include the convening of an Andean drug summit. Additionally, it calls for improved counterdrug efforts in the coca transportation areas of Central America, Mexico, and the Caribbean.

While the strategy identifies heroin as a major threat, it acknowledges that influencing the principal opium-producing countries to decrease heroin production will be difficult. Efforts to curtail the supply of heroin to the United States require the cooperation of countries that do influence opium-growing countries to assist in supply-reduction efforts.

International efforts to decrease the foreign supply of marijuana are highlighted, along with the need to strengthen foreign enforcement efforts through training and logistical and intelligence support. The strategy also supports crop eradication programs, but notes that they may not be the most appropriate approach in all situations.

In addition to specific action targeting drug-producing countries, the strategy calls for foreign policy initiatives to gain the support of Western Europe, the Soviet Union, and Eastern Europe in destroying the international drug trade. Concerted international efforts with the above-mentioned foreign areas, as well as with other industrialized nations such as Japan, Australia, and Canada, are needed to change world opinion regarding drugs.

The international initiatives section concludes with a call for stringent controls on the export and diversion of chemicals used in the production of cocaine, heroin, and other drugs. Money laundering is the final area of concern discussed, and international cooperative agreements supporting strong measures to criminalize and penalize money-laundering activities are recommended.

INTERDICTION PRIORITIES

* Development of a comprehensive, information-based approach to federal air, maritime, land, and port-of-entry interdiction:
    —Upgraded intelligence support to interdiction through intensified interdiction-specific investigations and undercover operations.
    —Enhanced computer support to interdiction through acceleration of machine-readable documentation programs; installation of document machine readers at appropriate ports of entry; and development of the International Border Interdiction System (IBIS) and other computerized border information systems.
    —Creation of interagency/interdisciplinary teams to analyze and target smuggling models, methods, and routes.
* Concentration on high-value individuals and shipments:
    —Review of existing methods for deterring air smugglers.
    —Improved operations aimed at money couriers and shipments.
    —Improved container inspection techniques and intelligence.
* Enhanced border systems, operations, and activities:
    —Dramatically reduced document fraud, especially fraudulent use of U.S. birth certificates and other "breeder documents."
    —Expanded use of drug detection dogs, antivehicle barriers, and container inspections.

—Provision of automatic exclusion authority and general arrest authority to Immigration and Naturalization Service officers.

—Improved detection and monitoring systems and secure operations procedures.

—Expanded secure communications systems.

The strategy states that although postinterdiction efforts have resulted in the disruption of trafficking patterns and in the seizure of increased amounts of drugs, the supply of illegal drugs entering the United States has continued to grow. Despite this acknowledgment, the strategy maintains that interdiction "has major symbolic and practical value" (National Drug Control Strategy, 74).

Specific strategy recommendations are aimed at mid-level drug traffickers, including pilots, money couriers, and field managers who are purported to have knowledge of their organizations' structure, membership, and methods of operations. It was stated that low-level carriers, or "mules," do not possess sufficient operational knowledge to warrant full-scale efforts directed at them. At the other end of the drug trade organization, "kingpins" generally do not take part in actual drug transportation efforts and thus "have little to fear from ordinary interdiction measures" (National Drug Control Policy, 76).

Interdiction priorities include improved automated information and intelligence delivery systems to provide necessary data to aid interdiction efforts. Additionally, the strategy recommends stepped-up efforts to reduce production and use of fraudulent documents at border areas.

RESEARCH PRIORITIES

• Establishment of a Drug Control Research and Development Committee involving directors of research and evaluation and chief technology advisors to all appropriate drug supply- and demand-reduction agencies. This committee will

—Recommend to the Office of National Drug Control Policy policies and priorities for drug-related research and development.

—Review, monitor, and coordinate federal research, data collection, and evaluation activities.

—Eliminate duplication and gaps in current data collection and generate accurate and useful information on which to base national drug control policies.

—Assist agencies in effectively acquiring and using new technologies to prevent and treat drug use and to detect and suppress the flow of illegal drugs and related commodities.

• Better and more frequent data collection and analysis, including flexible, quick-response data collection instruments.

• Increased basic and clinical research on drug use and addiction.

• Development of new technologies or innovative adaptation of existing technologies for use against illegal drugs.

- Development of a comprehensive information base about "what works" in controlling drug use through support for public and private evaluation of drug enforcement, drug prevention, and drug treatment programs.
- Archived and disseminated information, research, and evaluation results through an appropriate mechanism that combines prevention, treatment, and criminal justice data.

The strategy's research priorities target three specific areas, including the need to fill information gaps by expanding current data collection activities; the need to learn more about effective criminal justice prevention and treatment programs; and the need to better coordinate data collection efforts and to more widely disseminate research findings.

Regarding current data collection efforts, the strategy recommends more frequent use of surveys such as the National Household Survey and the National Drug and Alcoholism Treatment Unit Survey conducted by the National Institutes on Drug Abuse and on Alcohol Abuse and Alcoholism. On the drug enforcement side, more information is needed on the impact of drug availability and price fluctuations, stiffer drug penalties, and other deterrents.

INTELLIGENCE PRIORITIES

- Increased intelligence efforts to concentrate on the infrastructure of trafficking organizations and their allied enterprises, particularly money laundering.
- Improved drug automation and information systems to allow swifter, better, and more cost-effective drug law enforcement, prosecutions, and interdictions.
- Sharing of intelligence developed in the course of investigations and intelligence operations and dissemination of finished, analyzed intelligence to appropriate federal law enforcement and intelligence agencies.
- Establishment of an interagency working group chaired by the Office of National Drug Control Policy to develop plans for an intelligence center to unite U.S. drug-related analytical capabilities and to improve intelligence capabilities. Results will be presented to the appropriate cabinet council.

The national strategy recommendations regarding intelligence efforts highlight the need to "know the enemy far better than we do now" (National Drug Control Strategy, 87). In order to achieve better information, the strategy supports increased intelligence efforts by the federal agencies currently involved in such activities—the Drug Enforcement Administration (DEA), the Central Intelligence Agency (CIA), the Departments of Defense and State, and the Customs Service.

The strategy also recommends the sharing of intelligence information with all appropriate federal, state, and local law enforcement agencies. Although particular care must be given to sensitive information and appropriate safeguards against unwarranted disclosure must be taken, it is believed that the "finished products of intelligence analysis must be shared among all participants in the war on drugs who have a need to know this vital information'' (National Drug Control Strategy, 88).

The strategy also calls for the establishment of an interagency working group to coordinate the collection of domestic and foreign information and to develop a federal center to facilitate this coordination.

Source: *National Drug Control Strategy*, The White House, September 1989.

Federal and State Controlled Substances Acts (CSAs)*

THE FEDERAL CONTROLLED SUBSTANCES ACT

Scheduling

The regulatory scheme of the federal controlled substances act classifies substances into five categories, or schedules, to facilitate administration and regulation of the manufacturing, distribution, and dispensing of narcotics and other dangerous drugs without interfering in the legitimate and necessary businesses of doctors, pharmacists, and manufacturers.

The categories are based upon such characteristics of drugs as potential for abuse, accepted medical use, and propensity to create a psychological or physiological dependency for users. Classifications of drugs and periodic updating and re-publication of lists of drugs included in each category are the responsibility of the U.S. Drug Enforcement Administration (DEA).

Drugs in the most strictly controlled category, listed in schedule I of the classification scheme, have a high potential for abuse, no currently accepted medical use in the United States, and no acceptable safe level of use under medical supervision. Many narcotics, such as heroin and other opiates and opium derivatives, fall into this category. In addition, many hallucinogenic drugs that have no recognized medicinal value in this country, such as marijuana, mescaline, peyote, psilocybin, and lysergic acid diethylamide (LSD), are listed in schedule I.

Schedule II drugs have a high potential for abuse, and their use may lead to severe psychological or physiological dependencies; however, they have some

*Reprinted from *A Guide to State Controlled Substances Acts* (Washington, D.C.: Bureau of Justice Assistance, U.S. Department of Justice, and the National Criminal Justice Association, 1988).

recognized medicinal value. Drugs in this category include cocaine, morphine, methamphetamine, and phensyclidine (PCP). Dronabinol, the synthetic equivalent of the active ingredient in marijuana, recently was moved from schedule I to schedule II in recognition of its growing medical uses in treating glaucoma and chemotherapy patients. The DEA has under consideration a petition for reclassification of marijuana from schedule I to schedule II for similar reasons.

Schedule III controlled substances have less potential for abuse than schedule I or II drugs and may lead to moderate or low physical dependence or high psychological dependence, but have some accepted medical use. Substances listed in schedule III include limited quantities of some narcotic drugs; amphetamines; and derivatives of barbituric acid.

Schedule IV controlled substances have a low potential for abuse compared to substances in schedule III, and, although they may lead to limited physical or psychological dependence, they have a currently accepted medical use. Substances in schedule IV include phenobarbital, chlordiazepoxide hydrochloride (librium), diazepam (valium), and propoxyphene hydrochloride (darvon).

Schedule V controlled substances have a low potential for abuse compared to substances in schedule IV and a currently accepted medical use; use may lead to limited physical or psychological dependence relative to schedule IV substances. Substances in schedule V are narcotic compounds containing a limited quantity of narcotic drugs together with one or more non-narcotic medicinal ingredients.

Penalty Provisions

The federal CSA separates violations of CSA provisions into two major categories of offenses: the possession of controlled substances and the manufacture, distribution, or dispensing of, or the possession with intent to manufacture, distribute, or dispense, controlled substances. (The second category is referred to collectively in this *Guide* as "manufacture, delivery, or sale" of controlled substances.) There is a flat penalty for possession offenses, but a graduated penalty structure for manufacture/delivery/sale offenses based on the type, amount, and purity of the substance involved in an offense. Penalties also differ depending upon whether the offense is committed by an "individual" or "other than individuals." Offenders in the latter category face much harsher fines than individuals.

Every possession offense carries a penalty of up to one year's incarceration and/or a fine of $1,000 to $5,000. Second offenses for possession are punishable by a minimum of 15 days' and a maximum of two years' incarceration, and/or a fine of $2,500 to $10,000. Third or subsequent offenses are punishable by three months' to three years' incarceration and/or a fine of $5,000 to $25,000. There is an exception to the general scheme for possession of piperidine, a precursor ingredient of PCP; a first offense carries a penalty of up to five years' incarceration and/or a $250,000 fine.

The basic penalty for the manufacture, delivery, or sale of any schedule I or

Table 1
Penalties for Manufacturing/Delivery/Sale

	Schedules I and II	
	First Offense	Second and Subsequent Offenses
	Incarceration/Fine	Incarceration/Fine
Individual:		
No death/bodily injury	0-20;$1 million	0-30;$2 million
Death/bodily injury	20-life;$1 million	life;$2 million
Others:	$5 million	$10 million

Table 2
Penalties for Manufacturing/Delivery/Sale

	Schedule III	
	First Offense	Second and Subsequent Offenses
	Incarceration/Fine	Incarceration/Fine
Individual:	0-5; $250,000	0-10; $500,000
Others:	$1 million	$2 million

schedule II drug, or between 50 and 100 kg. of marijuana, is a sentence of up to 20 years' imprisonment and/or a fine of up to $1 million for an individual or up to $5 million for other than individuals. If death or serious bodily injury results from the use of the drugs, the term of imprisonment can range from 20 years to life in prison. Second or subsequent violations of manufacture/delivery/ sale provisions are punishable by up to 30 years' imprisonment and/or up to $2 million in fines for individuals and up to $10 million for others. If death or serious bodily injury results from a sale and the offender has a felony drug conviction, there is a mandatory sentence of life imprisonment. (See Table 1.)

Offenses involving schedule III drugs or offenses involving less than 50 kg. of marijuana; 100 or more marijuana plants, regardless of weight; less than 10 kg. hashish; or less than one kg. hash oil are punishable by up to five years' incarceration and/or a $250,000 fine for individuals; the potential fine is $1 million for others. Second or subsequent offenses under this section are punishable by up to 10 years' incarceration and/or a $500,000 fine for individuals, $2 million for others. (See Table 2.)

Manufacture/delivery/sale offenses for schedule IV substances are punishable

Table 3
Penalties for Manufacturing/Delivery/Sale

Schedule IV

	First Offense	Second and Subsequent Offenses
	Incarceration/Fine	Incarceration/Fine
Individual:	0-3; $250,000	0-6; $500,000
Others:	$1 million	$2 million

Table 4
Penalties for Manufacturing/Delivery/Sale

Schedule V

	First Offense	Second and Subsequent Offenses
	Incarceration/Fine	Incarceration/Fine
Individual:	0-1; $100,000	0-2; $200,000
Others:	$250,000	$500,000

by up to three years' incarceration and/or a $250,000 fine for individuals, $1 million for others. Second or subsequent offenses under this section are punishable by up to six years' incarceration and/or a $500,000 fine for individuals, $2 million for others. (See Table 3.)

The manufacture/delivery/sale of a schedule V substance is punishable by up to one year's incarceration and/or a $100,000 fine for individuals, $250,000 for others. Second or subsequent offenses under this provision are punishable by up to two years' incarceration and/or a $200,000 fine for individuals, $500,000 for others. (See Table 4.)

Under a provision of the 1986 drug act, the CSA also includes a measure stipulating that an offense involving a controlled substance analog, a chemical substance substantially similar in chemical structure to a controlled substance, shall trigger penalties as if it were a controlled substance listed in schedule I. This section is designed to combat the proliferations of so-called "designer drugs," substances manufactured by chemists who slightly alter the chemical makeup of a controlled substance so that it retains the same psychotropic effect as the original substance but technically is not subject to regulation because it is a new compound not specifically listed in CSA schedules. The DEA has emergency scheduling power under which it may treat a given substance as "controlled" for enforcement purposes pending completion of hearings on whether to list the substance in the federal schedules.

Recent CSA amendments also have increased penalties for violations involving minimum amounts or more of heroin, cocaine, PCP, LSD, and marijuana. Any manufacture/delivery/sale offense involving more than the following quantities of drugs is punishable by a mandatory term of imprisonment of 10 years to life and/or a fine of up to $4 million for an individual, $10 million for others; one kg. of a mixture containing heroin, five kg. of a mixture containing cocaine, 50 g. of a mixture containing cocaine base, one kg. of a mixture containing PCP, 100 g. of PCP, 10 g. of a mixture containing LSD, and 1,000 kg. of a mixture containing marijuana. Second and subsequent offenses under this section are punishable by prison terms of 20 years to life and fines of up to $8 million for individuals, $20 million for others. If death or serious bodily injury results from a first offense, there is a mandatory sentence of 20 years to life in prison; if the offender has a previous felony drug conviction, the mandatory sentence is life imprisonment.

Forfeiture Provisions

In addition to progressively harsher sentences for initial and repeated drug laws offenses, the federal CSA provides for other sanctions against offenders who have profited from their illegal activity. Specifically, the statute permits the government to bring civil forfeiture actions against drug trafficking proceeds and other property used to facilitate CSA violations. Under § 881 of the CSA, the following items are forfeitable: all controlled substances manufactured, distributed, or possessed in violation of the CSA; raw materials or equipment used to manufacture, import, or export controlled substances; any property used as a container for controlled substances; all conveyances, including aircraft, vehicles, or vessels, used or intended for use to transport controlled substances; all books, records, and research used to violate the CSA; all moneys, negotiable instruments, securities, or other things of value furnished or intended to be furnished in exchange for controlled substances, or all such property traceable to such an exchange; and all real property used to facilitate violations of the CSA.

Forfeiture not only deprives criminals of the proceeds of their illegal activities, but also generates revenues to support drug law enforcement activity. Forfeited assets or proceeds from their sale are deposited into the U.S. Department of Justice's Assets Forfeiture Fund, administered by the U.S. Marshals Service, and may be used to buy equipment, refurbish conveyances, and pay awards for information, among other purposes. Monies deposited into the fund also may be shared with state and local law enforcement agencies that participate in cooperative investigations with federal agencies. (See ''U.S. Attorney General's Guidelines for Seized and Forfeited Property.'')

New Offenses

The CSA also includes special penalties for offenses involving minors. These provisions have been added in recent years in response to drug dealers' increased use of minors to sell drugs to other minors, particularly in or around schools, or to deliver drugs to other distributors. First, any person 18 years or older who distributes a controlled substance to a person under 18 is subject to a sentence of up to twice the term and fine otherwise authorized. In addition, the statute provides that any person who distributes a controlled substance in, on, or within 1,000 feet of real property of a public or private elementary, vocational, or secondary school or a public or private college, junior college, or university shall receive a sentence of three years to life in prison or up to three times the fine and term of incarceration otherwise authorized, whichever is greater. Finally, any person at least 18 who hires, employs, coerces, or uses anyone under 18 to violate any part of the CSA or to assist in avoiding apprehension by law enforcement officials faces up to twice the term and fine otherwise authorized for the offense, with the added stipulation that the term of incarceration be a minimum of one year. The recent amendments also include provisions establishing similar sanctions against any person who knowingly distributes controlled substances to a pregnant woman and establishing enhanced penalties for second or subsequent offenses involving minors.

Like provisions relating to minors, two other recently-added CSA provisions, both part of the 1986 anti-drug abuse act, are intended to address specific new developments in drug control efforts. The CSA now includes a drug paraphernalia provision making it unlawful to use the U.S. Postal Service or other interstate shippers to sell, offer for sale, import, or export drug paraphernalia; violations of this section are punishable by up to three years' incarceration and/or a $100,000 fine.

The other measure, a so-called "safehouse" provision, provides that anyone who maintains, rents, or leases any building, room, or other enclosure for the purpose of manufacturing, distributing, or using controlled substances faces up to 20 years' imprisonment and/or a $500,000 fine.

STATE CONTROLLED SUBSTANCE ACTS

Scheduling

Many states have adopted CSA schedules identical or similar to the federal schedules. In some instances, states have integrated the federal scheduling mechanism into state CSA statutes, but have adopted different mechanisms for the assignment of penalties. Those state CSA's that differ from the federal method and from other state CSA's do so primarily in the way they group drugs together for determining penalties.

Scheduling approaches in state CSA's fall broadly into five categories. The first group of states includes those that have adopted the federal scheduling method, including the same five schedules and the same criteria for determining a substance's classification. In addition, many of these CSA's include language that provides for the automatic addition, deletion, or re-classification of sub-

Table 5
Minnesota Penalties for Possession Offenses

	First Offense	Second Offense	Subsequent Offenses
I/II narcotics	0-5; $10,000	0-10; $20,000	same
I/II non-narcotics	0-3; $5,000	0-6; $10,000	same
III	0-3; $5,000	0-6; $10,000	same
IV	0-3; $5,000	0-6; $10,000	same
V	0-1; $5,000	0-2; $10,000	same

stances whenever such changes occur in the federal schedule. These CSA's generally have graduated penalties for offenses, with the heaviest penalties for offenses involving schedule I drugs; another, less severe set of penalties for offenses involving schedule II drugs; and so forth.

Like the CSA's in the first category, CSA's in the second group have scheduling schemes similar to that of the federal CSA, and most contain provisions for "automatic conformity" with federal scheduling actions. Unlike the first category, however, CSA's in the second group subdivide schedule categories according to some other distinguishing factor; in most CSA's that follow this scheduling approach, schedules I and II are divided into narcotics and non-narcotics for purposes of establishing penalties. In Minnesota, for example, schedules are set up as shown in Table 5.

The CSA's using the third scheduling method retain the five-schedule system of the federal CSA, but deviate from the federal system in their classification of specific drugs, generally in order to provide for more or less severe penalties for offenses involving those substances. For example, Louisiana has placed phencyclidine (PCP), which is under schedule II in the federal system, in schedule I to make use, possession, and manufacture/delivery/sale of PCP illegal under all circumstances. This type of classification approach differs from creation of an enhanced penalty, under which a CSA violation involving a specific drug in a given schedule triggers a penalty higher than would violations involving other substances similarly scheduled.

On the other hand, some states classify drugs in schedules carrying lower penalties in order to deal with the reality of cost and administrative constraints that can become considerations in a state's prosecution of frequently-committed offenses, such as use of certain drugs. Further, a state may deviate from set scheduling mechanisms in handling a specific drug without changing the overall CSA scheduling in order to avoid decriminalizing a drug offense or dealing with a complicated legislative process. For example, in Michigan, dimethyltryptamine, lysergic acid diethylamide (LSD), peyote, mescaline, psilocin, and psilocybin, found in schedule I, are listed separately from other schedule I substances for penalty purposes. The penalty for use of these drugs is up to six months' incarceration and/or a $1,000 fine, whereas the penalty otherwise would be up on one year's incarceration and/or a $1,000 fine for these offenses. (See Table

Table 6
Michigan Penalties for Use Offenses

	First Offense	Second Offense	Subsequent Offenses
I/II narcotics	0-1; $2,000	---------	---------
I/II non-narcotics	0-1; $1,000	---------	---------
III	---------	---------	---------
IV	---------	---------	---------
V	---------	---------	---------
marijuana	0-90 days; $100	---------	---------
other: LSD, peyote, mescaline, dimethyltrptamine, psilocin,psilocybin	0-6 mo.; $1,000	---------	---------

Table 7
North Carolina Penalties for Possession Offenses

	First Offense	Second Offense	Subsequent Offenses
I	0-5; $5,000	---------	---------
II	0-2; $2,000	0-5	same
III	0-2; $2,000	0-5	same
IV	0-2; $2,000	0-5	same
V	0-6 mo.; $500	0-2; $2,000	same
VI marijuana			
$^{1}/_{2}$ - $1^{1}/_{2}$ oz.	0-30 days; $100	---------	---------
> $1^{1}/_{2}$ oz.	0-5;$5,000	---------	---------

6.) This special scheme for penalty purposes applies only to use and possession offenses; manufacturing, delivery, and sale offenses involving the above drugs trigger the same penalties as do other substances in the same schedule.

A fourth scheduling method used by some states is to list marijuana separately from other schedule I substances and to specify lesser penalties for offenses involving marijuana than the offense would trigger under the penalty scheme for offenses involving schedule I substances generally. Under these statutes, states either include marijuana under schedule I but establish a lower penalty for marijuana offenses than for other schedule I substance offenses, or the states create a schedule VI specifically for marijuana offenses that includes the desired lower penalties. For example, North Carolina had adopted the latter method, assigning marijuana offense penalties as shown in Table 7.

States operating under the fifth scheduling method have developed scheduling

Table 8
Hawaii Penalties for Possession Offenses

	First Offense	Second Offense	Subsequent Offenses
dangerous drugs			
$< \frac{1}{2}$ oz.	0-5; $5,000	same	0-10; $5,000
$\frac{1}{2}$ - 2 oz.	0-10; $10,000	same	0-20; $10,000
$> = 2$ oz.	0-20; $10,000	same	0-life; $10,000
harmful drugs			
$< \frac{1}{8}$ oz.	0-1; $1,000	same	same
$\frac{1}{8}$ - 1 oz.	0-10; $10,000	same	0-20, $10,000
$> = 1$ oz.	0-20; $10,000	same	0-life; $10,000
detrimental drugs			
$< \frac{1}{8}$ oz.	0-30 days; $500	same	same
$\frac{1}{8}$ - 1 oz.	0-1; $1,000	same	same
$> = 1$ oz.	0-5; $5,000	same	0-10; $5,000
marijuana			
< 1 oz.	0-30 days; $500	same	same
1 oz. - 2.2 lbs.	0-1; $1,000	same	same
$> = 2.2$ lbs.	0-5; $5,000	same	0-10; $5,000

schemes for classifying drugs that differ considerably from the federal approach. Under this method, states classify drugs by type, or by characteristic, such as potential for harm. Hawaii, for example, classifies drugs as dangerous, harmful, or detrimental, with a separate category for marijuana, as shown in Table 8. Another state employing this kind of approach is Arizona. The Arizona CSA, however, contains seven scheduling categories, including dangerous drugs, narcotic drugs, prescription-only drugs, marijuana, peyote, vapor-releasing substances, and precursor chemicals.

A variation of this approach is to combine some aspects of the federal scheduling scheme with classes of drugs. For example, Kansas has three schedules. The first includes federal schedules I and II narcotics; the second includes depressants, stimulants, hallucinogens, and federal schedule IV drugs; and the third includes federal schedule V controlled substances.

Other states retain a scheduling system for classifying drugs that includes some aspects of the federal schedules, but that assigns drugs to schedules according to penalties. Maine and Massachusetts, for example, have followed this method by establishing alternatives to the usual I through V scheduling system and assigning names or letters to delineate the different penalty groups. In Maine, the highest schedule (W) includes amphetamine, methamphetamine, phencyclidine (PCP), barbituric acid and its derivatives, cocaine, and opiates and their derivatives. The second schedule (X) includes other depressants, such as methaqualone and chlorhexadol, and many hallucinogens that are schedule I substances in other systems. Schedule Y consists of some lower level depressants such as codeine and diazepam (valium). The last schedule (Z) includes marijuana and prescription drugs not listed in the other schedules.

Massachusetts has adopted a similar formula, under which schedule A includes narcotics that would be schedule I substances in other systems, while schedule B includes amphetamines, LSD, PCP, and methaqualone. Many other hallucinogens, including peyote, mescaline, psilocybin, and tetrahydrocannabinol (THC), all of which are classified in schedule I under the federal and some states' CSA's, are placed in schedule C in Massachusetts.

States' varying responses to the federal CSA scheduling scheme highlight the advantages and disadvantages in adopting the federal approach to classification. Many states have chosen to rely on the federal government's perceived expertise in analyzing and classifying substances more effectively or efficiently than some states are able to by adopting statutory provisions requiring "automatic conformity" between state schedules and any scheduling changes made on the federal level. This type of provision permits states to control new substances, such as analogs, that otherwise would fall outside the CSA regulatory scheme without having to approve a regulatory or statutory change in each instance. The state of Arkansas, in fact, repealed its own CSA scheduling lists in 1979 and now updates its schedules in accordance with annual updates received from the DEA.

On the other hand, federal provisions may conflict with states' own penalty or administrative policies. Moreover, there is some concern that the "automatic conformity" provisions in some state statutes may raise constitutional issues regarding delegation of state authority to the federal government. The NCCUSL, which has considered this problem in revising its model CSA, has proposed an alternative to the "automatic conformity" clause that would establish a 30-day grace period within which any interested party may object to the placement of a substance in a given schedule.

Penalty Provisions

Almost all states have adopted the mechanism used in the federal CSA to establish two general categories of offenses—"possession" offenses and "manufacturing, delivery, sale" offenses—for penalty purposes. However, state CSA's also contain a number of additional provisions establishing specific types of offenses not included in the federal CSA or in all other state CSA's. For example, many states have adopted separate provisions to distinguish offenses involving possession or controlled substances with intent to distribute from ordinary possession offenses. A person is charged with this type of offense if he possesses an amount equal to or greater than the statutorily-specified minimum. Arkansas, for example, has designated floor amounts of heroin, cocaine, morphine, marijuana, and LSD that constitute an "intent to distribute" offense; the charge against a person who has less than the floor amount is possession of a controlled substance. An "intent" offense usually carries a penalty similar to those for manufacturing, distributing, creating, or dispensing controlled substances.

Another category of offense in at least 12 state CSA's is that created by so-called "use provisions," which make it a crime to use or be under the influence of a controlled substance. In some states, a prosecutor need not prove that the offender was under the influence of a specific controlled substance in order to obtain a conviction under such a provision; he need only establish that the person manifested the physical and physiological symptoms or reactions caused by use of any controlled substance.

A state CSA also may create degrees of severity of offenses based on the purity of controlled substances involved. For example, New Jersey provides that a person who manufactures a schedule I/II narcotic with less than 3.5 g. of the pure free base schedule I/II narcotic drug is subject to imprisonment for not more than 12 years, a fine of $25,000, or both. A person who manufactures a schedule I/II narcotic with 3.5 g. or more of the pure free base schedule I/II narcotic drug is subject to imprisonment for life, a fine of $25,000, or both. Similarly, under the federal CSA, the penalty for delivery of 500 g. of a mixture containing cocaine is the same as it is for delivery of a substance containing five grams or more of cocaine "base," the pure, unadulterated form of cocaine, popularly known as "crack" or "freebase."

In addition to delineating specific penalties for certain offenses, a number of state CSA's, like the federal CSA, provide for enhanced penalties for offenses involving particular drugs that are "targets" for enforcement activity. At least 24 states have singled out specific drugs that will trigger enhanced penalties for offenses involving specified amounts or more of those drugs. Enhanced penalty formulas range from relatively simple provisions, such as those of Tennessee, to complex formulas, such as those of Illinois.

In Tennessee, the penalties are the same for all offenses involving all targeted drugs except marijuana; penalties for the manufacture, delivery, sale, or possession with intent to distribute targeted drugs are 10 years to life in prison and/or a fine of up to $200,000. Penalties for offenses involving non-targeted Schedule I controlled substances are five to 15 years' imprisonment and/or a fine of up to $18,000. Penalties for similar offenses involving 70 lbs. or more of marijuana are 10 to 20 years' imprisonment and/or a fine of up to $200,000; the penalties for 10 to 70 lbs. of marijuana are four to 10 years' imprisonment and a fine of up to $10,000. (See Table 9.)

Illinois, on the other hand, has a two-tier scheme of enhanced penalties for offenses involving the manufacture, delivery, or possession with intent to manufacture or deliver targeted drugs. For example, the penalties for manufacture of at least 30 g. of cocaine are six to 30 years' imprisonment and/or a fine of up to $500,000; the penalties for manufacture of 10–30 g. of cocaine are four to 15 years' imprisonment and/or a fine of up to $250,000. By contrast, the penalties for manufacture of non-targeted schedule I and II narcotic drugs or for manufacture of less than 10 g. of cocaine are three to seven years' imprisonment and/or a fine of up to $200,000.

Illinois also has enhanced penalty provisions for simple possession of targeted drugs. For example, a person convicted of possession of less than 30 g. of cocaine could receive a sentence of one to three years' imprisonment and/or a

Table 9
Enhanced Penalties under Tennessee CSA

Targeted Substance	Amount Necessary to Trigger Enhanced Penalties	Penalty
Heroin	> = 15 g.	10-life; $200,000
Morphine	> = 15 g.	"
Hydromorphone	> = 5 g.	"
Lysergic Acid Diethylamide (LSD)	> = 5 g.	"
Cocaine	> = 30 g.	"
Pentazocine/Tripelennamine	> = 5 g.	"
Phencyclidine (PCP)	> = 30 g.	"
Barbituric Acid	> = 100 g.	"
Phenmetrazine	> = 50 g.	"
Amphetamine/Methamphetamine	> = 100 g.	"
Peyote	> = 1000 g.	"
Marijuana	> = 70 lbs.	10-20; $200,000

Non-targeted Substances		
Schedule I		5-15; $18,000
Schedule II		4-10; $15,000
Schedule VI (marijuana)	10-70 lbs.	4-10; $10,000

fine of up to $15,000, while a person convicted of possession of 30 g. or more of cocaine could receive a sentence of four to 15 years' imprisonment and/or a fine of up to $200,000. Although these penalty ranges are the same as for other schedule I and II narcotic drugs, a non-targeted drug would trigger the greater penalties only if the offender possessed 200 g. or more of the non-targeted narcotic substance. (See Table 10.)

In the 24 jurisdictions providing for enhanced penalties for offenses involving specified controlled substances, the drugs most frequently targeted are heroin, cocaine, PCP, and methamphetamine and/or amphetamine. (See Appendix B.)

Forfeiture

In addition to seeking enhanced penalties to punish major drug laws violators, many state and local enforcement officials, like their federal counterparts, increasingly are looking to forfeiture as a means of depriving drug laws offenders of the profits of their illegal activity. Forfeiture provisions vary widely from state to state, but most states' CSA's have incorporated some forfeiture provisions similar to those of the federal statute. Most states' CSA forfeiture proceedings are civil "in rem" actions, in which the forfeiture is an action against the property. In such actions, the state proves by a preponderance of the evidence that the property facilitated a CSA violation or that the owner obtained the property as a result of illegal activity. A few states have criminal forfeiture

Table 10
Enhanced Penalties under Illinois CSA

Targeted Drugs

Manufacture, Delivery, or
Possession with Intent to
Manufacture or Deliver

Targeted Substance	Tier I		Tier II	
	Amount Necessary to Trigger Enhanced Penalty	Penalty	Amount Necessary to Trigger Enhanced Penalty	Penalty
Heroin	10-15 g.	4-15; $250,000	> = 15 g.	6-30; $500,000
Cocaine	10-30 g.	"	> = 30 g.	"
Morphine	10-15 g.	"	> = 15 g.	"
Peyote	50-200 g.	"	> = 200 g.	"
Barbituric Acid	50-200 g.	"	> = 200 g.	"
Lysergic Acid Diethylamide (LSD)	5-15 g.	"	> = 15 g.	"
Pentazocine	10-30 g.	"	> = 30 g.	"
Methaqualone	10-30 g.	"	> = 30 g.	"
Phencyclidine (PCP)	10-30 g.	"	> = 30 g.	"
Amphetamine/Methamphetamine	50-200 g.	"	> = 200 g.	"

Possession

Heroin	> = 30 g.	4-15; $200,000
Cocaine	> = 30 g.	"
Morphine	> = 30 g.	"
Peyote	> = 200 g.	"
Barbituric Acid	> = 200 g.	"
Lysergic Acid Diethylamide (LSD)	> = 15 g.	"
Pentazocine	> = 30 g.	"
Methaqualone	> = 30 g.	"
Phencyclidine (PCP)	> = 30 g.	"
Amphetamine/Methamphetamine	> = 200 g.	"

provisions, which require that a prosecutor prove his case beyond a reasonable doubt or that the property owner be found guilty of the underlying offense leading to the forfeiture before forfeiture can proceed. In most states, forfeiture is a judicial proceeding; however, some state CSA's, like the federal statute, authorize administrative forfeiture of property under a certain value if no interested party contests the proceedings.

In most state CSA's, the list of forfeitable assets, similar to that in the federal CSA, includes such items as drug containers, conveyances, drug records, money and valuables, and proceeds traceable to violations of the CSA. Other forfeiture provisions relating to forfeitable property vary considerably, however. For example, numerous state CSA's provide for forfeiture of drug paraphernalia and imitation controlled substances, items not forfeitable under the federal CSA. On the other hand, only 17 states have made real property subject to forfeiture, as the federal forfeiture statute does.

Many states have adopted forfeiture provisions different from those of the federal statute to address specific state concerns. For example, several states authorize the forfeiture of a conveyance only in a case where the underlying offense is a felony or involves more than a designated amount of a controlled substance. In California, no vehicle may be subject to a forfeiture action if it is the defendant's immediate family's sole means of transportation, nor may a conveyance be forfeited if the offense involved less than one-half ounce of heroin, one ounce or less of any other schedule I or II controlled substance, or one pound or less of marijuana, peyote, or psilocybin. Under federal law, by contrast, a conveyance may be forfeited in any case where any usable amount of a controlled substance is involved.

Another important difference among the forfeiture laws is the formulas for distribution of forfeited assets or their proceeds. Although all states that provide for forfeiture require that proceeds first be used to pay for costs of activity associated with forfeiture proceedings, such as the seizure of forfeited items, the storage and maintenance of the property, and the advertising and sale of the property, states differ in the ways that they allocate funds remaining after coverage of costs. Many jurisdictions provide that the remainder be deposited into the state or county general fund of the seizing agency. Others provide that the funds be applied towards specific programs, such as state drug education or drug rehabilitation programs, or for other purposes unrelated to drugs or law enforcement. Others have set up special drug enforcement funds, monies from which help pay for enforcement of CSA provisions. Some states have no provisions addressing distribution of proceeds.

Provisions Relating to Minors

In addition to forfeiture, a major focus of state drug laws enforcement activity in recent years has been offenses involving minors. Of the 51 jurisdictions covered in this *Guide*, all but four have modified CSA's recently to provide for increased penalties for offenses involving distribution to minors of some controlled substance or other contraband, such as imitation controlled substances or drug paraphernalia.

Penalty provisions for distribution to minors vary considerably from state to state. Many states have followed the guidance of the UCSA, under which increased penalties for sales to minors apply only when an offender is 18 years old or older and the buyer is under 18 and is at least three years the seller's junior. Others have made such provisions applicable to offenders over 21, or to offenders over 18 where the buyer is under 18, regardless of the age difference between buyer and seller. Under proposed changes in the UCSA, the model language would alter the age difference criteria slightly to make the distribution to minors provision applicable where the buyer is "at least two years the seller's junior."

Schemes for determining penalties also vary significantly among jurisdictions. Many states have differing penalties for offenders who distribute narcotics and those who distribute non-narcotics; others base penalties on the schedule placement of the drug involved in the offense, often authorizing a lesser sentence for offenses involving marijuana. Determining the applicability of such provisions can be complex. In Delaware, for example, the recommended statutory penalty for distribution of any non-narcotic to a person who is 16 years old is a sentence of incarceration of six months to 15 years. However, the statute also provides that if the seller is under 21, the buyer is over 15, the seller was not making a profit or assisting another to make a profit, and the buyer had been acquainted with the seller for at least one year prior to the incident, there is no mandatory minimum term of incarceration, and the maximum sentence is two years' incarceration and up to a $1,000 fine. Other states, like the federal government, double the term and fine that otherwise would be applicable for distribution of the substance; some establish set terms with stiff mandatory minimum terms and fines.

Provisions regarding distribution of drugs in or near schools, or so-called schoolhouse provisions, also are becoming popular in the states. At least 10 states—Alaska, California, Illinois, Louisiana, Minnesota, New York, South Carolina, Utah, Virginia, and Wisconsin—have adopted some type of "schoolyard" provision that provides for enhanced penalties for sale or distribution of drugs in or near schools. Although based on the federal or UCSA provisions, these provisions vary regarding the types of schools, the extent of the area near schools covered by the provisions, the drugs targeted, and the age groups involved. Wisconsin's provision, for example, applies only to those who distribute cocaine within 1,000 feet of a public or private school building, while Alaska's applies to any person over 18 years who possesses any controlled substance on school grounds. California's law covers distribution to minors on a school ground or at any school-related activity. Louisiana, like the federal statute, includes post-secondary schools in its law, but other states do not. South Carolina's law stipulates that any distribution of a controlled substance within a half mile of any elementary, middle, or high school is a separate offense unto itself; most other states either have limited applicability of schoolyard provisions to school grounds or have adopted language similar to that of the federal CSA and the UCSA, limiting the scope of the provision to activity "within 1,000 feet" of a school.

A number of states also have taken the extra step of providing for increased penalties for offenses involving distribution of imitation controlled substances and drug paraphernalia to minors. At least 18 states have provided for increased penalties for distribution of imitation controlled substances to minors, and 27 jurisdictions have done the same for distribution of drug paraphernalia to minors.

There has been less state activity to date to address the problem of drug dealers' use of minors to distribute controlled substances. Knowing that minors generally receive less severe sentences than adults for CSA violations and thus are unlikely to implicate suppliers in exchange for lighter sentences, an increasing number of drug traffickers are employing minors to sell and distribute their drugs. While federal provisions of the 1986 anti-drug abuse act address the problem by making it unlawful for any person 18 or older to hire or use any person under 18 to violate any part of the CSA or to assist in avoiding detection for any offense under the CSA, only three other jurisdictions—California, the District of Columbia, and Maryland—specifically prohibit the use of minors for distributing controlled substances. California's law applies to any adult who encourages or intimidates a minor to violate any part of the controlled substances act regarding all narcotics, methaqualone or mecloqualone, mescaline, peyote, marijuana, or tetrahydrocannabinol (THC). The District of Columbia's law applies to offenders who enlist, hire, or encourage anyone under 18 to sell or distribute controlled substances, and it calls for penalties equivalent to those applicable if the adult himself had sold the drugs, plus up to an additional 10 years' incarceration. Maryland's provision is similar to that of the District of Columbia, but the maximum permissible penalty under Maryland law is 10 years' imprisonment and a $10,000 fine.

Drug Paraphernalia Provisions

Provisions to counter the sale and distribution of drug paraphernalia also have been a significant part of recent changes in state CSA's. Since the DEA drafted the Model Drug Paraphernalia Act in 1979, 47 states have passed some type of paraphernalia provision, almost all following the language of the model act, and the Congress passed a federal paraphernalia act as part of the 1986 anti–drug abuse law. These acts typically prohibit the manufacture, sale, possession, distribution, or advertisement of drug paraphernalia, but few prohibit only distribution.

Although similar in many respects, states' provisions vary in the assessment of penalties for violations of the law. In Idaho, for example, distribution of paraphernalia is punishable by up to nine years' incarceration and/or up to a $30,000 fine, while a similar offense in Kentucky is punishable by up to 90 days' incarceration and/or up to a $250 fine, and in Maryland and South Carolina, by a fine of up to $500.

In the 27 states that have adopted enhanced penalties for offenses involving distribution of drug paraphernalia to minors, such penalties also vary widely, and some provisions permit avoidance of penalties altogether. In the state of Ohio, for example, the distribution of marijuana paraphernalia to a person under 18 is prohibited, and a violation is punishable by up to six months' incarceration and/or up to a $1,000 fine. However, if the violator can show that a parent accompanied the minor to whom the offender sold the contraband, there is no penalty.

Imitation Controlled Substances Provisions

Imitation controlled substances are non-controlled substances that are sold or otherwise distributed as controlled substances. Often the non-controlled substance is caffeine or ephedrine, found in diet pills and sold over the counter in drugstores. The imitation controlled substances often look like legitimate controlled substances, with the same shapes, sizes, colors, and manufacturer's markings found on the legitimate product.

All but four states have provisions addressing imitation controlled substances, and in developing these provisions, most states have followed the DEA's Model Imitation Controlled Substances Act. Although a few states have treated imitation and counterfeit controlled substances similarly for definition and penalty purposes, an important distinction between imitation and counterfeit controlled substances is that an imitation controlled substance is not a controlled substance at all, while a counterfeit controlled substance is a controlled, but illegally manufactured, substance. A prime example of a counterfeit controlled substance is the proliferation of illegally manufactured methaqualone (quaaludes) distributed in the form of tablets stamped with the legitimate manufacturer's markings.

Penalties generally are less severe for offenses involving imitation controlled substances than for those involving counterfeit controlled substances. In both Delaware and North Carolina, however, the penalty for delivery of imitation controlled substances is the same as it is for whatever controlled substance the seller represented the product to be. At least 18 states that have imitation controlled substance provisions have enhanced penalties for distribution of these substances to minors. For example, Rhode Island provides that any person at least 18 years of age who distributes an imitation controlled substance to a person at least three years his junior is subject to a term of incarceration twice that otherwise provided for in the statute.

Safehouse Provisions

States, like the federal government, also have had to contend with drug manufacturers' and distributors' increased use of so-called safehouses or rock houses in recent years. At least 10 states have adopted some type of safehouse provision, but a number of these differ from federal law in the scope of activities covered; some states, for example, prohibit only an individual's "presence" at a place where controlled substances are stored, manufactured, or used. California's rock house provision, on the other hand, goes one step further than federal law by establishing enhanced penalties for anyone who operates any such place and purposely fortifies the building, room, or house against law enforcement entry.

Education and Treatment Provisions

Prevention education for potential drug users and treatment for drug abusers have been a major focus of state legislators in recent years. In this area, many states have adopted the language of the UCSA, which provides for educational programs designed to prevent and deter misuse and abuse of controlled substances. The UCSA provision is intended to include educating the pharmaceutical industry, as well as interested groups and the general public, about the dangers of abuse and ways to reduce it. The majority of the provisions also encourage research on misuse and abuse.

A number of states have developed this concept further in attempts to stop drug abuse problems early. Under the CSA's of both Colorado and Delaware, for example, if a court finds that a person convicted of use is physically or psychologically dependent on the substance, the court must place him in a rehabilitation program. Under North Carolina law, a first offender convicted of possession may be placed in a drug education program as part of probation. In most instances, an offender who successfully completes such a program may have his record expunged.

In order to help fund these programs, some state CSA's provide for use of monies from state forfeiture funds to administer education and rehabilitation/ prevention programs.

Miscellaneous Provisions

Many jurisdictions have gone beyond what the federal law sets out as a model for controlling drug trafficking and drug-related activity by passing their own innovative provisions.

Several states provide that first offenders may escape from harsh mandatory minimum penalties if the defendant assists in the apprehension of any of his accomplices.

Maine recently passed a provision that anyone convicted of any drug offense shall be fined, in addition to the regular fine, an amount equal to the value of the drug.

Although generally found under revenue codes rather than in CSA's, stamp taxes on controlled substances that are possessed unlawfully have been approved in a few states. In Minnesota, for example, the tax is imposed at the rate of $3.50 for each gram of marijuana and $200 for each gram of any other controlled substance sold by weight, and $2,000 for each 50-dosage unit of a controlled substance not sold by weight. Failure to pay the tax results in a 100 percent penalty in addition to the tax, as well as liability for criminal penalties of not more than five years' incarceration and/or a fine up to $10,000. Illinois' provisions, enacted in fall 1987, are modelled after the Minnesota law. Arizona also has adopted a similar scheme under its tax laws, and South Dakota had a drug tax until the state supreme court declared it unconstitutional in 1986.

Nevada provides that if a death results from the sale of a controlled substance, the seller shall be prosecuted for murder, in addition to any drug-related offenses.

Rhode Island provides that any person who accepts a plea bargain in relation to an offense involving the sale of drugs shall be assessed an additional $1,000 fine, to be deposited into the state's forfeited property account.

Tennessee authorizes prosecutors to seek a ''habitual drug offender'' charge against any person convicted of engaging in repeated acts of manufacturing or distributing controlled substances. The punishment for conviction of the charge is 10 years to life in prison and a fine of not more than $200,000.

Washington authorizes parents of a minor to whom a controlled substance is sold to bring a cause of action against the seller of such drug to recover damages to the minor. Damages include the cost of treatment and rehabilitation of the minor's drug dependency, the proceeds received from the sale of the substance, and reasonable attorney fees.

Table 11
Comparison of Penalties for Use, Possession, Sale—First Offense

State/Schedule	Use Penalties	Possession Penalties	Sale Penalties
Alabama			
I	–	1-10;$5,000	2-20;$10,000
II	–	1-10;$5,000	2-20;$10,000
III	–	1-10;$5,000	2-20;$10,000
IV	–	1-10;$5,000	2-20;$10,000
V	–	1-10;$5,000	2-20;$10,000
marijuana	–	0-1;$2,000	2-20;$10,000
Alaska			
IA	–	0-5;$50,000	5-20;$50,000
IIA	–	0-5;$50,000	0-10;$50,000
IIIA	–	0-5;$5,000-$50,000	0-10;$50,000
IVA	–	0-5;$5,000-$50,000	0-5;$50,000
VA	–	0-5;$5,000-$50,000	0-5;$50,000
VIA	90 days;$1,000	0-5;$100-$50,000	0-5;$100-$50,000
Arizona			
dangerous drugs	2-5;$1,000-$150,000	2-5;$1,000-150,000	$3^{3}/_{4}$-10;$1,000-$150,000
narcotic drugs	2-5;$2,000-$150,000	2-5;$2,000-$150,000	$5^{1}/_{4}$-14;$2,000-$150,000
prescription-only drugs	0-6mo.;$1,000	0-6mo.;$1,000	$0-1^{9}/_{10}$;$1,000
marijuana	9mo.-5;$750-$150,000	9mo.-5;$750-$150,000	1-10;$750-$150,000
peyote	$9mo.-1^{9}/_{10}$;$150,000	$9mo.;1^{9}/_{10}$;$150,000	$9mo.-1^{9}/_{10}$;$150,000
vapor-releasing substances	$1-2^{1}/_{2}$;$150,000	$1-2^{1}/_{2}$;$150,000	$1-2^{1}/_{2}$;$150,000
precursor chemicals	$5^{1}/_{4}$-14;$150,000	$5^{1}/_{4}$-14;$150,000	$5^{1}/_{4}$-14;$150,000
Arkansas			
I/II narcotics	–	2-5;$10,000	10-40;$25,000-$250,000
I/II non-narcotics	–	2-5;$10,000	5-40;$15,000-$100,000
III	–	0-1;$1,000	5-40;$15,000-$100,000
IV	–	0-1;$1,000	3-40;$10,000-$50,000
V	–	0-1;$1,000	3-40;$10,000-$50,000
VI	–	0-1;$1,000	4-30;$15,000-$100,000
California			
I/II narcotics	–	16mo.-4;$20,000	3-5;$20,000
I/II non-narcotics	–	0-3	2-4
III/IV/V narcotics	–	16mo.-4;$20,000	3-5;$20,000
III/IV/V non-narcotics	–	0-3	2-4
marijuana	–	0-3;$100-$20,000	2-4;$100-$20,000
Colorado			
I	1-4;$1,000-$100,000	4-16;$3,000-$750,000	4-16;$3,000-$750,000
II	1-4;$1,000-$100,000	4-16;$3,000-$750,000	4-16;$3,000-$750,000
III	0-2;$500	2-8;$2,000-$500,000	2-8;$2,000-$500,000
IV	0-2;$500	1-4;$1,000-$100,000	1-4;$1,000-$100,000
V	0-2;$500	0-2;$500	0-2;$500
marijuana	1-4;$1,000-$100,000	15days-4;$100-$100,000	2-8;$2,000-$500,000
Connecticut			
I/II narcotics	–	0-7;$50,000	0-15;$50,000
I/II non-narcotics	–	0-1;$1,000	0-7;$25,000
III	–	0-1;$1,000	0-7;$25,000
IV	–	0-1;$1,000	0-7;$25,000
V	–	0-1;$1,000	0-7;$25,000
marijuana	–	0-5;$1,000-$2,000	0-7;$25,000
other hallucinogens	–	0-5;$2,000	0-15;$50,000

Table 11 (continued)

State/Schedule	Use Penalties	Possession Penalties	Sale Penalties
Delaware			
I/II narcotics	0-5;$3,000	0-5;$3,000	0-30;$5,000-$100,000
I/II non-narcotics	0-2;$500	0-2;$500	0-10;$1,000-$10,000
III	0-2;$500	0-2;$500	0-10;$1,000-$10,000
IV	0-2;$500	0-2;$500	0-10;$1,000-$10,000
V	0-2;$500	0-2;$500	0-10;$1,000-$10,000
marijuana	0-2;$500	0-2;$500	0-10;$1,000-$10,000
District of Columbia			
I/II narcotics	—	0-1;$1,000	4-15;$100,000
I/II non-narcotics	—	0-1;$1,000	20mo.-5;$50,000
III	—	0-1;$1,000	20mo.-5;$50,000
IV	—	0-1;$1,000	0-3;$25,000
V	—	0-1;$1,000	0-1;$10,000
PCP/PCP precursors	—	0-1;$1,000	4-25;$200,000
Florida			
I narcotics	—	0-30;$5,000-$10,000	0-30;$10,000
I non-narcotics	—	0-5;$5,000	0-5;$5,000
II	—	0-5;$5,000	0-15;$10,000
III	—	0-5;$5,000	0-5;$5,000
IV	—	0-5;$5,000	0-5;$5,000
V	—	0-5;$5,000	0-1;$1,000
marijuana	—	0-5;$1,000-$5,000	0-5;$5,000
Georgia			
I	—	2-15	5-30
II	—	2-15	5-30
III	—	1-5	1-10
IV	—	1-5	1-10
V	—	1-5	1-10
marijuana	—	0-10;$1,000	1-10
Hawaii			
dangerous drugs	—	0-20;$5,000-$10,000	0-20;$10,000
harmful drugs	—	0-20;$1,000-$10,000	0-20;$10,000
detrimental drugs	—	0-5;$500-$5,000	0-5;$1,000-$5,000
marijuana	—	0-5;$500-$5,000	0-5;$1,000-$5,000
Idaho			
I narcotics	—	0-3;$5,000	0-life;$25,000
I non-narcotics	—	0-1;$1,000	0-5;$15,000
II	—	0-3;$5,000	0-life;$25,000
III	—	0-1;$1,000	0-5;$15,000
IV	—	0-1;$1,000	0-3;$10,000
V	—	0-1;$1,000	0-1;$5,000
marijuana	—	0-5;$1,000-$10,000	0-5;$15,000
Illinois			
I/II narcotics	—	1-15;$15,000-$200,000	3-7;$200,000
I/II non-narcotics	—	1-3;$15,000	2-5;$150,000
III	—	1-3;$15,000	2-5;$125,000
IV	—	1-3;$15,000	2-5;$100,000
V	—	1-3;$15,000	2-5;$75,000
marijuana	—	30days-5;$500-$10,000	6mo.-7;$500-$100,000
Indiana			
I/II narcotics	—	2-5;$10,000	10-30;$10,000
I/II non-narcotics	—	2;$10,000	10;$10,000
III	—	2;$10,000	10;$10,000
IV	—	2;$10,000	5;$10,000
V	—	2;$10,000	2;$10,000
marijuana	—	0-2;$5,000-$10,000	0-5;$5,000-$10,000

369

Table 11 (continued)

State/Schedule	Use Penalties	Possession Penalties	Sale Penalties
Iowa			
I/II narcotics	–	0-1;$1,000	3$^1/_3$-10;$5,000
I/II non-narcotics	–	0-1;$1,000	1$^2/_3$-5;$1,000
III	–	0-1;$1,000	1$^2/_3$-5;$1,000
IV	–	0-1;$1,000	0-1;$1,000
V	–	0-1;$1,000	0-1;$1,000
marijuana	–	0-6mo.;$1,000	0-10;$1,000-$5,000
Kansas			
I/II narcotics	–	1-20;$10,000	1-20;$10,000
depressants,	–	0-1;$2,500	0-1;$2,500
stimulants,			
hallucinogens, and			
IV			
V	–	0-1;$2,500	0-20;$2,500-$10,000
Kentucky			
I/II narcotics	–	1-5;$3,000-$5,000	5-10;$5,000-$10,000
I/II non-narcotics	–	0-1;$500	1-5;$3,000-$5,000
III	–	0-1;$500	1-5;$3,000-$5,000
IV	–	0-1;$500	0-1;$500
V	–	0-1;$500	0-1;$500
marijuana	–	0-1;$250-$5,000	0-10;$500-$10,000
Louisiana			
I narcotics	–	4-10;$5,000	5-30;$15,000
I non-narcotics	–	0-10;$5,000	0-10;$15,000
II narcotics	–	0-5;$5,000	5-30;$15,000
II non-narcotics	–	0-5;$5,000	0-10;$15,000
III	–	0-5;$5,000	0-10;$15,000
IV	–	0-5;$5,000	0-10;$15,000
V	–	0-5;$5,000	0-5;$5,000
marijuana	–	0-10;$500-$5,000	0-10;$15,000
PCP	–	5-20;$5,000	0-10;$15,000
pentazocine	–	2-20;$5,000	7-10;$15,000
Maine			
W	–	0-1;$1,000	0-10;$2,500-$10,000
X	–	0-1;$1,000	0-5;$1,000-$2,500
Y	–	0-6mo.;$500	0-1;$1,000
Z	–	$50-$1,000	0-1;$1,000
marijuana	–	$50-$1,000	0-10;$1,000-$10,000
Maryland			
I/II narcotics	–	0-4;$25,000	0-20;$25,000
I/II non-narcotics	–	0-4;$25,000	0-5;$15,000
III	–	0-4;$25,000	0-5;$15,000
IV	–	0-4;$25,000	0-5;$15,000
V	–	0-4;$25,000	0-5;$15,000
marijuana	–	0-1;$1,000	0-5;$15,000
PCP	–	0-4;$25,000	0-20;$20,000
Massachusetts			
A	–	0-1;$1,000	10;$1,000-$10,000
B	–	0-1;$1,000	10;$1,000-$10,000
C	–	0-1;$1,000	5;$500-$5,000
D	–	0-1;$1,000	0-2;$500-$5,000
E	–	0-6mo.;$500	0-9mo.;$250-$2,500
marijuana	–	0-6mo.;$500	0-2;$500-$5,000

Table 11 (continued)

State/Schedule	Use Penalties	Possession Penalties	Sale Penalties
Michigan			
I/II narcotics	0–1;$2,000	0–life;$2,000	0–life;$25,000
I/II non-narcotics	0–1;$1,000	0–2;$2,000	0–7;$5,000
III	–	0–2;$2,000	0–7;$5,000
IV	–	0–2;$2,000	0–4;$2,000
V	–	0–2;$2,000	0–2;$2,000
marijuana	0–90days;$100	0–1;$1,000	0–7;$5,000
dimethyltrptamine	0–6mo.;$1,000	0–2;$2,000	0–7;$5,000
LSD, peyote, mescaline,psilocin psilocybin	0–6mo.;$1,000	0–1;$1,000	0–7;$5,000
Minnesota			
I/II narcotics	–	0–5;$10,000	0–20;$40,000–$60,000
I/II non-narcotics	–	0–3;$5,000	0–5;$30,000
III	–	0–3;$5,000	0–5;$30,000
IV	–	0–3;$5,000	0–3;$20,000
V	–	0–1;$5,000	0–1;$3,000
Mississippi			
I	–	0–3;$1,000–$30,000	0–30;$1,000–$1,000,000
II	–	0–3;$1,000–$30,000	0–30;$1,000–$1,000,000
III	–	0–1;$5,000	0–20;$1,000–$250,000
IV	–	0–1;$5,000	0–20;$1,000–$250,000
V	–	0–1;$5,000	0–10;$1,000–$150,000
marijuana	–	0–20;$1,000–$1,000,000	0–30;$1,000–$1,000,000
Missouri			
I	–	6mo.-20;$5,000	5-life;$5,000
II	–	6mo.-20;$5,000	5-life;$5,000
III	–	0–10;$5,000	0–10;$5,000
IV	–	0–10;$5,000	0–10;$5,000
V	–	0–10;$5,000	0–10;$5,000
marijuana	–	0–5;$1,000	5-life;$5,000
Montana			
I	–	0–5;$50,000	1-life;$50,000
II	–	0–5;$50,000	1-life;$50,000
III	–	0–5;$50,000	1-life;$50,000
IV	–	0–5;$50,000	1-life;$50,000
V	–	0–5;$50,000	1-life;$50,000
marijuana	–	6mo.-5;$100–$50,000	1-life;$50,000
opiates	–	2-5;$50,000	2-life;$50,000
Nebraska			
I	3mo.;$500	0–5;$10,000	0–20;$25,000
II	3mo.;$500	0–5;$10,000	0–20;$25,000
III	3mo.;$500	0–5;$10,000	0–20;$25,000
IV	3mo.;$500	0–5;$10,000	0–5;$10,000
V	3mo.;$500	0–5;$10,000	0–5;$10,000
marijuana	–	0–5;$100–$10,000	–
Nevada			
I	1–6;$5,000	1–6;$5,000	1-20 or life;$20,000
II	1–6;$5,000	1–6;$5,000	1-20 or life;$20,000
III	1–6;$5,000	1–6;$5,000	1-10 or life;$10,000
IV	1–6;$5,000	1–6;$5,000	1-10 or life;$10,000
V	0–1;$1,000	0–1;$1,000	1-10 or life;$10,000

Table 11 (continued)

State/Schedule	Use Penalties	Possession Penalties	Sale Penalties
New Hampshire			
I narcotics	—	0-7;$5,000	0-10;$125,000
I non-narcotics	—	0-1;$1,000	0-10;$125,000
II narcotics	—	0-7;$5,000	0-10;$125,000
II non-narcotics	—	0-1;$1,000	0-10;$125,000
III narcotics	—	0-7;$5,000	0-5;$50,000
III non-narcotics	—	0-1;$1,000	0-5;$50,000
IV narcotics	—	0-7;$5,000	0-3;$25,000
IV non-narcotics	—	0-1;$1,000	0-3;$25,000
V narcotics	—	0-7;$5,000	0-1;$10,000
V non-narcotics	—	0-1;$1,000	0-1;$10,000
marijuana	—	0-7;$2,000	0-10;$50,000-$125,000
New Jersey			
I/II narcotics	May have driver's license	0-7;$15,000	0-life;$25,000
I/II non-narcotics	suspended for up to two years.	0-5;$15,000	0-5;$15,000
III	•	0-5;$15,000	0-5;$15,000
IV	•	0-5;$15,000	0-5;$15,000
V	•	0-1;$5,000	0-1;$5,000
marijuana	•	0-6;$250-$15,000	0-5;$15,000
New Mexico			
I/II narcotics	—	0-18mo.;$5,000	0-9;$10,000
I/II non-narcotics	—	0-1;$500-$1,000	0-3;$5,000
III	—	0-1;$500-$1,000	0-3;$5,000
IV	—	0-1;$500-$1,000	0-3;$5,000
V	—	—	6mo.-1;$100-$500
marijuana	—	0-1;$50-$15,000	0-3;$5,000
New York			
I	—	0-1;$1,000	0-7;$5,000
II	—	0-1;$1,000	0-7;$5,000
III	—	0-1;$1,000	0-7;$5,000
IV	—	0-1;$1,000	0-7;$5,000
V	—	0-1;$1,000	0-7;$5,000
North Carolina			
I	—	0-5;$5,000	0-10;fine
II	—	0-2;$2,000	0-10;fine
III	—	0-2;$2,000	0-5;fine
IV	—	0-2;$2,000	0-5;fine
V	—	0-6mo.;$500	0-5;fine
VI	—	0-5;$100-$5,000	0-5;fine
North Dakota			
I/II narcotics	—	0-5;$5,000	0-20;$10,000
I/II non-narcotics	—	0-5;$5,000	0-10;$10,000
III	—	0-5;$5,000	0-10;$10,000
IV	—	0-5;$5,000	0-5;$5,000
V	—	0-5;$5,000	0-1;$1,000
marijuana	—	0-5;$1,000-$5,000	0-20;$10,000
Ohio			
I	—	0-6;$1,000	3-15;$7,500
II	—	0-6;$1,000	3-15;$7,500
III	—	0-60days;$500	1-10;$2,500
IV		0-60days;$500	1-10;$2,500
V	—	0-60days;$500	1-10;$2,500
marijuana	—	0-30days;$100-$250	$1/_2$-5;$2,000

Table 11 (continued)

State/Schedule	Use Penalties	Possession Penalties	Sale Penalties
Oklahoma			
I/II narcotics	–	2-10	5-20;$20,000
I/II non-narcotics	–	2-10	2-10;$5,000
III	–	0-1	2-10;$5,000
IV	–	0-1	2-10;$1,000
V	–	0-1	0-5;$1,000
marijuana	–	0-1	2-10;$5,000
Oregon			
I	–	0-10;$100,000	0-20;$10,000
II	–	0-5;$100,000	0-10;$100,000
III	–	0-1;$2,500	0-5;$100,000
IV	–	0-30days;$500	0-6mo.;$1,000
V	–	$250	0-30days;$500
marijuana	–	0-10;$100-$100,000	0-10;$100,000
Pennsylvania			
I/II narcotics	–	0-1;$5,000	0-15;$250,000
I/II non-narcotics	–	0-1;$5,000	0-5;$15,000
III	–	0-1;$5,000	0-5;$15,000
IV	–	0-1;$5,000	0-3;$10,000
V	–	0-1;$5,000	0-1;$5,000
marijuana	–	0-1;$500-$5,000	0-5;$15,000
Rhode Island			
I	–	0-3;$5,000	0-life;$500,000
II	–	0-3;$5,000	0-life;$500,000
III	–	0-3;$5,000	0-20;$40,000
IV	–	0-3;$5,000	0-20;$40,000
V	–	0-3;$5,000	0-1;$10,000
marijuana	–	0-1;$500	0-30;$100,000
South Carolina			
I/II narcotics	–	0-2;$5,000	0-5;$25,000
I/II non-narcotics	–	0-6mo.;$1,000	0-5;$5,000
III	–	0-6mo.;$1,000	0-5;$5,000
IV	–	0-6mo.;$1,000	0-3;$3,000
V	–	0-6mo.;$1,000	0-1;$1,000
marijuana	–	0-2;$100-$5,000	0-5;$5,000
South Dakota			
I	–	0-5;$5,000	30days-10;$10,000
II	–	0-5;$5,000	30days-10;$10,000
III	–	0-5;$5,000	30days-5;$5,000
IV	–	0-5;$5,000	30days-2;$2,000
marijuana	–	0-10;$100-$10,000	15days-10;$1,000-$10,000
Tennessee			
I	–	0-1;$1,000	5-15;$18,000
II	–	0-1;$1,000	4-10;$15,000
III	–	0-1;$1,000	3-8;$10,000
IV	–	0-1;$1,000	2-5;$7,000
V	–	0-1;$1,000	1-5;$5,000
VI	–	0-1;$1,000	1-10;$3,000-$10,000
VII	–	0-1;$1,000	1-5;$3,000
Texas			
group 1	–	2-99,life;$10,000-$100,000	5-99,life;$20,000-$250,000
group 2	–	2-99,life;$5,000-$100,000	2-99,life;$10,000-$100,000
group 3	–	0-99,life;$2,000-$100,000	2-99,life;$5,000-$100,000
group 4	–	0-99,life;$1,000-$100,000	2-99,life;$5,000-$100,000
marijuana	–	0-99,life;$1,000-$100,000	0-99,life;$1,000-$100,000

373

Table 11 (continued)

State/Schedule	Use Penalties	Possession Penalties	Sale Penalties
Utah			
I/II narcotics	—	0-6mo.;$299	1-15;$15,000
I/II non-narcotics	—	0-6mo.;$299	1-10;$10,000
III	—	0-6mo.;$299	0-10;$10,000
IV	—	0-6mo.;$299	0-5;$5,000
V	—	0-6mo.;$299	0-1;$1,000
marijuana	—	0-6mo.;$299	0-5;$5,000
Vermont			
depressants, stimulants,narcotics hallucinogens	—	0-1;$1,000	0-5;$10,000
V	—	0-6mo.;$500	0-5;$10,000
marijuana	—	0-6mo.;$500	0-5;$10,000
Virginia			
I/II	—	1-10;$1,000	5-40;$100,000
III	—	0-1;$1,000	0-1;$1,000
IV	—	0-6mo.;$500	0-1;$1,000
V	—	$500	0-1;$1,000
marijuana	—	0-10;$500-$1,000	0-30;$1,000-$10,000
Washington			
I/II narcotics	—	0-5;$10,000	0-10;$25,000
I/II non-narcotics	—	0-5;$10,000	0-5;$10,000
III	—	0-5;$10,000	0-5;$10,000
IV	—	0-5;$10,000	0-5;$10,000
V	—	0-5;$10,000	0-5;$10,000
marijuana	—	0-5;$250-$10,000	0-5;$10,000
West Virginia			
I/II narcotics	—	90days-6mo.;$1,000	1-15;$25,000
I/II non-narcotics	—	90days-6mo.;$1,000	1-5;$15,000
III	—	90days-6mo.;$1,000	1-5;$15,000
IV	—	90days-6mo.;$1,000	1-3;$10,000
V	—	90days-6mo.;$1,000	6mo.-1;$5,000
Wisconsin			
I/II narcotics	—	0-1;$5,000	0-15;$25,000
I/II non-narcotics	—	0-30days;$500	0-5;$15,000
III	—	0-30days;$500	0-5;$15,000
IV	—	0-30days;$500	0-3;$10,000
V	—	0-30days;$500	0-1;$5,000
Wyoming			
I/II narcotics	0-90days;$100	0-6mo.;$750	0-20;$25,000
I/II non-narcotics	0-90days;$100	0-6mo.;$750	0-10;$10,000
III	0-90days;$100	0-6mo.;$750	0-10;$10,000
IV	—	0-6mo.;$750	0-2;$2,500
V	—	0-6mo.;$750	0-1;$1,000

Table 12
Drugs Triggering Enhanced Penalties under Controlled Substances Acts

JURISDICTION	None	Heroin	Cocaine	Phencyclidine (PCP)	Meth-/Amphetamine	Meth-/Meclo-qualone	Marijuana	OTHER
ALABAMA		■	■			■	■	hydromorphone, opium
ALASKA	■							
ARIZONA	■							
ARKANSAS	■							
CALIFORNIA		■	■	■	■			
COLORADO			■					
CONNECTICUT	■							
DELAWARE		■	■	■	■		■	morphine
DISTRICT OF COLUMBIA				■				
FLORIDA		■	■	■			■	
GEORGIA		■	■			■		morphine, opium
HAWAII		■	■					morphine
IDAHO	■							
ILLINOIS		■	■	■	■	■		LSD, peyote, pentazocine
INDIANA	■							
IOWA	■							
KANSAS	■							
KENTUCKY	■							
LOUISIANA			■	■			■	pentazocine
MAINE		■						
MARYLAND		■	■	■	■	■	■	LSD, morphine
MASSACHUSETTS		■	■	■			■	
MICHIGAN	■							
MINNESOTA				■				schedule I hallucinogens (except marijuana)
MISSISSIPPI							■	
MISSOURI	■							
MONTANA	■							
NEBRASKA	■							
NEVADA	■							
NEW HAMPSHIRE		■	■	■			■	LSD
NEW JERSEY	■							
NEW MEXICO				■				
NEW YORK	■							
NORTH CAROLINA		■	■	■		■	■	opium derivatives
NORTH DAKOTA	■							
OHIO	■							
OKLAHOMA		■	■	■	■		■	LSD
OREGON	■							
PENNSYLVANIA			■			■		
RHODE ISLAND	■							
SOUTH CAROLINA		■	■			■	■	
SOUTH DAKOTA	■							
TENNESSEE		■	■	■	■		■	morphine, LSD, hydromorphone, pentazocine, tripelennamine
TEXAS	■							
UTAH	■							
VERMONT	■							
VIRGINIA	■							
WASHINGTON		■						
WEST VIRGINIA	■							
WISCONSIN			■					
WYOMING	■							
FEDERAL		■	■	■			■	LSD

Table 13
Forfeitable Assets under Controlled Substances Acts

JURISDICTION	Controlled Substances	Materials, products, equipment used for manufacturing, compounding, processing, delivering, dispensing, distributing, importing, or exporting any controlled substances	Books, records, research, including formulas, microfilm, tapes, and data used or intended for use in the manufacture or distribution of a controlled substance	Conveyances used to facilitate the manufacture, dispensing, or distribution of a controlled substance	Drug paraphernalia	Monies or things of value used or intended for use in the procurement, manufacture, compounding, processing, delivery, or distribution of any controlled substance	Proceeds from monies or sale of things of value used or intended for use in the procurement, manufacture, compounding, processing, delivery, or distribution of any controlled substance	Containers	Real estate used in the furtherance of illegal drug activity	Imitation controlled substances
ALABAMA	■	■	■	■	■	■		■		■
ALASKA	■	■	■	■		■		■		
ARIZONA	■	■		■	■	■		■	■	■
ARKANSAS	■	■		■	■	■	■	■	■	■
CALIFORNIA	■	■		■		■	■	■		
COLORADO	■	■		■	■	■		■		■
CONNECTICUT	■				■	■	■			
DELAWARE	■	■		■		■	■	■		
D. C.	■	■		■		■	■	■		
FLORIDA	■	■		■	■	■		■		
GEORGIA	■		■	■	■	■	■	■		
HAWAII	■	■		■		■		■		■
IDAHO	■	■		■	■	■		■		
ILLINOIS	■	■	■	■		■		■	■	
INDIANA	■			■		■				
IOWA	■	■		■	■	■		■	■	■
KANSAS	■	■	■	■	■	■		■	■	■
KENTUCKY	■	■	■	■		■		■	■	
LOUISIANA	■	■	■	■		■		■		
MAINE	■	■	■	■		■		■	■	
MARYLAND	■	■	■	■	■	■		■		
MASSACHUSETTS	■	■	■	■		■		■	■	
MICHIGAN	■	■	■	■		■		■		■
MINNESOTA	■	■	■	■	■	■		■		
MISSISSIPPI	■	■		■	■	■		■	■	
MISSOURI	■		■	■		■		■		■
MONTANA	■	■	■	■		■	■	■		
NEBRASKA	■	■	■	■	■	■		■		
NEVADA	■	■	■	■	■	■		■		■
NEW HAMPSHIRE	■	■		■		■		■	■	
NEW JERSEY	■				■	■	■			
NEW MEXICO	■		■	■	■	■		■	■	■
NEW YORK	■	■	■	■		■	■	■		■
NORTH CAROLINA	■	■	■	■		■		■		
NORTH DAKOTA	■	■	■	■	■	■	■	■		■
OHIO	■	■	■	■	■	■	■	■	■	
OKLAHOMA	■	■	■	■	■	■	■	■		
OREGON	■			■						
PENNSYLVANIA	■	■	■	■	■	■	■	■		
RHODE ISLAND	■	■	■	■	■	■		■	■	■
SOUTH CAROLINA	■	■		■		■	■	■		
SOUTH DAKOTA	■	■	■	■		■	■	■		
TENNESSEE	■	■		■		■		■		
TEXAS	■	■	■	■	■	■	■	■		
UTAH	■	■	■	■	■	■		■		■
VERMONT	■	■	■	■		■		■		
VIRGINIA	■	■		■		■		■	■	
WASHINGTON	■	■	■	■	■	■		■		
WEST VIRGINIA	■	■	■	■	■	■		■		
WISCONSIN	■	■	■	■		■	■	■	■	
WYOMING	■	■	■	■	■	■	■	■	■	
FEDERAL	■	■	■	■		■	■	■	■	

Sources of Information on Drug Abuse

AMERICAN COUNCIL FOR DRUG EDUCATION (ACDE)
Suite 110
204 Monroe Street
Rockville, MD 20850
301-294-0600

The American Council for Drug Education writes and publishes educational materials, reviews scientific findings, and develops educational media campaigns. The pamphlets, monographs, films, and other teaching aids on the health risks associated with drug and alcohol use are targeted at educators, parents, physicians, and employees.

AMERICAN PROSECUTORS RESEARCH INSTITUTE
Center for Local Prosecution of Drug Offenses
1033 North Fairfax Street
Suite 200
Alexandria, VA 22314
703-549-6790

The Center for Local Prosecution of Drug Offenses provides local prosecutors with training, technical assistance, and effective techniques for dealing with drug cases.

COMP CARE PUBLICATIONS
2415 Annapolis Lane
Minneapolis, MN 55441
1-800-328-3330

Comp Care Publications is a source for pamphlets, books, and charts on drug and alcohol use, chemical awareness, and self-help.

DRUG ENFORCEMENT ADMINISTRATION (DEA)
1405 Eye Street, N.W.
Washington, DC 20537
202-633-1000

The Drug Enforcement Administration offers a wide variety of information on how to implement drug programs including those for student athletes, the work place, and the community.

FAMILIES ANONYMOUS, INC.
P.O. Box 528
Van Nuys, CA 91408
818-989-7841

A self-supporting, self-help program for families facing problems at home, Families Anonymous, Inc., offers meetings for parents, relatives, and friends of individuals addicted to drugs or alcohol.

HAZELDEN EDUCATIONAL MATERIALS
P.O. Box 176
Center City, MN 55012
1-800-328-9000 (U.S. only)
1-800-257-0070 (Minnesota)
612-257-4010 (Alaska and outside U.S.)

Hazelden Educational Materials publishes and distributes a broad variety of materials on chemical dependency and recovery. A free catalog of materials can be obtained by calling the toll-free number.

"JUST SAY NO" CLUBS
Pacific Institute for Research and Evaluation
1777 North California Boulevard
Suite 200
Walnut Creek, CA 94596
415-939-6677

The institute serves as the international headquarters of the "Just Say No" clubs. On request, the organization will provide information on its history and current activities on the national and international levels. Information is also available on starting a "Just Say No" club, participating in the annual "Just Say No Walk Against Drugs," and obtaining an order sheet for other "Just Say No" materials.

KIWANIS INTERNATIONAL
Public Relations
3636 Woodview Trace
Indianapolis, IN 46268
317-875-8755

Kiwanis International has available for general distribution (in nine languages) public awareness/relations items for billboards, radio and TV public service announcement spots, and print ads. It has developed a teaching manual for grades four through six entitled *Choices About Drugs*.

NARCOTICS ANONYMOUS
World Service Office
P.O. Box 9999
Van Nuys, CA 91409
818-780-3951

Based on the twelve-step program originated by Alcoholics Anonymous, Narcotics Anonymous functions as a self-help group of and for recovering addicts. The group is open to any drug user and assesses no fees. Members rely on the therapeutic value of one addict helping another. Founded in 1953, Narcotics Anonymous has 12,000 chapters in the United States and chapters in forty other countries.

NATIONAL CLEARINGHOUSE FOR ALCOHOL AND DRUG INFORMATION (NCADI)
P.O. Box 2345
Rockville, MD 20852
301-468-2600

NCADI, which services the Office of Substance Abuse Prevention, has available a library that covers a range of alcohol and drug abuse issues and has a computerized research capability. The service responds to requests from community leaders, researchers, and others. Bulk quantities of informational materials are available to the general public.

NATIONAL COUNCIL OF JUVENILE AND FAMILY COURT JUDGES
P.O. Box 8970
University of Nevada/Reno
Judicial College Building #118
Reno, NV 89507
702-784-6012

The National Council of Juvenile and Family Court Judges provides the report *Juvenile and Family Substance Abuse: A Judicial Response*; technical assistance on issues of dependency, delinquency, and the substance abuse problem; and information on screening, prevention, identification, assessment, and evaluation.

NATIONAL COUNCIL ON ALCOHOLISM
12 West 21st Street
8th Floor
New York, NY 10010
212-206-6770 (office)
1-800-NCA-CALL (hotline)

The National Council on Alcoholism's two leading missions are to provide education and advocacy on behalf of alcoholics, other drug-dependent people, and their families. NCA has two hundred affiliates that provide information and referral in states and localities.

NATIONAL INSTITUTE ON DRUG ABUSE (NIDA)
U.S. Department of Health and Human Services
5600 Fishers Lane
Rockville, MD 20857
301-443-6245 (office)
1-800-662-HELP (hotline)

NIDA conducts and supports research on the causes, prevention, and treatment of drug abuse and produces a national directory of drug abuse and alcoholism treatment programs, leaflets, and drug abuse statistics. NIDA's toll-free confidential information and referral line directs callers to drug abuse treatment centers in the local community and provides free materials on illegal drug abuse on request.

NATIONAL ORGANIZATION ON LEGAL PROBLEMS OF EDUCATION
3601 Southwest 29th Street
Suite 223
Topeka, KS 66614
913-273-3550

The National Organization on Legal Problems of Education disseminates information on judicial decisions including those relating to drug use in education.

**NATIONAL PARENTS' RESOURCE INSTITUTE FOR
DRUG EDUCATION (PRIDE)**
50 Hurt Plaza
Suite 210
Atlanta, GA 30303
404-577-4500

Probably the best-known antidrug parent organization in the United States, PRIDE serves as a national and international clearinghouse to educate parents about drugs and drug abuse.

U.S. DEPARTMENT OF EDUCATION
Drug-Free Schools and Communities
400 Maryland Avenue, S.W.
Washington, DC 20202-6349
202-732-4599

Programs are designed (through state grants) to help local schools prevent and reduce drug and alcohol use and associated disruptive behavior. Five regional centers provide training and assistance to local school districts that apply.

U.S. DEPARTMENT OF JUSTICE
NATIONAL INSTITUTE OF JUSTICE
NATIONAL CRIMINAL JUSTICE REFERENCE SERVICE (NCJRS)
633 Indiana Avenue, N.W.
Washington, DC 20531
1-800-851-3420
301-251-5500

In addition to statistical abstracts and research reports on Department of Justice efforts, other available services include the following:

Data base searches. Closely defined by your subject and customized to your needs, these searches of the NCJRS data base of some 100,000 documents typically yield up to 200 citations and cost only $48 if sent to addresses in the United States. (Ask about data base searches on compact disk, available for reading and manipulation on your own personal computer.)

Electronic bulletin board. Free and available twenty-four hours a day, this electronic information service of NCJRS lets you log in by telephone and modem to view and download news, announcements, and publication briefs or to communicate via mail messages with other researchers and practitioners. Call for information.

Interlibrary loans. Ask for rules and rates that permit you to tap the resources of the NCJRS collection.

Microfiche. Ask for a copy of the microfiche catalog, and learn how to obtain, in this compact form, single works, collected publications of the National Institute of Justice, SLiMs (Selected Libraries in Microfiche), or even the 25,000-title NCJRS microfiche collection.

WASHINGTON LEGAL FOUNDATION
Courtwatch
1705 N Street, N.W.
Washington, DC 20036
202-857-0240

Courtwatch monitors what happens to drug dealers in the court system.

Selected Bibliography

Akins, Carl, and George Beschner, eds. *Ethnography: A Research Tool for Policymakers in the Drug and Alcohol Fields*. Rockville, Md.: National Institute on Drug Abuse, 1980.

Ausubel, David P. *Drug Addiction: Physiological, Psychological, and Sociological Aspects*. New York: Random House, 1958.

Battjes, Robert J., and Roy W. Pickens. *Needle Sharing Among Intravenous Drug Abusers*. Rockville, Md.: National Institute on Drug Abuse, 1988.

Berridge, Virginia, and Griffith Edwards. *Opium and the People: Opiate Use in Nineteenth-Century England*. New Haven, Conn.: Yale University Press, 1987.

Beschner, George M., and Alfred S. Friedman, eds. *Youth Drug Abuse: Problems, Issues, and Treatment*. Lexington, Mass.: Lexington Books, 1979.

Blum, Richard H., and Associates. *Students and Drugs*. San Francisco: Jossey-Bass, 1970.

Bonnie, Richard J., and Charles H. Whitebread. *The Marijuana Conviction: A History of Marijuana Prohibition in the United States*. Charlottesville: University Press of Virginia, 1974.

Byck, Robert, ed. *Cocaine Papers by Sigmund Freud*. New York: New American Library, 1975.

Chambers, Carl D., and John C. Ball, eds. *The Epidemiology of Opiate Addiction in the United States*. Springfield, Ill.: Charles C. Thomas, 1970.

Chambers, Carl D., and Leon Brill, eds. *Methadone: Experiences and Issues*. New York: Behavioral Publications, 1973.

Chein, Isador, Donald L. Gerard, Robert S. Lee, and Eva Rosenfeld. *The Road to H: Narcotics, Juvenile Delinquency, and Social Policy*. New York: Basic Books, 1964.

Courtwright, David T. *Dark Paradise: Opiate Addiction in America Before 1940*. Cambridge, Mass.: Harvard University Press, 1982.

Courtwright, David, Herman Joseph, and Don Des Jarlais. *Addicts Who Survived: An Oral History of Narcotic Use in America, 1923–1965*. Knoxville: University of Tennessee Press, 1989.

Dai, Bingham. *Opium Addiction in Chicago*. Shanghai: Commercial Press, 1937.

De Leon, George, and James T. Ziegenfuss, eds. *Therapeutic Communities for Addictions: Readings in Theory, Research, and Practice*. Springfield, Ill.: Charles C. Thomas, 1986.

DuPont, Robert L. *Getting Tough on Gateway Drugs*. Washington, D.C.: American Psychiatric Press, 1984.

DuPont, Robert L., Avram Goldstein, and John O'Donnell, eds. *Handbook on Drug Abuse*. Rockville, Md.: National Institute on Drug Abuse, 1979.

Galea, Robert P., Benjamin F. Lewis, and Lori A. Baker, eds. *AIDS and IV Drug Abusers: Current Perspectives*. Owings Mills, Md.: National Health Publishing, 1988.

Goldstein, Paul J. *Prostitution and Drugs*. Lexington, Mass.: Lexington Books, 1979.

Goldstein, Paul J. "Homicide Related to Drug Traffic." *Bulletin of the New York Academy of Medicine* 62 (June 1986): 509–16.

Gould, Leroy, Andrew L. Walker, Lansing E. Crane, and Charles W. Lidz. *Connections: Notes from the Heroin World*. New Haven, Conn.: Yale University Press, 1974.

Grabowski, John, ed. *Cocaine: Pharmacology, Effects, and Treatment of Abuse*. Rockville, Md.: National Institute on Drug Abuse, 1984.

Hanson, Bill, George Beschner, James M. Walters, and Elliott Bovelle, eds. *Life with Heroin: Voices from the Inner City*. Lexington, Mass.: Lexington Books, 1985.

Hawks, Richard L., and C. Nora Chiang, eds. *Urine Testing for Drugs of Abuse*. Rockville, Md.: National Institute on Drug Abuse, 1986.

Hendin, Herbert, Ann Pollinger Haas, Paul Singer, Melvin Ellner, and Richard Ulman. *Living High: Daily Marijuana Use Among Adults*. New York: Human Sciences Press, 1987.

Hubbard, Robert L., Mary Ellen Marsden, J. Valley Rachal, Henrick J. Harwood, Elizabeth R. Cavanaugh, and Harold M. Ginzburg. *Drug Abuse Treatment: A National Survey of Effectiveness*. Chapel Hill: University of North Carolina Press, 1989.

Inciardi, James A., ed. *The Drugs-Crime Connection*. Beverly Hills, Calif.: Sage, 1981.

Inciardi, James A. *The War on Drugs: Heroin, Cocaine, Crime, and Public Policy*. Palo Alto, Calif.: Mayfield, 1986.

Inciardi, James A. "Beyond Cocaine: Basuco, Crack, and Other Coca Products." *Contemporary Drug Problems* 14 (Fall 1987): 461–92.

Inciardi, James A., ed. *The Drug Legalization Debate*. Newbury Park, Calif.: Sage, 1990.

Johnson, Bruce D., Paul J. Goldstein, Edward Preble, James Schmeidler, Douglas S. Lipton, Barry Spunt, and Thomas Miller. *Taking Care of Business: The Economics of Crime by Heroin Abusers*. Lexington, Mass.: Lexington Books, 1985.

Kaplan, John. *The Hardest Drug: Heroin and Public Policy*. Chicago: University of Chicago Press, 1983.

Leary, Timothy. *Flashbacks: An Autobiography*. Los Angeles: J. P. Tarcher, 1983.

Lee, Rensselaer W. *The White Labyrinth: Cocaine and Political Power*. New Brunswick, N.J.: Transaction Publishers, 1989.

Lettieri, Dan J., Mollie Sayers, and Helen Wallenstein Pearson, eds. *Theories on Drug Abuse: Selected Contemporary Perspectives*. Rockville, Md.: National Institute on Drug Abuse, 1980.

Leukefeld, Carl G., and Frank M. Tims, eds. *Compulsory Treatment of Drug Abuse:*

Research and Clinical Practice. Rockville, Md.: National Institute on Drug Abuse, 1988.

Lindesmith, Alfred R. *Opiate Addiction*. Bloomington, Ind.: Principia Press, 1947.

Lindesmith, Alfred R. *The Addict and the Law*. Bloomington: Indiana University Press, 1965.

Milkman, Harvey, and Stanley Sunderwirth. *Craving for Ecstasy: The Consciousness and Chemistry of Escape*. Lexington, Mass.: Lexington Books, 1987.

Miller, William R., and Nick Heather, eds. *Treating Addictive Behaviors: Processes of Change*. New York: Plenum, 1986.

Morgan, H. Wayne. *Yesterday's Addicts: American Society and Drug Abuse, 1865–1920*. Norman: University of Oklahoma Press, 1974.

Morgan, H. Wayne. *Drugs in America: A Social History*. Syracuse, N.Y.: Syracuse University Press, 1981.

Musto, David F. *The American Disease: Origins of Narcotic Control*. New Haven, Conn.: Yale University Press, 1973.

National Commission on Marijuana and Drug Abuse. *Drug Abuse in America: Problem in Perspective*. Washington, D.C.: U.S. Government Printing Office, 1973.

National Drug Control Strategy. Washington, D.C.: The White House, 1989.

Nicholl, Charles. *The Fruit Palace: An Odyssey Through Colombia's Cocaine Underground*. New York: St. Martin's Press, 1985.

Nyswander, Marie. *The Drug Addict as a Patient*. New York: Grune & Stratton, 1956.

O'Brien, Robert, and Sidney Cohen. *The Encyclopedia of Drug Abuse*. New York: Facts on File, 1984.

Pacini, Deborah, and Christine Franquemont, eds. *Coca and Cocaine: Effects on People and Policy in Latin America*. Cambridge, Mass.: Cultural Survival, 1986.

Peele, Stanton. *The Meaning of Addiction*. Lexington, Mass.: Lexington Books, 1985.

Platt, Jerome J. *Heroin Addiction*. Malabar, Fla.: Robert E. Krieger, 1986.

Rettig, Richard P., Manual J. Torres, and Gerald R. Garrett. *Manny: A Criminal Addict's Story*. Boston: Houghton Mifflin, 1977.

Robins, Lee N., ed. *Studying Drug Abuse*. New Brunswick, N.J.: Rutgers University Press, 1985.

Rosenbaum, Marsha. *Women on Heroin*. New Brunswick, N.J.: Rutgers University Press, 1981.

Scarpitti, Frank R., and Susan K. Datesman, eds. *Drugs and the Youth Culture*. Beverly Hills, Calif.: Sage, 1980.

The Science of AIDS. New York: W. H. Freeman, 1989.

Shaffer, Howard, and Milton Earl Burglass, eds. *Classic Contributions in the Addictions*. New York: Brunner/Mazel, 1981.

Shellow, Robert, ed. *Drug Use and Crime: Report of the Panel on Drug Use and Criminal Behavior*. Springfield, Va.: National Technical Information Service, 1976.

Shilts, Randy. *And the Band Played On: Politics, People, and the AIDS Epidemic*. New York: St. Martin's Press, 1987.

Siegel, Ronald K. *Intoxication: Life in Pursuit of Artificial Paradise*. New York: E. P. Dutton, 1989.

Sloman, Larry. *Reefer Madness: A History of Marijuana in America*. Indianapolis: Bobbs-Merrill, 1979.

Smith, David E., and George R. Gay, eds. *"It's So Good, Don't Even Try It Once": Heroin in Perspective*. Englewood Cliffs, N.J.: Prentice-Hall, 1971.

Terry, Charles E., and Mildred Pellens. *The Opium Problem*. New York: Bureau of Social Hygiene, 1928.

Trebach, Arnold S. *The Heroin Solution*. New Haven, Conn.: Yale University Press, 1982.

Turner, Charles F., Heather G. Miller, and Lincoln E. Moses, eds. *AIDS: Sexual Behavior and Intravenous Drug Use*. Washington, D.C.: National Academy Press, 1989.

Weil, Andrew, and Winifred Rosen. *Chocolate to Morphine: Understanding Mind-Active Drugs*. Boston: Houghton Mifflin, 1983.

Weiss, Roger D., and Steven M. Mirin. *Cocaine*. Washington, D.C.: American Psychiatric Press, 1987.

Wickler, Abraham. *Opiate Addiction*. Springfield, Ill.: Charles C. Thomas, 1963.

Young, James Harvey. *The Toadstool Millionaires: A Social History of Patent Medicines in America Before Federal Regulation*. Princeton, N.J.: Princeton University Press, 1961.

Name Index

Subject Index

Contributors

M. DOUGLAS ANGLIN is Adjunct Associate Professor of Medical Psychology with the Neuropsychiatric Institute at the University of California, Los Angeles. He is also Director of the UCLA Drug Abuse Research Group. His research interests include drug abuse epidemiology, intervention, and social policy. He has been Principal Investigator for several long-term follow-up studies of narcotics and cocaine addicts.

JEROME BECK is a doctoral student in the Behavioral Sciences program in the School of Public Health at the University of California at Berkeley. He is also Project Director of a NIDA-funded study on "Exploring Ecstasy: A Descriptive Study of MDMA Users." Over the past fifteen years, he has been involved in most aspects of the drug field: prevention, treatment, education, and research. He has been following the MDMA phenomenon since its emergence in 1977 when he was employed at the University of Oregon Drug Information Center. Mr. Beck has published numerous articles on MDMA and other substances.

GEORGE BESCHNER has been until recently Chief of Community Research Branch, National Institute on Drug Abuse, U.S. Public Health Service. As an official of NIDA since 1971, he has planned, implemented, and coordinated research and demonstration projects designed to improve drug abuse rehabilitation services and to reduce the risks of AIDS. Previously he was on the faculty of the University of Maryland School of Social Work and Community Planning. He has served as a Training Director with the Office of Economic Opportunity. He has published numerous journal articles and monographs and is co-editor of five books on drug abuse problems.

JOSEPH R. BIDEN, JR., is the Democratic Senator from Delaware and the Chairman of the Senate Judiciary Committee. He was first elected to the Senate in 1972 at age twenty-nine and was re-elected in 1978 and 1984. The Senator is a graduate of the University of Delaware and the Syracuse University College of Law, A former trial lawyer, Senator Biden has been particularly active in efforts to combat illegal drug trafficking. He has been the leading advocate for improved coordination among drug enforcement agencies and for greater international efforts to stem the flow of drugs from abroad. Senator Biden played a key role in the passage of the Anti-Drug Abuse Act of 1988. The bill included a provision for a national drug coordinator in the Cabinet (the so-called ''Drug Czar''), an idea Senator Biden originated and advocated for eight years.

BARRY S. BROWN is Chief of the Treatment and Early Intervention Research Branch of the Addiction Research Center/National Institute on Drug Abuse located in Baltimore, Maryland. He received a Doctorate in Psychology from Western Reserve University in 1963 and, in the succeeding twenty-five years, has worked in both a clinical and a research capacity with drug abuse clients in correctional and treatment settings. He has published numerous articles, chapters, and books in the areas of drug abuse, mental health, and corrections.

WILLIAM J. BUKOSKI is a Research Psychologist with the Prevention Research Branch, National Institute on Drug Abuse, U.S. Public Health Service. He received his Ph.D. in Educational Psychology at the Catholic University of America. Dr. Bukoski has worked as an educational and health researcher for the past twenty years, with the last ten years focused on the development of a scientifically sound drug prevention research program at the National Institute on Drug Abuse. Special professional interest areas include the assessment of school- and community-based substance abuse prevention programs for youth and adolescents, and basic research in learning and social modeling theory and practices pertinent to the design of drug information and education programs. Dr. Bukoski is widely published in professional journals and technical texts devoted to health promotion and disease prevention.

DIANE M. CANOVA is Director of Public Policy with the National Association of State Alcohol and Drug Abuse Directors (NASADAD). She received her J.D. at the University of Louisville School of Law in 1983. Prior to coming to NASADAD, she worked as a Legislative Attorney for a Washington, D.C., law firm, handling a variety of health-related issues. Ms. Canova also spent several years on Capitol Hill, first as Counsel to a House subcommittee and then as Legislative Director for a member of Congress.

DALE D. CHITWOOD is Research Associate Professor of Medical Sociology, Department of Oncology, University of Miami School of Medicine; a member of the Sylvester Comprehensive Cancer Center and the Miami World Health Organization Collaborating Center for Mental Health, Alcohol and Drug Dependence; and Senior Investigator within the Center for the Biopsychosocial

Study of AIDS. Since 1974 he has been studying the patterns and consequences of drug use (particularly cocaine) in south Florida. Currently he is Principal Investigator of a five-year investigation of the epidemiology of HIV among intravenous drug users and Coprincipal Investigator of an evaluation of HIV risk-reduction programs among drug users and their sexual partners in Miami and Belle Glade, Florida. Dr. Chitwood is also a member of the South Florida AIDS Research Consortium.

RICHARD B. CRAIG is Professor of Political Science at Kent State University and author of *The Bracero Program* (1971). During recent years he has been engaged in research on the political implications of narcotics traffic and, more specifically, the impact of such activity on U.S. relations with Mexico and Colombia. Dr. Craig has published articles on U.S.–Latin American narcopolitics, Mexico's antidrug program, domestic and international dimensions of illicit Colombian narcotics, Turkey–United States drug diplomacy, and international efforts to control international drug traffic. He will soon publish a book on the impact of illicit narcotics on Mexican-American relations.

GEORGE DE LEON received his Doctorate in Psychology from Columbia University. He was associated with Phoenix House from its inception as Director of Research and Evaluation. Currently he is Director of Research and Training for Therapeutic Communities of America (TCA), is Visiting Research Scientist at Narcotic and Drug Research Inc., and is affiliated with several universities in New York. He is consultant to the National Institute on Drug Abuse, international governments, and industry and is editor on several journals. His numerous publications and papers address both research and treatment issues in the areas of substance abuse. In addition to his research he has maintained a private clinical practice for over twenty-five years and consults to major league baseball, drug treatment programs, parent organizations, community action groups, and schools.

MARY ANN FORNEY is Assistant Professor of Family Medicine at the Medical College of Georgia and Adjunct Professor at Augusta College in Augusta, Georgia. She received her Ph.D. in Education at the University of South Carolina in 1983 and has conducted federally supported research in the area of adolescent alcohol abuse. Dr. Forney is Principal Investigator for a national study examining substance abuse among medical students and Project Director for a grant researching intratreatment change among addicted veterans.

ALFRED S. FRIEDMAN is Director of Research and has directed drug treatment programs at the Philadelphia Psychiatric Center. He has served as President of the Family Institute of Philadelphia, Chairman of the American Psychological Association's Committee on Relations with the Social Work Profession, and Director of the Clinical School of Family Therapy, Family Institute of Philadelphia. Dr. Friedman has developed and directed large-scale federally funded research projects on schizophrenia, depression, drug therapy, marital therapy, juvenile delinquency, and youth drug abuse. He has published numerous clinical-research papers and books.

KENNETH C. HAAS is Associate Professor in the Division of Criminal Justice and the Department of Political Science at the University of Delaware where he has twice won the university's Excellence-in-Teaching Award. He specializes in criminal procedure and the law of corrections and postconviction remedies. His articles have appeared in both law reviews and social science journals, and he is co-editor of *Challenging Capital Punishment: Legal and Social Science Approaches* (1988), *The Dilemmas of Punishment* (1986), and *Crime and the Criminal Justice Process* (1978). His scholarly work has been cited in many law review articles and by the U.S. Supreme Court.

THOMAS E. HANLON is currently Associate Research Professor at the Maryland Psychiatric Research Center, Department of Psychiatry, University of Maryland Medical School. He is also consultant at the Friends Medical Science Research Center, Inc., an organization devoted exclusively to drug abuse research. Obtaining his Doctorate at the Catholic University of America in Washington, D.C., in 1958, Dr. Hanlon has since been involved full time in psychiatric research, largely psychopharmacologic evaluations on schizophrenia. His interest and involvement in drug abuse research date from the early 1970s. His initial work in the field was concerned with determining the efficacy of narcotic antagonists.

KERRY MURPHY HEALEY is a consultant to the Law and Justice Area of Abt Associates, Inc., Cambridge, Massachusetts, and a Ph.D. candidate in Law and Political Science at Trinity College, Dublin. She is a graduate of Harvard College in Government and has been Visiting Researcher in the International and Comparative Legal Studies Program at Harvard Law School. Ms. Healey is the author of *State and Local Experience with Drug Paraphernalia Laws* (1987).

YIH-ING HSER is a Research Psychologist with the Neuropsychiatric Institute at the University of California, Los Angeles. She is also Associate Director of the UCLA Drug Abuse Research Group. Her research interests cover human learning and memory, prevalence estimation modeling techniques and applications, drug abuse patterns and consequences, gender differences in narcotics addiction, and event history analysis of addict behaviors.

JAMES A. INCIARDI is Professor and Director of the Division of Criminal Justice at the University of Delaware. He received his Ph.D. in Sociology at

New York University and has extensive research, field, teaching, and clinical experience in the areas of drug abuse, criminal justice, and criminology. He has been Director of the National Center for the Study of Acute Drug Reactions at the University of Miami School of Medicine, Vice President of the Washington, D.C.–based Resource Planning Corporation, and Associate Director of Research for both the New York State Narcotic Addiction Control Commission and the Metropolitan Dade County (Florida) Comprehensive Drug Program. Dr. Inciardi has done extensive consulting work both nationally and internationally and has published more than one hundred articles, chapters, and books in the areas of substance abuse, history, folklore, criminology, criminal justice, medicine, law, public policy, and AIDS. Dr. Inciardi is also a member of the South Florida AIDS Research Consortium.

TIMOTHY W. KINLOCK is currently Research Associate at Friends Medical Science Research Center, Inc. For the past nine years, he has been involved in many aspects of drug abuse research at this organization, including interviewing narcotic addict respondents, analyzing data, and preparing manuscripts for publication. He received his B.A. degree from the University of Delaware in 1975 and his M.A. degree from Towson State University in Maryland in 1977. Among his most recent publications are those involving the derivation of criminal "types" and the relationship between criminal activity and drug use. His major research interests include drug abuse, criminal behavior, and evaluation of treatment for narcotic addicts.

RICHARD A. LINDBLAD, epidemiologist, clinician, and past Associate Director of the National Institute on Drug Abuse (NIDA), has worked in the field of drug abuse for the past twenty-eight years. His clinical experience was obtained at the Ft. Worth Public Health Service Drug Abuse Hospital and his program development, planning, and consultant experience though senior-level positions in NIDA. He has presented and published numerous papers and articles concerning the research, prevention, and epidemiology of drug abuse. He has served as a consultant on international drug abuse issues for the World Health Organization, the United Nations, the Organization of American States, and the U.S. State Department. He provided technical oversight to the Jamaican national epidemiology surveys and was a major contributor in the design of the United Nations International Drug Abuse Assessment System. Currently Dr. Lindblad directs international demand-reduction programs out of the Office of the Director, NIDA.

DUANE C. MCBRIDE is Professor in the Department of Behavioral Sciences and School of Business at Andrews University in Berrien Springs, Michigan; Chairman of his university's Institute of Alcoholism and Drug Dependency Research Center; and a member of the South Florida AIDS Research Consortium.

He received his Ph.D. in Sociology from the University of Kentucky and has published widely in the areas of criminology, criminal justice, substance abuse, and AIDS.

CLYDE B. MCCOY is Professor of Oncology, Associate Director of the Sylvester Comprehensive Cancer Center, and Chief of the Division of Cancer Control, Department of Oncology, University of Miami School of Medicine. Since 1973 he has been investigating the epidemiology of tobacco, alcohol, and drug use in Florida and has guided the development of computerized data collection systems for drug treatment programs. Currently he is Principal Investigator of an early detection program for breast cancer among economically disadvantaged women and Principal Investigator of an evaluation of HIV risk-reduction programs among drug users and their sexual partners in Miami and Belle Glade, Florida. Dr. McCoy is also a member of the South Florida AIDS Research Consortium.

JOHN C. MCWILLIAMS is Assistant Professor of American History at The Pennsylvania State University–DuBois where he also teaches courses in political science and criminal justice. He received his Ph.D. in American History at Penn State. During the past several years his research has focused on federal law enforcement and the intelligence community. His book *The Protectors: Commissioner Harry J. Anslinger and the Federal Bureau of Narcotics, 1930–1962* will be published by the University of Delaware Press in 1990. Currently he is working on a study of the relationship between organized crime and the Federal Bureau of Narcotics.

DAVID N. NURCO received his doctorate from the National Catholic School of Social Service in 1969. He is Research Professor, Department of Psychiatry, at the University of Maryland School of Medicine. His research interests focus on interdisciplinary planning and treatment for social and behavioral disorders. He has over twenty years of experience in supervising research projects involving many aspects of narcotic addiction. He is author or co-author of more than seventy-five scientific articles, chapters, monographs, and books. Among his most recent publications are several on the relationship between narcotic addiction and criminal activity.

J. BRYAN PAGE is Research Associate Professor in the Department of Psychiatry at the University of Miami School of Medicine and has studied patterns of drug use since 1973. His experience in this field ranges from field studies of chronic heavy marijuana consumption to evaluation of school-based prevention projects. He is currently Associate Director of the Center for the Biopsychosocial Study of AIDS and Senior Investigator on an ethnographic study of needle use. Dr. Page has preferred in his studies to conduct direct observation of drug use patterns in developing anthropological analyses of the place occupied by drug use in the lives of the users. Dr. Page is also a member of the South Florida AIDS Research Consortium.

MARSHA ROSENBAUM is Director of the Center for Substance Abuse Studies at the Institute for Scientific Analysis in San Francisco. She has been a NIDA-funded researcher for twelve years, having directed projects studying women and heroin addiction, methadone treatment, MDMA, and women and cocaine. Dr. Rosenbaum has authored and co-authored numerous articles and a book, *Women on Heroin* (1981).

BETH A. WEINMAN is presently Director of Criminal Justice Programs for the National Association of State Alcohol and Drug Abuse Directors, Inc. (NA-SADAD). She has over fifteen years of experience working in criminal justice system programming, including programs for juveniles, victims, judges, public defenders, probation and parole, corrections, offender case management, treatment/client matching, and drug treatment for the drug-dependent offender. Before joining the NASADAD staff, Ms. Weinman spent six years working directly with Treatment Alternatives to Street Crime (TASC) program operations in Illinois, New York, and Pennsylvania. She has written extensively on TASC program operations and case management theories.

ERIC D. WISH is a Senior Research Scientist at Narcotic and Drug Research, Inc., in New York City, currently on loan to the National Institute of Justice (NIJ) as a Visiting Fellow. At NIJ, Dr. Wish is establishing the Drug Use Forecasting (DUF) system, a national system for tracking recent drug use trends in arrestees in the largest cities in the country. He is also writing a manual for practitioners on drug testing of offenders. Dr. Wish has published numerous articles spanning the field of drug abuse, including relapse to heroin use in Vietnam veterans, problems for marijuana users seeking treatment, and the uses of drug tests for identifying the most active criminals and referring them to treatment or urine monitoring.